The *Phenomenology of Spirit* is both one of Hegel's most widely read books and one of his most obscure. This book is the most detailed commentary on Hegel's work available. It develops an independent philosophical account of the general theory of knowledge, culture, and history presented in the *Phenomenology*. In a clear and straightforward style, Terry Pinkard reconstructs Hegel's theoretical philosophy and shows its connection to ethical and political theory. He sets the work in a historical context and shows the contemporary relevance of Hegel's thought for European and Anglo-American philosophers.

The principal audience for the book is teachers and students of philosophy, but the great interest in Hegel's work and the clarity of Pinkard's exposition ensure that historians of ideas, political scientists, and literary theorists will also read it.

D0940935

Hegel's *Phenomenology*

Hegel's
Phenomenology
The Sociality of Reason

TERRY PINKARD

CAMBRIDGE
UNIVERSITY PRESS

Published by the Press Syndicate of the University of Cambridge
The Pitt Building, Trumpington Street, Cambridge CB2 1RP
40 West 20th Street, New York, NY 10011-4211, USA
10 Stamford Road, Oakleigh, Melbourne 3166, Australia

First published 1994
First paperback edition 1996

Printed in the United States of America

Library of Congress Cataloging-in-Publication Data
Pinkard, Terry P.
Hegel's *Phenomenology* : the sociality of reason / Terry Pinkard.
p.   cm.
Includes bibliographical references and index.
ISBN 0-521-45300-3
1. Hegel, Georg Wilhelm Friedrich, 1770–1831. Phänomenologie des
Geistes. I. Title.
B2929.P45   1994
193–dc20   94-32
                                                            CIP

A catalog record for this book is available from the British Library.

ISBN 0-521-45300-3 hardback
ISBN 0-521-56834-X paperback

Contents

v

CONTENTS

Acknowledgments

Several years ago I gathered up some articles I had written on Hegel and published them as a book. Shortly after that book appeared, several new books and articles on Hegel were published, which led me to fundamentally rethink many positions I had taken in that earlier work. Foremost among those pieces were Robert Pippin's works on Hegelianism, particularly his *Modernism as a Philosophical Problem* and the essays that came after that book. Pippin's work led me to reevaluate certain key ideas I had held; I had the good fortune to discuss many of those issues with him in print, at conferences, and through the modern means of electronic mail. The ideas contained here owe much to the dialectic of those conversations.

A number of individuals helped this manuscript along the way. Discussions with my wife Susan of the issues raised in the book were more helpful than I can say. Conversations about many of these ideas with Rüdiger Bubner and Otfried Höffe during my sabbatical stay at Tübingen University in Germany helped me to think through a number of issues. I would also like to thank those anonymous readers at Cambridge University Press who provided an extremely helpful set of criticisms and suggestions on an earlier draft of the manuscript.

The Alexander von Humboldt Foundation, the Graduate School at Georgetown University, and the School of Foreign Service at Georgetown University each provided research grants that assisted various parts of the writing.

Finally, I would like to thank my old teacher, Klaus Hartmann. I had the opportunity to discuss the general plan of this book with him about a year before his death. As always, he was encouraging and helpful even though the ideas in the project took issue with many of his own views. I always valued his support and good-natured criticism, and for that reason this book is dedicated to his memory.

Hegel's *Phenomenology*

I

Why the *Phenomenology of Spirit?*

1. The problem of the *Phenomenology*

The 1807 *Phenomenology of Spirit* is one of Hegel's most read, best known and least understood works. It has an air of mystery about it: at once profound yet obscure, detailed, important but only available to the initiated. It is written in an unmistakable style that identifies it as "Hegelian" both to its admirers and detractors. Even the tales of its creation have a bit of romance to them, with one story having Hegel supposedly writing the final parts on the night that the city in which he is living, Jena, is being shelled by Napoleon's troops in one of the climactic battles of the old regime in Europe. In one of the most celebrated interpretations of the *Phenomenology*, the Russian emigre to France, Alexandre Kojève, interpreted the book as giving philosophical voice to the "end of history" that was being given political voice by Napoleon's soldiers. Hegel himself was in dire straits at the time, having only recently entered academic life and having a job that seemed to be without a future. Had Hegel been hit by the proverbial horse cart at this point in his life, he would have been remembered (if at all) as one of the very minor figures in German idealism, a commentator on Schelling and Fichte. The book was written hurriedly by a fellow who could have easily been taken to be going nowhere in his life. Nonetheless, Hegel turned out a work more or less finished in its first draft that had no predecessors in its genre and (so some would say) also no successors, supposedly (as yet another story has it) fleeing with some of the pages in his pocket as Napoleon's troops entered the city.

There is even a dispute among Hegel's readers as to where the *Phenomenology* is supposed to fit within the overall architecture of Hegel's own thought. Hegel did not even originally give the book the title by which it has become famous. Its original title was the *Science of the Experience of Consciousness*, but Hegel changed his mind and renamed it the *Phenomenology of Spirit*, which was to be the "First Part of a System of Science." (Apparently he changed his mind during the negotiations with the printer, who, confused by the whole mess, printed both the old and the new titles on the cover pages of the first printing, so that some copies of the first edition were called the *System of Science. Part One: Phenomenology of Spirit*.) Moreover, Hegel did not leave us any completely clear indications about what role he thought the *Phenomenology of Spirit* was supposed to play in his later system. It is evident that he did not completely abandon the work; he continued, for example, to give friends copies of the book, and he continued to refer to it in his lectures and in his published work. Yet he did not offer lectures on it, and on a first glance at the structure of his overall later "system," it is hard for the Hegelian student to find a clear place in the "system" where it *could* fit. He did rework the themes of the opening sections of the Jena *Phenomenology of Spirit* ("Consciousness" and "Self-Consciousness") into a section of the later "Philosophy of Spirit" as a part of the *Encyclopedia* under the title "Phenomenology of Spirit," but the rest of the *Phenomenology* was omitted from that work, and, moreover, the "Phenomenology of Spirit" in the *Encyclopedia* version is only a short preliminary to his overall "Psychology." However, to complicate matters, Hegel was beginning to rework the longer Jena *Phenomenology of Spirit* shortly before his death, presumably for a new edition. What changes he might have made we do not know, although it seems as if he intended to republish it fairly well unchanged.

The *Phenomenology's* obscure style is notorious. One of the first books ever to be written in English on Hegel was James Stirling's *The Secret of Hegel*.[1] A reviewer commented that Stirling had succeeded in keeping the secret, and, for many contemporary readers, the feeling has been that the secret is still intact. It is still difficult to pick up the *Phenomenology* and simply begin reading it, even for a trained academic philosopher who has become thoroughly habituated to the kind of linguistic usage that characterizes much Western philosophy and that non-philosophers often find so puzzling. This initial obscurity of the *Phenomenology of Spirit* has invited upon itself various incompatible readings. Go to a university library and check out several works on the *Phenomenology of Spirit;* you will find that almost all of them say that the book is about different things. There are myriad readings of the *Phenomenology*, ranging from seeing it as a work of orthodox Christianity to seeing it as a full-scale attack on Christianity. To some, the *Phenomenology* has been taken to be something like a philosophical roller coaster that in certain passages suddenly roars down its tracks at high speed after having slowly rumbled up to certain heights, with no more rhyme or reason for any particular transition than that it struck Hegel that such a transition might be fun or illuminating. Others have seen it as a kind of philosophical *Bildungsroman*, in which the protagonist is something large and metaphysical called *Geist*, or "Spirit." Others have seen it as the work of a youthful revolutionary who gradually and unfortunately changed into a stodgy, officious professor in Berlin extolling the virtues of the Prussian state. Hegel's thought has been praised and blamed for the development of existentialism, communism, fascism, death of God theology, and historicist nihilism. Hegel has also been called the Aristotle of the modern world and the Aquinas of Protestantism. Indeed, given the differing reactions to Hegel, it would be an interesting piece of intellectual history to trace out all the various interpretations of this work (and of Hegel himself) that have surfaced in the world since its publication. It would be a history ranging from idolatry (Hegel as the man who had all the answers) to puzzlement to bewilderment to disgust to outright rejection as a charlatan (typical of the twentieth-century Anglo-American reaction to Hegel).

In this light, it might seem imprudent to be offering yet another interpretation of this book. (I have been tempted more than once to call this *Yet Another Book on Hegel's Phenomenology*.) Nonetheless, a good case can be made that we are finally in a position to begin assimilating what Hegel has to say to us. In the period after the Second World War, a set of German commentators began crafting an original, precise, and insightful interpretation of the Hegelian texts that can be fairly said to have demolished (one hopes forever) most of the old myths about Hegel. In the period from, roughly 1979 to the present, the seeds of that German debate have begun to flower in the Anglo-American world as a whole host of new interpretations of Hegel have been emerging that have taken that German scholarship (and the intervening French scholarship) in new directions. Moreover, the current situation in contemporary Anglo-American philosophy, with the kinds of problems that have come to the fore in analytic philosophy, has perhaps prepared a philosophical audience that is less likely to dismiss Hegel out of hand as antiquated humbug and more likely to look at him with fresh eyes. Even so, there is still widespread doubt that Hegel, at least in his full-blown form and not in some watered-down version, is too much tied in with the antiquated questions of the early nineteenth century to be of more than passing interest to us. The question is: Has Hegel really come back on to the intellectual agenda of contemporary thought? Or is his thought, however original and profound it might be, something that we study not for its insights but only to gain a kind of historical knowledge about how we came to have the problems that we do?[2]

My objective here is not to offer a commentary or a paraphrase of the book; there are already enough of those. Instead, I offer a reconstruction of Hegel's central theses and the central lines of thought in the *Phenomenology*. Instead of a commentary, I offer a kind of Hegelian analysis of Hegel's text itself. My idea is to pursue Hegel's arguments and to reconstruct them in a way that is both faithful to the text and that brings out what is at stake in Hegel's project and in the particular points he makes. Although my main hope is that this assessment can stand as a self-sufficient exposition on its own and be of independent philosophical value, I hope that this can nonetheless be of use for those who wish to read the *Phenomenology* or do a close study of it (even without being able to consult the German text). After having gone through the *Phenomenology*, I then conclude by relating it to Hegel's mature system, and show how certain developments in the mature system complete the project of the *Phenomenology*.

2. Hegelian preliminaries

What, then, is the *Phenomenology of Spirit* about? Hegel says quite clearly in his "Introduction" to the *Phenomenology* that the work is concerned with the theory of knowledge. In particular, he says that it is concerned with how the kinds of knowledge-claims that we make can be said to match up with the objects that they purport to be about. Thus, one might expect such a work to be concerned with problems of the evidence of the senses, induction, whether the justifying evidence for epistemic claims is "internal" or "external" to consciousness, and similar issues. However, the topics covered in the *Phenomenology* instead seem to range over items as varied as issues concerning the formation of character in early modern Europe, Kantian ethics, and the history and philosophy of religion, with there being only a short introductory chapter on what might at least look like epistemology to a modern philosophical reader. Understanding the general goal of the *Phenomenology* therefore requires us to see how Hegel takes the theory of knowledge to be connected with all these other issues.

The task of the theory of knowledge seems to be to offer an account that explains how our knowledge-claims (our ideas, our propositions, our sentences, whatever) could possibly match up with their purported objects. Hegel notes that putting the issue in this way seems to place the problem of skepticism at center stage in two ways. First, the basic issue of such a theory of knowledge would be with whether our knowledge-claims *do* or *can* match up with real things, in which case generalized skepticism – the doubt that our claims might *in general* fail to match up to "real" objects – becomes the main concern of such a theory of knowledge. Answering that kind of skeptic comes to be *the* problem of the theory of knowledge. Second, generalized skepticism is also the *result* of adopting such a view, in that once one understands the problem of knowledge to be that of matching up some "idea" with objects, these "ideas" become the intermediaries between the thinking subject and the world, and the problem thereby naturally arises as to how we could know that the intermediary is not giving us an illusory representation of its object.[3] Stated in those terms, it might seem impossible to answer the skeptic unless one therefore finds some kind of self-certifying idea (an idea that carries its own justification on its face, such as the property of being "certain" or being "infallibly known" or being "necessary") and a self-certifying procedure to move from that self-certifying idea to other non-self-certifying ideas.

Now, there are many candidates for what would count as self-certification (certainty, infallibility, indefeasibility, and so on), and the issue therefore seems to come down to which of these really would be the self-certifying "ground" of all other knowledge. The theory of such a "ground" would be a "science" in the German sense of *Wissenschaft* – that is, a kind of structured theoretical knowledge of some circumscribed domain. Is such a "science" possible? It seems not, for whatever shape this "science" may take, it is but itself only one more claim to knowledge, and it must therefore "ground" itself. There are, moreover, very conflicting claims to knowledge among different types of communities. Some religious types claim to know God with certainty and infallibility in their hearts; other more secular types claim to know the individual items of sense-experience with certainty or infallibility. The latter may claim to reject the former because they do not fit their canons of "scientific procedure" or the "commonly accepted standards" of rationality. The former may reject the latter because they substitute procedures of scientific rationality in places where only the "heart" can rule. Neither side, so it

4

seems, produces any real argument to convince the other, since both stances amount to simply taking certain standards or certain projects to be self-evident while rejecting the other side's claims simply because they fail to live up to the standards of their own point of view. Indeed, what each side takes as self-certifying is dependent, so it seems, on other assumptions that are certainly not so self-evident (such as issues concerning secular accounts versus religious accounts). At least from the standpoint of a theory of knowledge that would be a genuine *Wissenschaft,* we need more than the vague assurance that "our side" has really got it right simply because the "other side" has failed to live up to our standards. The other side is, after all, capable of making the same claims.[4]

Since each side in these disputes already makes a variety of assumptions in forming its accounts of knowledge-claims, each of these kinds of theories is, as Hegel puts it, itself only an *appearance* (*Erscheinung*), a historical phenomenon, alongside other claims to knowledge, and, *as* an "appearance," it can make no intrinsic claim to being true or even better than the others.[5] Indeed, if we are to take the problem of skepticism seriously, we must see all accounts, including the account we are giving of the other accounts, as "appearances," as merely one more set of claims as to what is real and true that stands alongside a host of other competing claims. An authentic skepticism must therefore be skeptical about itself; it must also take skepticism itself as only an "appearance."

But such a type of skepticism will, of course, seem corrosive, since it appears to offer no way to resolve such issues. How could, for example, the secularist come up with an account that is justifiable to the religious in terms that the religious can accept on their own terms or that give them reasons to change what they count as the "grounds" of belief? Yet, if Hegel is right, only a theory that does exactly that could claim to be an authentic *Wissenschaft,* a well-grounded, structured theoretical account of knowledge and not just a restatement or a refinement of principles that a given community (modern, ancient, religious, secular, whatever) already takes for granted. The task of a theory of knowledge must be to produce some way of evaluating what kinds of reasons for belief (or for action) can count as *authoritative* reasons, and it must be able to show that the reasons it gives for counting those reasons as authoritative reasons are *themselves* authoritative reasons, and it must do this while at the same time regarding all claims, including the ones it itself makes, as being only "appearances."[6] The theory of knowledge can therefore only adequately define its task if it is able to effectively delineate what it means to take everything as an "appearance" and to understand what it means to be genuinely skeptical.

To look at all such accounts as appearances, Hegel argues, is to look at them (in his words) as "formations (*Gestaltungen*) of consciousness," as forms of life that have come to take certain types of reasons as authoritative for themselves. Reasons appear as authoritative when they appear as mandatory, that is, as *necessary* for the agents for whom they are authoritative. In this way, Hegel continues the Kantian shift away from Cartesian issues about certainty (from the kind of hold that *we* have on certain norms) to necessity (the hold that certain norms have *on us*). A "formation of consciousness" in Hegel's sense is composed both of the ways in which a form of life takes certain types of reasons (or, to put it more generally, norms) as authoritative for itself and the ways in which it articulates to itself why it is legitimate for those reasons to count for it as authoritative, non-optional reasons. (A terminological point: In the *Phenomenology,* Hegel quite consistently refers to that set of "grounds" that people take as authoritative as the "essence," or the "absolute essence" of a formation of consciousness; he says of these "essences" that they are the "objects" of a consciousness that assumes that such and such is authoritative for it.) The *Phenomenology,* by and large, examines various "formations of consciousness" in terms of how they take these authoritative standards more or less as "given," as "objects" of consciousness that the participants in that form of life simply "find" in their social worlds ready at hand for them. To look at accounts *as appearances* is therefore to take them at their own word, to see how in their terms they take certain kinds of reasons to be authoritative, and how they attempt to legitimate that authoritativeness for themselves; it is not to *presuppose* that any one account or "appearance" is superior to another.

Since there can be a variety of different "formations of consciousness," it might seem that in taking each one as an appearance, the theory of knowledge is thereby destined from the outset to result in a kind of self-undermining relativism or some kind of pointless self-contradictory avowal that no statement of knowledge can be taken to be true. Taken this way, the attempt to produce an adequate theory of knowledge can, as Hegel puts it, only be seen "as the path of doubt, or, more authentically, as the path of despair."[7] If an adequate theory of knowledge must also therefore give a non-question-begging account of why it takes *its* own reasons to be *the* authoritative reasons for accepting the account of knowledge that it gives, then it seems not merely to have complicated its task but perhaps to have made it impossible. Those reasons themselves, so it would seem, would also have to be underwritten by other reasons, ad infinitum. Moreover, in order even to start, the theory of knowledge surely has to presuppose some kind of standard for counting some kinds of things as evidence, but this kind of methodological restriction seems to say that it can presuppose no such standard at all.[8] Thus, it seems that such strictures make it impossible to produce any kind of legitimate "science" – *Wissenschaft* – of knowledge at all.

Since we must start somewhere, it seems that we must simply take whatever standards of evaluation we happen to have and subject them to some kind of internal test. Indeed, Hegel recommends this solution as appropriate, given the general question with which modern considerations of the theory of knowledge already begin. That issue has to do with how we match up our "ideas" with the way things are "in themselves." Now it is trivially clear that whenever we attempt to go about doing this, we are always using some standard or another in terms of which we judge that something counts as the way in which things "really are" as opposed to the way they only seem to be.

Those standards, as Hegel says, are internal to consciousness in the sense that we are always taking things to be such and such in terms of the kinds of reasons that we have come to take as authoritative for ourselves. The major issue for the theory of knowledge must be to examine whether those reasons (or, more neutrally put, those "grounds") that we *take* as authoritative *really are* authoritative. It must show that what underwrites the "ground-rules" of our reason-giving activities is genuine and legitimate. If nothing else, we can look to see whether these authoritative reasons themselves are *within their own terms* satisfactory, not whether, for example, we find them satisfactory by the standards of another set of terms.[9] That is, we can examine the reasons that we or anyone else has come to take as authoritative, and we can reflect on whether those reasons can be shown to be adequate at least in terms of the goals that they set for themselves. In this way, perhaps, this kind of corrosive skepticism can become a "self-consummating skepticism."[10]

There are at least two types of doubts we may have about such reasons. We may have doubts about whether those reasons that we *take* as authoritative *really are* authoritative reasons and we may have doubts about whether the *account* that we have given of why they should (or should not) count as authoritative reasons is itself in order. Skepticism arises when either of these kinds of doubts occur; it arises, as Hegel likes to put it, out of the *negativity* of self-consciousness. The "negativity" of an account is its capacity to generate a self-undermining skepticism about itself when it is reflected upon within the terms that it sets for itself. The *negation* of an account, in Hegel's language, is always that set of self-undermining considerations that arise from within an account's own terms, and, for that reason, negation is always *determinate* negation, the *specific* set of self-undermining objections that come out of such accounts.[11] This kind of "negativity" – the capacity to generate a kind of skepticism about itself from its own terms – is a characteristic of those accounts that are the object of reflection, or, as Hegel puts it, of *self-consciousness*. The "science" (*Wissenschaft*) of knowledge must therefore also develop within itself some conception of the relation between authoritative reasons and self-conscious reflection.

Self-consciousness on the Hegelian model is not the awareness of a set of internal objects (sensations, mental occurrences, representations, whatever). To use a metaphor, self-consciousness is at least minimally the assumption of a position in "social space."[12] We locate ourselves in "social space" when, for example, we reason in various ways; or when we assume various roles; or when we demand a certain type of treatment because of who we think we are; or when we see some forms of behavior as appropriate to the type of person we think ourselves to be; or when we recognize others as having the right to make certain kinds of moves within their speech-community; or when we give a reason to another person to explain or to justify what we are doing; or when we give an account of what we are doing to others that we think affirms what we take to be a good reason for doing what we are doing. Within a "social space" individuals assert various things to each other and give what they take to be reasons for these assertions, and people impute certain reasons to them on the basis of the shared social norms that structure their "social space" – that is, on the basis of what they take the person to be committed to in light of what he does and their shared norms. All the various activities of reason-giving – for example, of telling someone why you take some belief to be justified, of giving a good reason to yourself for going ahead and doing something, or of narrating some story about yourself that you take to explain and justify the way you lead your life – are themselves forms of social practice in which we in turn mutually evaluate each other's actions, in which we each assume certain types of epistemic and ethical responsibilities, and in which we impute certain moral and epistemic responsibilities to others in light of their behavior. In the various social practices involving reason-giving, we also have principles of *criticism* for evaluating the reasons we give. Reason-giving, that is, is itself a social practice that goes on within a determinate form of "social space" that "licenses" some kinds of inferences and fails to "license" others.

A distinguishing feature of a particular "social space" is the set of what counts within that "social space" as the basic "ground-rules" for agents to justify their beliefs and to guide their actions. The structure of authoritative reasons within each "social space" thereby naturally appears to each agent to constitute not just the way that he and others contingently *happen* to reason but the way in which people in general *should* reason. That is, those sets of authoritative reasons appear as both certain and as structuring what is to count as truth, and as necessary, as something that is not optional for the kinds of agents they are. When a set of such reasons and the accounts given of them undermine themselves, they of course lose that appearance of necessity and they lose their link to truth for those agents. Part of the theory of knowledge, therefore, must be to see if there are any set of authoritative reasons that can generate their own necessity in a way that does not undermine itself.

This requires the construction of a self-conscious reflective account of those authoritative standards and norms themselves that can affirm for us which of them are genuine and legitimate. Any form of life will have certain reasons that it takes as authoritative; to the extent that it becomes *self-conscious* about these standards and norms, it will develop accounts of why what it *takes* as authoritative for itself *really is* authoritative. Becoming self-conscious about such norms is to become aware of the apparent paradoxes, incoherences, and conflicts within them.

All these forms of self-consciousness have a mediated (that is, inferential) structure.[13] Whenever there is mutual recognition among self-conscious subjects that is mediated by such a shared self-conscious understanding of what for them counts in general as an authoritative reason for belief and action – that is, mediated by *whom* they take themselves to be in light of what they count as being generally authoritative for themselves and why they take themselves to count those things as authoritative – we have a relation of what Hegel calls *spirit*. Spirit – *Geist* – is a *self-conscious* form of life – that is, it is a form of life that has developed various social practices for reflecting on what it takes to be authoritative for itself in terms of whether these practices live up to their own claims and achieve the aims that they set for themselves. Put more metaphorically, spirit is a form of "social space" reflecting on itself as to whether it is satisfactory within its own terms (with what it takes to be the "essence" of things, in Hegel's terms). "Spirit" therefore denotes for Hegel not a metaphysical entity but a fundamental *relation* among persons that mediates their *self-consciousness,* a way in which people reflect on what they have come to take as authoritative for themselves.[14]

Dilemmas arise within a given form of spirit when there are internal problems within that "social space" such that some of these taken-for-granted reasons seem to clash with each other, or when some ways of reasoning within that "social space" quite unexpectedly lead to skepticism about the whole system of reasons itself or about significant parts of it (for example, when a form of life sets certain basic aims for itself that it necessarily fails to satisfy, that is, when that form of life is unsuccessful in its own terms). In these cases, in order to stabilize their sense of who they are, agents seek to affirm for themselves that what they have come to *take* as authoritative reasons *really are* authoritative reasons. Moreover, this activity of affirming that things are in order and that our reason-giving practices are not flawed is aimed at satisfying the desire to affirm for ourselves that we are who we think we are, or that our self-identity is not terribly flawed and irrational, and that the world is therefore fundamentally as we take it to be. These social practices of affirmation and reassurance can take many different shapes – tragic drama, religious practice, philosophical reflection, acting within certain social roles – but they all function as practices through which individuals and communities reflect on their self-generated skeptical reproaches on their form of life and try to reassure themselves that their practices are in order (or with some revision can be put back in order) and that their "social space" is therefore internally lucid.[15]

Since we cannot assume that any one of these "forms of spirit" is correct – we must treat them all as "appearances" – and we cannot assume that we can take a vantage point *outside* any of these "social spaces," we must conduct the theory of knowledge "inside" each of these "formations of consciousness," which of course are also "formations of spirit." Since any putative theory of these reasons (any putative *Wissenschaft*) must itself be treated as *only* an "appearance," it must be treated as a historical phenomenon alongside other historical phenomena. Moreover, no such purely historical phenomenon can claim to be the correct theory (or to be the true *Wissenschaft*) simply by stating that it "works" within its own terms or "fits" better the contemporary scene or matches up to its participants' "intuitions," for that scene and those intuitions are themselves only "appearances" and are the result of many contingent factors.

But even this way of putting matters is itself not sufficiently skeptical, since it begs the question as to why it is *required* that philosophy should be such a *Wissenschaft* at all. (In effect, it makes being a *Wissenschaft* into a hypothetical rather than a categorical imperative.) The usual claims about philosophy's *need* to "ground" things cannot be satisfactory, nor can it be enough to simply *want* philosophy to be a *Wissenschaft* – to have a taste for large, architectural edifices rather than, say, desert landscapes. After all, why is it mandatory for there to be a "grounding" of thought and action at all? And why *that* type of grounding? Why should we not settle for something else, perhaps a kind of humanistic reflection in an essay oriented form, such as Montaigne offered? Or just aphoristic reflections, such as Pascal practiced? On Hegel's terms, to be genuinely skeptical, we should demand of philosophy that it give a non-question-begging account of why it must be a *Wissenschaft* at all, and in general how it can claim whatever authority it claims for itself.

Thus, in the terms that Hegel sets for his thought, he must be able to show why the kind of project that he is attempting – a theory of knowledge that treats everything, including itself, as an "appearance," a "formation of consciousness" – is itself a necessary project, something that "we" (the modern community, his readers) supposedly *require* because of some feature of ourselves. Moreover, not only must "we" be said to require it, this requirement itself must be intelligible to "us" as being more than something "we" just contingently happen to want or desire at this point in our history. Even if we do happen to want it or need it, that wanting and needing must be due to features of ourselves that are not optional for us.

It is therefore important for Hegel to show that alternative accounts of what is to count for us as authoritative are not merely deficient in respect of some particular aim or another; their deficiencies must somehow themselves *lead to* the kind of account that he thinks is the proper one.[16] That is, it would not be enough to gather up alternative explanations of what is to count as authoritative reasons for belief or action and then compare them on some scale of how well they all managed to satisfy some presupposed fundamental aim (for example, matching up with our intuitions in reflective equilibrium, or showing the rationality of science to be continuous with common-sense rationality). If nothing else, that would always leave it open as to the status of the presupposed aim itself, and whether that aim was optional for us. Instead, the other accounts must be shown to be *self-undermining* in such a way that they themselves require the Hegelian account to make sense of themselves. This may mean showing that there is indeed some *aim* that is operative in the practices of those alternative accounts that the Hegelian theory itself better fulfills. But that aim must be shown to *emerge* as a requirement itself, as something that those accounts themselves generate out of their own failures to make good on the terms that they have set for themselves.

Hegel's term for this way of looking at reason-giving activities is *dialectic*. Dialectic looks at *accounts* that forms of life give of what they take to be authoritative for themselves, and how those accounts are transformed in terms of considerations internal to the accounts themselves.[17] Forms of life as "spirit" are constituted by the kinds of self-conscious reflections on what is necessary in that form of life to explain and justify what for that form of life counts as an authoritative reason for belief and action. There is obviously much more in a form of life that does not fall under the category of reason-giving or justification, but the reasons for counting a form of life as a distinct form of "spirit" have to do with the accounts that the people within that form of life give of themselves, what they take to *affirm* for them that their self-conceptions are adequate, and what it is that they take to *reassure* themselves about what they as individuals and as a collective form of life do and accomplish. Thus, a crucial part of the story of these kinds of reflective forms of life concerns how and why it is that they come to take certain kinds of things as justifying what they do, how and why they take certain kinds of skeptical doubts about this to be more serious than others, and how and why *we,* the readers observing those reflective forms of life, can take our accounts as necessary to answer their skeptical doubts. When confronted with self-generated skepticism, a reflective form of life seeks reassurance in the accounts that it gives itself of what is authoritative for it. One of two things happens: either the reassurance is successful, and there is a renewal of that form of life; or it fails, and a new conception of what is authoritative – and thereby a new form of life – is required.

Although treating the theory of knowledge dialectically brings history into the theory of knowledge, doing so is not without its pitfalls. This would have been especially clear to Hegel, since he lived in a time of both growing historicism and of political movements that appealed for their legitimacy to alleged facts about traditions and to the way that, for example, the "Germans" or the "French" did things.[18] As Hegel clearly saw, however, if one explains our being the agents that we are *solely* in terms of historical forces or movements, then one will not be able to answer any questions about whether being these types of agents – whether having adopted these types of reasons – is itself justified. The most one could say is that this is what we have become. In that way, a purely historical argument taken as legitimating anything would only be an example of what Hegel called "positivity," and what Kant called "dogmatism." It would tell us that we are the agents for whom certain types of things and not others count as authoritative reasons, but it could not give us any reassurance that taking these reasons to be authoritative is not, for example, some massive act of self-deception or self-degradation, nor could it assist that form of life in dealing with its own internally generated skepticism about any of these things. If it appeals to something like "tradition" or just asserts *that* we have come to take such and such as authoritative reasons, it cannot even attempt to give an account of *itself* that can show why in any non-question-begging way its own accounts are "better" than other competing accounts. It would only be able to say that we have become these agents because of such and such contingent events in the past.[19]

Therefore, if history is to be brought into philosophy (and, in particular, the theory of knowledge) without its making philosophy into a new form of dogmatism or simply an apology for the status quo, then the purely historical account of the contingencies that have made us who we are must be supplemented by a philosophical – that is, a *dialectical* history of self-consciousness. A dialectical history tells a different story from that of the history of historians in that it does not concern itself primarily with how things came about – what social forces were at work, what contingencies were brought into play – but with showing how succeeding "social spaces" contained resources within themselves that were able to explain and justify themselves over and against earlier alternative accounts and to demonstrate and affirm for themselves that their own accounts of themselves were satisfactory. This dialectical history of self-consciousness is thus also a history of rationality itself. All forms of reason-giving must also be treated as "appearances," and the historical nature of rationality consists in the way in which forms of life develop not only practices for evaluating and criticizing other practices but also develop practices for reflecting on the practices of evaluation themselves.

Such a dialectical history does not claim that the later "formations of consciousness" were "fated" to succeed the earlier forms, or that the earlier forms were "aiming" at the later forms; it claims that only they (or something very much like them) can be seen in retrospect to have *completed* the earlier ones, to have provided a structure that in retrospect may be understood as having worked out the insufficiencies of the earlier ones in such a manner that this later form of life has the resources within it to justify its way of taking things as making up for the insufficiencies of the earlier reflective forms of life.

The very general form of a dialectical progression in the *Phenomenology of Spirit* therefore looks something like this. A reflective form of life takes such and such to be authoritative reasons for belief and action; those types of reasoning then generate within their own terms skeptical objections against themselves (as Hegel puts it, they generate their own "negation"); that form of reflective life, however, turns out to be unable to reassure itself about what it had taken as authoritative for itself; the new form of reflective life that replaces it and claims to complete it, however, takes *its* accounts of what *for it* have come to be authoritative reasons to be that which was necessary to successfully resolve the issues that were self-undermining for the older form of life; but this new reflective form of life in turn generates self-undermining skepticism about its own accounts, and the progression continues.[20] The necessity to be found in the dialectical history of self-consciousness therefore is not a causal necessity but something more like the necessity to be found in a line of argument. Just as only some kinds of things can complete a certain line of argument, only some types of things can complete a dialectical historical progression. The failures of certain accounts require that other very specific types of accounts be given, if those failures are to be avoided, and if the later account is to be said to be a resolution of the earlier account. Of course, for contingent reasons, the progression may not be completed. Just as I may fail to complete a certain line of thought for contingent reasons – I may die before I finish it, I may be rendered incapable of completing it, or I may come to find that completing that line of thought is not important to me anymore – a historical progression may for contingent reasons fail to be completed. Contingent failure to complete a line of thought does not, however, show that such and such was not therefore required to complete that line of thought.[21]

The *Phenomenology* offers a dialectical-historical narrative of how the European community has come to take what it does as authoritative and definitive for itself.[22] These other accounts are not confined to purely philosophical accounts but constitute all the ways in which "spirit" can appear: as art, as politics, as "high culture," as social critique, as religion, as science, and so on. In tracing out this dialectical history, Hegel also wishes to show how the tension between the ways individuals take things from their own personal point of view and how they take things to be justified from a more impersonal point of view lead them to revise their own self-conceptions and how they try to fit their personal accounts of their lives into the larger narrative that they take to be going on in their community.

Now it is clear that for Hegel, even something like this dialectical schema itself cannot simply be assumed without further question, for it rests on the idea that we *need* to give accounts of what we are doing, that we are *motivated* to alter those accounts when they generate self-undermining considerations and so on. But, again, for Hegel's program to remain true to the aims it sets for itself, it must pose the same kind of question: Why is dialectic not something optional for us? What is insufficient with our simply "carrying on in the same way," as it sometimes seems that Wittgenstein recommends, or with our not bothering as to whether all our reasons are in order, or with simply ignoring all the difficulties? For Hegel it would just beg the question to say that our "nature" demands answers to such questions, or that it is the "essence" of humanity to have such needs.

It is incumbent on Hegel therefore to provide an account that shows how such "carrying on in the same way," "giving reasons to others," and similar practices themselves necessarily lead to the kind of account-giving that dialectic seems to presuppose. This is indeed the main task of the first three sections of the *Phenomenology.* The work opens by showing how certain post-Enlightenment attempts at a description of our awareness of things in terms of some kind of direct awareness of the objects of consciousness undermine themselves, and within their own terms turn into quite different types of descriptions. It also tries to show how the attempt to salvage that idea by an appeal to the reflective "understanding's" description of supersensible entities itself becomes contradictory and antinomial, with the reflective "understanding's" claim that it consistently describes the world thereby also undermining itself. Since what "Consciousness" took to be a straightforward description of the world turned out to be antinomial, it finds that it must *reflect* on the accounts it gives itself. "Consciousness" thereby becomes *self-consciousness* in trying to give an account of how it could possibly grasp the world as it took it to be.

In each case, so Hegel tries to show in the *Phenomenology,* there is an element of teleology at work in that the schema of "skepticism, attempts at reassurance, and the ultimate insufficiency of the accounts" motivates a move to a different account that itself is justified only in terms of its overcoming the insufficiencies of the preceding ones. But at the beginning of the *Phenomenology* (in the chapters on "Consciousness") it is necessarily stated as an epistemological and not a historical point. Hegel's argument for the necessity of a historical account arises only out of the self-undermining failures of these supposedly non-historical accounts. Those offered in terms of some kind of direct awareness of objects or self-sufficient practical activity turn out to be insufficient and require an appeal to "impersonal reason" – the "view from nowhere," to use Thomas Nagel's term[23] – but all the different kinds of appeals to an "impersonal reason" that supposedly transcends all particular social practices turn out to fail on the terms that they set for themselves and to imply that they themselves must be understood as historically embedded forms of reflective social practice – for example, the failure of the otherwise successful methods of modern science to provide foundational answers to social and personal conflicts; or the failure of those claims about individual belief and action that do not appeal self-consciously to *norms* but to some fixed "inner quality" of ourselves, such as Faustian self-determination, emotionalist religion, or the activities involving the character ideal of the detached yet sincere "gentleman," the *honnête homme* of early modern French culture. Each turns out not to be the consequence of the application of "impersonal reason." Instead each turns out to be a specific historical "formation of consciousness," something intelligible only when seen in its historical context and in terms of the ways it tried to redress the historical insufficiencies of its predecessors, to realize their aims without falling prey to the ways they undermined themselves.

In the opening chapters of the *Phenomenology,* therefore, Hegel takes himself to have given an account of how spirit comes to see itself as *necessarily* being historical without at the outset *presupposing* that it must be historical. Or to put it a different way, we, the modern readers whom Hegel takes as his audience, come to see that the mandatory nature of some norms involves an account of their role in a complex set of reflective and non-reflective social practices – *Geist,* "spirit" – and that the attempt to explain the normative character of these social practices by appeal to some kind of direct awareness of objects, self-sufficient practice, impersonal reason or inner quality fails and must be supplanted by a historical account of those reflective social practices.

In this way, history, as a story of a sequence of events that are linked together in terms of their being parts of an overall account of how such and such came to be authoritative for a community, is possible only in terms of the development of *Geist* – that is, of the development of such reflective social practices. To understand the development of a social practice is to understand the development of its norms, and while there can certainly be causal accounts of how norms develop (in terms of historical causation, the diffusion of knowledge, the effects of new modes of production, and so on), an account of norms *as* norms is not causal but is itself normative. It is an account of how one set of norms fails at achieving its aims, how it undermines itself or is undermined by the acceptance of other norms – in other words, how it fails or succeeds on normative grounds itself. Indeed, we, the readers, thereby come to see that *Geist,* self-reflective social practice, makes *history* – as distinct from mere succession in time – *possible* through *Geist's* (spirit's) reflections on what in its past was insufficient and how those insufficiencies point in the direction of what could be authoritative about later sets of activities and practices.

Hegel's characterization of the problem of knowledge as that of taking all claims, even its own, as "appearances" thus comes full circle. The theory of knowledge must be historical, and the history of our claim-making activities must have developed within itself a series of practices for reflecting on the practices themselves, on what it means in general to be a legitimate ground of knowledge, and what it means to be a rational agent. This historicized theory of knowledge, which takes itself as simply an "appearance," is thus self-referential, and it must therefore be able to work out how it is that it can come to take itself as underwriting its own claims not by appeal to any transcendent entities or "essences" but only by appeal to its own free-standing practices and the way in which reason – as the principles for evaluating those practices in terms of their own internal normative structure – has itself historically developed.[24]

It is part of Hegel's thesis that reassurance about the intelligibility of those definitive norms is an especially difficult task for the late modern period. Whereas what was authoritative for earlier periods could be presented and justified through relatively succinct and compact accounts related, for example, to early religious practices, what is authoritative for moderns cannot be so neatly presented. Modern life's demands are also of sufficient complexity and its practices are sufficiently reflective so that its "spirit" cannot be fully presented in works of art or in religious rituals and symbols. Moreover, the complexity of modern practice makes it difficult to see how the terms of one practice do not simply conflict with and therefore undermine the terms of other practices (to see why, for example, the "demands" of career do not simply conflict with the "demands" of family life, and to see why one is not therefore simply forced to intuitively balance the claims of one over the other or simply to blindly choose one or the other). The intelligibility and justifiability of modern norms therefore always seem to be in question. This is the "negativity" of modern life.

In Hegel's own day, this "negativity" of modern life had itself been exacerbated by the image that had arisen among Hegel's immediate predecessors of an earlier form of life, the Athenian Greeks, as offering a clear, if unattainable, alternative to modern life. Competing alongside that idealized image of the Athenian Greeks was an idealized image of the Middle Ages as a time of tranquillity, reconciliatory religious faith, and a common purpose to life. For those who believed that neither a return to Athens nor to medieval Europe was in order, there was also a cacophony of other alternatives, many claiming to be distinctively "modern": post-Enlightenment social and religious thought, pietist religious revival, doctrines of revolutionary freedom, and romantic enthusiasms about the personal exploration of the "self."

Coming to terms with modern life therefore requires a dialectical history of European reflective social practice, of European *Geist* itself. This tracking of the history of the development of reflective social practice leads us, the readers, from the way that the form of life of the ancient Athenian Greeks undermined itself to the denouement of the classical world in Roman life. That denouement set the stage for the way in which medieval conceptions of faith and chivalry led to the self-undermining nature of the early modern aristocratic ethos and the ensuing experience of "groundlessness" in early modern European life. The movements of religious renewal in the seventeenth and eighteenth centuries and the eighteenth century intellectual movement known as the Enlightenment attempted to respond to the problems brought on by that early modern experience of "groundlessness," but the insufficiencies of both religious renewal and Enlightenment practice to resolve those problems necessitated the transformation of the early modern experience of "groundlessness" into the fully modern project of *self-grounding,* which itself then assumed several different forms: the French Revolution, modern subjectivistic accounts of autonomy and morality, and modern romantic inquiries into first-person experiences of the self.[25] In constructing the path that those various reflective forms of life have retrospectively been seen to have taken, we find not only that each such "formation of consciousness" is intelligible only in terms of the historical insufficiencies of the preceding "formations of consciousness," but that these "formations of consciousness" have left remnants of themselves in all the succeeding "formations of consciousness" such that the intelligibility of each – and of our own – is possible *only* in terms of the intelligibility of *all* of its predecessors.

Strikingly, Hegel argues that the modern European "spirit" can come to terms with the path it has taken and the place it has ended up only by understanding the sense of religiosity it has also developed along the way, and by finally understanding this sense of religiosity itself in terms of what he calls "absolute knowing": that culmination of the *Phenomenology of Spirit* in which a full reconciliation of modern humanity with itself is seen to be possible. Having come down the "path of despair," the modern community thus turns out to be the "self-consummating skepticism" that has within it the reflective resources to be able to continually renew itself against its own self-generated forms of skepticism.

The *Phenomenology* thus serves the task of forming and educating the modern European community into comprehending that its form of life is "spirit," that the European "spirit" has the shape it does only by virtue of the accounts that it has historically given to itself of what it has taken to be authoritative for itself, and that the kind of historicized account it must now give of itself is possible only because the historical insufficiencies of its previous accounts have themselves exhibited a kind of retrospectively understood teleology within its entire history. Accordingly, the *Phenomenology* is supposed to take its readers, the participants in the modern European community's form of life, through the past "formations of consciousness" of the European "spirit" – the ways in which that "spirit" has both taken the "essence" of things to be and the ways in which it has taken agents to be cognitively related to that "essence" – and demonstrate to them that *they require* the kind of account which the *Phenomenology* as a whole provides, that the *Phenomenology's* project is therefore not optional for them but intrinsic to their sense of who they are.[26] Thus, the *Phenomenology* serves as the *Bildung* (the education, formation, and cultivation) of its intended readership into coming to terms with what is entailed in their form of life and what kinds of alternatives are available to them. The conclusion of the *Phenomenology* thus originates for Hegel the project of showing how this is concretely to be carried out, and the "Berlin system" of Hegel's later days shows us how he attempted to fulfill this task.

The reconstruction of this ambitious Hegelian project is the goal of this book.

3. Notes on the text

One of the major difficulties in looking at the *Phenomenology* is the lack of an adequate translation of the book. Unlike Norman Kemp Smith's translation of Kant's *Critique of Pure Reason,* neither John Baillie's nor A.V. Miller's translation can be used for a close reading of the text unless one also consults the German original. There are too many technical terms in Hegel's work such as *Fürsichsein* (Being-for-self) and *Ansichsein* (Being-in-itself) that are translated in too many different ways for the reader to be able to mount a close reading of the English text. In Miller's translation (the one I am using here), *Ansichsein* is sometimes rendered as "being-in-itself," sometimes as "implicit," sometimes as "intrinsic being," and sometimes as "in principle." Likewise, Miller translates *Aufheben* alternately as (among others) "supersession," "do away with", "canceled," "nullify" (p. 133), "set aside" (p. 133), "lost" (p. 246), "not self-subsistent," (p. 393), "subordinated" (p. 313), "put aside" (p. 357), "stripped" (p. 433), "puts an end to" (p. 435), and "suspended" (p. 474). *Wirklichkeit* is sometimes rendered as "reality," sometimes as "actuality," while *Realität* is always rendered as "reality." *Wesen* is sometimes rendered as "essence," "essential Being," "entity," "Being," "divine Being," and "nature." Since "essence" is Hegel's term for what a particular *Gestaltung* of consciousness takes to be authoritative for itself, these differing translations of "essence" make it difficult for the English-speaking reader to follow how Hegel is arguing for changes in the conception of what a *Gestaltung* takes as authoritative. Every now and then, whole phrases are omitted. Miller's translation of both *Entgegengesetzte* and *Gegensatze* as "antithesis" unfortunately gives sustenance to the ongoing myth (started by the deservedly forgotten Heinrich Moritz Chalybäus) of Hegel's system as consisting of some oddly formal triumvirate of "Thesis, Antithesis and Synthesis" (terms that Hegel himself never uses and that also completely mischaracterize his thought).[27] Anybody trying therefore to pursue a close reading of the text only by relying on the English translation has a difficult task. This is surely enough to put off many people for good, as if one is telling them that either they have to learn German very well or they should not try. The sad fact, however, is that it is at the present impossible to do a really close reading of Hegel's *Phenomenology* without knowing some German (or at least consulting Jean Hyppolite's excellent French translation). Worse, there is no consistency of terminology among the various translations of Hegel's different books, and this makes a comparison of the *Phenomenology* with other English editions of Hegel's works especially difficult. It is fair to say that this seriously hampers both Hegel scholarship and the wider understanding of Hegel's thought.

I have therefore altered Miller's translation whenever I thought he got the meaning wrong and where a better meaning could be found. Sometimes these changes are enough to make the new sentence look quite a bit different from the old sentence; I have nonetheless continued to give the page on which Miller's translation can be found even when I have altered it quite a bit. (Since all citations to the Miller translation are to the paragraph number, the reader should have no difficulty locating these transformed sentences.) Sometimes I have opted for consistency of translation at the expense of literalness. For example, I try to translate *Gestalt* consistently as "formation", instead of "shape" or "form". The term *"Gestalt"* means "shape" or "form," but Hegel uses it in a sense in which Goethe uses it to denote a fundamental way in which individualities have a fundamental formation (or *Gestalt*) to them that gives the "parts" (or *moments,* in Hegel's terms) their characteristic determinateness. This is the sense in which "Gestalt" is used in the idea of "Gestalt Psychology." The English term "formation" has the connotation of being the external ordering of discrete parts, and thus in this way is not ideal; but neither is "shape." Thus, the reader is warned to look at the term "formation" as having this special sense. (In those few places where "formation" makes no sense, I have also supplied the German word in parentheses.) I have always rendered *Bestimmtheit* as "determinateness." *Bestimmtheit* is Hegel's general term for the *features* of anything; the term is meant to be neutral as to what type of feature is in question: qualitative, quantitative, relational, inferential, and so on. I have also altered Miller's translation in all cases where it was necessary to maintain terminological consistency. Thus, I have always rendered *Wesen* as "essence," *Fürsichsein* as "being-for-self," *Ansichsein* as "being-in-itself," and *Wirklichkeit* as "actuality." I have rendered all occurrences of *Aufheben* as "sublate," and noted the places where I do not.[28] In many cases where I have altered the Miller translation, I have supplied the German words in parentheses; in some cases even where I did not alter the translation, I supply the German term because I am uneasy about the translation but cannot come up with a better alternative. I hope that this satisfies the curiosity of those who, like me, often want to know what the relevant German terms are in these kind of instances. I have also taken the liberty of altering all other cited translations of Hegel's texts to maintain a terminological consistency.

I have almost completely avoided using quotations in the body of the book in order to keep the line of thought smooth and unbroken and thereby to make the text more readable. To indicate to the reader which of Hegel's texts I am discussing, I have supplied references in the notes. In the quotations from the *Phenomenology,* I give the paragraph number in the Miller translation and the German page number from the Hoffmeister edition (Felix Meiner Verlag) of the *Phänomenologie des Geistes* (abbreviated as *PG*). Often I cite one or more sentences from the passage in question, usually to help the reader get a sense of exactly to which point in the passage I am referring in the citation. This is not because I think that the sentence quoted is entirely on its own supposed to support the interpretation I am giving; it is rather to indicate the paragraph or the general place in the paragraph on which the reading is based.

I have tried to deal with the thorny problems of gender-neutral pronouns by simply using "he" and its cognates at some points. Having experimented with alternating the use of "he" and "she," I found that the results were simply too distracting for the reader. This decision is not intended to suggest (even subtly) that the actors in history really are just the "he's" (despite the fact that Hegel himself unfortunately held something like this view).

2

The claims to self-sufficient knowledge: sense-certainty, perception, understanding

1. Sense-certainty

What would immediate knowledge be?

It has often seemed puzzling to both the casual and the initiated reader of Hegel's *Phenomenology* that a book whose longest portions seem to concern themselves with cultural, social, and ethical issues begins with some very abstruse chapters on the nature of consciousness, perception, and theory-formation instead of simply beginning with various problems relating to social self-identity or problems in the philosophy of religion. Yet Hegel insists in the introduction to the *Phenomenology* that it offers a theory of knowledge, and that such a beginning is necessary for it.

The most obvious reason for Hegel to begin the *Phenomenology* with the chapters that he does is his professed belief that any philosophical system must begin without any presuppositions and develop everything out of that presuppositionless beginning. (Thus, just as the *Science of Logic* begins with "pure being," the *Phenomenology* begins with "sense-certainty.") However, the more basic and systemic reasons for the introductory sections to take the form that they do have to do with Hegel's general aim in the *Phenomenology* to show that a wide variety of things, ranging from the rituals involved in Greek religious cults to the French Revolution, are in fact best understood as forms of knowledge (as what Hegel calls "formations of consciousness" – that is, as ways in which forms of life take certain types of reasons to be authoritative, mandatory for themselves), and, likewise, that all claims to knowledge are best understood as historically situated forms of social practice in which agents seek to affirm for themselves that the structures of their own thought and practice really match up with the way things are, or have to be. This overall aim gives Hegel two basic reasons for beginning with the chapters that he does. First, this overall aim is by no means a self-evident truth, and there are in fact many very powerful philosophical tendencies to deny such a claim. Indeed, at first glance, this general aim would strike those of a more empiricist bent as being almost self-evidently false. From the standpoint of an empiricist point of view (or from that of the post-empiricist points of view present in Hegel's day), it surely seems that we do indeed *know* certain things quite independently of any particular social practice and, moreover, that this kind of knowledge-independent-of-social-practice can serve as a kind of "touchstone," "standard," or "foundation" (depending on which metaphor one chooses) for all our other claims to know something. Thus, it might seem, for example, that we are directly acquainted with certain types of sensory objects independently of whether we are ancient Greeks or nineteenth-century Germans, and that this direct acquaintance with such objects gives us a knowledge of them. Or that we directly perceive certain types of objects in our immediate environments whether we are French or Chinese, and that this perception gives us a knowledge of these objects. Or, finally, and maybe more ambitiously, that there is a basic metaphysical essence to the world that any human being possessing the powers of rational reflection could come to know independently of the social practices or even perhaps the historical situation in which he participates. However, Hegel wishes to show in his introductory sections that the major candidates for the kinds of knowledge that presumably could be secured independently of any historically definite social practice (which he calls "sense-certainty," "perception" and the "understanding") fail to provide *on their own terms* the kind of knowledge that their proponents claim that they provide.

Second, Hegel wishes to show that the basic candidates for such knowledge logically lead to and culminate in what we can call the subject/object model of knowledge and practice: a picture of our epistemic practices and our various practical endeavors that interprets them in terms of a subject, an independent object, and a representation (*Vorstellung*) that supposedly serves as a metaphysical intermediary between the subject and the object. On this view (which, following recent fashion, we can call the *representationalist* picture of knowledge), the so-called "problem of knowledge" comes to be the issue of how we might determine whether these representations "match up" with the world as it is. Hegel's second goal therefore in the three introductory sections is to show that such a picture also *on its own terms* fails to fulfill the goals that it sets for itself. Thus, by showing how the three available candidates for a kind of knowledge that would be independent of social practice break down, Hegel attempts to show how the view of ourselves as "metaphysical representers" of the world undermines itself and leads to the view of ourselves as organisms engaged in certain forms of historically mediated social practices whose general goal is the affirmation for ourselves that what we have historically come to *take* as true and right *really* is true and right. The problems intrinsic to a picture of ourselves as thinking substances inspecting the contents of our consciousness (our representations) to see if they match up with the world both leads to and gives way to a view of ourselves as being situated in a reflective form of life (or what Hegel calls *spirit*) that is in part constituted by a set of ends and beliefs that determine for the agents who participate in that form of life what is to count as knowledge, what is to count as a standard of right action and what is to count as a legitimate form of character. The rest of the *Phenomenology* then articulates and argues for the view that within various forms of life (of "spirit"), there are tensions and contradictions that in the historical development of that form of life come to the forefront of its practices and thereby appear in the self-consciousness of its members; and that out of this form of self-consciousness arise other types of practices whose purpose is to reflect on social practices in general, to see whether within the terms set by that form of life, the participants of that form of life can possibly affirm for themselves collectively and individually that what they take to be true, real, and right actually is what is true, real, and right. The view that Hegel defends in the *Phenomenology* – of ourselves as organisms dealing with the world in a variety of historically and socially mediated ways, in contrast to the view of ourselves as "thinking substances" who "represent" the world – allows Hegel to shift the basic epistemological task away from constructing metaphysical theories about how our representations might possibly match up with the world toward one in which the basic issue comes to be how we have come to *take ourselves* as being the agents that we have come to be, and how we come to take certain types of "grounds" as authoritative for belief and action. Thus, the overall goal of the first three sections is to motivate a shift of philosophical inquiry away from the kind of metaphysical epistemological concerns that have dominated much of modern philosophy toward the kind of social and historical epistemological concerns that Hegel thinks are more proper to a fully modernist philosophy.[1]

One way of beginning with the "immediate" would be to begin with those kinds of considerations that the readers of 1807 would have already taken for granted as authoritative for themselves. The *Phenomenology* would then begin with those considerations that count for its readers as obvious, certain, and as being the "essence" (in the sense of being the "authoritative grounds") of their beliefs. In Hegel's time, that would mean beginning with what certain post-Enlightenment theories of knowledge, perception, and theory construction took to be "certain," "obvious" (and therefore "immediate"). By beginning with these kinds of taken-for-granted considerations, Hegel is of course not denying or making himself blind to the ways in which these kinds of empiricist and post-empiricist conceptions have their own history. However, the *Phenomenology* cannot begin with their history, because given the terms that the *Phenomenology* has set for itself, such a beginning would beg the question. The *Phenomenology* cannot simply assume contrary to these post-Enlightenment conceptions that an account of knowledge *must* be historical; it must instead show that these non-historical conceptions of knowledge both undermine themselves and lead to a conception of knowledge as historical. Later in the *Phenomenology* (in the section on the Enlightenment that comes under the large section-heading titled "Spirit"), Hegel will show how what seemed obvious and immediate to the readers of 1807 – and what is therefore the "immediate" beginning of a chapter on "consciousness" – rests in fact on a conception of knowledge and rationality whose own plausibility is itself the result of the historical insufficiencies of preceding accounts.[2] On the terms that Hegel has set for the *Phenomenology,* however, it must begin as if the history of those conceptions were irrelevant or as if they had no history in order to motivate the account that will lead to our understanding their historical nature.

It thus is quite natural that the *Phenomenology of Spirit* would begin with an examination of some kind of claim to immediate knowledge that would grow out of a reflection on our natural awareness of ourselves and things.

This immediate (non-inferential) knowledge (if it is possible) would be an example of something that we know without having to know anything else; no inferences would be necessary in order to validate it, and it would therefore be knowledge that would be available to any agent independent of his social or historical setting. By a "natural consciousness," Hegel means a kind of pre-reflective view of ourselves in the world as one natural entity among others. Other ideas of ourselves – for example, as "subjects" of awareness – might be introduced later, but we cannot begin our reflections with such ideas, for that would involve importing some controversial conceptions into the discussion at the outset. Since ideas such as "subject of awareness" are introduced as theoretical constructions to explicate or explain how it is that such and such a form of life is possible, at the beginning of a work like the *Phenomenology* we should eschew such theoretical descriptions as much as possible. (It will turn out, as any reader of the *Phenomenology* knows, that Hegel believes such an eschewal to be in fact impossible; but it is a central Hegelian point that it must be shown and not assumed.) A description of our natural consciousness of the world would be something like the following: "We are aware of certain things such that we know them to be such and such." The first question to be asked therefore would be: What is it that we *know* in such awareness in "natural consciousness"? Better: Is there anything that we know in this "natural consciousness" *immediately* (non-inferentially) – that is, something that we can know without having to know anything else? If there were to be any knowledge that is independent of social practice or history, such immediate knowledge would be it. We must therefore begin with "a knowledge of the immediate or of the *existing* (*Seienden*)."[3] If there is anything in our awareness of the world that is immediate, then we would have an object of awareness from which no abstraction has been made; we would apprehend it as it really is, without any contribution from our own side.

Sense-certainty as immediate knowledge

Hegel calls this natural awareness of things in the world *sense-certainty*. In sense-certainty, we are certain that we are sensing an individual object, independently of whatever other claims that we might later wish to make about it, and this sensing of the object supposedly gives us a knowledge of it. Sense-certainty thus makes a claim to being a form of knowledge that is independent of social practice or historical context; it is immediate knowledge in that it involves knowing something without having to know about anything else. It should remain steadfast throughout the other changes that we make in our epistemic setup. We may come to believe, for example, that we should abandon Ptolemaic astronomy in favor of more Newtonian views, and we might come to believe that Jehovah is the real deity and Vishnu only a figment of our own construction; but throughout all these kinds of changes of our epistemic claims, we should never find that we have to alter any of our claims about what we are immediately aware of in sense-certainty.

Sense-certainty involves the following: I, an individual *sensor*, am sensorily aware of an individual object.[4] But what exactly are we certain of in sense-certainty? We are certain of the *object* that we sense in that we may be said to be *directly acquainted* with the individual object itself. But how should we describe this object?[5] What can we say with certainty about this individual item except that it *is* and that we are directly acquainted with it? To *say* anything about what the object is would involve us in ascribing various predicates to it, which we could not in turn assert with the same certainty. (We might say that it is round, only to find that it is really oblong, or that it is black, only to find that it is really blue.) It would seem, then, that the object of sense-certainty can only be a purely singular object, the kind of thing to which we can only refer with demonstratives such as "this," "here," and "now." The truth about sense-certainty, so it seems, is that it "contains nothing but the *being* of the thing [*Sache*]."[6]

It is all too easy at this point to misinterpret what Hegel is doing here by anachronistically reading into the argument certain twentieth-century Anglo-American philosophical themes about so-called non-inferential knowledge of sense-data. It would be only too easy to jump to the idea that the *object* of sense-certainty must be something like a sense-datum, an awareness of a specific mental object having certain sensuous qualities. While this understanding of sense-certainty might be compatible with many of Hegel's points, that is not the argument he is making there. The introduction of the idea of sense-data (as the authentic *objects* of sensuous consciousness) is the result of a theory of what the objects *must* be if there were to be the kind of immediate awareness that sense-certainty claims to provide. If we believe that there is indeed something of which we are immediately aware, then we might *postulate* sense-data (as a set of mental objects) as being the proper objects of sense-certainty in order to account for the possibility of such awareness. In the beginning of the *Phenomenology*, however, we are supposed to be describing natural consciousness as it immediately takes itself, and not yet postulating entities to explain it. At this point, we are only entitled to say: We are immediately aware of a singular object, this awareness seems to be both non-inferential and complete, and this consciousness *is* just its direct acquaintance with this singular object and nothing more. There is no expressible difference between our consciousness and the object of which we are conscious. Thus, it seems that what we have here is a relation between two items: an individual item (*eine Sache*) and an individual I.[7] It remains completely open as to *what* this individual object of awareness might be and what this "I" might be. Perhaps only a sense-datum would fill the role of "object" adequately; perhaps something else would fit the role better. Hegel takes the important point to be whether there even is such a role to be filled.

The object of sense-certainty thus seems only to be describable as an existent individual. We cannot even *say* of it that it is such and such, for we cannot be certain of that – or at least we cannot be certain of anything we *say* about it, since saying anything about it would involve using descriptions, which would violate the condition of immediacy; we can only say that it *is*. The object of sense-certainty therefore must be something simple and undescribable. Thus, the kind of immediate knowledge of which we are speaking must be (1) knowledge of pure individuals, and (2) knowledge construed as the immediate presence of an object to consciousness. Consciousness taken as sense-certainty is the awareness only of the *being* of things, and beyond that, we can say nothing about it.

Is this, however, an intelligible idea? Is sense-certainty even a *possible* form of consciousness? (If it is not, then we need not, for example, go to the trouble of postulating sense-data to explain *how* it is possible.) The problems with it begin to be clearly seen when one tries to characterize this immediate knowledge of an individual entity and to articulate in just what this knowledge consists. Assume that we are aware of existing individuals. If we describe the general form of this non-inferential awareness as "awareness of purely individual things," then it seems that it has at least two components to it: (1) the individual perceiver, and (2) the individual object perceived. Each – the "I" and the individual object – are equally pure singularities. We need not presume anything about what this "I" is or what this object is; we need not presume, for example, that the "I" is a mental substance, a subject of experience, or a natural organism, nor whether the object is a sense-datum or an entity in space and time.[8] We need only recognize that we have two types of singular objects: an "I" and an object of awareness.

Now it would seem, though, on reflection, that it is the *object* of awareness that is the crucial element here. After all, objects in themselves have a determinateness on their own, and we are aware of them truthfully when we are aware of them as they are in themselves.[9] The object is what is authoritative in this relation of knowledge; it is, in Hegel's terms, the "essence." However, in attempting to describe the pure individual object as it is in itself, we find that we can only directly *attend* to it without being able to *say* much about it. (That is, we can *mean* it, in the sense of the German, *"meinen,"* without being able to articulate it.)

Hegel offers two different accounts of this kind of direct attention. First, we can *point* at it through the use of what we nowadays would call indexicals (terms whose reference varies with the context of their utterance, such as "this," "here," and "now").[10] Hegel's discussion of indexicals in this context takes up the most room in the text and hence has been the subject of the most commentary.[11] In his discussion of these indexicals, Hegel has often been taken to be arguing that since the referent of "this" varies with the context, it follows that "this" must be a universal. Thus, if the content of sense-certainty is a "this," then "it is in fact the universal that is the truth (*das Wahre*) of sense-certainty."[12] This has led many people to criticize Hegel for seeming to argue that because their reference varies, indexicals are universals; the objection to this alleged Hegelian argument is that universals are things that can be *predicated* of many different individuals, whereas indexicals are not *predicates* at all. Thus, it is often concluded that Hegel had made a simple error here. The conclusion that indexicals are universals is not, however, Hegel's point. What is crucial for characterizing the object of "sense-certainty" is its *singularity,* its "this-here-nowness." As Willem deVries has argued, Hegel's point here is that the here-and-nowness of the object of "sense-certainty" is supposed to exhaust the object of awareness; there is no more to it other than its this-here-nowness.[13] The problem that Hegel sees with the arguments of "sense-certainty" is not that "indexicals are universals" but that the *object* of which sense-certainty is supposed to be aware alters according to the context of the utterance; "this" can pick out at this moment (at this "now") the page in front of me and then later pick out the pen I am holding. Because of the way in which the objects of sense-certainty vary, Hegel's point is that the use of demonstratives ("this," "here," and "now") share with the use of singular descriptive reference (such as "the cat in the hat") the features of being mediated by "universals" – that is, being linked up with other sets of descriptions and therefore being forms of mediate knowledge.[14]

Hegel later expressed some misgivings about this introduction of indexicals at this stage of the argument in the Jena *Phenomenology of Spirit*. Since the use of indexicals presupposes the inferential knowledge of space and time, using them to prove that this so-called immediate, non-inferential knowledge is really inferential knowledge would be circular.[15] Moreover, the objections concerning the use of indexicals could be easily avoided by the proponents of sense-certainty if they were to claim that the objects of sense-certainty (whatever they might be) are not in fact spatiotemporal objects at all (maybe they are sense-data), and therefore perhaps cannot be picked out by linguistic expressions at all.

But while that kind of move might meet some of the objections raised by Hegel in the first part of the section on sense-certainty, it would fail to meet his second and perhaps more crucial point, which has to do with the way in which this experiential attending to the singular objects of sense-certainty is an attending to ineffable individual *qualities*. Hegel speaks of the difference between what we *think* we are *saying* when we say that sense-certainty is an immediate awareness of individual objects and what we *really* are saying when we do so. If we cannot refer to or describe these things linguistically, then they must be beyond language and be completely unutterable, ineffable. Linguistic expression of this awareness is therefore impossible, since any linguistic expression of it will involve terms that link up with other terms or, as in the case of indexicals, with other forms of descriptions. If they cannot be referred to by means of demonstrative reference, perhaps they can be *named*. However, that will not work, since names have no cognitive content unless they are put into propositions to form judgments. If they cannot be expressed linguistically, then they cannot be put into propositional form, which means they cannot serve as premises for any argument. They would thus be without any cognitive significance. The upshot is that if the objects of sense-certainty are ineffable, then they cannot be expressed linguistically, and therefore they cannot preserve their status as objects of *immediate knowledge*. In stressing linguistic expression as a criterion of what we can be said to *know* (or to have a *cognitive* awareness of), Hegel is arguing that we are driven to the conclusion that we cannot be *cognitively* aware of these qualitative individuals in any non-inferential fashion; we are aware of them only as mediated through certain universals found in linguistic expression.[16] Thus, if we cannot be said to be cognitively aware of them, they cannot function as objects of non-inferential *knowledge*.[17]

The rest of the discussion of the chapter on sense-certainty repeats this argument with two other attempts at saving the idea of a cognitively significant awareness of individual objects. One such attempt is to see the object of awareness as the individual *awareness* itself, but that fails for the same reasons. Another is the attempt to see neither the object nor the individual awareness itself as the object of immediate knowledge, but the complex, "individual awareness of an individual object" as something that we non-inferentially know.[18] But this too fails for the same reasons.

In fact, the upshot of sense-certainty is that there is no *cognitively* significant *immediate* awareness of objects of any kind and therefore no immediate knowledge in the sense that "sense-certainty" originally claimed. Even if we could be said to be non-inferentially aware in some non-linguistic sense of any such objects, they would still be ineffable and thus be without any cognitive import. Of the idea that there might be an ineffable given element in experience with some cognitive import, Hegel says: "What is called the unutterable is nothing else than the untrue, the irrational, what is merely meant but is not actually expressed."[19]

Hegel's point here seems to be: If you can't *say* it or *show* it, you don't *know* it.[20] Sense-certainty turns out not to be so certain, and the most basic form of cognitively significant awareness thus turns out not to be an immediate awareness of singular objects whose nature is to be "this-here-now." It turns out to be a mediated awareness of individuals as having general properties. Sense-certainty, that is, turns out really to be what Hegel calls *perception*.

The determinateness of the purest form of awareness, it turns out, is already mediated by other factors than just what at first *seems* to be included in the awareness itself. The awareness of the pure *contents of sense* turns out really to be an awareness of *things*. If there were such an area of mental awareness that could be known non-inferentially, then it is conceivable that the contents of that awareness might remain the same whatever the state of the world might be; our experience of seeing a chair that actually exists might be qualitatively the same even if the chair were not to exist. This would lead, of course, to that kind of modern skepticism familiar to readers of modern philosophy in which the contents of the mind are conceived as having some determinateness that is independent of the world such that it makes sense to ask whether our various types of awareness of the world might be globally wrong – whether the world might be one thing, and the contents of our minds might be another thing. But if our knowledge of our purest form of awareness is already a mediated (inferential) knowledge – if awareness of sense-contents is just an abstraction from our awareness of things – then it makes no sense to imagine that we could vary the things of the world and still have the contents of our own awareness remain the same. Hegel's discussion of sense-certainty is intended to be the first step in his argument that the mind is not some self-illuminated sphere for which there is the basic metaphysical problem of how it could possibly be linked up with the world; in its most basic cognitive form, it is already linked to the objects of perception.

2. Perception

Individual things and general properties

The case for sense-certainty as an immediate knowledge of individuals turns out in fact to be the case for something else – namely, *perception* as a mediated awareness of individual objects having general properties. The claim that we are non-inferentially aware of pure individuals turns out not to be possible; what we really have is mediated knowledge of the objects of perception. We distinguish one object from another by means of inferential connections; in its most meager form, this involves designating something as "this" and "not that" (what Hegel will later call "pure difference," which is one of the "pure essentialities," the formal characteristics of thought[21]). Sense-certainty, or purely sensuous consciousness in general, turns out really to be an abstraction from the more determinate *perceptual* consciousness of objects.[22]

If perception is the mediated awareness of individuals via universals (such as "cubical," "green," and so on), then it would seem that the objects of perception would not be the pure singularities of sense-certainty but what we would ordinarily term individual *things* with many *properties*.[23] The basis of perceptual consciousness would therefore not be that of an individual sensor sensing a purely singular item; it would be the awareness of the objects of perception as a complex of general properties and individual things, and everything else would be just an abstraction from that complex. Sense consciousness itself would be only a special case of such perception.[24] Hegel's thesis is that this kind of characterization of perception, innocent as it may sound at first, ends up in a predicament very similar to that which we found in sense-certainty. "Perception" claims to offer a form of knowledge that is self-contained; those who claim that *purely* perceptual experience is a form of knowledge therefore must claim that this knowledge requires nothing else outside of perceptual experience itself, and that it is able to give a full account of itself by utilizing only the resources available in perceptual experience itself. In purely perceptual experience we should be able to *know* the individual objects of perception without having to know anything else; what will result from the dialectic of perception is, of course, the failure of perceptual experience to make good on that claim.

The arguments about perception begin with the conclusion reached at the end of the dialectic of sense-certainty – namely, that we are aware of individuals only as mediated by universals. We may now take this as the new "immediacy" – that is, as something that we can take for granted and accept without any further argumentation. (In the Hegelian dialectic, something that is mediated is said to become "immediate" again when it comes to function as an unquestioned starting point for other claims.) Accepting the conclusion of the arguments about sense-certainty thus preserves the original point of the idea that sense-certainty provides us a kind of knowledge that is available independently of determinate historical and social conditions, for even if sense-certainty is itself mediated knowledge, the inferences involved are so meager and so non-controversial that it is safe to say that the knowledge we get from perceptual acquaintance with the objects of experience is the kind of knowledge that we could have without also having to have much of a background in any kind of social practice outside of that of the use of language itself (something that is common to almost all kinds of social practice). The perception of individual objects can thus play the role of something that we know independently of any social practice other than that of speaking a language.

The discussion of perceptual experience as a form of knowledge must then begin with a description of what it claims to be. Perceptual consciousness (understood as what sense-certainty *really* was) consists of picking out individual objects by some kind of demonstrative ("this," "here," or "now"), but it is not understood as an awareness of any kind of pure singularity. Perceptual experience is a matter of perceiving *this* red thing *here,* right *now,* and it can be extended, no doubt, to identifying the perceptual object as the same red thing over time. This perceptual experience gives us a knowledge of the *things* of perceptual experience, and this knowledge is not dependent on anything other than the ability to refer to individuals with demonstratives and to characterize them by the general characteristics available to our perceptual experience itself; to be *aware* of this red sweet thing is to *know* that this thing is red and sweet, and it does not require us to know anything else.

What this description of perceptual experience seems to put forward is therefore something like this. We seem to be directly aware of two items: the *thing* and its universal *properties.* (For example, we could perceive a green x and a green y; x and y would be two distinct things, and the property they share – the greenness of both x and y – would be the universal – that is, something that is not an individual but is a property that more than one individual can share.) The issue at hand thus has to do with the way in which the awareness of these two items is combined into the perception of one determinate thing. It will, of course, be part of Hegel's thesis that there are not in fact two *items* – individuals and general properties – to be "combined" here at all, and the failure of the account given in "Perception" will be attributed in part to the incoherence of the idea that we are aware of two distinct items, which we then somehow combine into the perception of one determinate thing.

The questions then are: (1) If it is indeed such *things* that we perceive, how do we characterize these objects of perception, how do we characterize their properties, and how do we characterize our awareness of them? (2) Can we be said to *know* individual things through our perceptual experience of them, without our having to presuppose anything other than that found within perceptual experience itself?

The *properties* of the thing are the sensuous items of which sense consciousness was aware (inferentially, mediately).[25] So we might begin by asking what is the *thing* itself of which we claim to be aware. On the one hand, our description of the thing seems to be that it is the x that is red, that is round, that is sweet, and so on. The thing itself, however, does not seem to have any features of its own; it is merely what is referred to by some expression that picks it out, such as a name or an indexical. (Thus, we can characterize it here by the variable, "x.") But since that of which we seem to be directly aware is not the individual per se but its universal properties as *somehow* instantiated in an individual, it is therefore problematic as to how exactly we can be said to be directly aware of *the* thing at all. The failure of "sense-certainty," in which we were said to be aware of *the* individual object, led to "perception," in which we were said to be aware of *the* thing through the mediation of our awareness of its universal properties. The claims of the standpoint of "perception," as they work themselves out, are that we are directly aware of *this* green, *this* round shape, and so on, and that our awareness of the individual x is *only* our awareness of these individualized properties; it cannot be a direct awareness of the indeterminate "this," the "x" that *has* all these properties, at all.[26] The thing's properties are all logically distinct from each other (that the thing is red does not imply anything about its shape, about its taste, and so on). The thing itself, as the indeterminate x that *has* the properties, thus seems to be no more than the *collection* of these individualized properties, which themselves are (somehow) universal, capable of being instantiated in more than one thing.[27] The thing as determined by these properties seems therefore to be only "the indifferent also" of its properties, the conjunction of various individualized properties.[28] By this description, the awareness of the thing is no more than an awareness of a collection of such sensuous qualities. The thing itself is therefore nothing more than such a collection, a simple bundle of the properties ("a simple togetherness of a plurality," as Hegel puts it).[29] (Hegel remarks on a possible attempt at a naturalistic explanation for this view, citing some outdated eighteenth century physics to make his point: perhaps the thing itself can be conceived as being an "enclosing surface" that contains many otherwise independent individualized properties, which themselves would be some sort of "free matters" – *"freie Materie"* – collected in a spatiotemporal place.[30] This, however, will not work, because "free matters" are not properties of a thing; they are free floating individual things themselves that happen to coagulate around a region of space-time. Thus, this way out seems circular. If the various "matters" are individual things that themselves have general properties (such as redness), then the same kind of considerations that applied at the outset would apply to them, and we would be right back where we started. So this purported explanation cannot help us move the discussion forward in any significant way.)

Yet the claims of "perception" were not that we were not aware of individual things; it was that we were aware of particulars by virtue of their universal properties (that our knowledge of them was "mediated"). Yet the account given seems to suggest that we are not aware of particular things at all; we are aware only of bundles of particularized universal properties. If the standpoint of "perception" is to make good on its claims, then it must offer an account of how we are indeed aware of such individual things. Otherwise, it would be completely mysterious as to how we could be aware of particulars at all. A thing is one individual thing in distinction from other individual things, and *it* individualizes the properties (which are "somehow" universals) as belonging to itself. The thing is the indeterminate x that has the properties that we perceive. Therefore, if we are to be said actually to *perceive* the individual x, the thing itself, then the thing itself, as distinct from its properties, must be conceived as simply an individual unit, a "one," "a unity that excludes an other."[31] The thing as a "one," a unit that excludes other distinct units (other "ones") would be, to use Gustav Bergmann's phrase, a "bare particular." It would be a featureless (bare) unit that is different from all other units just by virtue of its very particularity. If we are to maintain that we have a knowledge of individual things in perceptual experience, then we must therefore claim to be directly acquainted with the bare particular itself (the "one") even though it is a featureless unity that is simply different from other bare particulars, and our direct acquaintance with it is always of it *as* instantiating certain properties. (As Hegel puts it, we perceive it only *insofar* as it has such and such sensuous properties, but it, the bare particular, is nonetheless something of which we are directly aware.) According to the account of perceptual experience as a form of immediate knowledge, the thing of perceptual experience thus seems to have two components: It is a bare particular and a universal. In perception, we are aware of these two components as combined into the sensuous awareness of an individualized property.[32]

If that is the case, however, then it would seem that we would be describing things from the standpoint once again of "sense certainty" – that is, on the basis of the idea that we are directly aware of pure singularities. If that is where we end up, then the same dialectic that brought us to "Perception" would simply begin again, and nothing would have been gained.[33] Therefore, if we are to be aware of the *things* of perceptions and not just their properties, it would seem that the thing itself cannot be a bare particular but must have some determinateness on its own.[34] This is one move that the standpoint of "perception" can make to salvage the idea that we have a knowledge of things by virtue of purely perceptual experience. We are directly aware of bare particulars, but we are directly aware of them only through their sensuous properties (which are instantiated universals).

However, the sensuous properties need not be the properties of the thing in itself. The thing in itself can have two different sets of properties: one set that it has in itself, the other that it has only for us. (This would correspond to the distinction between the primary and secondary qualities of the thing, although Hegel does not use those terms.) That things are red and sweet depends on our perceiving them in that way, on the fact that they affect our constitution in that manner. They are perhaps not really sweet or red in themselves but only for us. Thus, it at first seems that we ourselves as perceivers are the "universal medium" in which the sensuous properties are seen as belonging to the single thing.[35] The various sensuous properties of the thing would actually be features of our own consciousness of the thing, not of the thing itself. But if this account is true, then we cannot be said to *know* individual things through perceptual experience, for we could not experience the *things themselves,* since, on this account, we only perceptually experience the *sensuous properties* of the thing, the way it affects our constitution.

Therefore, if we know the individual thing through perceptual experience, the sensuous properties must be properties of the thing itself; although the thing is sweet "for us," its sweetness cannot be a free-floating property but something that the thing itself has. The individual thing (the x that is white and cubical) must be the true "universal medium" of the properties.[36] If perceptual experience, as a form of knowledge that depends only on its own resources, is to be possible, then we must somehow be able to give an account of how the features of the thing's being individual and the thing's having a determinateness on its own can be successfully combined with the idea that we can be aware of the individual thing itself without having to rely on anything outside of perceptual experience itself.

Moreover, if we are to have genuine *perceptual* knowledge, we must be able to distinguish within our own experience what is in fact genuine perceptual knowledge from what is simply an extrapolation by us or is something that we "read into" our experience that goes beyond what we can legitimately claim to *know* by virtue of our perceptual experience.[37] If we attend to perceptual experience carefully, we (supposedly) see that we are aware of singular things in our perceptual experience, and we are aware of their sensuous properties. The way therefore in which the thing seems to lose its individuality by being dissolved into a "bundle of properties" or into being merely an "enclosing surface" must be attributed simply to our own *reflections* on the matter, not to the way in which the thing as an object of perceptual knowledge is actually constituted.[38] In perceptual knowledge, therefore, the thing itself is *one* thing and thereby different from other things (that are also each "one" thing) even if our own reflections make this seem impossible; we must be said to be simply aware of singular things, of these bare particulars.[39]

The perceptual object as a metaphysical object

In this account of perceptual knowledge, the oneness of the thing is not a relational property of the thing itself: It is not one thing relative to other things; it is one thing on its own, a bare particular.[40] Yet, so it also seems, in our perceptual experience we can distinguish one thing from another thing *only* by way of contrasting it with other things.[41] Therefore, for this account, the oneness of the thing – its bare particularity – must be contrasted with its makeup (*Beschaffenheit*) in terms of its sensuous properties; this empirical makeup of the thing is the way in which we contrast and distinguish it from other things in our experience. Moreover, since a bare particular cannot exist without instantiating some sensuous properties, it is necessary to the thing that it have a sensuous makeup to it, even if that sensuous makeup is unessential to its oneness. The thing is thus *essentially* a bare particular that *necessarily* has an empirical makeup (that is, it necessarily instantiates certain sensuous properties). Its makeup is not essential to its particularity, but having a makeup is necessary to it.[42]

Like the previous conceptions of the thing of perceptual knowledge, this conception of the thing, however, fails to make good on the idea that we can know individual things with universal properties solely within perceptual experience itself – that is, without our having to go beyond that experience. Hegel notes that the distinction of something's being necessary but not essential to the thing is just playing with words.[43] Moreover, if this account of perceptual knowledge is to be maintained, it will not suffice simply to say that we see the thing *as* an individual and *as* a bundle of properties; we must be said to be directly acquainted with *two* different objects: the bare particular and the universal which it instantiates.[44] The dilemmas of the descriptions of perceptual knowledge may thus be seen to lie in the nature of the object of perception itself ; the object of perception is a "combination," a nexus of two different objects, and for perceptual knowledge to be possible, we must be directly acquainted with both objects in order for us to have the knowledge of the objects of perception that the proponents of this form of "immediate knowledge" have been claiming. This means, however, that the *knowledge* that was claimed for purely perceptual experience therefore fails on its own terms, for it turns out that in order to know the objects of perception, we must *somehow* know that the *two* objects (the bare particular and the universal) are "combined" into *one* object of perception, and that knowledge of the nexus of connection is not *itself* given in perception; we do not *perceive* the nexus, we only perceive the object that is the result of the two distinct "objects" being combined.[45]

The combinations of these two objects into the unity of the thing of perception, which is necessary for us to be able to be said to have immediate perceptual knowledge, is therefore not present in purely perceptual experience itself. It is rather something *posited* as being there in order to make perceptual experience possible. That implies, of course, that perceptual knowledge is not complete in itself; it requires a kind of knowledge that transcends perceptual knowledge per se. At this juncture in the argument, we seem to be required to conclude that we do not *directly* perceive the object of perception at all; what we perceive are its sensuous properties and its singularity, which are only the *manifestations* to us of its "inner" nature. The object of perception as a nexus of individuality and universality is the basis of these manifestations to us. Our perceptions of things thus do not seem to be a direct acquaintance with the things themselves that cause our perceptions; rather, at best they offer a mediated knowledge of them that goes beyond perceptual experience itself.

We must therefore conclude that we are *not* directly acquainted with the objects of perception but *only* with our representations (*Vorstellungen*) of them. The proponents of the idea that there is nonetheless a form of "self-sufficient, self-contained knowledge" must therefore make their stand on the claim that the "understanding" brings together our direct acquaintance with these representations and inferentially combines them into a true picture of the world.[46] Perceptual experience was supposed to give us a knowledge of the objects of perception that relied on nothing other than what was available in purely perceptual experience itself; however, it has apparently turned out that all that is immediately available in purely perceptual experience is a direct acquaintance with our *representations* of things, and not the direct acquaintance with the things themselves. With that conclusion to the section on "Perception," Hegel turns his arguments now to whether this new version of a conception of self-sufficient knowledge can itself be sustained on its own terms.

3. Force and the understanding: appearance and the supersensible world

Reflective judgment

Perceptual experience was supposed to be self-contained, self-sufficient knowledge of sensible *objects,* but in fact it turned out to be only an awareness of two different types of *representations* of objects – namely, representations of particulars and representations of universals. Perceptual experience cannot account for this combination by relying only on its own resources (on what is simply given to it in perception); such an account requires something more than perceptual experience itself, namely, the reflective "understanding." The "understanding" thus is based not on the claim that we have a direct consciousness of objects in the world but on the idea that the immediate objects of our awareness are our *representations* of particulars and universals, and that the unity of the representations of the universals and particulars is to be explained by something non-perceptible, an underlying supersensible metaphysical essence. The underlying metaphysical essence is the seat of "powers" or "forces" whose function is to explain the unity of perceptual experience in terms of its being an experience of particulars having individualized universal properties. This requires more than simply an empirical explanation because it is not the empirical relations between observed entities that we are trying to explain; the object of explanation is the way in which two ontologically distinct "objects" ("bare particulars" and "universals") can be combined into the unity of one object of perception. Since what we immediately perceive are our representations of the things in themselves (and not the "things themselves"), we must therefore *infer* on the basis of these representations to the things themselves in such a way that we have knowledge of the things themselves that does not depend on anything other than our acquaintance with the representations themselves and our own powers of reasoning – that is, on nothing that is dependent on any historically determinate social practice. Knowledge of things in themselves is not perceptual knowledge; it is mediated knowledge that comes from our own rational capacities to go beyond perceptual experience in order to arrive at a reflective knowledge of things in themselves.

Hegel's terms for the reflective judgmental activity that deals with these representations is "the understanding." The question is thus whether the kinds of concerns appropriate to the "understanding" themselves undermine themselves; Hegel argues that they do, and that this self-undermining leads to the kinds of accounts that are appropriate to "self-consciousness."[47]

Hegel calls the standpoint at which the argument now plays itself out the "unconditioned universal."[48] This is Hegel's rather abstract name for that conception of a metaphysical – that is, a supersensible – basis for the resolution of the problems that confronted "sense-certainty" and "perception." The "unconditioned universal" is the supersensible essence that supposedly underlies our perceptual acquaintance with our representations of objects and which has nothing underlying it. Whereas the proponents of "sense-certainty" and "perception" took us to be directly aware of *objects* in the world, the proponents of the "understanding" take us to be directly acquainted only with our *representations* of those objects. Our representations, in this view, can therefore only be the sensuous *manifestations* of that underlying supersensible essence. That supersensible essence should reconcile the contradictory aspects of the "thing" of perceptual experience: its being a "one" independently of its relation to other "ones" (that is, what seemed to be a bare particular) *and* its being a collection of many sensuous properties (that is, being simply a medium in which many sensuous properties subsist and consequently being only a singularity whose identity is determined by whichever contingent sensuous properties it happens to have).[49]

If the thing is not to be simply a bare particular, a featureless "one," then it must have some determinateness on its own that is different from the sensuous properties that it has in appearance. To the extent, therefore, that the thing itself has some determinateness that is not a matter of sensuous properties, the thing itself, so it seems, cannot *appear* to us as it is.[50] What explains the appearances, which are themselves sensuous, must therefore be something supersensible. If the two – the thing in itself and its appearances – are indeed linked in a non-causal manner – if the appearances are to be the appearances *of* a thing in itself – then the "understanding" must form some judgment about how the appearances are in fact linked to the supersensible essence of appearance. The questions are: What is the nature of the supersensible thing, and can we be said to know it?

Force

If we can be said to *know* the underlying supersensible essence by means of the reflective "understanding" (that is, if we can be said to know the essence without having any direct acquaintance with it), then we must have some way of linking that underlying supersensible essence with the appearances themselves such that the essence would be knowable *in* the appearances themselves. The appearance, therefore, must be the *expression* (*Äusserung*) of the underlying essence. This notion of the essence "expressing" itself is not a causal conception of the relation between the essence and the appearance, and thus it is not subject to a naturalistic, scientific explanation. The essence is not some one thing that could be linked causally to another thing; rather, the appearance is the way in which the essence expresses itself and therefore appears to us such that we can be said to know it.[51] The thing in itself – the "unconditioned universal" – is thus the seat of certain powers or forces (*Kräfte*) that manifest themselves to us in appearance.[52] We *know* these forces *in* their appearances (their "expressions") to us, and, as knowable, what the force is in itself should be *manifested* to us in its expressions in appearance.[53]

In his treatment of the nature of force, Hegel discusses two different concerns present in his time. First, and least important for him at this stage in the argument of the *Phenomenology,* is his discussion of the science (or, perhaps more properly, the philosophy of science) of his day as to what the relation of forces were to their appearances in the world. In that discussion, Hegel is attempting to argue for a non-substantialist theory of force; a force, so he argues, is not an entity that stands in some relation to the entities of appearance. For example, in his *Encyclopedia,* Hegel uses the example of magnetic force and its bearers in iron: The *movement* of a piece of iron in the direction of the magnetic force is the *expression* of the force.[54] It is not as if there are two different entities – the force and its expression – with the problem being how they relate to each other. Rather, one sees something in appearance (the movement of a piece of iron) as an expression of an underlying force.[55] The movement of the piece of iron and the magnetic force are not two *things* soliciting each other; indeed, it is the *whole* (the postulated magnetic force and its expression in the movement of iron) that is force itself. A force that does not express itself would not play the role it must play in this account of knowledge; a force that did not express itself would be an unknowable thing-in-itself. Throughout this part of the discussion, Hegel makes reference to certain debates during his time, such as the relation between centrifugal and centripetal forces in planetary motion, or the relation between inertial and accelerative forces. Each of these forces (centrifugal and centripetal, inertial and accelerative forces) exists only if the other does, and one of the questions concerning, for example, centripetal and centrifugal force has to do with whether they are two independent forces or are only manifestations of one force. (Unfortunately, however, Hegel himself apparently misunderstands some of the ideas at issue, although it makes no difference here to the point he is making.[56])

More important for Hegel's concerns at this stage in the *Phenomenology,* however, is the *metaphysical* idea of force, which had been introduced by various contemporaries in order to solve the metaphysical problems raised by the attempts to give an account of perceptual knowledge. In this light, Hegel probably has Johann Herder in mind in his discussion of *Kraft* (force). In some places, he has Schelling in mind.[57] He links this metaphysical idea of force with the kinds of discussions in the emerging idealist philosophy of his time concerning what the alleged implications of the natural scientific conceptions of force were. Since this force is not to be conceived as an entity that is related to another set of entities (as a metaphysical "one" relating to the multiplicity of the elements of experience), it must be conceived from the "understanding's" point of view as *necessarily* expressing itself. Moreover, since the force is the "medium" of the elements of appearance (which Hegel, continuing to use the terminology of an older eighteenth-century physics, calls "matters"), it is the reason for their appearing as they do. Without the underlying force, the elements of appearance would not exist as the elements they are. Such a force supposedly explains why appearance has the ontological structure that it does, and we are supposedly aware of it through its manifestations to us in a similar manner to the way in which we are aware of other non-metaphysical forces through their manifestations in appearance.

The underlying metaphysical force is a "one" that accounts for the multiplicity of appearance. Since this force is a metaphysical, supersensible entity, nothing can *cause* the force to express itself; rather, it must express itself because of something internal to the makeup of such a force. Therefore what solicits a force to express itself must be a force itself, either the force soliciting itself or another force soliciting it.[58] The question then would be whether there is a better reason to hold that there is only one metaphysical force that solicits itself into expressing itself or whether there must be a play of multiple metaphysical forces each soliciting the other. Although Hegel scatters references to the science of his day throughout his discussion of this metaphysical force, what is important for the argument that he is presenting is not the details of this science but the overall issue as to whether the kind of claim to knowledge being offered here – that we can know the supersensible things in themselves by virtue of a series of inferences made on the basis of our direct acquaintance with our representations of the things – can be sustained. For this to count as the kind of knowledge that the "understanding" claims it is, it should be a form of a priori knowledge. Thus, if there is a necessity for there being more than one force – for there being, for example, in every particular case always at least two forces, one soliciting and one being solicited – then that necessity must arise out of conceptual considerations about the nature of force and not out of any observations of forces manifesting themselves.

Hegel notes that there seems to be a formal argument, at least within this point of view, for there being two forces, namely, that the concept of solicitation involves a passive and an active element. If a force is solicited, it must be passive, whereas a soliciting force must be active.[59] Unless a force can be both passive and active, it cannot solicit itself; therefore, there must be at least two independent forces. Each is the force that it is only in its relation to the other force. Moreover, the independence of the forces is not the independence of two entities, for a force, as we have seen, is not one entity standing in some relation to another entity (however that relation might be characterized); a force is the kind of thing that manifests itself in its appearances.[60] The importance of this argument (which Hegel of course rejects as wholly spurious) is that it seems to be a logical, conceptual claim, something that the

37

"understanding" can determine without having to any empirical research.[61]

On the basis of perceptual experience, empirical science extrapolates to the nature of the forces and how they are related. But, so the argument now goes, for the purposes of resolving the issues raised by the claims of purely perceptual knowledge, we must look beyond the forces that are studied by the empirical sciences of nature to the metaphysical forces (or essences) that are the grounds of the determinateness of appearance. These metaphysical forces, being related conceptually to each other, can supposedly be known by virtue of the "understanding's" reflecting on the representations that are their expressions.[62] Although we cannot have any direct acquaintance with the objects themselves (as was erroneously claimed in "Sense-Certainty" and "Perception"), we may nonetheless be said to know what things are in themselves by virtue of *reflecting* on our representations of them as to what is necessarily manifested to us in these representations. As Hegel puts it, "[T]his true essence of things has been determined so that it is not immediately for consciousness; on the contrary, consciousness now has a mediated relationship to that which is internal and, as the understanding, *looks through this mediating play of forces into the true background of things.*"[63]

We thus have a curtain of sorts between us and the world, and the "understanding" is capable of getting behind the curtain and gaining knowledge of the things in themselves.[64] This curtain is the world of appearance (*Erscheinung*), the mediating point between the world of the things in themselves (the essences that are the determining grounds of appearance) and the "understanding" (or perhaps more prosaically, the reflecting person). As genuine knowledge, this world of appearance (as reflectively understood) is not the way things only *seem* to be but may not be in themselves; it is the gateway for the "understanding" to the way things actually *are*. (It is appearance, *Erscheinung,* and not just seeming, *Schein.*)[65] The way in which things are in themselves is, of course, not to be identified with the world of appearance; the domain of things in themselves is a distinct realm that is *expressed* in the world of appearance, in perceptual experience, with these expressions being the means through which we reflectively grasp the supersensible determining grounds of appearance that are manifested within them.[66] If this conception is sustainable, then the knowledge that would be thus gained would be independent of history and social practice; it would be a knowledge available in principle to any rational agent who wishes to reflect on the world as it appears to him.

The supersensible world is thus the "truth" of the sensuous world of appearance in that the conception of such a supersensible world is developed out of the difficulties inherent in the conceptions of purely perceptual knowledge. This supersensible world (supposedly) explains the determinateness of the appearing world; the structure of appearance in perception is (supposedly) due to the determining essences "behind" or "beyond" appearance.[67] This world of appearance is the domain of our representations, and the world of things in themselves is (supposedly) expressed in our representations.

What appears to the "understanding" is the "play of forces," the way in which the structure of appearance is explained in terms of the underlying plurality of metaphysical forces, with one force soliciting the other into expressing itself in appearance. We infer from the play of forces in appearance, the way in which we perceive concatenations of sensuous properties as forming one individual, to the metaphysical essence of appearance (the "inner" of the world of appearance, in Hegel's terms.) In seeking to infer to this metaphysical essence, the "understanding" seeks to uncover the unity behind the multiplicity of perceptual experience. It thus must hold that the apparent difference between the various forces that seem to manifest themselves in appearance is *only* apparent. The earlier so-called conceptual argument for there being two forces saw the whole basis for the asserted difference as resting in the differences between the "form" and the "content" of the different forces (the formal difference being that between soliciting and being solicited, and the difference of content being that between force as the "medium of properties" and the force as a "one"). However, the different forces are not conceptually independent of each other; the two forces can only be identified and described in terms of each other. The two different forces, x and y, are the forces that they are (they have the determinateness that they do) only by virtue of the *unity* in which they are separately identified; the x can be the x it is *only* in standing in the relation of soliciting or being solicited with some other y, which in turn can be the y it is *only* by standing in the relation of soliciting or being solicited by x. The true essence is thus not the play of independent forces themselves manifesting themselves in appearance; it is the *unity* of the forces that determines them as being the forces that they are. It is therefore this unity that is the true object of the "understanding"; and in inferring to this unity, that manifests itself in the play of forces, we supposedly thereby gain the knowledge which this point of view has promised. The "understanding" therefore believes itself to be licensed to say that we know the world both as it appears (in our immediate knowledge of our representations) and as the way it really is "in itself."

Laws

Hegel calls this unity the "law of force."[68] For "the understanding," this is the true "unconditioned universality"; it explains the world of appearance but requires nothing further to explain itself. As a domain of such laws (or as one Grand Law), the supersensible world is, in Hegel's metaphorical phrase, the "tranquil image" of the flux of the appearing world.[69]

Unfortunately, this conception of law makes it difficult to specify any content for such laws. On the one hand, the more humdrum laws of appearance are full of content; they are the observed regularities of the world that we extrapolate from experience (sugar dissolves in water, stones fall to earth when dropped, and so on). But what is the content of the more general "law of force"? If it is to play the role that it is supposed to play – to give us a knowledge of things in themselves by virtue of our inferring from the appearances – then it must be determinable by the "understanding" itself and not be the result of contingent empirical observations. (Hegel spends a few pages discussing all the various moves that might be made to bolster this claim before he discards it, and his discussion is rendered somewhat more obscure than it need be by virtue of his various references to the rather extravagant philosophical claims that were being made about the status of scientific laws in the philosophical climate prevalent at the time in which he wrote. Hegel's discussion of the idea of a metaphysical force in these sections is probably directed not only to Herder's conception of force but also to Schelling's discussions of the concept of force – for example, to Schelling's claims to "deduce" the concept of opposed forces from considerations appropriate only to "the understanding."[70])

The "principle of the understanding" cannot be satisfied with the plurality of laws, for it demands a unitary ground for the multiplicity of appearance.[71] The "understanding" is driven to seek *one* metaphysical law for the same kind of reasons that it is driven to reduce all phenomenal laws to one law in the natural sciences. (As an example of a reduction of many phenomenal laws to one general law, Hegel obliquely refers to the Newtonian unification of the laws of terrestrial motion with those of celestial motion, that is, Newton's showing that the same laws of motion apply to ordinary things – such as throwing a ball – as apply to the movement of planets.[72]) The "understanding" must therefore seek *one* metaphysical law from which all the other more particular physical laws may be (somehow) derived. However, the more generally stated this law is, the more empty it becomes. If it is general enough to be *the* law governing the so-called supersensible forces (and out of which the phenomenal laws are to be constructed), then it will have no content. If it is particular enough to have any content, it will not be general enough to be the "law of force" per se and will only be one phenomenally manifested force among many. The demands of the "understanding" to produce a metaphysical ground outside of appearance to explain the determinateness of appearance seem to lead only to progressively more empty statements. Therefore, for this metaphysical conception of force to work as an object of knowledge, it must be conceived not just as a progressive *abstraction* from more particular laws; rather, this law must exhibit some form of conceptual necessity to it such that the more particular laws can be seen to be *necessary* consequences of this more general law; in this way, the "understanding" may deduce the more particular laws from it in ways that it cannot simply "deduce" the regularities of appearance.[73]

This kind of metaphysical law could as well be called "force" (the ultimate metaphysical "force" of the world, similar to Herder's idea of a basic metaphysical *Urkraft*). Moreover, those who argue for this kind of metaphysical force could find what might seem like intellectual support for this view in some of the science of Hegel's time, which tended to divide various powers into opposites (for example, the opposition of north and south poles to explain magnetism, positive and negative electricity to explain lightning – it was even a fashionable scientific opinion that all tastes were combinations of sweet and sour).[74] But that general law, however it might be stated (perhaps as something to the effect that there is a general metaphysical law to the effect that nature's basic force must divide itself into positive and negative sides) is too general and indifferent to any particular law to have any real cognitive content. The so-called necessity for this (for the deduction of the division of nature into sweet and sour, positive and negative electricity, and so on, on the basis of some unitary and fundamental metaphysical factor such as a basic force) is spurious. For example, in many so-called natural laws dealing with forces, such as (to use Hegel's own example) the law of motion, there is not one item (for example, motion) out of which we then *logically* derive the constituent elements (space, time, distance, velocity). At best we can develop these constituent moments of motion out of motion itself only by an *analysis* of the *concept* of motion, in which case we would not have an instance of a basic force (or whatever) "dividing itself up" into positive and negative elements but only the articulation (the analysis) of what was already contained in the concept as it was being used in some particular scientific theory.[75]

The "understanding" thus cannot make good on its claim that nature's differentiating itself into positive and negative elements or forces is something that the "understanding" can deduce out of some more general law, such that the "understanding" can be said to know things in themselves purely by some kind of a priori reflection. In fact, it seems to be quite the opposite: It seems to be something that "the understanding" imposes on nature; it is the result of a theory that the "understanding" constructs about the way nature "must be" in itself. Rather than being the result of a special insight that goes behind the curtain of appearance to the world of supersensible things in themselves, it seems to be the "understanding" itself demanding that nature conform to a theory that it has laid down.[76] (Hegel gives an example of the emptiness of such spurious explanation: One states a law and then postulates a ground for that law in some kind of "force," which on closer inspection just turns out to be the law restated in a substantialized manner; for example, lightning is explained by reference to laws of electricity, which are themselves then "explained" by reference to "electrical force." But "electrical force" turns out just to be a restatement of what was already contained in the "laws of electricity." These kinds of tautologous explanations serve no genuine cognitive purposes.[77])

This account of what we can know therefore threatens to undermine itself just as the accounts in "Sense-Certainty" and "Perception" did. Rather than giving us a knowledge of the inner metaphysical necessities of things in themselves, this point of view seems to give us a knowledge only of the necessities in the way in which the "understanding" works; it seems more to study the way in which we *think* of things rather than the way in which things really are.[78]

There is, however, another move available to the proponents of the point of view of the "understanding" to deny that this failure to establish that there is one metaphysical force shows that the "understanding" necessarily fails to provide a knowledge of things in themselves. They can argue that these results show only that the "understanding" should not be so "monistic" but

instead should be more "pluralistic." Thus, they can draw the opposite conclusion than had originally been drawn: it is a mistake to hold that there is
one force; rather, there is a basic *duality* of forces; and modeling metaphysics
on the success of mechanics (which had reduced the laws of terrestrial and
celestial motion to one law) was a mistake.[79]

If one were to take seriously the idea that the world metaphysically requires
these negativities of forces (as Schelling apparently did), then one would have
to conclude, Hegel argues, that the supersensible world would therefore have
to be the opposite of the world of appearance in order for its forces to elicit
the structure of appearance as we experience it. We must therefore imagine a
kind of supersensible world that functions like a negative pole to the positive
pole of appearance. This is intended as a kind of *reductio ad absurdum* of the
kind of way in which the "understanding" posits metaphysical substructures
as explanations of the determinateness of appearance (especially in terms of
these kind of imposed "oppositions"), and is one of the many places in the
Phenomenology in which Hegel is simply having fun with what he takes to be
the flawed ideas of some of his contemporaries.

This constructed, opposite world is called by Hegel the "inverted world."[80]
The term applied in Hegel's day to a very popular type of engraving, in which
the normal world was shown as having gone topsy-turvy (the hare is grilling
the huntsman, children are lecturing professors, the mouse is pursuing the
cat, and so on); it also formed part of some Carnival celebrations.[81] Hegel
picked up the popular term, the "inverted world," to describe this fanciful
supersensible world in what is a genuinely sardonic section of the *Phenomenology*. His point is that the very absurdity of this idea should motivate those
who have this kind of conceptualization to think about what is going on in
such a case – to think, that is, about the *nature of their conceptualizing
activity* rather than about the particular oppositions that arise.

The point of view of the "understanding" originally claims that it is capable
of knowing the internal essence of the world by reflecting on our representations of that world, that it can correctly infer to what is behind the curtain of
our representations to what the world is in itself. The "understanding's"
claim to *know* the things in themselves, however, is completely undermined
by the fact that it can assert both that the "unconditioned universal" is a
unitary force lying behind appearance and that it is a plurality of forces lying
behind appearance and, worse, that not only is each assertion equally valid,
each is equally riddled with the same kinds of dilemmas and contradictions.
(The resemblance here to Kant's "Antinomies" in the *Critique of Pure Reason*
is probably not accidental.[82]) What this shows is that the "understanding's"
concern with the "unconditioned universal" is not in fact adequate to the
claims that the "understanding" makes about it. What is truly going on in the
"understanding's" claims about the nature of this metaphysical supersensible
world is that the "understanding" is making claims only about *its own activities* of construing the world. It is not so much describing a supersensible
world beyond appearance as it is describing its own structure for describing
the world. (To use Wittgenstein's metaphor, it is describing the frame around

the picture all the while thinking that it is describing the picture itself.) The "understanding" took itself to be determined in its structure by the "things themselves" – that is, it took the nature of the object to be authoritative for it. However, it has turned out that what is authoritative for it is its own conceptualizing activity; in setting its own terms, the "understanding" turns out thereby to be free from determination by the "things themselves." The "understanding" took the oppositions that are really a feature of its own conceptual activity as being the structure of things in themselves; thus, it took the logical structure of conceptual opposition to be a relation between two kinds of entities (the sensuous entities of the appearing world and the supersensible entities of the world of things in themselves.)[83] The true "essence" at play here is, however, not a supersensible entity that is different from and lies behind the entities of appearance; it is the work of the "understanding" itself. The oppositions at work of universal and particular, of inner world and outer appearance, are in fact aspects of the way in which the "understanding" conceives the world, not features of some entity (the supersensible metaphysical ground) that stands behind appearance. In following out the vicissitudes of "the understanding," we, the readers, come to see (under the guidance of our narrator, Hegel) that it is only by thinking of our cognitive and practical relations to the world in terms of some set of mediating *representations* that such an idea would be engendered in the first place; if we think of the realm of our consciousness as a realm of mental objects (representations) that are then related in some way to another realm of objects (the domain of things in themselves), we will always be caught in the dilemmas of trying to match the mental objects with the other kind of objects, and we will find that all the proposed matches ultimately undermine themselves.[84]

Self-consciousness

The true object of "the understanding," therefore, is the "understanding" itself. (Hegel also calls this an "infinity," meaning a structure that sets its own conditions.[85]) The oppositions that the "understanding" originally claimed to have found in things in themselves are in fact really just part of the structure of our inferential system, of the "social space" in which we operate. In coming to have its own activity for its object, the "understanding" comes to have an object that is *in itself as it appears* to "the understanding"; the "understanding" can thus claim to know what it is as it really is, rather than claiming to know what these metaphysical things in themselves are.

The contradictory nature of the accounts that the "understanding" has given of its "objects" has compelled it to reflect on the nature of those accounts. In this way, the subject/object model (that of "consciousness") is replaced by the more complex idea of *self-consciousness*. The conception of "consciousness" that informs the first three sections of the *Phenomenology* is that picture of ourselves in relation to the world that sees that relation in terms of a dualism between subject and object, a dualism underpinned by taking that relation to be mediated by *representations* that serve as the metaphysical "mediums" that stand between the subject and the object.[86] The contradictions intrinsic to this representationalist understanding of our relation to the world (which have emerged in the dialectical give and take of "Sense-Certainty," "Perception," and "Force and the Understanding") have thereby put us, the readers, into a position to see that the subject/object model of "consciousness" is not the natural metaphysical structure of our conscious lives but a way in which we have historically come to *understand ourselves.* In putting the issue in terms of self-consciousness, of the way in which we take ourselves to be, Hegel puts us in a position to shift away from asking the question, "How do we *represent* the world?" and to ask instead another question, "What must *we* be like, in our historically developing social practices, in order to make such a claim?" This shift moves us away from the subject/object model of knowledge to an understanding of *self-consciousness* – that is, to understanding that the question of how "we" relate to the world depends on how "we" understand ourselves to be. If we take ourselves to be metaphysical representers, then we will understand our relation to the world in one way; if we take ourselves to be something other than metaphysical representers, we will take our relation to the world in some other fashion. Thus, once the subject/object model of knowledge is replaced by that of "self-consciousness," we will be in the position to see that our claims to knowledge do not involve a metaphysically understood *representation* of reality but rather a way in which we *take ourselves* to be dealing with the world and each other. In this move to a view of ourselves as "forming views of ourselves as a component part of claiming to know things," we will drop entirely the picture of ourselves as *representing* the world, and we will come to see ourselves as social creatures forming *concepts* of ourselves as already world-related. By shifting the issue in this way, we come to see that the old question of how we represent the world is to be replaced by the new question of how we are to understand the self-conscious sociality of the organisms that we are.

The effect of beginning the *Phenomenology* with three sections on "Consciousness" and with problems involved in a post-empiricist understanding of knowledge is that it motivates our discarding the representationalist picture of our relation to the world and replacing it with a reflection on the kinds of social creatures we are. Knowledge, as Hegel understands it in the rest of the *Phenomenology,* is not to be understood as a metaphysical relation between a "subject" and an "object" but as a way in which the peculiarly social organisms that we are establish a relation with the world and ourselves that involves both the kinds of ends we pursue and the kinds of subjects we take ourselves to be. To understand what we take to be valid claims to *knowledge* is to come to understand the kinds of *persons* we take ourselves to have become. To put it another way: We move away from a representationalist picture of knowledge to the idea of socially situated reason-giving activities; we thus move away from a picture of ourselves as "subjects" *representing* the world to an understanding of ourselves as *participants* in various historically determinate social practices.

But this abstract sketch of what knowledge is can here only be a kind of promissory note; the filling out of this very general claim requires the rest of the *Phenomenology of Spirit*. Nonetheless, with the closing of the section on "Consciousness," Hegel completes part of the task of an introductory section to a book with the title the *Phenomenology of Spirit*. As a *phenomenology*, it must be a study of "consciousness," of how we take certain thing as authoritative for ourselves (in Hegel's terms, how we see ourselves in relation to the "essence" of things). This must begin with the theories taken for granted in Hegel's own day and the subject/object models of knowledge and action that they entail. Hegel has shown that "consciousness" is not a self-enclosed, self-illuminated sphere that must somehow be linked up with the world in some metaphysical fashion; it is already world-involving at its most basic levels, and it involves a form of *self*-relating.[87] "Consciousness" can only be understood in terms of various "formations of consciousness," of the ways in which certain historically determinate communities take certain kinds of things and practices as authoritative for themselves in determining what counts as knowledge. The next step, therefore, is to develop a conception of *spirit*. This is the goal of the next section, "Self-Consciousness." In that section, Hegel looks at an alternative version of self-sufficient knowledge. Instead of the conception of ourselves as self-illuminated minds who could know something about the world without having to know anything about anything other than what was contained in "sense-certainty," "perception," or "the understanding," we come to a view of ourselves as self-sufficient practical agents who attempt to deal with the world solely in terms of our own desires and to establish relations to it and even to our social context that need not take into account our sociality. The failure of those attempts at self-sufficiency sets the stage for the rest of the *phenomenology* of *spirit,* the dialectical history of the accounts that the European community has given of what could be authoritative for itself.

3

The claims of self-sufficient agency: freedom and self-consciousness

1. Self-consciousness and the desire for recognition

Self-consciousness and practice

The claim of the preceding sections was that it was possible for there to be a form of self-sufficient knowledge – that is, some way of knowing things that did not depend on anything outside of some small circle of beliefs that were all either established non-inferentially or were established by making only the most meager of assumptions (such as the assumption that knowers speak a language). The three candidates for such knowledge, however, have been shown to be internally self-defeating; judged on the terms that they set for their own success, they fail to make good on their claims. Moreover, in tracing out the structure of this so-called self-contained knowledge, the proponents of this point of view find that in fact they are only tracing out the structure of "the understanding" itself – that is, they are not tracing out the structure of *things* but instead the structure of our own conceptualizing activities. Thus, the standpoint of "consciousness" is integrated into this new, more reflective conception of what counts as knowledge, which Hegel terms quite generally, "self-consciousness." It is characterized by a reflection not on the structure of the things about which we are conscious, but on the structure of our conscious attendings and takings themselves.

In this new, reflective view, the goal of showing that what we *take* as authoritative *really* is so seems more readily achievable because the objects of reflection are our reflective activities themselves. Whereas in the original claims to self-sufficient knowledge, it had seemed that we were attending only to the things themselves (the individuals of "sense-certainty," the unities of particulars and universals in "perception," and the inner essence of things for "the understanding"), it has turned out that there were *no such things* in the first place – that is, no such things as pure singularities that could be non-inferentially known, no such things as unities of universal "objects" and particular "objects" that could be directly perceived, and no such things as essences lying behind the curtain of appearance. In tracing out the structure of our own way of *taking* these things, however, we are not tracing out the contours of something about which we could decide later that it did not exist; reflection on reflection cannot show that reflection does not exist. (We might find, of course, that we had characterized it wrongly, but not that it did not exist.) Our "certainty" about this thus *seems* to be identical with the "truth" about it; the object of reflection, as being the structure of the way we take things, is now taken to be fully present to our own reflections.[1]

The various determinations of objects as they have been taken in the first three sections are thereby seen not to be ontological features of the world in itself but only features of the way in which we describe, classify, and explain that world.[2] This new conception does not deny that there are indeed independent objects that we perceive or to which we infer; it does not, that is, replace the earlier kind of realism with some form of subjective idealism. The conception of the independent *existence* of the sensuous objects remains intact in this conception; the object of reflection, however, now is the structure of *our taking* these objects as such and such – that is, the set of inferences (the "social space") in terms of which we describe, classify, and explain those objects, and not the objects themselves.[3] Self-consciousness is this awareness of our taking things *as* such and such; in terms of our original metaphor, it is assuming a position in "social space," that is, assuming a whole set of inferences that license the agent to move from one position in that space to another. A "move" in a "social space" is an inference licensed by that space. To know oneself in this sense is knowing one's position in that "social space" – that is, knowing where one stands in terms of what one is licensed to believe. Consciousness requires that we have a position in "social space," and self-consciousness is the awareness of this position, of what we are and are not licensed to infer.

Self-consciousness thus has two moments: A self-conscious agent is conscious of a world of sensuously perceived objects that exist independently of him, and he is aware of himself as a position in "social space," as *taking* these things *as* such and such. The form that self-consciousness takes, Hegel says, is a relating of itself to itself. By this he means that although in consciousness there is a relation between a conscious subject and a world of putatively independent objects, in self-consciousness the terms of the relation are not independent of each other. This is constituted, as Hegel puts it, by the "I" relating itself to itself. Self-consciousness is the awareness of one's conceptual activity, even though this awareness may not be adequate to what is really going on in such activity. (We can, for example, misinterpret our conceptual activity as being a direct acquaintance with pure singularities or universals, as was done in the section, "Consciousness.") In self-consciousness, the "I" is *taking itself* as occupying a position in a determinate "social space"; this space is constituted by a series of inferential licenses that permit, demand, or prohibit various types of inferential moves (for example, from the characterization of something as a "now" it permits the inference to the claim that we are talking about something temporal). Thus, unless the "I" assumes some set of inferences – unless it comes to occupy a position in some "social space" – it cannot be said to be *knowing* anything at all. There is no pure acquaintance with objects (either pure singularities or universals). All consciousness is therefore self-consciousness in the sense that any awareness of any object is already mediated by the organism's assuming a position in some normative "social space."[4] In more concrete terms, all consciousness involves situating

47

oneself within a determinate historical community with its standards for what counts as authoritative for belief and action.

In coming to this view, an agent participating in this particular "formation of consciousness" does not abandon the idea that he is conscious of a world of independently existing objects in space and time, but he does forsake the idea that he knows this world in the supposedly self-contained manner of "Consciousness." In its place, he has come to see that his knowledge of this world is mediated by his self-consciousness, by his awareness of himself as taking things as such and such. The oppositions that were encountered earlier in the preceding sections are understood not as the result of some metaphysical "force" dividing itself up into fundamental dualities but simply as the result of the contrastive work of our own cognitive capacities (involving such oppositions as truth versus falsity, appearance versus reality, and so on). The so-called essence of things is not therefore any kind of metaphysical force, as "the understanding" had taken it to be. In fact, it is not a metaphysical essence at all; it is our own conceptualizing activity, contrasting itself as a normative order with the world of independently existing objects.

The subject of these experiences originally understood himself purely as an *apprehending* subject, someone who stood in the relation of acquaintance with the objects of knowledge. The guiding metaphor there is that of a subject *viewing* the object. With the collapse of that idea, however, an alternative picture of the subject has emerged – namely, that of a practical, living subject who deals with objects in terms of his cognitive capacities and for whom his concepts are more like *tools* with which he can deal with his environment. Hegel calls this "life." "Life" is expressed in our various desires. Organic life itself is self-maintaining; the organism deals with its environment so as to regulate itself and to maintain its life, and it does this in a purposive manner, even if its dealings with it are not necessarily cognitively formed. Life itself is a fluid process continuously renewing itself on both the individual and generic level.[5] But living individuals emerge from the process of life and assert themselves against it, maintaining themselves as individual organisms against their environment and dealing with their environment in terms of what satisfies their desires.[6] Agents are organisms dealing with their environments, and as an organism, an agent has various desires and attempts to maintain itself as an independent organism by satisfying these desires. The organism thus stands in an implicit self-relation in that its active dealing with the world is always in terms of what is necessary *for it* or its species to survive. The objects of the world count *for it* as having such and such properties only in terms of how they contribute to the satisfaction of the organism's desires.

To see the subject as part of life is to see the object of knowledge not as being like the kind of metaphysically construed objects of "sense-certainty" or "perception" that we can only *apprehend;* it is rather to see how these objects fit into the demands of the life of the subject himself – that is, into his various practical projects. Put in cognitive terms: What counts as a reason for belief for the subject depends on his life's various desires and demands – that is, on what it is that he needs and wants to do. On this model, the agent's relation to the sensuous objects of the world is therefore primarily practical and not primarily theoretical. Our conceptualizing activities are not to be construed on the model of our *apprehending* objects; knowing something is construed instead as a form of *acting*. The agent has various desires that demand satisfaction, and his conceptualizing activities are *tools* for the satisfaction of those desires. Like all tools, their adequacy is determined by how well they contribute to the task for which they are devised. Given this conception of what is authoritative for the subject, his knowledge of all the other things in the world may thus be said to be mediated by considerations of what is required to satisfy his desires.[7] As knowing himself as this kind of self-conscious organism, the agent as a knowing subject appears to himself as self-contained – that is, independent of determination by the object. He, not the objects of knowledge, sets the terms on which something is to count as knowledge – that is, he determines what is to count as an authoritative reason for him to believe something or to do something – in terms of how these things satisfy the demands of his personal projects. Conceptual activity results in knowledge if it assists in the satisfaction of the agent's desires and projects.

What we come to take as an authoritative reason for acting therefore depends on what best satisfies these desires and projects. Whatever contrasts we may make in describing the world are sustainable only to the extent that they function to satisfy these desires better than some alternative set of contrasts. There is no "essence" of the world that imposes one set of descriptions on us rather than another; instead, we classify, describe, and explain the world in terms of what best makes sense to us given what it is we want to do and accomplish. But in understanding himself in this way, the agent sets up a new opposition, that between self-consciousness and "life" itself. On the one hand, there is life itself and the world of objects with which the agent must deal if he is to satisfy his desires. On the other hand, there is the self-conscious subject making certain contrasts, setting them up, saving some and discarding others, altering what he earlier took to be true because of the failure of some claim to knowledge to succeed in satisfying desire – that is, in general, electing to *count* something as a reason for him. This view does not deny the independent existence of the objects of the natural world, nor does it deny their independent causal properties. It says that something comes to count as an authoritative reason for acting or believing because the subject himself *comes to count it* as an authoritative reason, and his principle for counting some things as authoritative reasons for belief and action have to do with whether they help to accomplish what it is he wants to do.

Knowledge and practice

The picture that emerges is that of an organism-subject with certain desires, but who is also a self-conscious agent, who understands that the putative objects of knowledge cannot impose upon him what can count for him as an authoritative reason for belief or action. This gives us a new picture of self-contained knowledge. That he has certain desires is given to the subject by "life." Yet he takes himself to be "self-conscious" – that is, to determine for himself what is to count as an authoritative reason for belief or action. Since what counts as an authoritative reason depends on how that reason helps to satisfy the subject's system of desires, the subject may know things only as they are related to his own plans and projects (that is, his system of desires). The object *exists* independently of the agent, but it cannot be said to have any independent essence (of which we could be directly aware or to which we could infer); the subject's reasons for taking the object to be one way as opposed to the other has to do with how this overall claim-making activity can be seen to fit into his projects and systems of desires. In this way, the agent understands himself as the truly *independent* member of the relation between "subject" and "object."[8] The object does not *make* our claims true; we *elect* to count certain reasons as good reasons in terms of whether they contribute to the satisfaction of our desires and projects in a certain way. The object, as Hegel calls it, is a "nothingness" for the self-conscious organism; it is something that is known by virtue of standards that the subject himself has come to accept as valid standards for knowing something, not something that imposes itself on us and that we can only apprehend. Which descriptions fit the objects of knowledge (or how we take them when we practically deal with them or when we consume them) has to do with which set of descriptions most efficiently satisfies our system of desires and projects.

In the sections having to do with "Consciousness," the knowledge-claims themselves were supposed to be self-contained, to presuppose nothing outside of themselves; now it is the *individual agent himself* who is supposed to be independent, who presupposes nothing outside of his own self-conscious awareness of the world in terms of the needs of his own life – in other words, his awareness of his cognitive activity as a living organism – in order to be able to know the way the world is. The subject is taken to have certain desires and projects independently of his relation to the world; and what counts for him is how things fit into those independently established and known desires and projects. The question is whether this new conception of knowledge can make good on the claims that it makes, or whether it too fails on the terms that it sets for itself.

It is, however, clear that an organic agent is dependent in a quite obvious sense on certain natural conditions in the world. The agent who thinks of himself as independent quickly finds that the putative dependence of the object on his own cognitive dealings with it cannot be complete in any straightforward *natural* sense. Although, as "self-consciousness," he takes himself to determine for himself what can count as a *reason* for him, and thus to be independent, as an organic subject, he finds that his *desires* are often simply given to him, and that he is completely dependent on his organic nature (on "life") to determine what desires he will have and which ones demand satisfaction. Moreover, once a desire is satisfied, it or another springs up again, and there is nothing that the agent can do about this; this is simply a given element in his life, something that is indifferent to all the alternative arrangements of his cognitive activities and that imposes itself on his conceptualizing activity. However, acting on the principle, "satisfy your desires," will not affirm his independence for the subject, since the nature of organic desire is to spring up again and again. Any full natural independence of the agent with regard to organic desire and the natural world is impossible to achieve; as soon as it seems to be achieved – whenever the agent has satisfied his desires by dealing with the world in whatever way best does this (whether it be knowing the world or consuming parts of it for nutrition) – "life" again makes its claims on the individual in terms of his having new desires which demand satisfaction.[9]

However, the subject as "self-consciousness" takes himself to be independent in that he determines for himself which desires are to *count* for him as authoritative reasons for action, even if he cannot determine *which* desires he will actually have (as "life"). The subject elects those desires to count for him as good reasons for action only in terms of how they fit in with his independently established projects. What is authoritative for him is not the object nor even the desire for the object but his own overall projects and thus his own overall desires about what he wishes to accomplish. In acting on desire, the subject is said to "negate" the object in that he affirms for himself that what is to be done with the object (letting it be or consuming it) is determined by him. That is, he elects for himself whether to let his desire to consume it be a good reason for him to act on the object; the object itself cannot impose any such *reason* on him, although it can pose itself as a "lure" for him. But whatever he does with the object is determined not by the object but by *his projects,* by what he wishes to do.

Thus, the subject finds that he is caught in a peculiarly conflicting self-understanding. On the one hand, he takes himself (as "self-consciousness") to be independent; yet on the other hand, he is dependent on the structure of "life" and its given desires. He determines for himself whether acting on this or that desire is an authoritative reason to act in terms of his more basic desire about what he wants to do, but he finds that the material of his deliberations is simply given to him. He determines for himself on the basis of his own projects what is a good reason for action, but as an organic agent he seems to be acting only on the principle that he is to satisfy desires, and his desires are simply given, thus making his independence only a very abstract notion even for him. Therefore, if he is to be able to integrate for himself his opposed views of himself as "self-consciousness" (as independent, as determining for himself what counts for him) and as "life" (as being dependent on the given structure of organic desire), he must be able to find some desire that is not simply given but is a desire that comes out of his nature as a self-conscious independent agent per se. Only the satisfaction of such a desire could affirm for him that his conception of himself as independent is indeed true. For this to be possible, he must be able to encounter an object of desire that affirms for him that he does indeed determine what will count as an authoritative reason (as "the truth") for him in terms of *his own* projects, which themselves are independent of determination by the world.

These requirements are met by the subject's having a *desire for recognition* (*Anerkennung*) as an independent agent by another self-conscious agent.[10] This particular desire is satisfied when another self-conscious agent *recognizes* the former as that *point of view* of the world that determines what counts as an authoritative reason per se for belief or action – as that point of view whose projects are his own and determine for him what counts as a good reason. Why this is the case emerges through the following reflections.[11] In encountering another self-conscious agent, the subject encounters a different type of "object" in his world. Natural objects can satisfy desire in a straightforward way: Water quenches thirst, apples quench hunger. If the subject is to achieve satisfaction from an "object," there must be something that the "object" *does* that *affirms* for the subject that it is indeed *he,* as the desiring subject, and not the object of desire who makes something into an authoritative reason for belief or action. If the subject is to maintain his independence, the object cannot *impose* reasons on the subject; the object cannot make the subject's reasons for belief and action into authoritative reasons. The subject seeks affirmation that this view of himself is indeed the true view, and he finds that *he* cannot do this purely in terms of desiring natural objects and fulfilling those desires, for he cannot determine which objects are to be there *for* him. It is only the "object" itself that *can* affirm this for him, and to do this, the "object" would have to present itself as something *other* than the subject, while at the same time also presenting itself as *dependent* on the subject for its conferral of recognition. That is, its dependence must be such therefore that it *makes itself* dependent on the subject. This "object," as Hegel puts it, must "perform the negation on itself": Since the subject cannot fully "negate" the *natural* object – that is, deal with it in such a way that the subject's sense of his own independence is preserved, the "object" must perform its own "negation" of itself for the subject to be able to realize this conception of himself as an independent agent. This "object" must be an "other" to the subject, something that at first appears to him as independent (his "negation"), and it must at the same time present itself as "negating" its own independence, as abdicating any claim it has to independence, presenting itself as fully determinable by the subject.

Thus, this new "object" can *only* be another self-conscious *subject* (1) who presents himself to the first subject as *making himself* dependent on the first subject's demand for recognition from him (that is, as performing the "negation" on himself), and (2) who thereby in this act of making himself dependent on the first subject *affirms* for the first subject his conception of himself as independent.[12] The person who seeks to have his conception of himself affirmed as an independent agent by satisfying his desire for recognition must confront another self-conscious person who *takes himself* to be dependent on the first person, and who, through his act of taking himself to be dependent, thereby affirms that first person's self-understanding. The other person must make himself dependent on the other in that he recognizes the other's projects as authoritative for himself, as determining what for him counts as a good reason for belief or action. It is crucial that the other person do this to himself; he must *determine himself as* dependent, for only in his coming to understand himself in this way can he offer the first person the kind of recognition that he desires.

The kind of dependence and independence that are in question here have to do with the dependence and independence of *points of view;* the "object" must take its point of view on what *really* counts as an authoritative reason for belief or action to be set by the subject demanding recognition. That is, the "object" (the other person) must understand his own projects as having validity only to the extent that they satisfy the first subject's projects.

The subject's self-conception as an independent agent can thus only be truly affirmed by his satisfying his desire for recognition from another subject.[13] The objects of the world that are not self-conscious have no projects; they cannot certify for the subject that his own projects are indeed authoritative. Only another agent with his own projects can do this. It thus seems that an agent's self-consciousness as *independent* is only possible – that is, is only sustainable, does not undermine itself – by having his conception of himself mirrored back to him in the acts of recognition from another agent.[14]

2. Masters, slaves, and the subjective point of view

Independence and recognition

The upshot of this is that the agent takes himself to be an independent agent only in taking himself to be *recognized* by another *as* independent. In being recognized as independent, his self-understanding (his being-for-self) is *affirmed for him* as being true, as being in line with what he really is (his being-in-itself).[15] The subject's seeking recognition from another agent is thus an instance of the more general way in which agents seek reassurances that what they take to be authoritative *really* is authoritative, and much of the dialectic of master and slave will turn on what is required for this kind of reassurance to be possible. Out of the dialectic of recognition between master and slave, Hegel will develop his conception of the *social* nature of knowledge – that is, his idea that the standards for what counts as authoritative reasons should be seen as the outcome of a process of a community's collectively coming to take certain types of claims as counting *for them* as authoritative, a process best understood in historical and institutional terms – that is, in terms of participation in social practices, not in terms of its being anchored in any kind of metaphysical relation between "subjects" and "objects" at all.

Taking this standpoint allows us (the readers assisted by our commentator, Hegel), to redescribe the picture of the agent that was earlier presented in the dialectic of "Consciousness" as that of the agent looking only within his own subjectively apprehended cognitive activities for affirmation that what he counts as authoritative really is so. The collapse of that attempt has led to the more practically oriented criterion that the agent now has, which itself has come to require not an inquiry into his own subjective experiences or a reliance only upon his cognitive skills, but a reliance on another subject for the recognition that would affirm that what he takes to be authoritative – namely, his *own* projects – *really are* authoritative not just for him but per se. In coming to understand that in holding a view of himself as independent he can only be satisfied by another agent's conferring recognition on him, the first agent seeking affirmation of his viewpoint "goes out of himself," as Hegel puts it, in that he comes to understand that the desired affirmation of his self-understanding can only come from another, not from himself.[16] This kind of *dependence* on the other for recognition is a matter of conceptual necessity; it is not the kind of contingent dependence on others that is, for example, constituted by the dependence on others to produce certain goods. We may depend on others for a variety of things because we cannot, for fully contingent reasons, produce them ourselves; I may not have the skills or time to produce my own shoes or produce my own wine, and thus I depend on others to produce those things for me (for which I can exchange something in return). But it is not a contingent fact about this agent that he alone cannot affirm his conception of himself for himself; it is part of the concept of what it means to be an agent, at least insofar as Hegel has developed that concept thus far, that the agent requires others to reassure him that what he *takes* as authoritative *really* is so.

The relation to the other is thus double-edged in that the other both *affirms* and *undermines* the subject's sense of himself, and it is this double-edged quality that leads to the dialectic of dependence and independence that structures the discussion of mastery and servitude. On the one hand, the subject (at this point in the development of Hegel's argument) would find his self-conception affirmed through the other agent's recognition of him, and thus he would find "only himself" in the other; he would find not the other's projects but *his* own projects affirmed in the other. On the other hand, he finds that his sense of himself as independent is *dependent* on the recognition conferred by the other agent, which seems to undermine any affirmation of himself as *independent*. If he is therefore to maintain this sense of himself as independent, he must integrate this kind of dependency on the other into a conception of himself that can preserve his sense of his independence while at the same time allowing for an acknowledgment of his dependence on the other for recognition. He must therefore give some more content (that is, more determinateness) to the conception of independence that he claims for himself.[17] This is complicated by the fact that in doing so, he must be also able to preserve the conception of the *other* as dependent on him, in the sense that the other must *take himself to be* dependent on him.

The dialectical complexities of this are luxuriant: The subject must secure his independence by becoming dependent on the recognition by an "other" such that the subject finds his independence affirmed by virtue of being dependent on an "other" who confers this recognition by virtue of affirming his own dependence on the subject. This complexity is intensified by the fact that the other would necessarily hold the same conception and would be involved in the same complexities.[18]

Could the agents resolve this complexity by simply *mutually* recognizing each other as independent – that is, each recognizing that the other's projects determine what will count as authoritative, what will count as being of value and so on? Part of the force of Hegel's argument will be that this is not possible for *these* agents (whom we are imagining as abstracted out of all developed social relationships, since they each take their projects to be identifiable independently of their social relations).[19] Hegel describes the mutual demands for recognition that the two agents make on each other as an encounter between people who each hold an *abstract* idea of themselves. Each conceives of himself as a "simple being-for-self." That is, the agent is aware of himself as having a *subjective point of view* on the world. This emerged from the dialectic of "Consciousness," in which the subject went from an understanding of himself as simply *apprehending* objects (pure singularities or perceptual objects) to an understanding of himself as knowing objects only by being engaged in conceptualizing *activity*. In taking himself as an essentially self-conscious agent, the subject developed a view of knowledge as being primarily an elaboration of more practical endeavors – namely, the satisfaction of desire. The subject thus takes his subjective point of view as his own perspective on the world – that is, how he sees things from within his own set of beliefs, expectations, and the like, and how he experiences things as being. The subjective point of view, taken abstractly (that is, taken out of the full context of all the mediating factors in it) appears to the agent therefore simply as his own *individual* point of view on the world, as something that *he* has, in distinction from the viewpoint that had characterized "consciousness," in which the objects were supposedly apprehended from no point of view at all – they were supposedly apprehended simply as they were in themselves. He also takes this subjective point of view to be self-sufficient; he, as an individual, can identify what this point of view is and what desires and projects he sets for himself without having to know anything else.[20]

Independence and subjective points of view

To be a *subject* is not only to be aware of things in the world but also to be aware of oneself as having a *point of view* on that world. If we imagine that the subject's basic point of view on the world is practical, such that what he counts as an authoritative reason has to do with what is necessary for the satisfaction of his desires and projects, then he confronts that world, as we might call it, as a "practical field." To *know* something is to be able to integrate it into this practical field, to see it as fitting in with the reasons that are generated out of what is necessary to fulfill his desires and projects and to fit them together with each other. Each subject therefore encounters the other first as an "object" in this practical field, as a "thing" to be integrated into the first subject's plans and projects. Each is "certain of himself" as being the kind of practical-knowing subject that he is, for whom the world is known as a practical field to be integrated into *his* own concerns and projects.

However, to see the other agent simply as an "object" in the practical field cannot be satisfying for the subject (it can have no "truth" for him), since in order to see the other as capable of bestowing *recognition*, he must see the other not simply as an "object" in the world like other things but as a self-conscious *subject*, who also has *his own* subjective point of view on the world. Each therefore presents himself to the other in the encounter as this type of practical-knowing agent who takes himself to *know* things when he knows them in terms of how well they fit into his own projects and desires – that is, into his subjective point of view.[21] In Hegel's terms, each presents himself to the other as a "pure abstraction of being-for-self."[22] The subject understands himself as a point of view on the world, specifically, as an independent agent whose knowledge of things consists in fitting them into his practical field; although he can neither determine which desires he might have nor what might satisfy those desires, he nonetheless understands his *independence* to lie in his *subjectively taking* certain things to count or not to count as authoritative for him, with the standards for his doing so being whether they fit into his desires and projects. Since each wishes to affirm for himself that his view of himself as independent is indeed true, each demands that the other recognize him as this kind of independent agent. Each agent from his own subjective point of view therefore encounters the other as an agent also having a subjective point of view and seeks to incorporate that fact – that the other has his own subjective point of view – into his own point of view. Each agent therefore comes to have a subjective, personal point of view that has as a component the idea of the other as also having a subjective, personal point of view.

From the standpoint of these agents, however, there is no way to reconcile these two subjective points of view into a third, more objective point of view, for at this stage, no such impersonal (or "objective" or what Hegel often simply calls, "universal") point of view could exist. Or, as we might put it, there can be no common, social project for these agents that could count as something into which they must reconcile their own projects. At this stage in the argument, neither of the agents could correlate his own point of view and that of the other with that of such an objective point of view. Instead each has his own subjective point of view, and incorporates the idea of the "other *as having* a subjective point of view" into his own point of view. Each takes his own subjective point of view as being the truth, and he simply maps the other's point of view into his own, denying the validity of the other's point of view when it conflicts with his own. Neither is in a position to assume an impersonal point of view that would incorporate within itself the subjective points of view of each agent, for the possibility of that impersonal point of view has not, at this point in the argument, been developed.[23] The encounter between the two agents is thus an encounter between two agents who cannot have any grounds to admit that any other point of view other than their own subjective point of view has any validity (or could take priority over their own point of view), even though each is supposed to recognize that the other has a point of view.

Each therefore demands that the other recognize him as an agent who is more than an organism *in* the world; he is also a subject having a point of view *on* that world and whose point of view is authoritative. For each to affirm this for himself, each must demonstrate *to himself* that he is more than just an organism by being recognized as such by the *other agent*. Risking his life by engaging in some isolated, dangerous action will not suffice; this could only show that he is willing to run certain risks for certain ends and would only affirm for him at best that he is a practical agent. It could not affirm for him the primacy of his subjective point of view; only recognition by another of the primacy of his subjective point of view could do that. (Simply wrestling a lion will not therefore suffice.) Recognition can only come from an "other" whom one takes to be a self-conscious agent (an agent who has a point of view on the world and therefore his own practical projects), and who *confers* that recognition on one. Each therefore makes a conflicting demand on the other. Each knows the other as a "thing" in the practical field, who is known only in terms of his integration into the former's own projects and desires. Yet each also demands that the other recognize him as independent – that is, as an agent for whom the other is known only in terms of his being integrated into his own projects. That is, each denies to the other that he is a "thing" and instead demands affirmation that *his* subjective point of view on the world is correct and the other's point of view is false to the extent that it conflicts with the former.

The result of this would at first be a struggle to the death. Hegel's argument for this is quite ingeniously couched in terms of a problem in the theory of knowledge. Both have a point of view on the world on the basis of which they make judgments as to what counts as true or false, as appearance or reality and so on. The general principle of the point of view of these agents (as it has been developed up to this point) is a very generally pragmatic principle: The activities of making knowledge-claims is a part of our overall practice of dealing with the world so as to satisfy the system of desires that make up our various projects; and we know things by integrating our conceptions of what counts as an authoritative reason for believing or acting into these overall projects and desires. Since two points of view can clash, there will be problems with conciliating one individual's claims with the conflicting claims of others. But a genuine conciliation could come about only if the parties could assume an objective, impersonal point of view from which they could then judge the conflicting claims made by themselves – that is, only if they could judge their own claims not completely *internally* to their own points of view and experience but could judge them in terms of something that would *transcend* that subjective experience. However, this objective point of view is not something which the agents themselves can simply acquire by dispassionately looking at the world and then simply reading off the determinateness of the objects in that world; the dialectic of "Consciousness" has shown that not to be possible. Since the objective, impersonal point of view cannot therefore be *discovered,* it must be itself *constructed* out of social practice; the agents themselves must construct a *social* point of view on the basis of which they will be able to reconcile the various conflicting judgments and beliefs generated out of their personal points of view. Moreover, for this social, impersonal point of view to play the role it is supposed to play, the agents must be able to learn to map their own personal points of view on to that objective point of view, and thus the objective, impersonal point of view must itself so constructed that it permits such a mapping. (To the extent that they cannot do this, there must remain a gulf, if not an outright contradiction, between the two points of view.) At this point in the *Phenomenology,* however, no such universal, objective point of view is available for these agents, and the "movement of self-consciousness" is the movement of what is involved in constructing an objective point of view that would integrate within itself the conflicting subjective points of view.

Given that there is no objective point of view for these agents, and no objective point of view could be simply "discovered" by them, each must attempt to redescribe the other in terms of his own subjective point of view. Each must assert that everything outside of his own subjective point of view is for him, as Hegel puts it, only a "negative" – that is, something that he claims to know only as it fits into his own personal point of view and that itself cannot impose any conditions of knowledge upon him.[24] Each therefore has a subjective point of view into which he integrates the idea of the other *as having* a subjective point of view. But each takes his own subjective point of view to be the *objective* point of view, to be the "truth," that to which the other's point of view must accommodate itself whenever there are conflicts.

Neither can therefore accept the other's description of him as a "thing" in the other's practical field, nor can either accept that the other exclusively sets the terms of what can be known and what can be permitted to be done. Since for these agents there can be no objective point of view in terms of which they could conciliate their desires – they cannot appeal, for example, to some general abstraction such as "a system of desires" that would incorporate both points of view – they cannot thereby reconcile their competing desires for recognition. Each subject claims primacy for his own point of view; in Hegel's terms, the "being-for-self" and the "being-for-other" of the two agents conflict. To the extent, then, that each understands himself in this way – that is, understands that in holding such a view he is not just an object *in* the world but a subject who has a point of view *on* the world, and he holds that point of view to be the "true" point of view (that something counts as knowledge only in terms of its being integrated into his projects) – each stakes his life in the struggle for affirmation of his being a "subject" and not an "object" (for being an independent point of view on the world and not simply an organism in the world). Moreover, to succeed in having one's view of oneself affirmed would also affirm for the agent that he is *free* in the sense that he is able to "do what he wants" and in the sense that he determines what he is to do.[25]

Although each stakes his life in the struggle for recognition, the death of one of the participants in the struggle cannot resolve this problem. If both stake their lives and struggle to the death, with the result that one survives and the other dies, then although the survivor has indeed demonstrated that he values independence above life itself, his victory will be nonetheless empty. The encounter between the two self-conscious agents is the attempt on the part of each to impose his own subjective point of view on the other and to claim for his own *subjective* point of view the status of being the "true," the *objective,* impersonal point of view. The struggle is therefore not just over the satisfaction of desire but over what is to count as the objective point of view and thus what is to count as the truth. The death of one of the participants implies that this point of view cannot then be achieved.[26] (This argument, as it plays itself out in the *Phenomenology,* ultimately aims at establishing that rational self-consciousness is only possible when one subject can fully integrate the *objective* point of view into his own *subjective* point of view. But that is only the aim; it is not achieved here.)

Mastery, servitude and an "objective" point of view

Therefore, the life of the participants must be preserved in order for the desired resolution to come about. Moreover, for this resolution to come about, the two must construct some kind of shared point of view that could serve to mediate their conflict. But, as we have seen, there are no conceptual resources at hand for either of these agents to construct a truly impersonal point of view. The encounter is therefore between two agents, each understanding himself as "being-for-self" (as having a subjective point of view on the world), and it can have a resolution only when the lives of each are preserved in the struggle for recognition. The only possible resolution therefore is for one to opt for life over recognition and simply to accept the other's point of view as the truth. The one who opts for life becomes the slave, the other becomes the master. The master is the agent whose subjective point of view, whose own projects, are accepted by the slave as the truth, and the slave therefore becomes a "being-for-another" in that he accepts that his own subjectivity – that what for him is an authoritative reason for belief or action – counts only in terms of how well it contributes to satisfying the master's desires and projects.[27]

The master therefore achieves what he desires, recognition from the other, his slave. The master thus thinks that he has successfully integrated the two opposing demands on him – namely, that he affirm for himself that he is independent while at the same time being dependent on the recognition by another. The question is whether this resolution can be satisfactory for the master on the terms that he has himself accepted. For him, what counts as a good reason has to do with its fit with his own projects and desires (which are for him authoritative), and he can affirm this conception of what counts as a good reason only by being given recognition by the slave. The master therefore knows who he is, and he knows what things are only by having his self-conception affirmed by the slave. What he claims to know about himself and the world is therefore mediated by the slave. The slave further supposedly affirms the master's self-conception by working for the master on the things of the world. The master is thus able to enjoy these things as the satisfaction of his desires, for they affirm for him that indeed what counts as a good reason has to do with what fits into what is authoritative for him – namely, *his* own system of desires and projects.[28] The slave, on the other hand, understands that his desires count as good reasons to act only to the extent that their satisfaction can be integrated into a scheme of satisfying the master's desires (for example, that it is appropriate to pursue his own desires only to the extent that they fit in with the master's projects and desires), and he understands that the things of the world can count for him as values or as things to be appropriated by him only insofar as such valuings and appropriations can be integrated into the master's projects and desires. The slave thus understands his own subjective life completely in terms of the master's projects; as we might put it, he maps his own point of view completely on to that of the master's. The master's subjective point of view thus comes to function *as* the impersonal point of view for the slave, the standpoint that he can assume in order to evaluate the correctness of his own personal point of view.[29]

The slave works on things for the master, and thereby affirms for him that what counts in the world is what satisfies the master's desires. But most importantly, the slave *recognizes* the master as the master and adjusts his own subjective point of view to fit the master's point of view; he thus affirms for the master that his viewpoint on the world is true and that his self-conception as an independent agent is valid. But this has another side to it. The master's point of view – understanding that what counts as an authoritative reason has to do with what satisfies *his* desires and projects – has come to be *the* point of view in terms of which any conflicts (either epistemic or practical) between the two agents are to be adjudicated. It is this acceptance of *his* point of view as *the* point of view that affirms for him that he is indeed an independent agent. However, this point of view can play that role only to the extent that the slave, as a self-conscious agent, *has come to accept* that point of view as authoritative. The dominance of the master's point of view is thus dependent on the slave's *having come to accept it* as dominant – that is, the dominance of the master's point of view is fully dependent on the slave's *contingently* coming to accept it and on his *continuing* to accept it.

The master's point of view thus proves to have no metaphysical or epistemic priority over the slave's point of view; its dominance turns out to be a *social fact,* something completely constituted out of the one-sided type of social recognition that makes up the relationship of master and slave, by the slave's coming to accept that point of view as his own.[30] To the extent that the master comes to realize this, he realizes that on his own terms he has failed. He has not established his own subjective point of view as the truth; he has merely managed for contingent reasons to have the slave *accept* it as the truth, with there being no further ground for the acceptance than the *contingent* fact that out of fear for his life, the slave opted to submit to the master.

Likewise, the slave's self-consciousness turns out to be different than it first appeared. The slave's self-consciousness is determined by the master's; what counts as a reason for the slave is a function of what he takes to count as a reason for the master. The slave identified his own projects as having validity only in terms of fitting in with the master's projects.[31] But if the slave comes to an awareness that this is the case – that he takes the master's point of view as his own only because of *contingencies* in the past relationship between the two – then that awareness itself will transform the slave's own self-consciousness, since it shows him that what he takes as authoritative for himself is only contingently authoritative. The contingency that made the slave into a slave was his fear for his life and his willingness to submit to the other rather than to die – for him to take the other to be the master and to *take himself as* the dependent person, the slave – in other words, to *make himself* dependent. This experience, Hegel suggests, had thrown everything into question for him; everything that had appeared as stable and true had been thrown into question by the fact that he faced death and chose to live by submitting to the other agent.[32] He thus faces the contingency of everything, including his own deepest beliefs as to what he regarded as true. But this experience of the full contingency of everything is implicitly what puts him into the position to see the contingency of the master's dominance over him. In submitting to the master and becoming the slave, he beholds in the master that "pure being-for-self" that he had also sought – namely, the master's subjective point of view in terms of which the master takes something to count as an authoritative reason for him only to the extent that it fits into *his* overall projects and desires; and the master's taking his own personal point of view to be *the* point of view, seeing things as counting per se only to the extent that *he* has come to accept them as counting. The slave comes to be in the position, however, to understand that this acceptance on his part of the master's point of view is not based on any metaphysical difference between him and the master but only on the fact that, out of fear, he accepted the status of slave in relation to the other, who became the master.

The master has appeared to satisfy his desires in having the slave work over the things of the world for him. The slave, however, in his working on things in order to satisfy the desires of the master, comes to see his own point of view embodied in the artifacts of his work. Whereas the master can only find his satisfactions in the contingent social facts of his dominance – quite literally in the *objects* which the slave prepares for him because of the slave's continuing *recognition* of him – the slave can find his satisfactions in working over and forming the objects of the natural world. Purely natural objects cannot, as we have seen, count for the master as affirming his sense of himself as an independent agent, since natural desire is something that simply *imposes* itself on him, that he has these desires whether he elects to have them or not; natural objects can affirm the master's sense of himself only if they have been worked over and formed *for* him *by* the slave (by someone who recognizes him as master and, out of this recognition, works on the objects for him in order to satisfy the master's projects).

Because the slave has internalized the master's *subjective* point of view on things as the "true," as the *objective* point of view in terms of which he must judge his own subjective point of view, he understands that these objects count as something of value only to the extent that *he*, the slave, works on them; without *his* working on them, they count for nothing for the master and hence count for nothing per se. However, this gives the slave an unintended form of independence, for the slave is now in a position to reflect on his own activity and to see that the natural objects of the world count as things of value only to the extent that *he,* the slave, integrates them into *a* scheme of satisfying desire (even if that scheme of desires is not his own).[33] To the extent that the slave comes to understand this – that he is a slave by contingency only and that his own activity is also constitutive of something's counting as a thing of value – he sheds the complete hold that the master had over his self-consciousness. In doing so, the slave will have thus turned out to have achieved the more nearly "objective" point of view of the two agents; the slave thus succeeds in doing that at which the master failed, namely, to construct a social, quasi-objective point of view out of his subjective point of view through his encounter with the other. The master must thus come to acknowledge this in the slave and learn to map his own point of view on to that of the slave who is emerging as independent.[34] Instead of having his own point of view as clearly dominant, as being the "true" view, the master must now learn to coordinate his own views with those of the slave and understand that his mastery over the slave is only a contingency, and not a function of the "intrinsic superiority" of his own point of view, or a mirror of some metaphysical truth supposedly "out there." Thus, neither the master nor the slave ends up where he had intended. The dialectic of master and slave was initiated by each identifying his own projects as authoritative for what counted as good reasons for belief and action, but each has now found that he cannot identify what is *his own* without reference to the other's point of view – without, that is, reference to the *sociality* common to both. What counts as *his own* projects for the master cannot be unambiguously identified without incorporating some reference to the slave's projects and vice versa.

The *necessity* of a common, "objective" point of view is thus established out of the dialectic of master and slave, although that common point of view has not yet been fully achieved. What has been created instead are two subjective points of view, each coordinating itself with the other, each as it were mapping itself on to the other's point of view. This result does not imply any change in the social relations of dominance between the master and the slave, for the slave may contingently lack the necessary practical means to free himself from the master, and the master may not relinquish his political or practical hold on the slave. What has unalterably changed between them, however, is that the master's point of view can no longer be the dominant point of view to which the slave immediately adapts his own point of view. A new, more nearly common point of view, has emerged; this new point of view will make new claims, and, so Hegel will further argue, these new claims – those involved with stoicism, skepticism and what he calls the "unhappy consciousness" – will also fail to make good on the aims that they set for themselves. But their failures make possible the point of view of modern life, which is the goal in which Hegel thinks the phenomenology of the European community can find itself completed, even if it has never actually aimed at that goal.

3. Stoicism, skepticism, and the unhappy consciousness

Freedom of thought

The dialectic of master and slave has created the possibility for the slave to understand that his status as a slave is the result of his contingently having come to accept the subjective point of view of the master as normative for *his own* point of view. The master's point of view becomes dominant because the slave *comes to count it* as dominant, and the reason for the slave's coming to do that has to do with the fear and anxiety he felt for his life in the initial struggle for recognition. The slave thus comes to be in the position to understand that it is his bestowal of mastery on the master (and his potential withdrawal of it) that sustains that relationship; the slave, as Hegel puts it, comes to understand that he has a certain type of freedom within himself. This freedom consists of his acknowledgement that what counts as knowledge has to do with how certain standards have come to be accepted by the community as defining what kinds of things can count as warrants for belief. (In this case, the "community" in question was only two people, the master and the slave.) The "truth" of the dialectic of master and slave was that what had come to count as authoritative was the result of contingent circumstances governing the social acceptance of certain standards of warranted belief; these standards had to do with what worked for the agents in question: What had "worked" for the slave was his having valued life as higher than recognition, and what had "worked" for the master was his willingness to die for the recognition he desired. However, with the understanding that the basis for what counts as warranted is the kind of contingency at work in the dialectic of master and slave, a new possibility of self-consciousness is created. The agents are now in a position to see that what counts has to do with their having *contingently come to count* it, and that outside of the historical contingencies of life (of, for example, one person having more fear than another), there is nothing that compels us to accept one standard over another. The sense of everything fixed being thrown into question, which the slave had experienced when he feared for his life, is now taken as defining the relation between subjects and their world.[35] Nothing is fixed, and the only stable point in the world is the agent's *freedom* to think about that world, to assume for himself what is to count *for him* as true. Not his practical projects, which can be thwarted by others, but his ability to freely elect for himself the standards for what is to count for him as authoritative in determining what is a warrant for belief.

This freedom is therefore at first understood as freedom in *thinking* about things, in the way we take them. One may not be free in the sense that one is not able to "do what one wants" (the slave cannot free himself, the master cannot *compel* the slave to believe what the master believes), but one is free in the sense that nothing can count as authoritative for oneself unless one has freely elected it for oneself. The master had sought to have his subjective viewpoint affirmed for himself by having the slave affirm it for him in the slave's act of recognition. However, that point of view, which had failed on the terms it had set for itself, is now redescribed in different terms: The master found that he could not determine the slave to accept his point of view (he could only naturally compel him), and the slave now sees that nobody can determine *him* to accept the other's point of view. He himself has to come to accept it. We thus still do not have a fully objective point of view; we have various individuals recognizing others as having their own subjective points of view but affirming for themselves that they are independent in having their own subjective point of view and in affirming that it is up to them as *thinking* beings to accept or deny other points of view. To *know* something is to *affirm for oneself* that such and such are the standards by which the truth is to be determined. The independence which the master had sought is now transformed into the "independence of thinking."[36] Once again, the issue is whether this conception of knowledge can satisfy itself on the terms that it sets for itself.

Stoicism

Hegel identifies classical stoicism in the *Phenomenology* with this conception of freedom as independence in thought. The move from the struggles over mastership and slavery to the considerations of stoicism (and then to skepticism and the "unhappy consciousness") has struck more than a few readers as puzzling. It seems to move quite abruptly and without much explanation from very abstract arguments about what a hypothetical encounter between two self-conscious agents in something like a state of nature would look like to a quite obviously historical discussion about some issues in late antiquity. The reason for this otherwise odd move from conceptual argument to history has to do with the connection between self-consciousness and history itself. History (or at least the history with which a "dialectical history" is concerned) becomes possible only when later stages can be seen as completions of earlier stages, such that the later stages may be seen to be teleological progressions from earlier stages.

This teleology itself is possible only in the following sort of way. Forms of life become *reflective* forms of life (become, that is, "spirit") when they develop practices for reassuring themselves and affirming (or failing to affirm) that what that form.of life has come to count as an authoritative reason for belief or action *really* is an authoritative reason. (In late modernity – the time in which we, the readers of the *Phenomenology,* are living – this overall reflective practice is differentiated into the distinct practices of art, religion, and philosophy.) However, these reflective accounts develop within the terms they set for themselves skeptical doubts about themselves; reflection on what has been affirmed as an authoritative reason shows that it is possible – given the kinds of accounts that have been offered of why those reasons really count as authoritative reasons – to doubt that these reasons really are authoritative reasons. These reflective forms of life produce, in Hegel's terms, their own "negatives" – that is, their own skepticism about themselves. It is out of the failures of attempts to construct an affirmative account of why certain reasons are authoritative reasons that a new set of reasons – and thus a new form of collective self-identity – emerges. Unless a form of life can develop such a reflection on itself, it cannot be completed by later stages, for the idea of a later stage completing an earlier stage is possible only if the later stage can be seen to resolve some kind of problem in the earlier stage.

It was in coming to see that his slavery rests on the contingency of his having chosen life over recognition – in fearing for his life and coming to see that nothing was fixed – that the slave acquired the possibility of becoming a stoic or a skeptic. That is, only when the practice of offering an affirmative account of what counts as an authoritative reason was set up and skepticism about it was engendered out by the very account that was given – a "negation" of the "affirmation" – were the slave and the master, as it were, ready to move on to another stage. (It should be emphasized that in speaking that way, Hegel does not mean that any two identifiable individuals, such as the "master" and "slave," are now themselves ready to become stoics; it is "formations of consciousness" that Hegel has in mind.) Hegel holds that this possibility was first fully realized in classical Greek culture (although adumbrated by Egyptian religion) in which "spirit" as such a *reflective* form of life first emerged. The structure of the argument that Hegel develops in the move from mastery and slavery has to do with his claim that the classical Greek form of life first realized in an institutional form the *possibility* present in self-consciousness – namely, that of offering reflective accounts of whether what we have come to count as authoritative reasons really are authoritative reasons. Previous forms of life, so Hegel thought, had certainly possessed activities of reason-giving and the like; but they did not develop a self-consciousness about it in the form of social practices that evaluated whether what they had come to accept as authoritative for themselves was in fact justified. The possibility of the kind of history that is the subject of a dialectical account depends on these reflective practices having been developed. For that reason, a social history of slavery in the ancient world, for example, would not satisfy Hegel's project; it is only when there is a reflection on the institution of mastership and servitude as insufficient forms of independence that history in the sense in which the dialectical philosopher is interested can begin. Thus, since Greece first developed the reflective practices in this sense, in Hegel's view it would be completely appropriate to jump from the rather abstract speculations about mastership and slavery to an examination of the historical practices of stoicism and skepticism, for it is in those accounts of the issues involved in the Greek institutions of mastership and slavery that history can truly begin. Hegel is thus ready to move from the abstract considerations of the encounter between two self-conscious agents seeking independence to the way in which the kind of reflections engendered out of that encounter would produce a historical movement of progressively more complex "affirmations" answering to progressively more complex "negations." Stoicism is historically and conceptually the first of these attempted affirmations that emerge out of the kinds of reflections on mastership and slavery.[37]

The doctrines of stoicism are the kinds of accounts that seem to satisfy the skepticism that both the master and the slave would arrive at as the result of their encounter. Nothing counts for the stoic as true or good unless he can affirm it within his own thought as true and good. The stoic does this by retreating from the concerns of everyday life – that is, the objects of desire and work. The rationale for the stoic's doing this can be described in terms of the insufficiencies revealed in the dialectic of master and slave. Seeking the satisfaction of desire had led neither the master nor the slave to establish their independence. In everyday life, one is ruled by others in society and by desire in one's own life, and it is impossible to identify what is genuinely a desire of one's own outside of social life. The stoic's solution is to become indifferent to whether he is a master or slave, for if true independence lies in the freedom of thought, then one's independence cannot be a matter of either mastery or servitude, for such things cannot affect one's real independence. For the stoic, the master can be truly free only to the extent that he can affirm for himself that such and such counts as an authoritative reason for him because *he* counts it, and the slave can be truly free only when he can do the same thing. Who is the master and who is the slave is a matter of contingency and is not in the agent's control; however, whether one retains one's independence of thought is completely up to the agent himself.

In this way, the stoic constructs something closer to a genuinely impersonal point of view than was possible for the "formation of consciousness" delineated in the dialectic of master and slave. The stoic comes to believe that the independence of thought for which he strives is not the imposition of his own *subjective* point of view on things but rather an attempt to become indifferent to all particular things and to assume the point of view of a "rational being in general."[38] Unlike the master, the stoic does not attempt to make his own subjective point of view normative for others; rather, he seeks to detach himself from his subjective point of view and take a detached, universalistic point of view. Unlike the agents at the conclusion of the dialectic of master and the slave, who *coordinate* their two points of view, the stoic is not interested in coordinating his point of view with another at all but with abstracting from all that is personal in his point of view. The stoic thus seeks to do in thought what the master and slave failed to do in practice. What counts as an authoritative reason is not a matter of its being integrated into our projects and desires, for those are too personal; rather, what counts as an authoritative reason is what can be integrated into our system of thought. The stoic is thus not dominated by any "other": neither by another person imposing his point of view on him nor by his desires, which are too personal and too determined by chance.

For the stoic, therefore, nothing counts for him unless he can bring it into some scheme of rational thought. However, this turns out for the stoic to be only a very *abstractly* impersonal point of view. By defining itself in opposition to the particularities of everyday life (which it sees as a realm of non-freedom and dependence), the stoic puts himself in a position of not being able to give any content to the impersonal point of view except to claim that it is "rational." To adopt a truly impersonal point of view according to the terms in which he has framed the issue, the stoic must abstract from all the particularities of everyday life but even from particular thoughts, for these too may have been given to him by others. Because of this, stoicism buys its independence at the cost of excessive abstractness and formality.[39] Because of its formality, the stoic point of view cannot give any account of what the *individual* stoic is actually to take as counting as knowledge or as being valuable. The stoic point of view was supposed to make good on the idea that true independence was to be found in freedom of thought, in deciding for oneself what was to count for one as true by virtue of counting as knowledge only that which meets the impersonal criteria of rationality; and the stoics claimed to have found this independence in their conception of a "criterion" of rationality by which they could decide for themselves what was true or valuable. However, the formalism of their principles cannot provide this criterion, since a purely formal criterion can only rule out the internally self-contradictory claims; it cannot decide between any claims that contradict each other but that are not themselves self-contradictory.

Skepticism

If followed out, the stoical point of view would lead to skepticism; or, as Hegel puts it, the "truth" of stoicism is skepticism. In his fear for his life, the slave had experienced the contingency of his own point of view; the skeptic transforms this into the contingency of *all* points of view, including his own. Anything that looks fixed and true can be shown, so the skeptic argues, to be only relative to a particular *subjective* point of view, including even that subjective point of view's view of itself.[40] The independence of reflective thought that had animated the stoic is made into a true independence of thought by the skeptic, for the skeptic applies the kind of reflections which for the stoic constituted independence of thought to thought itself, showing that what was taken as fixed and known by the stoics is in fact relative and open to question. We cannot know the things of the world with certainty, but we also cannot know our own thoughts with certainty. The skeptic's point is that when applied to itself, the impersonal point of view assumed by the stoic turns out to be self-undermining. Assuming the stoical impersonal point of view drives to the conclusion that any point of view is always the point of view of an individual person, and that any individual person's point of view is always subject to all kinds of relativizing doubts. Thus, the attempts at fulfilling the general aim to take the impersonal point of view lead to the view that there really is *no* impersonal point of view at all and that there are only subjective and relative points of view.[41] True independence of thought thus requires one to be a skeptic.[42]

67

Skepticism is thus the self-conscious expression of what was demonstrated in the earlier dialectical moves that have gone from the breakdown of the claims of sense-certainty to the failure of the relation between master and slave and its replacement by stoicism. By being skeptical about all these claims to knowledge, the skeptic thereby seemingly achieves a true freedom of self-consciousness. Nothing can count for him unless he *takes* it as counting, and the skeptic understands that nothing *can* count as knowledge for him, since he subjects all putative claims to knowledge to a series of dialectical moves (or "tropes") that shows them to be relative to the person making the claim, to the circumstances under which the claim is made, or even to be in themselves relative to other claims, which in themselves are relative to other claims and so on.[43] The skeptic thus focuses on his own activity of "taking things to be such and such". Skepticism is thus, as Hegel characterizes it, the "negative," a subjective point of view taking itself and itself alone to be that which sets the standards for what is to count as a claim to knowledge, taking itself to have shown that all putatively universal points of view are really only subjective points of view, and then arguing that no subjective point of view can succeed on its own terms.[44]

Nothing can therefore count as stable and independent for this type of skeptic except the skeptic's own *consciousness* of the relativity of everything else. Stoicism had sought independence in assuming the universal point of view, in seeing things from the standpoint of "rational thought"; skepticism claims that the rigorous application of the supposedly universal point of view to itself in fact shows that there was no such thing as *the* universal point of view. Viewed dispassionately, all claims to knowledge will come to be seen as relative to the subjective point of view of the individual person making the claim.[45] In taking this position, the skeptic thus seems himself to have achieved the adequate form of rational independence at which the stoic aimed.[46]

It is evident to the skeptic that this point of view has a tension within itself: the skeptic claims that *all* claims to knowledge are relative to the subjective point of view of *one* contingent individual, and his assertion of the primacy of the subjective point of view is based on his taking the universal point of view to be self-defeating. Yet in order to make the claims he does, it would seem that the skeptic himself must assume the detached universal point of view to see that all claims to knowledge are themselves relative to a subjective point of view. The true skeptic thus finds himself in what *seems* to be an elementary contradiction from which he cannot extricate himself; he assumes that all his claims to knowledge are contingent, are the result of whatever accidental factors have made him have the beliefs that he has. On the other hand, by seeing everything as contingent, he distances himself from them, seeing them as relative to some point of view or the other, and thus he implicitly assumes the detached, impersonal point of view. Ancient skepticism is not just a theoretical understanding of the world but a way of living. Thus, the skeptic finds that he can preserve his independence not by affirming any particular claim to knowledge but only by affirming only his own *reflective activity* itself. The skeptic is thus a divided form of consciousness, caught between the two points of view that he finds within himself: the contingent, purely personal point of view, and the detached, impersonal point of view. The skeptic thus does not give up his central beliefs about himself or the world; he continues to hold certain views quite strongly. He simply reflectively distances himself from them, knowing that however strongly he may believe something, it is not "objectively" true, not something that has any validity outside of him or his community *having made it valid* on the basis of a contingently formed point of view. His independence, the one non-contingent feature of his life, is his skeptical activity itself. Yet a true skeptic knows that even though he presupposes this view of himself as independent, he cannot justify it within the terms that skepticism sets for itself.

The "unhappy consciousness"

When the skeptic owns up to this division within himself, he ceases to be a skeptic, for now he owns up to the centrality of certain views for himself, owns up to the idea that there are certain things that he claims to know and certain values that he accepts that he cannot willingly change nor would want to change; he simply admits that he has no way of justifying those beliefs outside of his own contingently held point of view. Hegel calls this the *unhappy consciousness*.

The "unhappy consciousness" is the way in which the skeptic must live his life. The skeptic holds that only his own *activity* of evaluating all claims to knowledge is authoritative; he thus holds that he achieves independence in taking that detached attitude to every kind of claim-making activity. Yet he also holds that there is nothing that *can be* affirmed, including this affirmation of his own independence, because any such affirmation would require a non-contingent, universal point of view that is itself impossible to attain. Yet in making that claim, the skeptic seems to be assuming some kind of impersonal view on knowledge itself and on his own claim-making activity. The "unhappy consciousness" is distinguished from the skeptic in that the skeptic wishes to assert the supreme validity of *no* point of view and thus finds himself wavering between both the subjective and the objective points of view, whereas the "unhappy consciousness" takes that wavering to be an essential feature of itself and the world.[47] The participants in the "unhappy consciousness" are thus not *skeptical* about their claims to knowledge; they believe things, but they do not see how those beliefs can be justified, given the standards that they accept for justification.

The way in which a participant in the "unhappy consciousness" is divided within himself is not simply that of a person who finds that he holds some kind of particular self-reflexive contradiction that might be resolved simply by dropping one side of the contradiction or by tweaking his philosophical system so that the contradiction can be avoided. It is rather the self-conception of an agent who finds (1) that he *must* hold both sides of the contradiction, (2) that there is no way out of the contradiction, and (3) that he must therefore live with it rather than merely avoid it in his philosophical theories. The "unhappy consciousness" is thus not in the position of the self-refuting lying Cretan who announces that everything he says is false, for (presumably) the lying Cretan can view this as not really touching anything else he believes. The lying Cretan can continue to hold that all his beliefs are in order, with the exception of this particular, peculiar self-refuting statement, and it is only a matter of fine-tuning some philosophical theory to see how that particular paradox might be resolved. The "unhappy consciousness" however finds that his own conception of *everything* that he claims to know and to be is burdened with that kind of apparent contradiction. The "unhappy consciousness" thus finds that he cannot affirm within his own terms those things that he finds that he *must* believe. The "unhappy consciousness" *takes* certain things as authoritative but cannot quite *believe* in their authoritativeness. He embodies what Kierkegaard simply later called "despair."

The "unhappy consciousness" thus describes a particular form of life in which people's conception of themselves and of what they claim to know exists in an enduring state of crisis. The basic principles of that form of life have their hold on people and define who they are, yet there exists within that form of life a great skepticism about the viability of these principles or their ultimate justification. Thus, the participants in the "unhappy consciousness" find that they have a certain self-conception rooted in a set of social practices that for them is authoritative, but for which they can neither see any justification nor envision any concrete alternative. Hegel uses the idea of the "unhappy consciousness" to describe both medieval Christianity and the Hellenic and pre-Christian worlds in which the older Greek gods were gone with nothing yet having arisen to take their place. In the Hellenic world, for example, the "unhappy consciousness" appears as a longing for the lost Greek divinities, since the beliefs surrounding the Greek gods were central to the Greek form of life, but the belief in them had ceased to have any real hold on the participants of that form of life.

The "unhappy consciousness" is thus divided *within itself,* for it necessarily assumes both points of view. Assuming the universal point of view is necessary for it to justify its claims to knowledge. It still takes itself as incapable of assuming that point of view, since it takes itself to be capable only of achieving a relative and limited subjective point of view. The "unhappy consciousness" must therefore take the two points of view as fully *opposing* points of view: What is justified from one point of view is unjustified from the other point of view. That is, the impersonal point of view is understood to be the point of view that if it *could* be attained would manifest a non-contingent viewpoint on the world, whereas the "unhappy consciousness" itself can only live within its own subjective point of view. At first, therefore, the "unhappy consciousness" takes the impersonal point of view to be that which is essential to justifying the claims that it makes, and takes its own individual point of view to be fully contingent and to play no role in justifying things. In Hegel's terms, the "unhappy consciousness" takes the impersonal point of view to represent the *unchangeable* view on things (to be that point of view on the unchanging "essence" of things), whereas it takes its own subjective point of view to be the contingent, *changeable* (unessential) point of view.[48] The "unchangeable" is that which is both authoritative and unobtainable for the "unhappy consciousness." The "unhappy consciousness" embodies, of course, both points of view at once: It is "unhappy" because it cannot take those two points of view to be indifferent to each other; each is essential, and each contradicts the other. Any attempt to reduce the one to the other is bound to fail, for both are essential to the self-understanding of the "unhappy consciousness."[49] What is thus important about the two points of view for the "unhappy consciousness" is not only that they are *his* two points of view but that they seem to be *irreconcilable* with each other.[50]

The task for the "unhappy consciousness" is thus the attempt to conciliate or integrate the competing claims of the two points of view. The impersonal, detached, objective point of view is the true view for the participant in the "unhappy consciousness." His own subjective, personal point of view is too determined by contingencies for it to be able to affirm that what appears to him or what he takes to be true and valuable really is true and valuable. The only possible affirmation of his views would have to come from the objective point of view itself (the "unchangeable," as Hegel refers to it), and this point of view is impossible for him to attain. Thus, he must represent this objective, authoritative point of view to himself as something *beyond* his capacities, which he only knows well enough to know that he cannot attain it. That "beyond" is hypostatized as "the truth" and is interpreted as being "out there," external to human desires or wishes.

Having this view of the objective, impersonal point of view as something he cannot attain, the "unhappy consciousness" represents that point of view to himself as something like a "God's eye" view, which, if one could attain it, would be able to affirm for him what is indeed true and valuable and what is not. The historical transition involved in the transformation of the abstract ideas of the neo-Platonists – of the "unhappy consciousness" of late Hellenism – into the ideas of early Christianity clearly forms the basis of much of Hegel's discussion here.[51] This "God's eye" view can be represented as itself an abstract individual entity of sorts, as the neo-Platonists did. Even more so, it can be represented as the appearance of Christianity with the person of Jesus assuming the "God's eye" point of view from within the human (subjective) point of view itself.[52] But even this appearance of "the truth" in human form can only appear at first to these agents as something that has simply *happened* to them, something that the "unchangeable" (represented as a force or an entity) has done *for* them; it puts them in the passive position of not being able to do anything on their own to justify their subjective points of view but as having only to accept that something has simply befallen them. Although this appears to them at first as a reconciliation of the two points of view – of the deity's revealing the "truth" to fallible, one-sided people – it cannot serve as anything but a short-term affirmation for these people, for the appearance of "the truth" in the form of an individual person makes that affirmation as contingent as the people for whom it is supposed to serve as an affirmation. Jesus dies, and the Christian community begins to await his return, which more and more recedes into an indeterminate future.[53]

Since having the truth appear for them in the form of a person who promises to return proves to be only a short-term solution, the object of striving to integrate the apparent incompatibilities of the two points of view takes on the form of a kind of *practice* of trying to *fuse* one's own point of view into that of the impersonal point of view itself, of lifting oneself up to the heights of the "unchangeable." The "unchangeable" itself (the world seen from the impersonal point of view as a timeless set of essences) cannot do that for the agents; they must do it for themselves.[54] They must strive to bring their own view of the world in line with the "true view" by elevating themselves in thought to the divine point of view. They must alienate their own subjective points of view in order to attain to the mystical objective point of view (for example, through the contemplation of the eternal truths coupled with a metaphoric rise to the level of the absolute, as the neo-Platonists attempted.) The kind of unclarity and wooliness of the various attempts at resolving the dilemmas of the "unhappy consciousness" are, Hegel argues, a necessary feature of what is required to effect such a resolution, since the ideas under consideration by these agents are to them so riddled with tensions and contradictions. In such a time of transition, the ideas involved are bound to be themselves unclear.[55]

The stoic radicalized the standpoint of the master and the slave by seeking true independence in thought, in electing to count nothing as knowledge that he himself could not affirm *for himself* from the detached, universal standpoint; the skeptic consummated the stoic's project by applying the detached, dispassionate standpoint to the detached standpoint itself and showing that, dispassionately viewed, there are no detached, universal standpoints available to finite, contingent humans. The skeptic thus displays the full "freedom of self-consciousness" in that he is free to refuse to accept anything that he cannot affirm for himself, and, by the application of the various skeptical tropes, he finds that there is nothing that he in fact can affirm as being true except his own independent activity of accepting and rejecting things. The "unhappy consciousness" accepts that skeptical result but realizes that it cannot abandon the universal point of view, since it is the paradoxical application of the universal point of view to itself that makes skepticism possible in the first place.[56] It is therefore faced with two alternatives for reconciling its contradiction. First, it can accept that the universal point of view (the "truth") simply comes to it by some action not its own (through some doctrine such as Plotinean "emanations" from the eternal or, more concretely, by some form of Christian revelation). This tactic necessarily fails, so it must therefore return to the original guiding idea of skepticism, that it is its own thinking activity that allows things to count for it. The "unhappy consciousness" thus moves from a conception of itself as passive and as simply receiving the "truth" to that of being active, of preparing itself so that it can "receive the truth."[57] This is crucial, for it means that the "unhappy consciousness" assumes that there is a detached point of view to be achieved, but that its own activity is required for it to work itself up to that point of view. The move from a somewhat passive skepticism to an active attempt at working up to a fusion of the objective and subjective points of view amounts to a *social project* of transforming humanity (which Hegel sees as the crucial transition from the "ancients" to the "moderns").

The first stage of this attempt at transforming humanity so that it is ready to "receive" the truth is through devotional activity.[58] The agents wish to achieve the objective standpoint, and they believe that they must do this through their own activity. That is, they try to learn to put their own individuality (the subjective point of view) aside and remake themselves into agents capable of assuming the proper, authoritative standpoint. The various practices involving devotional activity and reflection are the first means for achieving this self-elevation. Hegel's point is that this kind of devotional activity makes more sense for *these types* of agents with *this type* of self-consciousness than merely thinking or reflecting on things in a more purely "philosophical" mode would do; the goal is to affirm that what they take as true really is true through some practice that will achieve the goal of fusing their subjective points of view with the objective ("true") point of view. (This is part of Hegel's overall view that apparently different things like devotional activity and philosophy are to be understood as different forms of social practice in which subjects reflect on themselves and seek reassurance and affirmation for what they take to be true and real.) This kind of devotional activity is composed of rites, of chants, of the smell of incense, and all the other trappings of the early Christian church. Through it, people get a vague understanding (Hegel calls it a "feeling") of what it means to distance themselves from their own limited, contingent points of view, and see things from an objective perspective that is nonetheless fused with their point of view; devotional activity leads them to conceive of the "truth" (the objective view of things, the "God's eye" view of the world) not as something that is foreign to their own subjective point of view but as essentially linked to it.[59] The idea that God is personal, and that He recognizes individual agents forms the basis for believing that it is also possible for humanity to elevate itself at least partially to that standpoint. By attending to the revelations in the proper attitude and engaging in the practice that constitutes "devotion," one prepares oneself for reception of that "truth." But, of course, it is impossible *actually* to assume the "God's eye" standpoint, for that would require that one be more than one can possibly be. Agents are finite, contingent people, and if the true standpoint on the world is only available to an infinite deity, then it is impossible to ever actually achieve that standpoint. The "God's eye" view must remain something always beyond us.

Hegel notes two failed attempts at overcoming the gulf between the subjective and objective points of view and uniting them. First, there is the mystic's idea that one can only achieve the integration of one's own view with that of the "true" view through some sort of mystical, ineffable experience that fuses one's own point of view with that of the divine point of view. But the mystic's idea – that one beholds in a pure experience the oneness of the divine within one's own experience – is really just a repetition of the dialectic of "sense-certainty," the idea that one can have an immediate experience of pure singularities.[60] Second, there is the search for the reality of the divine in the here and now, something evidenced in the Crusaders' attempt at conquering the Holy Land, as if anything further could be gained by conquering the lands on which Jesus once walked or by finding the grave from which he had supposedly arisen (as if one could gain authority in reason-giving activities or in devotional practices by seizing some ground on which Jesus had been). Success in taking these lands is not success in the intended sense; one is no closer to the "truth" by having done so than one was when one started out.

The attempt to bring oneself closer to the divine point of view by virtue of conquering the Holy Land (or, more generally, by virtue of trying to find any *place* that is supposedly closer to the divine) necessarily fails at what it is really trying to do. Reacquiring the land on which Jesus's supposed grave was located could not *affirm* for these agents that what they count as true and valuable is in fact what is true and valuable; it could get them no closer to the putatively authoritative divine point of view. In order to achieve the affirmation that they seek, they are thus driven back into reliance on their own activities, which must take a different form from that of gaining some kind of closer physical proximity to the divine point of view.[61] They must, that is, engage in some form of activity through which they feel they are brought out of their contingent, individual lives more into proximity with the divine point of view.

The vague feelings of unity with the divine point of view expressed in the social practices of devotion and the practices of the cults are only vague intimations of what is in actuality only an aspect of the true form of self-consciousness itself as a unity of the personal and the detached point of view, something that only completely occurs in late modernity. This unity is, however, only "for us," the readers, not for the participants in the "unhappy consciousness" themselves; we, as enlightened by our commentator (Hegel), see that what is going on is the gradual construction of the idea that the universal point of view is a *socially constructed* point of view, something to which we, the participants in modern life, must eventually own up, even if these pre-modern agents themselves *could not* have understood it in that fashion.[62] But the idea that it is *up to them,* to their own activities to achieve the union of the objective, universal point of view and the subjective, individual point of view within themselves is for us, the readers, a step on the way to the fully modern conception of "spirit" in which the two ideas are put in a comprehensible unity with each other.

The agents come to rely on their own activities to accomplish their union with the divine point of view; they thus come to see the possibility of this union as arising not simply from pure devotion (as something wholly within their own consciousness) nor by their coming into some kind of physical proximity with divine places (as in the Crusades) but as something that can only come about through their own activities. But if their own everyday activities are for them to count as being in any way authoritative, it must be because in such everyday activities (of "work" and "desire," as Hegel puts it) a proximity to the universal divine point of view is achieved. This, however, is possible only if these everyday activities themselves can be seen as somehow being connected with the divine, such that participation in them *counts* for something authoritative. The *world* itself for these people thereby becomes divided within itself just as their own form of self-consciousness is divided within itself. They had earlier taken the divine point of view to have revealed itself to them in their own individual consciousness in the mystical practices and reflections of devotional activity, but that revelation turned out to be insufficient in accomplishing the aims they had set for it. These agents therefore attempt to find that union of the universal and the individual points of view (that affirmation of their claims to knowledge and valuation) within the activities of everyday life. The world thus comes to be seen as a *redeemed* world in which their longings are in principle satisfied, as a world in which the ordinary happenings of everyday life are mirrored in a divine world.[63]

This reliance on their own labors within their ordinary activities to reassure them that what they take to be authoritative is in fact so is nonetheless not a true self-reliance, nor could it be so for these agents. For them, the universal, objective point of view is something that must be always just beyond their reach. Thus, they cannot see their own experienced enjoyments as being something for which they themselves can be fully responsible, for they view themselves and everything in the world as a set of fully contingent events. Therefore, they must view whatever satisfactions there are in everyday life as somehow being contingently bestowed on them by this "higher power," the "unchangeable." Even their own abilities must be seen as a gift from God, not something for which they themselves could have been fully responsible. Since they see themselves and the world around them as dependent on the "unchangeable" for whatever limited authority that world and activities have for them, they cannot see the authority of these activities as being really up to them – that is, they cannot see themselves as independent.[64] What occurs in the world as the result of human labor must be seen as something that essentially is a result of the power of the divine realm. In this way, the "unhappy consciousness" maintains a self-conception as a divided self: on the one hand, as contingent and incapable of affirming for himself that what he takes to be true really is true; and on the other hand, as having some access to the truth by virtue of his interaction with the realm of the divine.

The proper attitude, given these presuppositions about the world, can only be that of giving thanks to the divine for whatever satisfactions and whatever glimpses of the truth have been bestowed on one.[65] Such a viewpoint makes possible the affirmation for these agents that they are indeed in touch with the universal point of view (the "truth"). On the one hand, they see the divine as getting in touch with them through its bestowal of worldly gifts and humanity's talents; on the other hand, they see their giving thanks as that contribution on their part that makes possible the attainment for them of some small portion of the "truth."[66] The activity of giving thanks is the

75

affirming activity for these agents that they do indeed know something of the "truth."

The social practices of thanks-giving offer those agents a context and a means in which they are able to reflect on their essential self-identities, on what it is that they are doing. (Again, Hegel's thesis that there are many different social practices in which such reflection can take place – not merely the more modern social practice of academic philosophy – is apparent here.) But such reflection can only underscore for them their own lack of affirmative power; they can *only* give thanks. The "truth" is beyond their contingent, finite reach, and whatever grasp they have on it cannot be due to them. They are thus without intrinsic worth themselves, and have worth only insofar as it is bestowed upon them. What looked like an affirmation of their claims to knowledge becomes the opposite, a *disavowal* of their own selves and their basic individuality.[67] What they as contingent individuals count as valuable can turn out not to be so, and everything they believe to be true can turn out not to be true, unless they are reassured by the divine. Their independence completely vanishes,· for they take everything that can count for them as authoritative to come from outside their own activities.

The issue for these agents, therefore, has to do with how they can reassure themselves that skepticism is not the answer and affirm for themselves that what they count as true is indeed true. They have the belief that the stand-point of the "truth" is possible, is "out there" beyond their own consciousness and contingent lives, and the participants in the "unhappy consciousness" have come to count those claims to knowledge and value that they have constructed out of their own contingent perspectives to be "untrue." Their disavowal of their own lives as giving them any access to this "truth" indeed makes sense only in terms of their belief that this "God's eye" point of view is the *only* point of view that could be said to be "true" – that is, that only someone assuming the universal point of view *could* be in a position to affirm that such and such can legitimately count as knowledge and as goodness.[68]

For them to be able to affirm any contact between their limited, contingent lives and the divine point of view, they must therefore *represent* something as *mediating* between them as contingent individuals and the universal, divine point of view. This is represented as a priest, someone who has been given certain powers by the divine, but who is a contingent individual like themselves. The function of the mediator-priest is to affirm for these agents that what they have come to count as authoritative (the "God's eye" point of view) and what they come to disavow (their own finite claims to knowledge) are the ways that the "true" point of view would describe them.[69] The acceptance of such priest-mediators means for the participants in the "unhappy conscious-ness" that they alienate themselves from their own subjective point of view and its activities in favor of the putatively objective, "God's eye" point of view; but by virtue of such priest-mediators, the participants in the "unhappy consciousness" find themselves reassured that they are indeed at least par-tially in touch with the "truth." What seemed to them to be something that they had to disavow is thus brought into congruence with what they took to be the only possibilities for affirming what they believed. (Hegel also notes how this allows them to throw off their guilt, thereby affirming for them that each in his individuality counts as something valuable.)

In coming to understand the affirmation from their point of view of who they are and what they count as authoritative as dependent on a mediator-priest, the participants in the "unhappy consciousness" disavow their individuality, their subjective points of view, as having any intrinsic authoritativeness but as capable of being "in contact" with that which is authoritative. As the successors to skepticism, the participants in the "unhappy consciousness" find that the logical development of their form of life has led them to the opposite of the skeptical point of view. The skeptic affirmed the validity of the subjective point of view by applying the stoic's universal point of view to itself; the result was that the skeptic could only affirm the subjective point of view, which meant paradoxically that the skeptic then had to deny that the subjective point of view *could* make any valid claims to knowledge at all. The skeptic's independence consisted in the affirmation of his own reflective (skeptical) activity, but once the skeptic comes to realize that paradox, he becomes the "unhappy consciousness." The participants in the "unhappy consciousness," on the other hand, find that they must abandon the subjective point of view altogether, not in order to get out of skepticism by returning to the stoical standpoint, but to attain a more concrete understanding of themselves and the world from within the universal point of view. Thus, the result of the "unhappy consciousness" is to disavow the pretensions to affirmation and reassurance that come from within the subjective point of view and to replace it with the idea that individuals can only attain the "true," impersonal point of view by somehow *reconciling* their own individual points of view with the objective, universal point of view. The reconciliation that the "unhappy consciousness" finds is, of course, incomplete and unstable, for it depends on the idea that the detached, universal point of view is forever out of reach and is only partially attainable through the mediator-priest. Indeed, the participants in the "unhappy consciousness" implicitly come to that same conclusion in their realization that it is *their* decision to elevate themselves to that point of view and that *they* determine the value that they shall place on the words of the mediator-priest.[70]

The participants in the "unhappy consciousness" thus find that they have constructed out of the results of stoicism and skepticism the concept of a "universal will" – that is, a conception of a *shared* point of view that is affirmed not by passive contemplation but by human activity.[71] The pursuit of independence now takes the form not of trying to bend other subjects to one's own projects, nor in completely disavowing one's own subjective point of view in favor of a forever distant, "God's eye" objective point of view, but in fusing the two points of view into a unity. This transforms that form of life that is the "unhappy consciousness" into a different project than it originally was. It is not the project of *waiting* to be redeemed by some distant, divine point of view (when "all shall be revealed") but of actively *bringing* their subjective points of view into line with the impersonal God's eye view. The "faculty" that allows them to do this is *reason*. In acquiring the idea that even the truths of nature can be known by human agents provided that they bring their subjective points of view into line with what the impersonal point of view requires, the "unhappy consciousness" in the form of late medieval European culture arrives at a different understanding of itself than that with which it began: the idea that by appealing to impersonal reason alone human agents can discover what truly counts for them as knowledge, and that they have the means to affirm for themselves that what counts *for them* really is what counts *in itself,* and that *reason* – not pure faith or reliance on mediator-priests – can give an account of itself that, unlike its predecessors, does not undermine itself. Not only can these agents bring their subjective points of view into line with what the impersonal point of view requires, when this impersonal point of view is understood as that of *reason,* it is capable of reassuring these agents of its authoritativeness that the older view of the "unchangeable" could not. The participants of the "unhappy consciousness" had to simply *accept* the teachings of the mediator-priest; the participants of the culture of reason, however, can expect an account by reason that reassures those agents of its authoritativeness. This is the project of modern life, a reliance on reason to replace an insufficient, dogmatic theological foundation for life and culture; modern life sheds its old faith in favor of new trust in reason, a conviction that it can succeed where the past reliance on dogmatic faith had failed.

4

Modern life's project of self-justification

1. Reason, science, and modern affirmations

The transition to "Reason"

After concluding the section on the "unhappy consciousness," Hegel begins an entirely new section titled "Reason." Hegel's reasons for this transition have proved puzzling to some commentators, leading some to hypothesize that the book indeed has no coherent structure and that the section on "Reason" in particular shows that Hegel changed his mind about the composition of the book while he was writing it and did not have the time to revise the whole manuscript in light of this change of plan.[1] Other commentators, noting the differences between the transition in the 1807 *Phenomenology* and in the later works, particularly the *Encyclopedia,* have concluded that Hegel in his later Heidelberg and Berlin years simply abandoned the *Phenomenology's* approach to things.[2]

However, Hegel's reasons for making this transition can be elicited both from the structure of the *Phenomenology* and by attention to his later writings. There are good, systemic reasons within the structure of the text of the *Phenomenology* itself for the move. In the section on "Consciousness," the issue of what counts as knowledge is treated as having to do with a kind of unreflective fusion of both the subjective and the objective points of view and a failure to distinguish them. In "Consciousness," we have an account of knowledge in terms of some kind of direct awareness of the objects of consciousness; this account undermines itself as it follows out its own logic: The direct awareness of objects in "sense-certainty" turns out really to be a perceptual awareness of objects, which itself turns out to be a more reflected awareness of supersensible entities "behind" appearance that determine the structure of perception. However, the reflective "understanding's" description of supersensible entities itself becomes contradictory and antinomial, and "the understanding's" claim that it consistently describes the world thereby also undermines itself. "Consciousness" thereby becomes *self-consciousness* in trying to give an account of how it could possibly grasp the world as it really is; rather than taking an account of knowledge as a kind of passive, direct awareness of objects as authoritative, it must instead *reflect* on the accounts it gives itself.

In "Self-Consciousness," the issue of what we take to be an authoritative reason is at first explicated from the subjective point of view, and its insufficiencies then generate the objective point of view. After the two distinct points of view have been generated, they are then understood as being in opposition to each other in the sections that deal with stoicism, skepticism, and the "unhappy consciousness." The "unhappy consciousness," however, ends with the possibility of a unity of the objective and the subjective point of view in which the reasons that we take to be authoritative reasons are seen as subjectively determined by us but nonetheless as valid principles governing the world both in theory and in practice when seen from the detached, objective point of view.[3] That is, it creates the *possibility* for the individual thinker of having it affirmed for him that the world as viewed from the standpoint of principles that he endorses from his own *individual* point of view is the same as the world as seen in terms of principles that he would adopt from a more detached standpoint, with no conception of a metaphysical "beyond" being needed to affirm for him these principles that he *takes as* valid *really are* valid. This unity of the two points of view is called "reason" by Hegel, for it signifies that the capacity to affirm that "this is the way the world is" is based not on our "matching up" our representations with the world "in itself" – not, that is, based on any kind of metaphysical relation between our representations and reality – but on our capacity to construct explanatory accounts about ourselves and the world that are then tested internally to see if they can make good on their claims within the terms that they set for themselves.[4] At first, of course, this belief in "reason" is no more than a matter of faith; it is a historical *project,* an attempt to affirm a certain conception of the relation between human thought and reality that at the outset must be simply presumed and that in its development can later be demonstrated.

This is linked with the historical reasons for making the move from "Self-Consciousness" to "Reason": If the progression of history begins with the Greek attempts to work out the problems inherent in relationships of mastership and slavery such that self-generated skeptical doubts about what the Greeks themselves had come to count as authoritative reasons were to be answered by the doctrines found in late antiquity, then what follows should be the later conceptions that historically emerged out of the earlier attempts to work out the problems inherent in the Greeks' (and the Romans') own attempts to affirm for themselves that their reasons were good ones. The various attempts found in stoicism and skepticism led of course to the "unhappy consciousness" of late antiquity and early Christianity, which were incorporated into the medieval Christian period's reflection on the problems of the "unhappy consciousness." The move to modern life, however, gets underway with the post-medieval conception of the investigation of nature through the empirical sciences, what Hegel calls in both the *Phenomenology* and elsewhere the "observation" of nature.[5] The beginnings of experimental science in the period preceding and following the Reformation exhibited the idea that rational agents could in fact unlock the secrets of nature provided they were to follow a *method* that would be determined by their own rational powers and the force of which would provide them with a knowledge of nature that would be useful to humanity (in other words, Francis Bacon's ideal of science).[6] The result of the emphasis by early modernity on scientific *method* is the affirmation that humanity has within its power the capacity to determine for itself that what it takes as an authoritative reason can in fact be shown to be an authoritative reason, to be something that reveals to us the way the world is. That is, it affirms a conception of human agents' having a certain power – namely, that on their own they can develop a method that forces nature to give up its secrets. This kind of "power" spills over into the fields of social life and leads to political self-determination and, so Hegel argues, eventually to his own system of self-determining concepts.[7]

The results of the attempt to apply these methods of reason to nature and to society thus result in the formulations of the laws of nature and the laws of society, which culminate in that period of European life called "the Enlightenment." By constructing rational methods for the observation of nature, people find that they are then led to construct a view of themselves as rational independent agents. This view of ourselves as independent agents gives rise to modern life's idea that its form of life can be completely self-justifying, that it can affirm its social and political institutions for itself without appeal to anything other than that which is demanded by human reason itself. Based on the success of the sciences of nature, modern life attempts to establish a science of human social life that would uncover the heretofore hidden laws of human social and political organization. The idea of there being a "method" appeals to a conception of impersonal reason, "the view from nowhere," something that itself is supposedly independent of all social practices, which itself transcends history. (As the conception of impersonal reason, the "view from nowhere" thus replaces the idea advanced in the "unhappy consciousness" of the "unchangeable.") The section on reason attempts to narrate the dialectical history of that attempt at establishing a self-justifying form of life by the application of various "methods" in order to discover the general laws of nature and social life.

Science as "observing reason"

Hegel's discussion of scientific method and the rationale of the search for various laws of nature differs from his discussion of "sense-certainty" and "perception" in that the latter concerns itself with attempts to construct forms of self-sufficient knowledge that we could in principle have independently of any social practice or historical period, and with the failures of those attempts. Hegel's discussion of modern science, on the other hand, does not treat it as a form of self-sufficient knowledge but as a form of knowledge that presupposes the background of antiquity and the "unhappy consciousness" for its own possibility. The dialectic of the "unhappy consciousness" results in a "faith" that the nature of the world is not something intrinsically alien to our own ways of thinking. That kind of "faith" is the basis of a project of extending the powers of human thought. The rise of humanism, which presupposes the outcome of the "unhappy consciousness," gives rise to a conception of knowledge as serving human interests in which agents see themselves

81

as determining *for themselves* what may count as authoritative reasons for belief and action rather than thinking of the world itself as somehow making certain reasons count for them.

The idea of a self-determined "method" that underlies modern science makes possible the break from the ancients' idea that the ends of life and knowledge are set by nature or by the cosmos – more generally, it makes possible the shift from a conception of "fate" to a conception of freedom. The world is not merely to be contemplated but studied in terms of *human* reason, that is, in terms of how well it satisfies human desires and interests, with the presumption being that by constructing a proper *method,* human agents can discover the way the world is in itself such that they can reshape that world into something that better satisfies human desires and fits human projects. In order to do this, the agents must be content not merely to describe and to classify things (even supposing that the classifications match up with natural kinds); they must get at the nature of things, their essence, and this means describing them as falling under laws – in Hegel's terms, as bringing them to the universal.[8] Basic to this method is observation, observing things as they are, not as we would wish them to be, and constructing our system of laws out of these observations. By making careful, controlled observation central to its method, the scientific community affirms for itself that its rational methods are indeed appropriate to the reality being studied.[9] (Hegel seems to be describing basically what he takes to be Baconian procedures, noting all the while that many philosophers, including Bacon, take themselves *only* to be observing and describing, when in fact they are doing something more – namely, actively constructing theories and postulating entities to explain the correlations observed in their observations.)

The section on "observing reason" is the place in the *Phenomenology* in which Hegel attempts to outline his views on modern science and to come to terms with it (something he attempted later in a slightly different fashion in his *Encyclopedia* in what we now call his "Philosophy of Nature.") Several things about Hegel's treatment stand out. First, he does not go into much detail in the *Phenomenology* (and even less so in his later "Philosophy of Nature") about many themes that have come to be identified with philosophy of science in our time. He does not discuss scientific method in any real detail, and he does not offer any extended philosophical treatment of the problems of induction, on questions of theory construction, on the role of theoretical terms versus observational terms in scientific theory, on the logic of discovery versus the logic of justification, although a judicious reading of the section in the *Phenomenology* could arguably find some things that at least look like a discussion of each of these topics. This is because Hegel did not think that a philosophical theory could *prescribe* to working scientists what their method should be. In that sense, he apparently did not think that questions of scientific method were per se philosophical questions. At best, philosophy can enter into a debate with the scientific community about what are the proper procedures of scientific method, and it certainly can reflect on the role that science and scientific method play in the historical and philosophical development of our conception of ourselves. But the nature of scientific method is best left to the working scientists to determine for themselves; it is up to the *scientific community* (the community of researchers) to determine what is to count as a scientific reason *for them*. Philosophy can no more dictate to the scientific community what counts as an authoritative reason for them than it can dictate to painters what counts as a valid application of paint to canvas or to composers what counts as a valid construction of musical notes. Philosophy can, however, seek to understand the connections between the basic conceptions arrived at by the scientific community and the rest of our conceptions; this is what Hegel takes to be the major task of the kind of philosophy that he is pursuing, for this task helps to situate science within the larger question of the philosophical project of constructing an account of what it means for us to take something as authoritative for ourselves. Philosophy can ask why it is that we have come to accept scientific reasons as *authoritative* reasons or why the kinds of reasoning that the scientific community itself has come to accept have also come to count for the larger community as models of what we should count as authoritative reasons. That is, the Hegelian philosophy of science aims to see scientific practice as part of the overall development of reflective social practice, of "spirit." (Needless to say, it is also part of the legitimate task of philosophy to debate with the scientific community when it starts formulating, perhaps unwittingly, metaphysical or very generally philosophical theses about what it is doing.)[10]

Physics and biology

Hegel argues that science, especially in the form of what we now call classical mechanics, strives for necessity and not just statistical regularity in its laws – that is, it strives for more than the kinds of statistical regularities discovered by inductive observation. Hegel also thinks, however, that what gives the necessity to the laws is that they express the essence of the things they study – for example, that stones fall to earth is a statistical regularity, but that they *necessarily* fall to earth has to do with the intrinsic nature of stones, which is their weight. (The Newtonian view, of course, sees weight as an accidental property of bodies.) Because they have weight "in and for themselves," stones have a necessary relation to the earth. (These kinds of views of weight as an essential property account for some of Hegel's misunderstanding of certain key Newtonian concepts.[11]) However, Hegel's point – which is independent of the somewhat peculiar mixture of modern and pre-modern scientific views in his conception of nature – is that modern science cannot be content with mere Baconian induction but must strive to formulate theories that lend a certain necessity to the laws they come up with. This is done in several ways. The first way in which the agents affirm these findings as adequate is through experimentation. Second, scientists introduce theoretical terms, such as "matter," to explain the various ways in which what might look like different things and different laws can be subsumed under more general cases, thereby fitting what would otherwise only be disconnected observations into a richer conceptual apparatus. The introduction of theoretical terms thus allows for a richer and tighter set of inferences than would be possible if the scientific accounts were left simply at the stage of inductive generalization.[12] (As modern philosophers such as Wilfrid Sellars have argued, mere collections of inductive generalizations cannot explain why the generalizations sometimes do not hold.[13]) The third way is through the construction of *theories* in which the various inductive laws are reformulated in *mathematical* form. (This is not mentioned explicitly in the *Phenomenology*, but it is implicit in Hegel's discussions there, and it later becomes explicit in his mature philosophy of nature in the Heidelberg and Berlin years.) The mathematical form of the laws gives them a necessity that they could not have as mere generalizations from experience. Situating the laws within theories of mathematical form gives them a conceptual status that a mere series of observations could not have. The mathematical formulations of the sciences of nature, along with the generalizations and inferential possibilities offered by the introduction of theoretical terms, thus serve to affirm for modern agents that their own constructions (those of mathematics) are in fact adequate to know the workings of nature, and that therefore what they count as reasons can be shown to be authoritative reasons since mathematics is a human construction that can be shown to be justified and consistent. Scientific practice in early modernity does not, of course, formulate its results in this way. Instead, it takes itself to be offering only an "observational proof" that human reason and reality are not alien to each other; it takes itself, that is, to have formulated a method for "taking in" the world as it really is.

Hegel's reflections on the role of mathematics in scientific law also led him to the belief that the science of organisms would have to take a form different from that of mechanics, since the conditions that allow the formulation of mathematical laws are not present in the study of organisms. The entities of mechanical nature are only "externally" related to each other in purely quantitative and qualitative ways; thus, mathematics is the proper language in which to give a rigorous description of them. Organisms, however, are *self-maintaining* wholes. The proper language to describe them is therefore not mathematics but the language of teleology, of purposiveness. One cannot find any purposiveness, for example, in the solar system; the planets do not orbit the sun to serve any kind of purpose. As a mechanical system, the solar system is held together by sets of countervailing forces, none of which need make reference to any sort of purpose.[14] However, when one describes the system that is an organism, one must employ purposive descriptions (for example, that the heart beats in order to circulate blood, not that it just happens to circulate blood). The kinds of teleological descriptions appropriate to the description of organisms are what we would nowadays call *functional* descriptions. They are not the purposiveness of someone intentionally doing something (such as "going to the university in order to hear Hegel's lectures"). No beliefs or desires need be attributed to the organism when we describe it functionally – we say, for example, that the heart beats in order to circulate the blood, not that the heart "desires" to circulate the blood and therefore it beats, or that the heart "believes" it must beat in order to circulate the blood.[15] Because organisms require these teleological functionalist explanations, which are completely out of place in the physical explanation of inorganic nature, it follows for Hegel that biology must be a science separate from that of physics.[16]

Like physics, biology is based on observation, but, so Hegel argues, it is even less plausible that it could be a purely inductive science than it is that physics could be such a purely inductive science. The kind of functionalist teleology that is necessary for understanding an organism is not something that one simply observes; in order to understand an organism as an organism, one must make some extrapolations and infer to the various purposes that are served by this and that arrangement of organs. Like physics, biology looks for necessities in its subject matter, but in its case, the necessities that it reveals are the necessities to be found in functionalist teleological laws. Such laws assume the general purpose of the organism, which is that of its maintaining itself as an individual and maintaining its species, and then show that certain organs and processes can be seen to serve the attainment of those ends, even though we cannot deduce the exact nature of those organs from the functions which they serve. For example, we understand that the heart beats in order to circulate the blood only when we understand how the circulation of blood plays such and such a role within the self-maintenance of the organism.[17] Everything from the heavy fur of northern animals to the nature of the internal organs can thus be understood in this fashion, even if they cannot be deduced from knowing the general ends of the organism. The success of biology, which shows that even the sphere of life may be treated scientifically, serves further to affirm for modern agents that their point of view on the world is adequate to grasp the way the world is in itself – that is, is at one with an objective point of view. (In all his discussions, Hegel argues that the reason that such laws cannot be given a mathematical formulation is because they are not mechanical but teleological, but he seems simply to assume all along that functionalist teleological laws simply cannot be given a mathematical expression, an assumption that we nowadays need not make.)

Hegel reconstructs the way in which the biological sciences of his day tried to develop the basic ends (or functions) in terms of which all organisms took on their shape (*Gestaltung*) – namely, sensibility, irritability, and reproduction (which Hegel sees as serving the logical structures of universality, particularity, and individuality). These functions flow from the general function of the organism as a self-maintaining system, and they are subsidiary functions that serve this larger function. Sensibility refers to the internal structures of feeling within the organism, irritability refers to the structures by which it can be stimulated or provoked by its environment into some kind of action or reaction, and reproduction refers to those structures that regenerate the organism on a daily basis as an individual and also serve to regenerate the species.[18] (Typically for him, Hegel holds that reproduction is the unity of sensibility and irritability.) These three functions themselves then are specifiable into more detailed functional subsystems, such as the nervous system as serving the functions of sensibility, the musculature system as serving the functions of irritability, and the intestinal system as serving the ends of reproduction. (These subsystems must be seen as serving the more general ends of the organism and not as being identical with them; moreover, taken outside of the ends they serve, they can appear only as merely inert pieces of matter, for what is important in them is not the "stuff" of which they are made, but how this "stuff" plays its role in the organism – that is, satisfies the functions that it does.[19]) Once again, Hegel argues that there cannot be genuine laws at work in the biological sciences (at least not in the sense that physics has laws), for one can neither deduce nor predict from the general end of sensibility, for example, that it must be specified in a nervous system, especially if some other system could serve the same end as well.[20]

Hegel takes the so-called laws of biology as supposedly stating the necessity of the "outer" as being only the expression of the "inner." These laws are the kinds of so-called laws of development discussed by, among others, Lamarck and Buffon, in which there are "inner forms" that receive modification by the external circumstances but that effectively determine the course of development of an organism. Lamarck, for example, thought that just as there were laws of human development from child to youth to adult to elderly, animal and plant life went through a similar "law-like" development in which whole species could be seen as the "youthful" and others as the "adult" stages of animal life in general. But there can be no such laws, so Hegel argues, for what he calls the "universal individual, the earth" determines the organization of species in accidental ways that does not allow for there to be any genuine laws governing the distribution and kind of species – that is, anything like a system of laws specifying the necessity for there being such and such types of species.[21] The arrangement of nature as a system of living things existing within a context of non-organic material factors is too full of contingency to permit us to formulate any necessary laws for it.

The sciences of biology and physics (Hegel was later to add chemistry) are, however, unsuited to treat human reality, the social world of agents, because, as Hegel puts it, that world is essentially *historical*, whereas nature has no genuine history.[22] It obviously has a past, and there are obviously causal accounts of it that can be given, but it has no history because it is unintelligible how there could be any narratives that could be told of its developments that show how some later set of events can be said to be *completing* what came before them in the way that a later set of events in history can be said to be the completion of earlier events, even though the earlier events were not aiming at those later events. The teleology found in history has to do with the way in which the internal insufficiencies of a form of life's accounts of what has come to be taken as authoritative for it – the insufficiencies that generate skepticism about themselves – are resolved by those accounts given by the form of life that succeeds it; the narratives that make up history can only be understood in terms of the way in which these later accounts (as being essential to the self-identity of an age) overcome or fail to overcome the deficiencies of earlier accounts. The functional teleology inherent in biological nature is insuffi-

86

cient to provide the kind of narrative connection – of something's completing something else, of bringing a story to a close – that is necessary for there to be any genuine history. History is about stories that have at least potential completions, whereas in nature there are merely endless successions about which it makes no sense to say that this or that succession of events is now complete. The French Revolution, for example, may be seen as the consummation of a series of events leading up to it in the way that a new geological formation is not the fruition of anything but simply the accidental result of a series of past causal chains that have resulted in it. Hegel argues that human agents cannot therefore find that their sense of themselves *as agents* to be completely affirmed by the rise of modern science. Modern science teaches modern agents that what they construct with their own powers of thinking – what emerges from the human, subjective point of view – is in fact in accordance with the way things are and can thus be affirmed for them as knowledge; the practice of modern science affirms for modern agents that their own "subjective" capacities of reason are in fact in harmony with the "objective" nature of the world. But it cannot affirm for them that they know themselves *as agents,* and therefore really as human.

The "science" of self-identity

The question is thus whether their own nature *as agents* is something beyond the reach of science, or whether it too can be brought under the purview of inductive and postulational science. Since the answer to this question is not obvious, it is thus logical and certainly not surprising that at a certain point in early modern history, the European community would have tried to apply the idea of scientific method to itself in order to determine the laws of social life, and, to paraphrase Kant's description of Rousseau, to produce a "Newton of the moral world" who would thereby demonstrate the rationality of certain ways of thinking about human social life and the irrationality of others. It is this attempt that Hegel claims leads to the great crisis of modern life in its effort to justify itself by appeal to the methods of modern science.

In order to get to that point, Hegel takes a somewhat idiosyncratic detour through some contemporary (to him) attempts to apply the methods of natural science directly to human life, attempts that he thinks are not even remotely adequate for understanding the kind of historical and social character of human agency. Life, so he argues, exhibits an analogous structure to human agency in that the individual organism has, as it were, a subjective point of view, a set of drives and impulses that function together with each other that have as their goal the preservation of the organism; likewise, there is, as it were, an objective point of view on the organism, in that its various functions and drives serve to perpetuate the species without the organism's "knowing" this. But these "as it weres" mean only that the organism does not really have anything like a unity of the subjective and the objective point of view. Such a characterization of the organism is done from *our* point of view. The various functional teleologies in nature are there *for us,* not for the organisms themselves. We can see the various adaptive strategies exhibited by spiders, for example, as serving the purpose of preserving the individual and propagating the species, but this is not "for" the spider, any more than the function of circulating blood is "for" the heart (something that the heart is aware of).[23]

The question, though, is whether there are also *laws* that govern the way in which things are *for us* – that is, whether there are the same kind of functional teleologies within our own system of thought that govern how the world can be for us without our necessarily being aware of those laws. Candidates for such laws would be inductively established psychological laws of association. Hegel alludes to what in his time was a lively attempt to construct such laws, and the logic books of his day were full of attempts to explain various laws of logic as inviolable laws of human thought in that they were taken to be the ironclad necessities of the way in which humans (as opposed to cats or monkeys) had to think. Hegel's objection to this is fairly straightforward: Even if we could demonstrate some kind of typical association of thoughts (which he does not deny), we would still not have explained one of the most distinctive aspects of human thinking – namely, that the nature of thoughts is such that they can be reflectively criticized and reformulated in terms of other thoughts. Any associationist doctrine misunderstands both the normative character of thought and its reflexivity, the way in which it is capable of modifying itself. Thought, as Hegel likes to put it, is in movement not because it consists of a set of events following each other (as an inductive characterization of "associations" would have to have it) but because it is forever modifying itself by supplying itself with new concepts and new contexts for old concepts. The nature of a thought has to do with its relationships – particularly, its normative, inferential relationships – with other thoughts, and this normative structure itself is historical and social in character. Moreover, the reflexive structure of thought is such that it can always throw into question any particular association in terms of its adequacy or fit with other thoughts. Introducing new "thoughts" (such as the divine right of kings, the principle of entropy, syncopated rhythms, or whatever) can change the context of all the other thoughts such that any previous association ceases to be valid. The various thoughts that a person can have do not come in little sacks that prevent them from being modified by the introduction of new thoughts and of new connections with other thoughts. Moreover, the attempt at prescribing some kind of associationist laws for thought is bound to confuse simple idiosyncrasy – as when one person always associates Kantianism with Lutheran piety whereas another always associates it with egalitarian humanism – with what are the genuine inferential connections among those thoughts themselves. Those latter inferential connections are not idiosyncratic to the individuals involved; they are part of the *spirit,* of the common shared set of principles, vocabularies, and beliefs that individuals as members of a determinate historical community share.[24] The world may impinge on *individuals* such that it creates certain associations for them; but the world's impinging on individuals does not determine the inferential connections of human thought, which are normative, reflexive, and ultimately social in character, and which structure the community in terms of which the individual agent is a member. Thus, although we may be able to formulate associative laws for our consciousness, we cannot do so for *self-* consciousness, for self-consciousness is possible only by locating oneself in "social space," and there are no associative laws for the way in which the historical insufficiencies of certain kinds of inferential structures give way and are seen to be justifiably replaced by other forms of authoritative reasons. The world does not determine that for human agents; they collectively and historically determine it for themselves.[25]

Hegel also takes up various pseudo-sciences of his time – handwriting analysis, physiognomy (the attempt to correlate character with particular anatomical features such as the length and the shape of the nose), and phrenology (the attempt to correlate character and intelligence with the shape of the skull and with the bumps on the skull) – in order to show how these could not be sciences and thus how the attempt to construct a "science of self-identity" would be a false start. The "science of self-identity" could not affirm for modern agents that who they took themselves to be was in fact who they are because it rests on the wrong assumptions about the nature of character and self-identity. Individual self-consciousness is one's taking oneself to be located in a determinate "social space"; an individual's self-identity is made up of his actions in that "social space" and how those actions are taken by others. The "social space" is both the basis of the principles on which actions are taken and the basis of the interpretations of those actions by others. Self-identity cannot be something determinate and "fixed" that an individual could have outside of acting in any determinate "social space." The pseudo-sciences of self-identity however, see it as exactly that: as something that is completely formed and is then *expressed* in actions. For these pseudo-sciences, self-identity (or "character") is taken by them as something formed, fixed, and *inner,* whereas its expressions are taken as something that is *outer,* something available for observation. The pseudo-sciences of self-identity thus hope to find the laws that correlate the ways in which "inner character" is necessarily expressed in outer observable behavior.

On the one hand, this might seem unexceptionable. We might take certain behavior to be explicable only as being the outward expression of the internal process of thought. For example, we might see a person look at two things on a counter in a store, wrinkle his brow, then pick out one of them, and conclude that he was thinking about which one he wanted, which was better, or whatnot. But this already imputes a public conception of thought to the person being observed, and without using this public conception, we cannot hope to conclude what "inner processes" were transpiring in the person's mind. We might postulate, that is, that he was *thinking* about such and such and that this was linked with his behavior. But the pseudo-sciences of self-identity went farther; they reasoned that since there is a necessary connection between internal process and external appearance, the connection must be such that can find determinate laws that necessarily correlate external appearance with these fixed "inner processes." They claimed to find these correlations in facial shapes, handwriting, and the shapes and bumps of skulls. Behind their various proposals was the assumption that a person's character is something fixed and indifferent to its social expression such that it would be what it is without its being expressed in any actions at all. Because the pseudo-sciences of self-identity take character to be this kind of fixed, independently describable and identifiable entity, they concluded that it could be correlated with other fixed, independently describable and identifiable items like the shape and length of noses or the shape of skulls. Indeed, for there to be a lawlike connection between the two – between the "inner" and the "outer" – each would have to be independently identifiable, for only if the law correlates some independently identifiable X with some independently identifiable Y can it count as a genuine correlation. The idea that there could be such laws is thus the idea that there is some "inner" thing (one's character) that necessarily causes some "outer" thing (a shape of the face, a bump on the skull) to come into existence; in that way, the necessities of the correlations can be maintained.[26] However, the nature of action is such that its expression in various actions (such as a grimace) is a matter of *interpretation* by both the agent himself and by others in light of certain social norms. A person's character is inseparable from what he does, and what he does is a matter of interpretation.[27] Character cannot be a "thing" that exists independently of its expressions in various actions. Even what might look like a prime candidate for such "inner" things – namely, one's feelings – are themselves subject to interpretation; one must interpret one's feelings in order to know what one is feeling.[28] Thus, the ideal of finding lawlike correlations between the "inner facts" of one's character and its "outward expression" in the shape of the face is wrong-headed from the outset. In fact, there is no incontrovertible knowledge of character available either through introspection to the agent himself or to the observer of the agent's face or skull. Neither the agent himself nor his observers can be in a position to say indubitably that this is "who" he is outside of any social context. Each is making an interpretation based on the norms of his time, and each interpretation is fallible.[29] To say that it is an interpretation, however, should not suggest that there is some fixed "thing" that is being interpreted; rather, the "self" that is being interpreted is itself a *project,* something that the agent constructs within a social context and which he is not able fully to control. (In my own eyes, I might be selflessly devoted to the welfare of others, but in seeking the political power necessary to accomplish the ends connected with that I find instead that others regard me as a dangerous demagogue; or I might take myself to be devoted to the improvement of the lot of the disadvantaged only to find that I have become an arrogant paternalist.)

This necessity of this kind of interpretation in "social space" and of the self being more of a project than a fixed "thing" makes it impossible to have the kind of observational science for humanity that is possible for inorganic and organic nature. Agents do not have a character that is formed and fixed such that it can be observed and correlated with external occurrences in such a way that one can come up with a science of character that would provide us with the laws of character. Human agents have the possibility of reflection and thus deliberation; because of this, they may be said to *act* in a genuine sense. This is not to deny that human actions are not predictable. A "person of character" is precisely a person whose actions *are* predictable. He acts "in character" when he does things that are predictable in light of what we know about what he has done in the past and the circumstances in which he did it (in short, he is predictable in light of details of his biography). A person's character is thus a *historical* matter in that it involves knowledge of his past and how he responded in that past. This past, however, is the kind of thing that can be completed by later events; it is also a past that itself requires an interpretation by the agents confronting it, for they act in light of what they take the present situation to be, and that present situation cannot be construed except in terms of its links with its historical past and how they take that past. One cannot understand, for example, how a nineteenth-century German intellectual reacts to his time unless one also knows a bit about the Napoleonic wars, the stories that the Germans told themselves about these wars, and what the list of relevant possibilities for the future appeared to be for those people. In short, one cannot understand the person's actions unless one has some idea of how he *takes* himself and his situation to be, and understanding that "taking" is not a matter of correlating "inner" things with "outer" things. Of course, this also implies that one cannot simply observe one's rational agency within oneself as a datum of experience; one's rational agency is not some internally introspectible object. To be a rational agent is to be a *self-conscious* agent, which is to assume a position in "social space." Self-consciousness, that is, is a *doing* of something, not a *reporting* about oneself. One can report on others by taking them to be self-conscious – that is, by locating them in some kind of "social space" – but one's own self-consciousness is neither itself a reporting on one's inner life, nor is it imputing something to oneself; it is *doing* something.

The force of modern science was that it allowed modern agents to construct a view of themselves as capable of determining their own destinies through the application of "reason." That is, by appeal to their own rational powers they were capable of determining for themselves what would count as authoritative for them; the success of modern science affirms for them that this is indeed a true view of themselves. Yet, so it would seem, they cannot apply the *methods* of study to themselves that they applied to nature. Thus, if they are to be able to affirm for themselves that what they take to be authoritative really is so, then they must somehow be able to affirm for themselves that they are indeed these rational agents, and they must be able to do this by appeal only to their own powers of reason, not by appeal to any kind of "fate" external to themselves. The only way in which they could do this, consistent with the historical situation in which they found themselves, is not to look for some kind of observationally based inductive science of themselves but to look to themselves to construct themselves as rational agents. By appealing only to their own powers of reason – that is, without appeal to anything simply "given" – they must transform the "social space" in which they live and in terms of which they act and think into a properly rational set of principles and supporting institutions such that they can indeed affirm for themselves that they are indeed the independent agents they take themselves to be.[30] The early modern emphasis on reflective independence thus emerges with the early modern emphasis on reason and science, and the European community comes to be engaged in a political and social project of trying to show that its form of life can be justified in terms of the modern standards of reason it has set for itself. That is, it comes to be engaged in the project of showing that its form of life is rationally *self-justifying* and that the participants in that form of life are therefore truly independent.

2. Early modernity's social construction of individualism: Faustianism, sentimentalism, and natural virtue

In affirming for themselves that their form of life is itself self-justifying in terms of reason, modern agents are led to a view of themselves as independent individuals, whose own lives and values must themselves be justified purely by appeal to reason. Just as modern culture supposedly need not accept anything outside of its own resources in order to be able to justify itself, the modern individual need accept no reason that cannot count *for him*, as a rational agent, as an authoritative reason. Although reason itself as a general reflective capacity to evaluate and criticize our practices, including the practices of reason-giving itself, is something that itself has a history, for these early modern individuals it appears as something itself that is simply present within each individual. If nothing counts for an individual as an authoritative reason unless he can come to count it *for himself* as an authoritative reason, then the individual (or his "reason") must remain the ultimate locus of authority for what does and does not count as authoritative for belief or for action. For example, early modern political theorists were led to the idea that political legitimacy must come from reason, and it must be such that each rational agent could affirm for himself that the actions and form of life generated out of this set of institutions constitute for him authoritative reasons to act in such and such a way, to feel in such and such a way, and to think in such and such a way. They were also led to present this as a kind of fictional history of how man emerged from a natural state into a political state. Moreover, the impact of modern science made it seem that individuals need only apply the *methods* of reason to human affairs in order to bring about a state of affairs in which agents could rationally affirm for themselves their view of themselves as independent agents who need accept no ends that they cannot rationally affirm for themselves.

In that context, it would be logical to take the *social* concept of individuals as a *natural* category.[31] For example, Hobbes, one of the preeminent thinkers of the new individualism, understood the individuals of which he was speaking to be natural individuals who could be described and explained in terms continuous with the categories of natural science, as simply endowed with natural desires that led them to do predictable things in certain types of circumstances. Given this knowledge of individuals, Hobbes argued that we could therefore rationally set up a better social order. But the Hobbesian theory could only serve as a mediating point between the culture of the past and the emerging modern self-consciousness, for it could offer no way in which these modern individuals could affirm for themselves that they really were independent, since for him they were ultimately pushed by their given desires for power and security. However, Hobbes expressed the view that what had counted as a *traditional* reason for action no longer could count as such a reason simply because it was traditional. All particular reasons for action would have to be submitted to scrutiny by "reason" itself; individuals must affirm for themselves what will henceforth count for them as valid reasons for belief and action, and something's being the traditional "way things are done" was no longer sufficient to underwrite the normative force of any particular reason.

The Faustian project

Hegel uses Goethe's story of Faust to illustrate the immediate way in which the self-understanding of this kind of individuality is constructed.[32] Faust, a scholar offended by the fact that "theory" has not given him what he thinks it should, turns his back on science and goes forth into life to seek his pleasure, forging a kind of agreement with Mephistopheles to provide him with the powers he needs to pursue this kind of life and to affirm for himself that he is master of his own fate. Taking a witch's brew that makes him younger and rouses his passions, by chance he runs into a young woman, Gretchen, on the street and decides that he will have her. He then seduces Gretchen and abandons her. Faust passes from his life as a scholar to the life of a hedonist, from the pursuit of science to the pursuit of pleasure.[33] Goethe's version of the character of Faust offers a paradigm of this type of modern agent: Faust, a scientist-scholar, has found both that the practices of modern science cannot completely affirm for him what he takes himself to be (someone for whom nothing counts unless he, *as an individual,* elects to have it count for him) and that therefore neither past traditions nor contemporary mores can per se count for him as authoritative reasons. Merely describing and understanding the world in the terms of modern theory cannot satisfy Faust; not content to passively record the world, Faust attempts to establish that he is indeed independent, that he, as Faust the individual, is capable of doing as he pleases in that world. Faust takes the ideal of independence and transforms it into a pre-romantic program of self-realization and self-assertion: He will sample life and take what he elects to take. For Faust, independence is thus simply unimpeded freedom to do "as he pleases" unconstrained by past convention or mores. Faust desires to see himself affirmed as free in the sense of being unimpeded in his doing what he wants. In this way, Faust stands for the darkly self-realizational romantic side of modern self-understanding, the desire to cast away the past and push all limits simply in order to have it affirmed for himself that he *can* do so, that there is nothing in the past or in current mores that *could* count as a reason against his doing anything. In living this life, Faust takes himself to be expanding his self, to be encompassing more possibilities in it than would be possible by adherence to tradition, contemporary mores or by being bound to "scientific method."

The scientists of modernity affirmed the modern standpoint by showing that human constructions (the theories of modern science) capture the world as it is; they demonstrate through scientific practice that there is nothing in nature that is in principle impervious to human reason. They "force" nature to yield its secrets. Faust takes this a step farther and, as a scholar turning his back on science, attempts to show that his agency itself is capable of full independence without limits, that he can force the world to give him what *he* wants. If there are no intrinsic limits to human reason in theory (that is, in science), Faust reckons that there should be no limits to the human will, or at least his (the individual's) will, in action. Although rationality in *thought* finds that it simply must take some things in nature as given (must attend to them in observation and experiment), the rational *will* finds that it has no limits of principle, that it need not take *anything* as given.

But Faust's conception of independence as "self-realization" is empty, for there is nothing specific that Faust is trying to realize. Faust is not trying to realize any determinate conception of himself: he does not wish to become a member of a just political order, a great researcher, a truly moral individual, or whatever. He has no other end than that he should be able to do as he pleases and that he should push at the limits of things. Indeed, independence for Faust seems to him only to be possible *if* there are no intrinsic limits of history or morals to what he can do, *if* nothing could count as a reason for him unless *he makes it* a reason. But he has nothing to go on except the terribly abstract (and therefore almost fully empty) idea of "making it his own," without there being any further way of specifying what belongs on the list of things that he should evaluate in order to elect some reason as his own. Gretchen, who embodies the social world of custom and piety from which Faust, the "modern individual," believes himself to be emancipated, becomes simply a vehicle for Faust's search for self-affirmation; Faust takes Gretchen out of that established world, seduces her, and in the process leads her to unwittingly kill her mother (with a sleeping potion given to her by Faust so that her mother will sleep while Faust seduces Gretchen) and then later to kill their illegitimate child after she has gone mad, the result of which is Gretchen's being condemned to execution. But for Faust, his pleasures with Gretchen at first count as affirmative for him in that they show him that he is for himself the master of his fate and that he alone determines which pleasures he will try to satisfy; using Mephistopheles' magic, he is even able to kill Gretchen's brother, Valentin, who challenges Faust before Gretchen's door. He uses Gretchen for his own pleasure, and he abandons her. However, when Faust later tries to save Gretchen from her execution (again employing Mephisto's help), she refuses, and he finds himself powerless to do anything. Faust thus eventually comes up against limits he cannot override.

One way of taking the tragedy of Faust is to see it as the tragic clash between the old and the new: the old world of established values and its sense of "the way things are to be done" and the new world of unlimited freedom to do as one pleases, to challenge all accepted orthodoxy. (This reading perhaps fits Goethe's earlier version of the play – what we now call the *Urfaust* – but it does not fit the later revised version very well at all.) Hegel sees the tragedy in more general terms, as concerning itself with the *internal* conflicts within the conception of the independent subjective life that Faust embodies, not as a clash between the "old" and the "new." The Faustian agent's idea of being the "master of his own fate" is hollow and deceptive, for the tragedy of Faust lies in his discovering that he is exactly the opposite. This form of self-understanding understands there to be no moral, religious, or social limits to what it can do. The modern Faustian individual understands that since there is nothing *in the world* that sets any moral, religious, or social limits to his willing, there can be nothing beyond his own willing that can set any limits to his will, and he understands that he is under no obligation except that of realizing this conception of himself. But, having discarded the idea that the *world* can set any moral limits to his willing, the Faustian agent finds no inherent limits *within* his own willing that could set such limits. Faust thus necessarily becomes a hedonist, for having no determinate conception of a good, of a form of life, or of any specific role to play, he can only find his conception of himself confirmed in the satisfaction of his desires, in particular, the pursuit of pleasure. The content for his willing is furnished completely by desire, by what he happens to want to do.[34] Faust takes his subjective point of view to be the truth of the matter; Gretchen (who embodies the ethos of the pre-modern world) has a subjective point of view that Faust thinks can be simply dismissed. In this way, Faust's use of Gretchen is a modern variant on the master/slave dialectic. (The relations of power are reinforced by Faust's aristocratic looks and demeanor that contrast with Gretchen's ordinary, *bürgerlich* status, leading Gretchen to wonder how such a man could be attracted to her.) Faust seduces Gretchen, then discards her, for as a paradigmatic form of modern individuality, Faust can see no value in anything that is not for him a new "experiment" in living, that is not a means to his own self-realization.

The Faustian agent's conception of himself is thus necessarily empty.[35] The actualization of the form of willing *can only* be the illusory freedom and independence of hedonism; it is illusory because eventually the Faustian agent finds that his earlier acts themselves have in fact created limits to what he can now do. (Faust finds that he cannot later rescue Gretchen from prison on the night before she is to be executed, nor undo what he now regrets.) Willing in terms of a conception of lacking limits of principle in fact creates limits of principle to the willing agent, for the agent's deeds create a self-identity for himself that he cannot then disown. (When Faust learns of Gretchen's fate, he bitterly accuses Mephisto of having tricked him into it.

Mephisto answers: "I cannot undo the avenger's bonds, nor open his bolted door. – save her! – Who was it who threw her down into corruption? I or you?" Goethe's stage directions at this point simply say: "Faust looks about himself wildly."[36]) Thus, the Faustian agent inevitably finds that he cannot undo what he has done, and that his so-called freedom eventually entraps him in a form of necessity. Rather than being the master of own fate, free of all moral and social limits, he is in fact a mere slave of desire, or, as it is put in the play, a mere slave of Mephisto, who has lured him to his downfall and, through him, Gretchen to her execution. Faust, the grand "experimenter in life," finds out that things have not worked out as he intended them, that not everything is under his control. Faust takes himself to be freely determining what he will do in his demand to have Gretchen; but Mephisto has always known this is not the case, and Faust, who had in some sense realized this earlier, now fully realizes it only when it is too late. On Hegel's view, this is not accidental to Faust nor is it simply a psychological feature of some modern individuals; it is a logical consequence of this form of self-understanding.[37]

The freedom the Faustian agent thinks that he is to find in hedonism thus turns into a form of compulsion, of necessity. The freedom that follows from simply being an "individual" cut free from any social background or any determinate set of ends, who is absolutely free to do what he pleases and whose goal is to flout all such limits, to sample all the "experiences" that human life has to offer, is a life without direction, for the Faustian agent has only a fully empty concept of what it is to be an individual and thus an equally empty idea of what it would mean to "realize" his individuality. He seeks to actualize himself in the world as an individual, but he can give no content to that conception, since his conception both of rationality and of what it is to be an individual are so very general (so very "abstract," as Hegel puts it) that they can be filled in with anything, and, since he eschews all social and traditional limits, can in fact only be filled in by the individual's pursuing whatever desire he for whatever reason just happens to have. If science, as a human construct, can only give us truths that still take something as given, the Faustian agent reasons that practical agency can create its own truth without having to take anything other than the purely natural limitations of agency as something given. (The Faustian agent, that is, understands that he cannot fly or make himself disappear, but he also understands that there is no principled limit to what can be a legitimate object of willing.) Seeing the traditional roles of the past or the current set of mores simply as something given from outside the structure of his own willing, as something externally imposed on him, the Faustian agent concludes that what one *really* ought to do – seen from the objective point of view (from the standpoint of the "universal") – is therefore to realize one's nature as an individual, to set one's ends for oneself, and that boils down to acting out of whatever desires one has as an "individual" (with no more definiteness to the idea of "individuality" being possible for it than that). There can therefore be no desires that such an individual can identify as "his own" other than the desires that he just happens to have. (For example, Faust is perhaps given certain desires by Mephisto in the witch's brew, and after seeing the lovely forms in the witches' mirror, he goes off in pursuit of some woman, contingently meeting Gretchen along the way, thus setting the stage for her downfall.[38])

What he really is as just "an individual" (what is, as Hegel puts it, his "abstract *being-in-itself*") is thus simply a person who happens to have such and such a desire, who happens to do such and such – he is no more than that. The high-sounding talk, therefore, of "realizing himself" can amount to no more than simply doing whatever it is that he happens to desire.[39] But this cannot give him a coherent conception of himself. Faust, for example, finds that not all the desires that simply occur to him are jointly satisfiable – he wishes to have Gretchen, then he wishes to undo what he has done. Faust also finds that he is not free from the traditions which he had claimed to throw off, that he has a certain remorse for what he has done, and that he longs for Gretchen not simply as a vehicle for satisfying a particular sexual desire but in terms of wishing to reestablish their union. For the Faustian agent himself, this outcome must always appear incomprehensible. He wishes to sample life's experiences and thereby to actualize himself as an independent individual, but he always finds that rather than being independent, he has in fact been led by *contingent* desire, such that, the world being what it is, certain things that he has not *himself* willed *necessarily* follow from his actions. The direction of his life, which he had taken to be his to determine, turns out to appear to him to be in the grip of other forces. Taking himself to be the master of his own fate means that he takes the ends that he pursues as the ends that he has *given himself,* and that the pursuit of these ends and their satisfaction is that in which his *fate* consists. However, the relation between his so-called independently determined ends and his fate split from one another; in giving himself the ends he has chosen, he finds that his fate is after all *not* chosen, and he cannot, within this form of self-understanding, understand how that could even be possible. If, after all, he chose all his ends himself, how could it be that his fate, his life, has itself not turned out to be that which he determined it to be?[40] Faust's fate – the man who has led Gretchen to be condemned to death by beheading – is not what Faust willed. By taking himself to be free from all tradition and social mores, Faust thought he had thereby made himself master of his own fate; but he finds that the social world that he nonetheless inhabits imposes a fate on him, which for him is unintelligible only because he has no concept of how anything could be imposed on him without his actually having willed it. Faust thus ends up completely *alienated* from himself, finding no way in which he can identify with who he has become. His acts do not seem to be his own, for he himself had not willed Gretchen's condemnation or the death of her brother. The pure experimentalist individualism of modern life – the casting off of everything traditional and the attempt to encompass within oneself all human possibilities by "realizing one's individuality" – not only turns out to be empty; those individuals turn out to be the opposite of what they had taken themselves to be.

Rather than the bold experiment in living it had seen itself as being,

Faustian individualism had turned out to be only empty hedonism because of its excessively abstract conception of individuality and what therefore "realizing" one's individuality actually turned out to mean. The insufficiencies of Faustian hedonism to do what it claimed to do – to provide the basis for an actualization of individuality – motivates the construction of another conception that promises to make good on that claim.[41] Since Faustian hedonism cannot work, a successful form of individualism must be able to show that modern "individuals" – liberated from tradition and contemporary mores and electing to count as authoritative reasons only what each can count on his *own* terms as an authoritative reason – can indeed discover something within themselves that is only "potential" and that if "actualized" would bring to the light of day their individuality. The transition from Faustian hedonism to this other form of individualism parallels the move towards eighteenth-century sentimentalism or to the character known in that time as "the man of feeling."[42]

Sentimentalism and emotionalism

Faustian striving thus turns into *sentimentalism,* with its emphasis on the picturesque and on such favored objects as children, peasants, and appropriately likeable animals (domestic animals, bunnies, and so on). Sentimentalism is the logical result of demanding that the "individual" must be shown to have something "within" him that he can realize as an individual and that will nonetheless be justifiable from the objective point of view. The Faustian character had thought he had done this by showing that *reason* had shown that the past per se could not be binding on him; the Faustian agent took himself to be thereby required to discard the idea that past traditions on their own could offer him any authoritative reasons for action and, in casting off the past, to accept no end that he had not willed for himself. In doing so, Faustian individualism did not think of this as any kind of idiosyncratic task but as something of universal value, of doing in practice what science had done in theory. By adopting the Baconian injunction to frame theories that will satisfy humanity's interests, and by having succeeded thereby in gradually uncovering the "secrets" of nature, the scientists of early modernity had seemingly succeeded in affirming for modern agents that not merely their *intellects* were in harmony with nature, but that their *desires* were also in harmony with it. By constructing theories for the purpose of satisfying desire, the community of scientists had affirmed that intellect and desire themselves had within their own terms produced an internally coherent picture of the way the world was in itself. Faustian agents had sought to realize that supposed harmony of desire, intellect, and the world in the kind of experimentation in living that Faust embodied. If that ideal was to succeed, therefore, there would have to be something that could be discovered within such individuals such that in realizing it they would also be realizing the professed harmony between intellect, desire, and the world, and would thereby be affirming for themselves that it was *themselves* and not something else that set their ends for them.

98

The participants in the form of life of early modernity therefore came to a conception of themselves as having the *laws* of feeling and pleasure within themselves as part of their natural constitution. Since nature had constructed them to have certain feelings, in following the dictates of *genuine* feeling they would provide themselves with ends that were valid for all agents (since all agents had been so similarly constructed). Just as the community of scientists had discovered the laws of nature, the sentimentalists believed themselves to have discovered the laws of the "heart." The laws of genuine feeling express something internal to ourselves as rational agents that are unlike the blind laws of animal nature but that are nonetheless natural to us as "individuals.' Therefore, in acting on our genuine and natural feelings, we are acting on something that is *within* us and part of us, not *external* and alien to us; we are no longer caught in the throes of a blind necessity but are *expressing* ourselves and are therefore free.

The modern rejection of the idea that authoritative reasons for belief and action could be based solely on either "tradition" or "authority" (with the main target of that skepticism being, of course, church "authority") historically came to be echoed in both popular literature and in religion by a turn toward the cult of feeling as a new source for such reasons. Religious practices such as the pietist movement in Germany (originating in the late seventeenth century and flourishing in the eighteenth) managed to build a new form of orthodoxy around the idea that the source of both belief and the motivations of action lay in attending to one's feelings. These emotionalists rejected even the minor kinds of rapprochement which the churches had established with modern life in favor of what they took to be a more authentic form of Christianity with a grounding in the idea that individual, personal experience and a kind of emotional immediacy in faith was the key to religious life and to true morality.[43] These emotionalist religious movements thus shared the modern sense of authoritativeness being detached from tradition and authority and being located instead "within" the individual believer.

The failures of Faustian *hedonism* thus seem to be corrected by the doctrine of *emotionalism*. Emotionalism seemingly completes the modern idea of independence as determination by impersonal ("universal") standards that are at the same time also deeply personal. Hegel calls this the "law of heart."[44] The "law of the heart" – of doing that which one's genuine emotions dictate to you – is both something that comes from within the individual (and is thus part of his *subjective* point of view) and is also something that is a *law* – that is, it is the same for all naturally constituted rational agents, and is thus something that is justifiable from the *objective* (rational) point of view.[45] As an "inner quality," it is something that individuals can only discover by looking within themselves but that, once discovered and acted upon, has universal validity for all such rational agents. These individuals thus seem capable of doing what Faust failed at doing: realizing in their actions some part of their individuality (the "law of the heart," emotionalism) that comes from within themselves. (The use of the phrase, "the law of the heart" is most likely an oblique reference to Pascal and his involvement with Jansenism, a

99

movement within the Catholic church that shared some of the emotionalist predilections of the pietists, although the two movements – Jansenism and pietism – are historically unrelated, whatever the conceptual ties between them may be.[46] Unlike the pietists, the Jansenists stressed science, thus showing themselves to be more "modern." In the hands of Pascal, the demands of emotionalist religion were even supposed to be shown as that which "reason" itself comes to see as necessary to complement itself.[47] Pascal's notion of reason's recognition of its limits in the "law of the heart" thus fits the model of agency and authoritativeness that Hegel discusses.)

What had therefore seemed like *external* necessity for the Faustians now appears to their successors as *freedom* since it has been transformed into an *internal* necessity. Conceived as doing what comes from oneself, freedom is compatible with necessity, provided the necessity is internal to the self and not something imposed on the self from outside. Laws that are outside the self thus appear as alien intrusions on the freedom and independence of the individual, whereas those that come from within the self appear as freedom. Moreover, in acting on his internal freedom, his "law of the heart," the agent appears to himself to be acting on something that is valid for all people. The *Faustian agent* acted on the basis of whatever contingent desire he happened to have; the *emotionalist,* on the other hand, seems to be acting on something valid for all agents, since it comes not just from his own idiosyncratic desires but from human *nature* itself (something that reason can affirm even if it itself cannot produce the content of these laws). The failures of the hedonistic pursuit of pleasure are corrected by an emotionalist moral calling: By following the "law of the heart," I act not only to satisfy my desire, I act for the interests of mankind. Moreover, as a modern individual (and like the Faustian), the emotionalist is not bound by tradition or contemporary mores; what counts as an authoritative reason for him to act cannot be dictated by accepted mores and traditions but must instead be dictated (or at least affirmed) by something within him, within *his* feelings. Indeed, for the emotionalist just as much as the Faustian, the past or contemporary mores are a burden to be thrown off, since they are things imposed on him from outside his own subjectivity, not things he has willed for himself.[48] To the extent that the social laws are not identical with what the "laws of the heart" command, they can only appear as unjustifiable constraints preventing individuals both from enjoyment and from doing the right thing. The existing laws and mores of any given social order can only contingently have validity, that is, only to the extent that they happen to agree with what the "laws of the heart" command. The pietists, for example, fused the idea of individualism – a Faustian modern conception – with the idea of emotionalism as a source of reasons for belief and action, and they thus came to insist that the only truly authentic expression of piety is the production of good works (such as the founding of hospitals, orphanages, and the like), not adherence to any traditional doctrines.

The *law* of the heart is thus supposedly both universal (as being the kind of thing that people are "naturally" constituted to feel) and personal (as something that the individual can only find by looking within *his own* heart). To the extent, however, that the individual claims any kind of *general* validity for the "laws" that he finds in his own heart, he cannot make this claim as a purely personal statement. Rather, he claims to speak from the universal, objective point of view: this is what one ought to feel, not just how I happen to feel. That is, he takes his own *subjective* point of view (what *he* feels) to be normative for or revelatory of what the *universal* point of view ought to be.[49] These individuals thus naturally find themselves alienated from their social surroundings, since the laws and mores around them, even to the extent that they even contingently happen to coincide with the "laws of the heart," are nonetheless something *imposed* on them, not something they have willed themselves from within their own hearts.[50] (Thus, the pietists always had to contend with their submission to external church and secular authority and their deeply felt alienation from such authority.) Given their conception of the "law of the heart," it follows that as soon as one puts the "law of the heart" into effect – that is, as soon as it actually becomes a positive law or a valid custom – it necessarily ceases to be a law of one's *own* heart, since it now becomes a commandment from outside of oneself, something that "society" imposes on one.[51] Even if the content of some established law or custom is the same as what one's "heart" tells one to do, it is still an imposition because it is not coming from within oneself, out of one's own emotions. Only that which can be freely vouched for by individuals for themselves – that is, only that which these individuals can elect to be a reason for themselves – can legitimately count for them as a reason. (Thus, pietism can be seen as an attempt to assert the "traditional" faith in terms wholly appropriate to modern life, even though the pietists would almost certainly not have put it in those terms; rather than affirm the traditional dependence of human agents on the world, they affirm the power of human agents to change and improve the world by relying on the "law of the heart.")

Not only are these people necessarily alienated from the social order around them, they are necessarily alienated from the other individuals around them. Each claims to be expressing a universal law – each finds that his emotions, for example, tell him to be kind to peasants or whatever – but each by necessity cannot take the other's assertions to be *law,* for taking whatever they say to be law would be to have the law imposed on oneself from outside one's own heart. Thus, even if two sentimentalist individuals in fact agree on something, such as charity to the peasantry, neither can take the other's pronouncement as to what *one* ought to do (or feel) to be valid simply by virtue of the fact that the other expressed it; each must feel it *for himself* for it to be valid as a law *for him.* Thus, the claims of others' "hearts" are always invalid as claims on oneself, even when they happen to be identical in content to the claims of one's own "heart."[52]

But, on the other hand, the individual sentimentalist also must see the existing social order as springing out of the harmony engendered in him by nature. Nature, or more generally the divine order of things, produces a kind of harmony within human agents, such that each in consulting and acting on his (subjective) emotions naturally is led to doing what from the objective point of view is the right thing. In this respect, the "law of the heart" would seem to be necessarily in harmony with the "order of things" and could not be alienated from it.[53] For the sentimentalists of the early eighteenth century, of whom Hegel is speaking, an attunement to one's emotions (what constituted one's "sensibility") was necessary for knowing what was (objectively) right, and it was necessary to indulge fully in those feelings if one was to be truly virtuous; a failure to indulge in those feelings was evidence even to oneself of one's lack of knowledge of the right and the good, since it disclosed one's lack of "true sensibility," which was a precondition of moral knowledge. These emotions were implanted in one by a benevolent Providence (or Nature, or whatever), and one needed to attend to them in order to be able to count something as a true moral claim. Thus, the "law of the heart" was not only something subjective, within oneself, it was also something objective, part of the order of things.

Thus, on the one hand, the "man of feeling" must take all demands others make on him to believe something or to act in a certain way to be alien to him, to be thereby invalid claims, since a claim can be valid only if it comes from *his* heart. On the other hand, the existing order of things is what gives the "law of the heart" its validity in the first place. The feelings of love for one's fellow humans and one's charitable empathy with their misfortunes were, for the sentimentalists, reflections within human hearts of divine qualities, particularly of God's love. (Leibniz's theodicy as reconciling the existing order of things with God's perfection played a role in this conception.) Thus, the "man of feeling" finds his self-conception burdened with an odd contradiction. He must see the existing order of things as something that is the basis of the "law of the heart," that gives it its validity, yet he must also see any claim made by anybody else on him as invalid because it does not come from *his* "heart."[54]

Living with this kind of contradiction made these sentimentalist, emotionalist agents into slightly mad moralists. Each had to display himself to others and to himself as realizing his nature as an independent agent by displaying his sensibility in the form of indulging in certain emotions. Yet he could not find himself affirmed in any social ordering, since any such social order would necessarily be imposing its dictates on him. For such an agent, the public world must therefore seem to be devoid of feeling, alien to what he knows to be right; the only explanation for the lack of feeling in the public world would have to lie in its corruption by those who govern.[55] These agents take an authoritative reason to be one which the individual elects for himself to count as an authoritative reason, and for the sentimentalist emotionalists an authoritative reason can only be that which comes from the "heart." It can, however, only affirm for itself that its own "law of the heart" is indeed an authoritative reason by supposing that such laws are implanted in us by the objective order of things (benevolent Providence or whatever). Whereas the Faustian agent had no conception of exactly what he was trying to realize in realizing himself as an "individual," the sentimentalist has a more determinate but nonetheless fully contradictory conception: He is trying to realize his nature as an individual by displaying his sensibility, all the while rejecting the justifications which he himself accepts for why he can claim any validity at all for these subjective, emotionalist "laws of the heart." The sentimentalist thus is always turning things around on himself: He is claiming that only what counts for *him* – what comes out of his "heart" – counts at all, and that what comes from his "heart" counts because an objective order has made it that way.

A world populated by such individuals actualizing their individuality by displaying their sensibility would be a world in which such individuals would be constantly clashing with each other irrespective of whether they happened to be in substantial agreement. Each seeks to actualize himself as an independent individual by each actualizing in his or her actions and feelings his conception of themselves as "men and women of feeling." What seems to each as something deep and emotional, and, moreover, which substantiates what counts as a universal reason for action – what Hegel calls the "heartthrob for humanity" – is in reality a form of self-conceit (*Eigendünkel*), a way of taking one's own subjective point of view to be normative for others, to determine what the objective point of view would certify. In such a world, each would be battling with each other as to whose will, whose emotions, and whose feelings *really* counted.

Hegel's discussion alludes to the historically less cheerful aspects of the cult of emotionalism. Although the pietist movement's calls to action had indeed led to its founding various orphanages, workhouses, and the like, there was also in the sixteenth through the eighteenth centuries an emotionalist-based set of witchcraft trials and hunts for heretics.[56] During this period in France, the cult of the *devots,* both Jesuit and Jansenist, reached high levels, and there was, for example, a hotly debated matter concerning the construction of a general "hospital" in Paris, which in effect was established as a cross between a hospital and a prison in which beggars and other vagabonds – in other words, those people believed to be completely lacking in "virtue" and whose poverty was to be explained by their lack of such "virtue" – were to be forcibly housed, given exhortational religious and moral lectures, and fed and clothed badly in order to "reform" them, all in the name of Christian charity and a concern for the welfare of mankind. The cult of charity, which in France earlier had been the province of the "new saints" like de Sales, had been thereby transformed into a repressive, puritanical means of social control. The *devots* may therefore be among the examples of the "insane self-conceit" that Hegel has in mind. In any event, Hegel no doubt had in mind the Jansenist version of emotionalist religion, which in the eighteenth century became associated with reactionary aristocratic movements tied into the defense of the privileges of the aristocracy, the support of a national church against papal authority, and the incitement to mob actions having to do with hunting down of Jesuits, who were the great enemies of the Jansenists in part because they were also the great defenders of the authority of the papacy.[57] (Pascal's appeal to the "law of the heart" was conceived in part as a defense of certain Jansenist ideas, particularly against what he saw as the Jesuits' overly secularized and corrupt conceptions of free will and reason.)

Hegel's use of Hobbesian imagery to characterize the social order of the emotionalists is also almost certainly deliberate. The emotionalists of the eighteenth century all saw Hobbes as the enemy and themselves as the proper defenders of true humanity; in their own eyes, they were the true champions of true, warm, caring humanity who were out to prove that Hobbes was wrong in his pessimistic views of human nature as selfish and desirous only of power and security. The unintended irony of their position was that in fact the logic of their views led exactly to the Hobbesian conclusions that they publicly abhorred and condemned and against which they thought they had positioned themselves.

For these early modern agents, it seems that their individualism is something that is located "potentially" within them and that they need to actualize by casting away the fetters of the past and bringing that individuality to fruition and the light of day. They operate, that is, with a sense that there is some "core" within them that only needs to be actualized. Faustianism accepts the scientific account of the world as adequate to give us knowledge of nature but finds it inadequate to guide an individual into becoming an independent agent; Faustian individualism fails to do this because of its empty conception of both what it means to be an individual and what it means to have a self-chosen reason for doing something. Sentimentalism offers a more concrete conception of what it means to choose something for oneself – namely, to consult one's "heart" and act in terms of one's cultivated sensibility – but it fails as an account of practical knowledge, since its own account of what it means to have a self-chosen reason – namely, one that the individual can endorse because it comes from within him and expresses his true, "inner self" – conflicts with its own account of why such subjective reasons could count as practical *knowledge,* as something valid for all such agents.

The sentimentalists professed Hobbes to be their enemy, but they turned out to have led themselves on their own terms (at least in that form of sentimentalism that relies on the "law of the heart") to Hobbesian conclusions. The issue for these agents, therefore, was whether their conception of *individualism* itself was viable. For it to be viable in the broad terms in which it has been framed, they would have to find some "core" within themselves that had been restrained or prevented by the weight of past religious and moral tradition from being realized. It must moreover be something that belongs to the individual himself, something that is not imposed on him by any social or divine order. Although the "law of the heart" seemed at first well-suited for this task, for it provided some definite content for the individual's thoughts and beliefs, it turned out to be inadequate in its own terms, and came to look more like a case of slightly mad self-conceit rather than as a viable form of individualism.

Sentiment and virtue

What was necessary was to unite the sentimentalist conception of feeling with the Faustian acceptance of a modern, scientific/observationalist account of nature by a transformation of the "law of the heart" into the sentiments of "natural virtue." The account given of independent action by appeal to a "law of the heart" had failed on its own terms; therefore, if the "law of the heart" was to be an adequate account of authoritative reasons for belief and action, it needed to be amended so as to bring it into line with the modern conception of reason. Historically, this was echoed in the cultural shift towards to the later Enlightenment and its culture of the *philosophe* – the period that flowered after the expulsion of the Jesuit order from France and the consequent waning of the Jansenist movement (whose strength, after all, had resided mostly in its vehement opposition to the Jesuits). The *philosophes* of the Enlightenment tried to combine a conception of modern impartial reason with the stress on sentiment and the emotions that had been constructed in the period of the preceding Jansenist controversy.

The idea was that a rational ("scientific") observation of nature would show that the "law of the heart" and "reason" were not really at odds, that the "law of the heart" was indeed an authoritative reason for belief and action, provided it was correctly understood as an echo of that which was truly natural within us. Thus, it was argued that a rational observer would note that nature has constructed various species in such a way that their natural passions incline them to serve the common good of their "communities," and that if one extended these observations to humanity, one would have to conclude that the *natural* thing to do (which is what leads to the individual's own happiness) would *also* be that which benefits the community. It would follow then that the *natural* person would also be the *virtuous* person, who would also be the *happy* person. The virtuous person would then act in accordance with the natural passions, provided those natural passions had not been deformed by the social world around him. Thus, people like the Earl of Shaftesbury (Anthony Ashley Cooper), a figure revered among many figures of the Enlightenment, argued that insofar as one ordered one's passions in accordance with nature, one would act virtuously (for the benefit of the common good), and one would be happy in doing so.[58] In general terms, this became a cornerstone of many Enlightenment views: Reason, emotion (particularly, sympathy), and the common good (generally taken as "utility") were all compatible since each of them were principles "natural" to mankind. "Reason" thus showed that itself, emotion, and sociality were compatible with individualism and independence in that it demonstrated that each was natural to people.

The kind of conception embodied in the Earl of Shaftesbury's idea of natural virtue was countered by an opposing view of what was natural to people, which seemed to trace a path back to Hobbes. Hegel calls this view the "way of the world" – namely, the idea that an impartial view of humanity shows that by nature individuals only act in terms of rather narrowly construed self-interested passions. The partisans of virtue, like the Earl of Shaftesbury, thus attempted to show that the proponents of the "way of the world" (the Hobbesians) simply misunderstood what it meant both to act in accordance with nature and to act *self-interestedly.* The "champions of natural virtue" accused the proponents of the "way of the world" of confusing "acting in terms of one's interests" with "acting *selfishly,*" for they thought they could show that in fact acting in terms of one's interests requires one to act benevolently. The "man of virtue" is indeed acting out of a desire for pleasure, but contrary to the claims of the partisans of the "way of the world," he realizes that true pleasure comes from acting benevolently rather than selfishly.[59] Doing the *natural* thing (pursuing one's pleasure) leads one to self-sacrificing virtue, not to selfish vice.

This conception of "natural virtue" is reconstructed within the *Phenomenology* as the correction to the insufficiencies of the "law of the heart" (independently of whether any of the proponents of "natural virtue" actually took themselves to be doing that). The proponents of the "law of the heart" had thought that for the "law" to count for them, it had to come from "within" them. The proponents of "natural virtue," on the other hand, held that since that "law" itself is validated by something external to the subjective point of view of the agents (by Nature, or by benevolent Providence), the individual must therefore learn to subject his subjective point of view to that of the objective law.[60] The *sentimentalism* of the "law of the heart" is thus preserved within this new conception of "natural virtue."

It is thus no accident that people like the Earl of Shaftesbury found themselves very attracted to the neo-stoicism of the day, for it offered a concrete model of what it would mean to subject one's personal point of view to the objective point of view. The individual can only know something by distancing himself from his subjective point of view and assuming the impersonal point of view (for many figures of this period, this would amount to assuming the point of view of "Nature"). Nonetheless, for these champions of "sentimentalist natural virtue," this should not entail any deep opposition between the personal and the impersonal point of view. What is virtuous from the objective point of view – namely, acting for the common good – is also what is most pleasing from the subjective point of view because the nature of human agency is such that acting on the virtues produces the best and most lasting kinds of pleasures. For example, the Earl of Shaftesbury held that the act of self-sacrifice without any hope of reward is one of the highest forms of pleasure.[61] The sentimentalist person of virtue takes the validity of the laws of virtue to rest on the fact that they come from his feelings, and their nature is such that they will in fact bring him pleasure. In acting on the basis of these feelings, moreover, the individual is independent in that he is acting on the basis of something *within* himself that he can nonetheless take as authoritative for him because of its justifiability from the more *objective* point of view.

Virtue and self-interest

The "champion of natural virtue," however, finds himself confronted with the "way of the world" that is constituted by those individuals who egoistically put their own individual interests above the common good. As noted, the "champion of natural virtue" argues that this is a mistake on their part, since by acting *selfishly,* they actually thereby fail to act *self-interestedly.* To act *truly* self-interestedly would be to act according to the principles of virtue which bring about the greatest and most enduring pleasures. The "way of the world" claims that the world consists in self-interested people selfishly pursuing their own personal ends; the "champion of natural virtue" conceives of himself as a person pursuing impersonal ends but who by doing so is actually acting in a way that satisfies his own interests better than the partisan of the "way of the world" does by acting selfishly. Indeed, the whole conception of the "champion of natural virtue" arises out of what is taken to be the insufficiencies of both the Faustian account and the "law of the heart." Those earlier accounts had operated with the idea that there is an "individuality" (a kind of essence) within agents that needs to be "actualized," and this "individuality" can only be actualized by discarding the weight of tradition and even contemporary mores – that is, by distancing oneself from one's social relations in order to bring out one's "true individuality." The "champion of natural virtue" takes this to be wrong only in the sense that he takes these agents' views to be self-defeating in bringing about what they claim they wish to bring about – namely, a state of affairs in which they as individuals find themselves satisfied and in which their individuality is expressed or "realized." "True pleasure" (and the satisfaction of the desire for individuality) comes from accepting one's sociality.[62]

The partisans of the "way of the world" and the "champions of natural virtue" understand themselves to be at loggerheads with each other, but the question is whether there is any real difference between these two points of view. The partisans of the "way of the world" take the *subjective* point of view to be that which determines what is an authoritative reason for them to act; they act for pleasure (like the Faustian agents) or from the basis of their own emotions (like those who act out of the "law of the heart"). For the partisan of "the way of the world," it is important that he realize *his* individuality, that his "self-conceit" be actualized in the world independently of its effect on the community at large; he takes his own individuality to be the "law" that is to be obeyed.[63] The "men and women of virtue," on the other hand, take the *objective* point of view to be that which determines what is to count for them as an authoritative reason; they thus supposedly act for the sake of the common good. Both, however, take the subjective point of view – that point of view that focuses on one's feelings and emotions – as the basis for action and belief in the practical realm. On that basis, the "champion of natural virtue" wishes to show to the egoist professing "the way of the world" that according to his own principles he should strive for self-sacrificing virtue instead of selfish goals, since only such a pursuit would in fact achieve for him that which he wants to achieve – namely, self-satisfaction and affirmation as an individual. The "champion of natural virtue," that is, wishes to show the egoist that the "true essence" of the world – to which the egoist appeals when making his arguments – is actually on the side of virtue.[64]

The struggle between the "champions of virtue" and the partisans of the "way of the world," (the so-called egoists) was echoed in the debate over the merits of a Shaftesbury-like account of virtue with its emphasis on sacrifice and benevolence, and the merits of the more seemingly cynical view of the way of the world, typified by Bernard Mandeville's *The Fable of the Bees*. Mandeville argued against Shaftesbury's notions of virtue and benevolence, arguing that in the "way of the world," private vice is actually public virtue. Selfishness, a vice, turns out in free markets to be a virtue, since it produces more wealth for all concerned. Mandeville's fable concerns a prosperous and productive hive of bees in which all measure of vice flourished. Jove, tiring of the bees' vice (and of the ongoing complaints coming from the bees themselves about how corrupt they were), made all of the bees into virtuous, benevolent individuals. But after giving up all their vices, the bees then found that their hive was no longer as prosperous as before. All the bee merchants who had trafficked in luxury and vice went out of business, and the economic well-being of the hive precipitously declined. Mandeville's moral was clear (even in the subtitle of his reissued version: *Private Vices, Public Benefits*): The well-being of society is best served by egoistic acts, and any attempt to make us more virtuous is bound to have contrary and deleterious effects on us. In the eighteenth-century version of the debate, as we noted, the shadow of Hobbes loomed over the whole enterprise; since for many Enlightenment figures, Hobbes was taken to be the primary enemy to be refuted, Mandeville was naturally seen as the latest reincarnation of the Hobbesian view. In order to refute the Hobbesian-Mandevillean line, it thereby became important to show that what was *natural* to humanity was something more noble than the pursuit of individual gain, and the writings of the Earl of Shaftesbury became the focal point for those who wished to discredit Hobbesian views. The debate extended widely throughout the eighteenth century, and it turned on whether humanity's essence was "naturally good" or "naturally bad" (which obviously played into many Christian concerns about whether we should regard humanity as fallen and inherently sinful – and therefore Hobbesian – or whether we should regard human agents as having certain divine qualities within them – such as those sentiments of virtue such as sympathy that mirror God's love – and being therefore more Shaftesburyian).

For the "champion of natural virtue" to defeat the partisans of the "way of the world," he must therefore be able to show that if we follow our natural inclinations, we will be led to perform virtuous acts, just as the partisans of "the way of the world" must show that following our natural inclinations leads us to perform narrowly egoistic acts. The "champion of natural virtue" must therefore be able to show the egoist that internal to the egoist's own self-interested structure of willing and desiring is an inclination to virtue that only needs to be actualized.[65] Moreover, what Hegel calls the "knight of virtue" – referring no doubt to Cervantes' character of Don Quixote, the paradigmatic figure representing those who try to resurrect an outdated conception of virtue in modern conditions – must claim to know that the egoist does not actually act virtuously (that is, benevolently); otherwise, there would be no need to convince him. Thus, the idea of the natural disposition to virtue, to the Good, seems to be only a theoretical term (an "abstraction") that the champion of natural virtue has introduced as something to be actualized, not as a fixed feature of agents that is already in place. If there were such fixed features already in place in the hearts of everyone, then any reflective, sincere egoist would already have become a virtuous agent.[66]

What would these potentials for virtue be? They would generally be benevolent dispositions or talents within the agent that need to be realized in the agent's actions and that from the objective point of view would be justified as authoritative reasons to act because of the good consequences produced by such actions. Behind these general dispositions is the desire for the agent's satisfaction; it is therefore up to the agent himself to put these desires into effect, to act naturally. When the individual acts rationally, for the sake of his self-interest, he will act benevolently; when he acts irrationally, he will act egoistically. But this seems to mean that this desire to satisfy one's self-interest is not enough on its own to prompt virtuous actions, since the egoist apparently *misuses* the same desire (the desire to satisfy his self-interest) to direct his actions to egoistic ends. Something else besides "natural desire" must therefore be operating to get the egoist to see that he is not in fact satisfying his natural desire to be satisfied by his egoistic actions or feelings. Thus, on the "champion of natural virtue's" own terms, the idea of a "natural" desire to act benevolently or selfishly cannot be the full story here. The "champion of natural virtue" must therefore give some other reason to the egoist than the idea that he should act according to his natural dispositions, for that is exactly what the egoist claims to be doing.[67]

Hegel argues that the "champions of natural virtue" are only engaged in "shadow-boxing" (*Spiegelfechterei*) or pretense, since they share the same assumptions as the partisans of the "way of the world." The "champion of natural virtue" must assume that what the world is *in-itself* is something that has implanted natural desires in people to pursue their own interests. He shares with the egoist the view that people are only driven to act by "natural" desires to further their own interests; the two sides differ only in what they take to be a person's interests and therefore what they take to be natural. Furthermore, the champion of natural virtue must believe that since virtue is *natural,* it will "naturally" win out. If, after all, it will not naturally win out, then in what sense could it be said to be natural in the first place? But if it will naturally win out, then what is there for the champion of natural virtue to do in this battle between virtue and egoism?[68]

Indeed, in the debate between the egoists and the champions of virtue (with the latter being forced to the position that people are by nature benevolent and therefore will naturally do benevolent acts), the egoists will always have the upper hand. They have no incentive to defend or to subscribe to any of the traditional virtues except as any of them assists their egoistically conceived interests. They take the idea of acting in accordance with nature as seriously as the champions of virtue, and take equally seriously the idea that there is indeed a natural way to act, interference with which leads to unhappiness. (Thus, in Mandeville's *Fable of the Bees,* the conversion of the bees into virtuous citizens who do not lie and do not lust for objects to satisfy their pride destroys the prosperity and the livability of the hive.) Indeed, it seems that the "champion of natural virtue" is insisting on importing a conception of virtue into nature; he believes that, for example, human agents are created in the image of God's loving and thus are by nature benevolent, such that they will find their satisfaction in benevolent actions. The "champion of natural virtue" insists, therefore, just as much as does the egoist, that there is indeed a natural way to act, and that it is lodged deep within the individual's nature. Both sides hold that to gain moral knowledge, the individual must consult his feelings. The "champion of natural virtue" is thereby put into the position of having to accuse the egoist of not knowing his real feelings or mistaking them for something else. The "champion of natural virtue" originally rested his claim on the idea that moral knowledge – if this should be called "knowledge" at all – was available to an individual by virtue of his consulting his feelings, but this is exactly what the egoist claims to be doing (along with calculating his self-interest). The "champion of natural virtue's" conception of nature thus turns out not to rest on the careful *observation* of nature that he thinks is found in the practice of modern science (on which this view tries to model itself and from which it parasitically draws its authority). Rather, it is the result of *importing* into the concept of the "natural" a whole set of assumed normative concerns; not the "natural" per se but a certain abstract normative conception of the "natural" is at work there.[69] It denies that what can *actually* be observed around it – namely, the individuals of the emerging market societies of modern life acting in what seem to be egoistic ways – is in fact what "really" is the case. That is, it does not *observe* human behavior so much as it posits an underlying essence (which it calls "Nature"), which it then uses to explain how people *would* behave if indeed this *were* the essence of things.[70] The egoist takes the "champion of natural virtue's" own terms (such as "acting in accordance with nature") and then uses them in a way to defeat him, since the egoist's descriptions actually fit the way in which these people in fact act, not just the way they *would* act if they were to be fully "natural."

The egoist thus shows the "champion of natural virtue" to be not so much giving an explanation of virtue as offering a series of exhortations to get people to change their beliefs and actions, to become less self-centered and more benevolent. While this may serve certain edifying purposes, it cannot serve as an account of human behavior. The talk of "natural virtue" turns out just to be talk, and the neo-stoicism of the eighteenth century turns out not to be a revival of stoicism at all. Indeed, the attempt to revive an ancient conception of virtue in the conditions of modern emerging market societies is bound to fail, for it fails to take into account the new "social space" in terms of which people form their desires and their self-conceptions. The ancient world's conception of virtue did not have any room within it for any kind of modern individualism; instead, people's ends were given to them by the social roles in which they found themselves.[71] There was no "way of the world" to combat with any high-sounding conception of "virtue" as being that which is most natural to people. The ancient world, that is, had a social conception of "the way things are done" that was shared by its citizens such that past tradition and contemporary mores were in fact *authoritative reasons* for those people. The whole point of this form of modern individualism, however, is that it rejects the idea that there is such a *social* order that includes within itself a shared conception of "the way things are done," and that even if it did, such a conception could not serve the same function as it did for the ancient world, for the driving force of modern life is that "the way things are done," taken as an appeal to tradition or ecclesiastical authority, *cannot* count as an authoritative reason. For something to count as an author-itative reason, it must be such that the individual can self-consciously come to count it as an authoritative reason – that is, be *independent* in what he takes to be an authoritative ground for action and belief. The modern "champions of virtue," therefore, took a concept that was essentially social – a concept that such and such is correct simply because it is "the way things are done" – and tried to transpose it into the idiom of modern conceptions of nature, to show that people naturally act virtuously because that is just "the way that they are."[72]

Indeed, as the emerging market economies were showing, the so-called egoist who non-benevolently looks out for his own interests may actually be doing something that is more beneficial to the public good than the so-called "champion of natural virtue" who cultivates his feelings and claims to be acting benevolently. The Scottish economists – for example, Steuart, Fer-guson, and Smith, whom Hegel studied intensely in his youth – offered a theory that showed how this transformation of private self-interest into public benefit could in fact be achieved without having to make any assumptions at all about what was "natural" in human behavior. What turned out to be at stake at this point in modern life was therefore not what was "natural" to human agency but which set of social institutions best suited modern life's conception of itself as an independent form of life. What the debate between the so-called egoists and the so-called "champions of virtue" turned out to be about was the historical development of a new set of modern *social* institu-tions – the free market foremost among them – that both expressed and supported this emerging idea of independent individualism itself. What had seemed to the participants to be a debate about nature had turned out to be a debate about modern life and the direction of modern history.

III

3. The rational individual

The "fact" of individualism

The early forms of individualism in modern life, from Faustian experimentalism to that of natural virtue, had presumed that for individual agents to be independent (to be the moral agents within the "formation of consciousness" of modern *individualism*), they had to bring this about by actualizing some kind of determinate potential within them, and that the only way to do this was to free themselves both from the past and from the constraints of contemporary mores. Having taken the practices of modern science to show them that the "essence" of nature was disclosable by constructing various theories for the purpose of satisfying *human* interests, they concluded that their own individual agency should therefore be discloseable to them by their own construction of a practical world and a personal set of mores. The Faustian agent, the paradigmatic figure of early modern life, thus sets off on a voyage of self-discovery by throwing off all constraints of the past and sampling the various "experiences" that life has to offer, seeking to bring out what had been supposedly repressed by the constraints of the past. But because the Faustian agent's conception of his individual essence was too general and abstract, it therefore ended up in little more than self-defeating hedonism. The "law of the heart," with its conception of emotionalism as authoritative, undermined its own claims to authority by ending up in a self-contradictory account of why electing some particular feeling or emotion to count as a "reason" for belief and action was justifiable from the objective point of view. Finally, the "champions of virtue" of early modern life in their attempt to revivify ancient conceptions of virtue by showing that certain motives of benevolence were "natural" to individuals ended up losing the argument to the market-oriented egoists, who seemed to have a much better understanding of what it meant in modern conditions to speak of an individual satisfying himself and nonetheless promoting a common good (that is, that the followers of Mandeville won their argument with the followers of Shaftesbury).

The result of the victory of the "way of the world" over the "champions of virtue" was that individualism for these agents became secured within their self-understanding as an ineluctable feature of human agency. The project of this early modern form of life had to do with the application of reason to the observation of nature and to human social life. The underlying "faith" of that project was the belief that just as the application of reason in modern science has affirmed that human theoretical constructions can capture nature as it is, the application of modern practical reason to ourselves could capture *human* nature as it is. Because the earlier individualists had found the world confronting them as having no place for such individualism, they were led to see themselves as having to bring out this "implicit" individualism within themselves through either Faustian experimentalism, emotionalism, or by living in accordance with the precepts of a sentimentally construed nature. However, now that the Mandevillean individuals have found that the world – the emerging social world of modern market-oriented social institutions – not only has a place for such individuals in it but also affirms for them that they are in fact such individuals, they no longer must understand themselves as having to bring something only implicit or potential within them to fruition.[73] The idea that there is something already potentially "in" them that has to be actualized implies that there is something about them that is simply given (their potential), and that they are self-directing only to the extent that they guide that pre-formed potential to its adequate realization. But if the nature of human agency is such that we really are independent individuals, then there is no need to construe ourselves as having to live up to some ideal of Faustian individualism, emotionalist doctrine, or an ideal of natural virtue in order to be "true" individuals; it should be enough simply to *express* the individuality within each of us.

The result of the modern constructions of individualism thus thoroughly undermines that claim that individuals "find" a potential within them that is "given" and that they must then actualize; instead, it seems to require acknowledgment of the idea that they *already are* such individuals, and social life must orient itself around this "fact" of individualism. What Faustianism, emotionalism, and sentimentalism had understood as a potential comes to be seen instead as a fixed actuality. The Faustian, emotionalist, and sentimentalist agents had understood themselves as divided within themselves; they took their self-consciousness to be structured by their social context, which in order to be "true" individuals they believed they needed to discard or transcend.[74] But the historical insufficiencies of those early modern accounts generates an account of individuals as not primarily social, "inauthentic" agents who must *make* themselves into individuals by actualizing a potential within them, or living up to an ideal; they already are such individuals, and their project must be to properly express this individuality rather than to construct it.[75]

The project for this conception of individualism is to determine that part of the individual that transcends circumstances and remains constant throughout different acts and environments, since there must be some "pre-formed" part of individuality that makes it individual.[76] For this view, the past had repressed the development of individuality by submitting it to various social and religious pressures that in this view also appear as impositions on the "true nature" of humanity. Thus, true *individuality,* so it would seem, cannot lie in any social construction, for that is precisely the difficulty with the past models of agency that modern life takes itself to be rejecting. (As we might put it, it is a passage from the early modern idea of *individualism,* with its conception of each individual having an identical set of interests and liberties, to the pre-romantic idea of *individuality* – namely, the conception that each individual has a unique "nature" that cannot be commensurated with the other individual's "natures.")

Expressions of individuality: sincerity

Hegel's model of such a conception of individuality is most likely the seventeenth and eighteenth-century conception of the *honnête homme* (or, in En-

113

gland, the "gentleman"). The *honnête homme* was considered to be a more rational way of living, more in keeping with "nature" than were previous aristocratic models of life.[77] Not an aristocrat (a *gentilhomme*), the *honnête homme* was, as his name implied, an honest or sincere person, who expressed his nature but whose reason counseled him to prudence and to accept the existing social order. Moreover, the *honnête homme* was not a specialist; he went from one subject to another without having any overall view of how the various *things* with which he was concerned fit together, seeing them only in terms of how they expressed his "sincere" wishes and plans.[78] He had to display a studied unconcern with the issues concerning the overall coherence of his various interests. The "gentleman" is sincere, and he is rational (at least in the sense of being temperate); but he is not overly concerned with whether what he says or does is rational in any deeper sense, since he is primarily concerned with expressing his individuality in a sincere manner. In the English version, the "gentleman's" origins are also obscure; he may be an aristocrat, he may be the third son of an aristocrat (and thus not be able to assume the title under the English laws of inheritance), or he may be simply a merchant or the son of one; the English "gentleman" represents the way in which one can be a "true individual" independently of one's past.

Another model for Hegel's discussion would be Rousseau as he presents himself in his autobiography, *Confessions,* a work that may be said to complete the development of that ideal of character that has to do with sincerity. The idea of the "gentleman" is a man of uncertain ancestry, who is nonetheless "sincere" and "honorable" in what he undertakes. Rousseau, of course, rejects the ideal of the "gentleman" in large part because of what he sees precisely as his *insincerity;* but Rousseau is perhaps the paradigm of the true *honnête homme,* the really "sincere," "honorable" person who only does what in his heart he takes to be best. In his *Confessions,* Rousseau attempts to show how there was a certain "nature" (himself, Jean-Jacques), who, despite all the twists and turns in his life, remained the same person throughout and who always tried to bring that same person sincerely to the light of day.[79] Thus, Rousseau, for example, takes his individual "nature" to have been corrupted in part by his upbringing and by irrational social institutions in which he was "forced" to live, even though he takes that individual "nature" to have remained constant throughout his development; he also remains convinced that by displaying his "true nature" to all, he will vindicate himself in the eyes of the public. He tries to show that even in what appear to be iniquitous acts (such as his abandonment of his five children at the door of an orphanage immediately after each one was born) really were done from good, even if misguided, intentions, and that the "self" behind all these acts was itself basically good and well-intentioned and would have to be seen as such by his readers.

Rousseau's book, *Confessions* is a particularly good model for this case, since it represents a distinctly modern turn in the writing of autobiography. Earlier models of autobiography, such as Augustine's *Confessions,* had the author talking to God; Rousseau, on the other hand, talks only to his fellow humans. Other earlier models – for example, and perhaps most strikingly, Peter Abelard's autobiographical account in his *The Story of My Misfortunes* – take Augustine's own work as their model and try to fit the story of their life into the framework provided by Augustine: a key event, a falling away from God's favor, followed by a gradual return to true faith. These earlier works thus have the authors presenting their lives as examples of a more general framework. But Rousseau explicitly takes no model for himself, declaring that the world has never heard such a story such as he will tell, that he is absolutely unique, and that there can therefore be no prior model for the story of his life. Thus, Rousseau's *Confessions* represents a crucial literary manifestation of this turning point in the development of individualism to the idea that "an individual" is unique and is not just an instance of some more general pattern.[80] In Hegel's phrase, it marks the idea of an "individuality that takes itself to be real in and for itself."[81]

The goal of the individual cannot be to *become* an individual (like Faust) since he already is an individual; he must come to know himself *as* the individual he is and to express and pursue those ends that are consistent with such individuality. Indeed, because the individuality of each person is thus conceived as a "quality," something like a simple property, within them, the relation of the individual's acts to this simple quality can *only* be that of *expression,* of somehow bringing that which is subjective and "inner" into that which is "outer," into a publicly available form.[82] The circumstances of the person's actions cannot affect the intrinsic self-identity (the "inner quality") of the agent nor his true moral character. For example, Rousseau claims that although many things he did *seemed* to be bad, once one understood the "true" self and the intentions that were behind these actions, one would see that in fact both his self and his intentions were basically well-meaning and good. Since Rousseau claimed to know that his heart was pure and his intentions only well-meaning, it followed that their expression in what seemed to be otherwise reprehensible acts had to be the result not of his "inner nature" but of the corrupting social world around him. The truth of the matter with regard to the agent's self-identity and the nature of his action would thus supposedly only have something to do with this "inner self;" the way in which his actions appear to others (the public circumstances of the actions) can therefore also only be a "mere appearance" (*Schein*), a kind of facade for or semblance of this real truth of the matter. What the action *really* is (what it is in-itself) is an expression of this "inner self;" the action is not what it appears to be in the public world.[83] The individual therefore thinks of himself not as having some "unique nature" within himself as a *potential* that needs to be actualized but as something already there that fits all the particular elements of the story of his life into one story and that remains constant throughout it, being *expressed* only well or badly in different circumstances.

A major issue for this view is how the individual himself can know who he is. The actions that an individual performs can be good or bad expressions of his inner nature. Bad social circumstances can inhibit or deform one's actions so that one is not expressing who one really is (the inner self); for example, in one of the more celebrated scenes in Rousseau's *Confessions,* Rousseau relates how as a youth he got a servant girl into trouble by blaming her for stealing a ribbon that he himself had stolen, and he laments what he sees as the social pressures that, to him, forced him to do such a thing. On the one hand, therefore, it would seem that the individual must already know who he really is in order to be able to understand his own actions, in order to be able to see, for example, as Rousseau thought he had done, that blaming the servant girl for his own act of theft (and, he acknowledges, probably wrecking her life, since she would be unable to get the necessary letters of reference from her employers) was not the "real" Rousseau. Yet on the other hand, it would seem that even the individual would not be able to find out who he is except by looking at the expressions of his self-identity in his own actions, in which case it would seem that he would not be able to separate out the real from the merely apparent self. It thus seems as if such an agent might be caught in an odd circle, unable ever even himself to find out who he really is.[84]

This difficulty, though, is resolved for such individuals by the concept of *interest.* The individual looks to see what in the world interests him and attracts him, assuming that this will be revelatory of what it is that he truly is "within himself." (Thus, Rousseau looks to past events to see how they appealed to him, arguing that by his paying attention to the sentiments he attached to such things, he thereby knows what he was really up to in those episodes.) The *means* of expression are the other natural attributes of the person: his abilities, talents, character, and so on. The general defining *purpose* that the individual pursues is to express his individuality. The world can either be opposed to this purpose (by thwarting the expression or deforming it), or it can be in harmony with this purpose, but it cannot define that purpose.

In acting, the agent *expresses* this inner nature in some public outward fashion, perhaps through the production of some work (such as one of Rousseau's many books). The work, of course, is a limited, determinate thing and only therefore a limited, determinate and one-sided expression of the author's true nature. (For example, Rousseau complains that he has been misunderstood by the readers of his books, who have not had the insight of seeing the author's true nature, which was only partially expressed in the books.) This view of individuality thus curiously inverts the subjective and objective points of view. The subjective point of view – one's awareness of one's individuality through attention.to one's sentiments – is that which gives one authoritative reasons for belief and action (it is the "universal," in Hegel's terms), while the public world – the world as seen from an impersonal point of view – is understood as being only a world of particular things, of one-sided or incomplete (or, worse, false) expressions of one's "inner self." (Thus, Rousseau complains that even those acts that he came to regret and to admit to being wrong – such as his abandoning his five children – have been "misunderstood" because those who have accused him of being a bad man have not understood the so-called goodness of heart behind these acts.[85]) The public world cannot give one an authoritative reason for belief or for action.

(Rousseau knows that many in the public world have condemned him for what naturally *seem* like selfish or hard-hearted actions, but he knows that this widespread condemnation cannot count for him as an authoritative reason for *anyone* to judge his actions to be bad, since *he* knows in his heart that his intentions were always good.) What counts as an authoritative reason for such individuals has to be that which they know "in their heart" to be true about themselves – that is, what their sentiments disclose to them of their "original, determinate nature." The work itself cannot be judged as good or bad on its own without knowing how well it expresses or fails to express the "true, inner self" of the fabricator. Works can be bad only if the "self" that they express is itself a bad "self"; on its own, any given work is neither good nor bad.[86] To call a work bad is really to condemn the author of a work as being a bad person – for example, to decry a work as being too sentimental is really to say that the fabricator is a sentimental person and that being a sentimental person is a bad thing to be. (Voltaire, for example, attacked Rousseau for being a bad person, concluding that because of his badness, Rousseau's claims to being a reformer could not be taken seriously.)

This is a logical development of the principle of reason that animated so much of the early modern project. To modern agents, it seemed that science had affirmed for them that their system of thoughts and desires could be structured so as to disclose the secrets of nature, that reason and reality were intrinsically one. Modern science affirmed that no claims or reasons derived from past science needed to be preserved unless they could meet the new independent criteria of induction, experiment, and the postulation of imperceptible entities to explain the correlations and regularities that induction establishes. Modern practical agents thus sought to affirm for themselves that nothing from past traditions or contemporary mores needed to be preserved for them as reasons for belief or action unless they could meet the criteria of what was necessary to "actualize" the inherent "potential" of individuality in each agent. This idea of self-realization then itself logically developed into the idea not of actualizing a potential but of *expressing* the individuality that was already there. It would thus be logical that somebody *like* Rousseau, if not exactly Rousseau himself, would have to appear on the scene to argue that it was indeed the inherited traditions and the repressive current practices of civilization that prohibited or corrupted the expressions of natural selfhood. In this view, individuality is something that is already there, fully formed more or less within each individual, and nothing can count as an authoritative reason for belief or action unless this individual can affirm it for himself as fitting who he really is "within." It would be impossible for the individual to discover that he has turned out to be somebody different from who he originally was; the agent must be the same throughout his experiences, and although he may do many things out of keeping with his "inner nature," he will do those things only when his actions have been forced or corrupted by a surrounding world that is hostile to the expression of that nature.[87]

The issue is whether this self-conception can be *satisfactory* for the individuals who hold it – whether it can function within a structure of mutual recognition to affirm for them who they think they are. This seems to be difficult, given the logic of this self-conception. The work (the book, the poem, the play, whatever) is the expression of the agent's individuality; it is the means by which the agent acquires a presence to others as *this* individual in the public world. *Who* he is becomes expressed to others in the work, although *who* he is must be completely independent from any of these appearances and remain constant throughout the different circumstances in which the work appears. However, the work itself, unlike the "true self" behind it, is necessarily subject to different interpretations by other agents. The work exists only in public space; it has no individuality to it other than that which is conferred on it by others. Others, in confronting the work, must interpret it in terms of their own intentions, interests, and sentiments – in short, in terms of who they are in their own "inner selves."

It follows that if the creator of the work must act according to reasons that are valid for him as the particular individual he is "in himself" (reasons that are disclosed to him by his sentiments), then others must act on the reasons valid for them in terms of the particular individuals they are "in themselves."[88] As soon as the work appears in a public space, it (or any expressive act by the individual) therefore ceases to be only the expression of the individual who authored it or created it. Having no nature of its own, it becomes only what others make of it, which, given their own distinct individualities, will be different from the way in which the creator himself had intended it.[89] The *being* of the creator (who he is in-himself) thus is necessarily opposed to what he is *doing,* even when, from his own subjective point of view, his "doings" perfectly fit his "original, determinate nature," since others must necessarily take what he does (his work) in terms of their own "inner natures," and there can be nothing *in the work itself* that can put any constraints on how these others can take it.[90] For the work itself to be able to put any constraints on its own interpretation would imply on this account that the interpreters of the work were not themselves independent individuals but could have reasons imposed on them. Thus, the work *cannot* express fully and adequately the individuality of the creator in the public world, for the determinateness of the work (what it is) is *determined* by others' interpretation of it, whereas the determinateness of the *self* of the individual (who he is, his intentions, and so on) is supposedly independent of interpretation (that is, *determination*) by others.

Each self is taken to be free of determination by anything except its own given nature, whereas its public expressions are what they are in terms of the interpretations given to them by others.[91] Although the agent may wish or may try to structure his work so that it would be impossible for others to take it in ways that would lead to (doubtlessly wicked and false) interpretations of who he is, the logic of this self-conception makes that attempt impossible. There can be nothing that the creator of the work can do that would make it impossible for the work (and thereby for him) not to be taken "wrongly" by others. It can only be a matter of pure contingency if others take both the work and the author as the author intends himself and the work to be taken.[92] If he is to be a "true" individual, the author of the work therefore cannot concern himself with others' reception of his own work since only he can "sincerely" decide for himself what is to count for him as a good criticism or as a just piece of praise. How he is taken by others depends on contingent factors; who he is, however, should remain steadfast in all the various circumstances in which he finds himself.

The "real thing"

The agent must therefore concern himself not with the contingencies of his reception by others but with the "real thing," the *Sache selbst* – namely, the unity of who he *really* is in his "inner self" and his *expressions* of who he is.[93] The "real thing" is the "true work," what the work "really means" from the standpoint of what the creator of the work intended it to mean as an expression of who he is, as opposed to the way in which the work and the author might *actually* be taken by others.[94] To be concerned with the "real thing" is to be concerned with what one is actually "sincerely" expressing, as opposed to what others take one to be expressing.

The question is, however: What *really is* the "real thing," the "fact of the matter" at work here? The "real thing" would appear to be an individual sincerely expressing his own interests, desires, projects, and cares, and there can always be a difference between the individual self (or "original determinate nature") and the way in which he is taken by others. The underlying belief for this account of the "gentleman's" individuality is that there is a "real thing" that remains fixed and determinate throughout the contingent play of public recognition – namely, who the individual *really* is and what his works therefore *really* express. It is what binds the disparate elements of his self-identity (his talents, which ends he pursues, what he does) into a unity, as the doings and expressions of this particular individual with this particular self-identity; it is the "truth of the matter" about all these things.[95]

The individual who is only concerned with the "real thing" cannot be concerned with the various contingencies that determine his description by others; only his own "sincerity" can be an issue for him. Others may take him wrongly, but if he is sincere in his expressions of himself, then he cannot be faulted for misleading anyone.[96] This preserves the non-contingency of the self (its fixed and determinate nature) from the contingent and variable surroundings in which it finds itself. Things may turn out badly for the individual, or he may commit awful acts because of various contingencies – for example, Rousseau's claim that he blames the servant for stealing the ribbon because of his (good) desire to please and society's (bad) compulsion to adopt false explanations – but his sincerity cannot be itself a matter of contingency. The agent himself is in full control over whether he is sincere. For contingent reasons, he may not *actually* succeed in doing good things, but he can be *sincere* about having *wished* to do the right thing (a frequent claim made by Rousseau). Indeed, the agent can affirm for himself that it is in fact his (laudable) sincerity that provokes others of ill will to condemn him (another frequent claim made by Rousseau).

One of the problems with such a view of the "real thing" is of course its manifestly self-serving nature. Whatever happens – the individual commits a dreadful act, or the individual does nothing at all – the particular agent can always defend himself in his own eyes and to others by claiming that his inaction or his less than laudatory deed was not as it appeared and that in fact the "real fact of the matter" was something else (his good intentions coupled with various worldly contingencies that produced the wayward act, or the contingencies of the world that prevented him from acting, and social pressures that deformed his good intentions into bad expressions, and so on). This view seems to take nothing in particular to be essentially part of the "real thing" – neither the individual's willing nor his acting nor his inaction nor his circumstances nor his talents. What counts as the "real thing" is thus not any particular action, intention, or work, for any of these may fail to match up the "real, inner self" that constitutes the individuality of the agent.[97] Whatever intention the individual forms or action that he takes can for reasons external to his "self" be an inadequate expression of his real "self." The "real thing," the "truth of the matter," must appear therefore only as a kind of indeterminate ground of the individual's actions, what all these actions and expressions "really" are in themselves and not just as they appear to others; only the agent himself can know what these actions are *in themselves* because only he can know in his "heart" who he is.

In a community of such individual *honnêtes hommes,* each would present himself to the other as being only concerned with what his actions *really* meant. Each would profess to be concerned only with whether he was expressing his own "inner self," not with whether he is getting the other's intentions right. For example: one person professes an interest in social theory or music and does something (engages in a discussion, writes a piece of music, writes a book on social contract theory, whatever), which is then taken up by others. But, given the terms of this self-conception, he *cannot* be interested in the work on social contract theory per se; he can only be interested in it as it functions as a *sincere* expression of his "inner self," as expressing *his* interests. The supposed interest that he shows in the matter at hand (the book, the piece of music, the conversation, whatever) can have a significance for him only as it expresses, brings to the light of day, his own self. Thus, what may at first appear as a social or shared interest in something can in fact only be a *self*-interest, an interest in expressing one's self. This would hold not merely for the individual performing the act; it would also hold for the other participants. A conversation among such individuals over, for example, social theory might at first appear as an interchange between individuals over some matter about which they both cared; but such an appearance would be deceptive, for none of the parties *could* have a detached interest in social theory for its own sake, since the significance of social theory for each party can only be a function of how well it captures what *his* interests are. It cannot be social theory (or music or whatever) that is the main object of concern for any of the parties; it has to be the self and what counts as an expression of the self that is the object of concern. What one has then is not so much a conversation but a series of people each simply waiting for their turn to talk, to "express themselves," with the "self" in question being something that is defined independently of this social interchange – the "spiritual kingdom of animals," as Hegel titles such a community.[98] One can therefore have only a serial presentation of such expressions, with none of them really affecting the other. The fate of what gets expressed, of course, escapes the individual's control, but, by this account, that cannot be of any real concern to him; he is concerned with who he is, with what ideas, intentions, plans are really *his own,* not with what is not his own – namely, the contingent ways his expressions get taken up by others. The true "gentleman" (or *honnête homme*) is concerned with his real self, not with the contingent effects his actions may have. Moreover, for any of them to say that he, at least, was primarily concerned with the object under discussion (for example, social theory) would be deceptive, for he could not be concerned primarily with such an object but only with how well such an object expressed his own individuality.

The question is why any of these individuals should express anything to others at all. If their "original determinate natures" are independent of the contingent social circumstances in which they find themselves, then what role can *expression* play for them? If they know "in their hearts" who they are, to whom are they expressing this "inner self"? (This is problematic for Rousseau in his *Confessions,* for he claims to be telling the story of a unique life – "But I am made unlike any one I have ever met; I will even venture to say that I am like no one in the whole world"[99] – yet his story is also supposed to serve as a model for others that will enable them to discover their "true natural selves" within them; it thus functions both as *personal* expression and as a *universal* model for others.[100]) Indeed, the function of this kind of expression is to make oneself visible to others, to place oneself in the public world, not merely to cultivate one's own unique individuality; Rousseau, for example, writes his *Confessions* in order to make an apology and defense of his life *to others.* This concern with a so-called pure expression is deceptive, for the whole function of the expressive act is to place oneself in the public world, to translate one's subjective point of view into an objective setting. It is to put the subjective point of view into a public setting such that it does not cease to be a subjective point of view but nonetheless becomes something that others can take up according to shared criteria of appraisal.[101] What these agents take at first to be authoritative reasons – namely, those that have to do with determining what belongs to them as *their own* and what is only contingently "their own" (namely, the only contingently successful or unsuccessful expressions of that "inner self") – turns out to be impossible to specify on their own terms. If it is true that the "real thing" is the agent's individuality, his "self" as already formed and enduring independently of its contingent expressions, then he cannot be concerned at all with *expressing* it, for on this account, expression has no essential relation to that self. Yet, by this account, expressing his individuality is what is of interest to the agent. In this "spiritual kingdom of animals," each therefore claims to be unconcerned to others with what he expresses (since each is already who he is independently of that expression), yet each claims that his basic goal is expressing himself, since it is only in expressing the self, bringing it to public presence, that he fulfills his individuality. The account of the "real self" as something that transcends and is unaffected by social circumstance begins to evaporate.

In the "spiritual kingdom of animals," each agent takes himself to be the locus of a set of mediations with others, in which each has *his own* interests, capacities, and talents, and each thus enters into a negotiation with others to preserve that independence. Yet each finds that what even counts as an interest, as a capacity, as a talent, is something already out in public space. In making an assertion, the agent finds, for example, that it is not simply his intentions that determines the meaning of the assertion but the way the assertion is taken up by others in terms of their shared public space. But to the extent that what one means is something that is just as much for others as it is "for me" implies that there is no meaningful sense of "the real self" except as a part of that "social space." What counts as the "individuality" of the individual is not something that is the "real thing" (the *Sache selbst*) that transcends contingency or circumstance; it is as much a part of the pattern of social recognition as its expressions were taken to be. The attempts by each of the "spiritual animals" to preserve a part of himself as the "real thing" turns out to be a deceptive enterprise.

The account that these individuals would have to give of what they take as authoritative reasons for belief or action demands that they shift their original self-conception into a different self-conception. They cannot conceive of themselves as fully formed individuals who merely express their already formed natures to each other but as individuals who *become* who they are in making themselves visible in the public world. Or, to put it differently, the self becomes seen as a *project,* not as a fully formed "thing," something that is constructed in the processes of mutual recognition in social life. The affirmation of themselves as independent agents is carried out not in the disinterested expression of so-called inner selves but in seeing themselves as fully social entities; their independence is something to be achieved and negotiated, not something simply to be expressed.[102]

Sociality and normativity

The logical outcome of the dialectical to and fro involved in the "spiritual kingdom of animals" is therefore the development of the possibility for modern agents to form an account of spirit as reflective "social space," of their self-identities and of what they count as authoritative reasons for belief and action as being based in social practice, not as being based on any transcendent standards, or as parts of any kind of "substance."[103] The partial culmination of the development of the idea of reason in the self-undermining accounts of the "gentleman" makes it possible for the modern community itself to shift from a conception of reason as a fixed, transcendent standard – the "view from nowhere" – to a conception of reason as a form of *social practice* in which we appraise and criticize other actions that we take individually and collectively. It moves the modern community from an account of what gives authority to any kind of reason-giving practice in terms of "substance" (whether that be "mental substance" or whatever) to that of "subject," of collective social practice, or, as Hegel puts it, the "I" that is a "We," and the "We" that is an "I": that is, to understand the supporting structure of our beliefs and actions not in terms of some underlying metaphysical "essence" but in terms of the structure of self-consciousness, the assuming of a position in "social space."[104] The "real thing" (the *Sache selbst*) with which the agents took themselves to be concerned comes thereby to be understood not as the "inner self," which is detached and free from the contingencies of social interpretation in which it finds itself, but as the structure itself of this background "social space" in terms of which we are self-conscious. The "real thing" is thus *spirit* (or "spiritual substance" and "spiritual essence," as Hegel sometimes calls it). The agents who come to this conclusion thus come to understand themselves as "moments" of this "social space" – that is, as occupying positions in it. The search for the so-called laws of the social world thus ends in an understanding that these laws are the principles in terms of which agents come to think of themselves as *self-determining* and nonetheless *social* beings. (It was with reference to this kind of understanding of human agency and sociality that Kant remarked that just as Newton had discovered the laws of the physical world, Rousseau had discovered the laws of human agency.[105])

This "social space" is taken as a way of directing our actions and beliefs, for even beliefs now come to be seen as a form of action, a way in which we take things to be and that is structured by the norms governing this "social space." Significantly, Hegel calls it "ethical (*sittliche*) substance."[106] In calling it "ethical," Hegel is signaling his belief that both actions and beliefs are to be taken as *normative activities,* not as "expressions" (sincere or otherwise) of some "inner quality." Beliefs are not best understood in terms of the subject/object model of knowledge and action, as any kind of "matching up" of metaphysically construed representations (*Vorstellung*) with the world or as "states" in which a subject construed as "mental substance" can be said to be. Believing something is rather a normative activity of those organisms that are human subjects, and the development of the conception of rationality in early modern science and in ideas of individualist expressionism provided the historical and social background in terms of which the logical development of an understanding of this normative activity as *spirit,* as reflective social practice emerged as the account that was necessary for these agents to give of the modern lives that they had come to lead.

Thus, Hegel uses various terms that have *"Sitte"* as their core (for example, the adjective, *sittlich,* and the nominative, *Sittlichkeit*) to characterize a certain kind of structure of spirit. At least in its Hegelian use, *"Sittlichkeit"* means something slightly different from its usual translation as "ethical life." It signifies something more like an understanding within a form of life about

123

"the way things are done." To say that such and such is "the way things are done" in terms of *Sittlichkeit* is to acknowledge that this idea of "the way things are done" expresses something like a convention, but it is also to acknowledge that if it is a convention, it is nonetheless a *deep* convention, unlike the *mere* conventions of "driving on the left side of the road" or "tipping one's hat." These deep conventions have the stronger sense of being the way things *have* to be done in *this* form of life. To the members of that form of life, such deep conventions (their "ethics," their *Sitte*) non-reflectively appear to them as obvious and natural, as being second nature. On reflection, they can of course appear *as* conventions but they can never appear as *mere* conventions – that is, as conventions that could be changed overnight (such as changing the name of the national currency). They involve, moreover, not just the form that actions take but the kinds of feelings and emotions that are proper to those actions. They are the "conventions" that structure the subjective lives and expectations of the participants in that form of life.

To see the "real thing" (the *Sache selbst*) as a form of "social space" and to understand this "social space" as "ethical (*sittliche*) substance" is thus to understand that the baselines for the way one thinks and acts are indeed in one sense "conventional," but it is also to understand that one need not to be able to envision any concrete alternatives to this mode of acting and thinking, nor even to believe that such alternatives are *really* (as opposed, perhaps, to "logically") possible for oneself. Understanding that being rational does not consist in expressing some natural property of oneself or adhering to some timeless, transcendent, impersonal standard but in acting in terms of the norms of one's "social space" is therefore to come to understand *rationality* itself as a form of ethical life (*Sittlichkeit*), as a way of acting and thinking in terms of the "way things are done" understood as a background set of norms. The agents who understand themselves along such lines can be "at home with themselves" in their various activities; they need not be alienated from the activities structured by this form of "social space." (They would be "with themselves" – *bei sich selbst* – as Hegel puts it), and the agents would thus find their self-consciousness in such a form of self-understanding to be "satisfied." In Hegel's terms, an agent who understands himself as part of an "ethical life," of *Sittlichkeit,* will also come to understand himself as a "universal self;" his *personal* point of view on himself and the world will come to be fully congruent with his *impersonal* point of view on the same things.

Kant and the culmination of the Enlightenment

Hegel develops this idea of "ethical substance" out of a discussion of "reason as legislative" and "reason as testing laws," the final sections of Hegel's discussion of the role of reason in the development of modern life.[107] These sections have traditionally been a bit puzzling to many readers. They obviously concern themselves with a critique of the Kantian moral philosophy; yet they are both very short, Kant is never mentioned by name, some very non-Kantian themes are brought up, and the discussion more or less ends with a (slightly amended) quotation from Sophocles. The criticisms of Kant are the kind that are by now both commonplace and have also come to be rejected by a large body of Kant scholars. At first blush, Hegel's criticism simply seems to boil down to the claims that Kant is a formalist – that is, that Kant claims that the only source of moral law is the principle of non-contradiction – and that from such a formalism nothing material follows.[108] (Hegel's charge of formalism is not only made against Kant's ethics but against his theoretical philosophy as well.[109]) It thus can seem terribly haphazard, very unfair to Kant, and, even more puzzling, not necessary, since Kant comes in for longer criticisms in the later sections of the *Phenomenology* (specifically, in the section called "The Moral Worldview").

Hegel's discussion in these sections has to do, however, with the way in which the Kantian philosophy both completed the Enlightenment project and went beyond it, or, to put the same thing differently, with the way in which Kant remained a figure of the Enlightenment while at the same time pointing the way beyond it – namely, towards its and modern life's culmination in Hegelian idealism.[110] For Hegel, the Enlightenment was that penultimate point in the development of the role of reason in modern life that cleared the way for a fully modern self-understanding. Common to a wide body of thought in the Enlightenment was a very widespread and imprecise consensus that the seemingly different ideas of reason, happiness (sometimes identified as "utility"), sentiment (and later emotion) were all in fact in harmony with each other, and that only the vagaries and prejudices of tradition and (particularly priestly) authority had prevented this harmony from establishing itself. Part of the Enlightenment's faith was that the use of *reason*, unfettered by such tradition and authority and accompanied by a proper attention to "sentiment," would be enough to put things right. What had been only a *project* for the early modern period – that reason and reality are one – seemed to come to self-conscious fruition in the Enlightenment, which produced an account of itself that took reason, in Hegel's words, to be "certain of itself as being all reality."[111] Its various accounts led to the conclusion that taking an impersonal, observational point of view (which many Enlightenment figures identified as following the dictates of reason) would eventuate in some kind of overall social and even personal "harmony." In such an enlightened world, mankind would be "at home" with itself, satisfied in its social life, secure in its knowledge.[112] For such an Enlightenment faith, the various ways in which society was ordered into estates (agricultural, ecclesiastical, noble, and so on) could be seen to be the result of an implicit *rational* ordering that had *naturally* divided society into those estates. There was thus much debate within Enlightenment circles about what the basic estates were – for example, the physiocrats (early defenders of market systems of exchange) argued that it had to be the agricultural estate, since (so the physiocrats believed) it best fitted the Lockean conception of "mixing one's labor" with nature to produce property – but the conception was nonetheless widely held that the "natural" and the "rational" ways of organizing society were perfectly compatible (and that the traditional ways were also both unnatural and irrational).[113]

Many of the various sets of Enlightenment accounts were also held together by a belief in a beneficent Nature that had implanted certain natural passions in people, which if correctly followed would produce both a general social harmony and happiness (thus the popularity during the early Enlightenment of the writings of the Earl of Shaftesbury). The Leibnizian denial of radical evil in favor of the doctrine that this was the best of all possible worlds had been taken up as a matter of doctrine. In his *Essay on Man*, Alexander Pope succinctly rendered the Enlightenment's conception of the Leibnizian theodicy: "And spite of Pride, in erring Reasons' spite,/ One truth is clear; whatever is is right." This was not taken up as a call for quiescence but as an affirmation that the natural world was intrinsically a rational place, that Nature's "plan" for everything was fundamentally in order, and that *only* the perverting influences of tradition and authority prevented a rational (and therefore *happy*) world from coming to be.

To capture this sense of the world and nature being already "in order," the term "optimism" was coined in this period, and the Berlin Academy of Sciences announced a prize essay competition on the theme, "All is right." In 1755, they awarded the prize to Adolf Friederich Rheinhard. His name has been forgotten, but the event that occurred that year – the great Lisbon earthquake – has not.[114] The Lisbon earthquake, which destroyed the third busiest port in Europe and led to rioting and looting by the inhabitants of Lisbon themselves, caused many Enlightenment thinkers to begin questioning the wisdom of what before then had been matters of faith for them: that there was a beneficent Providence and that what was "natural" was also "harmonious." (Voltaire's *Candide* is one outcome of the disillusionment with the faith that harmony and goodness are part of the natural order.) To many Enlightenment figures, this seemed only to confirm for them that the *social* world should at least be put in order by reason even if the natural world was not as beneficent as had been supposed. However, Hume, a key figure in the Enlightenment, undermined the full faith in reason itself by seeming to have shown that what had been taken as pure deliverances of reason in fact amounted to little more than custom and habit or the result of the way in which human nature was contingently constituted to combine and associate its representations. (This is also coupled with Hume's famous dictum with regard to the role of reason in morality: "Reason is, and ought only to be the slave of the passions, and can never pretend to any other office than to serve and obey them."[115]) Finally, Rousseau had argued that self-love (*amour-propre*) leads to the domination of others and unhappiness for oneself if it is not properly socialized, and that by no means could the modern world be said to have properly socialized anybody – including, and maybe especially, Rousseau himself – and that therefore the Enlightenment's reliance on the idea that people's "natural" inclinations to self-interest would, if structured by "reason," lead to harmony was ill-founded. It seemed, therefore, that the project of modern life – of establishing a self-justifying form of life based on reason and of inhabiting that form of life with independent agents – was in danger of breaking down. Much was therefore riding on exactly what "reason" could and could not establish, and the person who determined that would thereby be overseeing the project of modern life itself.

In Hegel's view, Kant in his *Critiques* of pure and practical reason both rescued modern life's project and completed the Enlightenment's part of the project by producing an account of reason itself. However, in completing the Enlightenment project and by demonstrating the autonomy of the experiencing and acting subject, Kant did more than just bring it to fruition; in rescuing reason from Humean skepticism, the Kantian philosophy drove what seemed to be unbridgeable wedges between reason and nature and between morality and happiness, thus cutting off what had been a major part of the Enlightenment project. Indeed, it is the subject's active "taking up" of experience that gives experience its shape, and it is the subject's active "taking" something to be an authoritative reason for action that accounts for the moral nature of action and for the conditions under which people can live cooperative social lives.[116] Hume had seemingly shown that the way in which we combine our various ideas (*Vorstellungen,* as Hume's "ideas" were translated into German) had to do with habits and natural laws of association, and not with any metaphysical relations established by "reason." In the first *Critique,* Kant argued (1) that there are indeed determinate rules for the combination of our representations, (2) that the basic and foundationally authoritative rules come from self-grounding reason itself, and (3) that the activity of combination is the result of a self-grounding "spontaneity" on the part of the experiencing and thinking subject (although Kant was clear that part of the structure of knowledge comes from the a priori structure of the givenness of "intuition," a Kantian doctrine notoriously hard to make sense of, about which there is more literature than can be read, and whose difficulties are best ignored here).[117] Kant's claim was that those rules are necessary that are derivable from the conditions under which a thinker can become aware of his own representations as belonging to one unitary consciousness, as belonging to *his* consciousness as a single consciousness over time.[118] Nothing can therefore count *as a representation* at all for a subject unless the subject combines those representations according to the rules that are necessary for bringing all the representations to a unity of self-consciousness. This unity of self-consciousness is, as Kant argued, "synthetic" in character; it is not an "analytic truth" (not a tautology or a statement made true by virtue of what the words mean) that the "I" that "thinks" a particular representation is the same "I" that "thinks" another, different representation.[119] Moreover, since it is a condition of any representation's counting as a representation that it be possible that I be able to become reflectively aware of it as being *my* representation – as belonging to one consciousness – it is an a priori truth (something we know independently of experience) that we be aware of the identity of the "I." As such, then what Kant calls the "transcendental unity of apperception" – the possibility of the reflective awareness of my representations as being all "thought" by me – is the a priori condition of all representations and therefore of all knowledge. This unity of self-consciousness is something that cannot be established by "custom," "habit" or the psychological "laws of association" but is instead a condition of the possibility of there being any psychological "laws of association" at all.

The types of rules for combining representations that are necessary for the subject to be able self-consciously to take the unities of experience (the combinations of representations, the "synthetic unity of the manifold" as Kant calls it) as belonging to his consciousness are therefore those rules that are necessary "moments" of rationality itself. The basic rules for the combination of our representations would thereby be the *categories* of experience. However, as Hegel argues in the introductory section on "Reason" in the *Phenomenology,* among other deficiencies, Kant failed to provide the necessary derivation of the categories, gleaning them instead from the table of judgments found in contemporary logic books.[120] In that way, Kant's own theoretical philosophy fails on the terms it sets for itself. Moreover, Kant explicitly argued that we could only say that this was the way in which we necessarily had to combine our representations, not that these representations matched up with the way "things in themselves" were. Thus, the Kantian philosophy concluded that we could not know things "in themselves" and therefore ended the Enlightenment's hope that we could know the world as it really was by virtue of methodical observation aided by reason. Kant's theory of knowledge thus seems directly to contradict the idea that in Hegel's own words, reason is "certain of itself as being all reality," a claim, which Hegel argues, actually underlies the Kantian philosophy's pretensions to what it is doing.[121] The difficulties in which Kant's position had landed him led anti-Enlightenment figures such as F.H. Jacobi to charge Kant, that "pinnacle of Enlightenment thought" with having put himself in the paradoxical situation of claiming to know that "things in themselves" affect our intuitive faculties without us being able to say of them that they exist, and thus being forced to say that they "cause" representations to arise in us (as simply given) – which (in, for example, Jacobi's mind) is clearly to apply a category (causality) to them that on Kant's terms we cannot say applies to them.

Similar difficulties appear in Kant's moral philosophy. For Kant, the subject *acts* only to the extent that he spontaneously "takes" a maxim to be his own – that is, self-consciously takes a representation of a rule (for example, "tell no lies") as the motive that will count for him as a sufficient reason for acting. In a complex argument, Kant claims that since the agent self-consciously does this, he must be free, for there can be no external determination (determination from outside his own agency) that he take this and not that maxim as "his own" as constituting an authoritative reason for him to act. The subject chooses maxims, however, for a variety of reasons, and he chooses *autonomously* (instead of having the choice determined by something other than himself as a rational, thinking agent) when the criteria for his choice are those that he legislates for himself. Those criteria must be those of formal rationality, since no other set of criteria would be those that would fit the subject's conception of himself as a free agent. (Any material principle, Kant argues, would be a limitation on the subject's spontaneity.)

Hegel argues that this too fails on the terms that it sets for itself as an account of moral life, for formal reason cannot generate the kind of content that Kant claims. In fact, Kant must smuggle in moral content out of the accepted norms found in the form of life in which he lived. However, in extending the idea of the subject's spontaneously taking certain representations to count for him (in this case, to be the maxims that lead him to action), Kant broke with the Enlightenment idea that the rational choice of maxims was something that emerged out of our natural dispositions. It was, rather, an act of free self-determination independent of all external grounds. Likewise, in his conception of knowledge in the first *Critique,* Kant had tried to show that the combination of representations in the mind was self-authenticating in terms of being that which was necessary to provide a unity of self-consciousness; nothing except the act of combination itself as bringing representations to a unity of consciousness was required. Only reason, and not "nature," determined the necessary structure of the combination of representations. Nonetheless, there was still an element of "givenness" (or "immediacy," in Hegel's terms) to Kantian philosophy, which Kant in his second *Critique* strikingly called "the fact of reason," itself a "given" beyond which we could not go.[122] Since in making claims to knowledge we could only combine representations that were already given to us by our intuitive faculty, and we had no grounds for concluding that our intuitive faculty in any way gave us representations of things as they were in themselves, Kant argued in his first *Critique* that our knowledge was therefore *limited* to "appearance."[123] It was therefore illegitimate to ask for any further metaphysical or religious ground for the "fact of reason"; it simply had to be accepted and taken for what it was.

Nonetheless, it cannot be denied that Hegel's account of Kant in the short section of the *Phenomenology* titled "Reason as Testing Laws" is contentious and does not even approach being a detailed analysis of Kant's moral theory. Instead, Hegel seems to content himself in those passages with placing Kant in the context of the Enlightenment conception of reason and seeing where he fits into that context. Hegel takes the Kantian philosophy to be the midpoint between the earlier Enlightenment ideals of reason and harmony, and Hegel's own idealism, which he believes he can show develops directly out of the skeptical objections that Kantianism generates against itself.[124] (This is done in the later section of the *Phenomenology* entitled "The Moral Worldview.") The earlier Enlightenment conception of reason had turned out to be empty insofar as it was supposed to generate out of itself a determinate social order; the various concrete claims that early Enlightenment figures had supposedly derived from "reason and observation" had to do with the way in which they had rationalized already existing social practices or given very external critiques of those practices as failing to live up to some kinds of supposedly rational standards. Kant had seen, however, that the Enlightenment conception of reason could not withstand the internally generated skeptical objections against itself that had come from thinkers like Rousseau and Hume, and contingent events such as the Lisbon earthquake. In order to affirm what he took to be the core of the Enlightenment conception of reason, therefore, Kant was led to revise it and detach it from the idea of "natural harmony," instead making the use of reason into a self-certifying practice that relied on nothing that it itself could not for itself endorse and that therefore took nothing from "nature" as contributing to its affirmation of its own powers. Thus, Kant opposed both what he took to be pure empiricism and pure rationalism in his theoretical philosophy, and he opposed all forms of intuitionism – the idea that we can with some special moral sense intuit certain values – in his moral philosophy.

However, so Hegel argues, this new Kantian conception of reason shares with its earlier Enlightenment predecessors their inherent emptiness. The early Enlightenment did not see this because of its own "immediacy," the way in which it had simply *seemed* obvious to it – as something just "given" – that "reason" and "nature" were compatible (that what reason required of us in the way of belief and action was the same as what our passions and sentiments would impel us to do). The early Enlightenment therefore had simply maintained the modern faith in reason's being "certain of itself as being all reality." The charges by Hume and Rousseau, however, led the later Enlightenment to see that this faith needed some more vindication for itself. With his answers to Hume and Rousseau, Kant completed that part of the Enlightenment project. However, by detaching "reason" from "nature" – indeed from all forms of givenness (even "given" social practices) – Kant made the Enlightenment conception more reflective, but he left it just as impossible for reason to generate any content strictly out of itself. Without any appeal to what *has become* authoritative for a specific community, nor to what in that community's accounts of why what it has taken as authoritative really is *genuinely* authoritative, no determinate set of moral principles can be generated. Kant's achievement, therefore, was to show that reason-giving must be taken as a self-authenticating practice, as able to show that what it generates and legitimates is something that can be evaluated only in terms of the standards that it sets for itself (and not in terms of any external standards that might, for example, be "intuited"). The Kantian philosophy's insufficiencies were in making good on that claim. Hegel's way of situating Kant in the context of the Enlightenment is thus to say that Kant's conception of reason just *is* the Enlightenment's conception of reason deprived of all the external props about the "sentiments" and "nature" that had given the figures of the Enlightenment the merely apparent belief that they could produce various claims to know things purely by appeal to a combination of reason with empirical observation.[125]

In Hegel's eyes, Kant had shown that the rationality of what can count as authoritative for belief or action must be derived from what is necessary for a subject to take things as autonomously counting for him as knowledge or as a valid maxim for his action. However, Kant operates with only a "formal" and not a "material" conception of rationality. There is no room in Kant's

Critiques for a conception of a developing, historically situated rationality in terms of its consisting of those standards of evaluation that we have come to take as authoritative for ourselves because of the historical insufficiencies of earlier accounts. Instead, there is only the conception of Enlightenment reason itself, abstracted out of all social and historical contexts and in Kant's case even from "nature." With such a formal conception of reason, the Kantian philosophy cannot generate any determinate content for moral willing; it may rationalize existing relations, but it cannot give any finally self-authenticating account of them.

To illustrate this, Hegel discusses the example of whether it could be permitted to steal property. In a society with institutions of property and the related social practices of acquiring it, transferring it, and cultivating it, it is certainly contradictory to the very concept of property and its proper acquisition and transference that it might permissibly be stolen. However, the more basic question is whether there should be an institution of property at all – whether we should even have that concept – and there is certainly no self-contradiction in the claim that the entire institution of property should not exist. That various injunctions having to do with property are the kind of thing that would rationally count for agents living in a society with those institutions and practices is granted; but it does not seem that a merely formal conception of reason can generate purely out of itself the kinds of determinate institutions and practices necessary to satisfy the goals that the Kantian account of morality sets for itself. As a reconstruction of some moral ideals that European culture had come to hold in the late eighteenth century (and some of which it still holds), Kantianism may, Hegel grants, be remarkably successful. But in terms of having autonomously demonstrated these ideals out of formal reason itself, it fails. In Hegel's reading, Kant thus succeeds in showing that the earlier Enlightenment conceptions of reason failed to do what they claimed to do; he succeeds in showing what would be necessary to come up with a non-Humean account of subjectivity and reason and what would be necessary to come up with an account of the moral life that could answer Rousseau's criticisms; and he shows that if the modern project of establishing a self-justifying culture based on reason (an "enlightened" culture) is therefore to succeed, its principles would have to be shown to be derived from those conditions necessary for modern agents to understand themselves as rationally self-determining agents (which is another way of putting the Kantian idea that we are "spontaneously" self-conscious). Kant thus self-consciously shows that the modern project of establishing *independent* reason (and thereby independent agents) requires an account of reason and agency as *self-determining;* Hegel's dissatisfaction with Kant thus boils down to the charge that Kant failed to deliver what he promised.

The upshot is therefore that the Enlightenment conception of an "observing reason" carefully noting "human nature" cannot produce a set of self-authenticating principles of knowledge and evaluation, and the Kantian idea of reason as "testing" – as evaluating what is to count as a valid norm for knowing or acting while eschewing any appeal to "nature" or to "intuition" –

turns out to be equally formal and incapable of fulfilling the goal that it sets for itself.[126] Both the Kantian and the early Enlightenment conceptions of the relation of reason to what is to count for modern agents as authoritative for them are therefore each one-sided, each subject to skeptical reproach. (They have, as Hegel puts it, a "negative relation to ethical substance."[127]) The early Enlightenment idea of simply "reading off" the so-called rational laws from observation of the existing set of social practices is in reality taking a particular socially and historically formed set of desires and beliefs and positing them as "universal human nature" (which was also Rousseau's critique of the early Enlightenment project).[128] The Kantian project with its insistence on formal, self-authenticating reason detaching itself from all empirical natural and social relations finds, however, that it cannot determine any particular content at all.

If the project of modern life is to succeed, therefore, it needs a more complete integration of the early Enlightenment project and the Kantian completion of that project such that only those laws will count that can be shown to be part of actual social practice and that can be legitimated by an autonomous process of "reason." This amounts to transforming the modern project from an account of reason as a transcendent, enduring, ahistorical standard into an account of how those agents could come to evaluate these practices in terms of whether they fit the historically developing standards of rationality themselves, with "reason" being able to show that these putatively valid standards do not then within their own terms generate any further skepticism about themselves. Or, in more general Hegelian terms, existing social practices must be integrated into an account of what an autonomous self-conscious agent could come to count as valid for himself.[129] If this were to be done, modern life would have come to be constituted as an "ethical substance," as a form of life in which *Sittlichkeit,* "the way things are done," would be compatible with a sense of subjects taking the "way things are done" to be continuous with their own freely chosen ends. Moreover, "the way things are done" would then be capable of giving an account of itself that would neither be subject to the kinds of "negativity" – self-undermining skepticism about itself – that had characterized past forms of life, nor to the charge of "dogmatism," of taking certain standards of belief and evaluation as given.

If this project were to be successful, then it would show that this modern normative "social space" would be compatible with a conception of modern individuals as self-determining such that each could see the existing social practices as activities that each individual wills for himself as part of a common self-identity, rather than as being something imposed on each himself. The self-identity of each would be thereby continuous with the self-identities of others in the community, since the normative standards that make those practices into the practices that they are would be the standards that each would have come to accept as authoritative for himself; and the modern understanding of the *individuality* of agents would be preserved because these standards would count for these individuals as the standards that make up who they are as individuals. The Kantian conception of rationality as that which is common to all subjects and that makes them self-determining *subjects* and not *substances* determined from outside themselves can therefore only be fulfilled in terms of a conception of reason as *social practice,* not in terms of reason as a principle for combining representations into coherent experience. The *representationalist* model of knowledge – that of a subject inspecting its representations of a world – must give way to a model of knowledge as *participation* in social practice, as a set of historically situated claims that can only underwrite their own authoritativeness from within the terms of a concrete, historical community.

The standpoint of "reason" defines the impersonal point of view for modern agents, which is first worked out in the development of modern science; the Kantian theory of the subject as constituting for himself what is to count for him as authoritative in belief and action articulates a conception of how identifying the impersonal point of view with the standpoint of "reason" is necessary for a conception of subjects as self-determining. The other standpoint of modern "reason" is more subjectivistic: it sees modern agents as *individuals,* as each positing his *own* ends and standards and as accepting nothing unless he can himself certify it as authoritative for him. The personal point of view, as it is underwritten and expressed in the practices, institutions and accounts of early modern individualism, and the impersonal point of view, which finds its modern culmination in Kantian philosophy, are each, taken alone, insufficient accounts of what it means to be a rational, modern agent, for each fails to succeed at the goals it sets for itself. Taken together, however, they point to a social order in which a full union of the two points of view would be established. The question then is: Do they *merely* point to it as some idealized future task for European social life, or is there in fact a genuine account that could be given of such union within modern terms? Or is this idea of a "universal reason" simply the idiosyncratic understanding of a particular community at a particular time?

For many of the people of Hegel's generation, this question was particularly pressing, since it seemed to them that modern life's project had itself become only a new form of dogmatism; it had simply put an abstraction called "reason" in place of the deity and then taken on faith that this "reason" could provide the social institutions and the kind of unifying account that religion had always claimed to provide, with little more indication than the generalized Enlightenment "faith" that it could indeed achieve this goal. The idea of a union of the personal and the impersonal points of view, which Kantianism and modern individualism taken together point toward, thus began to seem to some like a project that modern life *could not* fulfill. As resting on the idea of "reason" as a kind of "universal method" by which all conflicting claims could be adjudicated, modern life's project seemed to be unable to justify itself within its own terms. Worse, there was, especially for Hegel's generation, the nagging doubt that not only might modern life's project not be successful, but that there was also in fact a clear theoretical alternative to it, which, although itself "dogmatic," seemed to lack many of modern life's problems. This was the Greek alternative, which even if it could not be achieved in the context of modern life, nonetheless showed what a successful version of the project of uniting the two points of view would look like. The elegiac nostalgia for Greek life – beautiful, lost and irrecoverable – was a weighty feature of the intellectual atmosphere of Hegel's time. The conversion of the project of accounting for modern life from that of reliance upon "reason" as an ahistorical, transcendent standard into a reliance on reason as historically situated social practice thus looked at the outset as if it could not succeed. Therefore, as Hegel clearly saw, any account of modern life's project had to come to terms with whether the Greek alternative was really what it seemed to be to so many of his time and, we might add, what it continues to be for many of us today.

5
Modern life's alternatives and modern life's possibilities

1. From Greek character to modern autonomy

To introduce the section on "Spirit," the *Phenomenology* develops a story about how a group of agents has moved from a conception of impersonal reason as providing them with a fixed standard by which they evaluate all their various contingent claims to a conception of rationality as a form of reflective social practice – that is, as "spirit."[1] Attempts at reassurance through accounts that appeal to impersonal reason or to the idea of a fixed, rational "self" have undermined themselves such that only some type of account that understands reason as a form of social practice would seem to be able to succeed. In seeking an affirmation from modern science and social practice, modern agents have found that the accounts that they must give of their practices of reason-giving and criticism have led them to the view that what they have come to count as authoritative for themselves has to do with an understanding of "the way things are done." The apparent success of the modern world in throwing off the constraints of tradition in science and in practice (and particularly the failure of those attempts by people like Shaftesbury to revive certain ancient traditions of virtue by relying on more modern doctrines of the observation of nature) helped to reassure the moderns that their conceptions were indeed correct.[2] But if to be rational is to act and think according to "the way things are done" – that is, is fundamentally a feature of sociality – then the issue for the moderns had to concern what kind of account they could give of this sociality, this "substance" of their lives, within the terms that this kind of modern self-understanding had set for itself.[3]

But why then should an appeal purely and simply to "the way things are done" not be good enough? Even if it is not good enough for those early moderns who had set themselves the project of accounting for their activities of reason-giving in terms of rational philosophy rather than that of faith and theology, it is not at all self-evident that the early modern project is the only rational or legitimate form of life. Even if the early modern project was the result of what was necessary to make up for the historical insufficiencies of its predecessors, it is not self-evident that it does not represent an intrinsically failed development of human history, perhaps an indication of a false path that history had taken. Indeed, people like Rousseau had come to throw much of the modern project into question, doubting whether the kinds of reasons that modern life had provided for itself could in fact be legitimated in their own terms and whether a return to "Sparta" or "Athens" would not be

135

more in order. In particular, modern life would be an internal failure if it were to fail to satisfy those criteria that on their own terms specify what counts as fulfilling the promises of the idea of a culture based on rationality. If modern life did fail on those terms, then it would quickly become another form of the "unhappy consciousness": It would be a form of life in which people would believe that such-and-such was necessary to justify what they were doing (that is, who would take something as necessary to affirm for themselves that what they *believed* was indeed *true* and that what they *did* was indeed *right*), but who did not believe that this standard could be met by them and who could not envision any concrete alternative project for themselves.

The issue was particularly disturbing for Hegel's generation, since they faced Rousseau's critique of the inauthenticity of modern life coupled with what at least seemed to be an alternative (at least in thought) to the modern project – namely, that embodied in the form of life of the ancient Greeks (as least as they had come to understand that form of life as it had been mediated to them by the great classical figures of German literature such as Goethe and Winckelmann). In a view widely shared in Hegel's time, the ancient Greeks had, at least for a very brief period in their history, a form of life in which "the way things are done" (*Sittlichkeit*) functioned to produce a fully harmonious, non-alienated social order and self-understanding, which, since it was consistent with their having attained the highest achievements in art and philosophy, could not be faulted as being somehow inferior to the alienated form of life of the early modern Europeans. Thus, even if it is not possible for us, the moderns, actually to return to that Greek form of life, it might nonetheless stand as a rebuke to modern life, to show just how far from the ideal it had descended.

In a way, the Greek form of life is the "natural" way of understanding the nature of spirit as "social space." The most natural way in which we would form a self-conscious conception of ourselves as social and cultural beings would be to understand the basic elements of the background social and cultural order of social life as both natural and also somehow necessary. That is, it would be to understand key elements of the given social and cultural world as embodying a kind of eternal necessity to them; "the way things are done" would be seen not as a feature of human idiosyncrasy but as part of the eternal order of things.[4] The Greeks expressed this in a rigid understanding of social roles: Men do one thing, women another; rulers do one thing, subjects another; masters do one thing, slaves another; that is just the way the world is, and, if the social world is to function correctly, it cannot be different. What one ultimately is to do is given to one by one's own social and cultural order, and that social order itself has a kind of self-certifying nature to it such that it appears immediately intelligible to its participants. One's social roles set one's ends before one, and in acting on these given ends, one also achieves the self-identity in the eyes of others that one thinks oneself to have. If one acts as a soldier, or as a son or daughter, or as a ruler is supposed to act, one finds that the meaning of one's actions and therefore one's self-

136

identity will be affirmed and recognized by others. The *ultimate* ends of life, just like the rules of thought, will seem given and unalterable, existing from time immemorial.[5] They will have a kind of immediate intelligibility and justification to them such each agent fully identifies with that social order and his place within it. At least as understood by many of Hegel's contemporaries, something like this view characterizes the form of life of ancient Greece, at least as reflected in the writings of its poets and tragedians.

It is not, however, the case that the Greeks saw everything about "the way things are done" as being both natural and immutable. Indeed, one of the striking features of Greek thought was its distinction between the artificial and the natural. Much of life was understood by them to be a social feature of themselves, a "way *they* did things" that was not universal but peculiarly Greek. Nevertheless, the Greeks also saw certain ultimate aspects of "the way things are done" – in everything from family life to the treatment of prisoners of war – as being expressions of what was natural and immutable, as resting on "laws" whose legitimacy was eternal. This distinction between what was peculiarly Greek and what was immutable is expressed as the difference between human and divine law.[6] Human law may be understood and altered, but divine law must be simply acknowledged and obeyed.

Hegel's analysis of Greek life does not challenge the widely held view in his day that the Greeks were a "happy" people who lived a "harmonious" life (although as he got older, he came less and less to share that rather buoyant view of Greek life, without, nonetheless, ever completely abandoning it). Unlike later historians, such as Jacob Burckhardt, who were to challenge this view of Greek life as historically inaccurate, Hegel took it for granted that the Greek form of life was in some sense harmonious, but he then inquired whether, given the descriptions that the Greeks gave of themselves, it could be said to be genuinely free of any deep and alienating contradictions in "social space," which many of his contemporaries (particularly his youthful friend in Tübingen, Hölderlin) took it to be. Hegel's concern therefore was not with the historical details of Greek life per se but with whether the idealized Greek life described by many of his contemporaries really could *on its own terms* be counted as a genuine alternative to modern life. Hegel's concern was therefore not with whether the Greeks violated some tenets of the kinds of self-understandings that *we*, the moderns, have but rather with whether their own form of self-understanding violated some of its own essential tenets. In other words, he was concerned with the way in which these idealized Greeks would have been "for themselves," not as they are "for us."

The Greek alternative

Hegel's treatment of Greek life occurs in two parts. In the first part, he sketches out the way in which this idealized Greek form of life could be understood to be harmonious and how it could be understood as an equally valid, if not better, alternative to the modern self-understanding. In the second part, he then tries to show that given what the Greek tragedians say about Greek life, it cannot *on its own terms* be understood to be as harmonious as some of Hegel's contemporaries had thought, and thus it fails to be the alternative they took it to be.[7]

As he had in his treatment of "Reason," Hegel uses the term "substance" to characterize the overall background normative order of thought and action. He uses this term in order not to prejudice the issue as to how this "substance" is to be taken: metaphysically, naturalistically, or as a structure of social practice. The use of the term "substance" is also meant to suggest that it is this background order that gives a "substantiality" to people's lives in the way that it fills out what their duties are, and it gives them an understanding of what their motives should be.

For the Greeks, this "substance" defined them as a people, as a distinct community apart from other communities. There was a recognition of "the way things were done" that was fully shared and that was determinate in the way it apportioned social roles and duties. But it was more than merely a shared way of life; the institutions of Greek life also provided them with various ways by which they could reflect both as individuals and collectively on who they were. As such, there was no discontinuity between how individuals understood themselves as individuals and how they understood the society. In part, this was because individuals did not understand themselves *individualistically* in the modern sense.[8] The Greek individual understood himself in terms of his social role; his individuality is filled out by his social role, not by any idiosyncratic and contingent features of himself.[9] The modern idea of *morality,* as expressed in a conception of inner conscience and self-conscious reflection on one's motives, could not therefore appear in Greek life.[10] The Greek individual would not therefore have any grounds, at least so it would seem, to be alienated from the social whole. He knows what is to be done, because the background order of things is determinate and clear on this point, and in acting in terms of this background order – in thinking and acting in terms of "the way things are done" – he also finds that his actions are harmonious with those of others. Unlike modern individuals, the Greek individual need not step back and reflect on whether what he is doing is really right; the alienating and self-distancing mode of reflection, which is so crucial to modern self-reflection, is absent for the idealized Greek agent, who can be fully at home in his actions.[11]

In one sense, then, the Greek form of life is characterized by a certain type of clarity of knowledge about what is to be done and believed. The doubts that plague the reflective, self-distancing moderns are not there for these idealized Greeks. They *know* ultimately what to believe and to think because there is a clear and determinate order for them of "the way things are done." They need not ask, "what reason is there for me to do this" because the reasons embodied in their social life are reason enough. The governing of the city for them by *human law* is thus merely one more way in which their "mores" and "ethics" (their *Sitte*) are put in practice. The government is the institution in the community in which a self-conscious reflection is carried out on what is to be done in order to keep this harmony and equilibrium intact; in its deliberations and legal enactments, the government presupposes this shared understanding of what counts as a proper goal of government, what counts as valuable, what public ends must, ought and need to be pursued, and so on.[12] It is the government's duty to preserve *justice* in the community, which in this case means apportioning benefits, honors and punishments in such a way that the harmony or equilibrium (*Gleichgewicht*) of the community is maintained. The most basic form of injustice, on this view, would be to let nature take over, that is, would be for the human community of the Greeks to cease to demonstrate to itself and to others how human law is effective in the life of the community.[13]

Self-conscious reflective life thus occurs within the context of a widely shared understanding of the "ethical life," the *Sittlichkeit*, of the community. In its political institutions, therefore, the public life of the community is always presupposing and confronting deeper assumptions that are simply taken for granted as being "the way things are done." These are understood by the community as the *divine law*, that set of very basic assumptions about the way things have to be and the way thought and action have to take place that one must simply acknowledge and to which one must simply submit, even if one cannot understand why the divine law is the way it is. Human law is constructed and intelligible; it is a proper object of rational deliberation. Divine law is given and immutable and must simply be accepted.[14]

Just as the government is the social institution in Greek life that embodies the kind of self-conscious reflection on what the community is to do to maintain itself as a particular and determinate people, the family is the institution in which the most basic assumptions about the natural or immediate character of the individuals in the community are realized and carried out. Whereas the government must deliberate about its policies (even though it formulates them in terms of a shared understanding of the goals of its policies), the members of the family simply know what to do. This is understood by the Greeks as being due to the family's having its basis in nature, in the natural facts of sex and reproduction. The Greeks took these natural facts (as facts about "the way things are") to specify determinate duties and social roles, "the way things are done." For the family, that is, they attached a specifically *ethical* significance to *natural* facts, and thus for them the social roles embodied in the Greek family seemed to be a feature of "the way things are done": Women have one set of roles, men have others, and this is immutable.[15] The family embodies ethical life, *Sittlichkeit*, in that it appears not as a feature entirely of "social space," but as a feature of nature.[16] This should, moreover, not be misunderstood as being an expression of some kind of elementary confusion on the part of the Greeks between "is" and "ought." For them, what they *ought* to do followed from the way things *are*, from the background understanding that this is "the way things are done," which for them was a *fact* about social life. By following out the determinate duties prescribed for them by their social institutions, they did what they *had* to do, and they did what they *ought* to do, all on the basis of their understanding of what *is* the case (on what is *required* of them by their social life).

Hegel's arguments about the nature of the Greek family are attempts to draw out its "logic" in terms of how it was presented in Greek art. He is not interested in doing a social history of the nature of the Greek family, for the object of his discussion in this section is Greek life in its idealized form, presented as an imaginative alternative to modern life by many of Hegel's contemporaries. Again, what is striking about Greek life taken in this way is the way in which its two basic institutions – governmental institutions and family life – together delineate how a self-sustaining *Sittlichkeit* – a form of understanding that "the is way things are done" – might be concretely possible. Indeed, in Hegelian terms, Greek *Sittlichkeit,* consisting as it does of the unity of "self-consciousness" and "immediacy" (that is, in an understanding that such and such is "the way things are done" taken in a *normative* sense and a self-conscious reflection on the normativity of these principles and how to implement them) defines the general possibility of there being a form of *Sittlichkeit* at all.[17]

The problem for the Greek understanding of family life had to do with how it could combine this conception of family life as *natural* with a conception of it as *ethical,* as embodying a set of norms rather than just being a natural fact about people. That is, it needed to construct a set of duties that would define the family as a social institution and not simply as a natural institution, which would also be consistent with its understanding of the social roles in the family being determined by the natural differences of the sexes. The issue for the Greeks therefore would concern what would be a necessary set of actions that family members could take (and that could only be taken by family members) that would also essentially concern only the family. These would be the duties to hold the family together as a social unit. But as a *natural* unit for the propagation and rearing of children, the family is in many respects a *contingent* affair. It is, for example, purely contingent that these two parents came together and had these particular children; likewise, it is desirable but also contingent whether the parents love each other, or whether when grown the children assist the parents (or even have the opportunity to assist their parents), and so on. If the family is to be more than *just* a natural unit, it must be maintained by something other than these contingent features.

The importance of performing the proper burial rites for deceased family members plays the important role in Greek tragedy that it does because of these considerations (or at least the role that it does in Sophocles' *Antigone,* the main object of Hegel's concern in his discussion of the Greek family). Holding the family together as a social unit means holding the memory of one's ancestors present before one, remembering that the family is a determinate *social* institution constituted by the *natural* facts of lineage. Since death is obviously a natural fact and not a social fact, in performing the proper burial rites, the family members are transforming this ultimately natural fact into one charged with a determinate social meaning. The non-rationality (or arationality) of death is given a rational significance by becoming a means by which the family maintains itself as a *social* unit (as "spirit"). One shows the proper respect for the deceased not in terms of his natural properties but in terms of *who* he was (his being-for-self, as Hegel puts it). Moreover, by carrying out the proper burial rites, the family members protect the standing of the deceased in the public community (the *Gemeinwesen*), for they signal by this that his *self*-identity remains important, not just his natural existence. Finally, they must perform these rites in order for the divinities of the underworld to be satisfied, even if they cannot understand why this is so. Since this is the basic means by which the family maintains its social, normative status, it constitutes an absolute duty for the family members, one of those things that just *has* to be done because it is "the way things *are* done" and for which no further reason need be given.[18]

The duties of the family toward the deceased thus constitute the *divine law*. It is simply something that has to be done, it need not be reflected upon, and whatever unintelligibility it has about itself just has to be accepted. Moreover, the human law cannot replace or supplant this; the goals of human law are just too different. The goals of human law are to take the person out of his raw, natural state and socialize him, teach him virtue, and provide him with the intellectual and social means to lead a communal life. Human law thus takes the individual away from nature, whereas divine law is the attempt to give a sense to otherwise non-rational natural facts such as those governing sexuality, birth and death.[19]

Indeed, because of the necessity of socializing people so that they are fit members of the public community, human law (through the institution of government) has to exert a certain force on the members of the community so that they do not "drift back into nature," into a more or less unsocialized form of life, and thereby disrupt the ethical harmony of the public community. One way of doing that for Greek life was the continual decision to go to war (something that the Greeks did often enough, but that the Grecophiles often tend to overlook). There is in fact a kind of logic to the fact of continual warfare in Greek life. By submitting the male members of the community to the threat of death in wartime, and by forcing them thereby to stake their natural lives for social glory, the government forced people out of their natural state into a social one, and in doing that thereby maintained the harmony of the community in which each played his part and contributed to the good of the whole, instead of falling into natural stubbornness or self-seeking.[20]

Part of the Greek solution to maintaining both the social harmony of this form of life and their understanding of how it was held together in terms of divine and human law was to apportion social duties accordingly. Although the Greeks understood part of their form of life in terms of its being non-natural – as being a matter of human artifice and social practice and thus the object of human law – they also understood part of their form of life to be determined by the immutable facts of nature and thus to be the object of divine law. The normativity of *human* law falls completely within the domain of human decision and action; *divine* law, on the other hand, has to do with those natural facts governing basic and universal questions of self-identity and humanity's most basic interests, namely, the facts of birth, death and sexuality. The basic *natural* difference between men and women therefore came for the Greeks to be a matter of great normative significance, even if this natural difference itself was just a given, something that need not be intelligible to be accepted. It is therefore not a completely contingent fact about the Greek form of life that it had such rigid gender roles, that it strictly saw men as destined for public life and women only for family life. Men were seen as the bearers of "spirit" and women as the bearers of "nature." The Greek *Sittlichkeit*, "the way things are done," divides itself into two parts, each to be fulfilled by one of the gender roles of Greek life. Thus, there arises the overall shared understanding of what counts in public life, and the shared understanding that there is a "way things are done" that is natural and therefore is not so much the object of *self-conscious reflection* as it is an object of *feeling*.[21] Women were considered to hold the family as a unity of feeling together, whereas the men were to participate in the self-conscious life of public affairs. The *natural* difference of the sexes is taken as determining the *social* difference of their roles.

Greek life is thus a mixture between the natural and social, functioning such that a harmony in the social order is thereby produced that is supposedly free of the self-distancing, alienating reflective stances of modern life. For this to be case, however, this harmony has to be a more or less spontaneous harmony between *free individuals*.[22] These free individuals become such free individuals through a process of mutual recognition. Each, freely and without compulsion, bestows a social status on the other, recognizing his great deeds or oratory or whatnot. This status of "free individuality" therefore is mutually conferred by citizens on each other for a certain excellence in public performance. Bound up with the ideal of "free individuality" is thus a certain *aesthetic* understanding of what the nature of such individuality is, and the idea that such recognition could only be conferred by equals, by the kinds of others whose recognition of one's great deeds counted for something.[23]

The kind of "free individuality," however, that is the hallmark of this idealized Greek life could *only* be attained within the public sphere, and not, so it would seem, within the family. The relation between the husband and wife in the family is partly a natural relation of sexual desire; it becomes an "ethical" relation only in terms of the duties involved in the having and rearing of children (without children, the "ethical" bond of marriage would have little reason for being within the Greek view of things). The relation between husband and wife is thus not completely a relation between "free individualities" since it is based in part on natural sexual desires from which neither is free, and on the natural fact that both are required for procreation. The relation between parents and children, moreover, is a relation between unequals, and cannot thereby serve as a basis for fully mutual recognition. Likewise, the children have as their goal to become progressively independent of their parents; they cannot become "free individualities" except by leaving the family and making their way in the public world.

It follows that neither men nor women could achieve the status of "free individuality" within the family. Women could do this neither *as* wife, nor *as* mother, nor *as* daughter, nor could men do this *as* husband, father, or son. However, because men would have the possibility of a life outside of the family in the public realm, it would be possible for them to develop themselves as such "free individualities" in this public, political realm. Women, on the other hand, who would be confined to the family by the Greek understanding of the way things had to be between the sexes, could not have the possibility, so it would seem, to develop themselves as "free individualities" at all. Women thus seem destined not to be *individuals* at all, but only to have an understanding of themselves as somewhat "generalized" particular agents. That is, they cannot see anything about their *self* as being individual; their individuality seems to be only the natural individuality of an organism, of being a single entity in space and time, not of being a single *self*.[24]

Within the context of the Greek understanding, therefore, the only possible relationship within which a woman could develop a sense of herself as having a *self* would be in the familial relationship of brother and sister (which is crucial for Hegel's interpretation of *Antigone*). Since women are confined to the natural realm, the domain of the family, if a woman is to be able to have a *self,* she must find some basis of recognition from someone to whom she stands in a *natural* relation but *from whom* such recognition would *count.* Brother and sister are naturally related, but they are free of desire for each other (which might not be the case were they unrelated); moreover, the brother's capability for leading a public life makes him the kind of agent who is capable of bestowing recognition. Likewise, the sister, who as a woman is someone on whom the brother could not otherwise confer any recognition, is, because she is his *sister,* the kind of person upon whom he can confer the recognition of being the bearer of the divine law. Since each can be recognized by the other, the sister can therefore stand in relation to her brother as a free individual, something she cannot do in a relation to her sister, for her sister would suffer under the same restrictions as she does. The sister is thus able to achieve selfhood in the process of mutual recognition between her and her brother, and thus the harmony of Greek life seems not to be threatened.[25]

It would be a mistake to take the issue here to be the incompatibility of this Greek view of the possibilities for men's and women's lives with modern, egalitarian views. For the purposes of Hegel's discussion, the only issue is whether this Greek understanding is *in its own terms* rational, not whether it fails to fit *our* modes of self-understanding. As an alternative to modern life, Greek life is not required to be consistent with modern life; it is only required to be consistent with itself, and for the Grecophiles of Hegel's day, it seemed to have succeeded (not that many of them worried about the status of women in Greek life). Greek life seems harmonious and complete in its separate acknowledgments of what can be an object of self-conscious reflection and what simply has to be accepted, and it seems to have combined all these elements into a consistent, coherent whole. The issue therefore is: Is Greek life really as complete as it seems to be?

Hegel relies on Greek tragedy and specifically on Sophocles' *Antigone* in order to analyze the way in which this mode of self-understanding must develop contradictions within itself. In the play *Antigone* we are presented with the family of Oedipus: two sons (Polyneices and Eteocles) and two daughters (Antigone and Ismene). Eteocles sits on the throne of Thebes, but Polyneices, who believes the throne should be his, attacks the city and is killed in the attempt, as is Eteocles in defending it. Their maternal uncle, Creon, assumes the royal power. He orders that Eteocles' body be given the proper burial rites, but because he believes Polyneices to be a traitor, he orders that these burial rites be denied to Polyneices' body. In defiance of this edict, Antigone performs the burial rites on her dead brother, Polyneices. She is caught at this, and Creon sentences Antigone to be entombed alive, the result of which is Antigone's suicide, Creon's son's suicide (who had been betrothed to Antigone), his wife's death, and his own ruin.

What makes this *tragic* is that each (Creon and Antigone) did what each *had* to do, *and* both sides were in the right: Creon as ruler of the city had the absolute obligation to protect it from attack by traitors (and he considered Polyneices to be a traitor), whereas Antigone had the absolute duty to perform the proper burial rites on her brother. Both Creon and Antigone are *ethical* characters in that each does things according to "the way things are done," and *because* each is an "ethical character," each *has* to do the things they do. Thus, the clash between Antigone and Creon is not something that could have been negotiated away or something that might have been avoided if one of the characters had reined in their feelings. (That is, the conflict cannot be understood as one of those more familiar modern clashes of "reason versus passion," or "conflicts of rights."[26]) It is rather a discord within Greek culture itself, between the two ethical powers that the Greek form of life recognizes as essential to itself: the divine law and the human law, embodied in the different individualities of men and women.

Since both Creon and Antigone are *ethical* individuals, each *knows* what he or she has to do, and each performs his or her duty in terms of "the way things are done." For each of them, therefore, it is the other person who is in the wrong. Antigone sees Creon as directly defying the divine law, and Creon sees Antigone as someone willfully and stubbornly violating the conditions under which the community can exist and flourish. The conflict between Antigone and Creon – in which each sees the other as being in the wrong – is really a conflict of both Antigone and Creon with the "substance," the normative basis, of Greek life. And because each is in conflict with the basis of Greek life, each is therefore guilty of having committed a crime: Antigone against the human law and Creon against the divine law. Each *knows* what he or she has to do, and each unwittingly provokes the other side into doing what the other has to do. Because neither of the two "ethical powers" of Greek life can claim to be more important than the other, both agents are at least equally guilty, with Antigone's guilt being perhaps a little greater.[27] (Creon acts as he does perhaps out of ignorance of the divine law or of its force; Antigone, on the other hand, seems to know that she is defying the human law and will suffer for it, and thus her guilt is perhaps even greater.[28]) The Greek conception of justice as preserving the harmony of the whole demands that both sides suffer, since both sides have damaged this harmony. Thus, with Antigone's destruction and Creon's ruin, it seems as if justice has been done. Since the Greeks conceived of their form of life as being *like* that of nature, which when disturbed comes to reestablish its own equilibrium, what would appear to the Greek spectators of this play would therefore be an affirmation that their understanding of what was the "essence" (was authoritative) in life was in order. Seeing justice done affirms their understanding that when the divine and human laws are violated, the system of the world (of Greek life) will be able to right itself and set itself in order again.

The Greek understanding would no doubt give a somewhat religious or metaphysical interpretation to this idea of the community's power of self-restoration by seeing the restoration of the equilibrium as the result of the divine elements themselves restoring the balance by their avenging themselves against their violation by human law. However, Hegel's point is that the real conflict here is Antigone's and Creon's clash with Greek life itself. The divine law and the human law are both essential to Greek life; the community is based in the life of the family and the way in which family life is maintained, and Greek family life requires just that kind of public community which it has. The conflict between Antigone and Creon is not just a conflict between two contingent individuals; it is an expression of a kind of essentially institutionalized clash between men and women in Greek life, which is itself an expression of a conflict between equally essential principles of Greek life. The public community (the *Gemeinwesen*) is the sphere of governmental action, that is, the sphere of *men*. Since its goal is to preserve the harmony of the whole, it maintains itself by swallowing up the familial sphere, presided over by women, and subordinating it to itself. Creon thus is ignorant of the force of the divine law. Likewise, such a public community necessarily makes its women into its enemies. As the keepers of the family and as barred from public life, women have no choice except to turn what are properly communal matters into ends that serve their familial interests, and in the extreme cases (as in *Antigone*) to actively act against the expressly stated (male) edicts of the human law. Women can become individuals only in the family, and there only in relation to their brothers, and it is the structure of Greek life that forces them into this position.[29]

This antagonistic position that Greek life must take against its women is revelatory of the much deeper contradictions at work in the idealized Greek form of life with its seeming harmony. Given the kind of "social space" that defines Greek life, women, who are barred from developing themselves as individuals by the very structure of Greek life, can develop their *selves* only in opposition to the public life of the community from which they are barred, and, given the role they are destined to play in that form of life, are also destined to develop exactly the type of individuality that the public community is destined to suppress. What makes this particularly problematic for Greek life is the fact that it also has to recognize and develop the same principle of individuality in its young men. The public community has to continually intervene in the lives of its members to exhort them to the public service that is necessary to hold Greek life together. It does this by its continual declarations of war against other communities, thus uprooting young men out of their "natural" state in the family and prompting them to put public glory above private enjoyment. It thus requires that its young men develop a sense of themselves as individuals at the same time that it tries to suppress the principle of individuality itself in those young men. It is a form of life that calls forth the type of agents whom, given its own self-understanding, it must also suppress.

Finally, by making its sustainability dependent on its waging wars, on its contradictory encouragement and discouragement of individuality, Greek life makes itself dependent on pure contingency, on the bravery, strength, luck, and contingent military skills of its young men. Because the Greeks (or at the least the adulated, idealized Greeks) conceived of their ethical life as quasi-natural, as something that naturally restored itself to a happy and just equilibrium, they could not come to understand that their success depended not so much on a *naturally* self-restoring form of life as on their own actions. That the equilibrium might be permanently destroyed or that it might be at odds with itself could not present itself to the Greek form of self-understanding. Underlying what looks like its happy harmony with itself is an opaqueness to itself that is similar to that opaqueness that the concluding part of the section on "Reason" in the *Phenomenology* characterizes modern life as having. Moreover, as the equilibrium of Greek life came to be more and more out of kilter, the participants in the Greek form of life would come to experience more and more a deep alienation in the activities that make up their form of life, and in its final stages, Hellenism, it would come to be characterized by what Hegel calls the "unhappy consciousness."

The idealized form of Greek life is thus not the alternative to modern life that those who venerated it believed it to be. The question is: Do any of the forms of life which historically follow it present any better alternatives? And can modern life discover the means within itself to integrate what has come before it and complete its own project?

Contingency of character and the interior self

The breakdown of the Greeks' account of themselves in terms of character as being fully constituted by the ethical life of the community, in which "the way things are done" is conceived as exhausting people's self-identities and as existing in a quasi-natural harmony, turns out to require the citizens of the ancient world to give a different account of themselves, one involving a conception of individuals as having no self-identity not contingently defined by their community. The community of late Hellenism thus turns out to be the "truth" of Greek life in that the accounts that the earlier community gave of itself turn out to require that later account in order for the later community to explain to itself how the various problems and incoherences in the earlier account took the shape that they did. With the collapse of that older form of self-understanding, the Greeks came to believe that the only valid account they can give of themselves is that of being a community held together by mutual recognition in which the self that is recognized is insubstantial.[30]

Individuals living in Greek ethical life took themselves to be following out the necessary ends in the life in their communities, and that this community existed in a kind of natural, self-restoring harmony with itself. They discovered, however, that those ends clashed with each other in irreconcilable ways. The breakdown of the Greek form of life thus created the "social space" in which individuals could only conceive of themselves as having basic ends determined purely contingently by a *legally* defined community. The Greek account of itself in terms of a naturally self-restoring whole thus came to be replaced by the Roman account of itself as a community held together only by custom and human law. To say that the self-identity of such a community could be determined only by human law required that the members of that community thought of themselves as having no deeper sense of self-identification with the community than the very abstract sense of belonging to this community by virtue of legally prescribed rules. Whereas in Greek life, the individual had thought that his sense of who he was flowed without rupture into his larger identification with the political community, the individual of the Roman form of life could understand his identification with the community only in the most abstract sort of way. Such a new form of life can thus only be seen as a structure of mutual recognition as *persons,* as bearers of legal rights (the human law), in which the individual's communal self-identity is fully exhausted by this legal status. The Roman citizen thus does what he does because that is "the way things are done," but this is no longer "the way things are done" in sense of being a form of *Sittlichkeit.* The "way things are done" is instead simply a form of legality, something decreed and not in any intimate way connected with the agent's subjectivity and system of desires. *He* is only accidentally identified with the activities prescribed by these legal rules, if he identifies with them at all.[31]

Whereas in earlier Greek life, the individual was *socially recognized* in terms of a network of interlocking social roles, in Roman life the individual can be given recognition only in terms of being a *legally* defined citizen and no more. Since to be a citizen of Rome was entirely an external, legal matter, and the basis of these legal rights was the possession of property, those lacking property were not really persons at all; they were therefore slaves. It is thus not accidental that *stoicism* arises in Hellenism and flourishes in Roman life. In stoicism, the content of the self is expressed in the idea that we are free in thought. In contrast to the life of the individual in Greek culture, in which the structure of mutual recognition provided a rich conception of character, the stoic conception of character has no defining end except that of indifference to everything. The empty social self that is constituted by the structure of mutual recognition as *legal persons* is mirrored in the stoic's reflective philosophy of indifference to existence. Stoicism is thereby a fitting response to the decline into Hellenism and the triumph of the Roman form of life. The essence underlying this form of agency is the abstract structure of mutual recognition among legally defined persons that produces these empty social selves. The ends of life for the individual are contingent; there can be no necessarily defining ends outside of this very abstract end of becoming a "legal person."

In this "social space," there is only the free play of individuals who understand themselves as persons bearing legal rights. There are, of course, social roles and norms, but these are understood as being contingently imposed by the social and legal order, not as having to do with the nature of agency itself. For the Greek form of life, the social roles seemed natural to the people inhabiting them, not arbitrary roles imposed by a surrounding social order. However, since in the Roman world there is no shared understanding of any ends that are necessary for human agency, the only way of holding this kind of "social space" together is through the imposition of some arbitrary power. Yet despite its atomism, the Roman community could not have thought of itself, for example, in modern liberal terms, as a collection of mutually self-interested rational individuals interested in securing stable social arrangements, for that would require a more developed sense of *reflective individualism* as a moral and political doctrine, not just the Roman sense of empty legal personality. Moreover, the project of liberal individualism, while having its early seeds in Roman stoicism and the Roman emphasis on law and property, was not yet, nor could it have been among the conceptual alternatives available to the Roman life. The Roman life was the successor to the breakdown of the ancient Greek self-understanding; the Greek world had discovered that life is contingent, that fate deals out different destinies for individuals, and that social harmony was not the natural state of the *polis*. They had thought that they were individuals with a determinate role to play in the world that had been prescribed by eternal laws, and they thought of this as both human practice and as divine, eternal law. They thought of themselves as *individuals,* who nonetheless had determinate, set roles to play. The Roman world therefore accepted that this was who they were: individuals tossed around by fate and fortune, whose essential self-identity was exhausted in the structure of recognition among legal persons.

The Greek form of life was held together by the shared ends of that form of life, which were found to be tragically at odds with each other. Out of the collapse of a sense of shared ends emerged the conception of agency as having only the contingent ends which characterizes the Roman form of life. In that form of life, there can therefore be no other means of holding the community together except simply that of coercing individuals into submitting to a more powerful force. The inequalities that fate deals out to various individuals and groups thus becomes the basis of authority. There is no natural basis for dominion over others except that of contingent inequality. This forms an opposition at the heart of Roman life, which first appears as the struggles between patricians and plebeians and later in full form as individuals pursuing private interest against the interests of the community.[32]

The harmony and stability of this community was therefore intrinsically a problem. Why should individuals adhere to such a community? Since the modern liberal answer, that it is in the mutual benefit of all that we cooperate, could not have been on the list of available alternatives because of who the Romans were, the structure could have only been understood as being held together by powerful individuals and families. The person holding all of this together is therefore the emperor, the "lord of the world," as Hegel calls him. The content to agency that is supplied by this type of mutual recognition is the arbitrary content supplied by the ruler – that is, the emperor. But, again, there is no natural harmony between the ruler and the ruled, so there is constant antagonism and the possibility of conflict. The ends of life pursued by these individuals vary, and there is no ultimate reason for pursuing one end as opposed to another. However, the resulting clashes between individuals were mirrored in the polytheistic religion of the Romans; they were seen as clashes of various elemental powers and fates fighting each other. There were no ends of life with which the individual as constituted in this "social space" could identify, and they thus remained profoundly alienated from each other and the community.[33]

Thus, these people discover that even their status as legal persons (as citizens of the Roman empire) is contingent, that is, that there is nothing essential to their social self-identity except the fact that they are recognized as being citizens, legal persons, and that if they failed to possess property, they will lack all social recognition and thus not be *persons* at all. Reflection on this pure contingency of their social self-identity leads, as we saw, to stoicism and skepticism, to the recognition that their social personality really is in essence empty, that only in their individual self-conscious reflections are they essentially anything at all. Stoicism, skepticism (and Hegel was later to include epicureanism) are the *accounts* that Roman life gives of itself. Earlier in the *Phenomenology*, those accounts were seen to be succeeded by the "unhappy consciousness," taken as an expression of a form of life in which the personal and universal points of view are at odds with each other such that the accounts that a form of life has given itself – the reasons it has come to accept as authoritative for itself – no longer have any hold on them, but in which there does not seem to be any acceptable or justifiable alternative set of practices or accounts. The conceptual formation of the "unhappy consciousness" is instanced in the development of the structure of mutual recognition that constitutes the "legal person." The self-consciousness of the "legal person," with its awareness of the contingency of social selfhood, thus leads out of the "unhappy consciousness" to the idea that its essence lies only in its self-conscious reflection on its own thoughts. The dialectic of master and slave showed that self-mastery had eluded both participants; it was thus succeeded by stoicism. Likewise, the Roman legal person finds that the only form of self-mastery available to him is the stoic retreat into oneself.[34]

This retreat into the self marks the appearance of what in his later lectures on the history of philosophy and the philosophy of history Hegel calls interiority (*Innerlichkeit*).[35] The agent acquires the possibility of reflection on his own inner life, his own motivations and passions. The idea of this form of subjective reflection had been articulated by Socrates in Athenian life, but the Greek form of life was such that the Socratic account could neither fit into the way it had understood itself, nor could its form of self-reflection be sustained by the institutional structures of Greek life since such self-reflection was inimical to the supposedly natural harmony of the Greek form of life itself. The Roman form of life created the institutional background for this to become a real possibility. Nonetheless, interiority for them necessarily has no essential content. The question now becomes for these agents what determinate content this new form of self-reflection, as reflection on their "inner lives," could have.

The Roman form of life thus creates the possibility for a new form of character in which the ends of life are set not by nature but by our own activity in terms of ends with which the individual can identify as a rational agent. By creating this "social space" for interiority, the Roman form of life thus created the possibility of the modern world.[36] (This comes out more clearly in the chapter on religion at the end of the *Phenomenology*.) The unhappy consciousness that marks the end of the Roman form of life thus marks a genuine turning point in the philosophical history of spirit in that it is the beginning point at which character as destiny is on the road to merging with character as *self*-determination.[37]

Early modern life: civilization and the loss of grounds

Out of the chaos of the collapsing economy in the West and the disintegration of many social institutions, the post-Roman European world gradually managed to institutionalize itself in a variety of ways that involved the creation of an estate of nobles. The early barbarian raiders and the necessity for providing common protection for communities, along with the heritage of Roman thought preserved in the culture, created a group of people who took themselves to be those who defended the ecclesiasticals and the ordinary people of their communities. These warriors took themselves not to be simply Roman *persons* having certain legal rights but spiritual descendants of the Roman patricians, *aristocrats* who had the duty to fashion themselves along the lines of what counted as a "noble" way of living. The social standards of nobility came to give these agents a new self-consciousness (a "self-image") both of what they *were* and what they *ought* to be. In this new account of self-consciousness, the Roman conception of the essentially contingent self was retained, but it came to be understood that this contingent self was capable of fashioning itself according to certain socially set standards of what counts as a valid form of noble life. Hegel's thesis is that what emerged as the historical insufficiency of the European nobility's form of self-understanding prepared the way for the fully modern conception of social life as based on a principle of freedom as self-determination.

Hegel argues that the post-Roman European understanding of nobility thus develops out of the ways in which Roman life had come to take the accounts offered by stoicism and skepticism as authoritative for itself. The stoical and skeptical accounts had led to a conception of the agent as free in his self-reflections, in his detaching himself from the surrounding social world.[38] In the post-Roman European world, this conception of freedom as detaching oneself from one's surroundings is transformed into an account of the agent as free to fashion himself according to externally set standards of aristocratic behavior. In the Roman conception, the person was only a legal entity, a bearer of rights determined by Roman law, who could be a Roman, a Teuton, or a Gaul. In the account that the Romans gave of themselves as to what counted in being a Roman, the agent's own particular character, taken from his own tradition and culture, was to be left unchallenged by Roman law. For these post-Roman agents, however, the particularities of character themselves are to be refashioned according to the external standards of what is to count as a noble. These standards are external in that they are not taken to be set by the individual agents themselves; they are simply *found* in the institutional structure of the world in which he lives. The issue, then, for such individuals has to do with how they understand these external standards (what Hegel calls the "universal") to be authoritative for them, to be standards to which they have good reasons to measure up. Everything that is particular to an agent (his "natural self" as Hegel calls it) is to be suppressed in favor of these externally (socially) set standards; the subjective point of view of the agent is to be brought in line by the agent himself to the objective (universal) point of view by his fashioning himself into an aristocrat. The agent thus becomes who he *ought* to be by suppressing what is particular to him in favor of becoming a certain *type* of person. To be a noble was to be a "type," to have cultivated oneself into measuring up to the standards of what counted as nobility.[39] To remain in the state of one's "natural self" was to be "base"; to become an aristocrat was therefore to *alienate* oneself into becoming that *type* of person who is "truly" noble.

Aristocracy and the ethic of honor. This process of becoming a type of person involves forming and cultivating oneself (*Bildung*).[40] The reasons that count as authoritative, therefore, have to do with what is necessary to become a cultivated individual, which for the Europeans of the late medieval and early modern periods had to do with a certain conception of nobility. Hegel's project in the *Phenomenology* does not concern itself with an account of the various contingent social forces that led to the European nobility's assuming the shape that it did. Rather, the project concerns the accounts (in the form of plays, poems, and philosophy) that European life gave of itself to reassure itself that the formation of an estate of nobles that was distinct from all other estates was "in order," that its reasons for belief and action were indeed good reasons. Hegel's point in doing so is to trace out the ways in which those accounts generated out of themselves a certain skepticism about the claims they were making, and how this account of nobility paved the way for what came to be called the Enlightenment.

One of the basic features of that account of nobility had to do with the way in which an aristocrat becomes and maintains himself as an aristocrat by becoming a *type* of person (a person who typically does such and such), and the ways in which in becoming such a type, he also thereby becomes a "true" individual, someone distinguished from the mass of others. By suppressing all aspects of his particular character and forming himself according to the socially accepted standards of what counts as nobility, he is thereby to become an individual distinct from and superior to others. The account is complicated in that it is the particular features of the agent himself – his bravery, his talents in battle, his willingness to face death – that enable him to measure up to the standards set by the social ideals of nobility. The individual is thus self-fashioning in a particular way: He utilizes his talents and character (something simply given to him by nature or "breeding") to perform the types of deeds and cultivate the types of emotions that are necessary for being a member of the nobility. Out of this demand to become a *type* of person and to feel and act only in the terms appropriate to such types emerges the outlines of an aristocratic ethics. What therefore counts as "good" is living nobly, which an aristocrat does by alienating his particular self in favor of living up to the standards of the "type" (nobility in general); what counts as "bad" is what is "base," living by the standards of commoners.[41]

The issue, then, has to do with how the nobles could reconcile these two aspects of their accounts of themselves. On the one hand, a noble is to sacrifice his *individual* desires by cultivating and fashioning himself into conforming to those external standards that determine what counts as a noble life; on the other hand, in doing so, he is to distinguish himself *as an individual,* to set himself off from the crowd of others through his pursuit and achievement of glory, which consists of acquiring honor in the eyes of others or defending his (inborn) honor before others. A noble is thus required to sacrifice his *particular* characteristics to make himself a *type* of person (who is such a type *only* in being recognized by others) and in doing so thereby making himself into an *individual*.[42] In practice, European nobles did this through the exercise of warfare. Risking death for glory, the late medieval knights, many of whom claimed to trace their ancestry to those who fought with Charlemagne, warred with each other, and often laid waste to the countryside in their pursuit of such glory. Glory was attained in gaining territory and status for oneself and one's family. In this way, the use of violence came to be idealized by the nobility, and the main objects of noble ambition thus came to be war and politics (which itself was generally taken as a means of enhancing their status by territorial and other gains). Moreover, the great civil wars in Europe in the 1600s had led to the renewal of the cult of aristocracy with its emphasis on glory and violence, despite the fact that by this time the various knights had long since learned the art of raising mercenary armies and no longer fit the chivalric descriptions they gave of themselves.[43]

The aristocrat who understands himself according to the chivalric code takes himself to be defending his honor (which is always honor in the eyes of others) by defending the honor of his lord (the noble who is above him). This constitutes politics, and the aristocrat takes himself to be who he is by virtue of his attachment to *state power*.[44] To be truly noble is to act for the interest of the "state" (or the authoritative political body or person). By the chivalric account that such people give to themselves, the man of true honor subordinates his own well-being to the good of the state (embodied in his ties to his feudal lord) and acts only out of that sense of honor. The *right* (that is, the *ethical*) thing to do is that which is required in order to defend one's honor, and that dictates that one selflessly serve the state by being willing to fight for it. (The medieval division of society into the estates of ecclesiasticals, nobles, and commoners had as its rationale the idea of a division of social functions: "I pray for you, I fight for you, I work for you.") But this so-called selfless service to the state is, like all pursuits of honor, a pursuit of something that *only* counts in the eyes of others. Honor unrecognized is not honor. The pursuit of honor in the eyes of others is thus a particular end, something that the individual may be expected to pursue out of concern for his own personal standing. Yet, peculiarly, so Hegel argues, the noble is supposed to take himself as pursuing this *self-interested* goal *selflessly*.

This constitutes the aristocratic "ethic of honor," one realization of which would be the ethos displayed by the seventeenth-century English cavaliers and their relation to Charles. For these nobles, there is nothing more important than duty to the king or queen, and the highest virtue for them is that of *honor*. Honor, especially for the cavaliers, was a matter of pure artifice. In making oneself a man of honor, one became a person who in his clothing, deportment and manner of life exhibited a lack of concern for the so-called petty details of individual life (thus separating himself off from the commoner-bourgeois). This aristocratic "ethic of honor" required great self-restraint and an overarching concern for one's reputation in the eyes of others. It required, that is, that this self-forming individual appear to act from an impersonal, detached point of view, while at the same time exhibiting a controlled passion in doing so. The cavalier both feigns indifference to normal things and claims passionate attachment to others; he claims to act from an impersonal code of honor, and he claims that this impersonal code is his deepest personal end. (This kind of ethic is nicely and concisely expressed by Richard Lovelace's well known lines, "I could not love thee, Deare, so much/ Lov'd I not honour more", as he explains to Lucasta that he must go to battle: "True; a new Mistresse now I chase/The first Foe in the Field; And with a stronger Faith embrace/A Sword, a Horse, a Shield."[45]) His bearing is expressed in his willingness to die in warfare for his king, for his honor. Thus, by the account that the cavalier gives to himself and to others, the cavalier has a set of ends, which include the attitude of nonchalance vis-à-vis all things, the necessity of self-restraint and avoidance of excessive or deep emotion, and the overwhelming duty to the king. Achievement of these ends is necessary for him to maintain his status as being a man of artifice.

In return for his services to his lord, the noble also thereby acquires *wealth,* which is a mark of his status and prestige, but which under the terms of the aristocratic ethic may not count as the end or motive for which he acts (which is to be honor itself). Nonetheless, honor requires wealth in that without having wealth (in the forms of lands or offices) bestowed on one, one has not acquired honor. Of course, there are those (for example, the merchants, who, along with the peasants, count as commoners) who pursue not honor but simply wealth itself, and who as a result may indeed be wealthier than the nobles.[46] However, they cannot be men of honor, for they do not act in the service of the state, and thus they cannot be truly noble. Since neither way of being (knight or merchant) is natural to anybody, the agent is free to choose which of these ends he shall pursue in the sense that there is no natural or external ground on which to make the choice. The individual must simply make the independent judgment himself. The noble, to be noble, must choose to subordinate his will to the will of the state (to his feudal lord); the merchant must choose to pursue his own self-interest and acquire wealth. Each must therefore choose the ends of service to the state or the pursuit of wealth on the basis of which one appears to them to be the proper (the good) choice and one that appears to be the inappropriate (the bad) the choice.[47] In the eyes of the merchant, the noble will be seen to be foolishly sacrificing himself for some chimerical idea, and the noble will see the merchant as acting only on the base motives of private gain. But since there can be no independent or natural basis of making that choice, the agent must therefore simply *opt* for pursuing one or the other, and whatever judgment the agent makes will also involve choosing at the same time the criteria that will make the other's choice appear to be the wrong one. Each has to make a *criterionless* choice – that is, a choice that involves choosing the criteria that then in turn justifies the choice itself. Because in making the judgment about which life he is to pursue, each also thereby necessarily chooses the criteria for making the choice itself, each will *necessarily* see the other's choice as bad, as the "negative," as not conforming to the "true" set of values.[48] What the spirit of this social world will seem to be – that is, what seems to be the only good account that this social world can give to itself of what counts as authoritative reasons for belief or action – will itself be constituted in the choices and judgments that these two types of agents make.

Each of these judgments does more than simply condemn the other's choice as bad. From the standpoint of each, the other judgment seems to be internally incoherent *on its own terms* in a way that validates the standpoint of the agent making the judgment. From the standpoint of the agent who only pursues wealth, for example, the noble's choice seems flatly contradictory. On the one hand, the aristocrat is free to choose the life of nobility. Indeed, it is his free choice, to lay everything on the line for the sake of that honor that supposedly gives him his noble character. Honor, however, is duty in the service of state power, which for a medieval knight is identical with fealty to his sovereign prince. This makes him an aristocrat, who in the scheme of things in the hierarchical social order of medieval and early modern European life thereby elevates himself above the "commoner," and especially the bourgeois, who act only for the sake of acquiring wealth: He "fights" whereas the bourgeois only "works" for him and the other aristocrats. However, in pursuing his honor, his own personal ends are completely subordinated to those of the lord above him in the feudal hierarchy. As subordinate to the lord above him in the hierarchy, he is thus formally no different from the bourgeois who is lower than him in the hierarchy. To be sure, his personal reward – the riches conferred on him that in turn enable him to live the extravagant life typical of an aristocrat – give free rein to his personal desires (those that do not involve honor but simply his own idiosyncratic wishes and wants). However, seen from the standpoint of the bourgeois-commoner, this only reinforces the similarity between the aristocrat and the bourgeois-commoner (in particular, with the bourgeois-commoner who apes the manners and styles of the aristocracy and who, to boot, has more wealth with which to do it). Indeed, as far as serving the state goes, the bourgeois-commoner can argue that what he does – produce wealth – is in fact of better service to the state, since it produces in turn more wealth for all, whereas the knightly aristocrat simply squanders wealth in the pursuit of glory and military conquest.

On the other hand, from the aristocrat's point of view, the merchant's judgment is equally incoherent. The merchant cannot look at things from anything other than his own subjective ("base") point of view, whereas the whole order of things – including the stability of the towns in which the merchant carries on his business – demands that the state keep that order with its laws and commands, which is impossible without the deeds of the aristocratic knights who subordinate their personal point of view to the objective point of view of state power from which honor and distinction flow. What counts in life is to cultivate oneself so that one may be distinguished in the eyes of others, and to concentrate only on wealth is to abandon oneself to what is only transitory in life, to cut oneself off from the possibility of establishing one's honor and glory in the eyes of others. The bourgeois-commoner effectively prevents himself from ever acting for the honor of things, since he is too imprisoned in the pursuit of his own satisfactions.[49]

The truth of the matter, though, is that both ways of making their judgments contain each other's principles, although this is hidden to each. Each takes his activity to be justified in terms of its serving the general good of state power – the bourgeois increases its wealth, the aristocrat achieves and defends its glory – and each takes his own personal satisfaction to be justified in terms of his serving this end. The bourgeois's self-seeking is justified (so he can claim) by his producing and increasing the wealth of the state; and the aristocrat's so-called selflessness (as he can understand it) is justified because of the way he thereby extends the glory of state power.[50] The aristocrat thereby identifies his ends with those of state power and despises the bourgeois, the man without honor; the aristocrat enjoys his wealth because it is a sign of his service to the state or to the lord, a reward that he takes himself fully to deserve because of his honor and his selfless devotion. The bourgeois, on the other hand, sees state power only in terms of the way it (to him) unjustifiably interferes with his own private pursuits, even when he understands his own private pursuits to be increasing the wealth of the state. In terms of the aristocratic ethics that constitutes this form of "spirit," the bourgeois will therefore experience himself as alienated from the state, since what counts in this form of life is honor, and the bourgeois by his own way of life and the virtues he espouses (for example, his industry, frugality and his attention to business) is excluded from ever acquiring such honor. The aristocratic ethos as the ethos of this form of life seems to make the aristocrat fully identify with his activities in the service of the state, and to compel the bourgeois to be fully alienated in his activities of seeking wealth.[51]

At this point, then, the bourgeois-commoner understands himself in the terms set by the aristocratic ethos. Only the internal inadequacy of that ethos, so Hegel will argue, will lead the bourgeois in modern life to a different, more affirmative, and non-alienated understanding of himself. In terms of the aristocratic ethos, though, it is assumed that self-worth (or inner respect, *innere Achtung,* as Hegel calls it[52]) is something that can only be bestowed by the opinion of others; although depending on the performance of certain deeds, honor or glory nonetheless only exists in others *taking one to be* possessed of honor or glory. In this way, the aristocrat can take himself to possess honor, since he can be recognized as having it, whereas the commoner-bourgeois must take himself to be necessarily lacking it. Each therefore is fully *alienated* in that each takes his self-identity to be dependent on that which is outside himself, the opinions of others. On its own, the self is empty; it is, as Hegel puts it, "pure consciousness," having no self-identity outside of that which it acquires in the recognition by others. The freedom that each acquires can therefore only be an alienated and not a fully realized form of freedom.

The feudal aristocrat thus takes himself to be the man of true *virtue,* which he identifies as his willingness to sacrifice himself for the sake of honor and as that strength of character that enables a truly noble character to triumph over others. This virtue is something to which the commoner-bourgeois cannot aspire, mired as he is in the pursuit of private ends. In terms of the accounts that this form of life gives to itself, he embodies, as Hegel says, the "heroism of *service*" to the "higher" callings, indeed, to honor itself.[53] In *cultivating* himself to display his loyalty to his overlord or to his political community, he rises above self-seeking concerns and achieves honor in the eyes of others and therefore for himself. (Honor is the "universal," that which is taken as authoritative from a detached, impersonal point of view) By taking this detached view toward himself, the aristocrat integrates his *self* into communal opinion, into a more objective point of view, and he produces thereby the social and political order that in turn affirms his sense of who he is. He exists for honor, for the service of the state; the commoner-bourgeois, on the other hand, exists only for his own ends, not the "higher" ends of service, honor, and glory. According to the story that the aristocrat tells himself, he does not think of his own good but only that of the good of others (thus, the popular tales of noblemen coming to the aid of women, commoners, and the meek). By this account, therefore, the noble is ideally suited for political life in a way that the commoner-bourgeois cannot be, for the latter seeks only his own ends and not the common good, whereas the knightly aristocrat puts aside his own private ends for the good of the state and for the honor of serving the community.

Hegel argues that the logic of this aristocratic self-conception leads to a conception of the legitimacy of a conception of absolutist monarchy. In making that claim, Hegel is again not asserting anything about the complex social causes that led from the loose associations of medieval feudalism to the absolutist monarchies of the seventeenth and eighteenth centuries. He is instead making a claim about the logic of the accounts that these forms of life gave of themselves in terms of how they tried to reassure themselves that the kinds of reasons that they had come to *take* as authoritative for themselves "really were" good reasons. The accounts that the nobles give of themselves – as men willing to risk death for the sake of honor and glory, who act not out of personal ends but out of their chivalric duties to the overlord or to others who need their help – served this purpose, and in turn generated its own kind of skepticism about itself. The aristocrats claim that they are suited for politics in ways that commoners (and especially the bourgeoisie) are not because the aristocrat is not concerned for his own private ends but for the public ends of the "state." However, the aristocrats who form the early versions of the "state of the estates" (the *Ständesstaat*) of early modern Europe in fact disagree vehemently among themselves as to what that public interest is in ways that undermine their claims to be acting only out of selfless interests. Each aristocrat gives his own counsel to the lord concerning how the state is to be run, and the counsel of different aristocrats conflicts with the counsels given by others. Indeed, in the "state of estates," it seems as if there is no real structure of government per se to mediate among the conflicting pieces of advice and counsel; instead, there seems to be only a loose collection of aristocrats each haughtily asserting his "privileges" against the others.[54] Yet to the extent that one noble asserts *his* "privileges" against another, he begins to appear more like the commoner-bourgeois than he is supposed to be, at least given the terms of the aristocratic ethic. To the extent that the nobles begin to appear to each other as agents simply asserting their own interests (in the form of their "privileges") against each other, they begin to doubt that the accounts they give of themselves – men who put honor and service above their own particular ends – can be correct.

Aristocracy and absolute monarchy. Since honor counts as honor only in the eyes of others, who must themselves be peers (for only a peer, a man of honor himself, can suitably bestow honor on another), it follows that if these aristocrats are to reassure themselves that their accounts of themselves are in order, they must therefore all be subordinate to some *one* aristocrat who is above all of them and on whom all honor depends. Honor consists in the "heroism of service," of acting for the good of the "state" and *being seen by one's peers* to be acting for the sake of such honor. However, if the "state" in question is only a collection of nobles, each asserting that he acts only for the good of the state while at the same time asserting his own "privileges" against the others, then each will fail to have honor even as he asserts it against others. The conflicts among the nobles thus require that the state, the political community, be embodied in *a* peer, who at the same time is above all the others, such that *his* interests simply *are* the state's interests. The absolute monarchy of Louis XIV, the "sun king," thus completes the logic of the self-understandings of the early modern European nobility, and serves to affirm the nobles' understanding of themselves.[55]

Hegel argues that this move to absolute monarchy, however, brings to the forefront what the aristocratic ethic actually entailed. Historically, this was accomplished by Louis XIV's undoing the nobility's traditional power in order to secure his own. The *Fronde,* a revolt against the king in the 1640s in which various elements of the nobility played key roles, occurred when Louis was about five years old, and it had left him with the conviction that he had to keep the nobles under control if he himself was to survive. The nobility, which had been a fractious and capricious element of French society, believed that it would cooperate with the king only if he would recognize their "privileges" and status. (Indeed, just what constituted nobility was itself a matter of great dispute in the French society of the seventeenth century, since the older nobility wished to draw distinctions between themselves and the newly ennobled.) For political reasons, Louis XIV moved his royal court out of Paris and into the new quarters of Versailles, and he required the chief nobility to take up residence there, more or less so that he could keep an eye on them. In place of the former cult of violence and glory, which had taken center stage for the Valois kings, the aristocrats under the reign of the Bourbon king, Louis XIV, were therefore to find honor by virtue of their *being* at the court and participating in the highly elaborate court rituals that centered around the king himself. (As has often been noted, the aristocratic ideal thus ceased to be that of glory through violent conquest and became instead that of glory in being allowed to hold Louis's coat as he dressed.) By gathering all the chief aristocrats around him at Versailles, Louis XIV was thereby able to defuse any potential rebellion on the part of the aristocracy. The artists of the day provided the requisite account of this new form of aristocracy. In particular, Pierre Corneille in his plays managed to transfer the old aristocratic ethos of violence, honor and glory to the stage, leaving the actual aristocrats to establish their honor through court intrigue and the fostering of the arts. The older aristocratic ethos of attaining glory and honor by triumphing over others in violent ways (for example, through warfare and duels) had no place at the court at Versailles. Hence, as the aristocratic images of violent and glorious triumph over others became displaced to the stage, the aristocrats in the court came to attempt their triumph over others by besting them in wordplay and wit.[56] The duels between aristocrats for the sake of honor thus came to be carried out with words, not with swords. Eventually, the style of court life at Versailles extended itself to the nobility living apart from Versailles, who began to gather at salons in order to display their own cultivation in "conversational warfare."

The project of the *Phenomenology* does not have to do with the social causes and conditions of Louis XIV's ability to consolidate power in himself alone but in the way in which the set of contingent events that eventuated in the mores and ethos of royal court life in Versailles had to be redescribed in the aristocracy's account of itself and the way in which the logic of that account (its attempts to reassure itself about the authority of the ground-rules it had come to accept) necessitated something like the kind of absolute monarchy that Louis XIV came to embody. Hegel's argument therefore does not have to do with the contingent reasons and social forces that are necessary to explain how the individual, Louis XIV, managed to amass all power to himself and to calm the aristocracy into obeying him; it is that the accounts that the European nobility had given of themselves dialectically required *something like* the social role of "absolute monarch" that Louis XIV stepped into and transformed in his own image.

Given the necessity to acquire honor in the eyes of others and thereby to be distinct from the commoner-bourgeois, the aristocrats needed some "peer" who was capable of bestowing such honor on them. The old aristocratic ethic of acquiring honor by triumphing over others in combat could not sustain itself, for it threatened to make the nobles into the same kind of person as the commoner-bourgeois – men in pursuit only of their own private ends. In practical terms, the pursuit of the old aristocratic ethos threatened to do away with the nobility itself, given the losses noble families inevitably suffered in the continual violence and struggles for supremacy and the conditions of modern warfare with its dependence on mercenary armies. In conceptual terms, it called into question the whole legitimacy of the reasons that the nobility had given as to why it was different from others and why this difference gave it alone the right to participate in political life.

The aristocrat who alienates himself by taking his self-identity to lie outside of him in the recognition of his aristocratic honor by others therefore needs some criterion of what is to count as honor in the eyes of others. At the royal court, it is the ability to act in terms of courtly behavior and to distinguish oneself in the eyes of others. Instead of being something demonstrated by "sword and shield," this must become primarily a *linguistic* activity, so Hegel argues, because only in that kind of activity of besting others through the brandishing of a sophisticated wit and the wielding of the sneering *bon mot* can an aristocrat display his *cultivated* manner as something that is not available to the commoner-bourgeois who must live outside the life of the royal court and who accordingly can never acquire the kind of cultivated manners of those who move within the royal orbit. The ability to dominate others through witty, barbed repartee thus becomes the standard by which honor comes to be measured. This form of self-presentation is particularly important for the nobles to be able to distinguish themselves from the commoner-bourgeoisie, since the latter can always acquire the proper clothes, hairstyles, and the like so that from the outside they may appear to be nobility. But, so the account goes, they will always be exposed as soon as they begin to speak. (Corneille's comedies, for example, often have to do with the way in which bourgeois pretenders to nobility give themselves away by their mannerisms or their cowardice.) This manner of self-presentation is a logical expression of the alienated self, which must always be reflecting on itself and foregoing other personal ends in order to become the "type" of person who is truly noble. What distinguishes the truly noble type of person is the way in which he can carry on conversation in the proper, witty, and ultimately triumphant manner. This new form of the aristocratic ethos requires not only the great amount of self-control that was needed for the earlier forms of the aristocratic ethos; it also requires a sophisticated kind of self-reflection about one's behavior in the face of others.

The aristocratic ethos thus comes to require that the agent distance himself from himself and observe himself carefully to insure that he live up to the ideals of nobility. The norms that structure the practices that inform the social institution of nobility consequently lead to a conception of the self as the "pure self," which both evaluates itself as to whether it measures up to the behavior and passions that are required of noble characters and that is distinct from and prior to any ends it may choose. In Hegel's terms, this self is "reflected out of" its practices and goals "into itself." It thereby constitutes itself as a kind of formal "point" from which the practices of criticism and evaluation are carried out.[57]

What holds these aristocrats together are the accounts that each accepts as authoritative for himself, the "spirit" of the Bourbon aristocracy. The social practice of dueling with words in the context of maintaining one's honor within the structures of court life – of displaying oneself to others as being a cultivated (*gebildete*) person *au courant* with the arts – creates a structure of mutual recognition in which the alienation of each party is manifest to the others, and in which such alienation is understood to be a condition of being a proper "type" of person. In these conversational duels and intrigues to see who has the upper hand in court life, each recognizes the other as a man or woman of honor, even as each seeks verbally to subdue the other; this recognition is mediated by the structure not merely of reasons that each has come to take as authoritative but in terms of the mutually acknowledged accounts that each gives. Thus, in the court of Louis XIV, life and theater began to merge. The nobles found out how they were to behave and feel, for example, by seeing the plays of Corneille, which also served to give them an account of why the reasons for belief and action that they accepted (that which distinguishes them as true nobility, *gentilhommes*) were in fact good reasons, and to give them the models of nobility which they were to imitate.[58] (In Corneille's plays, such as *Le Cid*, the action serves to affirm the idea that such truly noble people were indeed above the codes of ordinary morality, indeed, were different from all "ordinary" people in the nature of their passions and designs.[59])

The aristocrat as courtier. Corresponding to the purification of the conception of the self as being distinct from and prior to all its ends is an equally abstract conception of state power. The noble who understands himself as pursuing only honor makes a criterionless choice, and it is the nature of this type of choice that constitutes him as a pure self. There are no standards that exist prior to the choice of whether he is to be "noble" or "base" – that is, there is no natural hierarchy that determines whether he is to live the "base" life of a bourgeois or to pursue honor. The choice is groundless, and therefore *can* only be made by a "pure" self. But since honor can only be bestowed by others, the aristocrats require some *person* to bestow that honor. Since all honor therefore emanates from that person, the aristocrat has a duty as an aristocrat to serve him. In deferring to the absolute monarch, the noble constitutes the monarch as an absolute monarch. A non-absolute monarch is limited by the "privileges" of the estates, particularly the nobility; but by sacrificing all his "privileges" to the "state" – which in reality means sacrificing his "privileges" to another aristocrat – the noble constitutes that other person as unlimited in his authority. Independently of its social causes, the transformation of the Valois knights into the fawning courtiers of the Bourbon royal court of Louis XIV realized a certain logic of the self-understanding of the French nobility: "The heroism of silent service becomes the *heroism* of *flattery*."[60] In sacrificing everything of his *self* to the state as personified in the absolute monarch, the aristocrat-courtier constitutes the state itself as that which bestows honor upon him. Whereas previously he would have held a title and independence on his own (as the Duke of such-and-such), he now has his title as the Duke of such-and-such only when his having that title is recognized by the monarch. (Hegel's discussion of this obviously alludes to the development of French court life in which the titles of the nobility came to be seen as dependent on Louis's recognition of them; although this was historically false as an account of the origin and legitimacy of titles, in claiming this privilege Louis nonetheless portrayed himself to be doing only that which French kings had always done.[61]) By ceding the monarch this "privilege," the nobility constitutes him as the absolute monarch which the monarch claims to be.

The outlines of the master/slave dialectic are thereby repeated for the relationship between the king and his aristocrat-courtiers. The king gets his own point of view to be determinative for the point of view of others; for the aristocrat-courtiers, the king's ends are their ends, and they make him into the absolute monarch (the "master" of all) in their *accepting* the king's ends as their own. State power, which until then had been only an abstract conception of "that to which a chivalric man of honor was loyal," now becomes *sovereignty*, an authority from which all lesser authorities derive. A sovereign is the person or institution whose power cannot be limited by anything else. For the older nobility, state power was an ideal (in Hegel's terms, an "abstraction"), which they as chivalric men of honor both defended and "heroically seized" for themselves. However, as being constituted by them as that which bestows honor upon them, absolutist state power becomes something that constitutes them as the aristocrats they claim to be. Formerly, each noble was independent and claimed his traditional "privileges"; but in collectively ceding their claims to honor to the king, they lose that independence and in effect those "privileges" (although they continue to account for themselves in those terms).

Hegel, again, is offering this *not* as an explanation of the social forces that led to the loss of independence by the nobility under the reign of Louis XIV but as a dialectical reconstruction of the accounts that this form of life gave of itself (in other words, as a dialectical account of their "spirit" in terms of its being a "formation of consciousness"). Given their conceptions of themselves as men of honor and the skepticism about that status that the accounts generate, the nobility are led to give an account of themselves in terms of court life and the bestowal of honor upon them by the king. The set of "ancient laws" that had bestowed their "privileges" upon them thus becomes "reflected into itself" in becoming identified with the personal will of the monarch. The monarch becomes the absolute monarch not in subduing the other nobles by force but in having them alienate themselves and constitute him as the absolute monarch in their flattery of him, the sovereign "point" (the "empty name," as Hegel calls it) from which all "true honor" is dispensed.[62] The dialectical logic of this move is similar to other dialectical moves having to do with "spirit": An account is given of why certain reasons that had come to be taken as authoritative really are authoritative, a skeptical response is engendered out of those accounts, an attempt at reassurance and affirmation is pursued, and its failure necessitates a new set of authoritative reasons.

No longer Valois knight-aristocrats but now Bourbon aristocrat-courtiers, the nobles come to see their wealth not as a reward for service but as something they can manage to capture for themselves by shrewd maneuvering and wise investment. The aristocrat-courtiers thus become sharp-eyed men of commerce. (This parallels the way in which much of the traditional nobility that did not live at court became gradually impoverished; relying only on their traditional rents, they were unable to keep up with those astute urban investers residing at Versailles.) They become, that is, like the commoner-bourgeoisie from whom they had previously distinguished themselves in that they become pursuers of their own private ends. In the accounts of aristocratic life, the flattery of the monarch and the careful ballet of court life thereby becomes only a formality surrounding what *in its own terms* must be taken as a "base" pursuit – not the attainment of honor but the acquisition of personal wealth. This too follows out the logic of the accounts the nobility gives of itself. Honor is bestowed through the eyes of others; although all honor ultimately comes from the king, there must be intrigue to see who can persuade the king to bestow such honor and recognition. Each finds therefore that his honor is dependent on the whims of others and on their recognition of him as a man of honor. Deprived of any self-identity except that conferred by recognition at court, each realizes himself as therefore dependent on the others for recognition, and each therefore finds his self-identity to be "outside himself," to exist only in the view of others. Like the slave of the master/slave dialectic, the aristocrat-courtier finds that there is no natural hierarchy of ends that recommends itself to him; everything that he had taken to be true turns out to be a matter of contingency, and, as a "pure self" he finds himself living therefore in a groundless world in which the lack of criteria to choose ends becomes evident – that is, in which the criterionless judgments come to appear as they are: *criterionless*, without external supporting grounds.[63] Having thus constituted himself as a "pure self" (a self whose self-identity is completely external to him), the aristocrat-courtier finds that he can no longer identify with the ends of state power, for those ends can only be contingently his own ends. The reassurance that his transformation from a

Valois knight-aristocrat into a Bourbon courtier-aristocrat had provided in turn generates a self-undermining skepticism. His reflections on himself come to possess an internal contradictoriness in that what he takes to be defining for what is authoritative for himself (being a noble of the royal court and therefore having the "honor" and "privileges" of that nobility) turns out to be self-undermining: Life at the court is not spent in determining what is best for the community but in fawning over the king and engaging in verbal courtly intrigue with other courtiers as a way of marking one's "distinction," and it is *profitably* spent in making lucrative urban investments (which is to say, in pursuing ends incommensurate with the ideal of "honor"). For the aristocrat-courtier to take himself to be an aristocrat (and not merely a commoner-bourgeois) within the terms of the account he gives himself, he must therefore develop some new practice through which he can distinguish himself from the commoner-bourgeoisie. This necessity was realized in the aristocrat-courtier's becoming a *patron* of the arts (particularly of bourgeois artists), which was to affirm for him that he was indeed a noble, a man of honor who pursued the common good rather than his own private ends.

This is, of course, simply more groundless action, since there can be no natural hierarchy of ends that supports this self-conception. However, within the account that the noble has come to give of himself as a man of cultivation (*Bildung*), the practices involved in playing the role of "patron of the arts" has as its goal the affirmation for the nobles that they remain free and independent "masters" since their clients (the bourgeois artists and writers) are indeed dependent on them for sustenance. But there can be no real criteria for what would count as the kind of art that should be supported, since the traditional criteria have been fully called into question by the kinds of skepticism that the nobility's accounts of themselves have occasioned. Thus, the bourgeois client of the aristocrat-patron is aware of his dependence on the patron, while at the same time the aristocrat becomes aware of his dependence on the client to legitimate his claims to being a man of "honor" and "cultivation."

As the noble comes to understand himself as a dependent patron, a sycophant and (like the commoner-bourgeois) a person who pursues the private end of accumulating wealth, the "groundlessness" of this life becomes more apparent in the accounts that this form of life gives of itself. In its earlier accounts of what was authoritative for it, this form of life had accepted that there was a natural hierarchy of ends, and that these ends were "natural" to some personalities and not to others. Thus, the aristocrat would understand that his passion for "honor" and his flouting of conventional morality was a "natural" part of his self-identity, which he was both expressing and defending.[64] But with the logical development of the nobility's accounts of who it takes itself to be, any appeal to any "natural" self or to the "natural order" ceases to be authoritative.

The "groundless" self. Hegel takes Denis Diderot's *Rameau's Nephew* to be the most accurate portrayal of the logical conclusion to which this form of life leads. *Rameau's Nephew* is written in the form of a dialogue: An "I" (a *philosophe*) has a conversation with a "he" in the gardens of the *Palais Royale* about the way in which the "he" makes his living. The "he" is the supposed nephew of the popular composer Rameau; the nephew makes his living as a client of various wealthy families, supposedly teaching the members of the family musical skills, and during the dialogue he displays a wild oscillation from buffoonery to profundity as he explains how a man like himself makes a living in the houses of the rich and the aristocratic. *Rameau's Nephew* critically assesses one of the great conceits of the day – the idea that the "true" men and women of cultivation – the artists and writers – formed a kind of community that was independent of the prevarications of the nobles. The inhabitants of this community were not, however, the independent, free-spirited men and women of cultivation that they had taken themselves to be; they were just as much part of the patronage system and its culture of groundless selfhood as were anybody else. As Diderot constructs the character of Rameau's nephew, he is the man without substance, the cosmopolitan who attempts to live without any mediating institutions and to rely only on the force of his own talents or creativity in a world where the practices have to do with wealthy patrons dispensing various favors. Far from being an independent man, he is actually the highest form of servant. By detaching his *self* from everything, the nephew has sought to identify completely with whatever task he took on, and the result is a debased person who is fully conscious of his debasement and in fact both identifies with it and revels in it. The "I" of the dialogue – who represents at once the voice of "common sense" and of the character type of the eighteenth-century *philosophe* – is shocked by the nephew's self-conscious debasement and tries to offer him a series of arguments to show that it contravenes some basic or natural object of life. However, as the dialogue progresses, it becomes evident that the nephew is simply presenting to his noble and well-off employers only a mirror of the alienated, "pure selves" that they themselves are. He says that he appears to others as they wish him to appear: If it is better to appear virtuous, then he appears virtuous; if it is better to appear buffoonish, then he appears buffoonish. In short, the nephew is the bourgeois equivalent of an aristocrat at the royal court. The commonsensical "I" in the dialogue asserts, generally in short sentences or phrases, the accepted judgments about what is good and bad, virtuous and wicked, but he is almost always thwarted by the nephew who either gets him to admit that what the nephew says is true or at least leaves him without a reply.[65] The "I" insists that the nephew is leading a dishonorable life in so shamelessly degrading himself before others; but he cannot come up with a better account than the nephew has given as to why he should change. The "I" in the dialogue shares the "social space" of the nephew but deceives himself as to where the accounts that he gives of what is authoritative for both of them lead.[66]

The dialogue between the buffoonish musician and the "I" in *Rameau's Nephew* reveals that the musician is the character who speaks the truth about where the accounts of the culture of the aristocrat-courtiers (and its non-noble entourage of writers, thinkers, artists, and wealthy bourgeois-commoners) ultimately leads. There is no way to resolve the difficulties of this account within its own terms, for it has completed itself in its account of itself as internally self-undermining. The "pure self" that emerges out of the development of the culture of "cultivation" must therefore understand its surrounding social world as simply vanity, as a pretense in which each participates in order to pursue his own personal ends, all the while avowing only to be concerned for "higher things" or for "honor" itself. This "pure self" is distinct from and prior to all determinate ends. From the standpoint of this "pure self", all statements about hierarchies of ends (about some things being inherently better than other things) must be simply vanity embodied; such assertions could only really be the preferences and ends of one person or group disguised as the preferences and ends of "mankind" (or something like that) – that is, they can only be one person's or group's attempts to manipulate others for their own advantage by giving their actions a counterfeit patina of disinterestedness. Even the agent's own statements of ends have to be seen by the agent himself as vanity, as something to which he is not really committed. Not only is the "pure self" alienated from ends of others; he is also necessarily alienated from his own ends. Diderot's portrayal of the nephew, so Hegel argues, perfectly represents this alienated type of character.

The account that this form of life thus gives for itself logically develops from the account of aristocratic men and women of "honor" seeking only the "higher things" into an account of the vanity of all ends, including one's own. The only "grounds" that can count as authoritative are those that pertain to this "pure self" detached from its particular aims and its particular social world. This, of course, does not mean that these alienated agents cease to pursue the ends of power and wealth; it simply means that they can no longer see these as grounded in any particularly good account of themselves and their world. All that counts is the detached self itself that stands above all these ends.

For this kind of alienated agent to maintain any kind of coherent self-identity, therefore, he requires an account of what could be an authoritative reason that does not take as "given" any inherited or natural end. In order to be able to develop such an account, these agents must be able to discover within the self that is prior to all ends a set of ends that is somehow appropriate to that self. The groundless self that is the result of the development of European aristocracy thus must find its grounds, somehow, within itself.[67]

Modern life as Enlightenment and as faith

The aristocratic ethos that had provided a basis for European thought and action led to the collapse of that ethos in a kind of "groundlessness." The logic of the accounts that the aristocratic form of life gave of itself led to a complete skepticism toward the older assertions about there being a natural, discoverable hierarchy of ends that could provide an authoritative "ground" for belief and action. The "groundlessness" of European life that thus appeared seemed to require therefore that some account be given such that the newly "groundless" self could produce its own grounds. Unless the experience of "ground-lessness" was to lead to nihilism (which, as the culture of "vanity," the aristocratic account threatened to do), it had to be able to give an account of itself that showed how self-distancing individuals could discover or invent such grounds within the practices of "detached reflection" itself.

The rejection of tradition and authority. Two different movements emerged out of this experience of "groundlessness": the movement known as the "Enlightenment," with its characteristic emphasis on unbiased thought and observation and on a kind of "passionate naturalism," and a parallel set of emotionalist religious movements – Pietism in Germany, Jansenism and Quietism in France, Wesleyanism in Great Britain – that Hegel generically refers to as "faith." Both movements are characterized by the assumptions that (1) for an agent to know something is to submit it to certain authoritative grounds that are not themselves dependent on any transcendent source for their own authentication (although these authoritative grounds may themselves serve to authenticate belief in something transcendent); and that (2) for an agent to know something is to be in possession of "grounds of belief" that hold universally for all individuals. Each reacted to the "groundlessness" of European life brought on by the self-undermining nature of the aristocratic ethos by seeking universal "grounds" that would therefore not be dependent on the idiosyncrasies of particular cultures.

Although the two movements shared this conception of what are the authentic ground rules of knowledge and action, they nonetheless understood themselves to be unalterable opponents of each other's position. For example, whereas many Enlightenment figures disagreed among themselves about what would be the best or most rational social order, there was widespread agreement among the "republic of letters" and the *philosophes* that whatever form the better social order was to take, it would certainly not contain the past Christian religion in any clearly recognizable form, since that religion represented to them all that was superstitious and backward – in short, represented every practice that looked to discredited transcendent grounds to authenticate knowledge and action. Thus, the Enlightenment *philosophes'* main object of attack was religion in general and Christianity in particular, rather than many other aspects of the social order. Hegel argues that this attack on religion was in a deep sense a matter of self-deception on the part of the Enlightenment, since both the *philosophes* and the objects of their attacks shared a common conception of what it meant to know something, and thus shared a deeper self-identity than either of the antagonists in the dispute could admit to themselves.

Nor, so Hegel further argues, is it accidental that the main object of Enlightenment attack was Christian religion. Enlightenment thought is primarily "negative" in that it raises skeptical attacks on various accounts which European life had given of itself in the modern period. However, the Enlightenment did not raise these skeptical attacks with the purpose of undermining the project of modern life in any way (and returning, for example, to a premodern, medieval past) but rather for the purpose of cleansing modern life of what it took to be beliefs and practices extraneous to its project – namely, those that could not be supported by impartial, unbiased scrutiny (that is, "pure insight"). It thereby hoped to refashion modern life's project into a form more consistent with itself. For this purpose, there was little reason for the *philosophes* to concentrate their attacks on the vanity of court culture, for that culture itself and its chroniclers had already done a good job of exposing itself for what it was. Having become quite conscious to itself about its foibles, court life required no further assistance from the Enlightenment to become even more aware of its own "groundlessness," vanity, and self-undermining nature.[68] Instead, the proponents of the Enlightenment focused on what seemed to them to be their true opponent – namely, that which represented the appeal to spurious transcendent grounds and was therefore the true fount of all superstition: established Christian religion.

As a social movement, the Enlightenment thus understands itself as freeing itself from all authority and tradition and assuming thereby a detached viewpoint on all social practice for the purpose of seeing what could and could not be legitimated by an unbiased look at things. Hegel calls this the standpoint of "pure consciousness" – that is, a standpoint with regard to what counts as knowledge that is free from tradition, authority, fashion, indeed, from all social practice itself. As understanding itself in this way, the Enlightenment thereby *requires* opponents in order to have anything to say at all, since it begins with no content to its beliefs other than that of being unbiased by freeing itself from uncritical, inherited falsity and superstition. The Enlightenment therefore at first emerges as simply aimed at *exposing* the irrational prejudices of authority, tradition, and current practice for what they are.

Although the revival of religious orthodoxy at the end of the seventeenth century had provided many eighteenth-century Enlightenment figures with apt objects for their attacks, the emotionalist religious revival that was unfolding during the period contemporary with the Enlightenment offered them what seemed to be an even better target. This emotionalist movement in religion took its strength partly in opposition to the rationalism of the seventeenth century, and partly in opposition to the stultifying effects of inherited religious orthodoxy itself, but as it began to work itself out it began to take its strength perhaps most powerfully from its opposition to the growing Enlightenment movement itself. By taking emotion to be a "ground" of knowledge, this form of religion was also a form of "pure consciousness" since it held that one can truly know God *only* in an immediate manner (not mediated, for example, by priests or by any sophisticated theological doctrine). It is this set of practices that Hegel calls "faith." Like the Enlightenment, it too understood itself to be free from authority, tradition, fashion, and social practice. Logically enough, both sides understood the other to be the enemy. The Enlightenment, with its stress on "observing reason" as the ground of knowledge, had to understand itself as the complete opposite of "faith," just as the pietist "faith" had to understand itself as the complete opposite of Enlightenment.

Each ("faith" and Enlightenment) therefore contends with the other as to what kind of evidence can count for the *modern* individuals that emerged out of the historical insufficiencies of aristocratic culture. It is in its unremitting opposition to "faith" that the Enlightenment, so Hegel argues, is logically led to develop its own account of what counts for it as authoritative – namely, the principle of utility as a standard of moral action and of knowledge.[69] This point, however, can only be demonstrated by developing the dialectic between "faith" and the Enlightenment as a dispute over what can count as a "ground" of belief for such "groundless" modern individuals.

The proponents of Enlightenment (as "pure insight") understand that the only adequate ground of knowledge is a detached, unbiased view of things and oneself (often but not always identified with reason itself), and that this unbiased viewpoint is universally available to all men and women at all times. The first task for the Enlightenment therefore must be to give an account of why, if "faith" really is the embodiment of irrational superstition, so many people who have to be counted as at least *potentially* rational subscribe to it. Either reason is not universal (in which case the Enlightenment's program would have to come to a halt), or the otherwise inexplicable dimwittedness of the proponents of faith must be explained in terms of some *deception* that has been practiced on them. Echoing the curé Jean Meslier's charge against the church, the enlightened *philosophes* therefore at first could see "faith" *only* as the result of some kind of deception on the part of a lying priesthood in collusion with a corrupt, despotic, and cynical ruling elite that used this apparatus of superstition as a means for maintaining its unfounded despotic rule and for perpetuating the insidious idea that only the aristocrats are "fit" to play a role in political life.[70] The Enlightenment must therefore both attack what it sees as the irrational supporting beliefs of religion and focus on awakening the self-consciousness of those who have been so deceived by getting them to come to see those irrationalities for what they are.[71] This is also held to be possible for such deluded people, since a "pure insight" – the detached, unbiased observation of things or the exercise of the faculty of reason itself – is something within the capabilities of any self-conscious agent, provided only, as Kant puts it in his essay, "What is Enlightenment?", that he obey the injunction, "Have the courage to use your own reason," which means to take himself out of his "self-incurred tutelage".[72]

For both Enlightenment criticism and emotionalist "faith," what counts as a "ground" of knowledge is something available to any individual willing to assume a viewpoint detached from existing social practice, authority and tradition. For the Enlightenment, the possibility of determining what is authoritative for people lies in every individual's ability to assume an unbiased, detached viewpoint on things; for "faith," it lies in the individual's ability to detach himself from the sullying effects of (for example) orthodox theology, to look within his own heart and in the intense emotions encountered there to witness the presence of God himself. Both are contending for the allegiances of modern, "groundless" individuals in that both are offering replacements for inherited tradition and appealing to no grounds that individuals cannot discover within themselves. Therefore, as soon as the Enlightenment begins criticizing the standpoint of "faith," it logically finds its criticisms taken up by the proponents of "faith" since they recognize themselves in them.[73]

Faith" is of course no real match for Enlightenment criticism, since although they share the same general standpoint, the Enlightenment has the advantage in that it self-consciously seeks to *articulate* and to *state* its grounds, whereas "faith" is content simply to *accept* them. From the standpoint of the Enlightenment, therefore, it clearly seems that they have the upper hand. However, for the proponents of "faith," it is their *philosophe* opponents who so clearly seem to be the *real* deceivers that they accuse the proponents of "faith" of being. To them, the Enlightenment must appear as just more ill-founded dogmatism, since it seems that they have simply presupposed or assumed without any good grounds that their "pure insight" gives them better access to authoritative grounds than do the emotions of the faithful.

The development of the Enlightenment helps to support this charge, in that as "pure insight" begins, turns its critical instruments toward itself, it also begins to undermine the certainty of its own claims. Thus, in the unfolding of the Enlightenment, what had been a self-confident reliance on the authoritative nature of reason and unbiased observation became gradually undone and threatened by the arguments and observations of Enlightenment figures themselves, most notably, Diderot and Hume, who alternately pointed out the limits of detached observation and reason within the terms that the Enlightenment thinkers had set for themselves. Nonetheless, although this kind of self-criticism on the part of the Enlightenment helped to underwrite "faith's" claims that the Enlightenment criticism was itself just another dogmatism, even Diderot and Hume, the two great ironists of the Enlightenment movement, still understood themselves to be part of a movement whose unity was based on the idea of (in Hegel's terms) a "pure insight," on the idea that *only* a detached, unbiased approach to things – whether from the standpoint of detached, universalistic rationality, or from the more ironically detached personal standpoints of Hume or Diderot themselves – could provide the authoritative grounds for belief and action.[74] However little solace "faith" could ultimately find in the investigations of Diderot and Hume, their self-skeptical inquiries served to point out that the confidence in "pure insight" is merely the *project* of the Enlightenment, a matter of conviction (a "faith" of sorts, or perhaps just a "taste" for the non-dogmatic) that this way of proceeding will eventuate in knowledge and reform of society.

Indeed, because both the Enlightenment and "faith" share a conception of what certifies something's claim to be knowledge, many of the Enlightenment's criticisms of "faith" can with some logic be rejected by the proponents of "faith." For example, if the Enlightenment says that the object of belief for "faith" is only something that each believer finds in his own consciousness – with the Enlightenment meaning that it is therefore some kind of fanciful projection on his part – the men of "faith" will of course agree, since they have always claimed that they find the object of their belief (God) in the immediacy and intensity of their personal religious feelings. If the Enlightenment charges that they are just mired in their own subjective experiences, and that they need to transcend that merely personal point of view and submit their claims to an impartial test, the proponents of "faith" will point out that only in the immediacy of such religious experience could anyone manage to get at the "truth," to transcend their own limited point of view and arrive at the more universal point of view that God gives them. Both the Enlightenment and "faith" are committed to the idea that grounds of belief cannot be transcendent to the consciousness of the believer and that therefore the believer must be able to find the evidence for his belief within his own consciousness detached from all tradition and accepted social practice.[75]

Just as the Enlightenment does not understand that what makes "faith" seem valid to its proponents is roughly the same model as the Enlightenment's as to what counts as an authoritative "ground" of belief, "faith" too does not realize that it shares that conception with the Enlightenment. Likewise, just as the Enlightenment uses that model to reject the claims of "faith," "faith" uses that model to reject the Enlightenment's charges. The proponents of the Enlightenment argue that they achieve a non-dogmatic point of view in that they submit their claims to a detached, ironical standpoint or to the standards of impartial, universalistic rationality, and they accuse "faith" of only fabricating the purported object of their belief. The proponents of "faith" retort that the immediacy and intensity of their religious experience (which for them evidences the presence and certainty of God in their hearts) is not something they simply concoct: they do not, so they say, "produce" God in their hearts, they only *open* their hearts to him. On their view, *only* through the practices of a religious community that assists in bringing these feelings forth – for example, Count von Zinzendorf's Herrnhut Moravian Brethren, which seem to be the object of Hegel's remarks – can God become present to the hearts of the faithful.[76] For a pietist proponent of "faith," it is essential that the community perform its sacraments and bring forth the appropriate emotions in order for God to appear in the hearts of the faithful – that is the internal evidence of God's being in one's heart. But this appeal to immediate internal evidence cannot force a pietist, for example, to take that as evidence that God is therefore "only" a figment of his feelings. For the pietist, God (as transcendent, *external* to one's consciousness) produces an *internal* state of one's consciousness, but one has the *evidence* fully internally to one's consciousness itself that this state (the particular intense emotions) is indicative of the presence of God himself.[77] The pietist is, moreover, unconcerned with how his accounts of this form of emotional evidence conform to other "scientific" or "empiricist" accounts, since on his own account of what can count as authoritative, these other accounts employ criteria that are fully extrinsic to the real matter at hand, namely, the presence (or absence) of God in the hearts of the faithful.

The Enlightenment's initial charge, therefore, that the trappings and sacraments of religion are a deception foisted on an incredulous populace by a corrupt clergy and unscrupulous nobility is, within what the faithful take as authoritative in determining what counts as knowledge, a silly or maybe even a monstrous idea: Something that is evident, that fits the ground rules of what a community has come to take as authoritative cannot be the result of a *deception* of a group of people by another. What counts as a reason for belief is a function of the "social space," the basic vocabulary, in terms of which these beliefs are formed; the "social space" itself, however, is not a matter of individual *beliefs* in that it cannot be asked for its "grounds" in the same way that we can ask for the "grounds" of a particular belief. One can be deceived by the rulers about various facts – Hegel's example: battles won and lost – but it makes no sense to talk about being *deceived* about the grounds that one has come to take as authoritative for belief and action. One can later turn out to be mistaken, in that what one has come to take as authoritative turns out to be insupportable, but it makes little sense to think that somebody has tricked an entire form of life into accepting that account of itself.[78]

The charge made by some Enlightenment figures that the proponents of "faith" simply anthropomorphize certain feelings and call them "God" (that is, that they are only projecting certain anxieties into a fanciful notion of a deity) can also easily be rejected from within the "spirit" of the proponents of "faith." Some proponents of "pure insight" (for example, Voltaire) hold that all that exists is what can be perceived by the senses, since on the basis of what they take to count as evidence, this is all that there can be said to exist; they thus mistakenly charge the proponents of "faith" with investing statues of Mary or whatever with metaphysical properties. But of course the proponents of "faith" simply reject that as an account of what they experience in their emotionalist rituals when they claim to experience God's love, and they reject it because, once again, they reject it in the same general terms as the proponents of Enlightenment. The statues, the incense, and so on are ways in which the appropriate emotions are called forth, and those emotions bear within them the evidence that God is (or is not) present in the hearts of the believers. In that way, for the proponents of "faith," the Enlightenment is simply an *alternative* (something merely *different* from themselves) and not a genuine *challenge* to their point of view.

Of course, many of the things that proponents of "faith" said played into the hands of the Enlightenment. Those divines who tried to show that "faith" was based on scripture interpreted as an accurate report of past events only opened the door for the Enlightenment charge that since the scriptures are completely flawed, their mythologized accounts of past events cannot provide any grounds for "faith" at all. But, so Hegel argues, this is just a mistake on the part of some divines and does not go to the heart of the issue dividing "faith" from Enlightenment. Indeed, to the extent that the proponents of "faith" try to defend themselves by arguing that the scriptures are an accurate report of what happened (or that belief in miracles would be warranted on the basis of such and such "scientific" evidence, such as a "proof" that the Red Sea had historically actually parted), they are in fact actually abandoning what they have come to take as authoritative and coming to play the game strictly by the Enlightenment's rules (in which case they are also bound to lose). But the argument about the historical reliability of scripture misses the point, since (particularly) the pietist community's practices are based on the idea that such so-called scriptural evidence *cannot* count as underwriting religious practice: What *counts* is what one *feels* in one's heart, not what is written down in either scripture or (especially) in the learned books of theology.[79]

The Enlightenment's premature triumph. These kinds of disputes between the two camps simply obscured that deeper, shared sense of what each had come to take as authoritative – namely, a sense that the individual and the impartial points of view had to be fused into *one* viewpoint, that *individuals* had to be able to find grounds for belief within themselves that would be both authoritative for them as individuals and would be beliefs that they could hold as agents detached from tradition, history and accepted social practice. The aristocratic ethos's collapse and the consequent experience of "groundlessness" – that following the collapse of the traditional conceptions of discoverable natural and external hierarchies of ends – requires that *individuals* construct or find the "grounds" of belief somehow within themselves. The dispute between "faith" and the Enlightenment was thus over what *could* count as uniting these two points of view. For example, various religious communities renounced certain pleasures and forms of property in order to "purify their souls" and make themselves less dependent on the contingencies of their particular desires, and Enlightenment figures claimed that such a renunciation was absurd, arguing as they did that a *genuinely* unbiased approach to life would lead not to religiously based renunciation of earthly pleasures but instead to a "passionate naturalism." However, this so-called unbiased approach ("pure insight") is likewise a practice by which agents could reassure themselves that what they took as authoritative for themselves was not something contingent and idiosyncratic but something that was justifiable in terms of the standards of an ahistorical, detached, universalistic rationality. Each tried to shed what they took to be contingent, idiosyncratic elements that could prevent an individual from assessing the evidence present to him. Thus, from a formal point of view, both "faith" and the Enlightenment seemed to be after the same thing.[80]

In claiming to know God in the immediacy of feeling and emotion, "faith" could only take the trappings of ritual and sacrament to be auxiliaries to what it took to be the true knowledge of God. In claiming that whatever cannot be vouchsafed by "pure insight" is only auxiliary to true knowledge, the Enlightenment does something very similar. The Enlightenment appeals to the self-evidence of certain *thoughts,* whereas "faith" appeals to the self-evidence of certain *emotions.* But because it does this, the Enlightenment, unlike "faith," *must* become self-critical and come to require "enlightened" *theories* about itself. It is thus forced to ask itself how it can within its own general outlook underwrite its comprehensive appeals to "pure insight." The logical way to do this is to take "faith" on its own terms and show that one need not resort to "faith's" reassurance about itself – that the immediacy of feeling is the way in which God produces evidence of his presence in the heart of the believer – in order to speak of the way in which a transcendent deity can underwrite our claims to knowledge and social practices. Thus, to the extent that the Enlightenment attempted to offer any replacement for "faith" at all – and not just move directly to atheism, as did Diderot, D'Holbach, and Hume – it had to advance something like the doctrine of deism. The deist conception of God consists, roughly, in the idea that God created the world to behave in accordance with natural laws (and, correspondingly, also created a set of laws for human nature), and that there was little more to him than that. (Thus, the familiar deist metaphor of God as a clockmaker, creating and winding the universe up, then stepping back and letting it tick-tock on its own. Some Enlightenment figures went further, claiming that the deist God, being by nature beneficent, had thereby also created a beneficent natural order.) Moreover, as the architect of the order we perceive in the universe, God was really *only* knowable through reason and not through "faith." He could therefore be revered as the creator of the universe, as the source of order in the world, or as the wise architect of a beneficent natural order, but there was little point to any fully fledged religious observance having the forms of traditional ritual in order to honor him. There was also no need for any elaborate set of theological doctrines needed to explain or account for the mysteries of the divine since outside of his "watchmaking" functions, there was little more to him; indeed, the scientific study of the laws of his creation through reason and observation were a more fitting tribute to the grand clockmaker-demiurge than were the rituals and teachings of "faith." As the general creator of the universe, the deist God was understood as what was the general object of all religious belief – Christian, Confucian, Buddhist – once one abstracted away from the various external trappings of that object – that is, the various *representations* (*Vorstellungen*) attendant to those religions. Thus, in the wonderfully vacuous title that the Enlightenment gave to him, God is only the "supreme being."[81] Correspondingly, the so-called external trappings of religion – for example, the sacraments, the emphasis on revelation, or the cult of the saints – had to be regarded as superstition, contrary to reason and therefore something to be discarded.[82]

The Enlightenment's conception of authoritative reasons as those that form part of an unbiased, detached observation of things thereby led it to that conception of knowledge that Hegel had called "sense-certainty" in the first chapter of the *Phenomenology*. The dialectically historical account of how the Enlightenment came to hold this conception of what counts as authoritative reasons for belief explains the basis for what the first chapter of the *Phenomenology* is really about; it gives the social basis (the basis in "spirit") for what simply appears as self-sufficient, detached knowledge in the first chapters. On the Enlightenment conception of reasons for belief, we observe individual things whose features are independent of our observing them, and we "get it right" when we unbiasedly report on those things as they really are (as they are "in themselves"). Hegel thus takes himself to have shown how the Enlightenment's conception of "sense-certainty" would necessarily arise as the kind of account that those agents who have emerged from the world of cultivation would have to give of what kinds of reasons they must take as authoritative for themselves. (It is thus distinct from the way in which it is treated in the opening chapter of the section, "Consciousness," in which "sense-certainty" was taken as what appears to be "obvious," something simply taken for granted – without any consideration as to *how* it has come to be taken for granted – by the post-Enlightenment audience of Hegel's own day as constituting "immediate" knowledge.) For the participants in the Enlightenment, this appeal to "sense-certainty" is legitimized by its general claim to rectify the insufficiencies of earlier accounts of what could count as an authoritative reason, and in particular in its remedying the insufficiencies of the accounts supplied by "faith."[83] For the Enlightenment, what is thought to be real comes to be taken as what can be perceived by the senses and then brought into the orbit of rational thought.

What is to count as an authoritative reason for action must fulfill the same criteria as what counts as an authoritative reason for belief: It must be available to "pure insight" – that is, be independent of any kind of special religious revelation and not depend for its validity on any appeal to tradition. The moral order must therefore be discovered from within a "moral science," which itself would be constructed out of an unbiased "observing reason," and whose goal would be to determine which passions actually move people, which can be altered by education and environment, and which kinds of satisfactions are "natural" to people. Detached, unbiased "observing reason" (supposedly) establishes that people are naturally disposed to pursue their own happiness, and even to benefit (or at least display sympathy towards) others. By establishing through its observations what passions and forces actually move people to act, a moral science will thereby also set up what *really* count as authoritative reasons for action (which, of course, will be strongly contrasted with the ascetic, life-denying reasons given by traditional religion).

"Observing reason" moreover also (supposedly) establishes that the natural order is an interlocking system in which various parts have roles to play in maintaining the other parts.[84] The basic order of the world established by "observing reason," therefore, seems to be that of interlocking *utilities,* of the ways in which parts of the natural order are of use to other parts. Human agents have a special place in this interlocking system since their faculty of reason allows them to self-consciously order things for their own utility, which is itself a demonstration that they clearly are the "apex" of the natural world. Since the basic law of the natural order seems to be that each creature acts according to its own utility, and since it also seems to be that the natural order itself is so constructed such that it is a system of interlocking utilities, such that in acting in terms of its utility each creature also contributes to the utility of others, it will therefore seem that to the extent that an agent is to act naturally, he must therefore act in terms of what is of *utility* to him and to others. To do this, he must use his faculty of reason to insure that he acts "naturally" and not under the perverting influence of tradition and superstition (which have obscured the natural passions within each individual). Not surprisingly, a deist conception of a beneficent God creating such an order of interlocking utilities helps to underwrite such a view. An authoritative reason for action therefore must be that of making oneself useful for others and having others be of use for oneself. For the *philosophes,* a reformed religion, which would otherwise be damaging to human welfare, could perhaps be justified in terms of its utility toward leading people to better and happier lives.[85]

The conception of utility allows the type of character embodied by the *philosophe* to appear therefore as an authoritative ideal. The *philosophe* replaces the earlier European figures of the aristocratic knights of medieval lore (with their cult of honor); the witty, vain courtiers that these knights became in the pre-Enlightenment courts of the Bourbon kings; and the slightly later figure of the "gentleman" (or in France, the *honnête homme*), the well-behaved man, neither ostentatious nor vain, who, faced with the "groundlessness" of aristocratic life, is content to take society more or less as it is without himself ever valuing independent thought or trying to bring what he values from his subjective point of view in line with what he takes as authoritative from the objective point of view. The *philosophe* – to be distinguished from the academic "philosopher" – is the man or woman of reason, who organizes his or her life along the lines of unbiased, detached free thought, and who by virtue of exercising reason to keep himself within the bounds of a sensible yet passionate life is a voluptuary without being a debauchee.[86] (It is also, not incidentally, a modern character ideal that includes women as potential participants, in a way that, for example, the ideal of the "gentleman" obviously could not.)

The proponents of "faith" of course found this whole package to be beyond the Pale: The *philosophe* as an ideal of character, his alliance with the deist conception of God (or, worse, with atheism) and his disdainful attitude to both established and emotionalist religion – all this seemed to deny the full emotional significance of life's relation to the deity, to lose all that was real and immediate in the empty abstraction of a "supreme being" who is actually little more than the "Great Clockmaker." However, whatever horror the Enlightenment may have inspired in "faith," the Enlightenment's deist conception of the supreme being was actually only the mirror image of "faith's" conception of God, for "faith's" own conception of God as known only immediately in emotion is an equally abstract conception of the divine. In the dispute between "faith" and the Enlightenment, the Enlightenment is really drawing the logical consequences from "faith's" own practices, pointing out the difference between what the men of "faith" *take* themselves to believe and what they *really* believe (that is, what *follows* from their other beliefs). "Faith" thus finds itself caught up short in that the Enlightenment has only drawn the logical conclusions from what "faith" says, and thus mirrors back to "faith" the kinds of beliefs to which it has, perhaps unwittingly, committed itself. In Hegel's terms, the Enlightenment shows up the "negativity" of "faith" in that it shows how faith's account of what is authoritative on its own terms generates a series of skeptical antagonisms oriented against "faith" itself. Moreover, by eschewing critical thought and relying only on claims about the self-evidence of certain emotions, "faith" finds itself powerless to reply to the Enlightenment criticism of its views.[87]

Hegel charges, however, that although it demonstrated the "negativity" of "faith" by examining it in what it took to be "faith's" own terms, the Enlightenment failed to draw the conclusions of *its own* set of beliefs. The Enlightenment project is (at least at first) primarily negative in that it draws out the way in other practices are blinded by tradition and authority. It thus demonstrates to "faith" that something like a deist conception of God is the kind of belief to which the kind of modern agent who takes as authoritative only those reasons that are legitimated independently of the demands of either tradition or authority would be led. The men of "faith," by throwing off all the claims of orthodoxy and insisting that only the individual believer can know God in his own heart, are committed to the legitimacy of those *types* of accounts that are detached from tradition and authority that the Enlightenment itself gives. However, that the Enlightenment *shares* this conception of what counts as authoritative with "faith" is not a consequence that the Enlightenment, for understandable reasons, itself wishes to draw, since it regards "faith" as its complete "other," as the kind of practice which it wishes to "expose" as thoroughly unenlightened. The Enlightenment instead simply puts its trust in a hypostatized "rationality" or in some commitment to "pure insight," to the idea that a detached, unbiased agent can get to the truth of things. The Enlightenment, that is, ultimately fails to understand its own activity as historical social practice, as a way in which its reason-giving activity has developed out of the insufficiencies of the past as an answer to the crises and complications that past accounts of reason-giving had developed within their own accounts.[88] It instead sees itself simply as "pure insight," the unbiased, detached look at the world as it is; it thus takes itself to be an unbiased discarding of superstition, a paring down to what is "truly legitimate," and as a form of knowing that has freed itself from the obfuscations of irrational authority and illogical tradition.

Both the deists and the proponents of "faith" nonetheless posit a metaphysical entity as lying outside of consciousness (the "supreme being" of the deists, the "God of the heart" of the pietists), and they both accept that it is only in the ways that a detached agent takes himself to be related to this supersensible entity that any really authoritative reasons for belief can be certified. Each simply takes the other's *particular* reasons as faulty, while each accepts the *overall* picture of the *kind* of ground that can count as authoritative for them.[89] Indeed, each sees that only in this kind of modern, detached manner in which agents construct grounds for themselves can individuals find in their reason-giving practices a unity between the personal and the impersonal points of view. The men of "faith" find themselves as individuals affirmed by what they take to be God's presence in their hearts; their sense of themselves as individuals is affirmed by the intense emotional life they find in their religion. The *philosophes* find that the best life is that led in accordance with the kind of detached irony and attention to reason – the exemplary embodiments of which are Diderot and Hume – that allows them to stand outside tradition and to allow the natural passions and impulses in their lives to have their "proper," "rational" fulfillment. Each therefore *takes* his personal, natural life (the emotionality of the pietists and the passionate naturalism of the *philosophes*) to be integrated with the detached, impersonal point of view (that of God for the pietists, of unbiased free thought for the *philosophes*). The proponents of "faith," however, find that they are fighting a losing battle with the *philosophes,* for the kinds of reasons that underwrite their kind of "faith" are equally supported by the ideal character of the "philosophical" life, and they are unable to give an account of why what they *take* to be authoritative for them *really* is authoritative, such that the *philosophes* themselves could come to be convinced.[90]

Both, moreover, take the agent to be related to the world through the *representations* that he forms of that world. The proponents of "faith" take their feelings to be those "inner representations" that put them into an immediate contact with God. This allows the proponents of Enlightenment to argue convincingly that such feelings can be no guarantor that the putative object of the feelings exists, or that such feelings were in fact the way in which a detached agent could actually "get in touch" with the world. But because the Enlightenment shares with "faith" the picture of the agent representing the world to himself, the Enlightenment faces the same kind of problems that it accuses "faith" of having. It finds that it has the same kind of "negativity" (susceptibility to self-generated skepticism) as did "faith." On the one hand, it can deal with its self-generated skepticism about itself by just ironically continuing to believe that its approach is in order even if it must accept large parts of it, as it were, on faith. (One thinks of Hume's ironic skepticism in this regard.) For those for whom such an ironic stance of taking things "on faith" is not satisfactory, the Enlightenment must underwrite its claims to knowledge by positing some metaphysical support for itself – by positing some kind of metaphysical reassurance that its representations really match up with the world, that its authoritative reasons really are authoritative.[91]

The proponents of Enlightenment split over what the nature of this transcendent metaphysical support was supposed to be. On the one side were, for example, D'Alembert and Voltaire, arguing for a deist conception of God as the necessary metaphysical support; on the other side were, for example, Diderot, D'Holbach, and Helvetius, arguing for a conception of the underlying structure as consisting of (a rather metaphysically construed) matter. (The great ironist of the Enlightenment, Hume, is a special case and much harder to classify.) The materialists and the deists both have a structurally similar set of conceptions: Each posits something outside that set of representations of empirical reality (of "sensuous being," as Hegel calls it) as underwriting the adequacy of those representations. The deist conception of God is no more than the vacuous idea of a "supreme being" (a "pure abstraction," as Hegel calls it); but the conception of "matter" held by, for example, D'Holbach, is an equally vacuous idea (another "pure abstraction") endowed with various powers of producing thought within itself and so on. (Straddling

177

the two is the conception of Nature as a beneficent order, a frequently held view in the Enlightenment, according to which the natural tendencies of things if left to their own devices produce the greatest good; this is either seen as something constructed by a beneficent demiurge-deity, or it is simply a way of attributing to "matter" all the features of a beneficent deist God.) Since neither of the metaphysical groundworks that each advances for itself has any sensuous, empirical properties, both conceptions (matter and God-the-Clockmaker) are empty conceptions, posits made by agents trying to account for how their representations match up with things in themselves.[92]

The impasse between the deists and the materialists stems from the attempts by each to underwrite the authority of the *representationalist* view of the relation of agents to the world (the idea that the relation between agents and the world is to be understood in terms of a model of a subject, a representation, and a world-in-itself). The insufficiencies within both views drive the Enlightenment to extend the concept of *utility* beyond being only a criterion of moral *action;* it also becomes a criterion for evaluating *beliefs* – that is, a way of legitimating what the Enlightenment takes to be the ground rules of its critical practices.[93] This use of the concept of utility as a standard for evaluating beliefs allows the proponents of the Enlightenment thereby to jettison the search for a metaphysical validation of the authoritativeness of reason in favor of a "this-worldly" conception of accepting only those reasons that contribute to an increase in overall human utility (taken as pleasure or happiness). Since it is the agents themselves as unbiased, free agents (as participants in "pure insight") that posit these abstractions in the first place, they must ask themselves whether this kind of theoretical activity itself serves any purpose that is intrinsic to the kinds of purposes that a *philosophe* could find to be authoritative for himself. Since the purpose of a *philosophe's* life is to use his reason to think for himself and to indulge his "natural" passions and tastes, it makes sense to ask whether such in a view need be underwritten at all by such conceptions as "Matter" or "God-the-Clockmaker." The idea of "the underlying support for all there is" itself is little more than the idea of the "being" of everything, that human agents determine (or that they categorially "cut up") as they please for their own purposes. The *philosophe,* so it would seem, could fully lead a life of reason and natural passion without having to appeal to any such conception. To the extent that the this-worldly idea of utility is what is basic to this scheme of understanding, the further idea of a metaphysical support for such utility therefore need play no essential role in the life of a *philosophe;* it is apparently not required for the support of the practices that come to be definitive of the *philosophe* as an ideal of character that lays claim supplanting the character-ideals of the heroic knight, the courtier and the "gentleman." (Not surprisingly, the *philosophes* of the late Enlightenment came to see Voltaire, the hero of the earlier generation of *philosophes,* as being somewhat out of touch in his insistence on the necessity of some form of deism, and Voltaire himself also began to change his mind on those issues.)

The observing, enlightened subjects have, however, a particular place in this scheme: On the one hand, they understand themselves to be only parts of nature, of the overall interlocking nature of things, while on the other hand they are the determining power whose "utilities" determine the structure of that order.[94] As a precept for knowledge, the principle of utility holds that we have authoritative reasons for belief only to the extent that the beliefs that are generated out of them contribute to overall human happiness; this itself presupposes that things in themselves are such that following this principle yields knowledge of them. This faith in the knowability of things in themselves by appeal to various claims that are themselves based on utility is, moreover, buttressed by the success of modern Baconian science; modern agents have shown that by constructing theories of the world that answer to their own interests (to control nature in order to satisfy human interests), they are capable of knowing the world as it is (or at least those parts of the world that concern us). For the *philosophe,* the man or woman who lives a free, unbiased life based on a reasonable outlook on the world, this must seem like a reasonable assumption, even if it must remain for him only an assumption (or, perhaps, a postulate).[95] Still, it seems to have no self-defeating "negativity" within it, and, as Hegel puts it, it seems as if the certainty attached to that project that is the "rational self" (self-certainty, as Hegel calls it) and what really is authoritative ("truth") have coincided – that is, that the *philosophe's* project of constructing a form of self-identity centered around the ideals of "passionate naturalism," unbiased thought and free reason is based on an account of himself about whose authoritativeness he is fully capable of reassuring himself. Freed from the weight of the past and of history, the "new person" of "free reason" can look at things in a detached, unbiased manner and put the world into a rational order. Moreover, the Enlightenment seems to culminate in a kind of affirmative humanism: Humans as parts of nature nonetheless seem to have a dignity that transcends being "merely" a part of nature since it is their utilities that count. The Enlightenment project thus *seems* to be complete.

From groundlessness to self-grounding: Absolute freedom and social revolution

The authenticity of desire. The men who come to give an account of their practices in terms of the principle of utility have thereby transformed their account of what underwrites their practices away from both the Enlightenment's very abstract conception of a ground of belief that is the object of a "pure insight" (a detached, unbiased look at things), and "faith's" equally abstract conception of emotions as immediately disclosing God within the hearts of the faithful. Their account of what constitutes an authoritative reason for them instead has to do with what kinds of things satisfactorily satisfy their desires and needs, and there is thus no requirement to posit any kind of metaphysical essence to vouchsafe the rationality of their practices. In the doctrine of utility, modern agents seem to have a criterion that is both impersonal and well suited to them as rational, *desirous* agents, and that transcends any particular practice without apparently involving the postulation of any transcendent "essence" or hypostatized "reason."[96]

The criterion of utility therefore seems to be something that these enlightened agents can affirm for themselves by their own powers of rationality. In the appeal to utility, the "groundlessness" that had seemed to be the legacy of the collapse of the aristocratic ethos is taken to be satisfactorily replaced by a doctrine of "natural" grounds that dictates that agents are to pursue their own happiness and the happiness of others, and that this general end itself is the principle for establishing any hierarchy of ends and is also the highest end in any hierarchy of ends. The principle of utility ("maximize happiness") thus only requires that we determine which desires and which order of desires require satisfaction.

This conception ran up against Rousseau's charge that there can be no straightforwardly natural way to order our desires. If the principle of utility requires us to maximize happiness, and happiness is the satisfaction of desire, then there must be some criterion for evaluating which desires need to be satisfied, since some desires quite obviously conflict with other desires. Moreover, in order to make that evaluation, we need something more than simply the intensity of the desires themselves since equally intense desires can equally conflict with each other. Even if we form "desires about desires" (what are nowadays called "second-order desires"), we still need some criterion for determining which of those "second-order" desires should be satisfied. Either this criterion itself is an ungrounded, immediately known desire, a kind of third-order desire that certain second-order desires be satisfied, or it is not grounded at all but is only the expression of a "groundless" self, a self that orders his desires in terms of how well they express his own "groundless" hierarchy of ends. Since the former conception of an immediately known desire has been discredited, it thus seems that the self that chooses the principle of utility remains a self that is separate from and prior to the ends that the principle of utility claims to establish, however "natural" these ends (such as happiness) seem to be. The detached self is thus completely free – in the sense that it is not limited by any natural hierarchy of ends – to choose this or that ordering of desires, and the problem of "groundlessness" turns out therefore not to have been resolved by the principle of utility at all.[97]

Rousseau (the Enlightenment's great critic from within) saw that the problem for "groundless" agents in such an institutional setting had to be that of determining the way in which the self could be said to *freely* desire something. In his *Confessions,* his doctrine seemed to require a doctrine of the "true self" and the "corrupting influences" of society that distorted that "true self." In that work, Rousseau's description of himself as being in his own heart a truly natural and therefore good self (and also being a "sincere self") provided the basis for an account of how there might be some way in which the self could appeal to some "inner voice," some given, "true self" hidden beneath the socially constructed "false self" that would provide a set of hierarchical ends grounded in "nature." From the standpoint of the *Confessions,* Rousseau's problem was how he, with his desires and his self-proclaimed inability to be hypocritical, could satisfactorily live in a corrupt society. (Rousseau's answer was of course that he could not.) This suggested that the problem therefore was how to bring society in line with the desires of the given, "true self." However, in the chapter on "Reason," Hegel takes himself to have shown that the idea of there being a "fixed self" against which individuals can measure their projects and acts undermines itself as an account of the self; the supposedly "fixed" self turns out not to be so settled since what the meaning of what he *does* turns out to depend on the larger social context of which he is a part. The "gentleman's" account of himself in terms of his own "sincerity" and "fixed character" therefore turns out to require an account of social recognition; the self turns out not to be a settled and fixed thing amidst the world of contingent actions but is itself a project, something that the agent develops as part of his sociality, that is, within the context of "spirit." And the development of spirit – of the accounts that the European community has given to itself to legitimate to itself what it has come to take as authoritative – has led itself to the experience of "groundlessness." The "groundlessness" of the modern self cannot therefore be resolved by any appeal to a "natural" self that supposedly lies behind social appearances.

In *On the Social Contract,* Rousseau advances another idea: The groundless self can only be free in having all its desires structured by a social order that may legitimately be seen by individual agents to be the result of that agent's own free, unconditioned *will,* a faculty that is capable of initiating actions in a way that is radically undetermined by natural or social circumstances. To think of himself as being self-determining in terms of *willing* absolutely freely, therefore, such an agent will necessarily have to purge himself of all those desires that are *merely* given to him by others (for example, in the competition for "honor") in favor of a hierarchy of desires that can be said to have been elected for him by himself. Any social order creates a set of desires within individuals, and it was Rousseau's complaint in his *Confessions* that the corrupt social order had instilled desires in him that were not truly "his own." However, a social order established by such a *will* would shape the individual's desires and establish a socially sanctioned hierarchy of such desires in a way that would be compatible with the individual's coming to see that socially established hierarchy of desires as "his own." The hierarchy of desires would be "conventional" in the sense that it would be given to the individuals by the social order in which they lived and thus might at first seem as if it were imposed on them; but as coming from a social order established by a "groundless" will identical with their own will, it would be compatible with the hierarchy of desires that these individuals would choose for themselves. The central issue for these agents therefore becomes not how the agent best satisfies his *desires,* but the issue of which desires are really independently *his* – that is, which are the result of *his* will. These modern, "groundless" individuals' accounts of what would be authoritative reasons for acting thus move from that of determining what would be of greatest *utility* to that of what it means to be a *self-determining,* independent agent in a fashion that is compatible with all others being self-determining, independent agents, which requires that the agent have his desires formed by a social order that is as much his own will as it is the will of others.[98]

The project of self-determination. In this way, the early modern problem of *groundlessness* created by the self-undermining of the aristocratic ethos becomes transformed into the modern project of individual and collective *self-grounding;* and *modern life* truly begins with this project of self-grounding taken at first as a problem of *absolute freedom* – that is, freedom unconstrained by nature or any unreconstructed, merely inherited social roles. In "absolute freedom" the basic ends of life are instead to be set entirely by the agent himself in a way that is compatible with other agents similarly setting their own ends.[99] What had been for the Greek form of life freedom in terms of "the way things are done" becomes understood by these modern agents to be a completely open question of freedom, since there is no "way things *are* done" that could put any prior constraints on what for "absolutely free" agents is *to be* done. Neither the constraints simply of legal citizenship (as in the Roman form of life) nor the terms of honor in the eyes of others (as in the aristocratic ethos) can put any constraints on "absolute freedom." For these fully modern agents whose conception of the self has to with a conception of it in terms of "absolute freedom," an adequate account of authoritative reasons for belief and action must involve agents determining for themselves what is to be done, unconstrained by "nature," social roles, or history. This is, moreover, not a Faustian account, for the agent at least has a conception, however abstract it might be, of what the object of his willing is supposed to be – namely, willing its own freedom, affirming for himself his own independence – with the individual agent understanding that this willing is to be done from a union of the personal and the impersonal points of view – that is, as being *his own* (personal) willing that is equally an impersonally viewed willing by *others*.

The necessity of unifying the impersonal and the personal point of view (the project of both the "Enlightenment" and "faith") emerges from these general considerations. For a particular agent to be "absolutely free," he would have to legislate fully for himself what desires and directives are to count for him. However, since the particular will of any individual person is always a socialized will, that will cannot, so it seems, ever be "absolutely free." All individuals are socialized, and even the idea of a noble savage apart from society is only the idea of a person trapped in ignorance. Therefore, as Rousseau saw, if there is any true self-determination, then it can only come from a form of *socialization* that itself is (or can be legitimately viewed by the agent as) the result of *self-legislation*. Fully unconstrained willing can therefore only come about in a situation where the socialization of the individual by others is exactly that which the individual wills (or *would* will) for himself. A fully socialized will conceived as continuous with the groundless free will of each individual would be the "general will." "Absolute freedom" can therefore only come about by willing according to such a "general will."

The issue therefore is how the *individual* will is to relate to the *general* will – that is, how the personal and universal points of view with regard to unconditional free willing relate to each other within one agent in terms of the agent's having an integrated view of himself. The older solutions to resolving the split between the impersonal and the personal points of view cannot be satisfactory for these agents. For example, one of the classic functions of the estates, as corporate bodies with "privileges" (the nobles, the ecclesiasticals, and the commoners) was to provide ready-made, given roles for people; but in understanding themselves to be agents embodying "absolute freedom," these modern agents cannot accept any place for the estates in their individual and collective lives. The individuals who take the dictates of "absolute freedom" as authoritative for themselves are supposed to write their *own* scripts for their lives, not to fit themselves into predetermined scripts. They could not in principle be "at home" in any such predetermined scripts, for they could not identify themselves with some role that they had not determined for themselves. In his *Confessions,* Rousseau complains that one of the reasons for his inability to live a non-alienated life in his society was the way in which there was no place for him to be "at home" in such a world; the already determined social roles did not "fit" him, and he was determined therefore to create his own, uniquely individual role. But for the Rousseau of the *Social Contract,* the solution to the problem in terms of the idea of a "true self" is not available, since a conception of "absolute freedom" can presume no such "fixed self" as a benchmark by which to judge such roles. The "groundless self" thus stands apart from such predetermined roles and can identify only with what it can claim to have made on its own.[100]

By understanding themselves as absolutely free – that is, willing according to a "general will" – such agents would seem to be therefore necessarily alienated from any and all ends given to them by particular institutions, except for those cases in which they can see the structure of the institutions as having been determined by their own willing. What is problematic in this conception is what it means to say that the general will actually "does" anything, for it seems to boil down to the claim simply that particular individuals do things *in the name of* the general will. Each of these agents who take themselves to be "absolutely free" can therefore feel "at home" in an action taken by another individual (either purely as an individual or as the representative of some institution) only if each can see the willing of that other agent as fundamentally continuous with *his own* will – that is, see the willing of another as essentially only a manifestation of the general will and therefore continuous with his own willing. But what can count as evidence for such an identity of wills? When a multiplicity of wills in fact contingently coincides on a set of objects, this cannot be, by this account, authoritative evidence for there being an essential continuity between those wills; it can only be evidence that at this time, on this point, the different wills have just happened to coincide, not that they really are "identical" wills. To be able to see the willing of another as essentially continuous with one's own willing requires there to be some mediation between one's will and the other's will such that the agents can see themselves as essentially willing the same thing and not just as accidentally willing the same thing. To the extent, therefore, that the ends assigned to people by given institutions cannot be seen by the individuals as issuing from the general will (that is, the essential continuity between their self-grounding will and the self-grounding wills of others), then it can only be a matter of pure contingency for one agent actually to see the willing of another agent as a willing of the "general will," since whatever the second agent does and whatever ends the second agent pursues can only contingently be continuous with the ends set by the first agent.

To the extent that any given institution claims to be the result of the general will, and it cannot be seen by an individual or group of individuals as continuous with their own self-grounding wills, it must seem to them therefore to represent only the will of the particular group in power or of the majority in the community. Moreover, it seems actually impossible that any such institution could actually embody the general will, even contingently. For example, under the institution of absolute monarchy, it could be claimed that the *person* of the monarch (the actual flesh and blood king) represents everyone, since the country only has a unity by being united under the king; without a king, there would be only the non-unified assortment of the various estates. However, the logic that supported absolute monarchy collapses with the breakdown of the aristocratic ethos and the experience of "groundlessness." Moreover, the successor to the aristocratic ethos – the account of reasons for action in terms of "absolute freedom" – *cannot in principle* accept the king as giving unity to the community, for the "general will" *necessarily* cannot be continuous with the will of *any particular* person (such as the king).

The Revolution and the institutionalization of freedom. As the logic of this position is followed out, it becomes evident that if no *particular* person, such as the king, can represent the country, neither can a particular *group* of people represent the country. As Rousseau saw, only the society *taken as a whole* as the "sovereign person" could possibly represent the country as a whole. Society taken as a whole would therefore be the proper embodiment of the general will, and individual wills would only be "parts" of that "whole."[101] But that entails that in principle no particular *institution* can represent the community as a whole; it must always be the representation of only a section of the community.[102] For an institution to represent *the whole* community, it must represent it *as* a whole. (For this reason, the traditional Estates General in France, as a body consisting of representatives from each of the estates and limited in their representative powers to the mandate from their estates, was an unacceptable institutionalization of "absolute freedom"; in the Revolution, the logic of that situation led it in 1789 to dissolve itself and transform itself into the National Assembly with a claim thereby to represent the country as a whole.)

This conception of the general will is necessarily abstract, since it is conceived as the will of everyone but of nobody in particular. Abstractions, however, do not act; to be effective, they must be embodied in the actions of individual agents. This abstract general will must therefore be articulated into discrete social institutions in order for any of its directives to be carried out. That is, the agents who wish to carry out the general will must form a *government*.[103] (In his discussion of this, Hegel is making a historical reference to the formation within the French Revolution of the Jacobin government with Robespierre as its central figure.) In theory, the individual agent ought to be able to reconcile himself to any action taken by the government as "really" being the product of his own will, but any institutionalization of "absolute freedom" makes that impossible since there *cannot* be any criterion for what counts as *genuinely* willing from the standpoint of the general will – the individual agent can consult neither his own given nature (for there is none) nor any set of inherited public criteria. No particular government can therefore ever claim a fully rational assent to its policies; it will always appear to those who dissent from it as only a victorious *faction,* as in fact the various governments formed during the Revolution began to seem to their opponents.[104]

The logic of the revolutionary terror is not hard to decipher. Individuals are only *parts* of the whole that is the general will (society "as a whole"). A whole must excise those parts that threaten the integrity of the whole, and those threats will come from dissenters who oppose the general will. Therefore, some dissenters may be simply "deceived" about what they really will (that is, what the general will requires) and may therefore be cured by reeducation. Other dissenters, however, actively oppose the general will in that they call out for radically different policies; individually they will something at odds with the general will. However, as being part of the general will (as being a member of society "as a whole"), they have therefore freely and without constraint willed that people such as themselves require punishment to reinforce what the general will itself requires and to maintain the integrity of the "whole" against its "parts." If one augments that idea of freely willed punishment with a utilitarian principle that would justify the sacrifice of some for the greater good of all, then the logical step from there to the guillotine is short. The guillotine of revolutionary justice, Hegel says, is "the coldest and stalest of deaths, with no more significance than cutting off a head of cabbage or swallowing a mouthful of water."[105]

The general will thus turns out to be something different from what it was originally taken to be. The *groundlessness* that faced the early modern individual was to be overcome by a project of *self-grounding* for the fully modern agent. The general will is that conception of a social order whose institutions instill desires in its members that they will be able legitimately to understand as the kinds of desires they themselves would will to have; it will instill desires that they can legitimately see as "their own." By assuming the impersonal, *detached* standpoint of the general will, the modern self, as independent of and prior to all its particular ends, can therefore will ends that are identical with the particular ends it wills from its *subjective,* personal point of view. However, the institutionalization of the general will turns out to lead to an opposite account than that originally proposed for it. The general will becomes represented as a kind of higher-order particular person, who stands over and against the particular personalities of its members, and who themselves come to be seen as "parts" of this "whole" rather than being the *independent citizens* that they had taken themselves to be. The requirements of the general will, that is, must be taken by each of these agents as something *imposed* on them, except for those cases in which for contingent reasons the individual agent happens to identify with the agents doing the directing. In trying to understand the independence of their particular activities in terms of the general will, these agents find that this abstraction has in fact fully alienated them from its requirements, since the content of the general will is simply fleshed out by whatever faction happens to be in control.

The attempt by that form of life that attempts to account for itself in terms of the abstract conception of a "general will" as the realization of the idea of "absolute freedom" generates out of the logic of its own terms a destructive attack on itself in the form of revolutionary terror. The attempt at repudiating a set of established practices as historically insufficient in light of the criterion of "absolute freedom" shows the insufficiencies of the idea of the "general will" as a realization of "absolute freedom." In coming to doubt the satisfactoriness of the conception of a "general will" as the realization of "absolute freedom," the post-revolutionary agents thereby seek reassurance for themselves in clothing the idea of "absolute freedom" in the institutional trappings of what had come earlier – namely, in establishing a new set of practices which have the semblance of the roles and duties of the older, pre-revolutionary institutions.[106] With the experience of the Terror before it, the logic of this self-conception thereby leads to a reinstitutionalization of itself; it realizes that self-understanding in more stable institutional forms in which individuals play particular roles and have determinate duties according to those roles.

Although Hegel does not mention it explicitly, it is clear that he is talking about the consolidation of the Revolution under Napoleon. When Napoleon finally crowned himself emperor, it might have looked as if in fact the Revolution had regressed into what had come before it: aristocratic court life with its ethic of honor and its culture of artificiality. However, the historical experience of the Revolution and the rise of Napoleon himself had made such a return impossible. As the revolutionary French armies with their rational, meritocratic structure of personal advancement through the ranks swept away many of the old regimes of Europe, and as French institutions such as the Napoleonic civil code came to be adopted, modern life's self-understanding as *self-grounding* began to assume concrete, institutional form. Napoleon, the "little corporal," had shown that it was possible for a simple man of ambition and talent to make the hereditary nobles of European life tremble and to change the course of history. The historical role and the "glory" that had previously been reserved for aristocrats was now a possibility for anybody.[107] The possibility of "distinction" and becoming a "true individual" that had previously been thought to be reserved for the aristocracy (for people of "cultivated character") was now seen as a possibility for any ordinary citizen. As the consolidator of the Revolution, Napoleon solidified the institutions of the new bourgeois world even as he, as "Napoleon the emperor," took on the external trappings of the ancient aristocracy.

The form of self-understanding that relied on the distinction between the individual and the general will had been driven to conceive of self-determination as submitting to that which others (the "faction") contingently will. Its failure to provide an institutional setting commensurate with its conception of itself as "absolute freedom" created, however, the possibility of a form of self-understanding that took a willing of things *for oneself* as being equivalent to willing according to a detached, impersonal standard that transcended merely what others *contingently* happened to will. The French Revolution and the Napoleonic aftermath had put Rousseau's thought into practice and had almost completed it institutionally. But, so Hegel argues, it was German idealism that gave this form of self-understanding its full conceptual expression when Kant transformed Rousseau's account of the *volonté générale* into his own conception of the *rational autonomous will*. Kant saw that the abstract conception of a general will needed content, which had to be supplied by some kind of account of self-grounding rationality. In Kant's view, the general will construed as a *rational will* necessarily elects, absolutely freely, certain criteria for itself that in turn put necessary constraints on what it *may* will and which give it certain objects which it *must* will. It seemed, therefore, that the *practice* of the French Revolution as augmented by the *theories* of the German idealists would thereby enable absolute freedom to institutionalize itself in a way that would allow the participants in this new form of life to understand themselves as self-determining agents whose self-determination would consist in their *rationally* willing things. Kantian and post-Kantian idealist philosophy thus provides the outlines of how in the post-Napoleonic world, individuals can become truly self-determining only by incorporating into their conception of themselves the idea of a *rational, reflective morality,* the successor to the historical insufficiencies of the aristocratic ethos and the early stages of the attempt to institutionalize "absolute freedom."

2. Freedom and modern life

The political revolution in France (together with the more or less contemporaneous Industrial Revolution in England) had produced a very different world from the one in which people had previously lived; bringing the early modern world to fulfillment, it created the conditions for the realization of the fully modern world. The revolutions had created a world in which freedom had become a real possibility for all, but it also had created a world of social institutions in which people did not feel immediately "at home," and thereby experienced freedom as a possibility rather than as something already established. However, the new understanding of freedom had also created a new set of possibilities for individuals to make themselves a "new home" in and through their own acts of self-determination and thereby to realize freedom in their own lives.

Through the conception of "absolute freedom," which was put into practice by the French Revolution, individuals came to see themselves not merely as "enlightened" and therefore as unconstrained by nature or history in what they could do for themselves, but also as "absolutely free" in their thought and practices, in fashioning their social institutions, and, in the case of Napoleon, even in making history itself. The Revolution had thus ushered in a new form of self-understanding in terms of which individuals could self-consciously take themselves to be determining what *for them* would count as authoritative reasons for belief and action. In the Greek form of life, the agent had simply *found* himself in a world already "given" to him and in which he was already immediately "at home" and therefore free. The Greeks had a *grounded* form of life; each knew what counted as good reasons for belief and action because of the way in which the grounds of belief and action were embedded in the social practices and institutions that made up Greek life. The *groundlessness* of the early modern world had appeared therefore in stark contrast against the background of the *groundedness* of Greek life. This groundlessness of the early modern world had alienated the agents from their world; there was nothing in that world with which the agents could identify themselves, since it seemed to be contingent and subject to the whims of others. However, in the post-Revolutionary *modern* world, agents understand themselves as having the possibility individually and collectively of determining for themselves the new grounds of that world.

Modern life as *self-grounding* promises therefore to provide a non-alienated surrounding for these agents that will recapture what was appealing in the Greek spirit without succumbing to its failures.[108] The Greek conception of freedom, which for them was possible only within their form of *Sittlichkeit* (in their social sense that such and such is the "way things are done"), thus seems realizable in the modern world in an individualistic fashion, without the "givenness" that Greek *Sittlichkeit* demanded and allowing for the kind of detached reflectiveness that "absolute freedom" seems to demand. The Greek conception of freedom embodied three items: The individual was free because (1) he knew *what* it was he was doing (his actions were thus immediately intelligible to him), (2) he knew *why* he was doing it (he could cite the socially sanctioned reasons for the action), and (3) he *identified* himself with those actions (since he found his self-identity fully constituted by the social roles that he played). The post-revolutionary modern world seeks to realize this Greek conception of freedom in an individualistic form that dispenses with the Greek understanding of freedom as residing in the acceptance of given social roles. "Absolutely free" individuals are to determine *for themselves* what they ought to do, and in doing so fashion a rational world for themselves in which they can once again find themselves "at home." Greek freedom can thus be combined with the self-grounding post-revolutionary project; instead of simply discovering their grounds in the social world around them, modern post-revolutionary individuals must determine their grounds for themselves. It is this demand that leads the early stages of modern life to try to substitute modern reflective *morality* for what seems to be the all too narrow and insufficient sense of Greek *Sittlichkeit*.

German idealism and the Revolution

The issue then for the post-revolutionary world was in many ways similar to the three issues that Rousseau had raised for the immediately pre-revolutionary world: (1) what is it to be a self-determining agent?, (2) how can self-determining agents live together in a manner compatible with the self-determination of each and in which each recognizes the other as self-determining?, (3) what does it mean to say that an agent sets his own ends or that a people's social and political life is to be set by those people as freely binding themselves together, as taking upon themselves only what they freely elect to take upon themselves? Or, to put it more succinctly: what would it mean to *realize* the principle of freedom in the post-revolutionary world? The French Revolution had brought about the social conditions for the modern form of self-understanding as "absolute freedom," but it had been unable to provide the requisite account of itself that would enable it to understand what it was doing. Because of this failure to provide an adequate account of itself, it could not affirm for itself whether it was indeed a genuine alternative in history, a repeat of the past, or simply a mistake. German idealism took up this task and self-consciously endeavored to provide in *thought* what the French Revolution was to have done in *practice:* (1) to provide an account of what it would mean to realize freedom in the modern world by showing what it meant to be the kind of self-determining agent that had begun to take shape in that world, and (2) in doing that to show that the French Revolution was the necessary social movement to develop the institutions that would provide answers to the "groundlessness" of modern life.

This was neither an idle, foolish, nor arrogant task for the German idealists to assume for themselves.[109] Many contemporaries doubted whether the French Revolution's understanding of the possibilities for humanity were in fact defensible. (Edmund Burke's famous criticism of it as failing to understand the "organic" nature of social institutions and the way in which its idea of self-determination was really a chimera if not an evil is only the most prominent example.) Moreover, the forces of reaction, which were temporarily to triumph in 1815 at the Congress of Vienna, had already begun formulating attacks on the very ideas of "freedom" for which the Revolution had been a catalyst. The idealists therefore saw themselves as providing the necessary account of the revolutionary ideas of freedom and social life that would not only legitimate the Revolution but would also provide the tools for a valid criticism of its excesses.

Morality and modern life

The new form of self-understanding that the idealists articulated as completing the Revolution was that of *morality,* the idea that individuals spontaneously set their own ends both personally and collectively (to distinguish it from *Sittlichkeit,* ethical life, the "way things are done"). The idea of modern "morality" is bound up with the modern conception of what is authoritative for belief: that nothing can count as a good reason for belief unless we collectively or individually *come to take it* as counting and determine for ourselves what criteria are authoritative in adopting such reasons. In the Greek form of life with its "grounds" in "the way things are done," the agent simply acted in terms of a shared set of social self-understandings that he found present before him and into which he fit himself; in "morality," how-ever, the agent is *spontaneously* to set his own ends and *spontaneously* to determine what is to count for him as an authoritative reason for belief. "Morality" therefore also claims to be the practical realization of the task implicit in the early modern conception of "Reason": to provide a self-justifying, autonomous account of itself that can legitimately claim to com-plete the development of the kinds of accounts that the various "formations" of modern self-consciousness have given of what can be authoritative for them.

The development of German idealism in this direction is bound up with the other German reaction to the Revolution – namely, the religious move-ments associated with the historical development of German national con-sciousness in light of what were seen as various historical denigrations by the French. The pietist movement – the earlier German religious movement based on a view of the immediacy of feelings of faith and opposition to established orthodoxy – played a role in shaping this reaction to the French. With its stress on the necessity of turning inward and living a pure and authentic Christian life, Pietism became a focus for this nationalist sentiment against French culture. German clergymen and theologians began arguing that the Germans should eschew the temptations of French cultural and intellectual life in favor of being true Christians – that is, of keeping their German hearts and minds pure.[110] In Hegel's eyes, what Kant clearly saw was that the emphasis on duty in Pietism (with Pietism's rejection of authori-ty and tradition and its very modern emphasis therefore on the individual's assumption for himself of his duties) could only be adequately understood if it were to be linked up with the secular modern accounts of the subject as "absolutely free." (In Hegel's eyes, Kantianism amounts to the attempt to coherently combine Rousseau's conception of the absolutely free subject with the pietist conception of self-resolved duty – that is, it was the attempt to combine two different accounts that modern life had come to accept because of the historical insufficiencies of earlier accounts.) The Kantian explanation of what Hegel calls the "moral worldview" takes up those ideas of duty and obligation that had come to play such a central role in German thought, and gives a better account of them by appealing to a form of "absolute freedom" than they could have given on their own. Kant's account thereby transformed those ideas from being remnants of a pre-modern past into authentic expres-sions of a modern life.[111] It also seems to be Hegel's point that the defects of Kantian ethical thought, whatever its brilliance, are precisely the defects of the post-revolutionary "moral worldview" as such. (Whereas Hegel earlier treated Pietism as the mirror opposite of Enlightenment – as "faith" – he takes it now in terms of the ways in which it embodies and structures the post-revolutionary "moral worldview."[112])

The modern agent understands himself as determining for himself his own hierarchy of ends instead of understanding that hierarchy to have been set for him by nature. For this to be possible, the agent's *self* must therefore be free from any outside determination that he himself does not freely elect to count as a determination *for him*. Nothing can count for him as a good reason for belief unless he *takes it* as counting *for him;* nothing is to count for him as a good reason for acting (as constituting a duty for him) unless he *takes it* to be a duty. Moreover, the criteria for this taking something to be a good reason must come from "within" him, be spontaneously generated by himself. According to this view, it would seem to follow that such a *moral* agent could therefore be spontaneous only in *opposition* to purely "natural" determination. If the agent is to be self-determining, to be setting his own ends, he must somehow be subject not to a *natural* law (which would come from outside himself) but to a *self-imposed* law.

Kant claimed that it was the nature of the representations (*Vorstellungen*) that such a moral agent formed "within" himself that was the key to the proper account of the "moral worldview." Kant argued that something can be a representation only if it conforms to the conditions under which any representation can be *for* an agent, which, as Kant claims, is the spontaneous accompaniment of the "I think" with all one's representations. For representations to be *my* representations – to be the representations that *I* think – *I* must *take* them as mine. Taking these representations as mine is equivalent to ascribing them to one consciousness, a single "I," to me. This act of ascribing all my representations to myself is, however, "original" (as Kant calls it) – that is, "groundless" – in that no evidence external to the I's own self-ascribing activity is possible for determining what counts as the same "I." For natural objects of experience, there clearly can be such independent evidence: To know if the dog in the window is the same dog that I saw yesterday, I require some independent evidence for testing the claim. In the case of the "I," however, there is nowhere else to turn except to the "I's" activity of self-ascription itself. To put it another way: There can be no independent knowledge of the "I" as the *subject* of experience except the activity by which the "I" *makes itself* a subject. The "I" constitutes itself into being the subject of experience in its act of taking itself as the same "I" that is aware of different representations. It "synthesizes" itself, as Kant puts it, in taking itself to be the same "I" that is aware of X and is aware of Y – it is the "synthetic unity of apperception."

This "synthetic unity of apperception" is, moreover, a necessary condition of all experience. For there to be a *single* complex thought or a single complex intuition – that is, not just separate thoughts or intuitions of X and Y and Z but a single complex thought of (XYZ) or a single complex intuition of (XYZ) – there must be a *single* subject. If there were a non-unitary subject, there would only be different thoughts or different intuitions (for example, Johann would experience X, Paul would experience Y, and Georg would experience Z). This single subject is possible, however, only if the subject identifies itself as the *same* subject that has *different* experiences – that is, identifies the subject that experiences X as being the same subject that experiences Y. This identification of the subject that experiences X as being the *same subject* that experiences Y is *synthetic* in that it is not a matter of pure logic (that is, it is not an "analytic truth"). As necessary and as having no further grounds outside of itself, this self-identification of itself as the same subject is *self-grounding*. Or, to put it another way, there can be *no independent evidence* that the subject who experiences X is the same subject that experiences Y outside of the "synthetic" activities of that subject itself. The "synthetic unity of apperception" is therefore the necessary, self-grounding condition of all experience.

Something can therefore count as a representation for me only if it conforms to the conditions under which I can ascribe all these representations to one consciousness (that is, the conditions under which I can identify myself as the same subject of different experiences). Kant argues that these conditions are the "categories of the pure understanding," which he takes to be the rules of the logical form of judgments. The justification of the categories' claim to being necessary to any possible experience is that they express the necessary, rational rules for combining representations into the kinds of unities that can count as the representations belonging to *one* subject, to the synthetic unity of apperception. The categories, that is, are the principles that enable a self-conscious subject to ascribe its representations to itself.

These considerations about the subject as the "self-grounding ground" of knowledge also apply to the subject as the "self-grounding ground" of practices. Just as an agent spontaneously (groundlessly) takes given representations to be his own according to the self-generated rules of combination in logic, he spontaneously elects to have certain representations count for him as being sufficient motivations for action according to the self-generated rules of logic. The agent constitutes himself as a free agent by acting on his own *representation* of law, by electing for himself which representations of a rule of action are to count for him as the determining motives of his actions. The rational self is therefore self-constituting in both its claims to knowledge (although in knowledge it is also restricted to combining what can be given to it in sensuous intuition) and its claims to what counts as definitive reasons for action. Since an agent acts by directing himself towards certain ends, a self-determining agent must set his own ends and not have them set for him either by his social conditions (by tradition or authority) or by "nature." As self-constituting, the practical agent therefore sets his own ends and elects for himself what is to count as a rational hierarchy of ends.

This might make it seem as if there would therefore be two selves within each agent: a rational self that sets its own ends and a natural self that has its ends set for it by nature. But the natural self and the rational self do not inhabit two *worlds,* separate from each other; they are united in *one self,* and thus are only different *aspects* of the same self; they represent the same self described in two different ways – as a rational moral agent and as a natural organism.[113] To put it differently: the rational self and the natural self are two ways in which the agent takes himself to be. This unity of the natural self and the self-constituted self cannot therefore be itself a natural given but must be itself generated out of the rational self's own activity. The rational self combines its *self-given* determinations (the categories of knowledge, the pure imperatives of action) with its *externally given* determinations (intuitive sensibility in knowledge, various desires and impulses in action) into *one unity,* the unity of the embodied, thinking, acting agent himself. The agent as sensuous and the agent as self-synthesizing are *one* agent, and the identity of this agent is constituted by the activities of the rational agent himself. Nonetheless, these aspects of the unified self – the realm of rational, self-determining human agency and nature – are "indifferent" to each other in that the determinateness of one does not play a role in establishing the determinateness of the other.[114] Sensibility *cannot* play a role in the self-generated determinations of thought nor in the self-generated duties of action, and the self-generated determinations of the subject *cannot* play a role in the determinateness of the given elements of experience and desire.

If the post-revolutionary world is best articulated in the "moral world-view," that worldview itself is best articulated in the terms of some conception of *transcendental, subjective idealism,* of a view that the determining ground of appearance is "rational subjectivity," which itself is beyond appearance, posited in order to account for the determinateness which appearance is taken to have. That is, "absolutely free" subjects constitute a "world" for themselves by combining their representations in certain rule-guided ways; they thus occupy a special place in the world, since they are "points" outside of that world whose activities constitute the world into the shape it has. As such, they have a status and a worth (a "dignity" but no "price") that no other entity in the world can have. Given the way in which the post-revolutionary agents had come to understand themselves, subjective idealism therefore seems like the necessary explanation and articulation of who they had come to be. An idealist agent is "absolutely free" and can generate laws for his own actions. Each agent determines for himself what he is to do, but his determinations will essentially coincide with the determinations of others, since each is imposing the same rules of logic and rationality on themselves. The transcendental idealist account thus reassures us that the French revolutionaries who took history into their own hands were not deceived about what they were doing but were actually realizing in practice what the transcendental idealists took humanity to have always been about: the realization of freedom.

3. Rational autonomy: the moral worldview

Morality and nature

The moral worldview, whether in the form of Pietism or Kantianism, takes self-determined or self-resolved *duty* as its central conception. Duty is to be contrasted with all other motives that an agent might have, and an agent is to know his duty and to do his duty by consulting something within himself. No appeal to authority (especially theological authority) or tradition can legitimate this duty; the agent must elect it for himself on grounds that he finds "within" himself. For pietists this is done by consulting one's "heart"; it is something immediately known. For Kantians, one cannot immediately justify a rule as constituting a duty (that is, by consulting one's heart); one must rationally universalize one's maxims (the rules one gives to oneself that govern one's actions) to see if they are suitable for all rational beings. For both, the genuinely "moral" agent acts only out of a motive of duty, not for the sake of personal happiness; each seeks not necessarily to *be* happy but to make himself *worthy* of happiness. Without this moment of willing for oneself, of having one's *freedom* consist in determining for oneself both what one's duty is and what will be sufficient to move one to act, there can be no *morality* (in this modern, post-revolutionary sense) at all.[115] In the aristocratic ethos, the agent's duty is determined by externally set standards of honor, and he fulfills his duty only when he has honor in the eyes of others. However, in morality the agent wills his duty on the basis of a ground that he himself authenticates for himself, and he fulfills his duty in terms of criteria that he sets for himself. In the aristocratic ethos, the agent alienates himself to conform to the standards of honor in the eyes of others; he takes others' point of view as determinative for the kinds of reasons that are to count for him, and his personal freedom is thereby given over to others. In morality, on the other hand, the individual takes himself to be doing only that which he as an individual can authenticate for himself, and his freedom consists in this kind of self-authentication. Where he is correct in his assessment of his duty, his individual point of view is at one with the impersonal point of view so that what he chooses for himself is also universal. Thus, the moral agent is free only in his abstracting away from all particularistic aspects of himself.[116]

Although one can determine one's will to conform to one's duty, one obviously cannot determine one's natural constitution. Whether an individual is happy depends on his natural constitution (that is, it depends on what things contingently happen to give him satisfaction), and the individual's natural constitution is not something for which he can be responsible. Since the moral agent can only be responsible for those ends that he sets for himself, he cannot be responsible for those ends set by his natural constitution. Therefore, whether he achieves happiness because of what he does cannot lie within his power, and, within the conditions of the account given by the "moral worldview," the individual cannot therefore expect to find happiness in recognizing and doing his duty.

By the very terms of this account, though, it would seem that the individual would actually find satisfaction and happiness in doing his duty because the agent would find his self-conception affirmed in doing his duty. In doing his duty, he would be putting his conception of himself as a *"moral* agent" into practice; in Hegel's terms, he would be "actualizing" his self-conception. Moreover, since it is only as being willed *by him as an individual* that his duty can count as a duty (both for the Kantian and for the pietist), it should also be the case that his individual dispositions and sentiments (part of his "natural" makeup) would be involved in his willing to do his duty.

While this at first seems consistent with the "moral worldview," it also clearly seems to clash with that part of the moral worldview that holds that the "natural" aspects of the agent are indifferent, if not antagonistic, to his recognizing and doing his duty. In the account that the "moral worldview" at first gives of itself, it requires that the individual perform his moral duty *anonymously,* that he put aside his own idiosyncratic "natural" desires in favor of what the more generally valid duty demands of him, even though the grounds of that duty are to be discovered or constructed from "within" one-self. To claim something as one's duty cannot therefore involve an appeal to anything like the "natural passions tempered by reason," as some Enlighten-ment thinkers would have had it. It must involve knowing and doing one's duty *independently* of one's personal passions and natural dispositions. Yet to the extent that it is the *individual* who is to be the arbiter of what his duty is, the individual will find his self-conception and particular dispositions at work in the determining and carrying out of his duties. The "moral worldview" thus seems to have an antinomy located within its conception of itself.

This incorporation of the "natural individuality" of the agent into his moral willing exhibits the initial "negativity" of the "moral worldview" in that it shows how the "moral worldview" produces out of its own account of itself a set of skeptical doubts about itself. On the one hand, the genuinely moral agent does his duty independently of any inclinations or natural desires (which would otherwise compromise his freedom and which in any event can have nothing to do with establishing his duties). On the other hand, it is also a requirement of the way in which the "moral worldview" has accounted for itself that in acting morally the individual moral agent acts on reasons that he as an individual legitimates for himself. However, since individuality is insep-arable from one's natural characteristics, and happiness is the satisfaction of those desires that have been elected by an individual in terms of his self-conception (which itself is groundless), an individual performing his duties and thereby finding his self-conception as a moral agent affirmed in doing so will also find his happiness in performing his duties.[117] Whereas in the "moral worldview," happiness is supposed to pull us in one direction, and morality is supposed to pull us in another direction, it would nonetheless seem that a truly moral agent *thinking of himself* as a truly moral agent would be pulled by his duties in the direction of happiness. Yet the "moral worldview" holds that nature is indifferent to morality, which is only a matter of the individual's recognizing and doing his duty independently of whether "indifferent nature" arranges for him to be happy in doing so.

Consequently, in terms of the account that the "moral worldview" gives of itself, nature is taken as *necessarily* being indifferent to morality and is conceived in a way that implies that it cannot *actually* be indifferent. Thus, Hegel claims, the "moral worldview" must *postulate* that happiness and mo-rality are in harmony with each other in order to sidestep skepticism about its account of reasons for action.[118] The references to moral postulates in the *Phenomenology,* of course, has overtones of Kantian ethical theory and might suggest that in making those references, Hegel is alluding to some very specific Kantian texts. Kant, for example, notoriously claims that we must postulate the existence of God in order to account for how happiness could be disbursed to the virtuous. However, this specifically Kantian postulate (along with some others) is something that Hegel simply ignores in these passages, since he is not concerned with explicating Kantian texts at all but only with articulating what he takes to be the "moral worldview" for which he understands Kant to have been trying to give an account. Hegel's own postulate indeed ignores Kant's idea that we must postulate the existence of God to account for how happiness and morality could be in harmony. Furthermore, Hegel goes beyond Kant's idea that we have a duty to *strive* to achieve the highest good (the union of virtue and happiness) and instead argues that Kant did not go far enough: The "moral worldview" must postulate a harmony between nature and morality not as an end toward which we must strive but as an end already presupposed in the idea of the "moral worldview" as such.[119] The "moral worldview" is such that it both *denies* that there can be anything other than a purely contingent harmony between morality and happiness, and at the same time its account of moral action *requires* there to be something like a union of morality and natural happiness. The various techniques that Kant (or, for that matter, Schiller) uses to try to reconcile these claims are, for Hegel, doomed from the outset, because they can only be attempts to forestall the "negativity" of the moral worldview itself, to falteringly reassure the agents who hold to this account that the reasons they take to be authoritative really are in order. To do this, it must "postulate" all kinds of things as existing in order to make the account even passably work. Nor is he concerned about whether a more charitable reading of Kant could eliminate some of these problems in the Kantian texts (that is, whether a carefully articulated revisionist Kantianism could sidestep some of these charges against it). His point is not that there is no way in which to read more charitable doctrines concerning virtue and happiness into Kantian theory, but that any suitable modification of Kant will take Kant away from *Kantianism* and more in the direction of *Hegelianism,* a result that Hegel himself would of course find completely satisfactory. Whether one still calls it "Kantianism" would be irrelevant; in any event, it would no longer embody the "moral worldview."[120]

Nature appears again as a problem for the "moral worldview" in terms of the internal constitution of the agent himself, that is, in terms of the relation between his sensuous makeup and his rational character. The problem is roughly the following. For the "moral worldview," the moral agent must act out of duty, out of "pure" motives; yet this view must also hold that the agent has other than pure motives – namely, sensuous motives. Therefore, no matter how it is formulated, the "moral worldview" will always be burdened with the problem of accounting for how one set of motives (the pure motives of duty) override another set (the sensuous motives), given that it will seem that the agent always has two competing sets of motives. This is the problem of how the "universal," the impersonal point of view, which is taken as determining the "pure" duty, is to be reconciled with the individual, the personal point of view, in an account of what any given agent can reflectively and rationally take to be an authoritative reason for acting.

The "moral worldview" will thus be driven to something like the following account. It will identify the "non-pure" motives with the sensuous motives, and the "pure" motives with those that abstract away from the concrete ends of the non-pure motives (such as Kant's idea of the motive of respect for the moral law being sufficient to determine one's action). The sensuous aspect of the agent takes the form of various natural inclinations and drives that set their own "natural" ends and that may well conflict with the ends set by reason (whatever they turn out to be). The moral agent cannot take his duties from his passions; he must derive his duties purely, by recognizing them as God's law within his consciousness, or by recognizing them as universalizable maxims.

However, the two ends (the "natural" ends of the passions and the "pure" ends of reason) are each representations in *one* consciousness, as Kant's arguments about the synthetic unity of apperception establish. Moreover, this *one* consciousness is itself self-grounding; it is the "pure" aspect of consciousness ("thought" or, as Kant would put it, "the understanding") that unifies the pure and sensuous representations into one consciousness.[121] Morality consists in willing and acting according to those pure representations and in having the ends of action be determined by the pure representations rather than the natural representations. Indeed, the moral agent is precisely that agent who manages to have his actions determined by one kind of representation rather than another; indeed, what characterizes him as *moral* is that his duties (determined by the pure representations of law) prevail over his inclinations. (As Kant puts it, respect for the moral law alone is supposed to be a sufficient incentive to act.) To have his actions determined by something other than *pure* representations would mean that the agent would not be free and self-determining as the "moral worldview" holds that he must be. Thus, just as the thinking self *becomes* – or, in Hegel's language, as the self "actualizes" itself as – a thinking self by bringing the various representations into the unity of consciousness, the moral self becomes a moral self only by unifying its pure ends in a consciousness that both "rises above" and stands in opposition to those ends set by our natural impulses and inclinations.[122] If the agent acts out of "mixed motives" (acts out of desire for a natural end *and* out of a sense of duty), then the agent will not be moral; to be moral is to act solely out of a sense of duty. Yet all motives must be "mixed" since the agent is a natural individual and a dutiful (or, for Kantians, rational) self.

Since the empirical (sensuous) motives can conflict with the pure motives, the pure self must therefore not only elect as his motive the "pure" law of duty; he must apparently *eliminate* the other motives that have to do with sensuous ends so that only the "pure" motive can be determining for action. Since all actions on the account given by the "moral worldview" seem to have two motives – the pure and the sensuous – it would seem to follow therefore that for the agent to will something solely out of the motive of duty, the sensuous motives would have to be completely set aside.

However, the agent *cannot* simply set aside the sensuous motives; they are representations from his "natural" self that must be unified with the "pure" representations within *one* consciousness. To eliminate the sensuous motives from one's consciousness might make one into an angel, but it cannot make one into a moral agent because *moral* agents must always have the opposition of duty and desire present before them. Indeed, that opposition between universal duty and personal inclination is what makes them *moral* agents in the first place, since the *freedom* of the moral agent consists in determining for himself independently of any natural impulse what principles are to guide his maxims, and something counts as moral only to the extent that it is a realization of freedom for him. For other types of agents, this of course would not be a problem. For a Greek, *ethical* agent – an agent in *Sittlichkeit*, the social state where duties are a function of "the way things are done" – desires and duties coincide, and he finds his duties in the social roles with which he immediately identifies. Moreover, the Greek individual finds himself to be free in performing his duties since he both understands what he is doing and he identifies with it. In the aristocratic ethic, one's duties come from what is necessary to achieve honor in the eyes of others, and this is compatible with letting oneself be guided by the suitable "aristocratic" passions. The *moral* agent, however, must determine his duties for himself, and these duties cannot come from his passions, his social roles, or be motivated by the recognition that he gets from others. Instead, the moral agent (within the terms set by the "moral worldview") must have the right motives to be a *free, moral* agent at all.

Duties and motives

If all empirical actions have empirical motives (that is, sensuous motives), then there will always be potentially two different accounts of the same action. Moreover, the two types of motives are supposed to be in opposition to one another such that following one motive realizes freedom whereas following the other motive does not. Yet, as oppositions within *one* consciousness, they must be such that the account of the agent's empirical motives cannot make the account of the agent's pure motives impossible (for that would entail the agent could not be free). The "moral worldview" must therefore also postulate that sensuous motives in an individual *conform* to his pure motives such that they do not override the pure motives, or such that they do not make the dual account impossible. Since both types of motives are always present, and they are taken to be in opposition to one another, it would therefore seem that the moral agent has the always unfinished moral task of shaping his natural self so that his sensuous motives are brought into line with his pure duties. But if the agent is to act morally at all in the first place, it would also seem that he must be constituted so that his sensuous drives and his pure motives are already in line with each other; otherwise, the account of his action would be skewed since he would always have to give two competing accounts of what he was doing. Thus, the "moral worldview" must hold that the pure and the sensuous motives are in opposition to each other, and that the agent has the *task* of bringing them into conformity with each other; and that the sensuous motives and the pure motives are *already* in sufficient conformity with each other so that the agent can act in terms of the pure motives in the first place.

The general problem of the pure duties versus the non-pure sensuous duties reappears in the issue of how one derives specific determinate duties from the more general duty. There are cases involving trust, loyalty, deception, bravery, justice, duties to friends, duties to the state, professional duties, and so on.[123] In contrast with the universal "pure" duty (whether it simply be the duty to do that which is right or the more sophisticated Kantian injunction to act according to those maxims that can at the same time and always be willed as universal law), the specific duties are diverse and complex and have to do with various circumstances that are difficult to elaborate outside of the particularities of the case. Thus, the certainty with which an agent can approach one of these particular duties cannot be at the same level of the certainty with which he approaches his pure duty. What nonetheless counts as making a specific maxim or claim into a duty is that it be a *specification* of the more general, "pure" duty; it cannot be a duty that is simply more specific in its content and indifferent to the general duty (however the general "pure" duty is conceived). That is, it cannot be another duty *contrasted* with the pure duty; rather, it must be distinguished only by having more specific content than the universal, "pure" duty.[124]

The moral agent must see the specific duties and the general, "pure" duty in different ways. To him as a *moral agent,* the pure duty is absolute, not relative to anything else, and it is known with certainty. (The "pure" duty is taken, in Hegel's words, as something "in and for itself," not relative to anything else.) But to him *as an individual* with limited knowledge, any specific duty cannot carry with it the same certainty, since, given his limited knowledge, what *seems* to be his duty may in fact not be his duty, and thus it cannot be as certain. (A particular agent can, for example, simply be mistaken in his belief that he has a specific duty of loyalty to a particular person.) Yet *whatever* his specific duty is, he knows that it is in fact not relative but just as binding on him as the "pure" general duty.[125]

The issue for the moral agent is then how he reconciles what he takes to be the certainty, obligatoriness and even sacredness of a specific duty with what *to him* must appear as its relativity and uncertainty. This is all the more difficult if the "pure" duty is conceived formally, as Kant does in insisting that the categorical imperative must abstract away from all determinate ends. But however it is conceived, the "pure duty" has a different relation to the individual agent than the more specific duties. The individual can only view those duties from what to him must count as his *personal* point of view, no matter how detached he may be from the particularities of his situation.

To conceive of duties that are absolutely valid "in and for themselves" but which cannot be known to be valid from any finite individual's point of view is, however, to assume that there is an impersonal point of view from which these duties could be known. This idealized impersonal point of view is thus another necessary postulate of the "moral worldview."[126] Kant, for example, notoriously posited God as the divine legislator, and later proponents of the "moral worldview" postulated hypothetical "sympathetic observers." Indeed, given the *complexities* involved in going from the general pure duty (such as the categorical imperative) to the specific duty, it would seem that only a divine agent could possibly be in the position to manage those complexities well enough to be able to infer from the general, pure duty to the specific duty.

Hegel's point is that these incoherences and paradoxes are not accidental features of these types of accounts, since they are the kind of things to which they are inevitably led by virtue of the kind of account they must give of what counts as an authoritative reason within the "moral worldview." For example, in Kant's case, the posit of a divine legislator seems to be at odds with Kant's own stress on autonomy; if only those laws that have been autonomously willed by an agent count for that agent, then a law commanded by God is not a law that has been willed by that agent, and hence cannot count for him.[127] Kant is, however, led to this view because he has such difficulty deriving specific content from his formal categorical imperative, and he must hold that the specific duties are obligatory even if they are uncertain. Indeed, the need for Kant to posit God as the holy lawgiver is the same need for Kant to posit God as that which will bring together virtue and happiness; it is part of the self-undermining (in Hegel's terms, self-negating) structure of the general "moral worldview" which pushed Kant in those directions.[128] (Again, Hegel's point would also be that any attempt to rectify this through a revisionist description of Kantian philosophy will inevitably lead Kantianism away from the "moral worldview" toward something more like Hegelianism.)

The *idealized* point of view that would know all these duties with equal certainty is thus that formed by imagining the unity of the impersonal and the personal points of view. The conception of this idealized point of view involves the conception of knowing things in a detached, impersonal manner that would also be perfectly compatible with the kind of personal knowledge of the intricacies and complexities of life that seems to be available only to embodied, socially situated agents.[129] But it is very questionable whether this idealized subjective/objective point of view, within the terms set by the "moral worldview," could be available to actual agents. On the one hand, it would seem that it is not. An actual agent has to act, and one cannot act generally; all action is specific. The actual agent must therefore act without knowing with any certainty that what he does is his duty, while believing that there is a strict duty governing what he is to do. What *really* counts as his (specific) duty thus seems to be something that is determined *externally* to his own willing and consciousness. It is, however, difficult for the agent to accept this account of what counts as a good reason while adhering to the "moral worldview," for it means that the evidence for what counts as a duty is not something that falls "within" the individual's own consciousness. The agent thus cannot be free in doing his duty since he cannot understand what he is doing, and, yet, the "moral worldview" took its authority from its claim to be a realization of freedom. Nonetheless, this paradoxical view that the agent is radically free in performing actions in which he cannot be free is the account to which the "moral worldview" seems to lead.[130]

The "moral" agent must therefore take himself only to be able *contingently* to will the right thing, which means that he may not be acting in terms of his real, objective duty but only in terms of what he subjectively *takes* as his duty (and about which he therefore might be wrong). Since the agent cannot know with certainty what his specific duty is, he cannot be in control of whether he actually does his real, objective duty. Whether the agent is worthy of happiness is thus not up to him; it can only come to him at best as an act of grace by a beneficent deity who rewards him for trying. This too seems to be the kind of conclusion to which the "moral worldview" is led, yet it also seems to run contrary to the "moral worldview's" account of reasons for moral action, according to which it must be within the individual's powers at least to *know* his duty and to make himself worthy of happiness. It is not a matter, as it is with the aristocratic ethic, of luck in achieving honor. In the aristocratic ethic, only others can bestow honor on a person, and thus whether he has successfully done his duty is both dependent on the recognition by others and a variety of other contingent factors (his own strength, the turn of events, the available opportunities, his limited knowledge, and so on). For the "moral worldview," on the contrary, others can have no say in whether an agent is worthy of happiness, since that depends entirely on his virtue, which itself depends entirely on the willings of the agent himself. But the "moral worldview's" account of itself leads to the idea that the worthiness of happiness cannot depend solely on the agent's willings, and hence in this way the account also tends to undermine itself.

To sidestep this kind of negativity, the "moral worldview" can postulate something like a divine order that allots happiness in proportion to desert, with desert being determined in terms of purity of heart and of attempts in good faith to do the right thing. If there were such a divine order, then moral individuals would not need to know with any certainty what their duties are; those who sincerely try to will the right thing would be rewarded. In such a divine order, the discrepancies between willing for the sake of duty and willing for the sake of happiness would vanish, since the individual who tries to will the right thing will be rewarded with the happiness proportionate to his virtue. The individual who forswears his happiness for the sake of duty could thus be reconciled to such a state of affairs in that he would know his happiness would be forthcoming.[131]

Even such a positing of a divine order, however, would fail to sidestep the complete "negativity" of the "moral worldview," which comes from the way it seeks to realize the modern principle of freedom through its idea of a unity between the subjective and the impersonal points of view and its equal insistence on the sharp separation of the two. This itself, Hegel says, comes from taking a representationalist stance toward knowledge, of looking for something "within" the individual that is to match up with what is "outside" the individual; once that move is made, then there will always be questions about whether the evidence for something is present (internal) to the subject's consciousness or outside the subject. This will be particularly striking in moral issues, since the agent must possess some type of representation that *he* generates (or recognizes for himself within *his own* consciousness) that is nonetheless valid for *all* agents. (The "negativities" of the "moral worldview" thus operate around the way in which this type of account relies on oppositions and unities of "universal and particular" and "internal-to-the-subject" or "external-to-the-subject.")[132]

The paradoxes of the "moral worldview"

Indeed, because of these "negativities," the "moral worldview" becomes antinomial in that it generates within its own terms a set of mutually exclusive propositions for which there is equally good evidence. For example, in terms of the kind of description of moral agents given by the "moral worldview," we could conclude that there cannot be any *actual* moral agents, since any human agent would have to have a purity of willing that is impossible for him to have: To conform solely to duty would be to eliminate one's sensuous motives, and that would be impossible for any flesh and blood agent to do. Moreover, given the terms of the "moral worldview," it would seem to be impossible for anyone to actually achieve the kind of moral perfection (of acting solely out of a sense of duty) that would be necessary for him to be a genuinely *moral* agent. Yet on the other hand, since this consciousness, which is aware of its pure duty, *represents* it as an ideal, it knows it as something to which it can aspire but never reach. Thus, given the terms of the "moral worldview," one can show that there actually *are* actual moral agents who abstractly know what duty is and who *try* to achieve the highest goods of morality (of doing their duty, of trying to make themselves worthy of happiness by bringing their inclinations into line with duty so that they will only have virtuous inclinations that deserve reward).[133] Thus, the "moral worldview" tends to fall apart into two camps: those who believe that we actually can perform our duties and are at fault when we do not fully accomplish what is morally required of us, and those who believe that we cannot completely accomplish what is morally required of us, but we must always *try* to satisfy our moral duties.

The "negativity" of the "moral worldview" lies in the way it incorporates the subjective and the objective points of view within itself. On the one hand, it is intrinsic to the "moral worldview's" account of its reasons that authoritative reasons for action be found *within* the subject's consciousness, be internal to his own consciousness. In Kantian terms, the subject must be autonomous, self-legislating, giving itself its own laws. Thus, it would seem that what counts as an authoritative reason for action would be something intrinsic to the individual subject, to his own subjective point of view. On the other hand, what is taken to count as a good reason is to be a good reason for everyone – or for all rational beings, in Kant's formulation of the principle – and thus is something that is valid from the objective point of view. In making morality thus dependent on the objective point of view, however, the moral worldview takes away what originally prompted it – namely, the idea that what counts as an authoritative reason has to do with what an individual agent finds within his own consciousness. The various "ins and outs" of the ways in which the "moral worldview" can be formulated have to do with the need to reconcile the claims that what counts is what is posited from a subjective point of view and what counts is what is valid from an objective point of view. "Morality" is objective and valid for all agents; it is also something for the sake of which an individual is to put aside his own particularistic interests; yet moral reasons are supposed to be posited by the individual from his own subjective point of view. The "negativity" of the "moral worldview" results from trying to combine these opposing claims.

The "moral worldview" thus takes authoritative reasons both as transcending the individual and as not transcending the individual.[134] (Or, to put it differently, the "moral worldview" generates these opposing intuitions in those who participate in this worldview.) If there is no way within the terms set by the "moral worldview" to reconcile these kinds of opposing claims, then, in order to accommodate himself to this opposition, an agent participating in this worldview must dissemble about the point of view from which he is speaking and shift back and forth between the two points of view. That is, in giving an account of how he takes his representation (*Vorstellung*) "within" himself to be certified by himself as authoritative – that is, as being a representation of a moral law that transcends him and is valid independently of whether he *subjectively takes it* to be valid – the "moral agent" is led to shift and dissemble (*Verstellen*) in his accounts of just what it is that makes his moral reasons authoritative for him and others.[135] Hegel takes this as evidence that the "moral worldview" cannot be serious about its own account of itself, and is in fact pointing toward, if not actually already relying on, another account of itself that would not require such shifting and dissembling.

This shifting and dissembling is illustrated in the way in which the "moral worldview" tries to bolster its accounts through various kinds of postulates. The postulated harmony of morality and nature is such that the moral agent must take the actual world confronting him as not being in harmony with morality, as being in fact indifferent to it, since moral requirements have nothing to do with individual impulses and drives, and what counts as a moral reason transcends those impulses and drives. But nature is what gives human agents the impulses and drives that they have. Their impulses and drives can, so it seems, only contingently match up with what duty requires them to do. Thus, morality (as what duty requires) and nature are indifferent to each other. It therefore follows that happiness – the satisfaction of desire – cannot have anything to do with morality, since our desires come from nature. Yet in successfully acting out of a sense of duty, the individual moral agent actualizes a moral end. For example, if the individual assists another because he believes it is his duty to do so, he actualizes the moral end of beneficence. For any action to count as a realization of freedom – and the authority of the "moral worldview" comes from its claim to be *the* only adequate realization of freedom – the agent must *know* what he is doing. Therefore, such an agent must be *self-consciously* doing his duty for it to count as a moral act; otherwise, he would only be acting in conformity with duty (doing something without knowing what he is doing) rather than acting out of duty (acting because he knows that such and such is his duty).

A self-conscious agent necessarily has a certain self-conception; these moral agents have a self-conception as agents who wish to do the right thing. That is, they have a desire to *be* such moral agents. In giving himself a sufficient incentive to do the right thing, therefore, this agent will find his self-conception as a moral agent affirmed and actualized, and in doing so the individual satisfies those desires that follow from his image of himself as a moral agent. But since all desires are natural, it follows that nature and morality are in harmony for this agent, at least in all cases where the agent self-consciously does the right thing. Moreover, since happiness is the satisfaction of desire, the agent will also therefore find a certain happiness in doing his duty since it fulfills his desire to be a certain type of person. Thus, the "moral worldview" can maintain itself only by shifting between the objective standpoint of what is required by duty and the subjective standpoint of the acting individual. In the "moral worldview's" account of itself, nature and morality are opposed; a moral agent who accepts this account, however, acts in a way that presupposes that they are not opposed. In taking the objective point of view, the moral agent opposes nature to morality in that he can see himself as free only in acting in opposition to his natural impulses; in taking the subjective point of view and acting, however, he presupposes them as being in harmony.[136]

In the dialectical to and fro involved in the "moral worldview's" attempts to reassure itself that what it takes as authoritative for itself is satisfactory, it might seem as if all that is at issue is that the agent *practically* (subjectively, for himself) has to take nature and morality as being in harmony even though he cannot *theoretically* (objectively) satisfy himself that they are in harmony. But this subjective way of taking things is sabotaged by the account he gives himself of the value of what he is doing. In acting, he seeks to accomplish certain ends; however, the only end morally worth accomplishing is what (objective) reason can certify as being a fully justified end. Since his own actions are carried out from his subjective point of view, they cannot be counted by his own objective evaluations of his actions as essentially fulfilling this end. Yet he can subjectively view his own actions as arising out of the incentive of respect for the law (or some appropriate feeling of duty), and thus those actions do count for him as fitting the standards of moral action.[137] The agent must shift into the objective point of view in order to see his actions as only *contingently* measuring up to the claims of morality and then shift back to the subjective point of view to see his actions as *essentially* measuring up to his conception of what counts in morality.

The agent can also view a "highest good" as a union of virtue and happiness (that is, of morality and nature) and see it as an ideal, something for which the agent is supposed to strive. However, to the extent that the "moral world-view" understands morality to be a set of imperatives that finite agents impose on themselves, then it must see this idea of a "highest good" as implying that morality per se is no longer an issue. If virtue and happiness were to be united, then by this account morality would not be experienced as an imperative since there would be nothing "commanding" about it. An agent who always *wanted* to do the right thing could not experience moral norms as *imperatives*. The idea of a highest good, therefore, as a union of virtue and happiness, would be the idea of the abolition of *morality* as a distinct domain for human life and would be a substitution of something else – perhaps something resembling a form of Greek *Sittlichkeit* – in its stead. Thus, the duty to strive for the highest good would be the duty to strive for a state in which morality in this modern sense is no longer present. From the subjective point of view, the highest good seems like an ideal to work toward – that is, the ideal of bringing one's subjective life into conformity with what the objective point of view demands. From the objective point of view, though, the highest good represents a state of affairs in which modern morality per se plays no essential role.[138] The highest good, therefore, as an objective ideal represents not the fulfillment of the practice of modern morality but its abolition; as a subjective ideal, it represents a benchmark against which current attempts may be measured.

The question is whether this even makes sense as an ideal. At first, the ideal was of an agent who acts only out of duty and is thereby absolutely free; yet the so-called highest good has him acting also for the sake of happiness, which on the "moral worldview's" account makes him unfree. This is maintained as an ideal for the individual agent only by shifting and dissembling between the subjective and objective points of view. The conception embodied in the "moral worldview" of both the relation between duty and happiness and the opposition of *pure,* general duties to particular inclinations and impulses is further subverted by other accounts the "moral worldview" is forced to give of itself. That account must hold that something like "respect for the law" can be a sufficient incentive to action. Thus, for the "moral worldview" to be possible, it must be the case that even when there are opposing inclinations, this respect for the law is sufficient to override these opposing inclinations. But for a flesh and blood agent to act, he must act in terms of his empirical features. It is his natural, "sensuous" existence that puts his "pure consciousness" of duty into practice. For the agent to act, his "pure consciousness" of duty must supply a motivation for the agent to act. However, the pure motivations (the "pure consciousness," as Hegel calls it) must be translated into the real motivations of a self-conscious agent in order to result in an action.[139] The pure "respect for the law" therefore produces real actions only if it can be translated into the motivations that actually move a real agent; it must become an impulse to act for that flesh and blood agent. It would seem then that the "moral worldview" would have to hold one of two things: A non-empirical motivation is capable of directly motivating empirical action; or a "pure" motivation is an impulse to get other empirical impulses going (a kind of pure motivation for empirical motivations). The latter view certainly involves all kinds of oddities. It is intrinsic to the "moral worldview" that empirical motivations have their own set of laws that at best are only contingently related to the laws of morality. If that were not the case, then the whole account of *morality* in terms of freely doing one's duty even when it conflicts with one's desires and inclinations would be undermined, for if we were naturally inclined to do what duty requires, then this account of morality would have little point. But if that is the case, then for the pure motives to influence the sensuous non-pure motives (to be the motive of the motive), these non-pure motives would have to conform to the nature of the pure motives so that the pure motives could actually prompt the non-pure motives into motivating the action. Such a baroque idea (of motives having motives within them in order to be actual motives) seems to be required by the "moral worldview" if it is to hold to its central conception of "duty versus inclination." The "moral worldview" can reassure itself about its rather convoluted account of motivation only through a metaphysical doctrine like Kantian transcendental idealism (with its non-empirical noumenal self initiating actions in the empirical world) or through simply postulating that the domains of pure and non-pure motivation are "really" in conformity with each other (something that conflicts with its own account of what the experience of morality is supposed to be like.)[140]

Indeed, the moral worldview cannot be so concerned about its moral perfection as it claims it should be. If moral perfection involves not only always *doing* one's duty but also actually *wanting* to do one's duty, and one is obligated to *try* to achieve the "highest good" – that is, moral perfection (the union of virtue and happiness in which doing one's duty is also what makes one happy), then the issue arises as to why one would be morally obligated to desire happiness at all. It might be that the obligation to pursue one's happiness is only an *instrumental* obligation to insure that one will do one's duty; in linking personal happiness to moral duty, one would be insuring that one would have no competing inclinations threatening to take one in a different direction from duty's call. But an agent who always did his duty even in the face of competing inclinations would be as morally perfect as an agent who did them without competing inclinations; it would be odd, therefore, to call the union of virtue and happiness a "highest good," since the object of morality is doing one's duty – that is, attempting to realize the moral good, not achieving happiness. If the highest good is that which one should always seek to achieve at the expense of lesser goods, and the moral good is that which one should always attempt to achieve above all other goods (if the only thing, for example, that is good in itself is the good will), then the moral good is the highest good. How then can there be a highest good (the union of virtue and happiness) that is higher than the highest good? If the agent knows, more-over, that he cannot *achieve* the highest good (since it is an ideal), and he believes (as Kant seemed to) that God's apportioning of happiness to the deserving (that is, the virtuous) is part of the idea of the highest good, and he (the agent) moreover believes that being the frail, finite creature he is, he cannot be said to *deserve* it because of what he has *actually* willed but only for his sincerely *trying* to be virtuous (and that it therefore must come to him as an act of "grace"), then it follows that he is also shifting and dissembling about matters, since happiness and not duty would really be the direct object of his willing. That is, he knows he cannot do his duty, but he tries to do it because he believes that God will reward him for trying; he wants happiness and does his duty in order to achieve it. But if that is the case, then we are not making happiness instrumental to duty; doing (or trying to do) one's duty becomes *instrumental* to attaining happiness. (Indeed, Hegel suggests that this idea of the union of virtue and happiness is really based on the envy of those who are less happy of those who are more happy; it is really nothing more than the complaint that things have not gone as well for oneself and one's friends – the "truly deserving" – as one thinks they should. All the talk about happiness going to the less deserving is just a convenient psychological crutch for those who are envious of others.[141])

The "moral worldview," therefore, is burdened with a contradictory out-look from the outset. (Hegel accuses it of "syncretism."[142]) Worse, these contradictions seem intrinsic to it; they do not appear to be mere mistakes in its formulations that could be eliminated by a more thorough execution of the program. The "moral worldview," as embodied in modern religious move-ments and explicated brilliantly in the Kantian philosophy, therefore gradu-ally undermines its claim to be *the* realization of freedom in the modern world, and the modern world therefore requires therefore some new account of what can be authoritative for itself in the realization of freedom. That account was to come from the movement that took itself to be reacting to the "moral worldview" – namely, Romanticism – and it is in the union of the two – Kantianism and Romanticism – that the key to an adequate account of the realization of freedom in the modern world is to be found.

4. Personal autonomy: Romanticism, authenticity, and beautiful souls

The philosophers of the post-revolutionary period had self-consciously for-mulated the principle of the modern world as being a principle of self-determination. For this to be possible, the modern world should have two parts. First, they had seen that it should constitute itself as a rational, self-justifying form of life, dependent for its justification on nothing other than the accounts that it generates for itself; and, second, they had seen that this self-justifying form of life required each agent to constitute himself as "self-justifying subjectivity." Both these were necessary if the successes of the French Revolution were to be solidified, and if its failures (particularly the

Terror) were not to be repeated. For the modern world to hold good to its promise, it required not some very abstract conception of "absolute freedom" – which logically led to a form of practice in which a *faction* simply imposed its own views – but a conception of how people could be bound together in a free manner that both preserved a sense of the individual's own freedom and autonomy and established the actuality of a self-justifying form of life. The "moral worldview," most brilliantly worked out in Kant's writings, was the first post-revolutionary attempt at such a formulation.

Romanticism

Hegel takes *romanticism,* a movement contemporaneous with Hegel's own life (and with which Hegel's philosophy has often been mistakenly identified) to be the attempt to preserve the idea of self-determination while overcoming the difficulties in the "moral worldview's" account of what it would mean to realize freedom. In Hegel's eyes, romanticism partially completes the development of subjective idealism and the post-revolutionary world in that it both renders the contradictions of that world fully apparent and creates the "social space" in which the possibility of a resolution of those contradictions finally appears, even though romanticism itself does not offer that resolution on its own. Romanticism offers an account of the self-grounding self of modern life, an account that then undermines itself in its own terms and thereby opens up the possibility for a more adequate account of what modern institutions and life are about. Hegel's attitude toward romanticism is thus complex; on the one hand, he holds it to be a completion of a certain line of historical-conceptual development; on the other hand, he holds it to be deeply flawed, and often has difficulty concealing his disdain for what he regarded as its more extravagant expressions.

Hegel takes the romantic self-understanding to be an attempt to carry out the forms of the new post-revolutionary self-understanding articulated in the German idealist movement without that movement's assumption of the way in which *representations* mediated between the agent and "nature."[143] Hegel's argument is not to the effect that this is in fact the cause of romanticism, nor is he arguing that this is the way in which all romantics saw themselves; his argument is that the account offered by romanticism as to what may taken as authoritative grounds for belief and action may itself be reconstructed as being the type of account that was necessary to resolve the dilemmas generated within the idealist movement in its attempts to determine what it would mean to realize freedom in the modern world. In the case of the romantic movement in Germany, with which Hegel would naturally have been most acquainted, the influence of the movement of philosophical idealism on the romantic artists was indeed present and in some cases profound. Fichte played a large role in this development, inspiring not only younger philosophers such as Schelling and Hegel, but also exercising a large influence on younger artists and critics, who attempted to apply some Fichtean ideas to art and art criticism. Some, like Novalis and Friedrich von Schlegel, heard

Fichte's lectures and were deeply inspired by him. Hegel's youthful friend, the poet Hölderlin, also heard Fichte's lectures in Jena and was inspired by him to formulate some philosophical ideas that criticized Fichte's philosophy; those ideas in some very general ways also bear a strong similarity to some of Hegel's ideas.

The romantic project undertook to realize the principle of freedom by thinking of personal subjectivity not in terms of anonymous rational subjectivity (as the Kantians had done) but in terms of the existing, concrete subjectivity of particular individuals.[144] The post-revolutionary idealist movement had come to see an individual as free to the extent that he *determines for himself* what is to count for him as an authoritative reason for belief and action, and he can do that only by willing from an appropriately anonymous point of view; self-determination required the idealist agent to detach himself from all particular perspectives – both social and natural – in order to achieve the requisite independence necessary for self-determination. The idealists held that only by assuming that detached, impartial standpoint could the agent really be said to be free and to be able to make his beliefs and actions *his own;* the idealist movement had done that by focusing on the conditions under which the agent could make his *representations* his own. In opposition to this notion of freedom, the romantics turned away from the idealist account of making representations one's own in favor of a more concrete sense of making something's one's own by looking inward and exploring one's *own* subjectivity in the hope of finding therein the grounds for a truly free and non-alienated human life.

The romantics thus shift the conception of modern freedom away from the idea of rational, anonymous self-determination toward something more like the ideas of authenticity, irony, and true feeling. In particular, they shift moral consciousness away from the idea of obedience to a self-imposed *law* toward the idea of being "true to oneself." The idealist *transcendental* self that is beyond appearance is displaced in favor of the *actual, individual* self, which is available to certain forms of introspection and is best expressed in certain artistic treatments. The romantic self, so it seems, appears as it is in the actual empirical world. There is no anonymous self *in itself* that determines the way the world appears to an individual; there is only the existing, concrete self of the individual, with his full emotional makeup and his particular life-history. What is to bind free agents together in the world would not be an appeal to a common rational law, which each would freely impose on himself, but an appeal to *conscience,* to being true to oneself and one's convictions.[145] Genuine freedom for the transcendental idealist consists in bringing one's personal convictions into line with what was required from an impersonal ("universal") point of view (the standpoint of "reason"). Genuine freedom for the romantic consists in acting from the *personal* point of view, in acting in accord with one's deepest personal convictions; it consists not merely of acting in terms of what is impersonally rationally justifiable but in terms, for example, of the agent's religious views, his concrete conceptions of the good life, his own personal biography, and so on – provided that these conceptions can be said to be genuinely *his own*. The romantics had thus in one sense returned to one of Rousseau's questions: What really are my deepest personal convictions, and how can I know them?

There is, of course, a schoolbook objection to this, which the romantics themselves recognized: "What if two different consciences make contradictory demands?" The romantics took themselves to have an answer to that objection in their ideal of a free *community,* in which each individual would act only on the basis of his own conscience, each would freely recognize the right of conscience in the others, and, since each would be genuinely free, each would be acting in concert with the others. The genuinely free community would be one in which each would be allowed to go his own way, to explore his own self, knowing that others affirm this for him instead of forcing him into some social mold. The romantic who authentically looks inward and examines his emotional life and beliefs will then be able to act on the basis of ideas and emotions that are genuinely *his own*. He does his duty to others by reflecting on what kinds of actions are appropriate, that is, what in good faith he can do according to the convictions of his own conscience, and, in the community of romantics, he is *recognized* as a man of good faith and conviction in his actions. The community of romantics thus determines for itself *as a community* what is to count and what is not to count by virtue of each attempting to become an authentic individual and in each assisting the others through his acts of recognition to become such authentic individuals.

The moral worldview lacked this element of recognition. The subjective idealist agent acts on the basis of motives that he has elected to count for him as motives, that he has "let" determine his actions because he can see them as fitting a rational principle that he himself has (anonymously) accepted for himself. No social act of recognition is necessary for this election of motives, nor could one in any way assist it or be constitutive of it. Implicit in romanticism, however, is the idea that one finds one's true motives – that one is "true to oneself" – *only* in and through a process of mutual recognition within a community (or that one finds one's authentic self only in community with a romantic other, a theme very prominent in the poetry of romantic love). The romantic agent does his duty by acting authentically in terms of his conscience – by doing what he has elected to do in terms of his own deepest convictions – and he has thus determined the content of his action out of his own authentic self, but he understands himself as having done his duty because others bestow a certain *recognition* on his actions and thereby affirm his own self-understanding as an authentic individual.[146] The individual romantic agent can thus understand himself as acting in accord with the essence of things by virtue of acting in accordance with his own deepest and therefore most true feelings and convictions.

The romantic individual is not to be mistaken for the "man of sincerity" portrayed by Hegel in the section of the *Phenomenology* titled "The Spiritual Kingdom of Animals." The sincere individual can be sincere about anything; the "real thing" (the *Sache selbst*) about which the "sincere individual" claims to have an interest is in fact a fully empty conception. Moreover, the sincere person can *sincerely* believe something without *authentically* believing it; one can sincerely believe, for example, in the validity of some social rule without ever having considered whether that rule is defensible or whether it fits one's own deepest convictions. In the romantic conception, the "real thing" is the actual, subjective life of the individual himself, what the individual *authentically* feels, wants, and believes. The authentic individual cannot be authentic about anything as the sincere individual can; he can only be authentic about what comes from his true emotional life and convictions, what he has genuinely made or found to be his own, not just something he has found within himself and about which he is sincere.[147]

However, while it may not immediately fall prey to the schoolbook objection to it, the romantic solution still has trouble within its own terms. There is nothing in the appeal to conscience per se (in the appeal to one's authentic convictions) that seems to specify any determinate duty or action whatsoever. For the romantic, the determinateness of any action or duty cannot come from any general appeal to "reason" or to any generalized idea of "conscience"; it can only come from the individual's own concrete emotional life and from the acts of recognition on the part of the community. But in the last analysis, the individual himself must remain sovereign over his own decisions and actions; he must decide for himself whether some action that is demanded of him, or seems to be called for in some situation, is in fact one that he can do in good faith. The romantic agent who acts only in terms of his conscience thus takes his own determinate *self* (his "I") to be final, at least in the sense that duties are his to accept or reject, according to his convictions and his knowledge of the circumstances.[148] The community of moral romantics thus consists of each doing his duty by consulting his own deepest convictions and in that way constituting himself as a truly self-determining individual within a social life. However, since nobody's appeal to conscience can claim any superiority to any other's appeal to conscience, the romantic community is a community of equals.[149] What was the universality of rational agency for the subjective idealists is pictured by the romantics as the concrete unity of humanity united in its mutual respect for each other's own point of view, of each heeding their own consciences. Only in this way, the romantics thought, could each overcome the alienation present in non-romantic communities; since each acts only out of what he can with best conviction determine as being his own authentic beliefs, each will necessarily find himself identifying with his activities, "at home" in his world, and the community of romantic selves will thus overcome the alienation between the impersonal (communal) point of view and the subjective point of view. The romantic community can thus lay claim to genuinely realizing the principle of freedom in the modern world. (The community of romantics thus non-accidentally resembles a community of Fichtean "I's," each recognizing each other and being completely free in doing so.)

Since each is absolutely free to determine his own duty – since nothing can count for an individual unless it can answer to his own deepest convictions –

each is independent of determination by an "other" (whether it be another person or simply external circumstances). Therefore, no individual can recognize the declarations of conscience by another as in any way binding on him. Yet each demands that the other recognize him as a free person who acts on the basis of his own conscience. In these mutual declarations and in the complex ways in which the romantic agents socially deal with each other in such communities, the romantic *self* is constituted. The romantic self understands his freedom to consist in his looking into his own subjectivity and discovering therein his own deepest convictions, and by only acting on such convictions that he can count as *his own,* the romantic individual only does that which is true to his own self. But such a self-exploration makes sense only in a social context in which the declarations of conscience and conviction are set off against the requirements that others make of him; the romantic self thus actualizes himself only in these declarations to others of what his conscience requires.[150] Without a society of others *against* whom the romantic can declare his convictions, the romantic self has no room to exist. (The world of the romantic artist and his hangers-on, constantly baiting the more staid elements of the middle class, and the nineteenth-century discovery of "bohemia" also make their appearance with this form of self-understanding. What for the pietists had been the struggle of godly men and women against a world enmeshed in sin – and who by looking into their own hearts for God's commands, could triumph over wickedness – became for the romantics the person of deep conviction – like Rousseau – who finds that he cannot live within "society's" strictures because they conflict with his deepest convictions and his desires, with who he "really" is, but who, unlike Rousseau, can triumph over an inauthentic world by being true to himself and by becoming *authentic.*)

The deep problem with such a form of self-understanding is that although it is in these declarations of conscience and conviction to each other that such romantic individuals constitute themselves, each romantic agent understands himself as acting not in terms of anything constituted by "external" social institutions but only in terms of his own deepest self. In the terms of the romantic individual's self-understanding, if he is to act out of what are really *his own* motivations – if his *self* is to identify with his activities, if he is not to be alienated – then he must act from convictions that come from his "self," not from convictions that have been "imposed" on him by "society." The romantics are thus faced with the problem of how to unite the impersonal point of view of the community (the "universal") with their own deeply subjective point of view (the "individual"). This is partially accomplished by the linguistic and therefore public acts of "declarations of conviction" (or their more modern equivalents, the "protests in the name of conscience" by such individuals).[151] The function of the reciprocal declarations of conviction for the romantic individual is to provide an *assurance* to each that he is indeed acting in a self-determining manner.[152] Thus, in these reciprocal declarations to each other, the romantics form a community, a shared sense of who they are; they fashion themselves, that is, into a self-conscious formation of spirit.[153] The *assurances* that each individual gives to the other in an institutionalized system of mutual recognition unites, so it seems, the impersonal and personal point of view. This formation of spirit is best embodied in a form of *religious* community, of individuals bound together in a community by their declarations to each other of what lies deepest in their hearts about what counts as having inherent and absolute value.[154]

The "moral genius" and the "beautiful soul"

In this context, it is thus no accident that one of the most characteristic ideas of romanticism, that of the *genius,* would appear. The specifically "moral genius," who appears particularly in the writings of the German romantics, is that person who in his "inner voice" hears the divine voice; he thereby unites the impersonal point of view with his own personal point of view in that in simply his pursuing *his own* interests and desires he produces artifacts and utterances that are of interest to humanity as such.[155] The romantic community would thus logically think of itself (at least to the extent that it fully realized itself as a *romantic* community) as a community of such "moral geniuses," each expressing the universal divine truth by looking most deeply into what each as an individual believes, with each finding that in doing so, he has discovered a moral truth that others can now make their own. This "solitary worship service," as Hegel sarcastically calls the "moral genius's" exploration of his own subjectivity, would be in actuality also a *communal* worship service, with each declaring to the other the purity of his heart and the authenticity of his convictions, and the community existing in this reciprocal assurance of each other's conscientiousness.[156] For such a community, there would be no hidden metaphysical essence determining things for them; there would be only the immediately present truths of their own inner lives, which when authentically followed out would incorporate within themselves the impersonal point of view (what Hegel often calls the "in-itself," or the "essence" for this form of life).

In such a romantic religious community, individuals mutually pursue the goal of communal authenticity: of coming to know themselves as and coming to be authentic individuals, that is, as individuals, who, in acting on the basis of what in their deepest convictions they know to be *their own* desires, also express the life of the community and express what is of interest not only to each individually but also to humanity. The shared self-knowledge of such a community would consist in the fully public acts of "the community's speaking about its spirit," the ways in which the community articulates itself to itself in its social institutions.[157] The problem for the romantic form of self-consciousness is therefore: How would such a community be possible?

Such a community would consist of "beautiful souls."[158] There are three possibilities for the "beautiful soul" to develop his sense of himself and act on the basis of the way he takes himself. First, the "beautiful soul" can withdraw into himself and focus exclusively on his own subjectivity, withdrawing from the world and trying to find what is truly his own by attending exclusively to the purely personal and most subjective elements of his life. This possibility was actualized in the lives of some romantic artists. For example, the German romantic writer Novalis held that the best poems are those that are entirely personal. Indeed, Novalis came to embody this romantic possibility centering on the search the individual subjective life in its purity; in Novalis' *Heinrich von Ofterdingen*, the search for the "blue flower" in both dream and fable stands for this possibility of the "beautiful soul." However, this search for the purely personal, the purely subjective, leaves the "beautiful soul" with no room to act. To act would compromise the integrity of the "beautiful soul"; the result therefore of taking this possibility as an adequate account of what the beautiful soul's life should be is that the "beautiful soul's" inner life becomes empty. Deprived of all social content, it has nothing to it. In his search for the truly authentic as being the absolutely personal, the "beautiful soul" finds that there is no "core" to himself; he finds that searching for the self in the purely subjective parts of one's life is like peeling away the rings of the onion only to find that when all the rings have been peeled away, there is nothing there, that there is in fact no "core" to the self that supposedly lies at the end of such an activity of "paring down" to the "core." With nothing there at the end of the journey for self-knowledge, the "beautiful soul" wastes away, its subjective glow gradually dying out like an ember. And indeed actual poets such as Novalis and Keats end up "wasting away" just as does Rousseau's fictional "beautiful soul," Julie, in his *La Nouvelle Héloïse*.[159] Even when they do not succumb to tuberculosis (the romantic poet's disease par excellence) it is absurdly fitting that they die young, because there is nothing to sustain them into further life.[160]

The "beautiful soul" as ironist and as moralist

There are two other possibilities for the "beautiful soul" to work out some way in which the personal autonomy and authenticity of different agents can be compatible with the life of the community so that the romantic community does not simply deteriorate into a community of confrontation in which each individual challenges the others because of what *his* conscience demands, with there being no possible concord among such differing demands of conscience. One possibility is for the "beautiful soul" to become a romantic *ironist*. Hegel does not use the word "irony" here in the *Phenomenology,* but, given what he says about irony in his later works, it is clear that it is romantic irony that he has in mind in his discussion of the possibilities for the romantic self-understanding to work its account of itself out. (For example, in his *Philosophy of Right*, he links his treatment of the romantic community in the *Phenomenology of Spirit* more or less explicitly to his other views on the nature of irony.[161]) Nothing can count for such a "beautiful soul" unless he *lets* it count for him, and this election of what counts for him is something entirely personal, something that he must decide on his own to do in terms of *his own* basic convictions. This formation of the romantic authentic individual is thus logically led to taking an ironic attitude toward everything, including himself. Nothing can count as absolute, nothing as definitive unless he, *as an individual,* elects to count it as such; but the romantic, authentic individual knows that in principle this cannot be a sufficient ground for convincing others of the meritoriousness of what he has elected to count as worthy of belief or action because the others must elect to count it for themselves on the basis of their own convictions. (This also holds true, for romantics, for all the so-called principles of rationality.) Thus, the romantic agent knows that nothing can be final and definitive in a communal sense, and knowing that, he also knows that nothing can be final and definitive for himself, since whatever bonds he puts on his thoughts and actions can also be loosened and thrown off by him. The only appropriate attitude therefore is that of *irony,* the belief that whatever one believes and takes seriously cannot be final and definitive even for oneself.

The other possibility for the "beautiful soul" is to preserve his moral purity and stick to his convictions, demanding that the world take him on his own terms or not at all. This "beautiful soul" cannot be ironic, for that would mean for him that he should abandon his own deepest beliefs. However, a community of such "beautiful souls" would be unlikely to be able to sustain itself since it would quickly deteriorate into pure confrontation among uncompromising "men and women of conscience." But would it be possible for a set of such non-ironic "beautiful souls" to form a coherent community with a set of ironic "beautiful souls"? Each after all represents one of two real possibilities for a romantic community: (1) a community united by a set of firm convictions which each individual identifies as *his own* – that is, a community united around a set of basic truths which have been arrived at authentically and reflectively (in distinction from the idealized Greek form of life, in which these truths would be simply taken for granted); (2) an ironist community united by no common belief except that each individual is the locus of authority for what is to count for him as true and good, and that no individual can claim more than a subjective validity for his own beliefs (for what "works for him").[162] Moreover, each would see the other as a subordinate part of what he takes to be true. The ironist sees the determining "I" as the basis of everything (that is, that he as an individual must decide to *let* something count for him), and his knowledge of this therefore loosens the hold on him that these beliefs may have once had.

The ironist therefore must see the non-ironist as being deluded about what he believes he can really claim with authority. The non-ironist, on the other hand, must see the ironist's standpoint as parasitic on the general life and beliefs of the community, as a self-indulgent pretense of assuming a "higher" standpoint than the community out of which he takes his ideas. For the non-ironist, the ironist can only appear to be evil, for the non-ironist can only see the ironist as someone who sets himself apart from the basic self-evident truths to which any "rational" or "sane" or "intelligent" man or woman would assent. The ironist declares not only that he does not agree that the truths are so "self-evident" and not only that he must reserve the right for himself to decide whether these truths can possibly count for him – worse, he declares that these so-called truths *really have no* validity on their own unless some individual (such as himself) elects to count them as his own. The ironist thus seems to be denying outright what the non-ironist understands for all practical purposes to be the "commonsense" criteria of intelligence and rationality themselves. The ironist's account denies the very possibility of the validity of the non-ironist's account of what is authoritative; he thus challenges directly whom the non-ironist takes himself to be. Since the ironist does this knowingly and self-consciously, he thus seems to the non-ironist to be not just philosophically mistaken about a few abstruse issues in the theory of knowledge but to be *bad*. Moreover, he seems to express his contempt for what is true and virtuous by his insistence that *for him* all the so-called "self-evident truths" voiced by the non-ironist count for nothing unless by his own free act he (the ironist) *elects* to count them. The ironist also claims to do this out of only the most high-minded of motives: his refusal not be browbeaten into going against his own convictions. To the non-ironist, he thus also seems to be a *hypocrite,* since he pretends to take seriously things that on his own terms he cannot.[163]

To the non-ironist, it will seem obvious that at least the "commonsense" of any community will cluster around some set of beliefs that will seem obvious and self-evident to the members of that community, and to that extent there will always be a non-ironic consensus about what needs to be counted as true and valuable. Out of the institutions and practices of the community will emerge a set of beliefs that will be reciprocally recognized by the members of the community but against which the ironist will assert his own authority. The ironist will point out that whatever the set of beliefs may be, it has its force only in the practices of mutual recognition by the members of the community and has no definitive claim on anybody who does not participate in those practices. In reply, the non-ironist asserts against the ironist that all "intelligent" (or "rational" or "sane" or whatever other term of approval he uses) people in the community recognize in their hearts that such-and-such is just "the way things have to be done." (If the non-ironist is philosophically inclined, he might also claim that such-and-such form a set of "basic intuitions" against which all other moral claims or theories must be measured.) The ironist replies that it is not the case that all well intentioned, rational (or sane or intelligent or whatever) people share these beliefs, since he and his non-ironist friends do not or at least need not share them. (If the ironist is philosophically inclined, he can claim that these are only the basic intuitions of a single group, and even if he does contingently happen to share them, this nonetheless confers no special authority on them.) Moreover, the ironist takes the non-ironist's appeal to things like "the beliefs we all share" as all the more proof that what he, the ironist, says is correct. In fact, the ironist would claim, if anybody is a hypocrite it is the non-ironist who claims a universal validity for what he in practice admits are only the shared beliefs of a particular community (or maybe even just his own intuitions on the matter).[164]

The non-ironist thus represents the *judgmental* agent who condemns the ironist but does not act, whereas the ironist represents the agent who realizes that he must act even in the face of what he takes to be the contingency of all standards. When followed out to their logical conclusions, both the ironist and non-ironist transform into two common figures of modern life: (1) The judgmental agent becomes the person who does not act but only prattles on about the "absolute standards" that must be maintained and is forever moaning about the loss of such standards; (2) the ironist becomes the kind of casuistical agent who is always invoking the "complexity" of life to justify his own self-serving actions, and pointing out to others how they have "failed to understand" just how very complex is the situation he is in. In reality, both are hypocrites in that both make duty a matter merely of words, each claiming all the while the high moral ground for himself: the judgmental agent in terms of his insistence on purity and clean hands, the casuistical ironist in terms of his insistence that whatever he does (given how "complex" life is), he is doing his "duty."[165] One becomes the "beautiful soul" who is forever above actually doing anything and who is forever intoning against the corrupt world he always finds around him; the other becomes the "beautiful soul" of action, invoking his sterling conscientiousness, his fine intentions and the regrettable complexities of the situation to justify whatever it is he happens to do. The judgmental agent holds the acting ironist to be a hypocrite, since he can only see his claims as casuistical, ex post facto, self-serving legitimations of what is really just a matter of personal interest; able to understand only motives that are pure, he is unable to see any motives in the ironist's actions other than those that can only seem to him to be self-serving.[166] The acting casuistical ironist sees the judgmental non-ironist as the kind of hypocrite who claims purity only by avoiding ever actually *doing* anything.

This would seem to be an impasse in the romantic account of what constitutes an authoritative reason for belief and action, and it would seem to undermine the romantic's claim to have construed what would count as a realization of freedom. However, in confronting the various statements by the judgmental agent, the ironist becomes capable of seeing himself in the "other," the judgmental agent himself – that is, he becomes capable of understanding what he is really doing by reflecting on the other agent's practices, something that, after all, the ironist actually claims to do in his taking himself to be "above it all." By his own hypocrisy, by claiming to be "above it all" while never having to act, the judgmental agent actually holds up a mirror to the ironist, showing him that his own way of talking about what he is doing is, after all, just talk, often being simply a prop that he uses for convenient justifications of what he wants to do. Even on his own terms, the ironist himself must be able to separate what is merely an action that serves his own interests from what he takes to be an important action, even when both those aspects fall within the same action. Moreover, the ironist holds that his actions can have, given the institutions, practices and history of his community, great importance within the community, even while he also holds it to be true that there is no "metaphysical," definitive justification for those practices outside of the structure of mutual recognition within that community. He comes to see that the non-ironist has a point, for the non-ironist expresses the shared beliefs that give the community the shape that it has and that therefore structure the self that the ironist himself has. The ironist thus comes to give up his standpoint of being "above it all," for he now sees that even his own ironist self is a *social* self; without *this* past, in *this* community, the romantic ironist self would not and could not exist. The ironist thus sees that like the judgmental agent, he too held that there is one thing that any "enlightened" (or "rational" or whatever) agent must believe – namely, the primacy or superiority of the ironist *self*. However, in coming to that belief, he implicitly ceases being a romantic ironist, and thus ceases being a "beautiful soul."[167] Just as there is no immediate knowledge for "sense-certainty," there is no immediate knowledge even of oneself or one's own heart. All knowledge, even self-knowledge, even the "knowledge" of that which it seems that one "must" believe, is mediated. There is no fixed Archimedean point to which any agent can fasten his beliefs that is independent of all other points.

Hegel asks us to imagine the romantic ironist confessing this to the judgmental agent. The former ironist now sees his equality with the other, and in confessing to the other, expects a new form of mutual recognition (of spirit) to appear. But the other rebuffs him, for he remains a "beautiful soul," only now not really so beautiful; instead, he becomes the "hard-hearted" moralist, who refuses to identify himself with the former ironist.[168] But the same possibility exists for the hard-hearted moralist as did for the ironist; the ironist holds up a mirror to the judgmental consciousness, showing him that there are no truths that can be taken as metaphysical anchors independently of social practice, and that his own reliance on "the universal" (on "basic intuitions," or on "what we must all take for granted") is hypocrisy when it is expressed as what "any sound mind" must believe, for the judgmental consciousness is either dogmatically taking his *self*-selected standards to be *the* standards against which all these things are to be measured, or at best is representing the standards of a particular, historical community as if they expressed timeless truths, or, to the extent that he is aware of the contingency of his own beliefs, is actually no different from the ironist himself. If the judgmental consciousness follows up the confession made by the ironist, seeing the ironist's point and seeing his similarity to the ironist, then the judgmental agent also ceases to be what he was.[169] Each forgives the other, and in that way each comes to be reconciled to the other. Each comes to see that a depiction of what is authoritative for belief and action must take into account the historical contingency of those standards, and thus each comes to accept a key part of what the ironist intends; but each also comes to see that the ironic stance toward such contingency is not enough and that the community must work out within its own terms an account of why its standards have the authority they do in order for those standards to be satisfactory to the members of the community. In that way, the ironist and the judgmental agent come to see the "truth" of each other's viewpoints as they each abandon their own particular viewpoint.

In this reconciliation, the romantic community abandons its account of itself as a *romantic* community while preserving what it takes to have been the truths of such a community. Its members come to see that they are indeed held together by a set of shared beliefs; that all actions are motivated out of a complex of passions, interests and so on, and that the significance of what one does is a matter of its recognition by members of the community; and that action is complex, and wrongs can be done, but that the community can best realize its self-identity if it bases its practices not exclusively on praise and blame based on contingent and partial perspectives but on the reconciliation and forgiveness that becomes possible when those perspectives are seen for the partial, contingent perspectives they are.

The former romantics thus find themselves no longer in a romantic community but in a kind of community that is by virtue of its reflections on itself an *absolute* community: It is not mediated by any metaphysical "other" but only by the free-standing structures of social practice that make it up. This community now has the possibility of understanding and structuring its institutions and practices so that they are not alien impositions on its members but continuous with their sense of who they are. These institutions may then be rationally reconstructed to serve as supports and embodiments of its members' desires and their duties, such that in acting on the dictates of these institutions, individuals can find themselves *in* the activities they require and can be fully reconciled with the social world around them, thereby becoming genuinely free. Modern lives thus acquire the *possibility* of being non-alienated in communal life, of perhaps discovering a modern form of *Sittlichkeit*, of a form of life in which "the way things are done" is congruent with the modern sense of reflective distancing and of agents *electing* what is to count for them, with appeals to subjective conscience fitting together with moral certainty. Such *possible* social institutions would not be legitimated by an appeal to any transcendent values but only by appeal to the way in which those practices can show themselves to be satisfactory in light of the insufficiencies of past communities' accounts of what they took to be authoritative and in light of what it would mean for a modern form of life to realize the ideal of freedom.

At this point in the *Phenomenology,* Hegel argues that this form of community can only be a *modern religious* community – that is, a community that is oriented to reconciling its members with each other by reflecting on what it is that binds them together but which does not at the same time deny their distinctively modern sense of individuality.[170] In this modern religious community, humanity therefore acquires the possibility of *coming to terms with what it has come to be,* rather than seeking to create itself along the lines of any kind of metaphysically structured image. Hegel must now explain how this religiously bonded community brings us to such self-certainty and truth and why it will not break down as the other forms of self-understanding have done. It will turn out, so Hegel will argue, that the God of this religious community is not the transcendent metaphysical God of orthodox Christianity but is what is divinely immanent within human life itself as the human community has come to understand itself. What we take as *sacred* – the divine – are the things that for us have come to have absolute value (that is, in Hegel's words, what "exists in and for itself"). Humanity's highest interests are expressed in what it holds, as it were, to be beyond bargaining, to be what for it is the absolutely good; it is this "absolutely good" that counts as the sacred in human practice. It is Hegel's thesis that the reconciled community is held together by a definite and shared sense of what is sacred – of what is not simply important for it but what is of absolute value for it – and it is his further thesis that this element of the sacred is established in modern life as the principle of the sacred quality of rational, self-conscious *life,* of *spirit* itself as the self-conscious reflection of a community on what it takes as authoritative for itself. Hegel takes religion to be the institutional communal practice of such reflection and affirmation of what we have as a historical community come to take as sacred. It is also Hegel's thesis that the very concept of religion leads necessarily to the religious community's secularizing itself in the modern world, although without its thereby abandoning its sense of itself as religious.

6

The self-reflection of the human community

1. Religious practice as self-reflection

The reflections on the nature of religion begins to bring to a close that series of reflections on spirit as social practice – that is, on the series of self-understandings and accounts of what is taken as authoritative that began with the Greek alternative to modernity and ends with the fully modern self-understanding that structures the community that unites the post-revolutionary Kantian conception of autonomy as impersonal rationality with romantic discourse about personal self-choice. These various forms of self-understandings about the self-identity of the community have led to a conception of a form of social practice which is a form of "absolute reflection" – that is, what Hegel calls *absolute spirit:* a given community's reflection on its essential self-identity and its highest interests through the historical practices and institutions of art, religion, and philosophy.[1]

The section on "absolute spirit" is necessary to explain the kind of teleology that has occurred in the move from the Greek *Sittlichkeit* to the culmination of modern life in the uniting of Kantian and romantic conceptions of autonomy. Only when such "reflective institutions" are established – that is, when social practices are established whose function is to reflect on, and thereby to affirm or disaffirm that what a given form of life *takes* as authoritative reasons for belief and action *really are* authoritative reasons – can there be a *teleological* historical progression. Prior to that there can only be a historical "chronology," a set of changes and alterations without any inherent story to them. A form of life can change its reasons, perhaps in profound ways, for a variety of contingent social and historical reasons. However, unless a form of life develops some way of reflecting on its reason-giving activities, it cannot generate the kinds of self-undermining skeptical discreditings that then *require* and make possible their resolution in some later form of life having its own distinctive account of itself and its own set of reflective institutions. Unless a form of life develops these reflective institutions, it can change in its structure and in what it takes as authoritative for itself, but it cannot have an idea of teleology, of progress, within itself; its change can only be differences, not rational resolutions of earlier dilemmas. A form of life thus becomes *Geist,* "spirit," by developing the practices whose function is to reflect on what that form of life takes to be the "essence" for itself (to be authoritative for it). This type of reflection thereby introduces "negativity" into the form of life in that this type of reflection discovers within the terms that the form of life has set for itself certain contradictions and incoherences that engender a skepticism about what it had up until then simply taken for granted. By reflecting on what a form of life takes to be authoritative reasons for belief and action, these forms of reflective practice thereby put into question the self-identity of the agents within that form of life. This prompts a need for reassurance about the "essence," about what is definitive and supreme for that form of life. The series of reflections on "spirit" which lead to the chapter on religion have shown that not only were none of those reassurances successful, but that when they are seen from the standpoint of the succeeding accounts, it becomes clear that they *could not* have been successful within the terms each had set for itself.

In reflecting on what is the "essence" for itself, a form of life reflects on what for it is definitive of what it means to be a person, an agent in that form of life. All forms of absolute reflection are reflections on the forms of character and the highest interests of those forms of character – that is, those interests that have to do with what people take as definitive grounds for belief and action, in short, for living the lives they do. Earlier accounts of the various "formations of spirit" looked at both what people took to be authoritative for themselves (what they took to be the "essence" of things) and how the people in that form of life took themselves to be related to the "essence" (how they took themselves to *know* that which was authoritative for them – in Hegel's terms, what was the "object" of their consciousness). In many of those "formations of consciousness," a religious or quasi-religious conception was taken to be authoritative for people. Having run through the series of "formations of consciousness," however, Hegel has arrived at the point where he can focus on that authoritativeness itself, on what the European community's highest interests must be, given who that community has come to be.[2]

As a form of absolute spirit, that is, of the human community reflecting on its essential self-identity and therefore on the ultimate ends of life, the practice of religion is a form of communal reflection on the *absolute principles* governing human life. As the self-consciousness of a community, it is "authoritative reflection" on what is authoritative for that community – that is, it is a type of practice that has come to count in that community as being itself warranted to articulate what else in that community is definitive for it. Religion is a form of institutionalized social practice in which a community reflects on what it takes to be the "ground" of everything else that is basic to its beliefs and practices; it is the communal reflection on what for a community in Hegel's terms counts as "existing in and for itself."

For example, one basic problem for religious reflection is the reconciliation of two different aspects of humanity. People are part of the world of natural phenomena, and one of the basic natural facts about them is the crucial fact of their mortality. However, what makes natural humans into thinking, acting *agents* are not these natural facts about them, but their place in a "social space," in their symbolic, cultural world. The natural facts about humans are not, of course, irrelevant to how humans understand themselves in cultural space; the family, the economic system of production and so on are inconceivable apart from obvious natural facts about humanity. They are simply not determinative of what makes humans into thinking, acting *agents,* even if they make a difference to the form that their agency takes. This poses the issue of whether *nature* and *spirit* can be reconciled.

What makes this kind of reflection religious are both the *object* of the concern and the *form* that this concern takes. The objects of religious reflection are the absolute principles governing human life – that is, with what at all times has been understood as the *divine,* as that which is the ground of what is sacred, of ultimate and inherent value to humans, of what constitutes the point of life. The knowledge of the absolute principles governing human life is thus knowledge of what is divine, and it is this kind of knowledge with which all forms of absolute spirit including religion are concerned. Religion thus has a similar content to other forms of communal reflection – namely, human self-identity in terms of what it takes as authoritative in determining the grounds of belief and action. What distinguishes its type of knowledge from other forms of knowledge, so Hegel argues, is the *form* that religious reflection takes – namely, that of *Vorstellung,* which I have rendered here as "representation" and sometimes as "representational thought" to distinguish it from theoretical, conceptual thought. The idea is that religion gives us a self-reflection neither in terms of concepts and theories nor in terms of works of art but in terms of "representations" or, we might put it nowadays, in terms of *symbols,* stories and rites.[3] Religion gives us a self-reflection through various symbols and stories, not through conceptually articulated theories or artistically produced works. Nonetheless, it shares with all forms of absolute spirit the key idea that it is, as Hegel puts it, "the spirit that knows itself as spirit," that knows that it is authoritative as to what counts for it as a ground of belief or action.[4]

To *represent* something in this Hegelian sense is to try to make it present for consciousness in some intuitive sense so that it can be seen or grasped. For example, representational thought is a mode of conceiving of things in which we try to picture certain conceptual relations as relations among entities or even as entities themselves. As we have noted, representational thought can mislead us, since it can suggest to us that we look for substantives where there are none. But representational thought can also be a means of genuine knowledge; it can concretely present to us certain very abstract relations so that they are more easily intelligible. (For example, reflecting on life in terms of certain key religious stories can illuminate our highest interests in new and emotionally gripping forms better than any more dry accounting of fine theological points can do.) Hegel argues that there are genuine developments of thought that can only proceed in such representational form, and religious thought is one of them.

All religious practice is therefore a reflection in representational form on what is ultimately authoritative in human life. In that way, it symbolically presents to us what we take as that which "exists in and for itself." It tells stories and uses various images to mediate our reflections on who we essentially are and what is absolute in human life. Thus, we might represent God as a "loving father" (or perhaps better nowadays in our changed social circumstances as a "loving parent"); and for the purposes of this type of reflection on our essential self-identities, that would be fully adequate. Such representational thought helps to structure our more conceptual, discursive knowledge about ourselves and gives us paradigms around which to anchor certain types of claims about knowledge and practice. Whereas philosophy articulates matters in discursive abstract conceptual thought, religion presents matters in representations, in the form of concrete symbols and images. As representing what is ultimate in human life, religious practice moves individual agents out of their natural, egoistic state (their merely personal point of view) into a communal state in which they accept reasons, obligations and proscriptions that for them place objective limits on belief and action. Religion is thus a *representation* of the divine, of the "absolute ground of belief and action," of what "exists in and for itself," and the proper religious *attitude* is therefore that of awe and reverence toward the divine.

At the end of the section on morality and forgiveness, Hegel shows how a conception of a modern community that reconciles its members with each other by transcending the morality of praise and blame must be a religious community of a certain type – that is, not a community based on rigid responsibilities and on the finding of fault or on the idea of us as humans fully transcending the contingencies of our nature, but on a structure of mutual recognition that allows the members of the community to achieve a reconciliation both with each other and with themselves as individuals. The historical construction of self-identity in human communities becomes thereby transformed into the project of *coming to terms* with who we are. This transformation is brought about, so Hegel argues, by the modern community's having become a community in which a certain type of Judeo-Christian morality has come to play a formative role in the *secular* life of the community. In order to understand, however, how this form of a *religious* account of ourselves has come for us to be dialectically transformed into the rational *secular* account of ourselves in a modern community, it is necessary to see how this form of religion is to be understood as itself an answer to problems of self-identity. If a form of religious community – an understanding of ourselves in terms of certain basic tenets of Judeo-Christian morality – is the rational secular solution to problems of the character and the ultimate ends of life of the European community, then we must understand what it is about fully modern religious consciousness itself that gives it this place.

A fully *modern* form of religious consciousness would be a reflection on the absolute principles governing the forms and practices of the modern community, in which we reconcile the modern conception of ourselves as self-determining agents with both the facts of social life and the emerging scientific picture of people as merely natural phenomena governed by the same set of laws as the rest of nature. Hegel argues that modern life has made several failed attempts at establishing a fully modern religious consciousness, but each of these has failed. These forms may be seen in the preceding chapters of the *Phenomenology,* and he thus begins his reflections on religion with some very general remarks about why these early modern attempts have failed.

All forms of religion are representational reflections on the divine, on what we must regard as not merely valuable but *sacred* in the world. Until the explicit treatment of religion in the chapter dedicated to it, the *Phenomenology* treats religion only as a "form of consciousness" – that is, a way in which subjects take themselves to be aware of what is authoritative for them (the "absolute essence," as Hegel calls it). In each of these forms (for example, the "unhappy consciousness" and "faith"), there was discussion of an agent's taking something as "absolute" (as sacred), but the focus of the discussion had to do with the way in which that form of life's accounts of agents' taking this or that as "absolute" could be counted as legitimate. The focus of discussion in the chapter on religion, however, is with the sacred itself and how religious accounts of the sacred undermine themselves, break down, and thus require more complete religious accounts.

Religious consciousness is, moreover, not to be understood as a kind of truncated form of theory-building (that is, as a kind of primitive alternative to natural science or philosophy). Religion is not primarily concerned at all with positing supersensible entities to explain the phenomena of experience. It is concerned instead with formulating reflections and beliefs about what is the "absolute ground" of belief itself and therefore on what has "absolute value" for humans, what human agents must take as *sacred* to them. It is thus fully misunderstood if it is seen as a form of "the understanding," as an account of our awareness of things as grounded in supersensible determining grounds.[5] For example, accounts such as the argument from design – the idea that since the world exhibits an order, there must be a divine designer of that world – cannot function as fully *religious* reflections, for they focus on what they take to be a good explanations for the determinateness of appearance, not on what we must take to be of value "in and for itself." Nor could the "supreme being" function as an object of awe and reverence.[6] The "other" for "the understanding" is simply an abstract entity beyond consciousness, beyond appearance in general. Modern religious consciousness, however, requires an account of how its communal, reflective activity of taking something as authoritative can serve as a ground for taking something to be sacred. (Indeed, part of the historical maturation of religious consciousness involves the development of the separation of "the understanding's" accounts of appearance in terms of supersensible entities and religion's concern with what is of ultimate value in human life.)

Nor can the "unhappy consciousness" be a genuine form of fully *modern* religious consciousness. The form of life of the "unhappy consciousness" in late antiquity seeks to secure its self-identity both within its communities of devotion and in its communion with the transcendent supersensible beyond which it cannot attain. The "unhappy consciousness" is a form of life in which what has been taken as authoritative is no longer able to defend itself against skeptical discreditings but in which no alternative account has yet emerged. Thus, the "unhappy consciousness" represents a form of life that has lost faith in itself, that can no longer really believe in what it once took to be authoritative for itself, and that also has no alternative to its skeptically regarded accounts of itself. In its early medieval form, moreover, the form of life of the "unhappy consciousness" engendered a self-understanding that actually laid the ground for a fully non-religious, secular form of life, since its account of itself as coming to a knowledge of the "essence" of things through a mediator-priest helped to create a view of nature that opened the door for early modern natural science to seek an account of nature in human reason alone. That form of self-understanding that grows out of the early medieval form of the "unhappy consciousness" thus actually undermines many aspects of the religious view and leads to a non-religious, secular view of nature and a search for the ultimate values in human life in some form of naturalism and gratification of the senses.[7]

The "religion of morality" (Hegel's name for the kind of religion associated with the "moral worldview") comes the closest to developing a fully modern conception of religious consciousness, but it still cannot fully understand itself as religious. In the religion of morality, the agent understands himself as a completely autonomous being, divorced from nature. The essence of things is seen to lie in the noumenal willing subject, who does not (who actually *cannot*) surface in the appearing world and whose self-determination and purity of motive are its important features. The self-conception involved in the moral worldview, with its appeals to conscience and irony, leads to the harsh world of praise and blame that can only be lived through in a kind of ongoing mutual hypocrisy. This itself is overcome only by an adoption of a practice of forgiveness and reconciliation, in which people come to terms with their limitations by practicing a secularized version of certain Christian virtues. The practice of "religion as morality" undermines itself in that its own antinomies lead to a community of "beautiful souls" who, in their attempts to overcome the alienation and antinomies of the moral worldview (along with its envy of the happy and its incipient hypocrisy), themselves become a community of mutually accusatory ironists and hard-hearted judgmentalists. Only in realizing that each has presupposed a certain form of rational, self-conscious life as what is of utmost value – only as realizing that it holds such rational, self-conscious self-grounding life to be sacred, to be that which, as Kant held of the moral law itself, we must stand in awe – did the community of "beautiful souls" come to any reconciliation with itself. That is, the "beautiful souls" can come to the type of reconciliation that is needed to affirm that which both the ironists and the judgmental moralists hold as being of ultimate value by ceasing to be a purely *romantic* community and becoming instead a modern *religious* community.

A fully modern religious consciousness thus must articulate the kind of self-understanding that is constitutive of modern individuals, and it must be compatible with the secular worldview that Hegel will argue is in part generated by the kinds of accounts that religion has given of humanity. Moreover, in the ideal case, in modern religious practice each would understand himself to be acting out of a sense of who he is, and he would understand that who he is is not the result of some determination by a metaphysical entity beyond appearance but of the history that has structured his "social space" in the way that it is. Finally, not only must a fully modern religious consciousness articulate these ideas, if it is to be a fully modern *religious* consciousness, it must be the case that there is something about this fully modern *self-consciousness* that requires a *religious* component – that is, something which *only* religious reflection can perform in modern life.

That religion is a form of absolute spirit, of the human community reflecting on its self-identity without the mediation of a metaphysical other, does not mean that all religions understand themselves that way. In fact, so Hegel argues, because of the manner in which religious reflection is carried out – namely, by representational thought – religious reflection in its own terms tends toward the metaphysical; this is the case even in fully modern religious reflection in which the metaphysical element is in principle undermined. The particular historical institutionalization of any form of religion will thus not be in full congruence with the overall point of religion, although (so Hegel will argue) this can only be apparent to individuals living in and formed by a fully modern community.

Religion is necessarily implicit in any form of life, since any form of life will have certain norms and standards as authoritative for its reason-giving activities. But religion only becomes genuine religion when it is part of "spirit." A form of life becomes "spirit" when it develops reflective practices whose objects are the authoritativeness of the reason-giving activities of that form of life; as reflective practice, religion has for its objects what is ultimately authoritative in terms of what is of inherent and fundamental value and what is to count as sacred. Thus, the development of religious consciousness is itself a development of various "formations of consciousness," of the kinds of things that are taken as authoritative and the kinds of ways in which agents take themselves to know such things (that is, of the "authoritative objects" of consciousness and the ways in which agents take themselves to be related to those "objects"), and the development of religious consciousness thus will be subject in principle to the same kind of dialectical progression as the other "formations of consciousness." Religious consciousness, that is, is a mode by which agents individually and collectively try to develop a coherent self-understanding in coming to a coherent understanding of what is to count for them as ultimately definitive for belief and action.[8] As such, religious consciousness is internally linked to the "spirit" of a form of life (in Hegel's terms, to particular "formations of spirit"), and the teleology of religious consciousness is the same as the teleology of other "formations of consciousness." Thus, religious consciousness develops from a form of "immediate" knowledge, as a form of life taking what is definitive for itself to be based in a kind of non-inferential awareness of some divine, determining ground of belief and action; or as a form of self-conscious reflection in which the "object" of consciousness is taken to be the self's own determining powers of determining the "divine ground" to appear to the community; or finally as an awareness of the determining ground as "spirit" itself, as the structure of practices through which a form of life reflects on what has come to be definitive for itself and the ways in which those reflections renew and reassure or transform and splinter what that form of life has come to regard as definitive for itself.[9]

Since absolute spirit is the reflection on the essential self-identity of the human community, it makes some sense to say (as it does not, for example, of politics) that there is only *one* religion, one set of basic interests that tie members of the entire human community together.[10] These have to do with our understanding of ourselves as *finite* rational agents who are born and die and of our attempts at reconciliation with these facts. Unlike the politics of an earlier epoch, which can later appear as completely odd and foreign to us, the reflections of absolute spirit have a kind of timeless presence such that the truths articulated therein can be appropriated by people living in much different circumstances and times.[11]

Natural religion

The most immediate way in which a community would understand its essential self-identity would be similar to the way in which the human community would first understand itself as a community – that is, in terms of a kind of natural background of secure beliefs that the community's practices reflect a stable order of things that just are what they are, and that the ends of human life are set by this stable unchanging order. The form of religion corresponding to this would be *natural* religion, in which the community understands itself as a product of nature (with nature being understood in a more or less obscurely metaphysical sense by that community). The community's awareness of itself would be in terms of a set of beliefs and practices that would seem as natural to the members of the community as the behavior of animals seems natural to those animals. Both the cultural and the natural orders would be understood to be the same at their source, and the issue for such reflection would thus concern the articulation of what this source is and how it structures both the world of nature and human practice. Hegel takes an illustrative version of this conception of religion to be something like early Zoroastrianism, a religion of what Hegel calls "the luminous essence" (*das Lichtwesen*).[12] The community believes that its "natural" and embedded beliefs and practices must have some kind of ground that explains why their form of life is in accordance with the order of things, and it seeks to intuit that ground in nature. One readily available symbol for such a view would be that of sunrise and light; the essence of things could be seen in terms of their being grounded in the "luminous essence." The sunlight radiates things and brings out their features, whereas night tends to obliterate the individual features of things. Thus, both nature and human social practice have their source in a common "luminous essence." The appropriate symbol for this view of the ultimate determining ground of belief and action is thus that of a great white light that bestows determinateness on things (as a symbol for the way in which the great world-in-itself brings forth a phenomenal world of individually determinate entities).[13]

However, the very abstract metaphysical conception of the "luminous essence" has no space in it in which human agents can see themselves reflected. By reflecting on themselves through the representations of lightness and darkness, humanity can acquire no more than the most abstract understanding of its essential self-identity, of *who* it is. The divine is simply other than humanity; it is not intelligible to us, nor is it connected in any clear way with specifically human concerns. Although we may stand in the relation of awe and reverence to it, we cannot understand it, whether it has any purposes or how it is related to the appearing world for which it is the "ground." The underlying essence of all that exists is merely the indeterminate One, from which all is supposedly said to flow, and from this very abstract understanding flow only highly general pieces of so-called abstract "wisdom," such as "Everything has a common source" or "Everything is good." The "negativity" of self-consciousness – the development of norms of critical reflection on the kinds of reasons we take for granted – appears also in such religious reflection. If the "light" is what is good, and everything is bathed in light, then how do we explain evil (that is, those things that the religious consciousness on its own terms must accept as the contrary of what they take to be the good), except by denying it or seeing it as posited by some other anti-divine force (such as, of course, darkness).

Reflection on who we are that is mediated by such symbols naturally leads to a proliferation of deities, just as "sense-certainty" as a form of consciousness leads to the form of consciousness called "perception" with its attendant multiplicity of abstract entities and their properties. The kind of natural pantheism of the "luminous essence" tends toward polytheism. After all, if everything has a common source (say, in the luminous essence), then why is anything different from anything else? People likewise manifest many different types of concerns that have to do with the various facets of their natural and social lives. The most natural explanation for this fact of multiplicity is the idea that there are not just *one* source but *many* sources of determinateness. Natural religion thus quite intuitively becomes polytheistic.

Since in natural religion the aspects of cultural life are to be understood in terms of natural facts (of a sort), various basic human passions and conflicts will necessarily be pictured in this polytheism by representative natural entities (for example, various plants and animals) that themselves are naturally symbolic of these passions (for example, lions as natural symbols for courage, snakes as natural symbols for sneakiness and treachery, and so on). These symbolic forms embody and mediate this kind of reflection. People understand their virtues, for example, as coming from, say, eagles. Indeed, the passage from a symbolism of plants to a symbolism of animals entails a passage from a more quiescent understanding of the divine as that which develops itself in nature to a more aggressive understanding of the divine as engaged in a form of life and death struggle with various opposed elements (just as the eagle must struggle for existence against others[14]).

Natural religion thus tends to represent good and evil as opposed, as manichean forces (for example, light and darkness, or the conflict among different "animal spirits"). Natural religion, moreover, has the logical tendency to develop accounts of the determining ground of reason and belief (of appearance in general) as lying not in one abstract thing (such as the "luminous essence") but in the *process* of conflict itself between various divine forces represented by symbols of light and darkness or in terms of symbols of animal life. Because of this, it cannot offer any reconciliatory vision for humanity; it must see life as eternally unreconciled, as existing in a space of eternal conflict among competing powers or divinities. In natural religion, the divine powers can thus have no real interest in human concerns. Only the religious agents themselves have concern about the divine, about that which they take to be determining and definitive for them. However, the religious *consciousness* of this "eternal process of conflict" is that which *represents* the process to itself, and as the form of life comes to offer forms of reflection on the constant movement of the "eternal conflict" (for example, in practices of meditation or in certain rites), natural religion logically develops a form of self-consciousness about how the religious agent himself stands beyond the conflict. Natural religion, as reflective social practice, thus logically tends to dissolve itself as it tries to offer accounts of what it takes to be the divine – the inherently, ultimately valuable and determining in human life – in terms of these symbols of conflicts of light and darkness or between abstractly opposed powers.

Natural religion and its attendant problems are brought to a culmination, Hegel argues, in the religion of the Egyptians.[15] In ancient Egyptian religion, the human community learns to represent to itself what it takes as its essential truths by representing all of the different animal gods as expressing various realities about life. The gods, moreover, are *represented* by artifacts (for example, statues) produced by an *artisan (Werkmeister)*. The artisan is the result of the religious consciousness that becomes self-conscious as representing the process of conflict among the gods; the artisan is, however, not self-conscious of his representing activity *as representing* so much as he simply produces artifacts according to social norms as to how this or that god is to appear (as an owl, a falcon, or as a more mysterious mixture of animal and human forms).[16] The artisan is thus to be distinguished from an *artist*. The artisan understands himself as fashioning natural material that is already ready to hand in the way that simply fits conventional standards; that is, he simply fabricates various artifacts according to communally accepted norms as to what the artifact is supposed to look like. An artist, on the other hand, understands himself (and is understood by others in his community) *as an artist* to the extent that he understands his activity to be a reflection on that which the community takes as definitive for itself. The artist is *reflective* about the truth of what is ultimate for his community, and his artifacts are fashioned by him to present those truths; the artist's activity is thus inherently teleological, as involving a conception of fashioning things so that they better represent the truth about these ultimate values and beliefs. The artisan's activity is not teleological; he changes the shape of his objects as the community's norms change without any reference as to whether the later or earlier norms are "closer" or "further" from the truth. The artisan of religious consciousness thus simply accepts certain things about the divine as "given," as taken for granted, whereas the artist of religious consciousness takes the divine to be accessible only through an act of reflection.

In Egyptian religion, nature and spirit are both represented as having a common divine source in something that is itself *both* nature and spirit. The gods of ancient Egypt were the concrete reflections on this question of the self-identity of the Egyptian community, for they embodied in themselves the peculiar mixture of animal forms with each other and of human and animal forms together that nowhere appear in the phenomenal world but that symbolize what are taken to be the underlying hidden truths about that world. The underlying essence of things is seen as having a kind of self-consciousness that is something *like* human self-consciousness and is therefore partially intelligible to us, yet is also very different from human life and is therefore partially unintelligible to us. In order to express this conception of the "essence" of appearance as being something that is both a part of nature and also self-conscious, the artisan is led to mixing the natural forms into more human shape, and some of the familiar gods of Egypt appear with, for example, the heads of animals and the bodies of humans. Natural religion thus creates a kind of religious account of humanity in which it is possible to form an understanding of the metaphysical essence of things to be not nature per se, but a kind of mysterious union of nature and spirit. To the extent that humans are part of nature yet are not part of it – to the extent that the distinction of nature and spirit remain in this account only very crudely opposed – it makes sense to think of the hidden essence of things as itself mixing nature and spirit in strange and mysterious ways, toward which the attitudes of devotion and awe are appropriate. Thus, although the determining ground of appearance is depicted through the various statuaries, obelisks and the like, the actual determining ground itself comes to be understood as not actually appearing *in* them but as remaining *beyond* them and being mysterious and mostly unavailable for human thought. The works themselves are only *symbols* of an essential world beyond the realm of the appearance of the natural world.[17] (Hegel thinks that the paradigmatic form for this kind of self-understanding is architectural: planes and lines that enclose the body either as a habitat or as a grave.)

In doing this, however, the artisan comes to see *himself* symbolically mirrored in the work (for example, a statue) in the way that the other forms of natural religion with their attendant animal gods could not allow. In such a form of religious reflection, the artisan would understand himself (and would be understood by others in the practice of natural religion) to be fashioning natural shapes according to socially accepted, simply "given" principles. However, the kind of reflection on self-identity prompted by the artifacts of such artisanship leads to an account of such artifacts as being *symbolically representative* of an "inner essence" of things that involves something like human form. Once the move is made to understanding the artifacts as *symbolic* of some "deeper," "inner" truth that also has a human form (of sorts), religion itself becomes more self-conscious in its reflections on the principles governing humanity. But as natural religion, the object of its reflections must remain something "given," something that is apprehended by the religious consciousness and which cannot itself necessarily be comprehended.[18]

To understand his work in this way, however, changes the artificer's task for himself; the task ceases to be the merely technical problem of how to fashion, for example, a proper statue of a hawk but that of how the artisan's intuition of a set of "deeper" and "hidden" truths can be given adequate expression. This change in the understanding of the relation between a symbol and what it symbolizes has fundamental implications both with how the artisan and his community understand what he is doing and with understanding whether he should even be taken as an *artisan* at all. For example, it is a technical problem for the artisan as to how best to produce a statue of a hawk so that it better represents some favored natural quality (for example, prowess in hunting); fashions in this can change and develop, and different artisans can be better or worse at it. Underlying that view of the artisan's role is the understanding that a statue possesses a perfectly natural relation between itself (the statue of a hawk) and what it symbolizes (prowess in hunting).

However, once the inner truth being expressed is not seen as standing in a *natural* relation with the symbol – that is, once the problem is seen as lying precisely in the *indeterminate* relation between the symbol and what it symbolizes – then the problem can no longer be purely technical. The problem becomes instead how to unite the naturalistic and human prototypes with a form that is more conducive to expressing the so-called "deeper," "inner" truth. In order to do this, however, the artisan must be understood to be possessing special insight into these "hidden" truths about human life, for otherwise he could not even begin to know how to craft the proper statue.

The artisan and his community must therefore come to hold that he is not so much an *artisan* fashioning statues of natural entities (plants or animals) in the accepted style, instinctively shaping material into its proper form but someone who must possess an "insight" into a range of mysterious and hidden truths. In this way, the religious consciousness comes to understand him not as an artisan but as the *artist* of a cult who creates works that capture these "hidden" truths about what are the divine grounds of human life. Out of the possibilities created for them by natural religion, the ancient Egyptians themselves created an account of the relation between nature and spirit that made it possible to think of the opposition between them in a way that both played up their difference and that brought the divine closer to the human. They were thus able to move away from natural religion to a more reflective religion and thus historically enable a move into spirit – *Geist* – proper. The underlying sense or point of the religious practices of the Egyptians had to do with a reflection on what it is to be a human agent. The transformation within their religious practices of *artisanal* activity into self-conscious *artistic* activity created the possibility of *reflecting* on whether the "artist" was not just "getting it right" in terms of certain socially established norms of fabrication and symbolization but in terms of whether he was presenting a reflective version of what the community had come to take as definitive for itself. The *artisan* produces his artifacts in light of what has come to be taken as the norm for how, for example, a statue of Osiris should look; the *artist* begins to produce works that embody a communal reflection on whether what has been taken as a valid statue of Osiris is indeed *really* a valid portrayal of what is truly divine. With that creation of the social means for reflecting on what a community has come to take as authoritative for itself, a dialectical transition is effected to a different form of religious life that is historically exemplified in the passage from the world of ancient Egyptians to that of the ancient Greeks.

The religion of art: Greek life

Beauty, truth and divinity. The ancient Greek form of life with its characteristic self-understandings arose out of the religious accounts of human life created by Egyptian religion's completion of the accounts of life in terms of natural religion. Natural religion had depicted the divine grounds of belief and action in terms of some parts of nature abstracted and made into symbols, and Egyptian religion had transformed that symbolic natural ground into something that mixed both nature and spirit together. Egyptian religion therefore tacitly brought the difference between spirit and nature to the forefront of human reflection in the way it represented the metaphysical basis of human life as resting in something that was not simply nature but the mysterious complex of nature/spirit/humanity that constituted the Egyptian divinities. In the Greek form of life, this account is sharpened into a symbolic presentation of the gods as being very much human. Out of their earlier natural gods, the Greeks represented to themselves a more nearly human set of gods as evolving and eventually triumphing over the nature-gods. Thus, in the Greek form of life, the *divine* comes to assume a *human* form, and because of this, these gods and the self-understandings they represented were best expressed and understood in works of art. The gods are seen as fulfillments of human beauty and perfection, similar to us yet also radically unlike us. They are like us in that they assume human form; they are unlike us in their immortality and thus their incomprehension and indifference to many of the basic passions and motivations of humanity. As eternal, they are, unlike humans, untroubled by the natural facts of birth and death. The Greek form of life thus resolved in its own way the difficulties left over in the Egyptian fulfillment of natural religion in that it saw no need to conceive of a single source – nature/spirit – in order to give an account of the absolute principles of human life. It now conceived of the divine as very much like humanity and divine ends as thus more intelligible to us than the ends of an unintelligible natural world. In natural religion, the divine – the ground of what is sacred, of ultimate and inherent value to humans – is itself indifferent to human concerns; in Greek religion, the divine is conceived as somewhat closer to human concerns.

233

Greek religion and Greek art are combined in the presentation of the Greek understanding of the divine. The divine for the Greeks is represented as human perfection – specifically, of the Greek ideals of male and female beauty. Both art and religion are types of absolute spirit, that is, practices which offer reflections on what has come to be taken as authoritative for a community; in Greek life, art and religious practice coincide. Art is reflection on what is authoritative by means of the production of beautiful artifacts; beauty is, in Hegel's terms in his lectures on aesthetics, the "sensuous *appearance (Scheinen)* of the idea," the rational coherence of sensuous appearance.[19] For the Greek conception of divinity, the artist who produces a work of beauty therefore also presents the divine; the artist who wishes to craft a sculpture of, for example, Apollo or Aphrodite, need only concentrate on what a beautiful young man or woman would look like in order to present an accurate image of Apollo. Beauty and truth (at least about divinity) thus fuse together for the Greeks, and the Greek religion is therefore the *religion of art.* The serenity of the Greek gods, untroubled by the *natural* fact of mortality, is captured in the statues of them; philosophical reflections, for example, on their eternal nature must measure up to that understanding rather than evaluate the gods from the standpoint of independent thought. (For this reason, Hegel thinks, genuine philosophical reflection was profoundly destabilizing for Greek life.) Likewise, the conflicts between gods and humans are best captured in epic and tragic poetry, not in abstract speculations about the foundations of knowledge. It is this understanding of what was involved in Greek life and why it had to fail on its own terms that led Hegel to his belief that this kind of fulfillment of the practice of art was achieved only in ancient Greek art and indeed *could* only be achieved in Greek art.[20]

Hegel begins his discussion of Greek life by focusing on the way in which in the transition from Egypt to Greece, the artist's self-understanding necessarily must change because of the change in the conception of the divine. In coming to understand himself as an artist, the artisan of natural religion comes to see his task in a different light. He must create something out of natural material that expresses the "inner essence" of the community (what for it is authoritative) but is not itself simply a piece of nature. This would be the kind of art that seems to have an *immediate* presence to it, and it finds its expression in ancient Greek art. In such a work of religious art, one would supposedly behold the divine presence immediately in the work. The work would not be a *representation* of the divine through symbols, which would leave it to the beholder to infer the characteristics of the divine on the basis of the representation. Rather, it would actually *present* the divine fully before one. One would behold the divine in the work (for example, a statue of Apollo) without having to make any further inferences. Thus, the initial steps of the "religion of art" take over from natural religion the idea that the divine is an immediate object of religious consciousness, something directly apprehended without any further knowledge being necessary.

However, because in casting, say, a statue, the artist in the Greek form of life understands that statue as bringing the god forth without any intervention either on the artist's part or on the part of the beholders of the work, the artist at first cannot understand himself as fully creative. Although he understands that he is not merely an artisan putting things into their "natural" forms, he does not understand himself as putting anything of *his* own into the work any more than the beholders are putting something of themselves into it. Since (for example) Athena actually appears in the work, he is not constructing a work that is *his* understanding of how, for example, Athena is to be understood. The work of art is therefore an object that is independent of him, that depicts its truth without any contribution from him. Thus, the artist, although thinking of himself as an artist, still conceives of himself along the lines of being an artisan.

There is a conceptual development, however, from natural religion, and that concerns the form which religious art takes. The statue that represents the God assumes a human and not an animal form. In natural religion, divinity took on animal and plant forms. But the facts about spirit – the self-understandings involved in the practices of the community – are not natural facts. The "facts" about spirit are contained not in the natural facts about human life but in the kinds of practices and norms that together constitute the "social space" within which the self-identity of its members takes shape. In Greek art, this comes to the foreground of artistic representation. By representing the gods as human-like, the Greeks were able to articulate a different conception of themselves than would have been possible in natural religion. They were able to gain a more determinate (although still abstract) form of self-knowledge in thinking of the divine as human in shape.[21]

However, the representation of the god cannot be understood by this form of life (at least at this stage in the development of its self-understanding) *as a representation*. The statue is not a *representation* of the god; it is the presence of the god itself that is beheld by the members of the cult by virtue of the presence of the statue to them. The god is present in the statue, and we intuit him (or her) in seeing the statue. The artist therefore can only understand himself as a fabricator, someone who makes things, not someone who creates things. The statue must be seen as having, so to speak, inspired its own creation.[22] The god who is beheld in the statue is a perfect entity (he displays human qualities to perfection) and yet the god is also a non-human entity (he displays an indifference to human life that is also characteristic of nature's indifference to human life, while at the same time he sometimes takes pity on humans in a way typical of humanity itself).

If it is to provide a means of self-conscious reflection on self-identity, the work of art must be linked to human self-conscious activity; it must be understood as being an artifact, not a product of nature. If it is seen to animate itself, the work cannot proffer much of a means of mediating the reflections of individuals. If it is to be understood as *art* and not as a relapse into natural religion, the work must therefore be understood in its relation to the artist's activity. If the statue is seen as animating or ensouling (*beseelen*) itself, then it cannot be seen as coming to an appearance through any *human* mediation, however human the statue may look. If the presence of the god is to be in some way human, then it must be linked with self-conscious human activity, and it can only do this if the artist or the community itself plays a role in bringing the god to view. The god cannot simply appear on his own; he must be assisted in his appearance in some way by the act of the community. In seeing the divine – that which governs the absolute principles concerning human life – as approaching the human and as coming to understand human intervention as essential for the appearance of the divine, Greek religion revises its account of the divine, taking it in the direction of conceiving of the absolute principles directing human life as coming from humanity itself – that is, toward a conception of spirit as the human community self-consciously reflecting on its self-identity as a human community.

This signals a crucial change in the self-understanding of the community. The members of the community had understood themselves simply to be beholding the presence of the god. However, they come to see that only through their activity can the god be present. This change in self-understanding is part of the way in which the artist gradually comes to understand himself not just as an artisan but as an artist. As the community comes to have this self-understanding – that of creating a work in which the god can appear – it too comes to understand itself differently. It comes to see itself as playing a determining role in how what is definitive for itself takes the shape it does.

However, once it comes to see this as its role, it also comes to understand that statuary is an imperfect vehicle for this type of understanding. The reciprocal interplay between the community's activity and the appearance of the god demands a type of work in which the appearance of the god is reflective of both the self-conscious activity of the artist and the community in bringing about that appearance, and in which the self-conscious nature of the god is not tied into something so obviously lacking in self-consciousness as a statue. A form of art involving language is much more suited than statuary for this role, and, so Hegel argued, something like the hymn practiced by the cults of ancient Greek life stepped into the space of logical possibilities created by the development of this kind of reflective practice. Language is, after all, the major mode in which we appear to each other as agents and subjects. Language is fully intersubjective, and it nonetheless expresses the individuality of the person speaking. Language is also a complete expression of thought; the thoughts expressed by language are not hidden essences or entities standing "behind" the words; the language and its use *are* the meanings.[23]

The religious overcoming of alienation. In the hymn to the god, the community creates a work of art that helps it to understand its own determinative role in the appearance of the divine. Whereas natural religion had seen the divine as something outside of human life (in nature) that determined human life according to its own laws, the Greek form of life sees humanity's own acts as partially constitutive of the appearing of the divine. Not only do the gods partially resemble humanity, humanity's actions are necessary for the gods to appear. Humanity begins, that is, to see the absolute principles governing human life not as imposed by something alien to their concerns but as something that is intimately connected with their concerns.

In coming to this kind of understanding of the divine, the Greek religious consciousness fashions for itself an understanding of the divine with which it can be "at home," or "with itself."[24] Ultimately, the agent can only be "with himself" in a social situation in which the determining ground is constituted by the practices of his community, and those practices have a kind of internal rationality to them that makes it both appropriate and necessary for the agent to identify with them completely. But there is more to it than merely being "at home with oneself" in a community. Hegel also speaks of the agent's being *in* the action.[25] An agent is *in* his action if that action is such that the agent can identify with the action, see it as embodying who he takes himself to be, and if the agent is not *in* the action, then he may be said to be *alienated* from it. Only in acting does the subject acquire a self-identity and any concrete, visible presence in the world. (Thus, since the "beautiful soul" of romanticism refuses to act, he cannot have any concrete existence in the world of appearance.) A further sense of the subject's "being with himself" is thus that he not be alienated from his actions, which, as we have seen, is only possible in a "social space" in which there are no fundamental, essential irrationalities. In those forms of life (of spirit) in which the structure of "social space" is essentially contradictory, the subject will experience a deep sense of being alienated from himself or from his social environment.

In Greek life (on Hegel's view of it), the agent finds such an identification (at least at first) in that the institutions and practices of Greek life were internally rational enough to make a claim on his identifying with those practices, since in Greek ethical life the subjective certainty of self-identity and the affirming structures of mutual recognition meshed. In following out the demands of a social situation with its associated roles and duties, the agent is "with himself" to the extent that these socially determining factors characterize him as a rational agent, such that he does not take any of these social requirements as being in any sense alien to him.

The religion of the ancient Greeks embodied this idea of "being with oneself." The religious hymn unites the individual and the community in a practice that is understood as calling forth the appearance of the god. Each therefore finds that in participating in the hymn, he is encountering the divine – what is of ultimate and inherent value to that community – in himself and in the community as a whole. Each finds, that is, that in following out what the *community* determines he is to do, he is doing that which his personal point of view demands of him.[26]

Hegel contrasts the way in which the hymn is used to call forth the presence of the god and the Greek practice of consulting oracles. He argues that the role of oracles in Greek life and religion is to be understood as a holdover of the genesis of the Greek gods from the gods of nature (the titans of Greek mythology, who were vanquished by the Olympians). Oracles represent a conceptually more primitive formation of religious consciousness. Interpreting the throwing of dice or the reading of entrails comports well with the kind of self-understanding of natural religion, since in it the divine is taken as something ultimately unintelligible to us and which reveals itself in natural symbols. As the indeterminate ground of the determinateness of appearance (well represented by the light of sunrise), the divine has no basic commonality with human life that can be discerned. Being so different from us, it cannot be really understood by us; indeed, the nature of the difference cannot even be stated, since the divine is taken to be unknown. Thus, it follows that the utterances of the divine must be mysterious, in "another language" and the best one can do would be to learn to "read" its mysterious utterances (from bones or entrails) as best one can. The divine is supposed to be found in the mysteries of nature; therefore its utterances must themselves take the form of natural events (smoke, rustlings in the trees, etc.) Interestingly, rather than espousing the romantic view that was then beginning to be articulated in his own day, namely, that primitive people were less alienated than modern people and more in touch with nature, Hegel argued the opposite: Primitive forms of life are *more* alienated from each other and nature than are modern forms of life. The conception of divinity found in natural religion is fully alien even to the people who are most in its grasp.[27]

In early Greek life (in the abstract work of art), the god makes an appearance because of the activity of the community, and in the activity of the community, the god (not a representation of the god) is taken to be fully present to the participants. Certain truths about the essential self-identity of the participants are therefore manifested to them. But because the gods are represented as individuals and as the divinities governing a particular people, it is logical to understand their peculiar utterances as being similar to the contingencies of an individual's deliberations. Thus, the god is seen as deciding what is best for the community of which he is the god by deliberating in a fashion analogous to the way in which a person deliberates – for example, perhaps similar to the way in which Socrates claimed that he relied on his personal daemon, his own oracle, to make particular decisions about with whom he should keep company. (The example is Hegel's.) In this way, the utterances of the oracle become humanized in a way which is not possible for a purely natural religion. It is typical of the conceptual development of Greek religion that even its naturalistic holdovers, such as belief in oracles, would be transformed into a more human form. As being the god of a particular people, he takes a concern for that people's welfare, and his deliberations are about what to do with and for the people for whom he is the deity. The oracle, rather than being something mysterious lying behind appearance becomes instead something that is more congenial to human concerns.[28]

The cult. Speech and statuary – human participation and the god – come together in the Greek cult. In the cult, one sings hymns before the statue in order to behold the presence of the god. The cult is the practice in which the people reflect on the absolute principles of their lives. However, in its attempt to reveal the divine truth immediately in the minds of the participants, the form of self-reflection on the divine practiced in the cult is only a very abstract form of reflection on what is absolute in human life. In its understanding of what it is doing (bringing the god to presence in the minds of the participants), the cult attempts, however abstractly, to unite nature and spirit, but it does this by doing two very different things. On the one hand, the cult attempts to highlight the unessential, contingent aspects of human life in terms of the eternal divine necessities, yet on the other hand it attempts to show just how essential human self-conscious practice is in calling forth the presence of the divine. The practices of the cult bring out this contradiction fully. In natural religion, people simply acknowledged themselves to be at the mercy of the divine, to be themselves merely contingent, unessential aspects of the world, and the kind of self-knowledge gained was thus abstract and alienating. In the Greek cult, a richer and more determinate form of self-knowledge is gained, for in it the participants come to reflect on the nature of their own activity and to see that activity as itself essential to the bringing forth of the divine for human witness.[29]

It is therefore not completely accidental that the cult develops some mode of natural sacrifice, in which, for example, goats are sacrificed or the fruits of Ceres and Bacchus are consumed.[30] By sacrificing something that belongs to *nature,* the individual in effect displays a devaluing of what belongs to him as a contingently existing individual in favor of what he recognizes as the underlying universal essence of nature and spirit. The act of sacrifice is a kind of reflection on what is of absolute value in the world: not the purely contingent aspects of individual life nor the contingent effects of nature but the essential and abiding aspects of divinity in its quasi-human form. In the act of sacrifice, however, the individual participant brings himself into a kind of reflective unity with the essence of things. Moreover, in consuming the wines of Bacchus, the participants assimilate the divine into themselves and are capable therefore of displaying the divine in their own humanity.[31]

In natural religion, the underlying essence of things is seen as utterly distinct from human life. However, in the practices of the ancient Greek cults – in their acts of devotion and sacrifice – the divinities become conceived as more congenial to human life. Since the divine is that which is of absolute and not contingent value, as that which is necessary, the gods must be seen to have brought this about themselves, for they have assumed determinate forms of existence and have given part of themselves over to humanity. By making themselves into participants without whose participation the god could not appear, the members of the cult create the "social space" in which it will be possible for them to acknowledge their own determining power in the way in which things are conceived. They no longer take themselves to know the divine immediately but only in terms of the shared activity between the divine letting itself come to presence before them and their activity of calling forth the divinity.[32]

The practices of the cult thus lead to a transformed type of self-understanding. The individuals no longer value their own contingent lives below that of the unknown mysterious divine essence. Instead, they find their conscious lives affirmed by the practices of their religion, they find their self-conscious lives to be an ingredient in the determining essence of things (in the appearances of the gods), and they find the gods to be more like them than would have been possible in the earlier conceptions of natural religion. The people who reflected on their lives in terms of the earlier forms of religion had to conceive of themselves merely as subject to a kind of divine power about which they could know little. In the Greek cults, on the other hand, the human community and the gods are conceived as standing in something more like that of an affinity for each other. The so-called mysteries of the cults (particularly the mysteries of the Dionysian cults) express this understanding of the divine. Their mystical nature expresses the cryptically articulated consciousness of the unity of human self-consciousness with that which is divine in the world. This unity is the unity of the vaguely informed self-understanding of the human community as not being completely under the sway of unknowable metaphysical forces (represented typically in terms of lightness and darkness or in terms of animal deities) but as having some determinative power over its destiny. What is rational in these forms of mystical life is this belief, articulated through religious symbols, that the practices of the community are not metaphysically of a different order than the underlying essence of the world and that reflection on who we essentially are is not a reflection on anything fundamentally different from the meta-physical nature of things.[33]

The revelry of the bacchantes and the festivals in which these practices were refined all played a role in articulating for the ancient Greek form of life who they were. So Hegel argues, even the festivals at which athletes were admired had a religious significance for the Greeks, since the young athlete embodied for them a kind of human and yet fragile beauty that found its non-fragile expression in the statues of the gods.[34] The young athlete in this sense was the *living work of art,* a human who gave us some flesh and blood representation of the appearance of a god.[35] The Greek religion thus moves the Greeks fully away from a conception of the divine as something radically different from humanity toward a conception of the divine as being very much like humanity; indeed, the divine becomes conceived as having an affinity with the self-conscious life of a people.[36]

The development of Greek religion as a series of individual cults, each with its own god, lays the ground for a uniting of the various gods into a collection of gods, a pantheon, in which not just a single group of people but humanity as such can be represented. The development of the pantheon marks a crucial stage in Greek self-understanding. The story of the struggle among the gods results in the triumph of the more spiritual gods over those of nature; the titans lose out and are dethroned, and Zeus becomes the commanding deity.[37] The more human-like gods triumph over the purely natural forces, and in this way, the early Greek forms of religious practice enabled the Greek people to understand in representational form the emergence of "spirit" not as a *natural* phenomenon but as constituted by ways in which the community's social practices give shape to forms of self-consciousness.[38]

Religious practice is reflection on the divine, on what is ultimately of value for a form of life. It is thus a reflection on the essential self-identity of a people, on where they stand on the issues that for them are of fundamental importance. In uniting the gods into one pantheon and in moving away from the sheer "givenness" of natural religion, the Greek form of life fashioned itself as "spirit," as having essential to its self-conception its reflections on what is authoritative for itself. In making the Greek form of life into a reflective form of life (into "spirit"), Greek religion thereby created a need for itself to give an account of why it took the things it did to be authoritative for itself. It had to offer an account of how it was that this form of life could come to be such that these conceptions of the divine could be legitimated as being genuine. In other words, by creating a form of self-reflection, it also created a need for reassurance that what it took as authoritative *really* was authoritative – in short, that its self-identity as a form of life was what it claimed to be. If what is ultimate in life cannot be found in some kind of immediate, direct apprehension of the divine (such as natural religion thought it could do) but only in some type of reflective practice, then religious practice itself had to move toward a form in which it could offer a reflective account of why what it took to be definitive for life really was definitive. The teleology of the Greek practice of religion thus motivates it to move to a conception of religious practice as lying in a *spiritual* work of art – that is, a form of religious reflection in *art*.

Epic. The Greek form of life thus was led through its religious practices to affirm its sense of the divine in the construction of art, in the self-reflection on what is of ultimate value in terms of determining its self-identity. It does this in two ways: It determines its self-identity by self-consciously reflecting on its *differences* from other forms of life and how it conflicts with them; and it determines its self-identity by self-consciously reflecting on its own *internal* principles and the possible conflicts these principles can have with each other. The Greek form of life filled this in first through its *epics* (such as Homer's *Iliad* and *Odyssey*) and second through its *tragedies* (such as those written by Aeschylus, Sophocles and Euripides).

In an epic, as Hegel later explains in his *Aesthetics,* a form of life reflects on its essential self-identity by focusing on its conflicts with another form of life, particularly in war, and how it comes to an awareness of who it is by virtue of this conflict. An epic embodies the form of life's reflection on its self-identity not through the practices of the cult (the singing of hymns to the statue of the god in which the god appears) but in the construction of a poetic narrative of how that form of life came to determine itself and discover who it was. An epic tells the story of how a determinate group of people with their own form of life have come to self-consciousness about who they are because of a conflict with some other group of people that forced them to develop that sense of who they were. Because the outcome of an epic is a self-conscious affirmation of who they are as a people, it must therefore begin with a lack of such self-conscious awareness. Thus, the actions taken by the characters of epics must be taken without much or any reflection about self-identity on the part of the characters. They simply do what they have to do, given who they take themselves to be, and the result of their doing what they had to do is a people's coming to awareness of who they are even though this is not the aim of the protagonists. Thus, the epic tells the story of how certain individualities – the mythical heroes of the past – established the self-identity of a certain form of life by their acting as they did in circumstances in which they were challenged by another form of life.[39]

Epics thus tell the story not of a *founding* of a form of life by early heroes but of that point at which the form of life is itself already established but has not yet come to a full *self-consciousness* of who it is. The people in it are taken as knowing who they are, but they do not reflect on this self-identity; they simply are immediately who they are, and they act on the basis of that self-understanding. The more prosaic aspects of a people's life – its laws, its institutions for the administration of economic life and so on – have to be supposed not yet to exist; instead, the form of life must be seen to be seemingly natural to the people involved in it, to be something that informs each of their self-understandings without their having to think about it or administer it.[40] For this reason, epics can only be mythical remembrances of a fabled past time when the heroes knew who they were, did what they had to do, and in doing so laid the basis for the community's self-consciousness.

For the Greek form of life, the creation of its epics mark a conceptual break from its origins in natural religion. The Greek epics are structured around a reflection on the absolute principles governing Greek life; thus, they form a reflection on what is divine and on the relation between humanity and divinity. Such epics are possible only as the narration of a form of life that has developed a means of seeing the *self-consciousness* of its members reflected in their understanding of the divine. As long as the divine is represented simply as a dominant natural force, as indifferent to humanity and unintelligible to it, the divine cannot be understood as having a correspondence with humanity in any way. It is instead something alien to humanity, something that rules over humanity and nature but cannot itself be understood. The use of such representations does not give a people any means to reflect on themselves as self-conscious agents; they can only see themselves as contingent subjects of some divine power.[41]

In telling a narrative of how a people came to be who they are through their conflicts with other peoples, an epic tells a particular kind of story of the relation between humans and the divine. The humans strive to fulfill their plans and ambitions, and they act out of their passions (out of their sense of who they are). Since the epic is the story of a people and their form of life, the characters of the epic must be embodiments of that form of life in condensed form. They must thus be capable of *freely* acting on their own, of making their own decisions and of expressing their sense of who they are. Yet on the other hand, the circumstances of the epic must be such that the people involved really had no choice. They did what they *had* to do, given who they were and what the circumstances were.[42] The link between this conception of free personality, worldly circumstances and the gods is that of *fate*. The heroes of the epic act freely in that they act out of a sense of who they are and of the passions bound up with that sense of self-identity, yet what they do may be foreseen by them themselves since it has a necessary outcome to it.[43]

Thus, the Greek epics present what at first may appear to be a largely confused and contradictory picture. On the one hand, the epics tell a story of fate and necessity – that is, of what has been ordained. On the other hand, they tell a story of individuals freely pursuing certain goals, while at the same time acting out of certain passions related to who they are. The Greek epic thus seems to run the danger of becoming either a story in which humans become only the playthings of the gods (and thus collapsing back into a form of natural religion), or in becoming a purely secular story in which the gods play only a peripheral or no role at all. It is therefore unclear to whom the actions undertaken are to be ascribed. The individual heroes are necessary to the telling of the epic, for without them nothing happens, and without the hero the gods are powerless to effect their ends. Yet it might seem pointless for the heroes to try to effect their own ends, since fate determines what is to be. Moreover, the gods themselves enter the affairs of the world through the actions and passions of humans, yet because of their immortality, they are ultimately indifferent to these affairs. Even the gods themselves may be seen as confusedly drawn figures; like humans, they scheme, plan and act, yet their plans cannot have the same effect as humans, since for them there is no risk involved; nothing at stake for these gods, since they are eternal.

The world of the gods is linked to the world of humans through the singer (the minstrel).[44] What links the gods to the minstrel, so Hegel argues, are the heroes of legend (such as Achilles and Odysseus).[45] The heroes represent the people and their form of life, and acting on their sense of *who* they are, they do what they *must* do. Yet the heroes' actions are determined by the larger plan that the gods have thrown in their way. By arranging the circumstances in such and such a way, the gods have constructed things so that the heroes (such as Achilles) will freely act in an ordained fashion because of who they are. In this way, the independence of the gods and the independence of the actors is provisionally maintained.[46]

However, in arranging events so that the community will come to a self-consciousness about who it is, the gods evidence a concern for the community's coming to such an awareness. The epic thus presents a certain kind of mutual participation between humans and the gods, since without their joint participation, the epic cannot occur.[47] Indeed, the Greek conception of divinity and of human life implies a kind of necessity to the epic story. Epic is a remembrance of how a form of life came to be aware of having the self-identity it has by virtue of a conflict with another form of life, with its triumph in that conflict being a matter of fate. It must understand that in the conflicts that follow from its sense of who it is, the principles on which it is based have the *right* to triumph. They acquire this right because the gods have set up the circumstances surrounding the action such that a certain outcome is foreordained given the self-identity of the actors. Since what the gods ordain is just, the triumph of the Greek form of life over the Trojan form is also just, however cruel, arbitrary, and perhaps unintelligible it might at first seem to those who hear the epic being sung. For this reason, the minstrel must in telling the story unfold the events such that the events have an inexorable direction. In the minstrel's account of the events, it is even the case that the direction of the events may be known to some of the protagonists in the story. The hero may be both doomed and know that he is doomed, but he must do what he has to do and accept whatever happens.[48]

For the Greek epic, the problem was understanding the role of necessity in all this. On the one hand, the heroes' actions would seem pointless if the gods actually control everything. On the other hand, it is fated that the heroes will go off to perform their deeds and that the result will be a self-consciousness about the community's self-identity. Indeed, without this kind of necessity, the doomed heroes would seem foolish, since without the necessity of fate, they can only seem like obdurate and impulsive individuals, not like heroes. The necessity that drives the epic, therefore, is a *conceptual* requirement brought on by the Greek understanding of the relation of the divine and the human as it is presented first in the cults and later in the telling of the epic itself. Since the determinate, semi-human gods each have their *own* self-identity in terms of which *they* are required to act (Zeus doing what he has to do, Hera doing what she has to do), they thus seem also subject to a kind of background necessity. This necessity to which they gods are subject, however, cannot be understood by positing, for example, any more gods than determine that necessity. Thus, behind the world of the gods themselves there seems to stand a realm of unintelligible metaphysical necessity.[49]

This had to raise the question for the Greeks as to whether the actions taken in epic were in fact *just*. At first, these actions seem like they must be just, since they were provoked by the gods. By constructing the circumstances in the way they did, and knowing the self-identities of the actors involved, the gods foreordained a certain outcome. Since the gods do what is just, this outcome must also be just. However, if the gods themselves are acting out of a sense of who they are – if their actions are also necessary – how can what they foreordain be just? If the gods ordain the destruction of Troy because of who they are, why is this otherwise arbitrary destruction just? Homer's sympathetic treatment, for example, of the doomed Hector implicitly raises just this question.

From tragedy to comedy. This conceptual dynamic in Greek religious life required their construction of tragic drama. The unintelligibility of the idea of necessity can only be overcome by new type of reflection on the relation between the divine and the human in which the actions that individuals take make a difference to what happens. Tragedy is that form of art in which this reflection takes place. Just as epic reflects on self-identity of a form of life in its conflict with another form of life unrelated to it, tragedy reflects on the internal conflicts within a form of life itself (or, as in the case of modern tragedy, of conflicts within a character or between characters).[50] Moreover, tragedy represents a conceptual movement in the development of Greek self-understanding, since it offers an explicit reflection on necessity and self-identity. In Greek tragedy, the tragic element comes about because of characters who act out of their sense of self-identity, and who thus *necessarily* act in a manner that in turn *necessarily* leads them to their frightful culminations. The profundity of Greek tragedy and its greatness, according to Hegel's view of it, lies in its self-conscious reflection on these implications of self-identity as understood by the Greeks.[51]

In speaking of tragedy, Hegel is referring to it as a form of drama with actors on a stage.[52] In tragic drama, it is essential that instead of a minstrel impersonally relating the story of the epic, we have the *characters* speaking themselves. This is accomplished in the Greek form (as it is for us in the theater) by having actors play the roles.[53] Thus, instead of an impersonal minstrel reciting the tale for us, we have humans speaking the parts for us.[54] The work of art is present before us as it unfolds itself.[55]

What makes something tragic as opposed to being merely unfortunate (or simply terribly sad) is the idea that the characters who embody some basic aspect of the self-identity of a form of life, given who they are, do what they have to do, and this action on their part necessarily leads them to some terrible end.[56] The progress toward the tragic fate of the characters is grounded in actions that necessarily follow from who they are; there is no point at which, given who they are, they could alter the course of events. The idea of something's being tragic as opposed to being merely unfortunate is linked with the possibility of *reconciliation* in tragedy. Reconciliation is achieved in tragedy by the course of events turning out such that *justice* has been shown to have been done. Indeed, without some idea of justice or desert, it makes little sense to describe something as tragic, as opposed to being merely unfortunate. What the tragic character does is something he *must* do because of who he is. Moreover, he must be *right* in doing so (that is, his character must be in itself justified – the evil actions taken by a brigand because of who he is cannot lead to tragedy). Thus, for something to constitute a tragic course of affairs, the tragic character *must* undertake an action (because of who he is) which is *right* in itself but which leads him to commit a *wrong,* and justice requires this wrong itself to be righted – that is, for the character to suffer commensurate to the wrong that has been done. Since reconciliation in tragedy requires that the ethical world be set aright, it requires *either* the destruction of the character (or some form of appropriate suffering) *or* divine absolution for the wrong which was committed.[57] For there to be reconciliation in tragedy, there must therefore be some idea of a "substantial order" of things – a scheme of ethical justice – that can be shown to prevail. Reconciliation in tragedy is not, however, simply a matter of crime being punished. For there to be reconciliation in tragedy, it must be the case that the tragic heroes be seen to be in the right; what is tragic in their actions is a function of their doing something wrong as a direct corollary of their being in the right. Reconciliation therefore requires that the "substance" of things be seen to be in harmony with itself and that its harmony be restored by the denouement of the tragedy itself. The significance of tragedy thus lies in its showing how a form of life can be conflicted *within itself,* such that characters who embody some basic feature of that form of life are led to perform actions that, although right, are also nonetheless wrong, and for which the "substantial order" demands some type of atonement on their part in order for the "substantial order" to be set aright.

The necessity that was blind and incomprehensible in the epic is in tragedy shown to have a conceptual necessity to it, namely, in the exposure of what is internally contradictory in the Greek form of life. It is not simply that things turn out that way and had to turn out that way; they turn out that way *because* of the contradictory one-sided nature of the *roles* that Greeks found perfectly natural to assume. Nor could their conception of the gods be of much help to them in this context. The gods who contend among themselves cannot be expected to be able to resolve any of these conflicts. Moreover, given their nature, it is unclear why they would even care about them. Since there is no unitary nature to the gods, there can be no unifying overview of the basis of life.[58] When the gods do appear to assist the humans in tragedy, it is clearly a contrivance on the part of the author.

The Greek multiplication of gods was a reflection on their view of the world, which lacked a unifying focus of *principle*. Instead, the unifying focus, so Hegel argues, is that of *art*. (In his later lectures on the philosophy of religion, Hegel described Greek religion as the "religion of beauty.") The gods are depicted as being beautiful and serene, and the religious practices themselves come to be works of art. For the Greeks, tragedy therefore was a work of art in which their religious vision of the world was presented to them such that they were enabled to come to a self-conscious reflection on who they were. The chorus in Greek drama represents the voice of the common folk (as the embodiment of the Greek *Sittlichkeit*) expressing their view of the necessity that confronts the characters in the play.[59] From the standpoint of the chorus, this necessity must remain simply uncomprehended, and it can only express terror and compassion in light of the necessarily oncoming destruction of the parties whose actions it is witnessing. In order to provide the spectators with material for reflection, the characters in such a tragedy must represent one of the basic dimensions of the Greek form of life (such as the way in which Antigone represents the family and Creon the state). The protagonists, that is, must take upon themselves one of the dimensions of Greek life in order to expose the one-sidedness of that dimension and the terrible consequences of acting only according to that dimension in abstraction from the other. Their character is thus informed by one of the "powers" of the Greek form of life (for example, by one of the gods). This puts the characters in the position of acting on the certainty of who they are as the god has revealed it to them and finding that their destruction follows from this action.[60]

In tragedies such as *Antigone*, each character represents one of the basic ethical principles of the Greek form of life (one of the ways in which Greeks understood "the way things are done"). Each thus does what he believes he must do given who he is, with the result being that each brings about his own (and the other's) destruction because of the incompatibility of the principles themselves. Antigone finds that who she is, as the keeper of the rights of the family, is essentially at odds with who Creon is, as the keeper of the rights of the polity. The conflict between the two is not contingent, not a matter of the vagaries of two "personalities" who cannot get along with each other. Each character's self-identity conflicts with the other because the principles (or "powers," as Hegel calls them) that each embodies, which forms the *character* of each in Greek tragedy, is at odds with the other. In the case of *Antigone,* this conflict also presents a religious vision – namely, the equal power of the dark nether world with the luminous world of Zeus.[61] The result of such a clash of characters (which is always really a clash of Greek life with itself) is either destruction (as in *Antigone*) or divine absolution (as in Aeschylus' *Eumenides*).[62]

The reconciliation found in Greek tragedy cannot be therefore entirely satisfactory, for the self as portrayed in the tragedies is one-sided, having a "pathos" rather than a fully developed character.[63] The tragic figure completely embodies one of the powers of the form of life and is necessarily led to his destruction because of who he is. The only reconciliation that Greek tragedy offers is the view of necessity as *rational* necessity, as implied by the self-identity of the characters instead of just issuing from the blind fate found in the epic. It is the rationality of the "substantial ethical order" asserting itself against the wrongs that have been committed. For Greek tragedy to work, the laws that govern both humans and divinity must be presumed to be both eternal and rational. That is, for there to be a true reconciliation, the Greek spectators *must* presume that this fate is rational, that it is fundamentally that of a just cosmic order, even if (as in distinction from the later Christian view) the goals and aims of this order cannot be revealed to humans. Without this assumption, Greek tragedy could not make sense to the Greeks.[64] In this context, reconciliation in the tragedy can only come about through the acceptance of matters that fundamentally cannot be understood. This form of reconciliation must therefore be only partial; the form of self-consciousness on which it rests cannot fully understand itself. A kind of unintelligible irrationality still seems to hang over the whole background of Greek tragedy, since the freedom of individuals to act seems bounded not only by irrational struggles among the gods, but by a "power" or fate by which the gods themselves seem to be ruled.

In bringing this aspect of Greek thought to the foreground, however, Greek tragedy initiates the move away from Greek religion and thus from the whole Greek form of life, for by throwing into question the coherence of the pantheon – what Hegel calls "the unthinking mingling of individuality and essence"[65] – it throws into question the whole Greek conception of divinity and its relation to human life, and with that the general practices of that form of life itself. By focusing on what is essentially true about their form of life (of who they essentially were), the tragedians gave an account of Greek life that indicated certain basic contradictions within the Greek self-consciousness. The "fate," the background necessity of things, which drives the tragedies and on which the possibility of reconciliation rests, was thereby made the object of reflection for Greek religious art. (Hegel later argues that reflection on this background necessity cannot be adequately handled by art but by something more suited to it, namely, philosophy. It is thus not surprising that the same form of life that produced the tragedians would also produce Plato and Aristotle. The tragedians in fact help to pave the way both for that kind of philosophical reflection and for the recognition of what was impossible for the Greek form of life, the status of the self-reflective individual.[66])

In presenting the truths about the conflicts essentially inherent to the Greek form of life, tragedy presented the truths about the essential self-identity of that form of life. But in exposing the contradictions inherent in Greek life itself, Greek tragedy threw into question the idea that the individual could be exhaustively described in terms purely of social roles and duties. For the Greek agent, his form of life (his *Sittlichkeit*) gave him a set of norms that he understood himself intuitively to follow; to know the norm was just to know how one "goes on," to continue in the "same way" without having to reflect on it. Greek tragedy put the individual in the position of questioning whether his acting in terms of these roles without reflection on them was in itself a fitting reason for action. It thus presented the Greeks with skepticism about whether what the Greek individual had taken as authoritative for himself – as something just "given," as acting in accordance with Greek *Sittlichkeit*, of simply "going on" in the same ways – really was a good reason for belief and action. In becoming *self-conscious* in the form of art, Greek life could no longer simply accept the norms of Greek *Sittlichkeit* at face value, nor could it accept that what it had taken as divine really was so.

Because of this, Greek religious art had to develop an account of this skeptical individual – namely, the individual self-consciously *taking* himself to be acting in such and such a fashion, which it did with *comedy*. Greek comedy – like all genuine comedy – takes as its project the same concern with presenting truths about essential self-identity, but it does this by humorously mocking the "insubstantial" aspect of the various practices of a form of life in order to make what is genuinely true and essential come to the foreground of reflection. The major vehicle for such comedy is the humorous mocking and exposing of people's pretensions in order to bring out who they really are and what the society is really about. The fundamental core of comedy is thus the gap between people's *pretensions* about who they are and who they *really* are, between what people *say* they are doing and what they *really* are doing.[67] In comedy, so Hegel argues, the *individual* for the first time makes a genuine appearance; it is even possible in comedy for the actor as an individual person to appear from behind the mask. (In his discussion of this in the *Phenomenology*, Hegel is no doubt referring to Aristophanes making an appearance without a mask as himself in his own play, *The Clouds*. Indeed, Hegel's whole discussion about comedy in the *Phenomenology* is sprinkled with references to *The Clouds*, which at least there he seems to take as paradigmatic for Greek comedy, just as he took *Antigone* to be paradigmatic for tragedy.[68]) In comedy (specifically, in *The Clouds*), the mocking of the manner in which Greek life had conceived the gods shows that the Greek conception of the divine is incoherent, and it shows that way in which divinity was conceived to be open to all kinds of bamboozlement.[69]

The comedic mocking of the public conception of the gods and the tom-foolery attending to their adoration thus necessitates a *philosophical* conception of them. Although the move to a philosophical conception indicates conceptual progress for us (the readers), from the standpoint of the Greek form of life it actually marks a relapse into abstraction. Greek religion and practice were not well suited for purely philosophical reflection, however great that reflection ended up being, for the Greek religion of art was best suited for poetic rather than philosophical contemplation. For that reason, the philosophical attempts to reduce the multiplicity of gods to the very abstract philosophical conceptions of "*the* beautiful" and "*the* good" offered up a kind of wonderfully prepared raw material for the comedic writer. In *The Clouds*, Aristophanes does just that, lampooning Socrates and the entire sophistic movement as taking themselves to be deep and wise men, but who were actually just spouting what (for an Athenian tied to the old way of life) was just fashionable balderdash and high sounding poppycock. But however conservatively conceived, Greek comedy, particularly Aristophanes' comedy, actually exposed to the Greeks what was truly going on in their form of life. Greek life had discovered the *self* behind its various conceptions of fate and devotion. The self-evident and serene assurance in the validity of Greek *Sittlichkeit* that had provided the authoritative reasons for belief and action had been thrown into question by Greek tragedy, and Greek philosophy could offer no satisfactory reassurance within Greek terms that those reasons were indeed authoritative reasons. Greek comedy exposed the reflective individual behind the role, who now came to see himself as taking up the role in a self-conscious fashion. Although Aristophanes lampooned Socrates, the inventor of this new form of reflection, he seemed not to realize that he was actually parodying the Greek self-conception itself. The Socratic individual, unsure of what was true, turned out to be the truth of Greek life.

The revealed religion

Religious alienation. The dramatic practice of comedy turns an ironic eye to all established order in an effort to bring out what is substantial and basic in that order. What genuine comedy succeeds in doing is providing a means of reflection through which the individual person himself (the individual consciousness) can distance himself from all the established norms, authorities, even from the accepted pantheon of gods themselves. Even in the hands of a conservative such as Aristophanes, the comic outlook on the world ends up distancing itself from that world. The comic outlook undermines the kind of unity that an individual would feel with the community in which he lives in that it creates a kind of distanced self who ironically looks at all the currently received views about religion, morality, and politics from a more or less disengaged point of view and thus does not identify his *self* with the practices of that community. This places that person in a new relation to his world, for he now takes a more impersonal and an *alienated* stance toward that world, since this impersonal point of view is indifferent to his personal point of view. There comes to be nothing in that world with which he can fully identify, nothing with which he can say that its ends are fully his ends – that is, no way in which he could be said to be "at home with himself" while living out the duties of that form of life. The Greek comic view of life, while spelling the end of the classic Greek form of life and the beginning of "Hellenism," becomes actualized in the Roman form of life, in which legal personality and brute contingency become the ways in which the citizens of that form of life account for themselves and what they take as valid for them. The Roman self-understanding allowed that there was nothing essentially to agency except the contingently formed (and therefore *essentially* empty) self assuming whatever structure it needed to assume for expediency's sake. (In his later lectures on the philosophy of religion, Hegel therefore called the religion of the Romans "The Religion of Expediency.")

While this form of life is (from Hegel's point of view) not as rich or as admirable as the Greek form of life, it nonetheless begins to open up the possibilities for the kind of modern account of community and modern self. Given what it was, the Greek form of life had to splinter, for in its actions, it created the kind of self-distanced individuality that was incompatible with its sense of *Sittlichkeit*. However, by putting the gods into human, self-conscious form, Greek religion created the possibility of the Roman account of itself in terms of its own practices. In reflecting on itself – that is, in coming to see the internal incongruities within its own account of itself – the Greek form of life had reached the point at which it could no longer understand itself within its traditional terms. The "unhappy consciousness" – the alienation between a form of life that is not believed in by its adherents but to which there is no discernable rational alternative – is the *tragic fate* itself of Greece. It is tragic in its working out of a form of "character as destiny": because of who they collectively were (that is, because of the religious accounts which they had constructed for themselves), the Greek community worked out an account of itself as self-conscious human practice, and in doing so, left its gods behind without having anything to replace them. It is tragic in that the internal conflicts of communal *character* required a resolution that in turn led to the destruction of the whole form of life itself. This internal conflict appears in the creation of the dramatic form of comedy. The alienated self surfacing in comedy finds his self-identity to be anchored in practices for which he can find no justification within the terms of those practices themselves. The gap between what is officially taken to be authoritative in accepted practice and the actual world of self-distanced individuals is thus great, and comedy steps in to offer reflections on that gap. The absurdity that characterizes the gap between accepted practice and actuality – between what people take themselves to be doing and what they are actually doing – provokes laughter in comedy; comedy's laughter is the mirror image of the despair that the "unhappy consciousness" feels in the presence of that same absurdity.[70]

The Greek form of life with its epilogue in Roman legalism, stoicism, skepticism and finally the "unhappy consciousness" thus created the "social space" in which it became possible for the recognizably distinct social practices of art, religion, and philosophy to develop, such that what would have seemed at an earlier point to a Greek as only one kind of practice came to be seen as three distinct kinds of practice within the setting of absolute spirit, that is, as a set of practices and institutions in which the community reflects only on its own accounts of itself. The Greeks did not *cause* this form of self-reflection to come about, but only such a communal practice of self-reflection appearing in the institutional form in which it did would satisfactorily resolve the incoherences of Greek life.[71] The Greek form of life had initiated a teleological direction to history in that the Greeks found their own practices to be insufficient with respect to the norms needed for the kind of self-conscious reflection embodied in Greek religious practice. In Hegel's terms, the "substance" of their form of life had become self-conscious – had become "subject": Their form of life had developed institutions and practices of art, religion and philosophy in such a way that this type of communal self-conscious reflection on itself had become an essential part of how it had come to understand itself. However, as Hegel has argued, this necessarily led to these agents coming to understand the basic determining ground of their practices as lying within the structure of those practices themselves, in the ground rules for what is taken as authoritative by them, and what is taken as a criticism of those practices. In this way, the development of tragedy and comedy is basic to the history of *reason* itself, for it is in the development of these types of communal reflections that the conception of a criticism of the principles of criticism themselves unfolds, that reason's project of giving a satisfactory account of itself is both made possible and appears.

In the breakdown of Greek life, both the "substance" (a form of life's ground rules and what it takes as authoritative for it) and the self-identity of the individuals in that form of life have, as Hegel puts it, *externalized* themselves. By this, Hegel means that the "substance" has become embodied in the institutionalized practices of self-conscious reflections on the ground rules of that form of life itself. Whereas prior to the denouement of the Greek form of life, the "substance" had resided more or less unreflectively in the accepted practices of the culture, in the way people simply "went on" in the same way, after that denouement it becomes an object of reflection and criticism. (In this sense, the "substance" has become an object of external reflection.) Likewise, the individuals in that culture more and more find their self-identities not to be naturally *given* to them by the nature of things (by the "substance") but to be culturally *constructed* and therefore also fully open to reflection and criticism; in that sense, the individuals (or their "self-consciousness," their locating themselves in "social space") have become an *external* object of reflection and criticism. Both "substance" and "self-consciousness" moreover may be said to have externalized *themselves* since this is a necessary conceptual development out of the self-understandings involved in that form of life. This externalization of self-consciousness is the result of a developed form of reflexiveness within the "social space" of modern life, and it traces out the history of rationality itself. Rationality exists in those practices of appraisal and criticism according to normative standards. It is part of the inner teleology of reason that ultimately these standards of appraisal and criticism *themselves* come to be appraised and criticized, since it is in the development of the "criticism of criticism" that the practices of criticism complete themselves. The development of such a reflective practice of criticizing the standards of criticism (brought to its penultimate form in Kant's three *Critiques*) entails a new sense of reflective self-consciousness.[72]

Hegel makes it clear that he is not doing a purely historical study of this coming-to-be of the human community's awareness of its social practice as the foundation of what it takes as authoritative for itself. This is to be a dialectical history: It draws out the way in which a form of life's self-understanding rationally leads to its successors. It is not a causal account, and it offers no causal laws of historical development. It offers, that is, no law of the form "If event A occurs, then event B follows." (For example, "If the Greek form of life reaches a certain stage, then Roman life succeeds it, and modern life follows.") Hegel notes of his own account that if it is to be convincing, it must be shown that the awareness of spirit as spirit – of the human community's recognition that it is only the community's linguistic and cultural practices and the socially instituted structures of mutual recognition that provide the grounds for determining who one is – arises through a kind of conceptual necessity, not historical causality (which is not to say that it excludes or forbids any causal accounts of how that came about). It must be shown that a stage of self-understanding in the world's cultures (what Hegel only somewhat misleadingly calls the "world-spirit") has reached a type of self-awareness such that it understands itself in that way.[73]

Christianity. In this way, the ancient world created an account of itself that made it possible for a new religion – a new conception of what was divine – to arise with a set of rites and symbols in which humanity could see itself fully reflected. This particular *possibility* was realized in the historical appearance of Christianity.[74] Christianity represents the awareness of God as human, not in the form of a statue or a cult but as a living human being who fully represents in himself what is truly divine in human life and who extends this understanding of the absolute principles and highest interests of humanity to all who realize this. This human-divinity is not the idealization and transcendence of humanity as were the Greek gods; instead, it shares in all of humanity's features – its passions and even its mortality. The Greek gods were remote and relatively indifferent to human concerns because of their immortality; they were symbolic representations of humans with only an impersonal, detached point of view. The new representation of divinity in Christian thought, however, sees God as fully human, fully identified with the life of human beings, uniting the divine, impersonal point of view with the very subjective, personal point of view of the individual. This is the content of *absolute* religion, although the content can be given different forms (some of them inadequate). Hegel claims that this religion's claim to being *revealed* religion is appropriate, for it *reveals* in representational form (in the form of *Vorstellung*) what philosophy later articulates in discursive, conceptual thought.

Interestingly, Hegel does *not* seem to be arguing that Christianity per se was a necessary development. He is, however, arguing that something very much *like* Christianity is the proper fulfillment of the possibilities opened up by Greek life and its Roman aftermath; Christianity contingently happened to be the religion that stepped into the "social space" opened up by stoicism, skepticism, and the Hellenistic forms of the "unhappy consciousness." Hegel's arguments do not amount therefore to a kind of philosophical eschatology in which Christianity itself is understood as the meaning of history, that toward which history was aiming. Hegel is arguing a different point: dialectically understood, history is a succession of forms of self-understanding, of the teleological development of reason itself. It is not simply a succession or chronology of types of accounts that forms of life give themselves; rather, each of these types of accounts – and religious practice is one form of social self-reflection that is ingredient in these accounts – may be shown to raise questions for itself within what each takes as authoritative that retrospectively can be reconstructed to have been realized in the accounts that followed them. The kind of "absolute religion" that Christianity represents may be understood as a reflection on the way in which these forms of self-understanding are consummated. In its presentation of the incarnation (*Menschwerdung*) of God into man, Christianity presents in representational, symbolic form the idea that the divine is no longer to be sought outside of the life and practices of the human community itself. The truth that is gradually articulated in this religion is that God is known as spirit, that what is divine exists only in the human community's self-reflection on the absolute principles governing human life, not as some metaphysical essence lying beyond or behind appearance that determines the structure of our knowledge and action. The divine just *is* the human spirit reflecting on itself and establishing *for itself,* through its religious practices, the "absolute principles" governing human life and doing so necessarily according to the principles of rationality that it itself has historically developed.[75]

The conceptual possibility opened up by Greek religion and its successors is realized by Christianity, and with that the dialectical history of religious practice as communal self-reflection comes in principle to an end. In casting the gods into human form and reflecting on what that meant, the Greek form of life had created the "social space" in which a kind of full self-knowledge on the part of the human community became possible. This full self-knowledge would be expressed as the idea that there is no metaphysical determining *ground* of human consciousness that could affirm the legitimacy of these practices. There are only the free standing linguistic and cultural practices of communities themselves, which develop standards of criticism within themselves that in turn require reflective accounts of how certain norms can be maintained in the face of potentially self-undermining skepticism about themselves; the existence of such practices of self-conscious account-giving contain within themselves the ideal of a complete account – that is, an account of what is taken as authoritative that itself can renew itself in the face of self-generated skepticism about itself. Since there is nothing outside of the practices of the human community in these kinds of reflections, that which is divine in human life does not transcend human life itself, and the divine in human life can therefore be fully known as it is: this is, in Hegel's argument, the radical message that Christianity presents in symbolic form: God has been fully *revealed*.[76]

God in the Christian understanding is the *representation* of the conceptual idea that spirit knows itself as spirit – namely, that the human community comes to an awareness that it is in working out the internal requirements of its own reason-giving activity that it sets for itself what is to count for it as its absolute principles, and that its internal requirements are those that it itself has developed out of the insufficiencies of its earlier accounts of what it took to be definitive for itself, and that this activity of self-conscious spirit is what is divine, what is of absolute and inherent value, what is the "ground" of all belief and action. The representational trappings of this form of religion, however, need to be explicated in the community in terms of this revelation to itself about who it is. Hegel argues, for example, that in the "social space" created by the consummation of Greek religion, Christianity offers a series of steps by which the human community comes to a full awareness of itself. These steps, like all other types of dialectical development, do not come fully developed on to the scene; they must be first articulated, then their internal insufficiencies must be worked out and superseded by other accounts that make up for these insufficiencies. Thus, the representation of the divine as self-conscious spirit is at first taken as the relation between agents and an independent object – that is, the reflective community takes what is authoritative for it as what in Hegel's language in the *Phenomenology* is called the "essence," as an independent object of consciousness, as something different from itself that underwrites its claims to belief. Thus, not surprisingly, the divine is at first represented as a distant entity, "beyond" us in the heavens, far beyond the sky and so on. These representations of God as a distant entity are pictorial images of a still metaphysically conceived divinity.[77]

Hegel does not argue that we should *replace* the concept of God (or, in general, the divine) with the concept of humanity. Rather, we must find a place for the divine within the concept of humanity. That is, Hegel is not arguing, as many of his later students were to do, that we should see the divine as *only* a fanciful projection by humanity of itself and its highest interests, a kind of fiction and illusion that humanity needs now to cast off. For Hegel, the divine is real, not a fiction that we have made up and to which we now (in a more "enlightened" age) discard. The divine (the sacred) is that which we see as the "ground" of everything and as such having a value that transcends all other more relative values. The sacred is what *counts for us* as having an "absolute" value that is also incommensurable with other values. It is that to which Kant was alluding when he said of rational beings that they had "dignity," not a "price;" to use Hegel's language, it is that which we must take as genuinely "existing in and for itself." Although the divine can quite obviously be given a theistic interpretation, the concept of divinity (and therefore religious reflection) is not intrinsically tied to theistic conceptions. Hegel's point is that we regard as divine, as the object of awe and reverence, that which we take to be the "ground" of all belief and action, and that which we take to have absolute value; the concept of the divine is not at first identical with the concept of self-founding humanity, but in working out the insufficiencies of its previous accounts of itself, humanity as "self-conscious spirit" comes to realize that identity, to see the divine as implicit in its own activity of reflecting on what it can take as divine. To comprehend what is *divine* – that is, what is *sacred* to us, we must reflect on who we have come to be and why certain things *must* count for us as having such sacrosanct value *given who we have come to be* – that is, given what we have come to take as authoritative for ourselves. To call something sacred (or divine), therefore, is to count it as something which human agents are to value independently of whether they contingently happen to desire it, and to which they stand in awe and reverence. Indeed, the divine, the sacred is exactly that which makes a claim on human agents to change their desires and their inclinations if they find that they do *not* value it. The divine is that which calls on people to transform their lives in light of it, to alter their personal point of view in light of what is "truly" valuable. Religious reflection, therefore, is a historical community's reflection on what it *must* authoritatively count for itself as sacred.

Hegel illustrates a number of elements of the Christian story in terms of these basic ideas.[78] For example, God's creation of the world in seven days is a *representation* of certain *conceptual* truths. God takes seven days to create the world and has to create humans in that world, for without such a gradual creation, God cannot come to an awareness of Himself. Nature per se is amoral, cold, valueless. Sacred value therefore enters the world only with the introduction of rational agency. Thus, the story has God creating humanity in order to insert value into what would be an otherwise well constructed but valueless world and in order to come to know Himself as reflected in His "other," (in order, that is, to come to self-consciousness about His own sacred value).[79] God, that is, requires recognition from another in order to come to a full self-consciousness about Himself. Likewise, the story of the expulsion from paradise is the story of humanity's coming to be who it is as a community of *self-conscious* free agents. As living innocently in the garden, humanity is neither good nor evil. However, as having tasted the fruits of the forbidden tree, humanity acquires a self-consciousness about itself and becomes *like* God. Human life thereby comes to have a sacredness to it that makes it a value in and for itself. The punishment, however, for having done this is pain and labor. Humanity must now work for itself; it must become self-creating. Likewise, the newly self-conscious agents, Adam and Eve, are now self-consciously for each as self-conscious agents (thus, they become "aware" of their nakedness to each other). But humanity remains mortal; unlike the originally divine, individual people must die. Because of this, humanity becomes alienated from the divine and fails to note its own sacredness and instead sees the sacred as existing apart from humanity and perhaps as being indifferent to it. The existence of evil follows from humanity's combination of its natural existence and its self-consciousness. This is a symbolic version of the conceptual reflection that because of the possibility of self-consciousness itself, we acquire the possibility of *both* good and evil. Normative considerations come into play and at the same time the ability and (even for some people) the inclination to violate them. As natural creatures, we are capable of denying or being oblivious to that which is of absolute value about humanity – namely, its sacred capacity for self-conscious life; to be oblivious to what is of ultimate value in the world (rational, self-conscious life) is to see everything in the world as having only relative value and hence to be disposed to treat people as simply one more item of relative value in that world (to treat them, for example, only in terms of their usefulness to oneself or to one's community). Evil is the falling away from what is sacred about us – it is a falling away from God the divine – because of our own finite short-sightedness and our stubborn adherence to our own personal point of view, which in turn lead us to see ourselves and others as having only relative value. Good and evil, however, in representational thought are conceived as two different and opposed *entities,* and for this form of thought, it is natural that good and evil either become hypostatized into independent powers fighting for the allegiance of humanity (for example, God and the Devil), or that humanity itself is represented as having two independent "natures" inside it, one inclining it to good, the other to evil.[80]

Representational thought pictures the reconciliation of the divine and the human through the familiar Christian story. For Hegel's purposes, however, the point is to take the familiar story and reconstruct out of it the truths to be found in the story of Jesus' death and resurrection. The Christian story is one of the divine taking on human form and then dying in order to affirm its divinity. This is represented as the divinity's reflection into itself. The death of Jesus is the establishment of a religious community dedicated to the teachings of Jesus. But what are these? Christianity teaches that God has fully revealed himself, which, conceptually understood, means that he is fully present in the world of appearance. The Christian teaching that "The kingdom is upon us" is the representation (*Vorstellung*) of the idea that the divine is now to be taken as identical with self-conscious spirit, with the human community coming to an understanding that it must take its own rational self-conscious life as absolute, as having intrinsic value. The "kingdom of God" is thus not to be found in some transcendent metaphysical realm but in a set of reformed practices *within* the human community. Humanity can reconcile itself with itself in the religious *community* that understands certain basic truths about human life in both its "natural" and its "spiritual" form. The Christian religion thus representationally formulates an account of the divine as *present* in the human community provided that the community assume a certain reflective attitude toward itself.[81]

The basic *truth* that is thus revealed in the Christian religion is that the full "presence" of the divine within the human community means that rational, self-conscious human life *as spirit,* as determining for itself what is to count for it as authoritative, is divine. In the symbolic language – the *Vorstellung* – of religion, God had determined himself to die and thereby to unite with humanity. The awareness of the self-grounding nature of "spirit" is the awareness of the "ground" of all that we take as true and valuable; the proper attitude, therefore, is awe and reverence for the ways in which historical communal reflections on what we take to be authoritative for us generate accounts, undermine themselves, and succeed each other in a teleological fashion. Out of this awareness of the divinity of "spirit" comes a doctrine of what is therefore sacred for people living in such a community that has come to offer this account of itself. Seeing spirit as divine means that we must regard rational, self-conscious life as sacred, and that therefore we must regard treating rational, self-conscious human life as if it were of only relative importance to be a prima facie transgression against the sacred. Once the inherent sacredness of rational, self-conscious life comes to be seen, slavery, social practices involving petty humiliations of others, and refusals to acknowledge people's freedom also come to be seen as transgressions against the sacred value of *rational* self-conscious life. Indeed, in Hegel's view, even certain practices within a community can take on sacred value to the extent that they are the institutions that enable such self-conscious life to be possible. But what makes rational, self-conscious human life sacred is not some metaphysical, supersensible property within humans (such as an immaterial soul) but the way in which modern agents have come to be the kind of community for whom rational, self-conscious human life *must count as* sacred because of the history of that community's accounts of itself. To say that the divine is present "within" us is to say that by having come to accept that account of what is authoritative for us in terms of our being self-grounding agents, we have come to accept the idea that self-grounding humanity is ultimately authoritative for everything else, even for what it takes to be sacred (that is, divine) for itself and that the sacredness of human life cannot come from a divinity that is metaphysically outside this kind of human activity. If we were only self-grounding without being *rationally self-grounding* – that is, without developing the idea of self-grounding out of the historical development of the "practices of reason" itself – we would not be committed to human life as sacred, for there would be no "ground" to include all people rather than just those of the immediate community. Reason, which develops itself out of the communal practices of reason-giving, reflection, self-undermining attempts at reassurance and the development of new accounts, is the dynamic of divinity, the ground and source of all that we can value "in and for itself."

The sacrosanct character of communal, rational, self-conscious human life is the result of the history of the accounts that the human community has given of what is authoritative for us and the way in which those accounts have undermined themselves and thus necessitated other accounts. Christian religion is the account in representational form of how the "divine in human form" comes to be conceived as that which rational self-grounding agents *must take* as sacred, as being the kind of value that transcends contingent desire and comes to be valuable in and for itself for such agents. Rational self-conscious human life as self-grounding, though, is possible only within the forms of spirit, of those practices that offer reflections on what we have come to take as authoritative for ourselves and that examine the "negativity" of the accounts we give to reassure ourselves that what we take to be authoritative reasons really are authoritative reasons. Indeed, it is ultimately this idea of the sacredness of rational, self-conscious human life, so Hegel argues, that makes modern political community possible (as the idea that all people are "inherently free") and indeed makes modern life itself possible as a coherent form of self-consciousness. The attitudes of awe and reverence to the sacred as lying in the inherent value of rational, self-conscious life, so Hegel argues, is the condition of modern, non-alienated political life.

The alienation of humanity from God is represented as the alienation of naturally existing individuals from the divine community, from what is true and best in human life. The issue running through the development of religious accounts of the absolute principles of human life has to do with how humanity is to understand itself as both a phenomenon of nature and as a social, cultural form of life and how it is to come to terms with the natural, contingent parameters of its life. From the philosophical standpoint, it is the conceptual issue of how two different descriptions of humanity – the naturalistic and the spiritual – are to be coherently resolved in terms of each other: How would it be possible for humanity to reconcile itself with itself as both a natural phenomenon – humanity's understanding of its basis in the system of nature – and as a spiritual phenomenon – humanity's coming to understand itself in terms of its social and moral constitution? In representational thought, this is presented as a struggle between two different realms or "essences" (pictured as two entities). The human world in its pride falls away from God into a natural existence, and the divine world, being independent of humanity, beckons it to join it. In falling away from God, humanity is in its natural existence evil, for it is a forsaking of God's spiritual community in favor of a purely natural existence. This is represented as a turning inward of humanity (*Insichgehen*) away from God, and it can overcome this evil only by reuniting itself with God, by reuniting the spiritual and the natural. Seen in this way, the reconciliation is possible only if the divine bends to the human, and if humanity is willing to accept the divine.[82] Evil can only be vanquished by God's redeeming the world: The natural must be redeemed into the spiritual. This is accomplished in the Christian story, of course, by the appearance of Jesus and his transfiguring death. The individual, Jesus, is the symbolic representation of how this reconciliation is to be carried out: The divine is to be found directly in the human world, expressed in the Christian dictum, "the kingdom of God is upon us." The divine assumes fully human form and experiences humiliation and death. That which is divine, is sacred to us, comes to be taken as something not essentially different from human life at all. Christian religion teaches that rational, self-conscious human life itself, as structured in communities reflecting on the absolute principles of life, is the divine, and in this account of itself as legitimating that which it takes to be divine through its religious, artistic and philosophical practices, it is the reconciliation of nature and spirit.[83]

When conceived as the "luminous essence," the divine is taken to be wholly different from the human. Conceived as the Greek gods, the divine is *like* the human, but nonetheless remains both fundamentally different from humanity and more or less indifferent to human concerns; conceived as the Judaic God, the divine is both concerned with humanity and is *like* humanity in that it is in the form of "spirit" – it bestows a sacredness on human life, but is still transcendent to human life; in Christianity, Hegel claims, the divine *becomes* human, suffers, and dies. Thus, the divine and the human are reconciled as humanity comes to see that *as spirit,* humanity is self-grounding, self-legitimating activity, while individual humans are born and die. This remains in Hegel's view a *religious* conception in that rational, self-conscious human life *as spirit* becomes the object of religious awe and reverence – a doctrine that many of Hegel's followers were later to reject.[84]

As long as humanity's self-conception remains metaphysical – that is, as long as the legitimating ground of knowledge and action is understood as lying "beyond" appearance – it remains alienated from itself in its conception of itself. In the religious representation of itself as having two "natures" or as living in two worlds (a divine and a natural world), humanity can still only understand itself as bifurcated, at odds with itself. It is quite natural that in that "social space" constituted by the account of itself that had been made possible by the demise of the Greek religion, it would seem that what was needed was a divine-human mediator, a person sharing elements of both worlds. For contingent reasons, early Christianity was the religion that stepped in to fill out this logical space. In its picturing of a full reconciliation of humanity and the divine, the Christian account creates the possibility of a non-representational, conceptual understanding of the way in which what is taken as authoritative in human practices can be affirmed. In becoming Christianized, Europeans became the *kind of agents* for whom such a conceptual truth could appear as one of the available options. Just as the denouement of the Greek form of life creates the conceptual possibility for something like Christian religion, Christian religion creates the possibility of an account of what legitimates belief and action that relies on no external metaphysical grounds to legitimate itself but on the terms it develops for itself in its social and cultural practices. That which is divine, which governs human life, is no longer represented as indifferent to us, as it was in Greek life; instead, the divine is to be found *within* the human, in both its natural and non-natural aspects.

In his mature Berlin lectures on the philosophy of religion, Hegel augmented his earlier discussion in the *Phenomenology of Spirit* as to how the

Christian form of life necessarily developed into the modern form of secular self-understanding. In those lectures, he argued that the historical process of the formation of the modern self in Christian religion took the steps it did in order to work out within the terms it had set for itself what was necessary for it to come to a rational self-consciousness about itself. If indeed the natural world is seen as an evil place, then it would follow that the religious community would wish to withdraw from that world in order to preserve its holiness. Thus, the foundation of monasteries and the self-abnegation of the monkish life are logical developments out of the original Christian self-understanding. The monkish life, however, is only a reconciliation of the heart, and thus fails to live up to the promises of the Christian teachings since the world remains unreconciled, and only the monks in the religious community have any reconciliation with the divine. It would then be reasonable that the church would try to reconcile itself with the world by trying to redeem it through the imposition of church authority and the creation of "Christendom." In attempting a reconciliation of the world and spirit, however, the church secularizes itself (makes itself more worldly) at the same time that it spiritualizes the secular world. This creates the possibility for modern life, for a reconciliation of spirituality and worldliness in the creation of communities based on the principle of freedom and the recognition of the supreme value of rational, self-conscious life.[85]

However, religious practice cannot on its own give this kind of conceptual account of itself. In order to be a *religious* community, it must understand these truths in *representational* form. Representational thought, however, is inevitably led to picturing conceptual relations or structures of practices as substantive things. Thus, what we can conceptually understand as the structure of the practices of a determinate historical community will be pictured as entities (for example, as "God the Father" revealing His will to us). In that way, revealed religion (which historically turned out to be the Christian religion) necessarily remains at least quasi-metaphysical in that it takes the "essence" (that which is authoritative for itself) to be an independent object of consciousness; it is thus incapable of fully understanding what is required in its own account.[86] On its own, the form of life of revealed religion cannot break out of this picture, since it must remain dependent on a "revelation," not on a conceptual articulation of what it takes to be true. The result of the Christian community's account of itself is that in order to complete its account in the terms that it sets for itself it must become a *secular* community that nonetheless tries to understand itself in terms of the religious, metaphysical representations that have made that form of communal practice possible in the first place.[87]

However, for the Christian religious community, such a secularization of itself will appear to it like a new falling away from the central truths that made it the community that it is. For it to understand truly what it has become, it needs an account of itself in terms of conceptual thought, not symbolic representation. What revealed religion has done is to form the type of person who is now ready for that type of conceptual thought.

2. Philosophy as communal self-reflection

The modern European community has given an account of itself in terms of self-determination in thought and personal independence in practical affairs. It takes the former to be partially affirmed in the practices of modern science, for these seem to authenticate the claim that modern life has the capacity to set for itself authoritative ground rules for its theoretical practices such that they reveal what the world is in itself. It has also created a set of social practices and institutions in which the independence and self-determination of practical agents can be affirmed as (1) rational self-determination, as electing for oneself what is to count as an authoritative reason for action and what will move one to action in terms of evaluating those reasons by reference to universally valid rational criteria; and as (2) personal autonomy, as counting as reasons those that have to do with oneself, *as an individual,* incorporating one's personal emotions, character, convictions, and passions into the account of what can count as an authoritative reason for the individual agent. The community populated *only* with such romantic, personally autonomous individuals, however, threatens to break down into a community of dissembling hypocrites. In a form of life in which there can be no shared moral certainties (since everything is negotiable and indeterminate in the reciprocal appeals to legitimation through to "personal conscience"), there can be no "safe areas" of life that are beyond the charges of immorality, wrongfulness or hypocritical dissembling. In order to avoid this dissolution into a community of subterfuge and hypocrisy, there must be some conception of "the way things are done" that fits the modern account of agency and collective life as self-determining and self-justifying. For this community to be able to account for what it takes to be the principles of its practical life, it must move beyond these reciprocal charges of hypocrisy and pretense to a form of life that is able to reconcile within itself the "beautiful souls," the ironists, and the moralists by fashioning an account of itself that shows *how* it may take some practices as authoritative, as embodiments of "the way things are done" in such a way that it also shows that these practices *can* count as the "way things are done" for those agents who understand themselves in terms of the self-distancing practices of modern life. Hegel's argument for how this is done is one of the bolder claims of the *Phenomenology:* This can only be accomplished through a type of modern self-reflection that Hegel calls *absolute knowing.*

Absolute knowing is a reflection on the accounts that the modern community has given of what is authoritative for us and why these "ground rules" "really are" or "really should be" taken as authoritative. In absolute knowing, this "account of the accounts" is self-consciously understood as moving altogether and completely *within* the terms those accounts have already set for themselves. That is, absolute knowing does not see itself as offering an affirmation or justification or critique of social practices by appeal to anything that would be "external" to the practices themselves – for example, not by appealing to any kind of metaphysical essence that would somehow vouchsafe those practices.

Hegel claims that it is *absolute* in its being entirely self-mediating. Its status as absolute can be contrasted with other successful, although non-absolute, forms of knowing. The practice of natural science, for example, cannot be absolute in this sense. Natural science is dependent on its objects, on the way the world happens to display itself to the community of scientists – the natural world mediates the accounts that natural science gives of it. Modern natural science must accommodate itself to that world; it cannot determine *it*, although it can determine what for the scientific community counts as an authoritative reason (what counts as a successful experiment, as a confirmed theory, and so on). For this reason, the knowledge gained by natural science is *finite* – that is, dependent on its other for its determinateness. It thus cannot within its vocation as natural science understand how it is that the scientific community sets it own norms for what is to count for it as valid grounds of belief. (Hegel's criticism of natural scientific knowledge is *not* that it is "false" because it is "one-sided," or is not a part of a "whole" that is supposedly presented by Hegelian dialectic – a common enough picture of Hegel's view of natural scientific knowledge – but that it is limited by and partially determined by its "other," the natural world. It is not self-mediating as is philosophical knowledge.)

Modern philosophy, the institutional setting for absolute knowing, is, however, not confined to the way the natural world happens to present itself to the community of working scientists. Philosophy is the reflection on what the community as a whole has come to take as authoritative for its evaluation of those practices and its attempts at legitimations of those practices in terms of an appeal to standards of rationality that themselves historically have been developed within the history of that community's accounts of itself. It can therefore legitimate that account only within those historically generated terms, within that "social space," not by accommodating itself to any kind of object external to the historically developing set of practices of reason-giving and account-giving themselves. Absolute knowledge is *absolute* in that it has no "object" external to itself that mediates it in the way the natural world mediates the claims of natural science. Absolute *knowledge* is thus the way in which absolute *spirit* articulates itself in modern life; it is the practice through which the modern community thinks about itself without attempting to posit any metaphysical "other" or set of "natural constraints" that would underwrite those practices.[88] Absolute knowledge is the internal reflection on the social practices of a modern community that takes its authoritative standards to come only from within the structure of the practices it uses to legitimate and authenticate itself.

The development of the Christian religious account of humanity is essential for the possibility of such reflection, since in its reflection on the absolute principles of human life – on the divine – it has provided a way in which the European community has come to understand the absolute principles of its life as set not by something transcendent to human life itself but in terms of something both close to the human "heart" (the person's sense of his own finitude) and to the human "understanding" (the person's rational, reflective capacities). Humanity's reflection on itself as partially accomplished in these religious narrations, and the ways in which these narrations are continually reenacted in rite and ritual, provides the account by which men and women, individually and collectively, come to recognize that their capacity for evil and for good is a "power" lying solely within the human community itself, not in some metaphysical "entity." In this way, in the religious language of sin and redemption, the modern community holds out the possibility of reconciling itself with itself, of humanity's coming to terms with whom it has become.

However, religion on its own cannot perform this practice of reconciliation in modern life; it cannot serve alone as the integrating force for bringing these essential moments of modern life and itself together. Religion's inability to provide the integrating force of modern life is, moreover, not based on any contingent social facts about the plurality of religions in modern societies, the possibility of civil war, or the inability of modern communities to attain a full consensus on religious matters. Rather, it has to do with the implications of how modern agents can rationally comprehend the stories they have told about themselves. Religion is incapable of giving the "account of the accounts" in a way that meets the criteria for this form of life to conceive of itself as fully self-justifying, for that requires that no practice be accepted of which this kind of account cannot be given, and, as *representational* social reflection, religion cannot do that. The purely *religious* outlook must therefore be overcome, for the religious form of reflection through representationalist thought cannot fully articulate what it is about since it must see the "object" of its reflections as an independent object of consciousness.[89] In representational thought, we picture things as entities; the human community is thus necessarily conceived as an object of some sort, standing in a relation to some other object (the divine). But this type of representationalist thought at its best offers an emotional, intuitive understanding of the self-understandings of the modern community that cannot serve to unite the fragmented practices of modern life into one coherent account. In order that the modern community can come to that type of integrated self-consciousness, the type of self-knowledge that religion brings about must therefore be integrated into some form that can clearly articulate what religion merely symbolically shows.[90] This may be first done in theology, but theology, as it tries to realize the ideal of a rational account of itself, becomes philosophy, and thus the form of social practice of philosophy itself becomes the general task of developing a concrete theoretical reflection on what it is for modern life to be able to affirm *for itself* its own authoritative practices.[91]

The development of religious reflection to the point where it needs to be "overcome" is part of the history of rationality. What we count as rationality itself is built up out of the *practices* of appraisal and criticism. In applying these standards to actions and beliefs, the European community has been logically led to extend the practices of appraisal and criticism to the practices of appraisal and criticism themselves. In a final self-reflexive move, characteristic of Hegel's day, it is then led to ask both what it means in general to appraise and criticize and what kinds of agents we must be in order to have such reflective practices play such a central role in our self-conception. In thinking of its practices of criticism in this way, however, this practice of self-reflection must come to understand that rationality itself has a history that develops internally, and that the history of rationality is coextensive with the history of the community that is giving the account of itself at the end of the *Phenomenology*. The development of that form of practice leads to the development of the kind of philosophy found in the *Phenomenology*.[92]

Hegel argues that the kind of account that is needed for this type of reconciliation to occur has to do with the way in which the kind of social *action* necessary for the construction and sustainability of modern life must be united with a certain way of *thinking* about that life that is continuous with those actions if that form of life is to be able to give a coherent and sustainable account of itself. The first step is to note that this reconciliation is a practical affair that is accomplished not purely by thinking about it but in terms of the way in which the modern form of life has taken on a certain institutional form. The desired unification of the religious and the modern secular accounts of what legitimates human action has thus *already* occurred through the community's practicing a secularized version of Christian morality, even if the religious community cannot understand that secularization within its own terms.[93] Both forms of the "beautiful soul" – the character who is forever intoning against the world's corruptions and thus can never act, and the character who is always invoking his own conscientiousness and the regrettable complexity of the world to justify whatever it is he happens to do – are parts of this act of redemption; these "beautiful souls" come to realize that they are hypocrites. The reconciliation between the self-reflected "beautiful soul" and the ironist prefigures the reconciliation between two aspects of modern social practice: that between reflective thought and social action, the kind of reflections on the basic interests of humanity that occur in the form of absolute spirit, and the ways in which in social life in general and in politics in particular people must *act* in order to accomplish anything. The reconciliation is thus between *politics* and *reflection,* between the "doers" and the "thinkers" of modern social practice (between the "Napoleons" and the "Hegels" of modern life).

Modern life's claim to be a *self-justifying* culture is thus possible only through the reflective practices of "absolute spirit": Only in the self-mediating reflections on both the *kinds* of principles that we have come to take as authoritative for us and on how they *can be* authoritative for us – that is, in those reflections by the "thinkers" in which we autonomously and independently determine what will count as a reason for us – can modern life fulfill its task of constructing its justification of itself.[94] However, modern life also claims to be a form of life embodied in independent, self-determining *individuals*. To do this, it needs various social institutions and political reforms that the "thinkers" cannot provide. In the unreconciled form of modern life, the men and women of "thought" and the men and women of "action" condemn each other; the "beautiful soul" of thought and reflection condemns what he sees as the hypocrisy, if not evil, of the "doers" in society who are forever having to justify what they do in terms of the complexities and exigencies of the situation; likewise, the "doers" in society condemn the reflective beautiful souls for what they see as their hypocrisy in forever criticizing without ever actually doing anything. The reconciliation of modern life with itself is the reconciliation with the necessity of both action *and* reflection, and the necessity of institutionalizing both action and reflection such that the critical reflective accounts will be continuous with the kinds of things that need to be done. Both are necessary for modern life to be able to give a complete account of itself that is not subject to the kind of internally generated, destructive skeptical discreditings that characterized past forms of life. Nonetheless, this reconciliation between the actors and thinkers, although at first possible only from within the *language* of religious practice, is completed in the *dialectical* account given in the *Phenomenology* of how we may understand the absolute principles governing human life not as "given," as independent objects of consciousness but as internal to the ways in which we *have come to take* these principles as authoritative for us.[95]

Absolute knowing in the form of the historical practices and modern institutions of philosophy is the form of reflection on that "social space" in which the kinds of reasons and legitimations of the "ground rules" – of what is authoritative for us in thought and action and whether they *can* be authoritative for us – are rationally reconstructed to see if they can indeed affirm for us our sense of who we are.[96] This reflection is absolute in its being fully internal to this "social space." We cannot leap out of this "social space" to take a look at the "real world" in order to see if our concepts match up to that world – to see if, for example, our mathematical concepts and procedures "match up" with the Platonic forms, or to see if our roles as private individuals and public citizens "match up" with the Natural Law, not because we live behind a curtain of appearance that keeps us away from the things in themselves, but because we have come to understand that the only things that *could* count for us as authoritative have to do with our understanding ourselves as historical, social beings. In the modern account, there can be no room for the role that "matching up" our practices with "natural laws" or "Platonic forms" would have formerly supposedly played. The practices of modern science and the world of modern politics have participated in the development of a self-understanding of the "ground rules" of our practice as not linking up with a world as something "metaphysically beyond" our consciousness that we only "represent" to ourselves; our thought is already from the start world-involving. The issue is rather the structure of our self-consciousness: how we take ourselves to be, what we have thus come to count as valid claims to knowledge, and the social practices in which we try to reassure ourselves and affirm for ourselves that we are who we think we are and that we really do know what we claim to know.

Self-reflection on essential self-identity is necessarily social reflection, on the positioning of oneself in "social space" and on the possibilities of self-conceptions that are both opened and foreclosed by that "social space." This falls to the historical practice of philosophical reflection, which in its modern form is mostly carried out in the institutions of universities and faculties of philosophy. This is not to say, of course, that this is the understanding that the practice of philosophy has always had of itself. Indeed, in this Hegelian view, the historical institutions in which philosophical reflection is embodied will necessarily take on different forms depending on the differences of self-understanding. It is only when the form of life has incorporated into its essential self-understanding a conception of self-reflection on ourselves as cultural beings – only in a *self-grounding, reflective historicist* culture when the social practices of reason-giving have been turned on themselves – that such absolute reflection is possible and that this type of dialectical philosophical reflection can appear and can understand itself for what it is.[97] Whereas philosophers might have understood their task earlier to be primarily metaphysical – that is, to put us in touch with various kinds of supersensible entities that supposedly were necessary to underwrite our claims to knowledge and that supposedly could reassure us that what we were doing was in fact right – the social institutions and practices of modern life, including the way in which this life has secularized the Christian tradition within itself, have made it possible for modern agents to come to understand past philosophy historically, as having really been parts of the progressive developments of accounts of who we were that historically have attempted to affirm and to reassure us that we really were "in touch" with things. Modern Hegelian philosophy, understanding itself as engaged in such a historical practice, cannot therefore claim to go on *outside* of the rest of culture – as if philosophy looked at things from the purely impersonal standpoint, the "standpoint of eternity," uninfluenced by the life around it – but firmly *inside* it, part of it and its history, in a way similar to other ways in which that form of life has tried to reassure itself that it was on the right track.

Although the various forms of life portrayed in the *Phenomenology of Spirit* were not consciously aiming at such an outcome, the self-understandings developed by these forms of life made possible the modern self-conception in that this modern self-conception developed out of the kinds of conceptual moves necessary to accommodate the problems of affirmation, reassurance and legitimation that earlier periods had developed. Something very much *like* the current structures of modern life, if not those exact structures themselves, had to develop *if* a resolution of those earlier dilemmas was to be possible. One can discern the kind of conceptual necessity at work only when one abstracts from issues about historical *causality* – of what caused population movements, what caused agricultural communities to take such and such form, and so on – and reflects on the conceptual structure of the "social space" that the earlier forms of spirit inhabited. One looks at the accounts that they gave of the kinds of principles and practices that they took as underwriting their form of life, and one sees the internal conceptual flaws within those self-conceptions. Indeed, the past breakdowns of metaphysical accounts – of those accounts of knowledge and practice that understand their ultimate justification as lying in our contact (somehow) with abstract, supersensible entities – lead to the modern account in which one understands that even a concept itself is not a metaphysical entity but is itself a moment in "social space," a position in a system of inferences. It thereby becomes possible to study these forms of life in terms of the basic types of conceptual structures that distinguish them as forms of human *agency,* of spirit.[98]

Hegel does not claim that history is *caused* by relations of conceptual necessity but rather claims that these relations, by making human *organisms* into *agents,* are the enabling conditions for there to be history at all. For example, there is no conceptual necessity that Rome succeed Greece; however, only something *like* the Roman self-conception could have taken the Greek self-conception and its internal contradictions in a direction that could develop that account of agency and knowledge further in a way that could both sustain the kind of form of life that Rome developed and develop within itself the ways in which the Greek self-conception could be furthered and altered, although this can only be seen in retrospect. It might have happened for purely contingent reasons that the Roman tribes never acquired the power and territorial claims that they in fact acquired. It might even have been the case that European civilization never developed in the way it did. However, the relation between communal self-conceptions is such that the *contingency* of its coming about in the form it did nonetheless has a kind of internal logic to it, such that certain *types* of self-conceptions can *retrospectively* be seen to *complete* the development of earlier conceptions in the sense that they can give accounts that within their new terms answer the skeptical discreditings that occurred within the older conceptions. It is not "fated," however, that any of these new types of accounts in fact succeed each other, for the facts of such successions are purely contingent affairs. What is necessary is that in retrospect, we can see that only such a succession could have been the logical development of the earlier one. Moreover, that such and such was in fact the answer to those problems cannot be predicted; it can only be understood ex post facto.

The *Phenomenology of Spirit* is thus the philosophical reflection on who we are in modern life. It is the explanation of how we came to be the people for whom "absolute knowing" – that is, the human community's coming to a reflective non-metaphysical understanding of what it must take as authoritative grounds for belief and action – is not *just* a possibility but something that essentially characterizes our self-understanding. History alone cannot tell us this. History can only present a contingent story of movements of peoples, the rise and fall of political dynasties, a story perhaps of the lives of ordinary men and women, all with no internal rationality to them. Nor, it seems, could academic philosophy alone, as a reflection on conceptual possibility or as a transcendental science, explain to us why this type of reflection is for us now possible, and why the old-fashioned metaphysical explanations seem to have lost their force *for us.*

As we might put it, how is it even possible to write the *Phenomenology of Spirit?* Or why would such a philosophical-historical book seem like a viable possibility for a German academic to write in 1807? That *Hegel* was the person to write the book is a purely contingent fact; that such a book became possible in modern life is a feature of our contemporary conceptual furnishings that Hegel has traced out. If not the *Phenomenology of Spirit* itself, something *like* the *Phenomenology of Spirit* becomes possible in a community in which people have come to understand themselves as cultural artifacts, as constituted by their practices, as finding their forms of legitimation, of reassurance and affirmation coming only from the historical nature of norm-guided reflective activity trying to make those norms intelligible to itself. That such a book could appear as an option within the self-understandings of modern life cannot be understood by a form of reflection that abstracts itself from the history of that community. What is needed is a dialectical reflection on the series of self-understandings that traces out that history's "path of despair" to show how those self-understandings broke down because of their inability to account for themselves in ways that the agents could find satisfactory. From our standpoint, we, the readers of the *Phenomenology,* can understand that it was the failure of a satisfactory account of reflective agency and a form of life that integrated reflection and action within itself that explains the failures of these earlier self-conceptions. This is not because this was some "potentiality" lying deep within us that modern institutions have "actualized"; the history of this development, that is, is not analogous to the development of the child into the adult. It is rather because this type of account succeeds in *forming us into* such reflective agents that the success of the modern reflective account (in its being self-justifying) shows the failure of the past accounts to be failures exactly in the way in which they failed to create social institutions in which this kind of reflection could take root. This kind of reflection – comprehended history (*begriffne Geschichte*), as Hegel calls it – becomes the new paradigm for philosophy, one of whose goals is the explanation of its own possibility. But this possibility is part of the larger field of possibilities that make us who we are, and our reflections on them are themselves only part of that self-enclosed circle of human practices and the ways in which we have developed the practices of reflecting on them. Dialectic does not end in absolute knowing; it begins the task of renewing itself.

7

The essential structure of modern life

1. The post-phenomenological project

After the *Phenomenology*, Hegel began to work out what was later to become known as "the system," articulated in his *Encyclopedia of the Philosophical Sciences* (originally published in his Heidelberg years in 1817) and expanded in his lectures in Berlin from his arrival there in 1818 to his death there in 1831. During this period after the writing of the *Phenomenology* and the construction of the "system," Hegel apparently came to think that it was possible to say more about the structure of this modern community within the dialectical terms he had set for himself. The *Phenomenology* ends with the statement of the modern project: the creation of a reconciled community that would unite the *intellectual* project of modern life – the attempt to create a self-founding form of life – with the *practical* project of modern life, the attempt to create a form of life of self-determining individuals. However, in the *Phenomenology*, this remains as a project, for there is no theory offered there of which practices or institutions could accomplish it.

Among the kinds of watershed events in the European community's history that the *Phenomenology* had located, the most consequential for the post-phenomenological project was the sense of "groundlessness" in the European community after the decline of the aristocratic ethos. This "groundlessness" is the loss of the intelligibility of there being a natural or "given" hierarchy of ends for belief and action, a set of norms that, so it had been believed, could be "discovered" and inspected directly by conscious agents. Confronting its "groundlessness," the European community faced two alternatives: either it could go in the direction of nihilism – that is, it could come to the conclusion that there were no authoritative reasons at all – or it could transform the project of "groundlessness" into the project of *self-grounding*. It seems clear that Hegel never seriously considered the nihilistic alternative, since for him that would be stopping the teleological process of that community's giving a rational account of what was authoritative for itself; nihilism simply was not a rational alternative, for it could not resolve the dilemmas that the collapse of the aristocratic ethos had created, and it did not seem to be a necessary consequence of the experience of "groundlessness." Hegel did complain about what he thought was the growing subjectivism of his day, by which he meant the idea that what was authoritative for individuals was only what they could personally and idiosyncratically underwrite themselves out of their own feelings. (In other words, he found his romantic contemporaries' ideas of what counted as a good reason disturbing.)

Nonetheless, if the modern project were to avoid the slide into nihilism, it needed an account of itself that showed that the loss of the intelligibility of there being a natural or "given" hierarchy of ends could be transformed in the reflective practices of modern life into a self-grounded set of ends. Hegel's mature system was intended to accomplish that project. As a "science," a *Wissenschaft,* it was to explore the various ways in which such a project could be carried out in all the areas of modern life: logic (the science of thought), the philosophy of nature (to show that the practices of modern science were on sound logical footing and did not require any postulation of "given" meta-physical entities or modes of "immediate" knowledge), and modern life, with its various institutional structures. This was the famous (or, to many, infamous) "system" of Hegel's Berlin years. In keeping with the idea of this as a *project,* Hegel tended to elaborate it almost entirely in lectures and only occasionally in books. In his *Science of Logic,* the first systematic part of the "system," Hegel attempted to show that thought, taken on its own, could be self-grounding thought. Hegel himself thus took his *Logic* as crucial to his program, not in the sense that it gave him a "dialectical method" that he could then "apply" to other areas (as so many of his followers were later mistakenly to claim) but in the sense that in his view it was crucial for the modern project to show that the enterprise of self-grounding goes all the way down, that there is not some "object of consciousness" that we must simply take as "given" in order to make the kinds of claims that we do.[1]

Another major part of the project had to do with the institutional form of modern life. Indeed, part of the difficulty of that project is that from the standpoint of the *Phenomenology* itself, it seems especially difficult to bring it off, since it would seemingly require the kind of *Sittlichkeit* – a form of life embodying a firm sense of "the way things are done" – that the *Phenomenology* had intimated was ruled out for modern life. From the standpoint of the *Phenomenology,* the Greek form of ethical life, *Sittlichkeit,* was seemingly lost forever; the introduction of the kind of self-distancing moral reflection that is completed in the modern form of life had seemed to make its recapture impossible. Yet the *Phenomenology* had also seemed to suggest that something *like* this was required.[2] The issue, then, for Hegel was whether a more determinate account of agency and social life could be given that would provide more substance to the idea of a reconciled community than was possible with the *Phenomenology's* "abstract absolute" (as he later called the project of "absolute knowing" sketched out in the end of the *Phenomenology*).[3]

For Hegel to complete the *Phenomenology* therefore required him to ask whether there were within the practices of modern life a set of social institutions that could be dialectically reconstructed that would support a more determinate conception of practical agency such that something *like* the ancient Greek ethical life, *Sittlichkeit,* could be realized in the modern setting fundamentally characterized by the self-distancing, reflective, universalizing standpoint of "morality" and for which the basic norm had come to be that of *freedom* as self-determination. The *Phenomenology* shows that the reason why freedom comes to play the role of being *the* norm for modern life lies in the historical insufficiencies of those ways in which the initial responses to the early modern European experience of *groundlessness* failed to provide an adequate account of any authoritative reasons for belief and action that could make those reasons intelligible to modern agents. Those historical insufficiencies thus required the transformation of the experience of groundlessness into the modern project of *self-grounding* as the way in which an account of reasons could be made intelligible to modern agents. Freedom did not become *the* norm because it was a "good" that somehow won out over other competing "goods," but because it emerged as *the* principle necessary to make up for the historical insufficiencies of the early modern period. But to say that freedom is *the* norm of modern life raises the issue as to whether this norm can provide modern agents with a form of rational self-consciousness or whether it too is burdened with the kinds of insufficiencies that had developed within earlier norms. In effect this again raises the issue that was first brought up in the section in the *Phenomenology* that was concerned with "absolute knowing": whether the "doers" of the modern world have brought about a state of affairs that the "thinkers" of the modern world could demonstrate to have fulfilled the necessary conditions for counting as a modern form of *Sittlichkeit;* or, to put it differently, whether the kinds of institutions and social practices of modern life could be seen to provide agents with a knowledge about "the way things are done" that at the same time preserves the reflective independence of those agents.

In order to count as legitimate, moreover, any modern form of *Sittlichkeit* must be intelligible to the participants in modern life as a realization of freedom, not just as a form of "shared understanding" or as a form of "overlapping consensus." In order for a form of life to count as a genuine form of *Sittlichkeit,* the participants in that form of life must *identify* themselves with some social roles; those roles must form a constitutive part of each agent's self-identity. For this form of *Sittlichkeit* to be legitimate, therefore, each agent must rationally understand himself as *self-directing* in acting on the basis of these role-given ends even though the ultimate ends of action are not created by him as an individual. Only such a form of *Sittlichkeit* could legitimately be said to realize the norm of freedom, at least as it emerges from the development of the *Phenomenology* as a whole, in which to be free is to be "at home with oneself" (*bei sich,* "with oneself," as Hegel always phrases it).

Indeed, in the *Phenomenology* the norm of freedom emerges in its authentic form *only* in terms of certain structures of *Sittlichkeit* – namely, as the way in which actions become intelligible to agents in terms of the basic valuational structure of their lives, with this valuational structure itself being intelligible only as part of a larger kind of "ethical culture" that makes the agents into who they are. Ancient Greek life thus was free because the agents in it knew what they had to do and they identified with what they had to do. Deficient forms of freedom, on the other hand, were those found, for example, in stoicism, in which an alienated agent detached himself from the world in order to maintain a certain control over his thoughts and conscious life; the stoic could not be free in his actions because he could not identify himself with any action that was or threatened to be under the compulsion of something other than himself (which was true of all actions). Nor can freedom be adequately understood metaphysically – in the terms of "the understanding" – since the various systems that "the understanding" proposes ultimately turn out to be antinomial and therefore not to be intelligible to the agents themselves. (Or "the understanding" postulates different metaphysical realms for agency that split the agent into two agents – for example, an "empirical" and an "intelligible" subject of action – thus leaving the agent with both a divided self-understanding and with the need for a further account of how these realms could interact.) Freedom must instead be understood *socially* – that is, in terms of the way subjects *take themselves* to be located within their "social space." To say that one is free only to the extent that one is "at home with oneself" is thus to say that one is free when (1) what one does or thinks is intentional (such that one understands *what* one is doing), (2) what one does is characterized by a form of self-understanding (such that one knows *why* one is doing it), and (3) one rationally identifies one's self with what one is doing or thinking such that one's actions affirm one's self-conception. To say that one is free in terms of this Hegelian conception of being "at home with oneself" is thus not to say anything about one's psychological or causal history; it is to say that one's thoughts and actions fit into one's sense of self-identity in these ways. (Hegel thus avoids any reliance on a conception of freedom that requires any metaphysical conception of agency.) This is of course the Greek conception of freedom as Hegel reconstructs it in the *Phenomenology* and gives it a fully social, non-metaphysical form. Fully developed freedom is thus only possible in a form of *Sittlichkeit* in which certain social ends – what we can call *ethical ends* – exist within the "social space" of agents such that they can make these ends their own and that are fully intelligible to those agents (that is, ends that do not contradict each other, undermine each other, or are constituent parts of practices that themselves make it impossible to achieve those ends but whose criteria of success count as worthy or valid only those actions that achieve those ends). These ethical ends create *common projects* in terms of which an agent's *individual* projects can thereby be identified and evaluated.

The end of the *Phenomenology* shows that these kinds of ends cannot be adequately formulated as universal principles that are valid for *any* rational agent and to which the agent simply must "submit" himself; they must be ends that he *as an individual* would have good reason to incorporate into his concrete plans for action so that he *identifies* himself with acting on the basis of such ends. For them to be ethical ends for *modern* agents, they must be realizations of freedom, which requires them to be ends with which the agent as an *individual* and not merely as the place-holder for a social role can identify. What would these ends be, and how would these agents determine these ends? For the modern agent, they must be determined internally to the practices that constitute the agent's self-identity. They cannot be determined, for example, by deriving them from any given desires or impulses that an agent might have, for the legitimacy of any given set of desires would itself always be unresolved and tentative. Moreover, since for modern agents there can be no obviously natural way of ordering desires, any given sets of desires or impulses will on their own appear as only facts of nature, as mere presumptions, and thus cannot count as *self*-determined. Moreover, these ends also cannot be seen as realizing any kind of "potentiality" in human nature. They cannot, that is, be understood as lying latently in human nature, requiring only the correct social structure in order to bring them out. Thus, a prevalent early modern strategy – that of seeing humans as potentially free agents who only needed to be set loose from the constraints of the past and of "society" in order to achieve this potential – will also be unsatisfactory in specifying these ends for modern, self-determining, reflective agents. Nor could anything like a Kantian solution be available for this purpose; we cannot ask what are the *transcendental* conditions of the possibility of knowing and acting, for that always rests on some assumption about who we are. The transcendental option must rest on some presumption about the way we experience things and can only construct the conditions for the possibility of *that* experience, thus leaving the legitimacy of that "experience" unresolved and tentative. Thus, for example, in his practical philosophy Kant takes as given the moral experiential structure of certain types of modern agents – namely, that of feeling duty as a check on inclination and impulse and of the centrality of the emotion of guilt. That strategy, even if it were successful at delineating what those ends would be, would make the ethical ends of agency into a function simply of who we now are, and thus it would be unsatisfactory as an account for those agents, since it could at best establish these ends as being rational only if one takes the present standpoint as given.[4] It thus could not serve to legitimate to modern agents their identifying their own projects with these common projects that are the ethical ends.

The ethical ends of modern agency must be such that they *can* be understood by reflective agents to be determined by free-standing social practices, to be nonetheless rational, and to be authoritative for what it means to be an agent in modern "social space" (to be the kind of common projects that they nonetheless take as "their own"). They cannot be imported from outside human practice, neither from nature, nor from an idea of a human essence that needs to be actualized, nor even from an assumption about who we are now that must be taken for granted. Moreover, if this understanding of the ethical ends of modern agency is to issue from the absolute standpoint itself, it cannot be the result of some kind of external reflection on who we are. The kind of reflection on the ethical ends of modern agency that Hegel is proposing must therefore be continuous with the agents themselves of modern life; the "we" doing the reflecting on the ethical ends of modern agency must be continuous with the "we" who are the community of modern agents, for it is only by virtue of their signifying certain common projects of a community of modern agents that they can count as ethical ends. The ends that are proposed must therefore be compatible with and be seen to follow from the kinds of self-understandings that modern agents have. Finally, since the participants in modern life supposedly transcend the standpoint of the "unhappy consciousness," they must be capable of uniting their subjective points of view with an objective point of view. The "unhappy consciousness" is that form of life whose authoritative reasons have been sufficiently undermined by skeptical reproaches such that the participants can no longer really believe in them and thus in their form of life, even though they cannot envision an alternative to their form of life. In modern life, if Hegel's account is adequate, that form of alienation should be overcome. The ethical ends of modern agency should be such that a modern agent would be committed to them, yet on stepping back and reflecting on them, can also see their justification, can see how they are legitimate common projects that enable him to identify his own personal projects with those ethical ends (to see those general common projects as *his own* projects). The agent can be committed to a set of ends because they define *who* he is, and therefore in pursuing them be doing what he *wants* to do, and on reflection be capable of understanding those ends as justified – in short, be capable of understanding that not only it is what he *wants* to do, but that it is also *right* to do. *Self-reflection* thus plays an essential role in modern agency, which distinguishes it, for example, from the Greek form of life, where the pursuit of certain ends was combined with a naturalness about it that reflection could only undermine. Thus the ends of modern life must (1) be reflectively justifiable yet have a non-reflective subjective hold on the agents, (2) be internal to the history of modern agency such that they cannot be established outside of the free-standing social practices of modern life and have their intelligibility depend on how they are understood to have successfully made up for the insufficiencies of what historically preceded them, and (3) be such that they can be justified by the "absolute knowing," which is the result of the *Phenomenology of Spirit*.

These ends should, that is, combine the *subjectivity* of the agent – his basic desires, wants and ideals – with the *objectivity* of justification – with what counts as a justification in the social practice defined by those ends – and that objectivity should be generated by "absolute knowing." That is, the motivations of the agent – what actually impels him to act – should mesh with the justification for what he is doing, with whatever particular ends he is pursuing, and that justification should be reflectively available to the agent. Such ends would thereby enable freedom to be realized: Pursuing these ends would put agents in the position to understand what they are doing, why they are doing it, and to be able to rationally identify themselves with those actions.

2. Freedom and subjectivity in modern life

Modern life's self-understanding

Hegel's reflections on the structure of these ethical ends are found in that part of the system called "Objective Spirit" and expanded in his *Philosophy of*

Right, published in 1821. The issue concerns how in the "social space" of the modern world an agent is to understand himself. Hegel begins with a general reflection on the conception of modern agency per se. Each agent has a set of desires, wants, and so on, and each *thinks* of himself as free, self-determining. The most abstract way in which such an agent could think of himself without any further specification as this type of agent would therefore be simply as being *self-conscious* (that is, thinking of himself as an agent) but not as being conscious of himself as *positing* any of his ends as truly his own. Given such a self-conception, he would merely find whatever ends he was to pursue to be given to him by his various desires, inclinations, impulses. He would therefore be conscious of himself only as the entity to which experiences are ascribed, someone who, although determined in his choice of ends by which contingent desires he happens to have, is capable of stepping back and evaluating his experiences and thus *in his evaluation of them* is not determined by these desires and inclinations.[5] However, if the agent's self-conception were exhaustively described in this way, his ability to evaluate his ends would clearly not imply, at least in any straightforward sense, any determinate set of ends, any set of ends that would be derived simply from his own set of practical reasonings. His ends would be set externally by wants and desires, and he would only be free to evaluate them and to elect which of them will count for him as a determining motivation for action.

In order to conceive of himself as a self-determining agent, the agent must be able to integrate these given ends with his sense of himself as an independent, self-determining agent. If there is no natural hierarchy of ends – no hierarchy of ends that can be discovered, or can be taken as "given" – then the agent must construct his own hierarchy of ends. Faced with the "groundlessness" of any particular given hierarchy of ends, the agent must become *self-grounding* in determining which ends are to count for him. That is, he must be able to see the determinations of the will as coming from *his* will, not as coming from "nature" or from anything outside the will's own determinations. The will must be seen as a mode of *practical reasoning,* as a way of drawing practical inferences about ends that eventuate in actions. Even if it were possible that an agent could fortuitously find himself with a fully coherent set of desires such that each desire did not conflict with other desires, he would still not find himself with any rational *system* of the *will's* desires. The agent would merely find himself having these desires; he could not be said to have determined them. Whether those desires could still count for him as authoritative reasons could not be given by the set of desires themselves; the agent would still have to elect to count these and not those as sufficient motivations for action. Nor can the desires be seen as expressing the "essence" of the agent, for that would make the "essence" of the agent into something given, something that the agent merely finds and that therefore is not determined by the agent. Rather, the system of desires must be integrated into his *agency* and be understood as located within the agent's self-identity, which is itself structured by the "social space" in which that agent lives. In order even to be able to choose between various alternative sets of desires, the agent must have some self-determined ends in order to rank any of these systems of desires so that he may decide for which of them he will finally freely opt.

It might seem that *happiness* could serve as a given end in terms of which a natural hierarchy could be constructed in that one might be able to rank one's desires in terms of which ones would produce the most happiness. If happiness is the satisfaction of desire, then, so it would seem, one would need only to figure out which desires need to be satisfied. That issue, however, is not simple. People have a variety of different desires, and the agent will still need to have some way of ranking those desires so as to be able to resolve for himself *which* desires are to be satisfied. Moreover, the agent will not only find himself with a set of given desires for various kinds of states of affairs but also with a set of desires about which desires he should have (what we now call second-order desires) and whether therefore some of these second-order desires ought to be satisfied. The agent must therefore be able to rank his desires (including these second-order desires) as to which ones are worthy of satisfaction, and that ranking cannot itself be decided by appealing to the concept of happiness.[6] The agent must therefore independently evaluate his desires. Even the most seemingly natural way of ranking desires – namely, by their given intensity – cannot suffice to give an agent a *system* of desires in this sense. Given the multiplicity of various contingent ends that can occur to any agent – eat this, eat that, don't eat at all, go for a walk, stay inside, read a book, and so on – there will always be incompatible but consistent orderings of equally intense desires. Which of these alternative orderings of desires is to be chosen could not be done by appealing to the concept of intensity per se. Indeed, the notion of the "intensity" of a desire is most often really a shorthand for the idea of a desire that is central to an agent's understanding of who they are. The agent must order these desires in terms of some conception of who he is – that is, in terms of which of his desires can be integrated into his self-conception.

The problem is even more complex for modern agents. Even *if* the agent could come up with some criterion (for example, utility) to rank the various ends that are simply given to him by desire, he could still not count this as *self*-determination, since the ends themselves would remain merely given to him by features that are external to his own determinings. In order for the ends set by these various desires to be genuinely his, they must be such that he can see them as *his own* – that is, as fitting into his conception of his self-identity, of *who* he is. To merely accept any given ends would be self-undermining for the agent himself, for it would conflict with his sense of himself as self-determining and independent.

It is therefore necessary to begin with a conception of how a modern agent with this abstract picture of himself could arrive at the idea that he must order his desires and wants in terms of some prior self-conception. If the self-conception itself cannot be regarded as simply a "given," as something that the agent himself must discover, then the agent must regard his *freedom* as prior even to that self-conception. For example, the agent may have a given self-conception from which certain second-order desires follow that themselves are incompatible with each other. The agent cannot appeal to his self-conception to answer that question. There consequently can be nothing "given" – even the agent's own self-conception – that could underwrite the choice of which of these second-order desires is to be satisfied. The basis of ranking these desires must therefore be the agent's *freedom* itself.

The determination of freedom as "rights"

In thinking of himself very generally as a subject of experiences and actions and determining what he will do with himself, a modern agent must therefore abstractly think of himself as self-determining. If there is no more specification to it than this, then he must think of himself as self-determining in the sense of seeing himself as an *agent* who is "doing what *he* wants." In order to satisfy this self-conception as self-determining, each agent must assert against other agents the appropriateness of pursuing the satisfaction of his own desires. Each agent moves from an understanding of the appropriateness of "doing what he wants" to an understanding of its *rightness*. Thus, each agent must claim against others as a matter of *right* that he be allowed to "do what he wants." The most abstract and immediate form of mutual recognition for such agents would therefore be as agents possessing certain *rights* to this kind of self-determination. These rights would not come from "nature" but from the way in which agents thinking of themselves as self-determining, desiring agents would be led to structure their self-conceptions and the kind of social practice that would sustain that self-conception. These agents thus construct a kind of normative "social space" in which the practice of making certain types of claims against each other is authorized. The issue for these agents is therefore how such a practice can be institutionalized and supported.

The most immediate institutional manner in which such agents can be seen as rights-bearers would be as *property owners* – that is, as existing in a system of social practice structured by the mutual recognition involved in understanding each other to have claims to the use or benefit of "things" (*Sache*) to do with as they please. The things themselves can offer no opposition to our determining them as property; as parts of nature, they are indifferent to whatever normative titles we bestow on them. The opposition or affirmation of such claims to things can only come from other agents themselves.

The institution of property is thus the minimal setup in which "things" – which are morally neutral – can be fitted into an *agent's* plans and desires in the sense that they are not understood merely as means for the satisfaction of desire but are integrated into a complex of other conceptions with the idea of free agency at its core. To classify something as property is to presuppose that the agents already recognize each other as agents and see the things in each other's possession as having what Hegel would call an idealized existence – that is, as being described in such a way so as to lead to a series of licensed inferences, such as, "if X is my property, then I may do such and such with it, and I may exclude others from doing certain kinds of things with it." An apple to a hungry man is just a means to satisfy desire; to classify the apple as property is to locate it – to *idealize* it in Hegel's terminology – within a certain "social space."[7] In acquiring and transferring property, the agent comes to see his dealing with "things" as constitutive of his *agency,* not just as a feature of himself as a desiring organism. It becomes an affirmation of his independence from determining conditions outside those that he has chosen himself.

In this form of self-understanding – as juridical individuals possessing certain property rights – the agents think of themselves as bound together only by the abstract network of legalistic relations of property and contract, a network of relationships that is indifferent to their particularities and individual characters. There is a *mutual recognition* of each other as having a very general status and position, even though this form of recognition must ignore each other's particular features. Each comes to exist as a kind of "point" in this normative "social space"; outside of being located at these points in "social space," the individuals cannot exist as *these kinds* of agents at all.[8] The agents come to think of each other as occupying *identical* positions in "social space;" their distinctions from each other are only those of time, place and particular desire. In taking and exchanging property, each agent is uncoerced by the other agent at least in principle. Each determines for himself what to trade, what to keep back, and so on.[9]

In thinking of themselves in this manner, these agents therefore acquire very general and abstract *ends* of action (acquiring property, exchanging it and rectifying unjust takings) without acquiring any particular set of *motives* that define who they are to be. That is, the *ends* (of being a property owner) are defining of their agency, but there are no particular *motives* that are defining for their agency. Their motives for acquiring or exchanging property are indifferent to their status as bearers of rights and as property owners. They can pursue the acquisition of property for a variety of motives: because of particular interests that they have, because they believe it is a duty to their families, because of greed, because of a sense of "gamesmanship," or whatever. The motives that attach to property rights may be various and are thus indifferent to the justifiability (that is, the rationality) of abstract rights. There may even be certain empirical motives, such as anxiety about one's livelihood or fear of others, that are usually conjoined with the desire for property. But these *motives,* however frequent their conjunction with these ends may be, are not authoritative for this type of agency. The *end* of being a property owner defines one's agency independently of whether one has any of these fears or worries. One can be a proper property-owner without having any of these motives.

Taken as a form of social practice divorced from any other social practice, "abstract right" has a number of difficulties associated with the fact that such a form of practice would render particular motives contingent upon a variety of factors. First, any necessity for our having a determinate *motive* to actually respect the rights of other persons is missing from the account of agency given in "abstract right." If these agents were to have *only* an understanding of themselves as being rights-bearers-as-property-owners, they would come to find, as Hobbes well knew, that their own rights were subject to a kind of contingency outside the sphere of their self-determination. Others in the pursuit of their own desires may come to believe for a variety of reasons that they need your property. Why then should their recognition of you as a property owner give them any motive to postpone the satisfaction of their desire – whether the desire be simply for your property, or for the status and prestige that supposedly comes from owning the things that you have, or even for the status and prestige that could come from being a self-determining criminal whom others must, under threat of coercion, "respect"?

The structure and presumed objectivity of "abstract right" does not comport well with the contingency of motive that goes along with it. The agent who only thinks of himself as having abstract rights to pursue the objects of his desires will have difficulties reconciling the rights he claims with the contingent aspect of his motives – that is, reconciling the reasons he could give others as to why he should be allowed to pursue his desires with the reasons he could give others not to pursue their desires for his property. He finds himself asserting as a reason for his claim to a right to his property that he should be able to pursue his own desires because he takes himself to be independent, free of determination by an "other." Yet those same reasons, which seem on the one hand to support claims to "abstract right," also seem to support the claim that others may refuse to recognize his rights when it conflicts with their own pursuit of their desires and their independence. On the one hand, his freedom seems to consist of "doing what he wants" and having this affirmed by others as a right. Yet he finds that the motives associated with "doing what one wants" are not necessarily consistent with the status of the claims that he himself makes against others. Each makes claims of right against these others, yet each can find himself in the embarrassing situation of having no motive to respect others' rights. The agent is, after all, a particular self-conscious organism with determinate desires and wants; in this type of situation he can find the rational side of his nature at odds with his more particular, desirous side. His status as a rational agent would thus be at odds with his status as a particular being. The problem of mutual recognition that was framed in the section of the *Phenomenology* on the master and slave – how it is possible for a person to have a self-understanding as an independent agent that is compatible with others having a self-understanding as independent and with a mutual recognition of each as independent – is thus not resolved by "abstract right." The independence that one agent claims for himself – the right and appropriateness to pursue his own desires and to have his rights recognized by others – is not compatible with his recognizing others as equally independent and as in turn recognizing him as such.

Moreover, an understanding of ourselves merely as property owners does not have the necessary conceptual resources to make any distinction between negligence and intended wrongdoing, a distinction that is necessary to any coherent doctrine of individual rectification as distinct from just avenging one's honor or the honor of one's family. It cannot tell us the difference between criminal wrongdoing, mere negligence, and mere accidents. For

"Abstract Right" to count as a realization of freedom, it must therefore include some idea of personal responsibility within itself, which requires that it develop a conception of punishment as commensurate with the level of wrong-doing in wrongful action.

What is insufficient, therefore, *from the standpoint of the agents themselves* is that in considering themselves merely as participants in the "social space" of "abstract right," they cannot understand themselves to be fully self-determining. While each thinks of himself as an identical *person* (an entity to which experiences and actions are ascribed) who is free as a person from determination by an other, each finds that (1) his ends are simply *given* to him by his desires, and (2) the rights that he claims for himself against others depend on those others *actually recognizing* and respecting those rights. Although freedom at first seems to such an agent to be something "immediate," to consist only of "doing what he wants," what he wants must appear to his consciousness only as a *given,* as having no intrinsic connection to his agency, and what he claims as a right as something for which he is *dependent* on the recognition by others. His independence as a property-holder, therefore, is dependent on a variety of contingent factors, and, on its own, is not full independence at all.[10]

Persons and subjects

For such an agent to maintain his self-conception as a self-determining, independent agent, therefore, he needs to change or to augment his account of what is authoritative for him in order to be able to reassure himself that he is what he takes himself to be. In order to be fully self-determining, the agent must find some way to avoid having these ends simply given to him; rather, he must understand that some ends of action are to be set by himself such that they *count for him,* and that this being "set by him" would be a reason recognized by others as valid (that is, that others recognize him as having the right to set ends that they do not themselves necessarily recognize as valid). Only in that way can he integrate them into his conception of himself as a self-determining rational agent. But thinking of himself merely as a self-determining, rational agent will not be enough to do this. The agent of "abstract right" is only an entity to which actions and experiences are ascribed in terms of some normative "social space;" to be said to set *his own* ends, though, he must acquire a *self-identity* in terms of which some ends can be said to be *his own* in the sense of being more integral to that conception of self-identity than some other ends. The most immediate way of doing this would be to incorporate these ends into a conception of himself that he has himself determined. He must, that is, think of himself more determinately than as simply an independent person having certain rights and having certain desires. He may then reconcile or not reconcile his ends set by his various desires as to how well they fit into his conception of himself.[11]

An end thus becomes *his own* end in that he *identifies* with it as something that expresses who he is and he endorses that as fitting his self-conception;

in Hegel's terms, it becomes an end that is brought into his own self-consciousness. It thereby becomes more than an end that he merely *finds* himself having; it is made into an end of his own by virtue of his subjectively identifying it as *his own* end. This conception of actively taking up an end as one's end by identifying with it does not entail, of course, that the agent actually have any specifically different ends than the ones he naturally has as a bearer of rights. It only entails that he incorporate them into some sense of who he is, such that in pursuing these ends he is pursuing an end with which he identifies. From this standpoint, what is essential to this self-understanding is therefore not the content that is willed but that it is willed as an end with which the agent identifies and endorses. An agent who thinks of himself *only* as a rights-bearer need not concern himself with whether his ends are his own; he need only concern himself with whether they express what he "wants to do." In thus identifying with and endorsing some ends and not others, the agent comes to see himself as an *autonomous* agent, at least in a thin sense.[12]

This conception of willing one's own ends, as Hegel introduces it, does not prescribe any particular ends to the agent; it only prescribes that whatever they might be, the ends should be *his own* ends. Those particular ends that he decides to pursue must be those that express his sense of who he is and that he reflectively endorses. The ends themselves may come from his upbringing, from natural desire, or from whimsy. They are his own ends, however, to the extent that he identifies with them and reflectively endorses them as fitting his conception of who he is. Hegel calls this the "right of particularity," the right of the agent not to have to endorse any end that he cannot understand as expressing his own subjectivity – that is, his sense of who he is. This "right of particularity" is not something that Hegel merely assumes as a kind of "moral fact" about agency that must be taken into account in any adequate moral theory (as if it were some kind of "datum" that Kant and others had somehow overlooked in constructing their own theories). Rather, he develops it out of the concept of self-determining agency itself. The first step in developing such a conception of agency is, as we have seen, to be found in a conception of "abstract rights" in which the agent is given some very general ends that partially define what it is to be a (modern) agent; an agent, however, who thinks of himself as self-determining will find this account of himself undermined in that he will be led to see himself as being subject to certain types of contingency that are incompatible with his claims to be self-determining. To maintain his claim to be self-determining, he must therefore develop a conception of himself as making his ends into *his own* ends by accepting only those ends that he can reflectively endorse as fitting his *self*-conception.

This conception of pursuing one's own ends may be recast as the right to pursue one's own welfare, to lead one's life in terms that one sets for oneself. Happiness depends on which desires an individual can find to be worthy of satisfying – that is, which desires fit the agent's self-conception. The so-called right to pursue one's own welfare is derivative from the idea that one has a right (and it is appropriate) to seek to satisfy one's desires. To pursue one's own welfare acknowledges that prior to the conception of satisfying desire is the conception of the agent having a self-identity. If the ends that one pursues, therefore, are to count as genuinely one's own ends, one must be able to define who one is, how one is to lead one's life. The demands of "abstract right" put negative limits on what an individual may do and give the agent very general and abstract ends to pursue. The idea of forming oneself into an autonomous agent – an agent who reflectively identifies with and endorses a set of ends as fitting his self-conception – involves pursuing not simply the generally countenanced ends of "abstract right" (such as being a property owner) but one's own particular ends, such as reading novels instead of philosophy books, or learning Latin but not Greek, or becoming a plumber instead of an electrician. Modern agents come to an abstract sense of this self-determination in "Abstract Right" and this sense is further supplemented in "Morality." The right to pursue one's own welfare is thus not derived from any general principle or "given" fact about agency. It is a claim that agents will necessarily make against other agents in modern social life. To claim the rightness of one's attempt to become autonomous – to accept only those ends that one can reflectively endorse as one's own ends – forms the core idea of what Hegel calls "Morality."

In "Abstract Right," the agent's action is *his* in the formal sense of being attributed to him as an organism in space and time and being given a normative significance; in "Morality," the action becomes his *own* in the sense that he endorses the action as fitting in with his self-conception and thereby identifies himself with the action.[13] In "Morality," Hegel says, we transform the conception of the (legally conceived) *person* of "Abstract Right" into the conception of the agent as a *subject,* as a reflective *self-ascribing* entity (that is, an entity who is conscious of his activity of taking himself to be doing or experiencing things).[14] To use the metaphor of "social space": The "person" is the "point" in the normative "social space" to which these rights are ascribed (that is, within the system of "Abstract Right," it is said of the organism/person that it is both right and appropriate for him to pursue his desires); the *subject,* on the other hand, is the *self-reflective person,* that "point" in "social space" that comes to *take itself* as doing such and such, as experiencing such and such, and comes to take itself as the source of that which can legitimate his own actions as counting as exemplifications of doing the right thing. The subject is a self-conscious agent, determining for himself what is to count as his own ends in terms of his determination of who he is.

The person as a "point" in "social space" simply has certain rights and actions ascribed to him; he is simply the logical "location" or "site" of these rights and actions, the entity to which they are ascribed by virtue of the rules of the "social space" of which he is a member. For the person, therefore, what counts as *his* action is ascribed to him from an *impersonal* point of view (for example, by the legal rules of his society). For the subject, on the other hand, what counts as his action is ascribed to him by his own *personal* point of view, by what he *takes* himself to be doing.[15] This, of course, makes a big difference as to how responsibility for action is to be assessed. The person of "Abstract Right" has certain responsibilities ascribed to him by virtue of his "social space" – that is, by virtue of which responsibilities the rules of that "social space" ascribe to him. That is purely contingent, since those rules will depend on a great variety of different factors, including that of how a particular, given "social space" treats problems of contingency itself. For example, many pre-modern societies assign responsibility for making good on damages to whomever performed the action that was causally responsible for the damage, irrespective of whether the consequences of the action were intended or even foreseeable. Thus, the agent can find himself responsible for providing a remedy for a damage that is only contingently related to what he was doing.

Responsibility

An agent who takes what he is doing not to be determined impersonally by the "social space" in which he finds himself but personally by himself must have some criteria for selecting what in his actions properly belong to him and what do not. That is, he needs an account of his actions as issuing from him that does not end up being reducible to an account of his having his actions impersonally ascribed to him as a person in "social space."[16] The most general way in which an agent can be said to be determining for himself what he is doing is to consider that his actions are component parts of his adopting certain plans or projects (*Vorsätze*) in terms of which he carries out his actions. Plans, of course, are necessarily indeterminate and open; I may plan to go to the museum tomorrow in order to increase my knowledge of contemporary art, but that does not specify a particular time at which I shall go, which art I shall see, or whether I shall focus on the paintings and ignore the sculpture. If I adopt a plan, I then engage in certain actions that count as carrying out the plan, and the actions are mine precisely because they are parts of *my* plan. But in carrying out the plan, I act, and any action produces consequences. The issue therefore is whether and to what extent the consequences of my action can be said to be part of my plan. For which consequences am I therefore responsible? On the one hand, it seems correct that the consequences of the action would be imputable to me only if they are part of *my* plan – that is, if the production of these consequences are part of my plan (for example, I might plan to clear some land in order to grow vegetables, planning as a result of this to create more sunlit space). There can of course be consequences of my actions that are not included my plan: for example, in clearing the land, I might create drainage problems for myself and others. Moreover, others who are affected by these consequences may attribute them to my plan even if I myself did not actually include them in my plan. There is therefore a contradiction between my conception of myself as determining what I *do* according to a plan and what others *impute to me* as following from my plan. I find what I *do* therefore being determined by things other than my agency, by what accidentally happens as a result of my carrying out my plans and what others impute to my plans as a result of what I do. To the extent that we account for this autonomy only in terms of a conception of "setting our own plans," there is still an element of external contingency (of the contingency of circumstances and the contingency of what others impute to my plans) that this account is supposed to disallow. By this account of agency, I am responsible for what I *do,* and what I do is a function of what *my* plans are; however, what is part of my plan is, by this account, not entirely up to me but can be influenced by all sorts of external contingencies.

To be fully self-determining, I must therefore see my actions as determined not only by a general plan (*Vorsatz*) but by a more specific intention (*Absicht*) – that is, by what I concretely will to do. Those consequences are to be included in my action that I specifically intend or that can be *reasonably foreseen* by me. The passage from a conception of myself as a planning agent to that of an intending agent makes the agent's own particular point of view on what he is doing more central to the nature of the action.[17] An agent who conceives of himself in this way has a richer conception of himself as a self-determining agent. His particular intentions count as determining what it is that he is does. Following out what his own intentions dictate and being *morally* responsible only for what he intends – to be kept distinct from being *legally* responsible – he is more nearly autonomous, exhibiting what Hegel calls "subjective freedom."

Hegel's discussion of "subjective freedom" is meant to contrast the modern account of action and responsibility from (what he takes to be) the ancient account of action and responsibility. The ancients, in Hegel's eyes, took the agent to be responsible for all the consequences of his actions independently of whether the agent had intended those consequences.[18] Hegel explains this difference between ourselves and the ancients in terms of the ancients not having an account of agency in terms of self-determining subjectivity – a lack reflected in their tragedies – and the moderns having such a conception of self-determining agency as an essential component of their accounts of action and responsibility.[19]

Both the ancient and the modern accounts have to do with the status of agency in a world of contingency. The ancients make the agent responsible for the contingent *consequences* of his actions; the moderns make the agent responsible for what he contingently happens to *will.* Thus, by the modern account, the individual agent may not be morally responsible for unforeseeable consequences of his actions, whereas the ancients held the individual to be ethically responsible for exactly those things. However, the modern form of life parcels out responsibility for these contingencies to other social institutions. What makes the modern account possible, therefore, are the complex modern institutions that parcel out the responsibility for remedying damages that result from such contingencies (for example, the pooling of risk in insurance schemes, such as the "widows and orphans fund" to which Hegel was a contributor in Berlin). Because contingencies can be socially handled in these kinds of ways, it is possible for the moderns to restrict individual responsibility for the contingency of circumstances in a way that allows the modern account to remain consistent with itself. The ancients, on the other hand, did not have the kind of institutional support that would have made possible for them something like the modern account.

However, the modern account leads to certain paradoxes within itself of what is an authoritative reason for action. On the one hand, the consequences of actions belong to the action itself; they are not simply external trappings to the action. Yet the modern individual is said to be morally responsible only for what he wills, and some consequences will clearly fall outside of his intentions such that he cannot be said to have subjectively *willed* them. Yet for many moderns, it will seem nonetheless that he should be morally responsible for those actions, thus contradicting the account they give of his moral responsibility.[20] Hegel explains the paradoxes of modern accounts of authoritative reasons for action as arising out of a person's seeing willings and consequences (more generally, actions and deeds) as having nothing to do with each other in the determination of moral responsibility. The paradoxes of "consequentialist" versus non-consequentialist accounts arise out of this; the paradoxes arise by taking one of the two elements (willings and consequences) as *the* determining feature of the moral quality of an action and taking the other to be only incidental.[21] On the one hand, there is a consequentialist principle that counsels us to judge actions solely in terms of the goodness of the consequences of the actions; on the other hand, there is a non-consequentialist principle, which counsels us to judge the goodness of actions by criteria that are independent of the consequences (or, more weakly, to judge the actions in terms of something other than the consequences alone). The plausibility of each principle arises out of the implausibility of the other. The non-consequentialist seems to counsel a person to do something even though it brings about catastrophically bad consequences, and the non-consequentialist seems to counsel people to do evil things because in some convoluted way they produce a much greater good. The plausibility of each of these principles, however, arises out of fixating on either the aspect of the "willing" or the aspect of the "consequences" in an agent's action to determine how we are to judge the rightness of her actions, holding that element fast, and then using that fixed element to determine the rightness of the action. One element is held fixed, and the others are varied in hypothetical accounts of what makes an action right. Thus, the consequentialist holds that the goodness of the consequences may be held fixed in determining what the right act is, and the willings of the agent may therefore vary while the goodness of the action stays the same, whereas the non-consequentialist holds that the willing activity itself may be held fixed in determining what the right action is and the moral worth of the action may remain the same even though its consequences may vary. The so-called paradoxes that are generated out of this have to do with consequentialists having to hold that something is right because it produces good consequences but that is wrong because it seems to violate some ethical norm accepted on other equally good grounds; and with the non-consequentialists holding that something is right that produces such bad consequences that no ethical individual could be said to countenance such a thing.

The paradoxes are avoided, Hegel thinks, if one understands both elements – that of the agent's intentions (his willings) and the consequences – to be component parts of the overall moral judgment to be made about the action and the moral status of the agent. Hegel therefore holds that an agent must be (in his sense) *morally* responsible for the consequences of our actions, even when he does not explicitly *plan* or *intend* those consequences; and that his *moral status* (our judgments about whether the agent is a good or bad person) nonetheless cannot be a function *only* of those consequences but also of what the agent intends. Both the agent's intentions and the consequences of actions therefore must be kept in mind in giving a moral assessment of the agent, and Hegel thinks that in such cases, there can be only general guidelines and no fixed, rigid rules for doing so; it is a matter for continuous reflective deliberation, and the idea that one might have a rule that would overcome this dilemma is a chimera.[22] (It should be kept in mind that a central feature of Hegel's theory is his claim that in any event these paradoxes cannot be fully resolved in "Morality" and therefore also require an account of *Sittlichkeit*.) For the ancients, the agent was fully responsible for the consequences of the action, even if he had not willed them; for the moderns, the agent is partially responsible for those actions, such that at least some feeling of regret or some responsibility for atonement is still present even when the consequences were not explicitly willed by the agent.[23] Accordingly, the modern account should not be taken as simply the contrary of the ancient account, as if Hegel were saying that the ancients were "consequentialists" whereas the moderns are "non-consequentialists." It would be false, so Hegel thinks, to claim that the ancients *only* looked at the consequences, and it would be equally false to say that the moderns should *only* look at what is intended. Rather, the modern account must be seen as *adding* an element to the ancient account, which, of course, on its own terms the ancient account could neither develop nor accept, and that requires therefore something like the very different modern account of agency. That extra added element in the modern account is the idea that one can be morally obligated only to those principles to which one can self-consciously acknowledge obligation.

Fixing the issue of responsibility and moral deliberation in this way, however, does not specify what ends these agents should pursue, since the idea that the agent should pursue only those ends which are "his own" gives him no material criterion for deciding which ends he ought to pursue. Given an account of self-determining agency that operates only with the terms introduced thus far ("abstract right" and the idea of responsibility for action being partially determined by intentions), it would seem that the agent must simply take up whatever contingent ends he happens to have and test them to see whether they could be made his own.[24] As pursuing and bringing about *his own* ends, the agent achieves a sense of *satisfaction,* of self-assurance, in finding his self-conception authenticated in his actions.[25] (Thus, as Hegel notes, satisfaction can come both from honor and recognition and in relations of love, acts of conscience, and so on.[26]) The satisfaction that an individual achieves is related to his happiness. Happiness is the satisfaction of desire, but, as we have seen, which desires are to be satisfied must be determined by an ordering of desire in terms of how each fits an agent's self-conception (what Hegel calls their becoming part of the *system* of desires). The agent experiences *happiness* when he fulfills those desires that fit his self-conception; he experiences *satisfaction* in having that self-conception affirmed. The well-being (*Wohl*) of an individual consists of his happiness and his satisfaction. Well-being, therefore, consists not just in the simple satisfaction of desire, but in satisfaction and happiness; well-being therefore extends over an individual's life and is not a moment by moment affair.

Hegel uses these distinctions to link the "right" (taken as a principle of justified action) with the "good" (taken as a doctrine of what states of affairs are desirable or worthy), and he links both to "morality" in the following way.[27] The *right* thing for a "moral subject" to do would be to respect the claims of "Abstract Right" in a way that involves that subject's setting those ends for himself. The subject thus wills his own ends under the proviso that he not violate anyone's rights in doing so. In willing from his personal point of view, however, the subject wills his own *satisfaction:* his affirmation of his own self-conception. In willing his own satisfaction, the subject must have some criterion for selecting among the various possible objects of willing (or, put more loosely, to elect what he *will* do among all the things that he *might* do). Without any further account of what counts for him as an authoritative reason for action other than that bound up with being a "person" and a "subject," the criterion for such selection must be that of *well-being* – that is, of electing to do that which affirms his self-conception and leads to happiness.[28] The subject thus has a universal principle on which he can act: A moral subject should freely will the pursuit of his own well-being (the "good") while at the same time respecting the claims of "Abstract Right." As having a universal principle (something that counts for him from an impersonal point of view, as *right*), the subject should thereby be able to reflectively integrate his personal and his impersonal points of view. Each subject is thus to pursue his own welfare while respecting the claims of "Abstract Right." The principles of right action, as defined by "Abstract Right," would therefore put strict limits on what the subject may do in the pursuit of his good.[29] What *cannot* be settled by this principle, however, is how one is to adjudicate clashes between different subjects. It is, after all, a purely contingent affair if one's own well-being coincides with others, and this principle only counsels one to pursue the well-being of oneself and the well-being of others to the extent that their well-being contributes to one's well-being.[30] Moreover, since one's achieving a certain well-being is contingent on a variety of circumstances, and particularly on others' having projects that support one's own, one may find one's own well-being at the mercy of the plans, projects and decisions by others. (If one likes to discuss mythology but can find no books on the subject or conversation partners, then one's own happiness will be limited.) Nonetheless, this principle expresses the moral subject's conception of himself as an agent having certain very general (abstract) rights and as being an autonomous agent (freely willing his own ends).

Both the practices and institutions of "Abstract Right" and "Morality" are justified as specifications of the general norm of "freedom" – that is, as necessary developments of the way in which it is possible for agents to affirm their self-understanding as self-determining agents. Thinking of themselves in terms of being autonomous therefore is for them as much a matter of *right* as are the claims concerning property, contract, and the rectification of injustice in "Abstract Right." Without the *right* to do only that about which he can satisfy himself that it is *indeed* the right thing for him to do, for which he takes responsibility, the agent could not think of himself as a "subject." As a moral agent, the "subject" must *take* himself to have a right to be autonomous in his choices, even when those choices have nothing to do with morality itself. The idea of autonomous choice, considered merely on its own, is not exclusively a moral matter; there are many issues having to do with the autonomy of the individual that have nothing to do with anything connected with "morality." For example, a person might ask himself if his tastes are really "his own"; this is hardly a moral question, but it is a question of whether he is autonomous.

The "moral standpoint"

The necessary collision between the objective demands of "Abstract Right" and the claims of autonomous agency (or what Hegel calls the "rights of particularity") gives rise to the specifically modern *moral* standpoint, which emerges when the *objective* claims of abstract right, which put constraints on people's actions, are combined with the *subjective* demands of modern individuals to lead their own lives and to determine for themselves what counts as an authoritative reason for them to act. The individual's *right* to pursue his own ends – to do only for that for which he by his own lights can satisfy himself is valid – can clash with the *right* that others have in terms of "Abstract Right." The moral standpoint grows out of this clash of rights.

In both in the published text of the *Philosophy of Right* and in his lectures on the subject, Hegel displays the contradiction between the two requirements of autonomy and "Abstract Right" in terms of a collision between the claims of distress or emergency (in which there is a "moral right" to save oneself) and the claims of "Abstract Right."[31] (In the *Philosophy of Right,* he offers the standard example of a starving person stealing bread in order to survive.[32]) This shows, so he argues, that the claims of "Abstract Right" and of autonomy are at least potentially at odds with each other, and, within the terms of an account whose components are only those of "abstract right" and "autonomy," it can only be a contingent matter if they are not. In order for the agent to maintain a conception of himself as a self-determining *rational* agent, he must therefore find some way of integrating these two accounts of his willing into his self-conception. This means that in order to be adequate, such an account must be available to the agents themselves – that is, it must be an account that the agents themselves could endorse as fitting their own self-conceptions. (In the language of the *Phenomenology*, the resolution must be "for them" and not merely "for us.") Such a conception, so Hegel argues, is the account of the modern moral standpoint as involving an essential appeal to personal conscience.[33]

It is one of Hegel's original and controversial theses that this capacity to be a moral agent is historically recent and depends on the development of the modern community for it to be possible. Hegel continually argued in his career that the Greek form of life did not have this type of agency within it because it had no place in its account of itself for the idea of a self-determining subject.[34] Nor are the collisions to which this necessarily leads, Hegel argues, avoidable in modern moral life. It is a necessary feature of the form of life allied with this conception that one person's pursuit of his own ends can be at the expense of another's "abstract rights."

The account of ourselves as both "persons" and "subjects" is therefore unstable in that the demands of "persons" and "subjects" conflict with each other. This instability threatens to undermine modern life's claim to being a realization of freedom: If an agent is free only if he is in a position to be acting in such a way that he can know what he is doing, why he is doing it, and can identify himself with that action, then where necessarily there are these kind of conflicting demands, there will also be the inability to satisfy all three of these conditions. Modern agents therefore *require* some integrating account of themselves as "persons" and as "subjects." One of the major issues for modern life is precisely whether these features of life could be integrated in terms of an enriched *moral* standpoint itself, or whether the modern moral standpoint requires something beyond itself to make itself satisfactory. The conservatives of Hegel's day, of course, held that modern morality required replacement by some older scheme of religious ethics, or at least required some kind of supplementation by an ethical doctrine that did not rely on the idea of self-determination. Hegel certainly rejected the claims of those like Jacobi that we needed some kind of non-rational intuition of a religious "absolute" to provide a satisfactory account of moral life; his argument against those conservative critics is that the kinds of integrating attempts found, for example, in Kantian ethics point in the direction of how modern "morality" requires not some throwback to a pre-modern scheme but requires instead a specifically modern form of *Sittlichkeit* for its completion. Hegel calls this supposedly integrating *moral* standpoint that of the moral *good,* the standard by which both moral rightness and the quasi-legal rightness of "abstract right" are to be measured. It is a major part of his thesis that this supposedly integrating conception of the moral good is nonetheless necessarily empty, and that this emptiness of the moral good requires a supplementation through a doctrine of modern ethical life, *Sittlichkeit.*

The moral good must include the objectivity of the claims of "Abstract Right," and it must be autonomously willed by the subject. This gives the concept of the moral good the following contours. First, as a *good,* it is motivating for the subject; it is the kind of end whose recognition motivates the person to try to achieve it. The moral good is, however, different from the particular good of any person (what constitutes any particular person's well-being) in that it also must function, second, vis-à-vis any particular good as a principle of *right:* It must put restraints on what can count as a valid pursuit of one's own good. However, the moral good cannot be equivalent to "the right" in general because that it is that *end* in terms of which right action is to be determined: it is supposedly in willing that end that one does the right thing (not, it should be mentioned, in willing to maximize that end).[35] The moral good is thus that which is completely authoritative for – which is the "essence" of – all individual acts of will, the end that constrains all other particular ends that may be willed and that itself is sufficiently motivating so that the subject does not have to will it as a means to anything else but can will it simply for its own sake.[36] Moreover, for the authoritativeness of the moral good to be consistent with the self-conception of an autonomous "moral subject," the subject must be able autonomously to satisfy himself that this is a legitimate end of action (that is, that he be able to reflectively endorse it himself) and not merely accept it out of habit or upbringing. (It is not good because he endorses it, but it cannot count as an end of his action unless he is capable of endorsing it.[37]) As authoritative for the subject, the moral good therefore prescribes to the subject both a set of duties and the motivations to fulfill those duties. However, the conception of the moral good must be fleshed out and given more substance for it to do play this role in modern life. Merely calling it the integration of "Abstract Right" and autonomy only sets the problem; it does not resolve it.

This way of setting the problem, of course, is familiar to any student of Kantian ethics, and Hegel's argument about how the moral good would develop out of the kinds of considerations having to do with abstract right and autonomy quite obviously makes reference to Kantian ethical theory.[38] It would be a mistake, though, to see Hegel as offering any kind of detailed commentary on Kantian ethics in the sections where he deals with "good and conscience." Instead, he is reconstructing what kinds of considerations would have to count for modern agents in order for anything like Kantian ethics to come to be a suitable option for them, to come to have a place on their "conceptual menu"; and he is reconstructing what must follow from such a conception of agency, independently of all the Kantian textual twists and turns. Hegel's argument is that Kantian ethics can appear on the scene only when the claims of "Abstract Right" and autonomy have made their *social* appearance. The kinds of considerations that characterize the Kantian search for what will count as the unconditional good are possible only within the social structure of a certain form of modern life. Kantian ethics, so Hegel argues, must be understood as an attempt to make good on the conflicting claims of modern morality: the apparent necessity for a conception of a groundless, autonomous subject and the objectivity of modern conceptions of rights and the social institutions that sustain them.

Hegel's general claim against Kantian ethics is that because Kant's conception of the categorical imperative is necessarily empty, Kantian ethics collapses into little more than a kind of rhetorical and high-flown doctrine of duty for duty's sake.[39] This is a charge that Kantians have always denied, holding that Hegel simply misunderstood certain key elements of the Kantian theory, and to some extent every fair minded reader must agree that there is some truth to the charge. Hegel often says, for example, that Kant's conception of the categorical imperative is simply that of a maxim of action that is not self-contradictory, which if it were true would certainly make Hegel's criticism applicable. But Kantians have almost universally rejected that conception of the categorical imperative with a good basis in Kant's texts for doing so.[40]

But it is striking that Hegel never goes deeply into the Kantian texts themselves. This is no doubt partly true to historical reasons. Hegel goes no more deeply into Kant's texts than Kant went into Leibniz's texts; each took himself to be rejecting a certain very general position, and to both it seemed no doubt pedantic to attach themselves tightly to the texts, especially since there were so many other Kantians and Fichteans around in Hegel's day who, had he based his criticisms solely on the Kantian texts themselves, would have used that to claim that *their* statement of the problem was unaffected by Hegel's criticism. So Hegel wished to criticize the Kantian position in general as a *type* of position, and his criticisms should be taken with that aim in mind.

Hegel wishes to show that one cannot integrate the objectivity of the kinds of claims of "Abstract Right" with the demands of autonomy from within a *moral* theory itself – that is, an account of the moral good as being authoritative for us only in terms of our acknowledging it for ourselves. He rejects all forms of theories of the right and the good that are *exclusively* moral theories, with Kant's theory being only a subset of those. An exclusively moral theory holds that the determinations of the right and the good follow from what it means for agents to reflectively submit to the moral law as individual agents, and it uses the conception of an individual agent willing the right and/or the good as the basis for determining what the moral law is. Against this, Hegel wishes to claim that the moral ability to submit ourselves to the moral law is itself the result of a particular historical development and thus presupposes rather than establishes an ethical community (a form of *Sittlichkeit*). It is in the socialization processes of an ethical community that we learn to treat each other in ways that count, for example, as "respecting freedom," and since individual acts of will presuppose the existence of that community, they cannot establish it. The authoritativeness of "morality" (in this restricted sense) has to do with how and whether it necessarily realizes the general norm of freedom – that is, if it can be shown to give agents *ends* such that in acting on those ends those agents will know what they are doing, why they are doing it, and will be able to identify themselves with that action. An exclusively moral theory proposes that these "genuine" objects of the will – the objects with which we can identify and about which we can satisfy ourselves as to their rational legitimacy – can be derived in some sense from a conception of the free will itself.

More loosely put: From the moral point of view, we look at what we are doing in terms of whether we are freely submitting ourselves to some moral law, and an exclusively moral theory sees the moral law as following from some idea of what an individual agent would freely elect to will or could dispassionately discern to do. The dialectic of any exclusively moral theory thus must eventually push it to a conception of a pure act of willing by an individual agent (or to some act of "insight" by an individual agent into the realm of goods and values). That is, from the exclusively moral point of view, moral agents must will the moral good as something that is impersonally right, and they must be somehow motivated to do this so that it counts as a free act on their part. To be a moral agent, therefore, the individual must find the moral good to be something that *motivates* him, it must become the *end* of his actions (that for the sake of which he acts), and he must be able to *satisfy* himself that what is required by the moral good is indeed absolutely authoritative for him (as Hegel puts it, that the good is good "in and for itself"). Now, if the agent were only to will as a *personally* autonomous agent (that is, will only that which he as an individual with his own set of tastes, inclinations, and values could endorse), then the agent would not be willing the *moral* good, since, if nothing else, he would be neglecting the impersonal demands of "Abstract Right." For the agent to will the moral good, therefore, he must will it from the impersonal, universal point of view. For a modern, exclusively moral agent, the impersonal point of view must necessarily be the point of view of a generalized rational agent. The moral good must be something that is impersonally good for the agent (good from the standpoint of all agents) and also personally good for him in order for it to motivate him, and it must be something with which he *as* a rational agent can identify. It is this set of requirements that requires the invention of the modern conception of *conscience:* the possibility of moral agency itself requires that there be some faculty that each agent possesses such that the particular agent can satisfy himself that he is willing the moral good. That is, for moral agency to be possible, there must be something like the appeal to conscience, taken as the "disposition (*Gesinnung*) to will what is good in and for itself."[41] Any moral standpoint will therefore come to something like this conclusion: the moral good is that which a particular agent can will from an impersonal point of view (find to be right in his conscience), find motivating for himself (have his particular conscience be motivationally efficacious), and about which he can satisfy *himself* (in his conscience) that it is valid (universal) for all such agents.

The great strain in any exclusively moral theory appears in its account of the relation between the individual agent's willing and the moral good itself. If the moral good is taken as being some kind of entity (for example, as being a set of existent "values"), then the relation of the agent to the moral good will be that of a perceiver who simply "intuits" the good, and it will be impossible to explain how that good can have motivating force for him. Or, insofar as it is the *will* of the agent that is crucial, it will be impossible to give an adequate characterization of the relation of the moral will to the *individual* agent's will that can maintain the requisite impersonal distance and still be motivating. Indeed, the great strain in any exclusively moral theory has to do with (1) its necessarily conceiving the agent's willing as being prior to any determinate end, and (2) with the relation between the individual's will and the universal will (since as an exclusively moral theory, it must claim that the validity of the agent's willing has to be universal). Inevitably, an exclusively moral theory will have to explain how the moral order can be generated out of individual acts of autonomous willing.[42] However, from the idea of rational agency in general – from the very general idea of simply assuming a position in "social space" – one can derive no determinate ends at all, and one cannot explain how such general conceptions can be motivating for particular agents.[43]

Any exclusively moral theory thus will be burdened with the following dilemmas. The moral good will remain a hopelessly abstract and empty conception unless it is replaced by some kind of idea of a set of "values" that would then be "intuited" by the agent; but this presupposes a completely implausible theory of knowledge, and it will fail to explain how such agents could then be motivated to act on the basis of this "intuition." If an exclusively moral theory eschews intuitionism, and is more consistent with its own claims, then it will claim that the moral good is something impersonally willed by the agent and has validity only in being so willed. But the idea of a universally binding moral good on our wills is empty and must remain so, because nothing can follow from simply the idea of a "rational agent in general" or from the idea of an "agent willing universally valid norms." An exclusively moral theory can mitigate this charge by bringing in other considerations, and it can claim a certain amount of plausibility for itself if these other things are themselves relatively non-controversial. But this gain in intuitive plausibility undoes the claims of an exclusively moral theory to be exclusively *moral* (in this restricted sense of "moral"); it must then hold that there are other considerations than those willed by the agents themselves that put constraints on what the agent wills. In other words, it must hold that there are things that transcend the moral point of view in general, without which the moral point of view can itself have no authority. It thus cannot count as a realization of freedom, and it thus cannot count as an adequate theory for modern "subjects."

Finally, if the *individual* is taken as authoritative in the moral life, if what counts as right depends on the individual's *taking it as right,* and if the "moral good" as conceived from the exclusively moral standpoint really is empty, then from the social point of view, the possibility for evil masquerading as morality are great. Enormous crimes have been committed by people who took themselves to be "above it all," to be "setting their own standards."[44] The appeal to individual conscience always threatens to degenerate into a hypocritical stance or into a self-righteous self-satisfaction, a society ultimately composed of people striking moral poses, dissembling, accusing each other of hypocrisy, all the while paying lip service to traditionally authoritative principles while mocking them. Hegel's point is that an exclusively moral standpoint has no resources within itself to inhibit this.[45] Only a socially supported system of ethical life, some sense of "the way we do things" that puts some things as out of bounds, as being right or wrong, can do this.

A symptom of this, so Hegel argues is the popularity in his day of the specifically modern ironic attitude, which he distinguishes from the ancient sense of irony.[46] The ironic attitude consists in seeing the lack of truth or the lack of justification of otherwise accepted claims and at the same time seeing oneself as somehow being "above it all." It consists in accepting a claim, while at the same time seeing that one's acceptance is without foundation.[47] This kind of ironic attitude is of course natural to any view that sees individuals as solely authoritative for moral questions. On the one hand, there will be the various accepted claims of moral and ethical life at work in one's community; on the other hand, since the agent himself understands that only he can authorize such claims as valid for himself, he sees that the otherwise binding quality of these claims lies solely in there being bonds on him that he can untie at any time. To the extent that the agent continues to accept these claims, he can only do so with a sense of detachment, that is, with a sense of irony. Indeed, the prevalence of an ironic detachment from all things is a symptom usually that a form of life is losing its internal justification.[48]

3. Modern ethical life

Ethical ends

The exclusively moral standpoint frames the problem of modern life in terms of how we combine a view of ourselves as self-determining agents (with its pull towards relativism) with a view of morality as objective; however, the *exclusively* moral standpoint fails to resolve that problem on its own. Or to put it slightly looser terms, modern life is committed to a language of general rights (to life, liberty and property) and to a language of moral autonomy (to the idea that nothing can count for us as an obligation unless we can acknowledge it to be such), and these two "languages" conflict with each other. The resolution of that problem lies in what Hegel calls ethical life, *Sittlichkeit,* a specifically modern sense of "the way things are done." "Morality" is the result of integrating the claims of modern autonomous agency with those of the claims of the objectively founded rights of modern free agents, and "ethical life" is the result of integrating further the claims of morality itself with those of objective right, of fleshing out the conception of the moral good. The social practices and institutions of "ethical life" are thus necessary for the realization of freedom, for agents to be able to know what they are doing, why they are doing it and to be able to rationally identify with the activities involved in those practices. Or, to put it differently, the insufficiencies of the very *individualistic* standpoint of "morality" are resolved only within the very *social* standpoint of ethical life and the common projects that it provides for its participants.

"Ethical life" thus makes good on the claims of "morality" and completes the otherwise unfinished project outlined in the description of the modern *moral* community in the *Phenomenology*. Hegel came to believe that in the wake of the French Revolution and the development of the "moral world-view," modern life had (for contingent reasons) developed a set of basic social institutions that created the possibility for a renewal of *Sittlichkeit* (of acting according to norms that are experienced simply as "the way things are done," that specify a "common life," which count as *authoritative* for modern individuals) which would not only be compatible with the reflective, self-distancing practices of modern life but would make those practices themselves possible as a rational form of self-consciousness. For the individuals brought up within these basic social institutions, they generate not only a determinate set of desires and needs, but also a sense of what is and is not really possible in their own lives, and in leading their lives in terms of the desires, hopes and expectations engendered by these institutions, individuals develop a concrete sense of what they are to do in terms of "the way things are done." Hegel's thesis is that the various modern understandings of "the way things are done" that are generated by these modern institutions – specifically, the institutions of the modern companionate family, the modern market society and the modern constitutional state – can be shown to provide a form of rational self-consciousness that satisfactorily resolves the apparent contradictions between the claims of "abstract right" and "morality."

Part of what distinguishes this modern type of *ethical life* from *morality* is that ethical life presents the agent with certain determinate ends that a self-determining agent is required to will in order to affirm for himself that he is indeed a self-determining agent, and toward which that agent is required to have certain types of motives. These determinate ends count as genuine *ethical ends,* as signifying a set of authoritative, common projects for participants in a form of *Sittlichkeit,* ethical life. By remaining only with the self-understanding present in "morality," the agent can have no consistent self-understanding, since that understanding is caught in the contradiction between the objectivity of the rights he claims as a modern free individual and the subjectivity of the moral claims he makes as a modern autonomous individual. If ethical life is to fulfill its promise, it must resolve that contradiction. Moreover, the resolution cannot be "merely" philosophical but must be a resolution for the agents *from within their point of view.*[49] For this conception of ethical life to work, the agents must be able to affirm the ethical ends as adequately resolving this contradiction. (To use the language of the *Phenomenology of Spirit* again, the solution must be "for them," not merely "for us.") Finally, they must specify and inform activities with which the subject can identify himself, or, as Hegel puts it, *in which* he can find himself to be fully "present" – that is, activities in which the subject can find that his actions and desires, even his emotional life, accord with his sense of who he is. To be in such a position is to realize the norm of freedom: to be engaged in activities that are intentional (the agent must know what he is doing), reflective (he knows why he is doing it), and with which the agent rationally identifies himself. To the extent that the agent cannot rationally identify himself with achieving these ends, he will be alienated from them (they will not be *his* ends), and they will not therefore be sufficiently motivating. If these modern ethical ends are to constitute a genuine form of *Sittlichkeit*, it must be case that the individual experiences them as both "the way things are done" and as being harmonious with his own sense of who he is such that he will not be alienated from the social life around him.

It is important to see what is being ruled out here. The Hegelian argument is not appealing – indeed, *cannot* appeal – to any conception of "human nature" or a "human essence" to make this point. It cannot be saying anything to the effect that "You will be happier (or more authentic or more in keeping with your "essential nature") if you do this, even if you cannot see it yourself." Instead it must appeal to the kind of self-consciousness and self-understanding that a modern agent – the member of a given historical community – must possess and what that form of life must do to make that self-consciousness intelligible to itself in its reflections on who it has come to be. The kind of solution that would resolve the problems of "morality" and "abstract right" must be such that it would match up motivations and ends so that the two are not indifferent to each other, such that the norms that are in force for the social practices and institutions can be sustained by the agents. For that to be possible, each determinate ethical end must be matched up with a determinate type of motivation, such that failure to have *that* motive would imply that one cannot be pursuing or achieving *that* end. In "Abstract Right" there is no particular motivation that must be connected with the ownership of property in order to make that determinate end valid. In "Morality" there are determinate motives that the agent must have (acting out of a sense of duty) but no determinate ends that follow from that. (Instead, "Morality" has only the indeterminate end of the moral good.) In ethical life, however, the agent has a set of determinate ends that are matched with a determinate set of motives that go with them. Ethical life, as Hegel puts it, has both an *objective* and a *subjective* side.[50]

Ethical ends therefore must be such that a modern reflective individual (1) would *want* to pursue them; (2) would even see it as his *right* to pursue them, such that being forbidden to pursue them or somehow being prevented by social conditions would be considered to constitute a wrong against the individual; and (3) would at the same time see these ethical ends as the "right thing to do," as *duties,* as that which is *required* to be a participant in that form of life. They are both what he wants and what he feels incumbent on himself to do. These features constitute them as ethical ends of modern agency. Moreover, these ends must be consistent with the dictates of "Abstract Right" and "Morality" and must be seen to *complete* the dictates of "Abstract Right" and "Morality," in the sense that only in willing those ends can the agents be said to be genuinely free. They are not ends that are simply added on to the dictates of those two spheres, nor do they supplant the two spheres.[51]

As the ethical ends of modern agency, however, they are also ends that the agent understands to be consistent with his claims to self-determination. For them to function as such ends, therefore, they should not be understood by the agent as anything imposed on him. This has been confusing to many of Hegel's readers: On the one hand, Hegel seems to be saying that these ethical ends should be self-determined, yet on the other hand, he seems to be saying that they are independent of any agent's will. How can they be both independent of us and at the same time be the result of our free self-determination? This has led any number of commentators on Hegel to suppose that Hegel must have some version of a "true self" theory of agency. That is, he must have held that we have a "false self" and a "true self," and that we are free only when we act in ways that the "true self" can affirm. Common to all "true self" theories is the idea that the individual may be mistaken about who his "true self" is. In these cases, it may therefore be necessary, to use Rousseau's well known phrase, to "force him to be free" by forcing him to do things which he does not *actually* want to do on the curious ground that he *really* – that is, his "true self" really – wants to do them. Thus, people have supposed that Hegel must hold some such view to the effect such ends express our "essence" and thus in acting in accord with our "essence" we are really acting not only freely but in a self-determining manner. Such a move, however, cannot be open to a Hegelian. The Hegelian argument aims at showing that these ethical ends can be both the result of self-determining action and be objective without making any appeal to anything "given" or immediate (which would include any theory of a given "human nature" or of a given "human essence").

One sense in which these ends may be said to be the result of self-determination is that the individual agent *wants* them; they are not, from the subjective point of view, merely ideals to be reached but are actually objects of desire which are practically achievable. The ethical ends can also be said to be consistent with the agent's autonomy to the extent that if an agent identifies with those ends, sees them as filling out and affirming his sense of who he is, then he makes those ends *his own*. Thus, in this sense, the ends can be seen as consistent with the agent's autonomy even if they are presented to him from the outside – that is, as "found" by him in his social environment. These ends are what makes possible his individual willings in the first place; they form the common projects of a form of life that make possible the individual projects of different agents. If the agent actually identifies with those ends, in the sense of making them his own, then the ethical ends meet the conditions of being consistent with autonomy, even though they are not themselves the result of self-determination.

But even this cannot be sufficient to make Hegel's point, since it might seem as if Hegel would then only be trading on an ambiguity between "is my own" and "is determined by me." For these ethical ends to be properly seen to be the result of self-determination, two conditions must therefore be met: (1) The ends must be shown to be derivable from reason, that is, they must be shown to be essential moments of the system of reasons that make up the "social space" that itself makes modern agency possible. (2) It must be shown that the modern agent sees himself as drawing these conclusions himself. That these ends form the system of practical reasons is the basis for Hegel's claiming them to be the system of determinations of ethical life derived *a priori* from the "Idea" (that is, from "reason") itself.[52] The system of ethical ends should form a kind of enclosed set of practical inferences, and the basic propositions about the various ethical ends should have the status in practice of unconditionally assertible truths, even though their assertibility actually comes from their place in the system of reasons. They cannot be merely generalizations from experience, nor can they be the results of some kind of intuition into essences. Instead, they must be a part of the system of reasons that make up the agent's "social space" in terms of the social institutions and practices of which he is a part, and they are to be justified in terms of making that system of reasons coherent with the overall norm of "freedom as self-determination."[53]

In holding such a view, Hegel is ruling out a conception of these ethical ends as items that a rational agent could independently identify and then "decide" whether to adopt as his own, for the agent who identifies with these ethical ends cannot be an already fully formed agent with his own independently identifiable set of interests which would then enable him to make that kind of "decision." Rather, the agent is who he is only by *participating* in a form of life with its associated practices; the agent's "self" is not some fully formed, fixed entity that then "decides" whether these ends fit his already formed interests. Rather than being a kind of "fixed entity," the self arises out of a position in "social space," and its point of view is a way of projecting itself into the future, of assuming a practical standpoint that orients itself in the world. Ethical ends in turn manifest the kinds of projects that the "social space" of his practical world has for him and with which he identifies. The major question concerning such ethical ends thus concerns primarily their rationality – for example, whether they jointly support or undermine each other, and the way in which they combine the differing points of view, the personal and the impersonal, for the agent. The agent cannot thus independently "decide" to adopt or eschew these ethical ends by relying on some conception of rational choice as "maximizing" (or just satisfying) his "interests." Without these ethical ends, the agent *would have no* set of rational interests in the first place. Indeed, "rational choice" itself is possible only with a form of "social space," and as practical choice it presupposes some (however attenuated) form of "ethical life."

In "Abstract Right" the modern agent is to be shown to identify with certain claims about objectively established rights, so it is already shown that the agent as part of his self-identity incorporates the impersonal point of view. The modern agent, however, also incorporates the various demands of self-determining agency into his self-understanding. If they are to fulfill their role, the ethical ends must also reconcile the subjective and the objective points of view; they must provide the individual with a set of ends that seem objectively true, justifiable from an impersonal ("universal") point of view; and they must seem to him to be an essential part of his subjective life, to be a defining feature of his own agency. That is, they manifest common, social projects that the individual finds to be his own projects and to be rational (that is, they do not undermine themselves or each other and they fit the accounts which that reflective form of life gives itself as to what is authoritative for it). If they do not fail on any of these counts, then the ethical ends can be seen to be the result of self-determination. They would be subjectively, personally self-determined in that the agent actually wants, actually wills them as his own projects. They would also be objectively (impersonally) determined in that the agent could see them as justified and even as incumbent on him.

In this way, genuine ethical ends would combine what we might call *formal autonomy* and *situated freedom*. The ethical ends would meet the criterion of "formal autonomy" that is appropriate to the level of "morality." Formal autonomy consists in making the ends *one's own* ends; formal autonomy is thus indifferent to the content of the ends which are made "one's own." "Situated freedom" is the pursuit of the *determinate* ends of ethical life in which they are experienced both as objects of desire and of duty – that is, as objects of the will with which we identify ourselves and that we recognize as having this status because of their rationality. "Situated freedom" thus completes in a way the originally Kantian idea that certain determinate ends follow from the idea of formal autonomy: They are ends that we determine for ourselves as the ends we will pursue and whose content is determined by us as rational beings. These ends may be seen as self-determined in that they are determined both by our impersonal rational nature and by our subjective ("wanting") nature.[54] They thus accomplish the *Phenomenology's* goal of uniting the Kantian and the romantic self-understandings, and they function as realizations of freedom, providing the will with objects which affirm for the agent his sense of who he is (with which he can identify).

However, such a conception of ends as reconciling the personal and the impersonal points of view might seem as just so much happy talk, a kind of papering over of the real conflicts and contentions in modern life in favor of a kind of unrealistically sanguine view of it. But Hegel is quite consciously not downplaying any of the real disputes in modern life. Especially in his lectures, he stressed the ongoing nature of the collisions of duty in modern life and the way in which modern life's languages of "abstract right" and the "morality of conscience" necessarily involve certain types of conflict that can only be reconciled within the institutional structures of ethical life. In his nice metaphor, Hegel claims of the modern agent that he is an "amphibious animal," who "has to live in two worlds which contradict one another."[55] Hegel thus makes no attempt in his writings or in his lectures to present modern life as free of conflict. (For example, he thinks that the problem of poverty in modern market societies is especially severe.) Nor is Hegel arguing for the smugly communitarian view that is often popularly attributed to him – namely, that in order to lead a satisfying life, an individual must simply live in conformity with the standards of his time. We often see that the standards of our own time are morally inferior, and Hegel is not endorsing any kind of claim that, for example, the American abolitionists would have been wrong to oppose slavery when slavery was widely socially accepted in the United States. The independent and critical moral standpoint does not vanish in ethical life; only what Hegel calls "self-will" (*Eigenwilligkeit*), the idea that the individual subject alone is morally authoritative in his decisions as to what to do, vanishes.[56] As the *Phenomenology* has shown, ethical life can be justified only to the extent that it is a *rational realization* of freedom; it cannot be justified by an appeal simply to tradition or to "what we (the community) do."

This ethical life is deeply social; Hegel at one point refers to it as an "ethical common life (*sittliche Zusammenleben*)."[57] He also refers to it over and over again as a "liberation." The ends of ethical life are not merely ends that modern agents entertain or believe that they "ought" to be pursuing; they reach down into the structure of the agent's basic desires, and as part of "social space," they are moments of material rationality itself. Indeed, Hegel's point about the way in which "ethical life" supplements "morality" is not, as it has often been taken to be, that "reason" cannot deliver content for morality and thus requires supplementation by something else, such as an appeal to "tradition;" it is that *reason* itself is deeply *social*. In pursuing these ends, these agents are thus able both do what they *want*, and to see what they are doing as *justified*. Moreover, these ends are such that the agent cannot pursue them except in tandem with others, not because of any coordination problems or free-rider problems but because of more deeply held shared self-identities. The ends of ethical life – that is, if they are to be effective – cannot merely be ideals, things that we *ought* to be achieving but for various contingent reasons cannot or do not want to achieve. They must be expressive of the existent set of self-understandings present in the community, of the common and individual projects of constructing self-identity. They function thereby as basic roles into which an agent can step and in playing these roles acquire a kind of substantiality to his or her life that would not be possible otherwise. If they were not part of the mores of the existing form of life, they could not provide the tight link between the motives and ends that they are to provide. Moreover, they must be widely recognized and shared. That is, it must be the case that an individual in acting on the basis of these three basic ethical ends will come to have an understanding of who she is that will be affirmed in structures of mutual recognition by all those around her, and thus will come to understand herself as a rational agent. There will be no gap, that is, between what the individual *thinks* she is doing (who she thinks she is) and what she *really* is doing (who she really is).

As Hegel argued in the *Phenomenology of Spirit,* a system based purely on "morality" cannot do this; the kinds of affirmations required of people who take themselves to be acting simply on the basis of their conscience turns into a community based on dissemblance and hypocrisy. Those things are matters of conscience that can be recognized by others as "hard cases," areas of the moral life about which it is widely believed that reasonable people can differ. Conscience, that is, concerns all those areas of the moral life about which there can be no ethical *certainty*. Where a question is a moral question, and there can be no certainty, the modern world leaves it up to individuals to determine for themselves what it is that they are to do. If *everything*, though, is a matter of conscience – if nothing, that is, *counts* as widely recognized, as morally certain – then absolutely everything will be up for grabs. In order for the freedom of the appeal to conscience to be possible, there need to be "safe areas" of social life in which certain types of things are off limits. Without such "safe areas," the practice of appealing to conscience to settle issues would quickly degenerate into the practices of dissemblers and hypocrites. However, in modern ethical (*sittlich*) life in which people act on the basis of the ethical ends of modern family life, modern society, and the modern constitutional state – in which they are lovers, family members, job-holders, members of civic associations and good citizens – the structure of mutual affirmation of each others' self-identities will be stable, free from contradiction, and in which a core of moral certainty will be established that is the precondition of a non-self-undermining practice of the appeal to personal conscience. The common ethical life is constituted out of this complex set of mutual recognitions that gives each individual, in Hegel's nice metaphor, a "substantiality" to his life.[58]

The connection between the "morality of conscience" and "ethical life" goes even deeper. The modern "moral" principle is that individuals are obligated only to those principles which they themselves can somehow acknowledge as binding.[59] (To put it another way, individuals are not obligated to follow ethical principles whose obligatoriness is a complete mystery to them.) This is specified more fully as the modern "right of conscience," the right to be obligated only to those norms that one can affirm for oneself in one's own conscience. The problem, however, with the "morality of conscience" is that it can provide no determinate content for that conscience. Moreover, since our consciences are in fact formed by our social environment (by our family, by what counts as acceptable behavior in our community and so on), the *formation of conscience* – or, in Hegel's terms, its becoming more "determinate" – has obviously therefore to do with the manner in which the community itself takes shape in its various institutional structures. Conscience is, as it were, the voice of the community speaking authoritatively to individuals. It is therefore of crucial importance that the institutions and practices which actually shape the consciences of their members and participants be themselves justified. As we have seen, this poses a particular problem for Hegel, since on his account certain traditional ways of justifying such institutions have been ruled out for modern life. Evaluating the rightness of institutions by judging them in terms of some "transcendent" principle (such as the "natural law" or the "categorical imperative") has to be rejected by virtue of such an account of justification having shown itself to be historically insufficient. For Hegel, therefore, the rightness of institutions must instead be demonstrated through the ways in which those institutions can be shown to provide a form of rational, non-alienated self-consciousness. That is, the "formation of conscience" which those institutions provide must be such that it permits the participants in that form of life to achieve a non-alienated self-understanding; and, in the conditions of modern life, these institutional structures must also be shown to be adequate realizations of freedom. Modern *Sittlichkeit,* the sense of "the way things are done," must therefore be given an *institutional* shape that can sustain such a sense of "the way things are done" (that is, be authoritative for the participants in that form of life). In this way, Hegel sees ethical life (*Sittlichkeit*) as *completing* the modern moral project – not as *replacing* it – through its providing the shape and content for that conception of "conscience" to which the modern moral project had itself led.

The three basic roles of modern cooperative social life that fill out the system of ethical ends are constituted in our understanding ourselves to be: (1) members of modern families, (2) modern individuals, and (3) citizens. These three essential roles correspond to the three basic forms of social organization in modern life: the modern family, the modern market society, and the modern constitutional state, and they serve to justify those types of social organization as having an inherent rationality to them that depends neither on their being natural facts about the world, nor on ways in which human beings realize some "essence" that they have, nor on their being transcendental conditions of experience in general. They are the substantive, determinate ends that integrate the conceptions of "Abstract Right" and "Morality" into a coherent self-conception for modern agents. For contingent reasons the modern world has established a set of institutions that would enable these contradictions between objective rights and subjective autonomy to be mediated through a new form of *Sittlichkeit,* a communal sense of a set of practices that embody a shared understanding that "this is the way things are done" with which individuals nonetheless can identify (thus being free in their identification with the ends set by this sense of "the way things are done"). These institutions also serve *Bildung* functions (that is, functions of education, formation and cultivation of character). To put it in looser, non-Hegelian terms: The problem for modern agents is that they are supposed to be self-determining, to write their own "scripts," but "abstract right" and "morality" give them no determinate guidelines for which "scripts" to write. The three aspects of *Sittlichkeit* – family, civil society, state – give these agents general "scripts" that provide them with roles to play, and with which they can as self-determining agents identify. They do this because these "scripts" are realizations of freedom, of "ethical ends" with which agents in the modern world for historical and systemic reasons necessarily identify, and which structure both their wills and their emotional lives. (These "ethical ends" as unities of duty, desire, and right provide unities of efficacious motive and evaluation: They are things that are both good in themselves and that structure the self-identities of the agents for whom they are ethical ends.)

It is clear that Hegel does not see these ethical ends as simply specifying three different roles, each supplying a type of good that then has to be balanced off against the others. If that were what he was arguing, then it would be enough simply to descriptively distinguish them from each other in terms of what kinds of goods are available in each and perhaps provide some intuitive criterion as to how to balance them.[60] Rather, each succeeding form of *Sittlichkeit* is supposed to make up for the insufficiencies in the way the former functions as a realization of "freedom as self-determination." Nor, if we take Hegel at his word, can it be that any of them are optional such that if one opted out of family life, civil society, or the state, one would be said only to be worse off in the sense that one would failed to obtain some particular good.

Modern men and women

The first of these three ends concerns the modern family formed out of the union of companionate marriage – that is, marriage based on love instead of clan connections. Unlike families in antiquity, the modern family based on companionate marriage is started by an act of free choice, even though the bonds that supposedly hold such families together are those of affection and shared self-identity. However, although the family is founded on an act of free choice, its other crucial moments are such that the concept of "free choice" does not apply to them. For example, the children do not enter the family as a result of any free choice on their own part, and it is also incorrect to say that they were coerced into coming into existence. The family is in fact the basic way in which "nature" becomes "spirit" – that is, in which human beings as natural organisms transform their natural features into bearers of symbolic significance. As organisms, human beings have sexual desires, and, whatever else is the case, it is almost certain that on the whole they will mate and reproduce. The issue, however, is not the naturalness of the desire but the way in which the desire is taken up and understood by the participants in the practice and integrated into a system of reasons that make up the practical "social space" of the agents. In particular, it is important to ask how these natural desires can become one's own desires such that one is not alienated from them. If they are to become part of the structure of modern ethical ends, then they must be integrated into a system of desires that is consistent with both abstract right and the claims of autonomous agents. The modern family, Hegel argues, does just that: It takes a natural feature of human agents and integrates it into a sphere of reasons (into a "social space"), thereby giving individuals a *project* – a way of orienting themselves in the world and toward the future – in terms of which their otherwise natural desires can be integrated. By being based on free choice, moreover, the modern companionate marriage is consistent with the other demands of modern life that have to do with free choice. In integrating themselves into the structure of modern family life, individuals both find something that each *wants* – to get married to another person to whom each is romantically attached, to raise a family, and to have a secure self-identity as a member of a family – and that each finds is the *right* thing to do. The power of romantic love as an erotic enduring bond between oneself and another provides a powerful personal motive that sustains modern marriage. When linked to the duties that accompany the practice, it provides an enduring bond, and also appears to the individual as the *right* thing to do – namely, to fall in love, get married, and fulfill one's duties as a spouse and father or mother. The bond of romantic love thus partially realizes the ideal of independence: The lovers achieve their independence in the apparently paradoxical fashion of making themselves fully dependent on others in order to achieve their own independence, since one's independence can only be vouchsafed if others provide a *recognition* of one's independence, and romantic love provides the emotional recognition necessary for one to achieve one's own sense of being securely independent in the world.[61] (A social order that does not provide the institutional support for such recognition cannot therefore achieve that ideal.) The dependencies of romantic love within the family consist in the emotional sustenance each provides the other, which empowers each to be independent, and in which each is fully *dependent* on that type of emotional recognition that each receives from the other. Likewise, the emotional recognition given the children in the well functioning family is a condition of their being able to develop themselves into independent people.

Family life based on companionate marriage is thus a fully fledged ethical end. Its romantic basis and its ideals of child rearing (along with its difference from the extended family of the clan) can, from the personal point of view, all be seen as moments of a whole, as parts of a consistent and coherent pattern of reasoning about one's life.[62] Although the modern companionate family has a variety of historical causes and origins, not all of which are perhaps consistent with each other, its historical origins are irrelevant to its rationality – that is, to whether it provides a social and individual project that fits into the modern agent's conception of himself and herself as autonomous, moral beings and as possessing certain abstract rights; and with whether it coheres with the rest of the set of ethical ends of modern life – namely, being an individual in modern bourgeois society and being a citizen in the modern constitutional state. It thus realizes freedom in that it provides the agents with appropriate "objects" to will and appropriate motives to go along with them: It provides them with ends with which they can identify and with a clear practice that enables them to know both what they are doing and why they are doing it.

Hegel's basic understanding of the family is clearly in terms of its being a bourgeois, patriarchal social unity (although he continuously inveighs against what he calls the patriarchal political state, which he identifies with the states of antiquity). He holds forth on how the woman's place is in the home whereas the man's place is in the market, how women are not fit for the higher activities such as science and statecraft, and how sexual infidelities are not as important for men as they are for women (since men have a sphere of activity outside of the family whereas women do not). Now, it would be easy to be disdainful about this aspect of Hegel's thought, and it is certainly tempting to take the high ground and condemn Hegel's sexist views on men and women. Nonetheless, however much Hegel's views on these specific topics may seem amusingly quaint to some and downright odious to others, it is important to see why Hegel thought the bourgeois patriarchal family is so well suited to play an essential role in modern social life.

First, it is important to note how Hegel's thought about the family fits his overall project. Hegel *could not* think that the family was a natural unit; to be consistent with what he says, he must see it as a social unit. He thus could not think that male dominance of the family was justified in terms of any theory of the "natural" dominance of men over women. It is true that in bourgeois society the family is the institution through which children are propagated and reared, but it is not a natural fact that it be the institution for doing so. There are obviously countless other possibilities for both the procreation and rearing of children and for men and women to express and act on their sexual desires; there are different forms of family life that do this, and there are also non-familial alternatives for accomplishing the same goal. Nor is Hegel arguing that in family life, the natural aspect (that is, the sexual aspect) of people's lives must be severely repressed or "brought under the control" of the "spiritual." Such a view would be flatly inconsistent with his *reconciling* view of human agency, and he recognized that.[63] The ends of ethical life cannot be experienced merely as imperatives calling out against our sensuous nature; they must be directives that are also "wants," demands that are also desires. They must give the agents ends with which they can be "with themselves" – that is, with which they can identify. In sum: Hegel's argument has to be that the form of the bourgeois patriarchal family develops out of the kinds of reasonings appropriate to *modern* agents and not out of any sort of appeal to human "nature" or to some "essence" that is realized in this social form. Moreover, the various ends that are moments of the overall end of "marriage and the family" must be consistent with the other ethical ends of modern life. Thus, the education of children must be to form them into becoming full fledged independent members of modern social life, not into being appendages of their parents or into carrying on the life of the "clan."[64]

In this respect, Hegel's arguments about the role of men and women are particularly interesting. If one takes an inventory of what Hegel says about the differences between men and women, it looks almost like a feminist parody (or perhaps a feminist nightmare) of male sexist thinking.[65] Yet Hegel is not making these claims on the basis of any *natural* difference between men and women but on the basis of what is required for agents in general in the modern world to have a coherent self-understanding and to be free – indeed, on his own terms, these are the only claims he could be making. Moreover, even more interestingly, Hegel himself quite clearly understands himself, in his own quaint way, to be defending a version of women's equality, however strange his version sounds to contemporary ears.[66] First, he argues that the natural difference between the sexes carries no moral weight on its own. To have any moral weight, it must be transfigured into a social (or "spiritual") relationship, that is, it must be taken up into some scheme of understanding and be integrated into a pattern of practical reasons. Moreover, there are no natural features of women that make them incapable of doing the things that men do.[67] "Male" and "female" are natural differences that are given a social meaning. For Hegel, different forms of life (or cultures, as we would nowadays put it) may even have more male or female characteristics in them than other cultures.[68] For Hegel, the female character in modern life embodies the ideals of wholeness and relationships. Women therefore develop their sense of self-identity more harmoniously, whereas the male character must struggle to construct his self-identity. The male character, so Hegel says, is more abstract than the female character, less attuned to the concrete realities of life, and for that reason, men tend to gravitate more to those tasks that depend on abstract thinking and in which they can put their personal lives aside in order to focus on some definite but abstract task. (This is why Hegel thinks he can confidently assert that all great works of art, science, and politics have been created by men; in his saying so, Hegel shows that his rather prodigious knowledge of history was apparently not quite prodigious enough.) In short, the male character is competitive, struggling, and oriented toward abstract things likes rules and principles, whereas the female character is oriented toward those aspects of life that involve caring, an intuitive grasp of matters, and in which the maintenance of human relationships is important. In Hegel's view, the patriarchal bourgeois family therefore has things just right. The woman is sovereign over the household (the realm of caring), the man is the breadwinner (in the market, the realm of struggle and competition).

The justification for this division between male and female characters is the difference between two distinct functions of civil society. One is the function of the family in general as providing a distinct form of self-identity and a distinct ethical end. The family involves the individual in his or her most natural aspect (sexuality, reproduction), but it does so through a fully social construction of meanings that surround these natural facts about us. It also involves an institutional structure in which the person is recognized for *being* someone rather than in terms of what he *does*. The other function is that of doing rather than being, of society rather than family, of a completely socially mediated, non-natural sense of self-identity rather than one in terms of natural features of oneself. Hegel argues that both functions are necessary, and the bourgeois family's division of the sexes insures that both functions are rationally fulfilled (that is, they are fulfilled in ways that are neither self-contradictory nor contradictory of each other nor contradictory of the other aspects of self-identity in modern life). In the bourgeois family, men and women are each operating in a "social space" that secures recognition and dignity for their activities. By virtue of women managing the household and maintaining the emotional bonds of the family life, with the men working and securing the family's subsistence and capital, the ethical end of marriage and the family is supposedly secured. A consistent and rational social order is maintained in which both men and women can come to a fully rational and consistent self-understanding and have that self-understanding affirmed in their daily lives.

This line of thought is indicative of a general tendency that colors much of Hegel's mature thought. Whenever Hegel understands some social functions to be necessary to a form of life's continuance and maintenance, he tends to look for discrete job-holders for those functions. That is, he tends to portion out functions to discrete individuals or groups as fulfilling that particular function. (We shall see it later in his treatment of the traditional *Korporationen* and their role in modern life.) This tendency in Hegel's thought is not in any way essential to his thought. It is not a requirement of his dialectic nor is it an implication of any of his particular ideas. It is necessary to his scheme of thought that these very different aspects be understood in terms of their unity, but it is not necessary that in social terms each of these aspects necessarily be represented by discrete individuals or groups. It apparently did not occur to Hegel (or he had some obscure reason for ignoring) that there were other alternatives, such as the possibility of combining these two features of modern life into the same personalities – that is, to make men more oriented to maintaining the emotional life of the family and to make women more concerned about securing the family's subsistence and capital, an alternative that has not escaped some commentators on Hegel's thought.[69] Indeed, in his own terms, he seems to be denying women full participation in modern life as self-determining subjects on the basis of some *natural* features of themselves, something entirely at odds with his overall project.[70] Moreover, to the extent that women cannot identify with the ends of modern life – cannot find themselves identified with the activities that are constituted in the achieving of these ends – they will be alienated from them, and they therefore will not be free. The ends will thus fail *for them* to meet the criteria of being ethical ends.

But this is one of those cases in which Hegel's solution may not be acceptable in his own terms, even though his statement of the problem and the general direction may be on the right track.[71] In terms of being an ethical end, marriage and the family must combine personal and impersonal points of view (the particular and the universal) into itself. It must take the natural distinction of the sexes and the facts of human procreation and child rearing and integrate them into a pattern of meanings that is consistent with the overall pattern of meanings that makes up modern "social space" in such a way that the individuals (both men and women) can identify with them. Within that end, some room must therefore be found for the integration of emotional life and securing family existence, along with the exigencies that come with raising children. Hegel's argument is that because of contingent historical facts, the bourgeois patriarchal family has come to fulfill all these conceptual needs and thus can be seen in retrospect to have necessarily (or conceptually) completed part of the modern project. But, again, Hegel's argument does not – *cannot* – rule out other forms of marriage and the family, provided that they can also fulfill the same criteria for a successful form of social life that he argues the bourgeois patriarchal family does; and there are good Hegelian reasons for arguing that the bourgeois *patriarchal* family does not fulfill these goals as well as Hegel seems to think that it does. There thus might be good Hegelian reasons for discarding a *patriarchal* conception of the family, but, in any event, something like the (non-patriarchal) *bourgeois* family would be needed to fill this role. To the extent that the bourgeois family cannot satisfy the criteria that Hegel has set up, much more of the Hegelian project in social philosophy would have to be rethought.

The mutual dependencies of civil society

The second of these ethical ends has to do with the formation of oneself as a modern individual in civil society (literally, "bourgeois society," *die bür-gerliche Gesellschaft*). Again, the same strategy is used to justify this end. It is shown to have both a subjective and an objective side (that is, to fit both the personal and the impersonal points of view), and it is shown to fit in with the other ethical ends of modern life. It is also shown to follow from the ideal of the bourgeois family itself. Although the family incorporates a sense of self-identity in terms of who one *is* (as a family member), there are many such families, the children come to maturity and form their own families, and there is, of course, the natural fact of death that dissolves families. In any event, civil society emerges as a collection of families or, more particularly, as a collection of individuals. Self-determination is given a more determinate sense here in that individuals now see themselves as pursuing their own particular ends, as concentrating on their own utility. Rather than being seen in terms of who they *are,* they are seen in terms of what they, as individuals, *do.* As we might put it, in civil society, the individual pursues rational self-interest. In marriage, the individuals involved seek a mutual affirmation of themselves in romantic love. The bond between the two is that of an *emotional* recognition of each other. The romantic bond is thus not that of mutual self-interest but of a mutual dependency that nonetheless preserves the sense of independence of each of the members. (Hegel thus strongly objects to Kant's conception of marriage as a contract for the mutual and exclusive use of each other's sexual organs.[72]) In civil society, the mutual recognition conveyed by the parties is more in terms of what each member of civil society can do for the other.

Civil society offers a new realm of freedom that is very similar to that of "Abstract Right": individuals understanding themselves as free in that each is "doing what he wants" with his property within the "social space" created by the sphere of abstract rights that each individual brings with him. Within this "social space," each appears to be self-determining, for each appears to be setting his own particular ends, whatever those ends may be, and to be acting on those ends.[73] Each agent must deal with other people, so it seems, only on his own particular terms. The dealings of the couple involved in romantic marriage are not of this type, for in that union each is seeking and operating within a deeply emotional bond that gives them a common self-identity (each understanding him- or herself as a "moment" of the marriage). In civil society, each member does not seek a common self-identity but rather seeks to establish and affirm his own self-identity (thus expressing the general dialectical move from unity to difference). Whereas marriage is a genuine union of agents into something that is held together by emotional bonds, civil society is a union that is seemingly held together only by rational self-interest. The motive for the individual to join civil society is thus clearly a personal motive: He gets to do what he pleases and to follow out the dictates of his own personality.

However, this freedom is in large part illusory. Whereas each seems to be completely self-determining, to be setting his own ends, each is actually dependent on the other people such that the ends that can be set are dependent not merely on the physical contingencies of life but on the contingencies of other people's willings. Since it is a fact, especially within the context of modern market societies and the desires they create in their members, that the individual cannot satisfy all his desires by himself, the individual is dependent on others to assist him in satisfying them. This exposes the individual to the contingency of whether others actually are so disposed to help him. Since the individual cannot escape this contingency, he must therefore orient his life so that these others will *in fact* be disposed to help him. His so-called self-determination is thus subject to the exigency (*die Not*) and contingency of the market. Individuals find themselves having to structure their ends and actions around what they take to be the ends and actions of others. The apparently unlimited freedom of civil society is thus in truth actually a thoroughgoing form of dependency and necessity. The apparent difference of self-identities of the individuals in civil society also turns out to be partly illusory, for at a deeper level there is in fact a shared self-identity, that of being the modern rational self-interested agent thinking of his situation in terms of its utility.[74] This is the truth of civil – market – society. The necessity involved in this form of dependency has two aspects. It is first of all the commonsense necessity of coordinating one's actions with those of others in order to achieve whatever it is that one wants to achieve. In this way, one's own ability to achieve one's own ends is subject to the contingencies of others willing things that assist it or at least do not thwart it. Second, one's willing turns out not only to be subject to the *contingency* of others willing certain things but also to the deeper *necessity* of the laws of the market, which are explored in the science of economics. One thus finds oneself subject to the whims of others and at a deeper level to the laws of the market.

It thus might seem as if it is only the *contract* – the binding agreement struck between two or more rational self-interested individuals as a category of "Abstract Right" – that is the basic form of social bond at work here. By virtue of the complete dependency of each on the contingent willing of each and the necessity of the laws of the market, a system of mutual dependency is created that is the inevitable result, although not the conscious aim, of the actions taken on the part of the members of civil society and of the particular desires they have. The issue is then whether this end – to be a rational self-interested individual in bourgeois market society – can serve as a genuine ethical end, since it might seem that it would fail to meet the criteria for being such an end. That is, it would fail to be something with which the individual can identify and can see for himself as an authoritative reason *for him* to act. It would seem that the individual agent can identify with these ends only to the extent that he is in the dark about them. Once he realizes just how dependent he is and how subject to contingency his willings are, it would seem that he would lose whatever identification he might have had with them and instead become alienated from them. Hegel must therefore give some reason for reconciling the individual with this form of life that is acceptable to the individual from his own subjective point of view.

The system of mutual dependencies that arise out of this can subjectively appear at first to each agent as something simply imposed on him and as something that has value for him only in that he can manipulate that system for the achievement of his own ends. In fact, it actually serves an "ethical" (in Hegel's sense) purpose: it cultivates people into becoming modern autonomous agents who integrate this formal autonomy with substantive conceptions of what is right. This overall productive organization of market society thus creates a kind of common capital on which individuals may draw in order to satisfy their own desires and needs; it requires only of the individual that he cultivate his talents and acquire traits that can be useful in such a society. Each may satisfy himself only by making himself useful to others; each thus is socialized into the form of life that constitutes modern life.

As Hegel acknowledges, this presents a certain amount of difficulty for any argument for civil society as an ethical end. Supporting himself with observations based on his readings of Adam Smith and the other Scottish economists, Hegel notes that the division of labor, which is necessary for the greater productivity of civil society, also leads to the distress of the worker (something of which he speaks in the lectures but that is only mentioned in passing in the published *Philosophy of Right*). The worker can find himself being put out of work because of technological advancement or because of changes in taste concerning the products his industry makes. This aspect of civil society is quite obviously difficult to justify on Hegelian grounds. As forming an independent ethical end, it must be something with which a modern agent can personally (subjectively) identify. Yet on Hegel's own admission, there are many alienating aspects about civil society. Civil society represents an alienated ethical end; it is not something in which the individual can immediately (that is, in a taken-for-granted manner) find himself at home. Until they reflect on it, it appears more to the individuals as either an obligation, an end to which they must simply learn to submit their inclinations, or as a social "fact" imposed on them, something that they must simply accept. The personal motive for complying with the demands of civil society is, in a sense, the fear instilled in each person of his not being able to meet his natural and his socialized desires. Contrary inclinations are checked by the necessity for each to earn his own way, to adapt his desires and plans to the system of dependencies in order to satisfy himself. Fear, however, is not a good motive with which to get an agent to identify with his actions.

What is reconciliatory in this form of social life, so Hegel argues, lies in the laws of the market itself. In producing both greater prosperity and a complete system of mutual dependency, the market actually liberates individuals from other more crippling contingencies.[75] (It must be remembered that Hegel is writing during the early experience of the Industrial Revolution, something that began to happen during his lifetime. He was fully aware of the ways in which the world around him was transformed by this upheaval, particularly by the way in which it transformed the backwaters of Europe into cosmopolitan centers and offered up wholly new alternatives for the people in them.) Thus the market creates a new form of social life in which people can actually pursue ends that are more their own, can make choices about their lives and what they are to do with them. The market forces each to work for others in order to satisfy his own desires and needs; it also forces the individual to order his desires and decide what it is that he really wants and what he is willing to sacrifice. Most importantly, therefore, the market socializes its members (or rather leads them to come to understand themselves as socialized). In that way it performs the Rousseauian task of "forcing a person to become free," not by forcing him to conform to any so-called "true self" but rather by disciplining the "natural will" – that is, by forcing him to regulate and order his desires instead of simply going along with whatever occurrent desire he happens to have. In learning to order and regulate his desires, the individual is put into a position in which he becomes more free – that is, in which he can come to see his desires as "his own." Moreover, the market demonstrates to the members of civil society, perhaps more effectively than philosophy can do, just how deeply social they and their desires really are; the desire for luxury or for comfort, for example, may be clearly seen to be dependent on what others in fact take to be luxury or comfort. Thus, although from the subjective viewpoint, the exigencies of the market can at first seem onerous to the individual, in fact, he *can* even come to subjectively understand them as assisting in his freedom, in an analogous way that a child can find going to school to be a burden but nonetheless understand that this in fact is gradually freeing him to be "his own" person. The labors required of us by the market in fact are part of our education and cultivation – our *Bildung* – as modern agents.

However, this would not be enough on its own to make civil society as a system of mutual dependencies into a genuine ethical end, for it would not provide a common project to participants in this form of life. Instead, it would be only a system of pure individualism, in which individuals dealt with each other *only* as individuals, not as members of a common life. Although the individual in such a system of individualism might come to see that the system of mutual dependencies had an underlying rationale in that it forced him to become more socialized, he would still *experience* the system as a type of imposition, since, so it would seem, he cannot do what he "wants to do"; instead, he must continually adjust his behavior and expectations in terms of what others are doing and expect from him. If there were only the system of dependencies, then it would not be possible to overcome the kind of alienation that would be experienced by the participants in such a form of life – that is, of individuals doing things because they *have* to do them rather than because they identify themselves with the actions.

The resurrection of the estates

In order to block this kind of alienation, it is necessary that there be different estates (*Stände*) in society. The estates thus fulfill a certain teleology inherent in civil society: They are the kind of things that are necessary to resolve the irrationalities of the otherwise pure individualism of modern social life. Although this is not the historical reason why the estates themselves arise, the estates can nonetheless be understood as fulfilling a necessary place in a teleological ordering of social forms intended to present a form of social life in which agents can be "with themselves," with which they can identify, and that is justified as a realization of freedom. Although each agent is equal to all others as a rational agent, the contingent circumstances for each person (talents, desires, social standing) are different. Because people have different needs and desires, there will be correspondingly different social functions for satisfying those needs and desires.[76] (Once again, we see Hegel's characteristic move from "distinct function" to "discrete individual or class to fulfill the function.")

Hegel's invocation of the estates is both peculiar and penetrating. Historically, the estates had both political and social meanings; they had grown out of the organizations of medieval feudalism but were distinct from them. They were groupings according to legally recognized social rank (which tended to correlate with economic status) in that they tended to concern themselves with the rights and privileges of people in terms of the estate with which they were associated. In their older form, they provided the way in which an individual interacted with the ruler. (A ruler, for example, would not collect taxes from individuals but from the estates, and it was then up to estates to decide among their members how the funds within the estate were to be collected. Likewise, in meting out justice, the ruler was obligated to make sure that each individual received his proper due not as an individual *per se* but as an individual-as-member-of-a-particular-estate.) As such the early modern estates were a much more legalistically organized form of social organization and much less dependent on the vagaries of personal ties and "ancient custom" than the organizations of feudalism. In the state-of-estates (the *Ständesstaat*) people tended to confront the ruler (or the "state") not therefore as individuals but as members of a group – that is, an estate. Indeed, this feature of *confronting* the ruler was one of the major distinguishing features of the estates from the older forms of feudal social organization.[77] But the growing impact of the state as a whole on the economic fortunes of its members and the rising individualism of Hegel's own time were increasingly making the estates into an antiquated relic, since the individualism dominant in both the American revolt and the French Revolution, which was also being encouraged by the growing market economies, increasingly were making the estates into an irrelevant political entity. Thus, in Hegel's time the estates were already on the wane. It is therefore striking that Hegel nonetheless argues that the estates should have a social basis and a political role within the emerging form of post-revolutionary modern life and that he tries to give an argument for it in terms of its being necessary to the realization of the modern principle of freedom.

Hegel's argument for modern society's requiring at least three such forms of social organization into estates is something like the following. Humans are organisms who in modern life have come to think of themselves as self-determining agents existing in a social sphere of mutual dependency, and whose needs and interests are both fully social and can be indefinitely extended. That is, they have immediate (taken for granted) organismic needs, mediated needs for the social organization necessary for the system of mutual dependency, and mediated needs for the social practices and institutions that recognize the self-determination of the agent in his socialized existence. There will therefore be three estates: an immediate estate (agricultural workers providing food), a reflective estate (the businessmen and burghers of local communities who guide its local politics and practices and who provide the system of mutual dependency), and a universal estate (the great generalizers of society whose talents and jobs do not bind them to any particular community – namely, civil servants, intellectuals, and the men and women of international trade, who can take the larger interests of society into consideration).[78] These correspond, not surprisingly, to the categories of individuality, particularity, and universality.

Each of these three estates will exhibit a particular set of virtues – that is, a particular set of dispositions, inclinations, and desires that correspond to the duties and ends of that estate.[79] The agricultural estate is described by Hegel in terms appropriate to the European peasantry he knew, so that the peasant emerges as dependent on nature (with its winds, rains, droughts, and so on) and develops his appropriate virtues of simplicity, trust and obedience (even though Hegel explicitly took note of the growing industrialization of agriculture already beginning in his day, something that he thought would nonetheless not intrinsically transform those virtues).[80] The business estate (*Gewerbe*) has as its principle the transformation of natural products into manufactured products. It includes artisans, industrialists, and the men and women of trade (that is, financiers and merchants who do not actually produce anything but pursue trade in things and in money). The members of this class, by relying on their own hard work to exploit the system of dependencies, pursue the goal of becoming independent by accumulating enough wealth (that is, they enter the market with the goal of escaping from it). Consequently, as a "reflected estate," it has the virtues of respect for freedom and order. The mobile "universal class" exhibits fidelity to the objectivity of the law. In this way, more determinate ethical content is also given to the idea of an autonomous will that wills consistently with the claims of "Abstract Right" and "Morality" – namely, through the content incorporated in the rights and duties of the distinct estates.

Giving this prominence to the estates raises the same problem found in other aspects of civil society: It seems to contradict, at least superficially, the modern ideal of self-determination, since an agent's self-identity will be determined by his or her position in this or that estate. This is not obviated by the fact that in the modern world the estates cannot be anything like castes. The individual must be able to choose which estate he is to join, even if the range of his choices are limited by contingent factors (for example, the peasant's son may not have the educational background to go to university and join the mobile "universal class"). Nonetheless, like other elements of civil society, the status of something like this as an ethical end seems precarious. Hegel's argument for the necessity of the estates therefore rests on two claims: (1) A specific claim that the necessity of the division of labor requires something like a division into separate estates; the estates are necessary because not everybody can do everything. On its own, this would not be sufficient, since it need not require anything like *estates* – that is, social/legal entities whose members have a certain legal and social status by virtue of their membership in them. (2) A more general claim that people's self-identity is constituted by the webs of mutual recognition. The second claim has to do with the Hegelian thesis that it is necessary for individuals to have some institutional filling (some "substantiality") to their lives in order to have any coherent sense of who they are. People's self-identities are stable only when their own self-conceptions are affirmed by others, and this process of mutual affirmation is itself successful only when there are firm institutional structures that mediate it. (This is not a "psychological fact" about people but a conceptual point about the link between self-identity and social recognition.) Hegel's point is thus that without *something like* the estates, there could be no recognized and stable form of self-identity. Without something like the estates, so Hegel argues, each individual would instead find his self-identity to be continually up for grabs. Moreover, without something like the estates, there could be no determinate *formation of conscience* for individuals, and there would thus be no way of having, inculcating or arguing about anything like the virtues. There would be only the collection of natural traits that individuals acquire by virtue of their natural endowments, their upbringing, or whatever, and there would be no way to attach any socially recognized significance to any of those features. This would completely undermine the realization of the principle of freedom as self-determination, since the individual would find that his self-identity was subject to the complete contingency of what others took him to be, and that would be a matter of contingent desires, inclinations and projects on their own part. In order to acquire a self-identity that one can make *one's own,* one must therefore be a member of a recognized social estate and identify with it. In that way, the personal point of view would be integrated with the objective point of view: in pursuing the ends of one's estate and in cultivating the virtues appropriate to one's estate, one would be in a position of "doing what one wants" (being an artisan, being a farmer, whatever), being able to see that as justified, since it fulfills a necessary function in social life and is recognized by the rest of civil society as doing so, and in identifying oneself with the activities associated with one's estate. The estates express a fundamental form of self-identity for the members of civil society that transcends their status as "individuals."

The estates thus assist in transforming the system of dependencies found in civil society into a system of freedom. Without a system of estates, there would be only the system of dependencies, in both the economic sense and in the more general sense of individuals forming their self-identities according to what is needed by others. However, individuals who act on the basis of the virtues and honors of their estate find themselves to be recognized members of civil society; they can thus find themselves identified with the activities based on those motives that attach to being a member of this or that estate. In this way, being a member of an estate is a condition for avoiding the kind of alienation that would otherwise follow from a society composed simply of atomistic individuals.

Hegel appeals to the estates – and in particular to the "universal" estate among them – for a good reason. Even though he is often cited as a basic thinker in the "communitarian" school, Hegel does not in fact make much, if any, appeal to the rather amorphous conception of "community." If nothing else, the local communities that he knew were, in the historian Mack Walker's phrase, the "hometowns" of pre- and post-Napoleonic Germany.[81] Although these "hometowns" had in addition to their own very complex legal order many of the features that modern communitarians and champions of localism like to extol, they were fundamentally closed off to the world and were provincial in the derogatory senses of the word. Communities in the form of "hometowns" prevent the kind of universalistic point of view that is necessary to modern life and to having a non-alienated form of life, for the "home-towners" can ultimately only understand other hometowners. Unless there is a *universal* estate – people whose life and mores are more cosmopolitan than the "hometowners" – it is not possible for there to be anything like the fully objective point of view necessary for a non-alienated form of modern social life. (We shall see later how this supports Hegel's arguments for the rationality of the constitutionalist state.)

The importance of the consistent and fair administration of a rule of law, so Hegel argues, follows quite straightforwardly from the necessity of the estates. The rule of law is necessary not merely on practical grounds (because of free-rider problems, problems of coordination, and the like) but on deeper ethical grounds. The non-alienated self-identity gained by being a member of an estate in a market society is possible only in a stable system of mutual recognition, and the social institution that fills this demand of reason is that of the rule of law, since it guarantees to the various members of civil society that their rights as being this or that individual will be respected. If there were no estates, then the rule of law could be only the abstract rule of property and contract. Agents would have no secure self-identity other than that which they could gain by what they acquire in original acts of appropriation (so rare as not to count in modern markets) or in exchange. Since a system of pure exchange would be a system of complete mutual dependency, it would be an alienated system for modern agents. The rule of law requires a high degree of specification into distinct and unambiguous laws so that the members of civil society can assert their sense of self-determination (codified in their rights) in a determinate fashion.

The estates as ordered by a fair administration of justice based on the rule of law augment the market's system of dependencies such that some substantiality is given to the individual's sense of himself. The "social space" in which the individual assumes a position becomes more determinate, and it is possible for the individual to assume a standpoint in terms of which he can coherently think of himself as self-determining. However, this itself is not enough to provide the agent with a coherent self-understanding, for it provides only for the individual's thinking of himself as a member of civil society possessing certain determinate rights, duties and virtues. The individual agent thinks of himself as autonomous, and through these various types of social institutions, he further acquires the support for thinking of his own self-determination from a subjective as well as objective point of view; thus, his more particular forms of self-determination (of "doing what he wants") will be seen as consistent with doing what he wants from a more universalistic point of view. The individual's well-being consists in his ability to pursue *his own* determinate ends. In a civil society with a rule of law, the individual has the legally enforceable rights to follow these ends; these rights thus safeguard and thereby assist in the agent's exercising his self-determination.

The problems of the market: contingency and poverty

However, this set of social institutions cannot shield the individual from other contingencies, such as ill health or accidents of various kinds that could prevent him from achieving those ends which he has a right to pursue. Thus, the individual can still take himself not to be fully identified with those actions done on the basis of the virtues and duties of the estates, since he can be fully aware that his success in achieving whatever determinate ends he seeks *within his estate* are subject to these kinds of contingency. Even at the height of personal success, he can step back and reflect from a more objective, impersonal point of view on how this success is nonetheless up to chance. Moreover, the guarantee by a system of law of his rights to pursue his ends does not ensure that others will afford him the means or opportunities to exercise those rights. The system of dependencies rewards him only to the extent that he contributes in a way that others find useful; once he ceases to contribute in that way, it ceases to support him, for the dependency is then asymmetrical and not mutual.

The system of dependencies mediated by a collection of estates under the fair administration of law therefore needs to be augmented by some type of communal regulation, what Hegel (following the language of his day) calls the *Polizei,* the "police." These "police" are not the officers of the law with whom we associate the word but the kind of regulators, administrators, and policy makers that characterize any modern polity.[82] The overall role for these "policing functions" is to make up for the contingency of conditions under which individuals live and work – that is, to make sure that not only are their rights protected but that their ability to *exercise* their rights is also protected. The justification for the institutions that fulfill the "policing functions" is based on their providing the individual not with a guarantee that he actually achieve the ends he seeks but with the "human capital" in terms of which he can pursue the ends. That is, the proper goal of the "policing functions" is to guarantee that the individual have the education and acquire the aptitudes necessary to pursue the goals appropriate to his estate and that the social order be well regulated so that it is possible for those goals to be achieved.[83]

A "policing function" in the social order is necessary, and it cannot be left up to morality alone to put into place. It is true that moral agents have a duty to be beneficent and charitable to others, but one's ability to exercise one's rights (and in particular to exercise one's capacity to be one's own person) is, if left up completely to the moral assistance of others, a matter of contingency. For various reasons, others might not do their moral duty. Because of assorted kinds of problems of coordination (and of moral agents not wanting to be taken advantage of by virtue of their fulfilling their moral duties while others fail to fulfill their own duties), it will also be the case that the removal of limiting conditions on people's ability to exercise their rights is done more efficiently and less arbitrarily by these "policing" *institutions* than by unconnected moral agents. The "policing function" thus cares for the infrastructure of civil society: the building and maintenance of roads, bridges, hospitals, schools, and so on. These various aspects that make up the "policing function" of civil society form a kind of common, social capital for individual agents to draw upon. However, the necessity of the "policing functions" follows not simply from these pragmatic considerations about what is necessary to "make things work" but on what is necessary to ensure that these modern agents have a coherent form of self-understanding such that they can be "with themselves" in their actions. Without the assumption of the form of "social space" built out of the linkage between the conceptions of abstract rights and autonomous agency, there would be no ethical justification for such "policing functions." Further, without some assumptions about the nature of the family, the market, and the necessity of there being various estates, there could be no argument in principle about how far the "policing functions" should go, about just how much is appropriate for the "policing functions" to concern themselves.

Part of the purpose of the "policing functions" is to deal with the problem of poverty in civil society. In this kind of market society, so Hegel argues, poverty will *necessarily* arise, and this kind of poverty presents the most pressing and intractable problem for this form of life. The division of labor and the growing efficiency of production in market society (explained by Adam Smith) entails that work becomes ever more "abstract." The artisan learns a trade and the skills that go with it, but the factory worker learns how to do some generalized small task. The factory worker thus can be more easily replaced than the artisan; indeed, he can even be replaced by machines. Thus, the type of work employed in factories is more "abstract" in the sense that it involves less of an orientation to a determinate type of activity and its associated skills, and the factory workers are more interchangeable with each other than artisans are. Indeed, since their work can be replaced by machines, these workers themselves can replaced by machines – a development that, as Hegel notes, has in his time already been accomplished in England. Moreover, those with greater capital can accumulate even greater capital by investing it in these (for Hegel's time new) industrial enterprises, and they gradually swallow up smaller enterprises. This growing efficiency and monopolization of industry, however, results in many workers losing their jobs and being forced to seek employment elsewhere. The problem of joblessness is exacerbated by other necessary features of a market economy. In the market society there will always be overproduction of some goods. When there is a demand for some goods, entrepreneurs will flock to satisfy the demand. More goods will then be produced than can be consumed, and many of the entrepreneurs will go out of business or at least be forced to cut back on their labor force. Those workers will have to find new jobs. In the cases where the jobs involved required the workers to acquire certain determinate skills in order to fulfill the job requirements, it will be even more difficult for them to find new jobs that employ the skills they have acquired. The result is a growing distress and misery for one part of the population at the same time as there is a growing wealth for other parts, and the distance between the two can widen immensely.

This results in a growing *dependency* on the part of the working class; their fate is now tied to the decisions that others make and to the laws of the market. The industrial worker thus finds himself caught in the system of dependencies that others seem to escape, and this contradicts his understanding of what (modern) agency is. Whether he can formulate it philosophically is irrelevant: The "social space" he occupies is structured around the ideals of independence and self-determination, and he seems to have neither. As the problems of poverty grow worse, a class of rabble (*Pöbel*) is thus created. This "rabble" (or "underclass," as current sociological jargon would have it) lacks the human capital (the skills to take advantage of the opportunities presented by civil society) that would give them the means to sustain themselves by their own efforts. They lack the means to participate fully in the workings of modern civil society, and, thus failing to participate fully, they either do not acquire or they lose the virtues and dispositions that are necessary to being a member of such a form of life. The vicious circle that gets established with the "rabble" is that, lacking the human capital necessary to participate in civil society, the "rabble" fails to participate in civil society, and, by not participating it fails then to acquire the human capital necessary to rectify the situation. But as participants in that form of "social space," they continue to think of themselves as self-determining or at least as having a *right* to be self-determining and independent, a right that they see as being violated (even though no particular individual is actually violating this right). They come to believe therefore that they are due something from a society that from their point of view unjustly cuts them off from its advantages; however, because of their lack of the skills necessary for participation in civil society, they do nothing within the terms of that society to entitle themselves to such advantages. Others cannot therefore recognize them as entitled to anything, and they take those others to be depriving them of something to which they are entitled.

This "rabble" is a modern socialized invention. It is not as if some basic natural needs are not being met; it is rather that the socialized needs – in particular, the "need" to understand oneself as a modern individual – are not being met.[84] The individuals of the "rabble" therefore come to experience an indignation at the holdings of those who have more and therefore also come to see no need to cooperate with the better-off members of society. They quite naturally also attract little sympathy, since they do not play by the rules of civil society, yet (so it appears to the better off) they demand that things come to them without their having to work for them. This exacerbates the vicious circle in which they are caught. Criminality and moral degradation come to be the lot of the rabble. The rabble thus represents a distinct type of concrete threat to the stability of civil society and a distinct type of threat of ethical failure of modern institutions.

Interestingly, Hegel also thought that the same kind of rabble mentality grows up among the wealthy.[85] Because they see everything as purchasable, they too come to see themselves as not bound by the rules of civil society. As the mirror image of the rabble, who come to think that civil society owes them a living, the wealthy come to think that they owe nothing to civil society even though they demand from civil society protection of their interests. Both the rabble and the wealthy become obsessed with a version of what is their own "by right" and for which they do not see themselves as having to make any contribution; both, that is, think that they should have certain advantages without themselves making any contribution to the functioning of civil society. In that way too, the wealthy come to suffer from an arrogance and moral corruption completely analogous to that of the poverty-stricken rabble.[86]

The problem of solving these issues of poverty cannot be met by either pure market mechanisms or by simply using the "policing function" to redistribute wealth. Pure market mechanisms will not work since it is the workings of the market that brings about the creation of the "rabble." Interfering with the market (by guaranteeing jobs) will not solve the problem, since that will only lead to overproduction of goods, which aggravates the problem rather than solving it. Moreover, simply giving the poor subsistence payments will not work since that deprives them of the socializing aspect of work and thus fails to create the necessary set of dispositions for functioning in civil society.

Hegel sees only two ways out to resolve this problem. The first way is to expand national economies into world economies so as to produce a rate of growth that can insure enough economic expansion to provide enough jobs to absorb the poor and to reintegrate them into civil society. (Hegel also partially links this with an argument about colonization, which I am ignoring here.) Once again, Hegel is not arguing for international commerce as a pragmatic solution to achieve some fixed end. His argument is that the creation of a system of international commerce is necessary in order to maintain civil society as a genuine ethical end – that is, to maintain a form of social life in which freedom can be realized and in which modern life's self-understandings are made rationally sustainable. International trade also opens people's minds up to a more general system of recognition of the common humanity of others, and it assists the formation of a more objective (universal) point of view than is possible in limited national communities. A system of international commerce is justified to the extent that it does these things. This is of course not to say that the system of international commerce *historically* arises because of this need to develop and maintain a coherent set of self-understandings. In fact, as Hegel makes clear, it arises simply out of the desire for profit. The need to preserve a coherent set of self-understandings is not the *cause* of the rise of international commerce. It is rather the way in which the system of world trade is *justified,* specifically by being shown ex post facto to fulfill a certain teleology inherent in the logic of modern life.[87] As we might put it, the *legitimacy,* as distinct from the *efficacy,* of international trade lies in its fulfilling this teleology of ethical ends.

The problem for civil society as an ethical end is that the unity established between the individual's personal point of view and the objective point of view – more particularly, between the claims of autonomous agency and the claims of right – is not fully stable. Each tends to separate and stand in contradiction to the other; the unity of personal and impersonal (subjective and objective) that is defining for ethical ends is forever coming apart in this particular set of ethical ends. What Hegel thinks has happened in the modern discovery of market mechanisms as explained by the Scottish economists is that a relatively stable way has been found to harmonize the self-seeking tendencies of modern autonomous agency with the claims of right that these kinds of agents intrinsically make for themselves. But this harmony is, because of its own logic, forever in danger of shattering. This is particularly true in the business estate (which presumably included the workers involved in that estate): The danger of self-seeking covering itself in the mantle of invoking its "rights" is particularly likely there. (In holding that view, Hegel is perhaps also being a bit too optimistic about the other estates.)

The resurrection of the Korporation

One solution to this problem, traditionally identified with Rousseau, is to get the members of civil society to come to see themselves as part of something like a "national family," and to see the state as the social institution for accomplishing this. Hegel rejects this solution. The state, as we shall see, cannot be anything like a family, and the attempt to give it the kind of unity that a family has is both theoretical nonsense and ethically disastrous. However, he does accept that something *like* a family unity must be established, and the social institution that fills this criterion is something that he calls the *Korporation,* the corporation.

The corporation is also the second solution (in addition to the expansion of international trade) to the problem of alleviating poverty. The corporations of which Hegel speaks were social institutions which, like the estates, were for all practical purposes already dead in his own day. These corporations are not to be confused with the modern capitalist giants that we call corporations. They are an older form of social and legal life, which were "groups of persons joined together for their common benefit and at the same time pursuing purposes of public interest."[88] The early modern German *Zunft,* or guilds, were corporate bodies in this sense, but not all corporations were guilds. Corporations included universities, bodies of civic officials (such as judges), and commercial companies. The corporation controlled admission to itself, set standards and provided for the needs of its members. Hegel does not argue for the existence of the full panoply of medieval and early modern corporations. Rather, he argues that one particular estate, the business estate, should be organized into distinct corporations, and his argument for this is similar to the argument he gave for the necessity of the estates in general. The necessity for corporations is to provide a social institution to support a certain type of self-consciousness, to provide a means in which "social space" can be rationally (that is, coherently and consistently) ordered.

The bourgeois family provides a "substantial" basis for the individual's self-identity. Because of who one naturally is, one achieves a substantial form of self-identity within the family, and many of one's emotional and psychological needs are met within it. In the family, one has a shared self-identity. The corporation extends to the individual a similar type of satisfaction but without the natural basis that underlies the family. The shared self-identity that exists in the corporation is that of camaraderie (*Genossenschaft*), not familial identity.[89] As a professional organization that furthers the interests of its members and upholds certain public standards, the corporation also provides a sense of mutual dependence that checks the tendencies toward egoistic self-seeking that is forever threatening bourgeois society. Part of the force of corporations is that in a society that is organized around them, it is the corporation that licenses its members to practice their profession; corporations are not private bodies like clubs but relatively autonomous public institutions. Although membership in corporations is voluntary, there is a great motive provided to join one, since without membership one cannot practice one's profession. For one's own private ends, therefore, it is necessary to join a corporation that is empowered with a certain public responsibility. Corporate membership thus creates a union between personal interest and public responsibility. It serves as a relief from poverty in that the members of corporations are required to take care of their own members – to provide them with the equivalent of unemployment insurance, to insure that their children are educated, and so on. The stigma, so Hegel clearly argues, of accepting public relief is alleviated because in accepting relief from the corporation, one is accepting help from people who are like one's second family.

The necessity for corporations therefore is like that of the estates in general. They provide an institutional arrangement for the mutual recognition of their members such that (1) the sense of self-determination is preserved for each member, for in acting in accordance with the standards of the corporation, one is acting in accordance with who one is (the corporation as a second family); and (2) in acting in accordance with the standards of the corporation, one is acting in a publicly recognized and beneficial way. The corporations provide an institutional setting for mutual recognition and for a harmony between the objective and subjective points of view.

The alternative to corporations is pure individualism, which he recognized as a direction toward which the business estate seems to develop. To the extent that one's self-identity is not secured by the standards of a corporation, one has no stable self-identity, and one's understanding of oneself as a self-determining agent is thereby contradicted or undermined. The only way in which one could then establish any consistent and coherent understanding of self would be as a kind of free floating individual linking himself up with some external standard that is widely recognized in civil society. That would be, of course, the accumulation of status goods and the hedonistic pursuit of pleasure.[90] Hegel's argument against this is not a moralizing, finger-wagging denunciation of its "wrongness"; it has to do with the irrationality, the unsustainability of that way of living. Such free-floating individuals find themselves in an unintelligible morass; they cannot understand who they are or what they are to do next. Thinking of themselves as self-determining individuals, they are forever finding that their lives are in fact determined by all kinds of contingencies that according to their self-understanding should have no control over them. However much pleasure they might derive from such activities, such individuals are bound to have a life of succeeding disappointments, since they will forever be failing to be the people – the self-determining independent agents – that they think they ought to be. (It is then especially curious that Hegel thought that the corporation, restricted to the business class alone, could help alleviate poverty. His reasons for doing this no doubt had to do with what he saw to be the impoverishment of those artisans who found themselves out of work during the early stages of the Industrial Revolution; his solution obviously would not apply to those rural folk who later came to comprise a great number of the unemployed urban proletariat during the later phases of the Industrial Revolution.)

Corporations and the family, Hegel argues, are the cornerstones of civil society. The structure of these two social institutions constitutes a "social space" in which people can acquire ethical ends: ends that are rationally acceptable to agents from both the personal and impersonal point of view, while also being ends with which the agents can identify (that is, being ends from which the agent is not alienated). But civil society with its corporate structure and its collections of families cannot completely fulfill this task of articulating a "social space" in which a coherent and consistent set of ends exist. Both corporations and the family are limited forms of community. In them, people attend to each other's particular needs and in them people are provided with personal resources of material and non-material kinds that enables them to lead lives that match up to their understanding of who they are. However, they do not acquire anything other than a moral motive of general beneficence to attend to the needs of members of other families or communities. This puts the fates of families and corporations at the hands of various other social and natural contingencies. There is also the question of cooperation among the various families, individuals, and corporations and whether various corporations and families should compete with other corporations and families for resources and status, perhaps taking some away from others in order to provide for the well-being of their own members. In one clear sense, the structure of civil society itself logically solves this problem in its erection of a rule of law and a system for administering justice. The principles of cooperation thus can emerge out of idealized bargains among the various families and corporations as a way of maintaining a certain peacefulness and cooperative spirit for the purpose of mutual benefit. People agreeing to cooperate on a basis of mutual respect could then devise the appropriate institutions of regulation and administration for the conduct of affairs in civil society.[91]

Why, however, would people agree to cooperate on a basis of mutual respect? Each thinks of himself as possessing certain very general (abstract) rights and as being an autonomous agent. Seen in this way, we represent the individual as having certain goals (even very general goals such as keeping his self-identity consistent) and then start looking for ways to best secure those goals. But seen in that way, it becomes clear that it would be a contingent matter whether treating others with "respect" would serve to secure those goals. If there is no further determinateness to the structure of "social space" than that of "family" and "civil society," then the individuals have no reason other than calculations of personal and corporate interest to cooperate. The injunction to cooperate becomes simply a moral exhortation, something we *ought* to do but not something to which we are otherwise inclined to do. As with any moral exhortation, it may or may not be something with which we identify in terms of our conscience. We may obey it as an injunction (and if we are good Kantians, we may console ourselves with the thought that it is really our own rational will that is doing the imposing, however much we as individuals may not find ourselves identified with the acts of the rational will), or we may find that it clashes with too many personal projects. Nonetheless, mutual respect, if left to this basis, would depend on others consciously adopting that principle as a maxim, something that may or not happen. Moreover, to the extent that it is left up to individual conscience to decide the matter, it is less likely that it will get done for a variety of reasons. Finally, the structure of this mutual respect is always threatening to unravel into a schism between the personal and the impersonal point of view.

Political community and the common life

There must be a further determinateness in the "social space" that structures the self-consciousness of these agents if such contingencies are to be avoided and if the form of life in civil society itself is even to be possible. This further determinateness must consist in a set of reasons that license a further identification with the other individuals of one's community. In order for the administration of justice and the orderly workings of civil society to be possible, there must be a further set of inferences having to do with the ethical status of the others in the community. In civil society, others are fundamentally means to one's own projects. Even in the corporations – the "second families" of civil society – the motive remains one of mutual dependency, of each furthering the ends of the others. Even though the corporation manages to motivate the individual, however unwittingly and unconsciously, into incorporating at least part of the public welfare into his own private projects (and thus serves as a form of *Bildung*), the fundamental bond there nonetheless remains that of cooperation for mutual benefit. Even in the best ordered of civil societies, where people find genuine identification with their estates and corporations, the conflict of interests is always there, and it is entirely fortuitous if for some reason, all interests happen to coincide. For it to be possible for civil society to be a genuine ethical end, therefore, there must be more to "social space" than just a collection of families and a civil society composed of families, individuals, estates, corporations, and a set of legal institutions for administering the law and various public works. There must be a deeper ethical community, which Hegel, interestingly enough, calls the *state*.[92]

The Hegelian conception of a state is that of a social and political form of life that secures for its members a certain type of self-consciousness and that makes the other forms of social and political life possible as realizations of freedom. Self-consciousness is minimally the assumption of a position in "social space," and human *organisms* become *agents* when they are socialized through various processes of *Bildung* – education, formation, and cultivation – into assuming positions in such a "social space." The *state* is the name for that set of norms (of what Hegel calls *Recht*) that license various moves within a "social space" that enables the people assuming these positions to see each other as co-members of a type of *political* community. A political community is a group of people sharing a *common life* – that is, a common constitutive set of basic principles that are defining for their self-identity. Politics is fundamentally about this common life, or shared self-identity; it is about where the limits of our self-identities overlap. It is this common life that makes the unities of family and civil society possible *as* ethical ends, as realizations of freedom. Families and civil societies without such a state could obviously exist, but the people in them could not be said to be genuinely free, since there would be an overarching type of alienation that each would experience vis à vis others in that community. In the Hegelian conception, the "problem" of the state is thus the issue of what *kind of common life* satisfies the demands of reason for coherence and consistency and that thereby realizes the freedom of its members – or, to put it more concretely, of what the rational and proper domain of politics is. (After all, the most difficult issue in all politics is how far down politics goes into people's lives.)

The Hegelian conception of the state is therefore that of an ethical (*sittliche*) community that underlies the social institutions of the family and civil society, which is, in Hegel's metaphor, their "substance" – that part of "social space" that constitutes a people as a political community and that resolves the contradictions in the "social space" that constitutes the modern family and civil society. (Indeed, it is probably overly contentious on Hegel's part to use the term "state" here at all to make his point. "Political society" or "political community" would better capture the point he is trying to make.[93] I shall nonetheless continue for the most part to use Hegel's term, "state.") The state is different from the family, which is also a unity of shared self-identity. The unity of the family is based on love and affection; the unity of the state is a unity of common projects and principles. To the extent that these are projects and principles of a genuine state, however, they make up the "social space" of the agents in question, and they are thus not projects and principles imposed on the agents from the outside, something indifferent to their understanding of who they are. As such the state is best expressed as that *common point of view* in terms of which people see their lives. As a common point of view, it unites the subjective (the personal) and the objective (the impersonal) points of view. The individual sees his own life in terms of these projects and principles, and, in taking an objective look toward things, he can see these personal principles as being justified.

This is a conception of the state in terms of its *legitimacy,* not in terms of how historically it came about. Hegel's comments show how aware he is of the multifarious and usually violent origins of the modern state. The issue is not how the state came to be but whether it can claim any legitimacy in the face of its members. The legitimacy of the state has two sides: (1) The legitimacy of any particular state lies in its being a satisfactory expression of the underlying principles uniting a political community; (2) the legitimacy of the modern state lies in its being a form of life that enables a coherent and consistent self-understanding to be articulated, in its satisfactorily resolving the kinds of contradictions that would otherwise be present in the associations of families and in civil society such that freedom as self-determination can be realized. The state, as a form of political community, therefore has certain functions of *Bildung* (of education, formation, and cultivation) to produce and sustain a certain general *type* of character who is capable of sustaining the modern family and the institutions of civil society: who sees the family as embedded in a set of larger social projects, and who sees the private projects of civil society as embedded in a larger public "social space." Without an adequate form of political community, of shared identity, the individual would be withdrawn out of public life and into himself; he would become "egoistic," seeing all his projects as only his *private* projects, and the overall norm (*Recht*) of freedom could not be realized in any satisfactory form.

For the norm of freedom to be satisfactorily realized, it must be such that individuals can identify with the activities required of them in their private and public lives, and their activities must have a certain clarity of public meaning for them so that they can understand what they are doing and why they are doing it. All this is possible only if there is a common point of view, a kind of common political culture, that makes such clarity and self-identification possible. The complexity of modern life brings along with it a certain amount of self-reflectivity; the social practices of modern life require self-distancing moral reflection and the modern economy requires a good measure of private self-seeking, of reflective calculation of what is to one's own benefit. For individuals to be genuinely free in such circumstances, they must be able to understand the norms structuring their own activities as not being something unintelligibly imposed on them by some alien body or external forces such that they cannot understand them and cannot identify with them. For that to be possible, it must be possible for them as modern *self-conscious* agents to be able to give *accounts* to themselves of the relation between their private and their public lives – or, put more loosely, to be able tell themselves various intelligible stories about who they are and what they are doing. They must be able to give themselves and others various explanations and explications of what they are doing that make their actions intelligible to themselves such that they can be said to understand what they are doing and to identify with it. These kinds of accounts need not, of course, be full-fledged philosophical accounts; they can be evidenced in certain types of behavior, in certain religious rituals, be embodied in certain works of art and so on. Only in the common point of view embodied in a type of public, political culture – in the political community, what Hegel calls the *state* – are individuals provided with the resources for those types of accounts, with ways of making sense of their lives as familial and private (civil society) individuals. Without that type of public account, the unities of civil society in particular threaten to separate, since the only "publicly" available account within the structure of civil society itself is that of cooperation for mutual self-interest. Civil society on its own cannot be self-sustaining *as a realization* of freedom, even though it might be self-sustaining as a form of (alienated) life. Or, to put it in Hegel's terms, civil society cannot be sustainable as a form of rational self-consciousness. In this sense, a certain type of "state," of political community, makes the family and civil society possible as a rational, non-alienated form of life; it makes them possible as "ethical ends," as realizations of freedom, as social and personal projects with which individuals identify.

The institutions of modern political life

The expression of the political community's (the state's) unity is its *constitution,* which can be written or unwritten. If written, however, its legitimacy as a binding political document consists in its being an adequate expression of the *genuine* constitution of a people – namely, that common point of view that defines their lives together. As such a common point of view, the constitution of a state can never be created *ex nihil* by a people. Indeed, a people without a constitution would not be "a" people; it would be only a disconnected mass of individuals sharing no common point of view (or sharing one only contingently).[94] In this sense, a constitution can also never be imposed on a people. There is, of course, nothing impossible in imposing a written document specifying certain rights, duties and a structure of government on a people. However, such a constitution could only fortuitously have legitimacy for the people on whom it was imposed. Unless it quite serendipitously captured a sense of who they were, it would be a document that required actions and policies from which the citizens would be fully alienated. They might even be able to see those actions as "justified" in some appropriately "objective" fashion, but they could not find *themselves* "in" the actions they were required to take on the basis of that constitution. A written document that does not express the genuine constitution of a people can only lead to alienation on the part of the people and ultimately, in practical terms, to its own decay and dissolution.[95]

It is in this sense and only in this sense that the state in its constitutional order can be seen as the will of the people.[96] The Hegelian concern with the constitution must therefore be with the kinds of *political institutions* that have developed in modern life that can be understood to legitimately fulfill the teleology of ethical ends. That is, if the state is to be seen as that common point of view that makes a people into a political community, and the constitution is the organization of that state into public "ethical" principles and political institutions, then the concrete issue for the modern state has to do with *which* existing political institutions may be seen to rationally support and express the criteria for something's being an ethical end. This is, again, not a question of "what works" or what means best fulfill an independently specifiable end; it is a question of what political institutions best fit the unity of the personal and the impersonal points of view such that individuals in assuming that unified view can act in a non-alienated fashion, can be "with themselves." The legitimacy of these political institutions does not lie in their efficiency or even in their ancestry – not, that is, in their being some part of a "tradition" as some communitarians like to think.[97] It is in their formulating and expressing a coherent rational modern self-identity for the citizens of these states.

The political institutions – the institutions of government – for which Hegel argues are somewhat familiar to modern eyes. What is different is Hegel's ethical justification for them as embodiments of a determinate form of communal and personal self-understanding and as realizing the central norm of freedom. Hegel argues, for example, for a separation of powers that he says is a guarantee of the freedoms of the citizenry. However, to understand the justification of the separation of powers in terms of some pragmatic solution such as a system of "checks and balances" would be to overlook the basis of their legitimacy. We do not separate the powers so that each blocks the other; that would make the legitimacy of the separation of powers depend on contingent assumptions about corruption, about who happens to be in office and so on. The real point, he argues, is for the distinct functions of modern social and political life to be recognized and expressed. To fail to separate the powers would be to fail to insure that the various functions of modern political life are properly fulfilled.[98] The issue is not to pitch the representatives of the powers against each other so that we onlookers can experience a certain bit of *Schadenfreude* over watching the hapless government officials thwart each other's ambitions.[99] It is to insure that the functions of modern social life are carried out in a rational fashion. Thus, Hegel worries about the independent specification of the powers, not with whether in practice one spills over into another (as in the American example, in which the executive, the president, plays a partially legislative role). The important point is that the powers be understood as separate distinct powers and that distinct institutional support be there so as to see that those powers are fulfilled. Those powers, he argues, are those of the legislative, the executive, and the crown.

The crown, Hegel argues, should only be a constitutional monarch in something like the English fashion, simply dotting the i's on already finished legislation. However, in keeping with the principles of modern life, the monarchy's own legitimacy rests on the monarch's respecting the self-understandings present in civil society and (in Frederick the Great's self-description) being merely a "servant of the state." It is quite clear that absolute monarchy (which Frederick the Great nonetheless himself represented) is out of the question in modern life. The necessity of monarchy for Hegel (as opposed, for example, to a presidential system) lies in the crucial symbolic role that the monarch plays in the modern state: The monarch represents the political community in a clear, intuitive way, and the rituals attendant to monarchy give the citizens a kind of account of who they are that is much more "immediate" than any philosophical account could be. The modern state is, after all, complex, bureaucratic, and is not something that automatically inspires either loyalty or identification with it. Hence, allegiance to it must be mediated in a rational way, and the monarch offers a concrete symbol of the state toward whom such allegiance can be focused. In focusing on this symbolic role of the monarchy, Hegel notably omits discussion of the other important way in which modern states could promote identification on the part of their citizenry – namely, through nationalistic sentiment. Hegel's disregard for nationalism as a way of underwriting allegiance to the modern state is based on his view that citizenship in the modern state cannot be predicated on subscribing to a particular religious or ethnic commitment or to any such analogous commitments, a view that itself is the historical outcome of the French Revolution (the American Revolution apparently playing no substantial role in Hegel's imagination on this matter).[100] It also has no doubt to do with his aversion to the kinds of irrationalities involved in nationalism, since it predicates membership in the political community on features that have little to do with freedom and self-consciousness – with modern "spirit" – so much as it concerns itself with external, "natural" characteristics, such as ethnicity.[101] Constitutional monarchy for Hegel is important as a bulwark against those tendencies that make identification with the political community purely a matter of nationalistic "feeling" and not of rational self-consciousness.

Whatever form the political institutions of the modern political community take, they must be consistent with the set of self-understandings essential to the modern companionate family and to civil society so that they can satisfy the general norm of freedom which structures modern political communities. A *legitimate* modern state, therefore, may not violate these conditions, not because they express independently existing moral rights that individuals bring with them prior to all social organization, but because of the internal necessities of consistency and coherence with modern self-consciousness. Put another way: It is the requirements of "spirit," of the determinate modern community's self-consciousness and the kinds of accounts it can give itself of what counts for it as an authoritative set of reasons that puts limits on what the state in its *institutional, governmental* functions may and may not do. It is the appeal to the internal rationality of modern life and what is necessary to realize the principle of freedom that underlies the modern insistence on constitutionally protected rights; such ideas cannot rest on any appeal to a "human nature" or to any set of independently existing "values" for their support. For these reasons, Hegel endorses various forms of pluralism and quite obviously supports universal citizenship; in opposition to the prevailing Prussian mores of his time, he held, for example, that Jews should be given full civil rights in any modern state since excluding Jews from full citizenship was inconsistent with the principles of the modern state.[102] Nor does Hegel justify freedom of speech and the press on any kind of appeal to the "marketplace of ideas." (If anything, he has great scorn for such a marketplace, noting that public opinion "deserves to be as much respected as despised."[103]) Freedom of the press and of speech is justified because modern citizens cannot continue to regard themselves as autonomous and at the same time as permitting officials of the state decide for them what they may hear, read, and say. At another point in history, when people had a different self-understanding, freedom of speech would have been unthinkable; in modern life, being without it is inconceivable.

It is not surprising that Hegel argues that modern life requires some system of representative government; it is a little more surprising, however, that Hegel does not argue that it requires democracy. (Failure to look at Hegel's arguments for this have helped to perpetuate the myth that his political philosophy was authoritarian and reactionary even for his own time and hence not deserving a closer look.[104]) The argument for representative government takes the same form as the arguments for the necessity of the other basic political institutions. It is justified neither by a pragmatic argument that it is necessary to make things work, nor by arguments of efficiency, nor by appeals to anything like natural rights or any set of transcendent values. Instead, more or less existing institutions (although Prussia in Hegel's day had no representative government) are reconstructed so as to show how they can be seen to be logical implications of a certain form of communal self-understanding.

The state is the political organization of a people; the modern state is a political organization of modern families and civil society. As such, its government must have representative institutions, since the kind of agents who constitute the members of civil society will not find it intelligible that, for example, the funds for the running of the state should be taken from them without their having some say in the matter. The modern bourgeois who takes care of his own personal finances and creates new capital will not be in a position to understand it as being rational that he simply hand over his taxes to the officials of the government; a medieval merchant or a feudal lord, on the other hand, living in a non-market oriented economy, might have no such scruples.

The issue is what form this representation is to take. The government is a distinct institution to further the aims of the political community. As such, it is a particular body of people, and there is always the temptation to see it as a particular entity over and against other particular people or against "civil society" taken as a whole. The institution of representation in government is the way in which the government as a *particular* body of people is mediated with the bodies of civil society such that the *political community* (the state) of civil society is maintained. Representation is thus not some stopgap measure to make sure government works; it is a moment of the ethical end that is the state (the political community), and its legitimacy lies solely in its role in maintaining the coherence and consistency of this modern form of "social space" – that is, in the way it realizes the modern principle of freedom. Representative government mediates between the private freedoms of civil society and the common point of view that is the political community (the state). As such it follows that the function and goal of representative government for such a modern state must be both to formulate and to express the common point of view; the workings of representative government must therefore be to prevent merely the voicing of many private opinions and to encourage the formation of this common point of view. That is, out of the many different basic interests of civil society, a common interest must be formed that is consistent with the self-understanding of the political community.

Hegel's argument against democracy – or at least against universal suffrage as a means of choosing the representatives – is the following. In a system of universal suffrage, it is a contingent matter if one's interests are represented. It is contingent in that it is fully dependent on there being a majority of people on your side. If you happen to find yourself and your group in the minority, you are then excluded from representation, no matter how important or basic your interests are to the political community. You are therefore voiceless. It is moreover the case that an individual's vote will count for little. It is therefore necessary to insure that all basic points of view are represented in the body that is to form and express the common point of view. At best, using universal suffrage to immediately determine the delegates can do that only fortuitously. Some institutional support must therefore be found for insuring that basic interests are represented. One way to do this is to have a system of representation that gives a certain number of places to the various estates and the various corporations. Since it has already been shown (if one accepts Hegel's arguments) that the individuals of civil society living in a system of mutual dependency would be rationally required to organize themselves into estates and corporations, then the only institutional setup that would be consistent with such a form of social life and self-understanding would be some type of an assembly of the estates.[105] (Hegel has very specific proposals for a bicameral system, but even he seems to acknowledge that such a system is not strictly required by modern political communities – it is a pragmatic setup that is nonetheless consistent with them.) Hegel's point, very generally put, is that once one has accepted the principle of representation, one must find some kind of institutional setup such that the basic interests in society are indeed represented. Universal suffrage on its own, without assistance from any other mediating institutions, cannot be the properly representative institution.

4. The final stage of political history, the teleology of modern life, and absolute spirit's coda

The "end of history"?

On the one hand, Hegel's treatment of modern bourgeois social and political life is not a treatment of any *actual* social arrangement. For example, the Prussian state, on which Hegel late in his life had come to place such hope, was a state lacking in the representative institutions of the type that he thought to be necessary. Hegel's appraisal of modern bourgeois life is thus a theory of what is *possible* for modern bourgeois life, although it is nonetheless a theory based on *actually* existing institutions. In some ways, what Hegel has tried to show is that if one combined certain institutions from contemporary England, France, and Germany (along with the reinvigoration of some already deteriorated institutions, such as the *Korporationen* and the Estates), then one would actually arrive at a coherent form of modern life. This is not the depiction of some distant, theoretical ideal, for it is based on actually existing institutions; but it is also not the description of any single existing state (nor is it thus the ex post facto justification of any particular existing state). It takes various existing institutions of modern life and shows how an existing state could reform itself into more of an image of the ideal modern state.

However, although it only sketches the *possibility* in this sense of an adequately realized form of modern life, it does seem to suggest that there is little room for any conceptual improvement in its essential structure. The essential structure of modern life is such that it reconciles the subjective point of view and the objective point of view in a way that no previous form of life could do and it provides for a realization of freedom by giving individuals ends that they can will with full self-consciousness and with which they can identify. Whereas the *Phenomenology of Spirit* (1807) could only see a redeemed and non-alienated form of life in the reconciliatory institutions of art, religion and philosophy, the scheme presented in the much later *Philosophy of Right* (1821) fulfills part of the promise of the *Phenomenology* by its presentation of a concrete idealist theory of modern social institutions and ethical life that goes beyond a merely moral critique of institutions. Particular individuals –

such as utopians and romantic reactionaries – may feel the structure of modern life to be without justification and to long for something better (for example, for an idealized Christian medieval past or for an aesthetically more satisfying future), but if the possibilities of modern life were to be realized, we would have to evaluate this continuing alienation on their part as more a function of their own personal pathology rather than anything inherent in the structure of modern life itself. The "unhappy consciousness" – the way in which an entire form of life can find itself unjustified without its being able to envision any alternative to itself – can therefore for the Hegelian only be a contingent appearance among isolated individuals in modern life. Modern life in principle unites the two points of view such that people in acting on the basis of the "social space" of modern life need run into no essential contradictions in the structure of their agency. In their actions based on the rationality of this "social space," they may therefore be "at home with themselves," be fully identified with their actions. Modern life, properly understood, offers the actuality of the kind of reconciliation sketched at the end of the *Phenomenology of Spirit:* The participants in modern life see the determinateness of their subjectivity as coming not from any metaphysical structure or entity outside them but from the free-standing structure of their practices in such a way they can reconcile themselves to the social life around them because they identify with it.[106] Moreover, they come to inhabit a "social space" that is free from any essential contradictions, such that the essential alienation endured by the agents of the past is not present for them. Alienation for the moderns need be only a personal, idiosyncratic problem, not a problem of the irrationality of "social space" itself.

This conception of the potential internal coherence of bourgeois social and political life led Hegel to one of his most controversial and least understood theses, that having to do with the final stage of history (sometimes called the "end of history").[107] The reason for the lack of understanding is easy to see. More than any other part of Hegel's system, it gives the appearance of ascribing the movement of history to a metaphysical ground (usually taken to be God) that is causing the movement of history to go in a particular direction. It looks, that is, as if in his mature philosophy of history Hegel is claiming to have discovered some kind of special causal force in history – namely, spirit's push to come to a full self-consciousness – and to have created a new "science of history" that studies this special causal force.

Hegel's point is, of course, nothing of the sort. His mature philosophy of history, sketched at the end of the published *Philosophy of Right* and elaborated at length in his lectures in Berlin, is a reconstruction of the history of political communities (states). His point is that the narrative of the history of *political communities* has come to an end; it is a *story* that is over. The mature philosophy of history thus extends the kind of philosophical history that he practiced in the *Phenomenology of Spirit*. The kind of history practiced in the *Phenomenology* concerned how we came to be the people for whom something like the *Phenomenology* itself and the mature "system" could come to be on the conceptual menu. It was a reconstruction of the historical insufficiencies of various basic forms of "social space" such that it could be shown how one form of life may be seen to be the resolution of the kinds of problems that arose in an earlier form of life when it attempted to answer those skeptical objections it generated from within its own terms.

This is not a causal account of history; the account of the various social forces and contingent events that lead to the actual breakdown of one form of life and its domination or replacement by another is a topic for the historians, not the philosophers of history. *Philosophical* history is concerned not with what caused one form of life to supplant another (what caused Rome to supplant Greece) but with the ways in which what a later form of life takes to be authoritative for itself can be understood only in terms of how it came to see the accounts given by earlier forms of life as insufficient. It is not as if one form of life is *fated* to be replaced by another (as if a "scientific historian" with the right "predictive apparatus" living near the end of the Greek period could predict the rise of Rome and what its structures would look like). Some forms of life, for completely contingent reasons, come to have a certain structure and, for completely contingent reasons, come to exercise dominance during a certain period. What is of philosophical interest is not the contingent ways in which one form of life succeeds another but with whether one form of life may be seen as a *rational* successor to earlier forms, such that the passage from one to the other can be seen as fulfilling a certain teleology, that is, such that the former can be seen to be *completed* by the latter. The insufficiencies in the various types of reason-giving activities can be seen to be overcome in the accounts of reason-giving in the reflective institutions of the latter. Something is a rational successor as opposed to a mere replacement if it can in this way be seen to *complete* the former stage, to remove some of the internal contradictions and incoherences, to create a different "social space" in which those basic contradictions are removed; it completes the earlier form of life in that its accounts of what counts for it as authoritative reasons for belief and action may be seen to answer the kinds of skeptical objections that were internally generated out of the earlier form of life's accounts of what counted as authoritative reasons for it. When a form of life develops a certain set of reflective practices, such as occurred in ancient Greece, it generates a skepticism about its own practices and its own accounts of what counts for it as authoritative; these skeptical doubts are the self-generated "negations" of the accounts they had given themselves, and they motivate that form of life to try to reassure itself that what is has taken as authoritative is indeed true, is well founded. In trying to reassure itself, a form of life will deploy a set of strategies and new accounts. If they succeed in offering a satisfactory reply that allays these doubts, they *renew* their form of life; if they fail, then there is a breakdown of the reason-giving activity. In those cases, that form of life gradually ceases to have faith in what it is doing: its members become alienated and develop into what Hegel calls the "unhappy consciousness" and what Kierkegaard later simply called "despair". Once in despair, a form of life finds that its institutions and practices can no longer claim the allegiance of its participants; the agents can no longer understand what they are doing, they cannot find themselves "at home" in those institutions and therefore they cease to be free. This kind of breakdown of a form of life – its descent into despair – itself can then only be made good by the generation of new types of accounts whose internal aims are consistent with what the old account *actually* accomplished (which, for example, is what the Roman form of life does with Greek culture); or new accounts whose internal new aims supersede the old aims by including them as components of itself (which, for example, is what early European culture did with the older Roman form of life).

It is thus a contingent fact that the Romans came to possess a certain military spirit and technology that allowed them to triumph over neighboring tribes; it is a contingent fact that Roman life had such and such a structure so that it was able to absorb Greek culture and transform it into Roman folkways as it did. It is of normative significance if the formation and political success of Roman life, contingently brought about as it was, can be understood to be, in Hegel's terms, the "truth" of Greek life in the sense that what the Romans came to take as authoritative reasons could be seen to resolve the kinds of skeptical discreditings that the Greeks had generated for themselves. The alienation that the Greeks generated for themselves was made into a constitutive element of the Roman form of life. This "negativity" of the dialectic in history can only be grasped in a retrospective normative reconstruction of history. From the historian's point of view, what happened in the passage from Greece to Rome involved complex social forces, striking personalities, bloodshed and large elements of good and bad luck. From the dialectical point of view, what happened in the passage from Greece to Rome was the conceptual move from an immediate form of ethical life to an alienated form of life based on abstract rights and held together only by force – that is, from one form of reason-giving and account-giving that could not sustain itself in its own terms and that found itself replaced by another form of reason-giving and account-giving that could claim to be the better account of what the first form of life had been up to all along.

The *Phenomenology,* however, only studied how *we* moderns came to be the people who were in a position to reconstruct our past so that it made sense as a movement from one form of "social space" to another. The "we" of the *Phenomenology* is only the "we" of modern European culture. The history of political communities per se, however, must be a larger task. There are other political communities in the world besides the Western political community. Hegel thereby came to realize that for his project to be able to make the claims he made for it, he would have to answer two questions: (1) Is it possible to compare our political communities with those of other traditions? (2) Might a philosophical reconstruction of, say, East Asian history yield another incompatible set of such successions of one form of life by another? Could it be that by the standards inherent in East Asian history, one form of life (for example, China under the Sung) could be seen to be the rational successor to another form of life (for example, China under the Ming, with the Yuan period in between being philosophically insignificant), yet could it also be that the standards that allow us to say that the Ming "completes" the Sung themselves

334

would be *internal* to the development of Chinese history while being *external* to our own history? Or, can the forms of social and political organization of the modern West in fact be said to complete the teleology of even Chinese (and all other) history? Can the "we" of this type of reflection be rationally extended to all of humanity?

Hegel thus came to see that he needed a universal or world history if he was to be able to make his claims about the absolute, self-grounding structure of modern life work. His mature lectures therefore dealt with the history of whole world, not just the history of the West. The historical elements of his mature, Berlin lectures on world history, art, religion, and philosophy extended his phenomenology from being that of only the phenomenology of the West to being that of the phenomenology of the whole human community. The later historical parts of the mature system, presented in lectures but not published by Hegel himself, were thus conceptual extensions of the phenomenology practiced earlier, with the restriction being that they only concerned the reason-giving activities of parts of "spirit" overall (for example, the history of "objective spirit" – that is, political communities). Hegel came to see the issue as concerning whether it was possible to reconstruct world history so that it could be seen to be a development of an understanding of how social and political life may be embodied in institutions organized around the expression and development of freedom, or self-determination. He argued that in fact such a reconstruction could be done. In his famous shorthand for the progress of world history, he says, "The East knew and to the present day knows only that one is free; the Greek and Roman world, that some are free; the Germanic world knows that all are free."[108] That is, the development of world history could be rationally reconstructed as a story of the progressive realization of the social conditions for the full equality of freedom in a way that would show the development of a certain type of rationality and determinate form of self-consciousness to be completing what was lacking in all the cultural projects of the world.[109]

Hegel's frequently misunderstood talk of the "world spirit's" directing history for "its own ends" is not a nod on his part to some metaphysical supervisor directing the entire drama of history from off stage. The "world spirit" is just the human community taken as a whole, seen from the standpoint of humanity's gradually coming to terms with itself through its developing sets of social and political institutions which in retrospect can be reconstructed as gradual developments of a kind of rational understanding of what is essentially involved in social and political life. This dialectical reconstruction of the past shows that at certain times, certain determinate human communities play the role of the avant garde in this development. What leads a community into this status of being the avant garde is itself also based on contingent reasons. Rome does not enter the scene *in order* to complete Greece, but in the retrospective viewpoint given by dialectical history, it comes to be seen as having completed Greece. This is what makes some events and not others in world history crucial to this development of human self-understanding. The criterion for what counts as a world-historical event consists in its playing a

335

decisive role in the *story* of the rise of freedom. The usurpation of the Roman empire by the Christian barbarians, Luther's nailing his theses to the doors of the Wittenberg church, the French Revolution and other such events are of world-historical importance only because they contingently contributed to the establishment of new social and political conditions that "we moderns" (their successors) can in retrospect see as having produced a form of human self-understanding that is better able to account for itself than its predecessors. But this is important *only* for this kind of dialectical history. From a more purely historical viewpoint, other events may be significant that for a philosophical history are of no importance. The clashes between Bourbons and Hapsburgs are no doubt of some importance in understanding much of early modern European history, but from the viewpoint of dialectical history, they may only be a sideshow. Hegel sometimes speaks of the "world spirit's" moving from one place to another (from Greece to Rome to the Germanic peoples); he means by this only that whatever contingently developed institutions and self-understandings characterizing that form of life enable it to play the role of the avant garde vis-à-vis the understanding of political freedom at that period in time. Forms of life do not construct themselves in order to play this role; they simply find themselves in that role. We cannot ascribe any great wisdom or foresight to the Romans or to the early emperors of the later (humorously misnamed) Holy Roman Empire; they simply did what they had to do, given their form of life, and if they play crucial roles in world history, it is because their contingently acquired attributes enabled them to play a role that we, living much later, can reconstruct so that their roles can be understood as having completed a certain conceptual development.

Hegel's claim about the final stage of history is thus neither a metaphysical nor a theological, quasi-eschatological thesis. It is rather the view that insofar as the conceptualization of freedom is concerned, European modern life has reached a point at which there seems to be nothing in principle left to be developed. A modern constitutional state with representative political institutions, based on a market society with the appropriate mediating institutions and a companionate familial structure embodies for political communities what the *Phenomenology of Spirit* promised: a non-metaphysical, non-alienated, reconciled form of life.

Modern life thus *completes* the development of political history. It does this not by actualizing any "human essence" or by finally living up to some externally existing set of "values." Hegel's claims for the superiority of modern life are not like those of the early moderns who thought that mankind might finally achieve a form of social structure in harmony with its "nature."[110] For the Hegelian, there can be no predetermined "nature" that could do this. The superiority of modern life consists in the rationality that it brings to spirit – that is, in achieving an internal coherence of a "social space" such that a form of life is achieved in which there is no cleft between the objective and the subjective point of view, in which the type of systemic alienation that had characterized past forms of life – namely, alienation as a reflection of the irrationality of "social space" – vanishes, and in which that form of life is able to develop accounts of itself that can show to its members and to others that it is within its own terms fully intelligible and capable of explaining and justifying itself without internal incoherence. It thus counts as a realization of freedom, the "principle" of the modern world.

Did Hegel therefore argue for the "end of history," as Alexandre Kojève argued that he did? In one sense, this seems like the only logical conclusion. If modern life in general and bourgeois social life in particular resolves the tension between the subjective and the objective points of view, and if that form of life is such that human agents living in it are finally reconciled with themselves, what more is to be done? For a Hegelian, there is one clear sense in which history, however, cannot be said to have come to an end. The Hegelian cannot rule out that future developments in political and social life may be such as to prompt some future Hegelianesque philosophers to find in *their* retrospective surmise of the world's events a different teleology to be at work in the history of the world. For that to happen, though, either rationality itself would have to change in ways that show our current schemes of rationality to be only partial – that is, to be something to be completed by some future development in their social practices of criticism; or the practices that orient themselves around the central norm of modern life, freedom, would have to be shown to be self-undermining in such a way that they require some other set of practices that supported and expressed some different norm that made possible a form of rational self-consciousness for its participants. The Hegelian cannot rule that out, but if Hegel's *Logic* is anything even like the rough outline of self-justifying thought, that prospect cannot be very likely. There is, nonetheless, some evidence that Hegel might have entertained the idea of history taking a different direction (even though he denied that we could predict what that trajectory might be).[111]

Another possibility is that perhaps Hegel viewed the "end of history" in a similar way in which he viewed the "end of art."[112] The phrases "end of history" and "end of art" do not actually occur in the Hegelian corpus, but Hegel does speak of a "final stage" in history and of art's being a "thing of the past."[113] When Hegel says that art is a "thing of the past," he is obviously not making a prediction to the effect that in a few years after, for example, 1828, there will be no further creation of works of art or that people will cease to care about them. Rather, it is the claim that art can no longer play the unifying central role in our common life that it once did, a claim that he also made somewhat obliquely in the *Phenomenology of Spirit*. Art is that social practice by which we reflect on the essential self-identities of our common life through the medium of various sensuous works (and not, like religion, through symbols and activities of communal service, or, like philosophy, through conceptual theories). Art is the "sensuous seeming of the idea" (*"sinnliche Scheinen der Idee"*). It has its heights, so Hegel argues, in Greek religion, because only in the Greek form of life is art uniquely suited to express the central truths of that form of life. With the advent of Christianity and the modern formation of the reflective self-determining agent, the "truths" of social life transcend the capabilities of art to represent them. The

337

standards of truth go beyond art, and it comes to be criticized by standards external to itself (for example, by religious standards in the Middle Ages, by moral, political and often purely subjective standards in more modern periods). The so-called "end of art" is the fate of artistic practice in a form of life centered on self-determining, reflective rational subjectivity. Other forms of reflection, such as philosophy and religion, make an equal if no greater claim to be manifesting the truths about who we are. In Hegel's view, only in Greek life is there a match between determinate form and determinate content in which the categories of beauty and divinity coincide. Thus, art is over only in the sense that it can no longer play the central role it once did. Greek life represents the completion of art. Later aesthetic developments cannot be seen as completions of what was lacking in Greek art, even though later forms of life can be seen as completions of what was lacking in Greek life.

Perhaps Hegel held a similar view of bourgeois life and political history; from time to time, he was known to make rather brooding comments about the structure of modern life, since he perceived quite clearly the existing and growing irrationalities of his time.[114] The kind of teleology that the practitioner of dialectical history in retrospect can discover has nothing necessarily to do with how the future will turn out. The Hegelian system has no room in it for a conception of any kind of *fate* that could insure that things will always turn out to be more rational. Political history might be over in the sense that there could be no improvement in political life, but certainly nothing rules out the destruction of the possibilities of bourgeois life by some set of historically contingent events. Bourgeois life might well founder on some series of contingent happenings – the disruption of the supply of some basic type of resource, a fortuitously lost war, whatever – that would spell its end. The kind of teleology that shows in retrospect that the possibilities inherent in bourgeois life are the completion of a certain line of conceptual development in no way rules out what factually could happen to it in the future. It thus might be the case that this form of bourgeois life cannot for contingent reasons sustain itself. If so, then history will indeed go off in new directions, but these later directions would be declines from the high point of what bourgeois social life could have been (and implicitly already was), and they would signify the reintroduction of alienation into the human community. Future Hegelian philosophers could then only look back at that form of life in the same way that Hegel looked back on Greek art.

On the other hand, perhaps future Hegelian philosophers would look back not with nostalgia to nineteenth-century bourgeois life but instead with a regret about Hegel's misreading of some of the dynamics of modern life. He lived, after all, only at the beginning of the Industrial Revolution. The civil society he envisioned was populated with artisans and merchants, not with an industrial proletariat, international corporations, and the mechanization and routinization of work, and the form of the state that he championed did not base itself on nationalism. To put it somewhat prosaically: Hegel might simply have placed his hopes for the realization of freedom on the wrong set of institutions or on the wrong shape of those institutions. However, these kinds of considerations need not discredit the Hegelian *project,* even though they do indicate that the full realization of freedom in history had not yet been accomplished either philosophically or socially in the mid-nineteenth century. Thus, for these future Hegelian philosophers, the "story" that Hegel assigns to political history may well indeed be *the* "story" for that history – that only the development of institutions in which "all" are free *could* complete that line of political development that although begun by the European community, extends out to the entire human community – but that "story" may not be over in the sense that the institutions and practices developed by the European community in the post-revolutionary era did not fully realize the norm of freedom. If, however, the "story" of political freedom is not yet over, then those other cultures which in Hegel's own account had been shunted off to the sidelines as playing no essential role in the development of world history – for example, the Asian and African cultures – might turn out instead to have large speaking parts in that "story" after all. Future Hegelian philosophers might therefore take the project of the *Phenomenology* as still open and the "system" as only an incomplete guide to what yet needed to be done to complete that project.

The provisionality of Hegelianism

Yet a third possibility is that the Hegelian resolution of modern life's problems was also conceived by Hegel himself as only provisional and qualified. In the introduction to the *Philosophy of Right,* for example, he notes that "philosophy too is its own time apprehended in thoughts" and that "[w]hen philosophy paints its grey in grey, then has a shape of life grown old . . . The owl of Minerva spreads its wings only with the falling of the dusk."[115] Although admittedly the sayings are cryptic and do not unambiguously specify any definite line of interpretation, they seem to indicate that Hegel himself believed that the kind of reconciliation that he thought modern life was in principle capable of achieving for itself in the middle of the nineteenth century could itself only be provisional; that the accounts that it gave itself would undermine themselves by failing to live up to their own objectives both because of internal difficulties and because of the way in which the dynamics of that form of life would bring about circumstances in which the aims and general purposes of certain institutions would become impossible to realize, even though he could not predict what form those insufficiencies would take. For example, the development of the patriarchal family under the conditions of increasing political equality, and the openness of the market to nontraditional participants, eventually undermines the patriarchal family's own social possibility in ways that are already clearly foreshadowed in Hegel's own time, even if he failed to see it himself. Indeed, Hegel's own dialectical phenomenology would seem to indicate just that: The certification of any claim to knowledge or any assertion of a binding practical principle depends on the ways in which it answers to the historical insufficiencies of previous accounts; this points to the idea that any *allegedly* final account can itself only

339

be *provisionally* final, that it too must be expected to undermine itself as the conditions under which it is to be realized develop themselves (for example, that it will fail to accomplish the aims that it sets as definitive for whether it can count as a success). In that case, one could see the project of the realization of freedom as having been provisionally accomplished but the very terms of that project now calling for a new and different realization of freedom in different circumstances. Hegelian philosophy would then be the self-renewing account of what is reconciliatory in the modern world, of what institutions and practices can count as realizations of freedom, even if only provisionally and incompletely. (Hegel's own remarks about irony in the *Philosophy of Right* also hint at his belief in the provisional status of his solution.)

But if the project is still open in that way, then we need some account of what it would mean to talk about the way in which the project is indeed provisional and the ways therefore in which it might be completed. The project of realizing freedom in the modern world would have to take the form of a modern, rational *Sittlichkeit,* a set of institutions expressing and enabling a reflective, self-conscious sense of "the way things are done" within the social conditions of modern life itself, which itself should then reconcile modern agents with their world by providing a rationally justifiable set of common projects with which the participants in that form of life could both identify and could *understand* as being "right," as realizations of freedom. The political community itself, taken purely on its own, cannot resolve that issue of justification and intelligibility, for that requires a general reflection on whether modern life lives up to the terms it sets for itself. Although many of the various institutions of modern political life, such as general elections, can be seen as institutional supports and expressions for a kind of social self-reflection on who we are, these political reflections always take place against the background of an already taken-for-granted form of "ethical life," *Sittlichkeit.* That background of *Sittlichkeit* includes, for example, what we have come to count as authoritative reasons for granting authority to certain people, for why we think that engaging in certain forms of social activity is to be encouraged, why other engagements are to be frowned upon, with what appears to individuals as a calling and with what appears to them as entirely optional. *Political* community on its own cannot answer whether these taken-for-granted sets of reasons and reason-giving practices themselves can withstand the kinds of criticisms and reproaches that come from taking those practices at their word and drawing out what is implied in them, for although involved with reason-giving activities of a particular sort, political community is not the *kind* of practice in which those other practices and activities themselves come under criticism *as* practices. Political institutions (for example, a general election) offer us practices for reflecting on our collective self-identity but always as mediated through institutions such as the family, the economy, and the institutions of political life. As involved in such cooperative social life, we engage in a variety of reason-giving activities, ranging from the accounts we give of why a certain set of actions in the marketplace is justified to the accounts we give of why certain child-rearing practices are in order. These kinds of accounts are mediated by the institutional and practical background – in our time, the modern "way we do things," the modern *Sittlichkeit* – of our cooperative, social lives that seem to us like a "second nature," the *commonsense* of our life, the things that seem to us as just *obvious*.[116] In cooperative social life, we are acting, and we cannot be acting if we have to stop before each activity to give a fully articulated justified account of what we are doing. Commonsense and common political life have therefore only limited means within themselves for reflecting on whether they are capable of sustaining themselves in their own terms.

"The way we do things" in social and political life does not within itself offer any means for evaluating whether it itself can be sustained. For that, a more detached, impersonal point of view is required that is not compatible, so it would seem, with the exigencies of political action. This is not to argue that political action is or should be non-reflective; the practices of modern life in fact require it to be reflective and to be able to offer rational, public justifications for itself in terms of principles that are widely shared among the citizenry. It is only to say that the practice of giving reasons in the political realm will be necessarily unsatisfactory when viewed from the standards inherent in the modern practice of reflective religious practice, art, and philosophy. Nor is it at all clear how they could be "reformed" so as to include such things – to include, for example, genuine philosophical reflection as part of their institutional practice. Modern political life is indeed highly reflective; it involves far more than just accepting the way the community is structured and run, more, that is, than just acquiescing to assertions that certain practices simply are "the way things are done." But modern political community cannot have within its practices a component that puts this kind of practice itself into question. The candidates for office, the functionaries of the political parties, the societal apparatus, and the bureaucrats who run the large institutions of modern life cannot be put in the position where in order to do the things they need to do they must be able to continually give a *genuinely* philosophical account of what it is that they are doing (as opposed to reciting the basic ideas that develop out of more or less socially accepted accounts, such as the idea of basic rights, of freedom to choose paths of life for oneself, and so on). Indeed, any attempt to reform modern, complex, bureaucratic institutions to incorporate genuinely philosophical reflection within them would most likely be disastrous, for it would inevitably not make the political institutions more philosophical but would instead degrade philosophical reflection into simply becoming an ideological prop for those practices.

That more detached form of reflection in modern life must be carried out within the three institutions in which "absolute knowing," the final point of the *Phenomenology,* is realized as an ongoing social practice. "Absolute knowing" as institutionalized is what Hegel calls *absolute* spirit, the reflection on our basic self-identities in a completely free manner, independent of all external considerations about what is necessary for action. Absolute spirit in modern life is articulated into three distinct institutions: art, through which we reflect on our basic self-identities through the aesthetic sensuous works or artifacts; religion, through which we reflect on who we are and what are our highest interests (on the divine in human life) through communal and personal rite and ritual; and philosophy, an enterprise nowadays mostly cordoned off to another relatively modern institution, the university, in which we reflect on what counts as authoritative reasons, what it means to give a reason, and what it means in general to be an agent who accepts certain things as authoritative for himself – on what it means to be the people who we have come to be and whether our current *accepted* practices and accounts *really can* offer authoritative reasons and accounts. In modern absolute spirit – genuinely modern art, religion, and philosophy – modern life partially fulfills the modern ideal of independence and self-determination and can show *whether* the terms in which it articulates itself can be vindicated vis à vis its predecessors and its alternatives. With its highly reflective social structures and internal complexity of bureaucracies and legal mechanisms, modern life requires a set of practices that allow its agents to step outside of the "second nature" of social life and to evaluate the ends of that life in terms of the self-chosen criteria of modern life itself. Past forms of life developed practices for accounting for the accounts that they gave themselves in everyday life. The late modern world, with its rapid communications, its ability to put more of the world in front of ordinary people on a daily basis, and its own self-awareness of itself as a historical phenomenon, requires a set of reflective practices different from those of the humdrum of daily cooperative life in the market. Only in what seems to be the detached and alienated institutions of the "absolute spirit" of late modernity – in its somewhat alienated art, in its modern religious institutions with their apparently peripheral involvement in everyday political life, and in its philosophy, nowadays safely professionalized into distinct departments with their own budget lines in universities – can the participants in modern life assume the impersonal point of view necessary for critically evaluating whether they are truly setting their own ends. These institutions have as their object the sustaining of a reflective practice which requires its agents to step back from the exigencies of political life in order to construct the requisitely *impersonal* point of view on the modern form of life, which if modern life is to be successful in its account of itself, should also be continuous with the *personal* point of view. If the practices of "absolute spirit" are successful in modern life, then its "products" should put the agents in a position to see their world and themselves for what they are.[117]

In absolute spirit, the "we" that is doing the reflecting is the "we" that is the object of the reflection, and, if Hegel's account is correct, there should be a full continuity between the personal points of view that "we" take in our daily lives and impersonal point of view that "we" take in working within the practices of "absolute spirit." The artifacts of the modern institutions of art, religion, and philosophy are modern life's own reflections on whether "we" can find ourselves affirmed in those responses of modern institutions to the kinds of skeptical objections that come from its own reflections on its complex, bureaucratic, legalistic, rights-oriented, self-detached social and political life.

If modern "absolute spirit" (that is, the modern practices of art, religion, and philosophy) is that set of practices in which the self-renewing task of "absolute knowing" developed at the end of the *Phenomenology* is carried out, then by the Hegelian account of "absolute spirit" and modern life, the task of modern philosophy (as of modern art and modern religious life) will be to construct and evaluate those accounts of who we are and to continue to skeptically ask if – as the human community has done in the past – we aren't just fooling ourselves again. Taken in this way, Hegelianism would be what Hegel intended it to be: not a finished "system" done once and for all in Prussia in the 1820s, but an ongoing series of dialectical reflections on the possibilities available to the human community such that we can see what kinds of self-identities are open to us and how we might in turn account for the people that we would be.

NOTES

Chapter One

1. James Hutchison Stirling, *The Secret of Hegel: Being the Hegelian System in Origin, Principle, Form, and Matter.* (Edinburgh: Oliver & Boyd, 1898).

2. The most influential version of this idea of Hegel as an important but unacceptable precursor to our world is Charles Taylor's *Hegel* (Cambridge: Cambridge University Press, 1975) along with his *Hegel and Modern Society* (Cambridge: Cambridge University Press, 1979), an adaptation of the longer *Hegel,* In Taylor's view, by constructing a metaphysics based on the idea of a universe posited by a Spirit whose essence is rational necessity, Hegel tried to combine the rational, self-legislating freedom of the Kantian subject with the expressive unity within man and with nature (that is, the Enlightenment conception of rationality with Romanticism). But this attempted synthesis, however grand, is dead. Part of the reason for this, in Taylor's view, is that Hegel seriously misunderstood the dynamic of modern life, thinking both that the forces of dissolution at work in modern life could be contained in the form of the rational constitutional state that he developed (in a new form of ethical life), and that his philosophy of nature would unify the empirical sciences. The dynamic of modern society, especially since the period in which Hegel wrote, has shattered Hegel's dream of a new form of ethical life, and his idea of unifying the sciences has been shattered by their own explosive growth. Hegel's importance for Taylor is that he posed what Taylor takes to be *the* modern question – how to unite radical autonomy with the expressive unity with nature – even though his solution is untenable. The value of studying Hegel, therefore, for Taylor is to study the last great attempt at an overall synthesis of the grand oppositions of modern life.

3. See ¶73, pp. 46–47; *Die Phänomenologie des Geistes,* hereafter referred to as *PG,* pp. 63–64.

4. See ¶76, pp. 48–49; *PG,* p. 65–66. Hegel notes: "By the former *assurance,* science would be declaring its power to lie simply in its *being;* but the untrue knowledge likewise appeals to the fact that *it is,* and *assures* us that for it science is nothing. *One* bare assurance, however, counts for as just as much as another."

5. See ¶76, pp. 48–49; *PG,* pp. 65–66.

6. See ¶78, p. 49; *PG,* p. 67. Hegel notes that in a "science" (a *Wissenschaft*), one must have the general intention not "upon mere authority to give oneself over to the thoughts of others but to examine everything for oneself and to follow one's own convictions, or better still, to produce everything oneself and accept only one's own deed as what is true."

7. See ¶78, p. 49; *PG,* p. 67. Hegel makes a play on doubt (*Zweifel*) and despair (*Verzweiflung*).

8. See ¶81, p. 52; *PG,* p. 70.

9. See ¶84, pp. 53–54; *PG,* pp. 71–72.

10. See ¶78, p. 49; *PG,* p. 67. "Self-consummating skepticism" is *sich vollbringende Skeptizismus.*

11. Thus, early in his "Introduction," Hegel speaks of *"determinate* negation" as signalling the breakdown of some account of what counts as knowledge. See ¶79, pp. 50–51; *PG,* pp. 68–69.

12. For Hegel, the kinds of reasons that we take as authoritative include not only formal but also substantive, material reasons. To capture this sense of "substantive" reason, I use the metaphor of "social space," which I take from Jay Rosenberg's neo-Kantian work, *The Thinking Self* (Philadelphia: Temple University Press, 1986). A social space in Rosenberg's sense consists of a set of material and formal inferences. Hegel shares something like this view, since he thinks of these social spaces as having a logic – that is, as having an inferential structure, which can then be outlined by the dialectician. See also Willem A. deVries, *Hegel's Theory of Mental Activity* (Ithaca: Cornell University Press, 1988) for a development of Hegel's idea of self-consciousness along very similar lines to Rosenberg's theory. (Both deVries and Rosenberg are very influenced by Wilfrid Sellars on these points.) I have also drawn some of the points from J.C. Evans' discussion of the way in which the Kantian theory of subjectivity needs completing in his *The Metaphysics of Transcendental Subjectivity* (Amsterdam: Verlag R.R. Grüner, 1984) pp. 78–85, and his conclusion of that discussion, pp. 104–105, although Evans and I come to different conclusions on this. The difference between formal and material inference is roughly the following. The terms in a formal inference occur (in Quine's phrase) vacuously; the status of the inference is not affected by which terms are entered. A material inference is one in which the terms do not occur vacuously; the substantive terms involved make a difference to the validity of the inference. An example will best illustrate the distinction. Consider the proposition, "If Los Angeles is west of Washington, then Washington is east of Los Angeles." This statement is true, and it seems to be true in some kind of a priori manner. But how? It is not true as a purely formal logical inference unless one adds a suppressed premise, "For any x and for any y, if x is west of y, then y is east of x." With the addition of this premise, the argument follows, and the necessity of the original proposition is only a function of the general necessity of the way in which conclusions follow deductively from premises. However, this way of explaining the force of the proposition begs the question, since if it is true, then we would then need to know in what manner the general proposition (the supposedly suppressed premise), "For any x and for any y, if x is west of y, then y is east of x," is true. It might be taken to be analytic, to be true by virtue of the meaning of the words; however, the troubles with notions of analyticity are well known nowadays, since notions of analyticity presuppose the idea of there being determinate meanings, an idea that is as problematic as ideas get (and certainly not an idea that a Hegelian could accept). Or it could be taken as simply an unconditionally assertible truth, in which case one would have begged the question again. Sellarsians such as Rosenberg take this as partial evidence for its being therefore a marker of a *material* inference rule to the effect: "From x's being west of y, you may permissibly infer that y is east of x." The rule is material because its validity depends on the content of the terms (which distinguishes it from a formal inference rule, such as *modus ponens*).

13. Hegel's emphasis on inference is underlined by his use throughout both the *Phenomenology* and his later Heidelberg and Berlin writings of the language of the logic of syllogistic inference to explain the conceptual transitions he makes. In

doing so, Hegel is, however, relying on the older logic of terms, not on the modern understanding of deductive logic as consisting of those rules of inference that are truth-preserving. In classical logic, the validity of the inference was explained by looking at the terms in the inference (the *Schluss,* the syllogism). For example, take the syllogism: (1) All men are mortal; (2) Socrates is a man; (3) Therefore, Socrates is mortal. "Mortal" is the *major* term. "Socrates" is the *minor* term. "Man" is the *middle* term. The middle term is said to "mediate" between the major and minor term. In his *Science of Logic,* Hegel argues that there are only three types of terms: particular, universal and individual terms. Thus, his claim that everything exhibits the structure of a syllogism amounts to the claim that everything can be described and analyzed in terms of concepts of particularity, universality, or individuality, and the roles these concepts play in various inferential connections. The logic of syllogisms is thus very important for understanding Hegel's conception of *mediation,* since the concept itself is taken from the language of syllogistic logic. The term for mediation – *Vermittlung* – is derived from the idea of the *Mitte,* the middle term of a syllogism that mediates between the major and minor terms. Mediation is thus clearly for Hegel a *logical* process, not the *metaphysical* process that a long line of Hegel commentators have taken it to be.

14. In the literature on Hegel, this characterization of spirit is, of course, controversial. The more traditional interpretation of spirit sees it as some metaphysical entity, a kind of grand mind of which human beings as particular minds are somehow parts. Charles Taylor's *Hegel* is probably the most influential version of this traditional interpretation in contemporary literature. Michael Inwood in his *Hegel* (London: Routledge and Kegan Paul, 1983) offers a similarly metaphysical interpretation of spirit that differs from Taylor's self-described "expressivist" version. But Hegel himself notes that "[s]pirit. . . . is not an essence already finished prior to its appearances, an essence keeping itself back behind the mountains of its appearances but is only something actually true through the determinate forms of its necessary self-revealing – and is not . . . a soul-thing standing in only an external relation to the body but something internally bound up with the body through the unity of the concept." §378, *Encyclopedia.* *Chinese philosophy*

15. On the theme of reassurance in Hegelian thought, see Robert Pippin, " 'You Can't Get There from Here': Transition Problems in Hegel's Phenomenology of Spirit", in Frederick C. Beiser (ed.) *The Cambridge Companion to Hegel* (Cambridge: Cambridge University Press, 1993). I have drawn on Pippin's discussion of the way in which, for Hegel, subjects seek to reassure themselves of their independence in their mediated interactions with each other.

16. See ¶80, pp. 51–52; *PG,* pp. 69–70. Hegel notes: "The goal is as necessarily fixed for knowledge as the serial progression; it is the point where knowledge no longer needs to go over and beyond itself, where the concept corresponds to the object and the object to the concept."

17. See ¶86, p. 55; *PG,* p. 73. Hegel there speaks of dialectic as the "experience (*Erfahrung*) that consciousness exercises on itself," meaning that it has to do with the historical experience of having accounts undermine themselves, being replaced with better accounts that avoid the pitfalls of the earlier ones, and then falling prey to their own self-undermining skepticism.

18. A later contemporary of Hegel's at Berlin, the jurist Karl Friedrich von Savigny, for example, argued that legal systems should be understood primarily as to how they express the spirit of a people, and that this spirit changes historically. There

can be no progress in history, only change; each form of a people's spirit is complete in itself. In von Savigny's view, there could thus be no deep, rational criticism of the law except in so far as it expressed or failed to express some given form of the *Volksgeist*. For a good overview of the rise of this form of historicism and the various political movements that sought moral legitimacy in given historical fact, see Georg G. Iggers, *The German Conception of History: The National Tradition of Historical Thought From Herder to the Present* (Middletown: Wesleyan University Press, 1968). Talking about von Savigny in the context of the *Phenomenology,* is anachronistic, since it is not a confrontation with von Savigny that informs the use of history in the *Phenomenology.*

19. Consider Hegel's criticism of the historical school of law: "To consider particular laws as they appear and develop in time is a purely historical task. Like acquaintance with what can be logically deduced from a comparison of these laws with previously existing legal principles, this task is appreciated and rewarded in its own sphere and has no relation whatever to the philosophical study of the subject – unless of course the derivation of particular laws from historical events is confused with their derivation from the concept, and the historical explanation and justification is stretched to become an absolutely valid justification." *Philosophy of Right,* §3, Remark.

20. This is at least dialectic in the way it functions in the *Phenomenology of Spirit.* In other works, such as the *Science of Logic,* it functions in an analogous way. In the *Logic,* the subject is how "thought" explains itself, and the movement there progresses in terms of how each new category of the *Logic* serves to let thought explain and justify itself as an inferential system. At each stage, because of contradictions and incoherences, thought is forced to move on until at the end of the logical progression (in the "absolute idea") it is supposedly capable of giving an account of itself and its inferential method that it managed to construct in order to reach that point at which it can reflexively give such an account of itself. But in each case "thought" gives an account of itself as grasping the object of thought exhaustively and then "finds" that its account generates a skepticism against itself. (Thus a Parmenidean account of thought grasping "pure being" generates on its own terms the denial of the claim it originally makes, that "thought" grasps pure being as different from "nothing.") At the end of the dialectical movement in the *Logic,* such dialectical "thought" is supposedly to have demonstrated that it is both self-subsuming (that all the various moves within the system are moments of itself) and self-explanatory (that it explains the structure of the system of thought in terms internal to the logical system, not in terms of its matching up with any kind of metaphysical reality).

21. Hegel mentions an example of such a contingency in his lectures on the philosophy of history when he discusses how in the decisive battle between the ancient Greeks and the Persians, "the interest of the world's history hung in the balance," indicating that he thought that had the Greeks lost, the type of account they initiated would perhaps never have been completed. See *Philosophy of History,* pp. 257–258; *Werke,* 12, pp. 314–315.

22. Part of the notorious style of the *Phenomenology* has something to do with the way in which later "formations of spirit" are supposed to complete the earlier forms. The later formations complete the earlier formations in that they supply what is necessary to answer or avoid the skeptical doubts raised within the earlier formations in their accounts to themselves. While the *Phenomenology* thus traces out a clearly *historical* progression, it is written almost entirely in the present tense,

since its narrative is written from the standpoint of the conclusion of the work – "absolute knowing" – which sees the historical progression more like a line of thought rather than a historical, temporal progression.

23. Thomas Nagel, *The View From Nowhere* (Oxford: Oxford University Press, 1986).

24. In commenting on the free-standing nature of such reflective practices, Hegel notes: "In these surroundings, thought is free and withdrawn into itself, free from all material, purely at home with itself. This pure being at home with itself belongs to free thought, to that disembarking into the open where nothing is below us and nothing is above us, and we stand in solitude with ourselves alone." *Encyclopedia*, §31, Remark.

25. Robert Pippin in his *Modernism as a Philosophical Problem: On the Dissatisfactions of European High Culture* (Cambridge: Basil Blackwell, 1991) fits Hegel into the wider context of the debate about modernity, particularly as that story runs from Kant through Hegel to Nietzsche and Heidegger and concerns the way in which the modern European community tries to understand the role of self-determination. My discussion of Hegel and modernity has been strongly influenced by Pippin's account of the way in which the philosophical themes of self-determination play into a larger cultural development during this period.

26. In ¶78, pp. 49–50; *PG*, pp. 67–68. Hegel says, "The series of its formations which consciousness journeys through on this path is rather the complete history of the *cultivation and formation (Bildung)* of consciousness itself towards science."

27. This is exposed in G.E. Mueller's, "The Hegel Legend of 'Thesis-Antithesis-Synthesis,' *Journal of the History of Ideas* 19 (1958), pp. 411–414. It is also discussed by Allen Wood in his *Hegel's Ethical Thought* (Cambridge: Cambridge University Press, 1990). pp. 3–4.

28. Much (really too much) has been made of Hegel's use of the term, *Aufhebung*. There obviously is no natural term in English with which to translate *Aufheben*, and one must therefore make a clear self-conscious choice that will allow readers to make up their own minds as to what is being said without making the text unreadable. For that reason, "sublate," apparently coined as a translation of the Latin term "tollere" is probably the best of the bad choices. Michael Inwood gives a thorough historical and philological account of the term *"aufheben"* under its usual translation as "sublation," and discusses the ways in which the obsolete English term "sublate" is also inadequate in his *A Hegel Dictionary* (Cambridge, Mass.: Blackwell's Publishers, 1992), pp. 283–285. Inwood suggests "to kick upstairs" as the most adequate rendering but notes that "it is too colloquial to win general approval." The German term has a three sided meaning: (1) to raise up, (2) to preserve, and (3) to cancel (as in phrases like "Raise your hands up," "Save a copy of the newspaper for me," and "Your insurance policy has been canceled.") It might also be rendered as "set aside," which carries some of the ambiguity of *aufheben* (as when one sets aside some item to save it for someone else, and when one sets aside something in order to forget it). Hegel's use of *aufheben* also explains how "immediacy" is for Hegel a relative term. All concepts are mediated in that their determinateness (what they are) is constituted by their inferential connections with other concepts. Once the various moments of a concept (which themselves are other concepts) are sublated (*aufgehoben*) into a coherent inferential structure, that concept can serve as a starting point and therefore be immediate. For an agent, a piece of knowledge can, moreover, be an *immediate* piece of knowledge if it functions as a basic principle or premise that has at some earlier

time been sublated into the agent's understandings. Interestingly, Hegel himself used the term *Integration* instead of *Aufhebung* in his lectures on the philosophy of right in 1819–1820 to make the point about how concepts are brought together: *"Die Sittlichkeit is die Integration der beiden ersten Standpunkte, des einen durch den andern."* ("Ethical life is the integration of the two former standpoints, the one through the other.") Cited from *Hegel: Philosophie des Rechts: Die Vorlesungen von 1819/1820* (Edited by Dieter Henrich) (Frankfurt a.M.: Suhrkamp Verlag, 1983).

Chapter Two

1. Hegel has a third target in these three introductory sections that is linked to the first two (to the subject/object model of knowledge and the idea that there are things we can know independently of any social practice) – namely, the Cartesian picture of a mind that can stand in a self-relation without in principle standing in any relation to anything else. Hegel tries to show that this Cartesian picture is also not a tenable conception, again because of considerations internal to such a conception itself; Hegel's anti-Cartesian thesis is that our awareness of ourselves and our awareness of the world are essentially bound together, such that it is not possible for us to know the contents of our own minds without knowing something about the world with which those minds are linked.

2. Hegel makes this point in ¶558, pp. 340–341; *PG*, pp. 397–398.

3. ¶90, p. 58, *PG*, p. 79.

4. ¶91, p. 59, *PG*, p. 80: "The individual (*der Einzelne*) knows a pure 'This,' or the individual item (*das Einzelne*)."

5. See ¶90, pp. 58–59, *PG*, p. 79–80.

6. ¶91, p. 58, *PG*, p. 79. Later in the *Phenomenology*, Hegel characterizes sense-certainty in the following way: "For the positive truth of sense-certainty is in its own self the *non-mediated* being-for-self of the concept itself as object and that too in the form of otherness – the positive truth that very consciousness is *simply certain* that it *is*, and that there are other actual things outside of it, and that in its *natural* being it, like these things, is *in and for itself* or *absolute*." ¶558, p. 341, *PG*, p. 398.

7. See ¶92, p. 59; *PG*, p. 80.

8. Hegel makes this point in his own terms: "When we look carefully at this *pure being* which constitutes the essence of this certainty, and which this certainty pronounces to be its truth, we see that much more is involved. An actual sense-certainty is not merely this pure immediacy, but an *instance* of it. Among the countless differences cropping up here we find that the crucial one is that in sense-certainty, pure being at once splits up into what we have called the two 'thises', one 'this' as 'I' and the other 'this' as object." ¶92, p. 59, *PG*, p. 80.

9. ¶93, p. 59, *PG*, p. 81: "But the object *is*: it is what is true, or it is the essence. It is, regardless of whether it is known or not; and it remains, even if it is not known, whereas there is not knowledge if the object is not there."

10. See ¶96, p. 60; *PG*, pp. 81–82.

11. In an influential article on the topic, Charles Taylor makes much of Hegel's use of indexicals and interprets these passages as presenting a kind of Wittgenstein-Strawson type of transcendental argument about the use of terms and descriptions. See Charles Taylor, "The Opening Arguments of the *Phenomenology*," in Alasdair MacIntyre (ed.) *Hegel: A Collection of Critical Essays* (Garden City:

Doubleday & Co., 1972). pp. 151–188. This way of taking Hegel's arguments attributes a project to him that he himself clearly rejects. Hegel's argument is not an argument to the effect that "in order to use particular terms, I must be able to use general terms." It is that the claims to knowledge posed by "sense-certainty," "perception," and "the understanding" fail on *their own* terms. Hegel is not concerned to show here how in the taken-for-granted usage of our ordinary terms, certain types of relations of presupposition exist, such that using one set of terms presupposes the abilities to use others. In reading Hegel in this way, Taylor imposes on Hegel's argument a kind of latter day phenomenology that is foreign to Hegel's concerns. Taylor takes Hegel's arguments to turn on considerations about "what is undeniable in our experience," or "what we cannot do without in our experience" (considerations that have more to do with the approaches and concerns of twentieth century phenomenologists such as Merleau-Ponty than they have to do with Hegel's own phenomenology). The Hegelian project requires that his arguments state their own conditions; to rely on conceptions of what is "just there" or what "must be the case for our experience to be possible" would be for Hegel a form of dogmatism. Robert Pippin in his *Hegel's Idealism: the Satisfactions of Self-Consciousness* (Cambridge: Cambridge University Press, 1988) integrates Taylor's points without making Hegel's argument dependent on any such "dogmatic" assumptions. I follow Pippin's general way of taking the opening arguments, although the details of the exposition here and Pippin's exposition differ greatly, in particular with regard to how close Pippin stays to Taylor's reconstruction while rejecting Taylor's overall basis for his exegesis.

12. ¶96, p. 60, *PG,* p. 82.

13. See Willem deVries, "Hegel on Reference and Knowledge," *Journal of the History of Philosophy* (26) pp. 297–307. In my view, deVries there also successfully answers those critics, such as Ivan Soll (in his *Introduction to Hegel's Metaphysics* (Chicago: University of Chicago Press, 1969), who attribute the view to Hegel that we cannot successfully refer by means of language to individuals.

14. In "Hegel on Reference and Knowledge" pp. 302–303, deVries lists four such similarities (although not in this order): "(1) A change in context can produce a change in reference. (2) The definite description, the _____, requires some completion with a predicate. So does this _____. (3) Both definite descriptions and demonstratives can have plural forms; names cannot. (deVries notes that Hegel himself does not pick up on this third point.) (4) Descriptive reference invokes a conceptual scheme allowing one to make certain inferences about the object; so does demonstrative reference, although the inferences licensed by demonstrative reference are meager. deVries introduces the idea of the *cognitive content* of a concept to explicate this feature. The measure of the cognitive content for a concept is its role in a scheme of inferences; a concept with little cognitive content will play a small role in only a few explanatory inferences; a concept with a greater number of conceptual connections to other concepts will play an important role in a number of illuminating explanatory inferences. Thus, concepts but not proper names have cognitive content, for proper names have no senses, and thus cannot be linked up to any other set of inferences. (Proper names can play a role in knowledge only if they are linked up with sentences used to form judgments.) It follows therefore that only predicates have cognitive content. Singular descriptive reference clearly has cognitive content, and, as one sees in the various similarities which demonstratives share with singular descriptive reference, demonstratives also have cognitive content. But the kinds of inferences that are li-

censed by the use of demonstratives are of only the most minor sort, such as the ability to infer from the use of "now" to the idea that what is being talked about is a time. Demonstratives are thus the *limit case* of items having any cognitive content; they have as little as possible. In his discussion of Hegel's later post-*Phenomenology* theory of mind, deVries argues that there too Hegel assimilates indexical reference to descriptive reference. See *Hegel's Theory of Mental Activity*, pp. 90–92.

15. Hegel notes, for example, in his later *Encyclopedia*, §418: "The spatial and temporal individualities, here and now, as I determined the object of consciousness in the *Phenomenology of Spirit* . . . actually belong to intuition" Willem deVries also makes this point in his *Hegel's Theory of Mental Activity*, p. 112, note 3.

16. ¶97, p. 60, *PG*, p. 82: "It is as a universal too that we *express* (*sprechen . . . aus*) what the sensuous is. What we say is: *this*, i.e., the *universal this;* or *it is*, i.e., *being in general*. Of course we do not *represent* (*stellen . . . vor*) the universal this or being in general, but we *express* the universal. In other words, we do not strictly say what in sense-certainty we *mean*. But language, as we see, is the more truthful; in it we ourselves directly refute what we *mean* (*unsere Meinung*), and since the universal is the truth of sense-certainty and only language expresses this truth, it is just not possible for us ever to say of a sensuous being what we *mean*."

17. Johannes Heinrichs in his *Die Logik der ⟨Phänomenologie des Geistes⟩* (Bonn: Bouvier Verlag, 1974) uses what he takes to be the systemic connections between the *Phenomenology* and the later *Science of Logic* to argue that sense-certainty corresponds to the opening chapter in the *Logic* on "pure being," which would show that we are dealing here with individual qualities, since that is in fact that with which the opening chapter on "pure being" is concerned. Sense-certainty would be therefore the awareness of pure being. The *Science of Logic* tells us that such a concept is impossible, since it is impossible to differentiate the concept of pure being from that of pure nothing. (Both are indeterminate, and hence no difference between them can be stated.) One should therefore expect the same kind of conceptual impossibility to show up in the consideration of sense-certainty; no *expressible* differences among the individuals can be found. Heinrichs' point is buttressed by the following statement from the *Phenomenology:* "Again, therefore, the *this* shows itself to be a *mediated simplicity* or a *universality. Pure being* remains therefore the essence of this sense-certainty, since sense-certainty has demonstrated in its own self that the truth of its object is the universal. But this pure being is not an immediacy, but something to which negation and mediation are essential." ¶¶98–99, p. 61, *PG*, p. 82. Heinrichs' exposition suffers, however, by making the *Phenomenology's* transitions dependent on those of the *Logic*, thus undermining Hegel's claim that the *Phenomenology* is an autonomous work.

18. ¶103, pp. 62–63; *PG*, p. 84: "Thus we reach the stage where we have to posit the *whole* of sense-certainty itself as its *essence*, and no longer only one of its moments . . ."

19. ¶110, p. 66; *PG*, p. 88.

20. This shows that there is no non-inferential or immediate knowledge, since it would have to be of pure individuals. However, Hegel continues to talk about immediacy in the rest of the *Phenomenology*. After the opening chapter on "Sense-Certainty," however, "immediacy" takes on a relative meaning. It denotes from then on what are the starting points of the reasoning of the agents, what they take for granted. Thus, what appears to them as "immediate," as what need not be

defended, what can be taken for granted, can be seen by us, the readers informed by accompanying commentator, as involving a complex series of embedded inferential connections.

21. The three pure essentialities for the *Phenomenology* are those of unity, difference and relation. See ¶363, p. 219, *PG*, p. 264.

22. ¶111, p. 67; *PG*, p. 89: "Perception takes that which exists (*das Seiende*) for it as a universal."

23. See ¶112, pp. 67–68; *PG*, p. 90.

24. ¶112, p. 67, *PG*, p. 90: "Since the principle of the object, the universal, is in its simplicity a *mediated* universal, the object must express this as its nature in it. It does this by showing itself to be *the thing with many properties*. The wealth of sensuous knowledge belongs only to perception, not to immediate certainty, for which it played only a subsidiary role (*an der er nur das Beiherspeielende war*); for only perception contains *negation* – that is, difference or manifoldness, within its own essence".

25. ¶113, p. 68, *PG*, p. 90: "Consequently, the sense-element is still present, but not in the way it was supposed to be in immediate certainty: not as the individual that is meant but as a universal or as that which will be determined as a *property*."

26. See ¶113, p. 68; *PG*, pp. 90–91.

27. ¶113, p. 68; *PG*, p. 91, in which Hegel says that the thing is an "abstract universal medium . . . thinghood or pure essence."

28. See ¶113, pp. 68–69; *PG*, p. 91.

29. ¶113, p. 68, *PG*, p. 91.

30. ¶121, p. 74; *PG*, pp. 95–96: "The thing is in this way raised to the level of a genuine 'also,' since it becomes merely an enclosing surface." Charles Taylor in his "The Opening Arguments of the *Phenomenology*," p. 169, claims that this introduction of the idea of "free matters" is a reference to "a concept connected with one of the false starts of physics of the late-eighteenth century, e.g., the attempt to account for heat by 'calorific matter.' "

31. ¶114, p. 69; *PG*, p. 92.

32. ¶115, p. 69; *PG*, p. 92: "In these moments taken together the thing, as the truth of perception, is completed insofar as it is necessary to develop it here. It is (α) the indifferent, passive universality, the *also* of the many properties or rather *matters;* (β) negation likewise as simple; or the *one*, the *excluding* of opposed properties; and (γ) the many *properties* themselves, the relation of the two first moments – the negation, as it is related to that indifferent element, and in this relation expanding into a set of differences, the point of individuality in the medium of subsistence (*Bestehens*) radiating forth into plurality."

33. See ¶117, pp. 70–71; *PG*, pp. 93–94.

34. "Things themselves are thus determinate *in and for themselves;* they have properties by which they distinguish themselves from one another." ¶120, pp. 72–73; *PG*, p. 96.

35. This seems to be the point of his discussion in ¶119, p. 72; *PG*, p. 95: "So in point of fact, the thing is white only in *our eyes, also* tart to *our* tongue, *also* cubical to *our* touch, and so on. We get the entire diversity of these aspects not from the thing but from ourselves . . . We are thus the *universal medium* in which such moments separate themselves and are for themselves."

36. ¶120, pp. 72–73; *PG*, p. 96: "It is, then, in truth the thing itself which is white, and *also* cubical, and *also* tart, and so on; in other words, the *thing* is the 'also,' the general medium, in which the many properties subsist externally to one another,

without touching or affecting one another, and without integrating (*aufzuheben*) one another; and, so taken, the thing is taken as the truth (*das Wahre*)."

37. See ¶¶118-119, pp. 71-72; *PG*, pp. 94-95.

38. ¶119, p. 72; *PG*, p. 95: "To begin with, then, I am aware of the thing as a *one* and have to keep it fixed in this true determination. If in the movement of perception something comes forth contradicting that, then it is known to be due to my reflection. Now, in perception various different properties also turn up, which seem to be properties of the thing. But the thing is a one; and we are aware in ourselves that this diversity, by which the thing ceases to be a unity, falls in us."

39. As Hegel puts it, the thing is "reflected into itself; it is for itself, but it is also for others." ¶123, pp. 74-75; *PG*, p. 97.

40. Hegel's term for the non-relational feature of the thing's oneness is the thing's "absolute character." ¶125, pp. 75-76; *PG*, p. 99.

41. ¶123, p. 74; *PG*, p. 97: "The thing is a *one*, reflected into itself; it is *for itself*, but it is also *for an other;* and, further, it is an other for itself *as* it is for an other. The thing is hence for itself and *also* for another, a doubly differentiated being (*gedoppeltes verschiedenes Sein*), but it is also *one*."

42. This is the upshot of the discussion in ¶124, p. 75; *PG*, p. 98, in which the thing's oneness as its "being-for-self" is contrasted with its makeup or constitution (its *Beschaffenheit*).

43. ¶127, p. 76, *PG*, p. 99: "This however is a difference which only lies in the words."

44. ¶127, p. 76; *PG*, p. 99: "With this, the last 'insofar' falls away; on the contrary, the object *is in one and the same respect the opposite of itself: it is for itself, so far as it is for another, and it is for another, so far as it is for itself.*"

45. ¶130, p. 77; *PG*, p. 100: "But these two contradictory extremes are not merely *alongside each other* but in a single unity, or in other words, what is common to both, being-for-self, is burdened with opposition in general, i.e., it is at the same time *not* a being-for-self." ¶131, p. 77; *PG*, pp. 100-101: "These empty abstractions of individuality and a universality opposed to it, and of an essence that is linked with something unessential – a non-essential aspect which is necessary all the same – these are powers whose interplay is the perceptual understanding, often called 'sound common sense.'" In his piece, "Hegel on Reference and Knowledge," Willem deVries makes an illuminating comparison between Hegel's views of perceptual knowledge and Bertrand Russell's defense of the idea that we must be directly acquainted with things like universals in order for perceptual knowledge to be possible. See pp. 304-305.

46. In an influential article – "Predication and Hegel's Metaphysics," reprinted in Michael Inwood (ed.) *Hegel* (Oxford: Oxford University Press, 1985). pp. 67-84 – Richard Aquila holds that Hegel's metaphysics, including his views on the relation of universals and particulars, presupposes his theory of predication, which, of course, is developed and worked out in the *Science of Logic*. If that is true, then by extrapolation, the arguments in the *Phenomenology* should presuppose the arguments about predication in the *Logic*. But if Hegel's project is to work on the terms that Hegel sets for it, then the arguments in the *Phenomenology* should not presuppose any arguments about predication at all; at best they should rather help to develop them. In my reconstruction of Hegel's arguments, I have tried to show how the argument in, for example, "Perception," does not depend on any theory of predication but simply on what it would take for those who claim that we have immediate perceptual knowledge to make good on that claim – that

is, without presupposing anything except what the proponents of such a claim would themselves have to presuppose. Part of the point of my own exposition is to give an alternative to Aquila's views.

47. "Consciousness has not yet grasped the concept of the unconditioned as *concept* . . . consciousness is not yet *for itself* the concept, and consequently does not know (*erkennt*) itself in that reflected object." ¶132, p. 79, *PG*, p. 103.

48. ¶132, p. 79; *PG*, p. 103: "In the dialectic of sense-certainty, seeing and hearing, etc. have been lost to consciousness; and, as perception, consciousness has arrived at thoughts, which it brings together for the first time in the unconditioned universal." See also ¶134; *PG*, pp. 103–104.

49. See ¶¶134–135, pp. 80–81; *PG*, pp. 103–104.

50. ¶136, p. 83; *PG*, p. 106: "The movement which previously displayed itself as the self-destruction of contradictory concepts thus here has *objective* form and is the movement of force, the outcome of which is the unconditioned universal as something *non-objective*, or as the *internality* (*Innres*) of things." In his *Encyclopedia* (§418, *Anmerkung*), Hegel says in reference to the corresponding section: "there the object is lowered or raised to being the *appearance* (*Erscheinung*) of an internality existing for itself (*für sich seienden Inneren*)."

51. See ¶137, p. 83; *PG*, pp. 106–107.

52. ¶136, p. 81, *PG*, p. 105: "In other words, the matters posited as independent immediately pass over into their unity, and their unity immediately passes over into its development, and this development again passes back over into its reduction. But this movement is what is called *force*. One of its moments, the dispersal of the independent matters in their being, is the *expression* of force; but force, taken as that in which they have disappeared, is *authentic* force, force which has been driven back into itself from its expression."

53. ¶136, p. 82, *PG*, p. 105: "Force is the unconditioned universal which is equally in itself what it is *for an other;* or which contains the difference in it itself (*an ihm selbst*) – for difference is nothing else than being-*for-an-other*."

54. *Encyclopedia*, §136, *Remark*.

55. Part of Hegel's argument both in the *Phenomenology* and in the *Encyclopedia* is that the distinction of knowable expression and unknowable metaphysical force is untenable. In the *Encyclopedia*, for example, he notes: "One is accustomed to saying that the *nature of force* itself is *unknown* and only its expression is known. On the one hand, the whole *determination of content of force* is the same as that of the expression; the explanation of an appearance by a force is thus an empty tautology. What is supposed to remain unknown is therefore in fact nothing else than the empty form of reflection-in-self, by which alone the force is differentiated from the expression." (§135, my translation).

56. Apparently because of his longstanding and idiosyncratic desire to argue that Newton had only restated Kepler's laws in mathematical form – and thus to vindicate the originality of his fellow Swabian, Kepler, against the Englishman, Newton – Hegel consistently misunderstood Newton's explanation of motion. Hegel thought Newton explained planetary motion as the result of the combination of two forces, centripetal and centrifugal forces, one pulling the planet away from its orbit (away from the star), the other pulling it into its orbit (toward the star). But Newton did not believe that, holding as he did there is only one force, centripetal, which, combined with the principle of inertia, accounts for the orbits. (One need not postulate a force to explain why something continues in a uniform rectilinear motion; one need only explain why it does not. One need only explain,

that is, why the planet continues in its orbit, not why it would otherwise go off in a uniform rectilinear path.) Hegel apparently held on to a more or less Aristotelian conception of matter and motion, according to which weight is an essential property of matter, and a moving body requires some force to cause it to move, its natural state being that of rest. These misconceptions reappeared in Hegel's later "Philosophy of Nature," part of his mature *Encyclopedia of the Philosophical Sciences.* Hegel's mistakes in this regard as well as the intellectual influences of his time (including Newton's own ambiguous formulations of the idea of "force") that would have led Hegel to such a view are treated in William R. Shea, "Hegel's Celestial Mechanics" (pp. 30–44), and Franz H. van Lunteren, "Hegel and Gravitation" (pp. 45–53) in Rolf-Peter Horstmann and Michael J. Petry (editors) *Hegels Philosophie der Natur: Beziehungen zwischen empirischer und spekulativer Naturerkenntnis* (Stuttgart: Ernst Klett Verlag, 1986). For the ways in which Hegel attempted to conciliate the older view and what he understood of modern mechanics (which he valued quite highly), see Michael J. Petry's detailed commentary accompanying his translation of Hegel's philosophy of nature in: M.J. Petry, *Hegel's Philosophy of Nature* (London: George Allen and Unwin, 1970) Vol. I.

57. Johann Herder posited a very generalized metaphysical conception of force as the explanation of the determinateness of appearance. Hegel parenthetically discusses Herder's idea of force in his discussion of Jacobi in an early piece, *Faith and Knowledge (Glauben und Wissen,* in *Werke,* vol. 2, pp. 357–359). In Hegel's understanding, Herder posited a unitary primordial force (*Urkraft*) in place of Spinoza's substance. Hegel notes, "The concept of power, like the concepts of matter and thought, says Herder, develop into (i.e., are entangled in) a concept of a primordial force, all three, according to the Spinozistic system, collapsing into each other – the eternal primordial force, the force of all forces is only *one.*" (p. 358) Hegel also remarks on this in his *Encyclopedia* version of the *Logic* when he discusses force. There he notes that Herder errs in understanding God as a force whose expressions can be known but who cannot be known himself. (§136) That Herder is at least one of the main objects of Hegel's criticism in the *Phenomenology* may be seen by comparing what Hegel says about those who hold such a view of force with what Herder says, for example, in his *Ideen zur Philosophie der Geschichte der Menschheit,* in Herder, *Werke* (Frankfurt a.M.: Deutscher Klassiker Verlag, 1989), vol. 6, pp. 167–168: "Either we must view these things as nature's playing (and the nature belonging to the kingdom of understanding never senselessly plays), or we will be driven to accept a *kingdom of invisible forces,* which stand in the very same precise context and dense transitions as we perceive in external structures. The more we come to know nature, the more we note these *indwelling forces* even in the lowest creations, moss, fungi, etc."

58. The argument about force soliciting itself and also not being an "entity" occurs in ¶137, p. 83, *PG,* p. 106–107 in a very dense paragraph, part of which goes like this: "Force as it has been determined, since it is represented as such or as reflected into itself is one side of its concept, but it is posited as a substantialized extreme and indeed is posited as falling under the determinateness of being a 'one' (*unter der Bestimmtheit des Eins*). Consequently, the *subsistence* of the developed matters is thus excluded from force and is something other than force. Since it is necessary that force *itself* be this subsistence, or that it *express* itself, its expression presents itself in this manner, that the other approaches it and solicits it. But, as a matter of fact, since its expression is *necessary,* what is posited as

another essence is in force itself. It must be taken back that force is posited as a one (*Eins*), and that its essence is to express itself as an other which approaches it externally. Force is rather itself this universal medium in which the moments subsist as matters; or, in other words, force *has expressed itself,* and what was supposed to be something else soliciting it really is force itself . . . The 'being-one' (*Einssein*) disappears, *as* it appeared, namely as an *other; it is force itself,* it is the force driven back into itself." (Incidentally, this passage displays one of the ways in which Miller's translation of the *Phenomenology of Spirit* can occasionally be misleading, since in it he translates *"vorgestellt"* as "conceived," thus obliterating for the English language reader Hegel's careful distinction between representational understanding and conceptual understanding.)

59. This idea of passive and active forces apparently comes from Leibniz. The idea had to do with reconciling the presumed "inertness" of matter with the idea of inertia. Leibniz saw the division as necessary because of his belief that bodies are not indifferent to motion but resist it in proportion to their size (since it obviously takes more force to move a large body than a small one.) See William R. Shea, "Hegel's Celestial Mechanics." p. 38.

60. Hegel develops this so-called formal argument in one paragraph, although, as it turns out, several paragraphs later he retracts it; the point of making such an argument, only to retract it within a few pages, is to illustrate how this kind of move to a supersensible determining ground for appearance logically develops to look for more basic and "deeper" grounds for the determinateness of appearance. Hegel makes the argument in ¶¶140–141; he retracts it in ¶148, pp. 89–90; *PG,* pp. 113–114.

61. This argument occurs in ¶¶140–141, p. 85; *PG,* pp. 108–110. I call it a "formal argument" because Hegel notes in ¶140 that the differences between the forces are differences of form and differences of content. The differences of content are those of being "force reflected into itself" (that is, being a "one") and force as the "medium of the matters." The difference of form is that between active and passive, soliciting and solicited. The formal difference, he notes, makes the forces independent of each other.

62. See ¶141, pp. 85–86; *PG,* pp. 109–110. Hegel there even whimsically notes that this conception of force is "the loss of reality (*Realität*); it has therein become something wholly other, namely this universality, which the understanding first or immediately recognizes as its essence and which proves to be its essence in its striving to be a reality (*an ihrer seinsollenden Realität*), in its actual substances." As always, Hegel means by "essence" here "that which is authoritative for the understanding's claims to knowledge."

63. ¶143, p. 86; *PG,* p. 110.

64. Hegel uses the phrase, "curtain of appearance," in ¶165, p. 102–103; *PG,* pp. 128–129.

65. See the first half of ¶143, pp. 86–87; *PG,* p. 110.

66. ¶144, p. 87; *PG,* p. 111: ". . . there now opens up above the *sensuous* world, which is the world of *appearance,* a *supersensible* world, which henceforth is the true world . . ."

67. See ¶147, p. 89; *PG,* p. 113.

68. ¶148, p. 90; *PG,* p. 114. Hegel also calls it the "simple difference," because as a unity, it is different from *all* the multiplicity of appearance – that is, it is the "simple difference" because it expresses the difference between the "universal" (the unity) and the "particular" (the multiplicity of appearance).

69. ¶149, p. 91; *PG,* p. 115.
70. One obvious source for this for Hegel would have been Schelling's *System des transzendentalen Idealismus* published in 1800. In the section of that book entitled "Deduction of Matter," Schelling claims to deduce out of purely transcendental grounds the basic kinds of opposed forces necessary to "construct" matter. See Schelling, *Werke,* ed. by Manfred Schröter (Munich: E.B. Beck Verlagsbuchhandlung, 1927, vol. 2), pp. 440–450.
71. See ¶150, p. 91; *PG,* pp. 115.-116
72. "But this plurality is itself rather a defect; for it contradicts the principle of the understanding for which, as consciousness of the simple inner world, the true is the implicitly universal *unity.* It must therefore let the many laws collapse into *one* law, just as, e.g., the law by which a stone falls, and the law by which the heavenly bodies move, have been grasped as one law." ¶150, p. 91; *PG,* p. 115. Hegel's references are to the laws of attraction and to their relation to gravitation. (However, the reference here is perhaps also to Kant's construction of the concept of matter out of the laws of attraction and repulsion, a construction that Hegel criticizes in his *Science of Logic* and his "philosophy of nature.") See M.J. Petry's helpful notes to Hegel's discussion of Newton's laws in his translation and commentary on Hegel's philosophy of nature in M.J. Petry, *Hegel's Philosophy of Nature* (London: George Allen and Unwin Ltd., 1970).
73. See the closing sentence of ¶151, p.92; *PG,* p. 116: "The pure concept of law as universal attraction must, to get its true meaning, be grasped in such a way that in it, as the absolutely simple, the differences which are present in law as such themselves return again *into the internality (in das Innere) as a simple unity.* This unity is the inner *necessity* of the law." Once again, Hegel seems to be showing how the invocation of these metaphysical laws in the "philosophy of nature" of his day spuriously modeled itself on the way in which, for example, scientific mechanics had unified certain laws.
74. See M.J. Petry, *The Berlin Phenomenology,* (Dordrecht: D. Reidel Publishing Co., 1981). pp. 145–146 for examples of this.
75. See ¶153, pp. 93–94; *PG,* p. 118.
76. See ¶154, pp. 94–95; *PG,* p. 118–119, particularly the sentences: "The understanding *has* however the concept of *this difference-in-itself,* precisely in that the law on the one hand is the inner, the *existing-in-itself (Ansichseiende),* but *in it (an ihm)* is at the same time that which is differentiated. That this difference is consequently *inner* difference is present in that the law is *simple* force or, as the concept of it, is thus a difference belonging to the concept (*Unterschied des Begriffes*). But this inner difference at first only falls in the understanding, and it is not yet posited as being in the thing (*Sache*) itself. It is thus its *own* necessity that the understanding expresses."
77. See the last half of ¶154 and the first half of ¶155, pp. 94–95; *PG,* pp. 119–120. Hegel there also notes that this is the same kind of spurious argumentation that first claimed that conceptual grounds require that there be at least two forces, only to find later that it needed to retract that argument, again on so-called conceptual grounds.
78. ¶156, pp. 95–96, *PG,* p. 120: "The understanding thus *learns* that it is a *law* of *appearance* itself, that differences arise which are no differences, or that which is the same(*das Gleichnamige*) repels itself from itself; and similarly, the differences are only such as are in truth no differences, which integrate (*aufheben*) themselves; in other words, that which is not the same (*das Ungleichnamige*) attracts

itself." (Translating the term *"Gleichnamige"* is difficult; one of its meanings, however, is the mathematical sense of being the common denominator.) (Hegel is apparently referring in this passage to the law of electromagnetism, according to which similar poles will repel each other, and different poles will attract each other. This interpretation of the passage is given by Heinrichs, *Die Logik der ⟨Phänomenologie des Geistes⟩*, p. 158.)

79. Compare this with one of Schelling's basic theses: "Since these forces are forces of one and the same identical subject, nature, they must thus not be able to be merely relatively opposed to each other, they must be absolutely opposed." §6 of his *Allgemeine Deduktion des dynamischen Prozesses oder der Kategorien der Physik,* published in 1800, cited in Schelling, *Werke,* vol. 2, p. 639. (my translation.) (The work cited was conceived by Schelling as an extension of the arguments of his *System des transzendentalen Idealismus.*)

80. ¶157, p. 96; *PG,* p. 121.

81. See Roger Chartier, "The World Turned Upside Down," in *Cultural History,* transl. Lydia G. Cochrane (Ithaca: Cornell University Press, 1988). pp. 116–126. The themes pursued in the images of the inverted world were not merely for entertainment value but had a moral point to them. Chartier, for example, discusses how themes concerning sex-roles appear (the wife goes hunting, the husband stays home to care for the children), and he speculates that the point of these images were to reinforce the prevailing social roles by giving the impression that women doing men's tasks would be parallel to the hare hunting the hunter – that is, would be fully absurd. Donald Philip Verene in his *Hegel's Recollections: A Study of Images in the Phenomenology of Spirit* (Albany: State University of New York Press, 1985) hypothesizes that Hegel takes the name from an obscure and unperformed play by Ludwig Tieck in 1797. (See pp. 50–53.) There is, however, no need to think that he got it from this play, since the term was already in wide use as the name for the type of engravings and as a popular term for things felt to be "crazy."

82. Hegel was very taken with Kant's antinomies and how he thought they displayed the limits of philosophy based on the "understanding." Sally Sedgwick offers a detailed explanation and defense of Hegel's understanding of the Kantian antinomies in her "Hegel on Kant's Antinomies and Distinction Between General and Transcendental Logic," in *The Monist,* 74, no. 3, 1991. pp. 403–420.

83. See ¶164, p. 102; *PG,* p. 127: ". . . but once again the understanding falls short of infinity as such, since it again apportions to two worlds or to two substantial elements that which is a difference in itself – the self-repulsion of that which is the same *(des Gleichnamigen)* and the self-attraction of the unlike. To the understanding, the *movement,* as it is found in experience, is here a happening, and that which is the same and that which is unlike are *predicates,* whose essence is an existing substrate. What for the understanding is an object in a sensuous covering is for us in its essential formation as the pure concept."

84. See ¶160, pp. 98–99; *PG,* p. 124. Hegel announces in the first sentence of this paragraph his conclusion: "From the representation thus of inversion, which constitutes the essence of one aspect of the supersensible world, we must eliminate the sensuous representation of fixing the differences in a different element of subsistence *(Elemente des Bestehens)*; and this absolute concept of the difference must be presented and grasped as purely as inner difference, a repulsion from itself of that which is the same *(Gleichnamigen)* as that which is the same, and the equality *(Gleichsein)* of the unlike as unlike." In other words, the oppositions

which were taken to be features of things in themselves (for example, of "that which is the same" as dividing itself into two contrasting forces) are really features of "the understanding," of the way in which it describes and contrasts things.

85. "Infinite" in Hegel's sense (as he explains it, for example, in his *Science of Logic*) always refers to some self-enclosed "circle" of determinations such that an item's conditions are all present. The opposite of "infinite" is "finite" – that is, having the determinateness of an entity come from outside this circle, as having its conditions outside of itself. For example, a finite syllogism would be one whose soundness depends on other syllogisms. "Infinite" also stands in Hegel's parlance negatively for absence of determination by a metaphysical other and positively for the idea of self-determination. To be infinite in Hegel's sense is thus not to be "boundless" but to be *self-limiting*. His major thesis is, of course, that only conceptual structures can be infinite in this sense. Only in a self-enclosed system of inferences is true "infinity" in this sense achieved. This point about Hegel's sense of "infinity" is also made by Willem deVries, *Hegel's Theory of Mental Activity*, pp. 193-194, although deVries ties this into a more metaphysical interpretation of Hegel's thought than that given here.

86. Bound up with the view that our dealings with the world are mediated through these representations is the idea that the world is composed of substances and their accidents. This comes from reflecting on language as a representational *medium*. When that is done, the subject-predicate form of the proposition is then taken to be a representation – a *Vorstellung* – of a substance and an accident. For these reasons, Hegel thinks that ordinary reflection on language as a way of doing philosophy leads directly to the old metaphysics that he is trying to overcome. Hegel often expresses this idea somewhat misleadingly by saying that the proposition is inadequate for the expression of speculative thought, thus suggesting to some that he must be relying on some kind of dubious non-linguistic "intuition" to express some esoteric truth. However, by this he means that reflecting on the proposition as a *Vorstellung* of reality – something to which "the understanding" is prone – necessarily leads one to a substance/accident metaphysics. Both doctrines – the metaphysics of substance and accident and the idea that the subject/predicate proposition is a representation of reality – are riddled with incoherences and contradictions, which are developed both in the first three chapters of the *Phenomenology* and later in the section on essence in the *Science of Logic*. For example, if one reflects on what such a substance is, one is quickly led to the empty idea of an "I know not what"; if one reflects on how a subject term works, one is led to idea of terms that merely point to indeterminate individuals. Hegel's point is to move us away entirely from thinking about language as a *Vorstellung* and rather to understand it in terms of its embodying *concepts* – that is, to understand ourselves as social concept-users – as participants in social practice – rather than as individual "representers." By doing this, Hegel moves us away from understanding ourselves in terms of the dualisms of "Consciousness" (such as the dualism of "subject" and "object") and instead to understanding ourselves in terms of *spirit* – that is, in terms of the essential self-understandings involved in social space. In *Wahrheit aus dem Begriff: eine Einführung in Hegel* (Frankfurt a.M.: Anton Hain, 1990), Rolf-Peter Horstmann makes a similar point about Hegel's critique of the subject-predicate proposition having to do with his critique of representational thought (*Vorstellung*). But, so it would seem, Horstmann does not draw the conclusion that therefore we ought to give up a representationalist

model. (In making this point, I am playing on the distinction between the German word *"Vorstellung"* and the English word "representation.") Horstmann takes Hegel's project to be that of determining what "in truth" things are. The problem is that if one believes that the form of the judgment leads to a contradictory metaphysics, then one cannot rely on the judgmental form to produce a better metaphysics; but if one nonetheless has to express one's ontological conclusions in propositional form, then one has a certain dilemma: "If one does not wish to simply leave the dilemma at that and thereby abandon philosophy's claim to knowledge of what exists in truth, then with Hegel one has a possibility to solve that problem: one renounces the assumption of the ontological implications of the judgmental form *(des Urteils)*, then clarifies the question of what objects "in truth" are and what "in truth" there is, and then develops a thesis about the connection between ontology and judgments." (p. 40) Following this idea out, Horstmann argues that Hegel resolves this by developing a system in which "[t]hat which an object in truth is, is the concept of the object, not its representation *(Vorstellung)*" and "[c]oncepts must be thought of as unities of incompatible determinations, that is, as organismic *(Organismusartig)* and, to be sure, conforming to a model which asserts that the essential characteristic of organismic entities is what Hegel calls 'subjectivity.'" (p. 75) This ingenious reading of Hegel (whose carefully worked out steps I am obviously leaving out), however, assumes that what Hegel is intending is a better *representation* of reality than a mere "representation" *(Vorstellung)* of it could produce. But, so I have argued here, Hegel is trying, especially in the first three chapters of the *Phenomenology of Spirit,* to undermine *all* representationalist models. Language, judgements, and so on are all social means by which that peculiar organism, the human subject, deals with the world and with other subjects. Agents do not represent the world in any metaphysical sense of "representation"; rather, they deal with the world in terms of a complex self-understanding of where they fit into that world, both physically and socially. It is to the dialectic of those self-understandings (of spirit) that Hegel wishes to direct our philosophical reflections.

87. In his lectures on the history of philosophy, Hegel notes that the modern set of philosophical problems is dominated by a set of oppositions that philosophical theories seek to overcome or to reconcile. He mentions four such oppositions that play a central role in philosophical debate, which, he notes, do not play such a central role in ancient philosophy. They are (1) the existence of God and the concept of God; (2) the origin of evil, given God's supposed omniscience and omnipotence; (3) freedom and necessity (which itself is divided into problems of freedom versus God's omniscience, freedom versus natural necessity, and efficient versus formal causation); (4) the relation between mind and body. Hegel explains the domination of this kind of oppositional thought in modern philosophy as due to the influence of the Christian religion on the worldview of the moderns. It is with Christianity that these oppositions are either engendered or sharpened so that they become *the* philosophical problems of the culture. Likewise, the Christian promise of reconciliation *(Versöhnung)* is the basis for the philosophical community's belief that some kind of resolution of these problems is the major task of philosophical thought in the modern period. Also for this reason, modern philosophical theories tend to divide along the lines of realism or idealism. See *Vorlesungen über die Geschichte der Philosophie, Werke,* vol. 20, pp. 66–69.

Chapter Three

1. See ¶166, p. 104; *PG,* p. 133.
2. See ¶167, pp. 104–105; *PG,* p. 134: "The *being* appropriate to just attending to things (*Sein der Meinung*), the *individuality* and the *universality* set in opposition to it of perception, as well as the *empty internality* of the understanding no longer exist as essences but rather as moments of self-consciousness, i.e., as abstractions or differences which at the same time *for* consciousness itself are nothing or are no differences and are pure disappearing essences."
3. See ¶167, p. 105; *PG,* p. 134: "It seems thus that the principal moment itself is lost, namely, the *simple independent subsistence* for consciousness. However, in fact, self-consciousness is the reflection out of the being of the sensuous and perceived world and essentially the return out of *being-other* (*Anderssein*)."
4. For a similar understanding of Hegel's conception of self-consciousness, see Willem deVries, *Hegel's Theory of Mental Activity,* chapter 6, pp. 87–107.
5. Hegel's description of organic life in ¶169, pp. 106–107; *PG,* p. 135–136 is short and extremely metaphorical, but I take this to be the gist of it. Even he notes the brevity of his characterization, and, perhaps surprisingly for the reader, thinks that it is quite enough. He remarks that at the beginning of that paragraph, "The determination of life as it has issued from the concept or the general result with which we enter this sphere is sufficient to characterize it without having further to develop its nature."
6. See ¶171, p. 107; *PG,* pp. 137–138. In ¶173 and the first sentence of ¶174, p. 109; *PG,* pp. 138–139, Hegel also draws an analogy to the way in which life develops itself into genera and individuals and the way in which we develop a conception of the "I" in dealing with the world: the "I" is the "genus" of the various seemingly independent moments of consciousness.
7. I take this to be the argument of the first half of ¶168, p. 106; *PG,* p. 135.
8. See ¶174, p. 109; *PG,* p. 139.
9. This seems to be the argument of the first half of ¶175, p. 109; *PG,* p. 139.
10. It should be noted that the sense of "recognition" in the German term (*Anerkennung*) is not that of the psychological sense of recognition, such as that involved in recognizing an old friend walking down the street; it is the sense of recognition in the way that one state recognizes another, or the way in which we recognize somebody for his lofty achievements.
11. Hegel's argument for this is extremely condensed, occurring basically in half of a paragraph; my account here is a reconstruction of the following: "On account of the independence of the object, therefore, it can achieve satisfaction only when the object itself performs the negation on it (*"indem dieser selbst die Negation an ihm vollzieht"*); and it must perform the negation of itself in itself, for it is *in itself* the negative and must be *for* the other what it is. Since the object is in own itself (*an sich selbst*) negation, and therein is at the same time independent, it is consciousness. In the sphere of life, which is the object of desire, *negation* is present either *in an other,* namely, in desire or as a *determinateness* opposed to another indifferent form or as the inorganic universal nature of life. But this universal independent nature in which negation is present as absolute negation is the genus as such or the genus as *self-consciousness."* ¶175, pp. 109–110, *PG,* p. 139.
12. See ¶176, p. 110, *PG,* pp. 139–140. This is a reconstruction of Hegel's short three-point summary there of his argument for why self-consciousness can only be satisfied in another self-consciousness.

13. *"Self-consciousness achieves its satisfaction only in another self-consciousness."* ¶175, p. 110; *PG,* p. 139. (Hegel himself underscores the whole sentence.)
14. "A self-consciousness is *for a self-consciousness.* Only so is it in fact a self-consciousness; for only in this way does the unity of itself in its otherness (*Anderssein*) come to be for it . . . A self-consciousness, in being an object, is just as much an I as an object. With this, we already have before us the concept of *spirit.* What still lies ahead for consciousness is the experience of what spirit is – this absolute substance, which, in the complete freedom and independence of its opposites – namely different self-consciousnesses existing for themselves – is their unity: the *I* that is *We,* and the *We* that is *I.*" ¶177, p. 110, *PG,* p. 140. See also ¶178, p. 111; *PG,* p. 141: "Self-consciousness is *in* and *for itself* when and because it is in and for itself for an other; i.e., it *is* only as something recognized."
15. See ¶178, p. 111; *PG,* p. 140. Hegel gives his most succinct definition of being-for-self (*Fürsichsein*) as the following: "If we determine being-for-self as *simple self-maintaining relation to itself* (*einfache sich erhaltende Beziehung auf sich selbst*), then its being-other (*Anderssein*) is simple *negativity.*" ¶291, p. 175; *PG,* p. 216.
16. See ¶179, p. 111; *PG,* p. 141.
17. See ¶180, p. 111; *PG,* p. 141.
18. These complexities are developed in ¶¶182–185, pp. 11–113; *PG,* p. 142–143.
19. In his lectures on the corresponding section of his *Encyclopedia* – published as *The Berlin Phenomenology* (translated and edited by M. J. Petry) (Dordrecht: D. Reidel Publishing Co., 1981) – Hegel comments explicitly on the way this account abstracts from all social relations: "At this present standpoint we have to completely forget the relationships (*Verhältnisse*) we are used to thinking about. If we speak of right, ethicality, love, we know that in that we recognize the others, I recognize their complete personal independence. We know too that I do not suffer on this account, but have validity as a free being, that in that the others have rights I have them too, or that my right is also essentially that of the other i.e. that I am a free person, and that this is essentially the same as the others also being persons with rights. Benevolence or love does not involve the submergence of my personality. Here, however, there is as yet no such relationship, for one aspect of the determination is that of my still being, as a free self-consciousness, an immediate and single one. In so far as the immediate singularity of my self-consciousness and my freedom are not yet separated, I am unable to surrender anything of my particularity without surrendering my free independence." §431, p. 77.
20. See ¶186, p. 113; *PG,* p. 143, which begins with the statement: "Self-consciousness is at first simple being-for-self, identical with itself (*sichselbstgleich*) through the exclusion out of itself of everything *other.*"
21. See the last half of ¶186, p. 113; *PG,* pp. 143–144.
22. ¶186, p. 113; *PG,* p. 144.
23. This is how I understand what Hegel means when he says, ¶186, p. 113; *PG,* p. 143: "Each is indeed certain of its own self but not of the other, and therefore its own certainty of self still has no truth. For it would have truth only if its own being-for-self had confronted it as an independent object, or, what is the same thing, if the object had presented itself as this pure self-certainty."
24. ¶187, p. 114; *PG,* p. 144: ". . . rather that in it is nothing present that would not be for it a disappearing moment, that it is a pure *being-for-self.*"
25. ¶187, p. 114; *PG,* p. 144: "And it is only through staking one's life that freedom is won; only thus is it proved that for self-consciousness, its essence is not *being,* not

the *immediate* manner in which it makes its appearance, not its submergence in the expanse of life . . ."

26. See ¶188, p. 114; *PG*, p. 145. There Hegel claims that in the death of one of the participants, ". . . they are cancelled out (*aufgehoben*) as *extremes* wanting to be for-themselves. But with this there vanishes from their interplay the essential moment of splitting into extremes with opposed determinatenesses; and the middle term collapses into a lifeless unity which is split into dead, merely existing (*seiende*) non-opposed extremes." In this passage, Hegel is again, as he does throughout his system, relying on the model of the syllogism to explicate the argument he is making. The two self-conscious agents with their own subjective points of view are two "extremes," like the major and the minor terms of a syllogism, and they could be mediated only by a third term (which, in the case, would be the "universal," the objective point of view). But if they destroy the possibility of this "third term," then they also destroy the possibility of any mediation between them. Therefore, the death of one of the participants cannot function as a resolution of the problem.

27. See ¶189, p. 115; *PG*, p. 145. Hegel notes there that ". . . since they are at first unequal and opposed and their reflection into the unity has not yet been achieved . . ." I take the "reflection into the unity" as Hegel's reference to the "universal," that is, the impersonal point of view.

28. I take this to be the point of Hegel's talking about the slave's working over and preparing things for the master in the last third of ¶190, p. 116; *PG*, pp. 146–147.

29. This is Hegel's argument in ¶191, p. 116; *PG*, p. 147, which he concludes by noting that the recognition achieved between master and slave is "one-sided and unequal."

30. See ¶192, pp. 116–117; *PG*, p. 147.

31. Hegel says that the slave's consciousness "at first appears as *external* to itself and not as the truth of self-consciousness." This notion of its being "external" to itself is the Hegelian way of saying that the slave's subjectivity – his subjective point of view – appears to be dependent on something outside itself (the master's subjective point of view) for its criteria of what counts as a good reason for belief and action. ¶193, p. 117; *PG*, p. 147.

32. In confronting his anxiety about his existence and the fear of death, the slave's consciousness ". . . is therein inwardly (*innerlich*) broken up, it has throughout trembled within itself, and everything fixed has been shaken loose." ¶194, p. 117; *PG*, p. 148.

33. This is the point of the dense section in ¶195, pp. 117–118; *PG*, pp. 148–149. Hegel says that the master's satisfactions are "vanishing" because they lack the element of "subsistence." The slave's work, on the other hand, is "detained vanishing." Through the mediating activity of work, the slave acquires a being-for-self that is "external to him" in that work (that is, he sees that the natural things of the world count only to the extent that he forms them so that they count).

34. In his lectures on this transition in the corresponding sections of the later *Encyclopedia*, Hegel finesses this a bit. In order to preserve his dominant social role in light of the slave's growing independence, the master has to learn to give reasonable orders to the slave, thus implicitly recognizing the slave as an independent rational agent: "Whoever wants to command must do so reasonably, for only he who commands reasonably will be obeyed. . . . Command involves understanding how to avoid what is preposterous and absurd, and knowing what is universal

involves the renunciation of the singularity of self-consciousness." *Berlin Phenomenology*, §435.

35. See ¶194, p. 117; *PG*, p. 148.

36. See ¶197, pp. 119–121; *PG*, pp. 151–152. Hegel claims in that section that such thinking is not a matter of *representing* things (not a matter of *Vorstellungen*) but is rather a matter of *concepts* (*Begriffe*). I take this difference to be that between merely asserting statements as representations of the world ("The figs are ripe") and reflecting on what the ultimate standards are for whether something is to count as knowledge. The truth of *representations* is not something that the subject can determine; once he has decided on what is to count as a standard for deciding what is knowledge, he is not then free to say that he knows this and not that. But he is "free" in the way he can accept or reject what the standards are, and this is a matter of "concepts."

37. See ¶199, p. 121; *PG*, p. 153: "As a universal form of the world-spirit, stoicism could only appear on the scene in the time of universal fear and slavery (*Knechtschaft*), but also at a time of universal cultivation, a cultivating which had raised itself all the way up to thought."

38. In his lectures on the history of philosophy, Hegel is quite emphatic in stressing that for him the principle of stoicism is "[t]he *principle of thought,* that of *universality* itself, understood however as being determined within itself (*in sich*); thought is the criterion of truth, that which is determining." *Werke,* vol. 19, p. 253. He notes the empirical and naturalistic orientation of many stoic philosophers, claiming that this is consistent with his own view of them: "This is the general idea (*allgemeine Vorstellung*) of the stoics. The stoics stick with the universal. It is a universal end: each individual is grasped in one λογος, this is again grasped in a universal λογος, which is itself the κοσμος." (p. 266) Thus, "[T]he stoics held thereby the study of nature to be essential and *useful,* that we know (*erkennen*) the universal laws of nature, the universal reason, in order to know (*erkennen)* from them our duties, the law for people and to live in accordance with the λογος, the laws of nature, to make ourselves correspond to those universal laws." (p. 263) But Hegel attributes this part of stoicism (what he calls its physics) to other aspects of stoicism, particularly its logic and ethics. The highest good of stoic ethics was to live in accordance with nature, which for them is equivalent to living in accordance with reason. This is given a purely formal interpretation: "Thought should determine what is in accordance with nature; being in accordance with nature, however, is only that which is determined through the λογος. This is wholly formal. For what is being in accordance with nature? The λογος – what is the λογος? That which is in accordance with nature." (p. 278). Thus, he plays up stoic *logic,* which he thinks shows what stoicism is really about, namely, the development of the formal determinations of thought. In fact, it was the skeptics who saw that from the stoic formal logic, nothing determinate followed. (See p. 276.)

39. See ¶200, p. 122; *PG*, p. 154: "To the question, *What* is good and true, it again gave for an answer the *contentless* thought: the true and the good shall consist in rationality. But this self-identity (*Sichselbstgleichheit*) of thought is only again the pure form in which nothing is determined." Hegel uses the term *Sichselbstgleichheit* (self-identity) and its cognates almost always to mean, "lack of an apparent contradiction." He notes, for example, in his lectures on the history of philosophy (when he is discussing the stoics): "Their criterion is however formal,

it is the principle of non-contradiction. In the absolute essence there is thus also no contradiction; it is identical with itself (*sich selbst gleich*) but thereby hollow." *Werke,* vol. 19, p. 273. Interestingly, in the lectures on stoicism, Hegel explicitly links this criticism of stoicism with Kant's philosophy, making several paranthetical comparisons between Kant's views and the stoics' views.

40. This kind of skepticism that Hegel is discussing should be distinguished from the more modern type of skepticism familiar to twentieth century Anglo-American philosophers. The latter form of skepticism generally concerns itself with whether anything external to the thinking subject's thoughts can be demonstrated. It is accepted that we have a non-inferential relation to the contents of our own minds – that we know the contents of our own minds with certainty – and it is then doubted if we can be said to know the existence of anything external to those contents with the same certainty. Hegel argues that this is not as thoroughgoing as the more ancient form of skepticism about which he is speaking in the *Phenomenology,* for it places one set of items outside of the sphere of doubt. The modern skeptic presupposes that our self-relation in terms of thinking and reflecting can have a determinateness that is independent of our relation to the world. Thus in so many versions of modern skepticism from Descartes to the latest journals, we have an imagined situation in which the content of our thoughts is said to stay the same while imaginatively the world is seen to vary. However, the dialectical, Hegelian point established in the sections on the subject/object model of knowledge and action is that we cannot identify the contents of our thoughts except in terms of some involvement with the world. Concretely, if we actually varied the world, we would also vary our own thoughts. Thus, for Hegel this more modern form of skepticism rests on the easily acquired illusion that comes from an individual reflecting on his own mental states – namely, the illusion that he has some kind of direct and immediate access to those states, and that those states and his reflection on them can serve as the ground of the determinateness of the appearing world (that we can construct the existence of physical objects or of other minds on the basis of these states). This is an illusion, because the authority of these "internal states" is, like all forms of authority, socially conferred. Their *apparent* immediacy does not consist in some kind of non-inferential relation between the "subject" and a peculiar "object"; it consists in the authority conferred on individual subjects by the community when it comes to talking about their mental states – the community allows such assertions to go unchallenged in ways that it does not allow reports on physical objects to go unchallenged. However, this is not Hegel's concern in this section, so we need not go into it here. Hegel makes this comparison between ancient and modern skepticism quite apparent in his treatment of skepticism in his lectures on the history of philosophy. For example, he notes, "*Ancient* skepticism must be differentiated from the *modern* form; we are only dealing with the former. The new skepticism is rather *epicureanism;* i.e. Schulze in Göttingen and others lay the foundations thusly: one must take sensuous being as true, what sensuous consciousness gives us; we must doubt everything else; what we attend to (*meinen*) is to be the final point." *Werke,* vol. 19, p. 360.

41. See ¶202, p. 123; *PG,* p. 155: "The differences which in the pure thinking of self-consciousness are only the abstraction of differences here come to be *all* the differences, and all differentiated being comes to be a difference of self-consciousness." In other words, the various "differences" or claims to knowledge that, for example, the stoic might feel confident in asserting are seen by the skeptic to be purely contingent, relative claims.

42. See ¶202, p. 123; *PG*, pp. 154–155: "Skepticism is the realization of that of which stoicism was only the concept, and it is the actual experience of what the freedom of thought is . . . It is clear that just as stoicism corresponds to the *concept* of the *independent* consciousness which had appeared as the relationship of master and slave, so skepticism corresponds to its realization as a negative attitude towards being-other (*Anderssein*), to desire and work."

43. Hegel does not mention these "tropes" in the *Phenomenology*, but he greatly expands on this point in his lectures on the history of philosophy where he discusses the various tropes, that is, dialectical moves that skeptics generally make when presented with some claim to truth or certainty. (Hegel notes that he takes the tropes from the writings of Sextus Empiricus.) In classifying them, Hegel argues that the older tropes (for example, moves based on the idea that people of different cultures disagree about what is good or true) are more ad hoc and empirical: "We see in these moves that they really are not logical moves, they do not come from the concept, but rather proceed empirically – immediately against the empirical." *(Werke,* vol. 19, pp. 384–385.) The other later tropes are, however, truly dialectical, in that they concern those positions that "assert something determinate as the absolute" (p. 393), and they then show the logical insufficiency of any such assertion. These try to show that any attempt to set something up as just *given* or simply *presupposed* is bound to fail on its own terms, since one can always make a case for the other side (if by nothing else simply assuming the contrary for the sake of argument). Thus, all those philosophies that presume some set of beliefs, and then simply draw the logical conclusions from them are shown to be deficient in that they can give no better reason for their own system than other contrary systems. In fact, these systems must always depend on the truth of certain beliefs that cannot be justified from within that system itself, and thus Hegel notes: "In these tropes is contained what is deficient in all metaphysics of the understanding." (p. 394), and "[t]his is skepticism in general, the skeptical consciousness; its procedure is of the utmost importance, showing in everything immediately accepted that it is not fixed, that it is nothing in and for itself." (p. 395) These characterizations of the skeptical tropes, of course, fit Hegel's understanding of his own philosophy quite well. In the *Phenomenology*, Hegel refers to these various tropes which supposedly show the relativization of everything to something else in a somewhat oblique manner: "It contains nothing enduring in it and *must* vanish before thought, because that which has been differentiated (*das Unterschiedne*) is just this, not to be *in itself* (*an ihm selbst*) but to have its essentiality only in an other. Thinking, however, is the insight into this nature of that which has been differentiated (*des Unterschiednen*); it is the negative essence as simple." ¶204, p. 124; *PG*, p. 156.

44. See ¶202, p. 123; *PG*, pp. 154–155: Skepticism "is *in itself* the negative and must present itself as such." Hegel also notes that the skeptic's relativization of all claims to knowledge to a subjective point of view would seem at first to deny the subject's freedom, since it would seem to be saying that the agent is simply subject to the contingencies of whatever presents itself to him. However, as he notes, the skeptic holds that it is the freedom of the agent to accept or reject these claims to knowledge, that no external standards other than standards that he himself accepts can count for him and that therefore the agent is "that which in the certainty of its freedom lets that which is given as other and real itself to disappear; not only the objective as such but its own behavior to it, in which it is made into something which counts as and is valid as something objective (*als gegenständlich gilt und*

geltend).. through which self-conscious negation it produces itself the *certainty of its freedom for itself*, generates an experience of it and raises it to truth." ¶204, p. 124; *PG*, p. 156.

45. See ¶205, p. 125; *PG*, p. 157: "It owns up to being a wholly *contingent, individual* consciousness – a consciousness which is *empirical*, which is oriented according to what has no reality for it, which obeys what is for it not an *essence*, which does those things and brings to actuality what has no truth for it . . . it also, on the contrary, converts itself again into that which is universal self-identity."

46. Hegel speaks of the skeptical consciousness's "identity with itself" (*Sichselbstgleichheit*), which is Hegel's own way of referring to something's being non-self-contradictory. (See ¶205, p. 125; *PG*, p. 157.) He is thus characterizing the skeptical position as seeming (at this point in his dialectical development of it) to be fully rational – that is, to be free from internal contradictions.

47. See ¶207, pp. 126–127; *PG*, pp. 158–159: "This *unhappy* consciousness, *divided within itself* (*in sich entzweite*) must therefore, because for it this contradiction of its essence is *one* consciousness, ever have in one consciousness also the other consciousness, and thus it is immediately driven out of each consciousness when it thinks it has arrived at victory and at the peace of unity." Hegel's conception of the "unhappy consciousness" may be compared with the distinction of the subjective and the objective point of view made by Thomas Nagel in his *The View From Nowhere*. In identifying the two points of view as two opposing points of view for which there can be no unity, Nagel in effect takes the standpoint of the "unhappy consciousness" to be insurmountable, since it is the expression of a metaphysical feature of the nature of consciousness. Nagel argues that all philosophical problems arise out of the attempt to overcome or explain away this insurmountable opposition. Hegel's point, for which the *Phenomenology* is an extended argument, is that the objective point of view is itself *socially constructed* and may or may not be in conflict with the subjective point of view, depending on the historical context about which one is speaking. The complete opposition between the two points of view that is so characteristic of the "unhappy consciousness" is thus for Hegel a feature of the way in which a particular form of life is structured and not a metaphysical fact about the nature of consciousness.

48. See ¶208, pp. 126–127; *PG*, p. 159.

49. See ¶209, p. 127; *PG*, pp. 159–160: "Here then is present a struggle against an enemy, against whom a victory is really a defeat, where one side achieves victory only to lose itself in its opposite."

50. See ¶210, pp. 127–128; *PG*, p. 160: "*This unity* itself *becomes for him at first* such that in it the *difference* of both is still the dominant element."

51. Hegel speaks of the "unchangeable's receiving the formation (*Gestalt*) of individuality." ¶212, p. 129; *PG*, p. 161. In his lectures on the history of philosophy, he seems to equate the rise of the "unhappy consciousness" with the ascension of neoplatonism in philosophy in Alexandria, which itself followed the heyday of skepticism in Roman life. Out of skepticism, which expresses the alienating aspects of Roman life comes the "unhappy consciousness" – at one point Hegel says: "Roman power is the real skepticism." (*Werke*, vol. 19, p. 404.) Speaking of stoicism and skepticism (along with Epicureanism, which is not discussed in the *Phenomenology*), Hegel notes: "The flowering of these philosophies falls in the Roman world, where out of the external, dead world, out of the abstraction of the Roman principle (of the republican principle and the despotism of the emperor) spirit had fled within itself – *out* of an existence which could give no satisfaction for it *into* an

intellectuality. This is a complete *unhappiness,* a dividedness of the *world* within itself." *Werke,* vol. 19, p. 402. (The "intellectuality" of which he speaks is the neoplatonic speculation about the good and the eternal so adeptly represented for him by Plotinus).

52. In his lectures on the history of philosophy, Hegel notes of the actuality of the world for the people living at the end of the Roman period: "The people finding themselves in that actuality have here completely forgotten (*verlernt*) their seeing and hearing, in general forgotten their sense of actuality and the present. The sensuously true does not count for them any more, and they are constantly engaged in deception; for they are incapable of an apprehension of anything actual because it has lost all meaning for their spirit. Others abandon the world, because they can no longer find anything in it and find what is real only within themselves. As all gods are gathered up into *one* pantheon, all religions collapse into *one.* It is this, that self-consciousness – an actual person – is the absolute essence. What the absolute essence is, is now revealed to him: it is a person, not yet mankind (*der Mensch*) or self-consciousness in general." *Werke,* vol. 19, p. 407.

53. This seems to be what Hegel is obliquely referring to in ¶212, p. 129; *PG,* pp. 161–162.

54. In ¶210, Hegel discusses the way in which the "unchangeable" (the universal point of view) appears in relation to the agents who take themselves to be fully contingent agents incapable of arriving at the truth. At first, it appears that the "truth" (the world as seen from the objective point of view) is simply given to contingent finite agents. This is laid out in terms of three moves (the "unchangeable" as opposed to them, then as taking on the form of an individual person and then as thereby reconciling itself with them). ¶¶211–212 develop those moves and the problems attendant on them. ¶214 begins to develop a similar triadic set of moves for the agents to assume for themselves the task of taking on the universal point of view.

55. This seems to be the point of the somewhat difficult section, ¶216, pp. 130–131; *PG,* p. 163. Hegel there alludes to skepticism and stoicism as something that the "unhappy consciousness" has transcended. Stoicism is too abstract in its insistence on the formalities of reason, and skepticism is just the awareness of the contradictory position to which stoicism's pretended assumption of the universal point of view leads. (That is meant by Hegel as a logical point: He is not saying that historically skepticism was developed out of specific reactions to stoic texts, but that the standpoint of skepticism is such that it can be seen as embodying in more self-conscious form the contradiction to which stoic accounts lead.) The "unhappy consciousness" however now tries for a more concrete union of the two conflicting points of view by virtue of some kind of mystical union with the "One" or with God. In his lectures on the history of philosophy, Hegel discusses this. (See *Werke,* vol. 19, pp. 411–412.) Hegel argues in those later lectures that out of the experience of the Roman world, of which skepticism as the consciousness of the contingency of everything was the complete expression, comes the retreat into the purely intellectual world of the neo-platonists, who conceive of a nontemporal realm that metaphorically descends into the temporal itself. It is only logical that their followers would take that idea and use it to interpret the appearance of Jesus as a real manifestation of the unchangeable in the world of contingency. It is then also logical that people would attempt to accomplish by their own spiritual efforts a reunion with this unchangeable realm. Hegel's point is that the obscurities and darkness of such views is to be attributed to the transformation in

ideas which they are trying to accomplish. As he notes, "This is progress which spirit in its self-consciousness accomplishes; this is not only restricted to philosophical development. It is also a complete turn (*Umschlagen*) in world history, in that which is mysterious, in that which is innermost; in philosophy it must necessarily happen in the same way." (*Werke,* vol. 19, p. 408.) Later he notes: "The relation of people to God is determined now as orders of saints, cults, but in particular as philosophy, with the express consciousness that the purpose is to belong to this intelligible world, that the individual ought to make himself capable of doing that, of being in accordance with it." (*Werke,* vol. 19, p. 417.) But he notes that at least as this is worked out in Plotinus, one misses any really clear conceptual articulation of these issues, finding instead only "words . . . which in fact say nothing" and so-called "logical developments which are completely arbitrary." (See *Werke,* vol. 19, p. 463.)

56. In the lectures on the history of philosophy, Hegel notes: "This last stage which we have had, was that return of self-consciousness into itself, this infinite subjectivity without objectivity, skepticism, this purely negative comportment against all external existence, knowledge, against everything determinate, valid, firm, true . . . It is notable that the stoic and the epicurean system has the same result and goal; but in skepticism this externalization of everything determinate is completed and with that is posited the completed memory, making-inner (*Errinerung, Innerlichmachung*)." *Werke,* vol. 19, p. 404.

57. Hegel concludes ¶216 by noting: "However it is not *for it,* that its object, the unchangeable, which for him essentially has the shape (*Gestalt*) of individuality, is *it itself,* that it itself is the individuality of consciousness." p. 131; *PG,* p. 163. That is, the "unhappy consciousness" takes the objective point of view, which it identifies as the *true* point of view, as something different from itself, something in terms of which it must transform itself.

58. Hegel makes a play on the words for thinking, *Denken,* and for devotion, *Andacht.* ¶217, p. 131; *PG,* p. 163.

59. In the lectures on the history of philosophy, Hegel notes: "This idea that the absolute essence is not alien for self-consciousness, that nothing is the essence to him in which he does not have his immediate self-consciousness – we now see this principle appearing as the universal of the world spirit, as the universal faith and knowledge of all people." *Werke,* vol. 19, pp. 404–405.

60. See ¶217, p. 131; *PG,* p. 164.

61. See ¶218, p. 132; *PG,* pp. 164–165.

62. See ¶218, p. 132; *PG,* pp. 164–165.

63. See ¶219, p. 132; *PG,* p. 165. In the lectures on the history of philosophy, Hegel is more blunt, and he also attributes this early medieval view of the world to representational thought: "An intelligible world had thus fastened itself to people's representation (*Vorstellung*) in the same way as their actuality, as a land lying far away, which is actually represented as the land which we see, peopled and inhabited but which to us is somewhat as if it were hidden by a mountain . . . rather it is the highest negativity therein – the contradiction of actuality and that other world. This intellectual world expresses the nature of the real absolute essence." *Werke,* vol. 19, p. 512.

64. See ¶220, pp. 133–134; *PG,* pp. 165–166.

65. See ¶222, pp. 134–135; *PG,* pp. 166–167.

66. See the first part of ¶222, pp. 134–135; *PG,* pp. 166–167.

67. See ¶225, pp. 135–136; *PG,* pp. 168–169.

68. See ¶226, p. 136; *PG,* p. 169.
69. See ¶227, p. 136; *PG,* p. 169, in which Hegel once again invokes the figure of the syllogism to show that he is trying to make a logical point and not simply a sociological or purely historical observation. The mediator-priest plays the metaphorical role of the middle term in a syllogism, mediating between the major term (the universal, the divine) and the minor term (the individual, the participant in the "unhappy consciousness").
70. See ¶229, p. 137; *PG,* p. 170.
71. See ¶230, pp. 137–138; *PG,* p. 170–171.

Chapter Four

1. See Otto Pöggeler, "Die Komposition der Phänomenologie des Geistes," in Hans Friedrich Fulda and Dieter Henrich (editors), *Materialien zu Hegels ⟨Phänomenologie des Geistes⟩* (Frankfurt a.M.: Suhrkamp Verlag, 1973). pp. 329–390.
2. See Robert Pippin's helpful brief on the literature on this in his " 'You Can't Get There from Here': Transition Problems in Hegel's Phenomenology of Spirit", in Frederick C. Beiser (ed.) *The Cambridge Companion to Hegel* (Cambridge: Cambridge University Press, 1993). pp. 52–57. One of the major grounds for some of this skepticism is the similar transition in the later *Encyclopedia* version of the *Phenomenology,* which, like the 1807 *Phenomenology,* moves from "Consciousness" to "Self-consciousness," but which, unlike the 1807 *Phenomenology,* then makes a transition to something called "Universal Self-Consciousness," (which is the same term that Kant uses to describe the ground of all knowledge in §16 (B132) of his "Transcendental Deduction" in the *Critique of Pure Reason*). From "Universal Self-Consciousness," the dialectic then makes its transition to "Reason." The *Encyclopedia* version also leaves out all the historical detail of the "Reason" section of the 1807 *Phenomenology,* thus seemingly adding weight to the idea that Hegel himself abandoned the specific way in which the 1807 *Phenomenology* presented its material, preferring instead to present the historical material in the lectures on art, religion, and the history of philosophy as part of the "system." Nonetheless, in structure these two transitions are similar: both move to a conception of the structure of "reason" as involving a unity of the subjective and the objective. Moreover, the *Encyclopedia* is self-consciously *not* a work of philosophical history; it is concerned with reconstructing the current (roughly, 1817–1831) status of our way of thinking about the world. As such a "system," it still presupposes the philosophical-historical treatment of the *Phenomenology* to explain how it is possible that we came to be the kinds of agents for whom such a "system" would be possible. There is thus no reason to see any great gap between the two enterprises, since the later "system" builds on the earlier *Phenomenology.* The idea that the later "system" is in some fundamental way different from and discontinuous with the earlier *Phenomenology* has helped to perpetuate the myth of a young (perhaps even revolutionary) ironic, lively Hegel who stands opposed to an older, rather official and officious, stuffy, self-important Hegel. There is no doubt that Hegel's views matured and that some of his views changed, but it is also clear that Hegel never abandoned the *Phenomenology;* indeed, he was even working on a revision of it at the time of his death.
3. See ¶¶231–232, pp. 140; *PG,* pp. 175–176.
4. This shows more concretely how the *Encyclopedia* version of the *Phenomenology* and the 1807 version are not at odds with each other. The *Encyclopedia* version

moves from "Self-Consciousness" to "Universal Self-Consciousness" for the same reasons that the 1807 version moves through stoicism, skepticism, and the unhappy consciousness – namely, to develop a conception of a shared point of view among the agents (that is, the idea of universal self-consciousness) out of the problems of coordinating the two subjective points of view in the dialectic of master and slave. This idea of a shared point of view that is instanced in each agent's own subjective point of view is, of course, the same conception of reason that the 1807 *Phenomenology* develops. But since the phenomenology of the *Encyclopedia* plays a different role than the phenomenology of the 1807 book – the *Encyclopedia* version contents itself with the development of the subject/object conception of consciousness as part of an overall theory of mental activity – it has no need to go into the history of the development of the modern point of view, since it already presupposes that modern point of view, reconstructing as it does the complex inferential structure of modern life's self-understanding.

5. Compare, for example, Hegel's remarks in his lectures on the history of philosophy where he claims that after the reformation philosophy is able to take the two different directions of realism and idealism: "In that first direction, observation turns now foremost to physical nature, from the observation of which one extracts the universal, the laws, and on this basis grounds one's knowledge. This type of experience and observation was called and is still called philosophy, the type of the finite sciences which proceed through observation and inference, or what is now called the *sciences exactes* . . . In its infinity the idea itself is here itself not the object, not known, but, on the contrary, the object is its determinate content. This latter is raised up into the universal, law – the universal taken up into its intelligible (*verständigen*) determinateness out of observation (Kepler)" *Werke*, vol. 20, p. 66. He also points out there more succinctly than he does in the *Phenomenology* how this puts a new emphasis and importance on the secular: "We thus see that the finite, the inner and outer present, is grasped in experience and through the understanding is raised up to the universal; one wants to get to know the laws, the forces, i.e., to transform the individual of perception into the form of universality. The worldly wants to be judged in a worldly way; the judge is the thinking understanding." p. 63.

6. In his later lectures on the philosophy of history, Hegel was also much more clear in attributing part of the origin of this different self-understanding to the newly discovered interest in antiquity, which produced an interest in the humanities; to the flowering of the arts in the renaissance; and to contingent events such as the discovery of the Americas (the "new world") and the development of the technology of printing. The intellectual advances of modern science, Hegel argues, are unintelligible outside of that matrix of other cultural developments. See *Philosophy of History*, pp. 408–411; *Werke*, vol. 12, pp. 488–491. In his lectures on the history of philosophy, Hegel credits Francis Bacon with much of the development of the intellectual ideas of this period. With Bacon, Hegel says, we find ". . . reason's trust towards itself and towards nature, that if it turns itself in a thinking manner to nature, it will find the truth in it because they are in themselves in harmony." (*Werke*, vol. 20, p. 77.) Bacon's formulation of the experimental and inductive methods of science, whatever their shortcomings may be, is thus for Hegel of the greatest importance in understanding this transition: "Of Bacon can one say, as Cicero said of Socrates, he took philosophy down to worldly things, into people's houses." *Werke*, vol. 20, p. 78. Hegel's oblique references to Bacon's inductive methods in the *Phenomenology* are in ¶250, pp. 151–152; *PG*, pp. 190–

191. (The language used there in the *Phenomenology* is very similar to that used in his discussion of Bacon in his lectures on the history of philosophy, including the reference to induction as inference according to analogy)

7. This emerges clearly in Hegel's treatment of Bacon in his lectures on the history of philosophy, in which he says: "And without the education (*Ausbildung*) of the experiential sciences for themselves philosophy could have come no further than the ancients." *Werke*, vol. 20, p. 80.

8. See ¶¶245–246, pp. 147–150; *PG*, pp. 185–188.

9. See ¶249, p. 151; *PG*, pp. 189–190.

10. Hegel's discussion of scientific observation thus plays a crucial part in the section on "Reason." Part of the structure of modernity, especially in its Enlightenment and post-Enlightenment phase, relies on its claim that its institutions and practices can be legitimated by *reason,* not by appeal to tradition or authority (especially church authority). As Kant clearly saw, the determination therefore of what counts as "reason" is crucial for modern life. The implicit social importance of the *Critique of Pure Reason* and the *Critique of Practical Reason* has to do with Kant's attempt to determine what can be rationally authoritative and what therefore can count as valid for modern culture. How one determines the link between science and reason is crucial to that debate, and Kant made it a central part of his theoretical philosophy. Hegel's point is that the reliance on reason cannot be itself simply a "given"; that reliance, as well as reason itself, is part of a historical *project,* part of a development of reflective social practice and its various attempts to affirm for itself and reassure itself about what can count for it as authoritative. Moreover, Hegel sees no reason to identify the procedures of science with the procedures of rationality itself, as he tries to show in the chapter on "Reason."

11. Describing Hegel's views as non-modern is, of course, no argument against them. Hegel's own arguments in favor of this non-modern view have to do with his attempts to show that this non-modern view is in fact presupposed by the practices and results of modern science. That is, Hegel wishes to argue that the kind of necessity for which classical mechanics strove would be impossible to have without some kind of presupposition of weight as an essential feature of bodies. Thus, Hegel tried to show not only that the classical view of nature was *compatible* with modern science but that modern science as science actually *presupposes* such a view in the accounts that it tries to give of itself. Hegel is not simply trying to preserve intact the older conception of nature in the face of modern scientific developments; in making his arguments, he also tries to show how the ancient view must be amended in order to fit in with what he understands to be the key concepts and findings of modern mechanics and physics. His arguments on this, however, betray certain key misunderstandings of what is at work in various key concepts in the Newtonian program; his mistakes in this regard thus undermine his claim that the Newtonian program must incorporate parts of the ancient view of nature in order for itself to work *as science.* On this point, see the earlier mentioned critiques of Hegel's understanding of classical mechanics voiced by William R. Shea, "Hegel's Celestial Mechanics" (pp. 30–44), and Franz H. van Lunteren, "Hegel and Gravitation" (pp. 45–53) in Rolf-Peter Horstmann and Michael J. Petry (editors) *Hegels Philosophie der Natur.*

12. See ¶¶251–252, pp. 152–154; *PG*, pp. 191–192. In his lectures on the history of philosophy (again in the section concerning Bacon) Hegel also makes this point: "The other formal deficiency which all empiricists share is that they believe that they are sticking only with experience; they remain unaware that in their taking

up of these perceptions they are doing metaphysics (*metaphysizieren*). Man does not stand pat with the individual, and he cannot do this. He seeks the universal; these are thoughts, even if they are not concepts. The most striking thought-form (*Gedankenform*) is force; one has the force of electricity, of magnetism, of weight. Force is universal, not perceptible; the empiricists indulge in such determinations fully uncritically and without cognizance." *Werke*, vol. 20, p. 84.

13. See, for example, Wilfrid Sellars' discussion in "The Language of Theories," in his *Science, Perception and Reality* (London: Routledge and Kegan Paul, 1963). pp. 106–126.

14. See ¶290, pp. 174–175; *PG*, pp. 213–214.

15. This point is made by Willem deVries in his "The Dialectic of Teleology," in Willem A. deVries (editor) *Philosophical Topics* (vol. 19, no. 2), pp. 51–70. He also distinguishes functional from intentional teleology by arguing that intentional teleology can be a one-time event (for example, going to the bookstore in order to buy a book by Hegel): ". . . but whereas the intentional model attributes purposiveness directly to event-tokens, in functional teleology, event-tokens must inherit their purpose directly from their respective event-types. My heart is beating now in order to circulate my blood only because it is generically the case that hearts beat in order to circulate blood." p. 62.

16. See ¶255, pp. 154–156; *PG*, pp. 193–194.

17. See ¶¶256–257, pp. 156–157; *PG*, pp. 195–196.

18. See ¶¶265–266, pp. 160–161; *PG*, pp. 199–201. See also Dietrich von Engelhardt's very helpful presentation of Hegel's philosophy of biology as it appears in his mature philosophy of nature in his "Die biologischen Wissenschaften in Hegels Naturphilosophie," in Horstmann and Petry, *Hegels Philosophie der Natur*, pp. 121–137.

19. See ¶276, p. 166; *PG*, pp. 205–206.

20. See ¶279, pp. 167–168; *PG*, pp. 207–208.

21. See ¶295, pp. 178–179; *PG*, p. 219. It is unclear that Hegel held on to this view after the *Phenomenology*, tending in his mature Berlin philosophy of nature to see the distribution of species as following from basic forces which themselves arise from the relation between geology and biology; he also thought that these forces arranged themselves conceptually into triplicities. See Trevor H. Levere, "Hegel and the Earth Sciences," in Horstmann and Petry (eds.) *Hegels Philosophie der Natur*. pp. 103–120.

22. See ¶295, pp. 178–179; *PG*, p. 220: "It is thus that *consciousness* has for the middle term between universal spirit and its individuality or sense-consciousness the system of formations (*Gestaltungen*) of consciousness as a life of the spirit ordering itself into a whole – the system that we are considering here, and which has its objective existence (*gegenständliches Dasein*) as world history. But organic nature has no history; it falls from its universal, from life, directly into the individuality of existence and the moments of simple determinateness and individual animation (*Lebendigkeit*) united in this actuality produce the process of becoming merely as a contingent movement, in which each is active in its own part and the whole is maintained."

23. See ¶298, p. 180; *PG*, p. 221–222.

24. See ¶305, p. 183; *PG*, p. 225.

25. See ¶309, p. 185; *PG*, p. 227. This is how I take what Hegel says there about there being no law-governed connection between *self*-consciousness and "actuality."

26. See ¶324, p. 195; *PG*, p. 238.
27. See ¶322, pp. 193–195; *PG*, pp. 236–237: "The true being of a person is rather *his deed;* in it, individuality is actual, and it is that which integrates (*aufhebt*) what is interpreted (*das Gemeinte*) in both of its aspects . . . It [the deed] *is* this, and its being is not only a sign, it is on the contrary the 'real thing' (*die Sache selbst*). It *is* this, and the individual person *is* what *it is*."
28. See ¶334, pp. 201–202; *PG*, pp. 244–245.
29. See ¶314, p. 188; *PG*, pp. 230–231. Alasdair MacIntyre is also helpful in bringing out this aspect of Hegel's argument, in his "Hegel on Faces and Skulls," in Alasdair MacIntyre, (editor) *Hegel: A Collection of Critical Essays* (Garden City: Doubleday, 1972). pp. 219–236.
30. See the last few sentence of ¶344, pp. 208–209; *PG*, pp. 252–253: "Consciousness will no longer *immediately find* itself but rather generates itself through its activity. It itself is to itself the end of its doings, whereas as an observer it had only to do with things."
31. "To begin with, this active reason is aware of itself merely as an individual (*eines Individuums*) and as such must demand and produce its actuality in an other." ¶348, p. 211; *PG*, p. 256.
32. This is in the sections of the *Phenomenology of Spirit* called "Pleasure and Necessity," ¶¶360–366, pp. 217–221; *PG*, pp. 262–266.
33. As Hegel puts it, this kind of individuality "brings to realization (*bringt zur Ausführung*) the pure individuality in which it appears . . . It takes hold of life much as a ripe fruit is plucked, which readily offers itself to the hand that takes it." ¶361, p. 218; *PG*, pp. 262–263.
34. See ¶362, p. 218; *PG*, p. 263. This rather dense paragraph seems to be a re-description of the whole movement of Faust in terms of the categories of the Hegelian *Phenomenology*. Faust sees the other as "his own selfhood (*Selbstheit*)," he "achieves . . . his consciousness of his realization in a consciousness appearing as independent, achieves his intuition of the unity of both independent self-consciousnesses." That is, Faust finds that instead of having merely used Gretchen, he comes to care for her. Faust conceives of himself as "this individual essence existing for-itself" but he finds instead the "unity of himself and the other self-consciousness," finding himself therefore in a shared point of view, the "universal."
35. See the first half of ¶363, pp. 218–219; *PG*, p. 263–264. Hegel notes that the emptiness of this self-conception is such that he can only draw on the "pure essentialities" of unity, difference and relation to determine what it is he will do; or in other words, there are at best formal but no material limits to his willing.
36. "Ich kann die Bande des Rächers nicht lösen, seine Riegel nicht öffnen. – Rette sie! – Wer war's, der sie ins Verderben stürzte? Ich oder Du?" From Goethe's *Faust,* the section called, *"Trüber Tag,"* "Dismal Day."
37. This point is entirely lost to Werner Becker, in his *Hegels Phänomenologie des Geistes* (Stuttgart: W. Kohlhammer, 1971), who is intent on interpreting the book from a more metaphysically idealistic view of German idealism in general so that "each determinateness of an existing object or an objective state of affairs is produced through subjectivity, i.e., occurs through subjective concepts." p. 26. In taking Hegel like this, Becker makes Hegel, oddly enough, into a subjective idealist. Thus, on Becker's understanding, Hegel must necessarily overlook the tragedy of Faust and Gretchen, since (on Becker's view) he could only take the

theme of the chapter on Faustian individualism to have to do with the "I's" narcissistically satisfying itself. This, of course, is the standpoint that Hegel is actually criticizing. See Becker, pp. 104–105.

38. Mephistopheles cynically remarks in a stage whisper after he has convinced Faust to drink the potion, *"Du siehst mit diesem Trank in Leibe/Bald Helenen in jedem Weibe."* (You'll soon see with this drink in your body/Helen [of Troy] in every woman.")

39. See ¶364, p. 220; *PG*, p. 265.

40. ¶365, pp. 220–221; *PG*, pp. 265–266.

41. This is in the sections of the *Phenomenology of Spirit* called "The Law of the Heart and the Insanity *(Wahnsinn)* of Self-Conceit", ¶¶367–380, pp. 221–228; *PG*, pp. 266–274.

42. Although the prototype perhaps of all sentimentalist works is the novel *Pamela* by Samuel Richardson (1740) with its virtuous heroine fending off a long series of unwanted advances (perhaps more so than the earlier *Manon Lescaut* of 1731 by Antoine Prévost), the phrase itself, "the man of feeling" is taken from a work by Henry Mackenzie, called (appropriately) *The Man of Feeling,* published in 1771, a very popular book in its day, the hero of which "weeps on almost every page, and is bound to bore or annoy the modern reader with sententious moralizing and maudlin melancholy." Peter Gay, *The Enlightenment: An Interpretation: The Science of Freedom* (New York: W.W. Norton and Company, 1969). p. 44. (Gay argues that the "man of feeling's" weeping is the "harbinger of a more rational, humane social policy . . . humanity, to paraphrase, Hegel, has its cunning." pp. 44–45.) It is, however, important to note that the appropriate subjects of this kind of emotional response included both men and women. Witness Lady Louisa Stuart's reaction to her first reading of *The Man of Feeling* at fourteen: she was "secretly afraid lest she should not cry enough to gain the credit of a proper sensibility." Quoted in Colin Campbell, *The Romantic Ethic and the Spirit of Modern Consumerism* (London: Basil Blackwell, 1987), p. 141.

43. See Leonard Krieger, *Kings and Philosophers: 1689–1789* (New York: W.W. Norton and Company, 1970). pp. 143–152 ("The Orthodox Revival and the Cult of Sentiment"). A good short description of the influence of the pietist movement in Germany on German thought is also found in James J. Sheehan, *German History: 1770–1866.* (Oxford: Clarendon Press, 1989), pp. 176–177.

44. Self-consciousness "knows that it has the *universal* or *law immediately* within itself, and because the law is *immediately* present in the being-for-*self* of consciousness, it is called the *law* of the *heart.* This form is *for itself,* as *individuality (Einzelheit)*, essence like the previous form." ¶367, p. 221; *PG*, p. 266.

45. See ¶¶367–368, p. 221; *PG*, p. 266.

46. The reference is no doubt to Pascal's well known aphorism: "We know the truth not only through our reason but also through our heart. It is through the latter that we know first principles, and reason, which has nothing to do with it, tries in vain to refute them." *Pensées,* translated by A.J. Krailsheimer (Baltimore: Penguin Books, 1966). p. 58 (No. 110, Lafuma edition).

47. Jansenism was a seventeenth century movement within Catholicism that styled itself as a revival of Catholic Augustinianism and that sought to purify the Catholic faith. It professed doctrines about the frailty of man and of predestination that came close to those of Protestant Calvinism. Nonetheless, it also stressed the immediacy of religious experience and the way in which such personal, emotional experience cannot be undermined by reason. They also displayed a full emotional

fury in the way in which they attacked their opponents. The Jansenists attracted some of the better scientific minds of the time – such as Blaise Pascal – to their ranks, and they educated people such as d'Alembert, who later wrote a tract that went against Jansenist interests (*Sur la Destruction des Jésuites en France*). For the Jansenists, the real enemy were the Jesuits with their doctrines of free will, their allegiance to the international papacy, and what the Jansenists saw as their lax interpretation of the requirements of Christian morality. The Jansenist emotionalist fury was turned full force on the Jesuits. Nonetheless, the Jesuits had a remarkable, although perhaps not entirely desired, influence in the form of the Jesuit-trained students that emerged from their schools: Voltaire, Diderot, Malesherbes, Helvétius, and Turgot. Robespierre was also a Jesuit product. See Peter Gay, *The Enlightenment: An Interpretation: the Science of Freedom*, pp. 505–506. (Gay notes that "[t]hroughout Catholic Europe, the Jesuits trained their most intransigent enemies.") In the eighteenth century, Jansenism became a more powerful and somewhat reactionary doctrine. The rise of Jansenism as a political force, however, was crucial in the development of the doctrine of *rights*. The king of France, Louis XIV, banned the Jansenists. However, unlike the less fortunate protestant Huguenots, who had nobody to defend their interests when they were expelled from the country by Louis, the Jansenists had many powerful members of the Parisian *Parlement* on their side, and the Jansenists were thus able to make the issue of whether they were to be tolerated into a question of whether the king (with his Jesuit advisors) was a despot. The Jansenists, who saw their abbey at Port-Royal des Champs razed in 1709 on the orders of Louis were, however, to triumph over the Jesuits in 1762 with the king's banning the Jesuit order from France. On the complicated story of the relation between the Jesuits and the Jansenists, see Dale Van Kley, *The Jansenists and the Expulsion of the Jesuits from France: 1757–1765* (New Haven: Yale University Press, 1975). The particular appeal to the "heart" and the kind of fury that the Jansenists exhibited in their political activities are no doubt part of the inspiration for Hegel's chapter on the "Law of the Heart."

48. See ¶370, p. 222; *PG*, p. 267: "This individuality therefore directs its energies to getting rid of this necessity which contradicts the law of the heart, and also the suffering caused by it . . . What it realizes is itself the law, and its pleasure is therefore at the same time the universal pleasure of all hearts."

49. See the last half of ¶372, p. 223; *PG*, p. 269.

50. See ¶371, pp. 222–223; *PG*, p. 268.

51. See the first half of ¶372, p. 223; *PG*, p. 268.

52. See ¶373, p. 224; *PG*, pp. 269–270.

53. See ¶374, pp. 224–225; *PG*, p. 270.

54. See ¶375, p. 225; *PG*, pp. 270–271.

55. Hegel has been taken to be making an allusion to Baron D'Holbach's idea that this corruption is conceived as "a perversion invented by fanatical priests, gluttonous despots and their minions, who compensate themselves for their own degradation by degrading and oppressing others, a perversion which has led to the nameless misery of deluded humanity." ¶377, p. 226; *PG*, p. 272. He makes the same allusion later in the *Phenomenology* at ¶542, p. 330; *PG*, p. 386, where he is there alluding to D'Holbach's criticism of religion in general. The reference in ¶377, however, is perhaps ironically aimed at the Jansenists, since D'Holbach was an avowed atheist who was opposed to clerics of all kind. Although its theology was a self-styled Augustinianism, the Jansenist movement had nonetheless paved the

way for the later anti-clericalism of the Enlightenment because of their hatred of the Jesuit clergy and their identification with Gallicanism (taking the side of the church as the national church of France in opposition to the "internationalist" papacy). The Jansenists tended to underwrite the idea that the clerics (the Jesuits) were corrupt, that the king was a despot (since he had banned the Jansenists), and that the clergy (the Jesuits) should be limited in their influence on government. See Dale Van Kley, *The Jansenists and the Expulsion of the Jesuits From France,* pp. 234–237. Thus, the Jansenist criticism of *Jesuit* clerics could be seen to lay the groundwork for D'Holbach's attack on clerics in general. In any event, D'Holbach's sally against the priesthood and the depraved nobility was only a repetition of a well known indictment given by a curé, Jean Meslier, who left behind a testament saying the same thing, in which he also uttered his famous wish that "all the great ones of the earth, all the nobles, should be hanged and strangled with the guts of the priests." Quoted in Paul Hazard, *European Thought in the Eighteenth Century: From Montesquieu to Lessing,* (Cleveland: Meridian Books, The World Publishing Company, 1963), p. 55. Meslier's testament was widely circulated in a version edited by Voltaire in eighteenth century France, and Hegel could well have known of it.

56. See ¶377, p. 226; *PG,* p. 271: "The heartthrob for the welfare of humanity therefore passes into the ravings of an insane self-conceit, into the fury of consciousness to preserve itself from destruction." Hegel also comments on this in his lectures on the philosophy of history: "The most ingenuous souls, the most innocent natures were in the most melancholy manner guided to the most secret workings of their hearts in order to observe them truly. This duty was combined with that of its opposite: man should also know that the good spirit dwells in him . . . Mankind was driven into interiority (*ins Innerliche*), into that which is abstract, and that which was spiritual was held to be different from the worldly. That lively consciousness of the subjectivity of mankind, of the interiority of his will brought with it the belief in *evil* as a great power of the worldly . . . The belief in this abstract, special power of the worldly – in the devil and his cunning – occasioned an infinite number of *trials for witchcraft* both in Catholic and Protestant countries." *Philosophie der Geschichte,* pp. 505–506; *Philosophy of History,* pp. 425–426.

57. See Leonard Krieger, *Kings and Philosophers: 1689–1789,* p. 147.

58. "And to have this entire affection or integrity of mind is to live according to Nature, and the dictates and rules of supreme wisdom. This is morality, piety, and natural religion." The Earl of Shaftesbury, *"An Inquiry Concerning Virtue or Merit,"* (1711), reprinted in Jerome Schneewind, *Moral Philosophy from Montaigne to Kant* (Cambridge: Cambridge University Press, 1990). Vol. II, p. 498.

59. See ¶383, p. 230; *PG,* p. 276.

60. See ¶381, p. 228; *PG,* p. 274.

61. See Norman Hampson, *The Enlightenment* (New York: Penguin Books, 1968). Chapter 3: "Human Nature: Man and Society", p. 100.

62. See ¶382, pp. 229–230; *PG,* pp. 275–276.

63. See the second half of ¶382, pp. 229–230; *PG,* pp. 275–276.

64. In ¶383, p. 230; *PG,* p. 276, Hegel speaks of the "weapons" that each side uses in this struggle.

65. See ¶384, p. 230; *PG,* pp. 276–277. Hegel claims that while this is for the virtuous consciousness the *"end (Zweck),* in the 'way of the world' it is *that which is internal (als Inneres)."*

378

66. See ¶384, p. 230; *PG*, pp. 276–277. Hegel notes that the Good exists "for *an other*, as something that is not *in and for itself*," meaning that these dispositions are not apparently already in the "hearts" of the egoists (they are not "for him") but exist in the eyes of the "champion of natural virtue." The "champion of natural virtue" posits these as *having to be* there within the egoist, given the theory that the "champion of natural virtue" has about the world and about human nature, even if the egoist himself cannot find them. (Thus, they are "abstractions," theoretical terms posited to explain something.)

67. See ¶385, p. 231; *PG*, p. 277.

68. See ¶386, pp. 223–232; *PG*, pp. 277–278.

69. As Hegel puts it, "What is *in-itself* is at first the *abstraction of essence* vis à vis *actuality*." ¶389, p. 233; *PG*, p. 279.

70. See ¶389, p. 233; *PG*, pp. 279–280. Thus, Hegel refers to the "champion of natural virtue's" purpose as "the abstract non-actual essence," that is, a theoretical term posited simply in order to shore up his other beliefs. This "essence" is as Hegel puts it, "not true but rather is only *for consciousness*," meaning that the champion of natural virtue takes this to represent something actual and experienceable when in fact it is only a theoretical term that he introduces in order to make his other beliefs hold together.

71. That someone like the Earl of Shaftesbury's conception of virtue was far removed from the aristocratic virtues of the ancient Greeks is displayed in a letter that Shaftesbury wrote to a friend: "All fame is not alike. There is as much difference as between noise and music . . . But the fame that arises from the consent and harmony of wise and good men is music and a charm irresistible to a heroic soul. The fame of nobility, high station, warlike feats or conquests, make not a single note in the symphony. What love was ever gained by these? What hearts were ever won in this manner?" Quoted in Peter Gay, *The Enlightenment: An Interpretation: the Science of Freedom*, pp. 48–49. This fits in with the enlightenment's general condemnation of Homeric heroes and medieval aristocratic warriors as miscreants.

72. See ¶390, p. 233–234; *PG*, pp. 280–281.

73. See ¶394, p. 236; *PG*, pp. 283–284.

74. See ¶395, pp. 236–237; *PG*, p. 284.

75. See ¶396, p. 237; *PG*, pp. 284–285.

76. This is treated by Hegel in the section, "The Spiritual Kingdom of Animals and Deception, or the 'Real Thing' (*die Sache Selbst*)" ¶¶397–418, pp. 237–252; *PG*, pp. 285–301.

77. See Erich Auerbach, *Mimesis: the Representation of Reality in Western Literature* (transl. by Willard Trask) (New York: Doubleday Anchor Books, 1953), pp. 323–326. Auerbach there discusses how the *honnête homme* plays a key role in the plays of Molière, particularly in the way in which this ideal of a non-noble "gentleman" plays off against the older ideals of aristocracy.

78. In a later passage having to do with the ideals of aristocracy and the *courtier* of the courts of absolutist French kings, Hegel says, "The sincere (*ehrlich*) consciousness takes each moment as an enduring essentiality and is the uncultivated thoughtlessness, not knowing that what it is just as much doing the inverse." 521, pp. 316–317; *PG*, pp. 371–372.

79. See ¶396, p. 237; *PG*, pp. 284–285: "[T]he element in which individuality sets forth its formation (*Gestalt*) has the significance solely of taking up this formation; it is the daylight in which consciousness wants to display itself."

80. See Karl Joachim Weintraub, *The Value of the Individual: Self and Circumstance in Autobiography* (Chicago: University of Chicago Press, 1978).
81. This is the chapter heading in the *Phenomenology* before ¶394, p. 236; *PG,* p. 283.
82. "Accordingly, individuality appears on the scene as an original determinate nature: *original,* for it is in-itself; originally determinate, for the negative moment is present in the in-itself, and this latter is thus a quality." ¶398, p. 238; *PG,* p. 285.
83. See ¶401, pp. 239–401; *PG,* pp. 287–289.
84. See the second half of ¶401, pp. 240–241; *PG,* p. 288.
85. Rousseau's explanations of these events are well-known but still extraordinary: "If I were one of those low-born men, deaf to the gentle voice of Nature, a man in whose breast no real feeling of justice and humanity ever arose, this hardness of heart would have been quite easy to explain. But my warm-heartedness, my acute sensibility, the ease with which I formed friendships, the hold they exercised over me, and the cruel wrench when they had to be broken; my innate goodwill towards my fellow men; my burning love for the great, the true, the beautiful, and the just; my horror of evil in every form, my inability to hate, to hurt or even to wish to; that softening, that sharp and sweet emotion I feel at the sight of all that is virtuous, generous, and lovable: is it possible that all these can ever swell in the same soul along with depravity which, quite unscrupulously, tramples the dearest of obligations underfoot? No, I feel, and boldly declare – it is impossible. Never for a moment in his life could Jean-Jacques have been a man without feelings or compassion, an unnatural father. I may have been mistaken but I could never be callous." *The Confessions of Jean-Jacques Rousseau,* translated by J.M. Cohen (London: Penguin Books, 1953) pp. 332–333. This is in part a complaint against Voltaire's charge of immorality against him, which shocked Rousseau; see Karl Weintraub, *The Value of the Individual,* p. 297.
86. See ¶403, pp. 241–142; *PG,* pp. 289–290.
87. See ¶404, p. 242; *PG,* p. 290, in which Hegel relates this to the overall theme of the section on "Reason."
88. See ¶407, p. 244; *PG,* pp. 291–292.
89. Rousseau, for example, complains often of people possessed of evil hearts who are out to discredit him because of their own depraved natures. Rousseau's suspicions (perhaps paranoia) about those around him which appear throughout the *Confessions* (such as his living under an assumed name in France for a while in the fear that Hume was searching for him) are well known. To take, however, one example of this, consider the passage at the end of Book Eight of the *Confessions,* when he tells why he must write the book: "But the attempts made by my powerful oppressors, who dread the truth, to destroy every trace of it, compel me to make every effort consonant with the strictest justice and the most scrupulous fairness, in order to preserve them . . . But since my name is fated to live, I must endeavor to transmit with it the memory of that unfortunate man who bore it, as he actually was and not as his unjust enemies unremittingly endeavor to paint him." *Confessions,* p. 373.
90. See ¶406, p. 244; *PG,* p. 292.
91. Thus, Hegel says that it does not matter which side (work or "inner self") is called "concept" and which is called "reality," since each will be opposed to the other in this way. See ¶406, p. 244; *PG,* p. 292.
92. See ¶407, pp. 244–245; *PG,* pp. 292–293.
93. The phrase, *die Sache selbst,* is nearly impossible to translate. A *Sache* (thing) is

not, Hegel stresses, a *Ding* (a thing): "The *Sache selbst* (the thing itself) expresses thus the *spiritual* essentiality in which all these moments are integrated (*aufgehoben*) as counting for themselves – therefore only counting as universal – and in which the certainty consciousness has of itself is an objective essence, a *thing* (*Sache*), an object born out of self-consciousness as its *own*, without ceasing to be a free authentic object. The *thing* (*Ding*) of sense certainty and perception now has its meaning for self-consciousness only through self-consciousness; on this rests the difference between a *thing* (*Ding*) and a *thing* (*Sache*)." ¶410, p. 246, *PG*, pp. 294–295. A *Sache* in Hegel's sense is a thing in the most general sense: a poem, a thought, a mental process, a symphony and a joke could all be a *Sache;* but they would not be things (*Ding*) of perception. A *Sache* is also the *point* of something, as in the injunction, "get to the point." It can also be a "matter" in the sense of "how the matter stands." (See also Michael Inwood's discussion in his *A Hegel Dictionary* of the various meanings of the term, *Sache selbst,* and its relations to the term, *Ding.*)

94. See ¶409, pp. 245–246; *PG*, pp. 293–294.
95. See ¶411, pp. 246–247; *PG*, pp. 295–296. Hegel there speaks of the *Sache selbst* as the "universal," which is present in all the individual moments and binds them together as moments of one whole. It is also, he says, "simple essence," and it is the "simple, abstract *Sache selbst*," meaning that for this type of self-conception, the "real thing" is a very general, not terribly determinate concept of what does bind all these elements together, and it is something postulated as having to be there in order for this conception to be able to give a reasonable account of itself.
96. See ¶412, p. 247; *PG*, p. 296. Compare this with, for example, Rousseau's well known opening to the *Confessions:* "So let the numberless legion of my fellow men gather round me, and hear my confessions. Let them groan at my depravities, and blush for my misdeeds. But let each one of them reveal his heart at the foot of Thy throne with equal sincerity, and may any man who dares, say, 'I was a better man than he.'" p. 17. *Ehrlich* is rendered by Miller and others as "honest," but "sincere" seems better to capture what Hegel is up to here, especially with regard to the comparison with Rousseau.
97. See ¶414, p. 248; *PG*, p. 297.
98. Emmanuel Hirsch claims that the phrase may be taken from a passage in Hölderlin's novel, *Hyperion,* in which he discusses being among the learned (*Gebildeten*) in such a way "as if human nature had been dissolved into a manifold of the animal kingdom". See Emannuel Hirsch, "Die Beisetzung der Romantiker in Hegels Phänomenologie" reprinted in Hans Friederich Fulda and Dieter Henrich (eds.) *Materialien zu Hegels ⟨Phänomenologie des Geistes⟩* (Frankfurt a.M.: Suhrkamp Verlag, 1973). p. 273, note 53.
99. Rousseau, *Confessions,* p. 17.
100. See Karl Weintraub, *The Value of the Individual,* p. 308.
101. See ¶417, pp. 250–251; *PG*, pp. 298–300.
102. See ¶418, pp. 251–252; *PG*, pp. 300–301.
103. See ¶418, pp. 251–252; *PG*, p. 300.
104. This well known passage occurs in ¶17, pp. 9–10; *PG*, p. 19: "In my view, which can be justified only by the exposition of the system itself, everything turns on grasping and expressing the true not only as *substance* but equally as *subject.*" The passage about the "I" being a "We" occurs in ¶177, p. 110, *PG*, p. 140.
105. See Ernst Cassirer's discussion of the point of Kant's comparison of Rousseau to

Newton in his *The Philosophy of the Enlightenment* (translated by Fritz C. A. Koelln and James P. Pettegrove) (Princeton: Princeton University Press, 1951). pp. 153–160.

106. ¶420, p. 253; *PG*, p. 302.

107. I am referring to the sections, "Reason as Legislative" and "Reason as Testing Laws." ¶¶419–437, pp. 252–262; *PG*, pp. 301–312.

108. One obvious reason for construing some of these passages as criticisms of Kantian moral philosophy has to do with Hegel's choice of examples. Hegel discusses, for example, the commandment about stealing property, and he argues that the commandment against stealing property already presupposes that there is an institution of property with its associated rights. He then argues that although it is perfectly consistent to claim that there should be such an institution, it is also perfectly consistent to say that there should be no property. Hence, the principle of non-contradiction will not settle the issue of whether we should have an institution of property. The same example of property occurs in his lectures on the history of philosophy at a point at which Hegel is explicitly discussing Kant; it is thus fair to conclude that Kant is at least one of the targets of the criticism in this section.

109. The Hegelian inspired critique of Kant as a formalist in the theory of knowledge is elegantly developed by Robert Pippin in his *Kant's Theory of Form* (New Haven: Yale University Press, 1982).

110. In the lectures on the history of philosophy, Hegel is clear on this: "Kantian philosophy is theoretically the enlightenment methodically worked out, namely, that what can be known is not that which is true, but, on the contrary, that which is only appearance." *Werke*, 20, p. 333.

111. ¶233, pp. 140–141;*PG*, p. 176. The same phrase appears in Hegel's lectures on the history of philosophy when he is discussing the transitional period from early modern to enlightenment philosophy. See *Werke*, 20, p. 266.

112. ¶420, p. 253; *PG*, p. 302: "Its object counts for it likewise as the true, for it unites self-consciousness and being in a single unity. It [the true] counts as the *absolute*, for self-consciousness cannot and does not want any more to go beyond this object, for in it, it is with itself (*bei sich selbst*); it [self-consciousness] *cannot*, for it [the object] is all being and all power; it does not *want* to, for it [the object] is the *self* or the will of this self."

113. Hegel's description of the way in which the Enlightenment saw an immediate unity between happiness, nature, reason and sentiment – the way in which it was poised between a conception of spirit as normative and a conception of spirit as natural – is developed in ¶¶419–428, *PG*, pp. 301–306, under the title "Legislative Reason." He characterizes this Enlightenment faith in the unity of reason, nature, and sentiment as follows: "The object is on its own (*an ihm selbst*) real as object, for it contains on its own (*an ihm*) the difference of consciousness; it divides itself into organically related groupings of people (*Massen*) which are the *determinate laws* of the absolute essence. These organically related groupings of people, however, do not obscure the concept, for the moments of being and pure consciousness and of the self remain enclosed within it – a unity which constitutes the essence of these overarching groupings of people and which in this difference no longer lets these moments step apart from one another." ¶420, p. 253; *PG*, p. 302. (I translated *Massen* as "organically related groupings of people" in order to capture the sense, as the *Wahrig Deutsches Wörterbuch* has it, of

its meaning as "a multiplicity of people who have partially or wholly given up their individuality in favor of the whole.")

114. See Paul Hazard, *European Thought in the Eighteenth Century: From Montesquieu to Lessing*, p. 316. Hazard claims that the term "optimism" first appears in 1737.

115. David Hume, *Treatise on Human Nature*, p. 415. In other Enlightenment figures (particularly Diderot), the skepticism about the scope of reason's powers was curiously combined with the corresponding faith in observing reason to solve various epistemological, social and moral problems. Peter Gay argues that this was the result of those Enlightenment figures' attempt to create a new "passionate naturalism," a doctrine that would avoid the rigidities of past Christian doctrine and what they regarded as its profound anti-rational tendencies. See Peter Gay, *The Enlightenment: An Interpretation: the Science of Freedom*, pp. 187–207. (For his claim about "passionate naturalism," see p. 204.)

116. This conception about the way in which the Kantian subject spontaneously "takes" things up in a certain way is skillfully set forth in Robert Pippin, "Kant on the Spontaneity of Mind," *Canadian Journal of Philosophy*, 17, 1987, pp. 449–476.

117. Curiously, Hegel discusses Kant's theoretical philosophy (although, again, only in passing and very obliquely) in the introductory chapter to the section on "Reason." (¶¶231–239, pp. 139–145; *PG*, pp. 175–182), not in the chapters on "Reason as Lawgiver" and "Reason as Testing Laws," in which the emphasis is on Kant's moral theory.

118. Kant says in §16 of the 1787 (B) edition of the *Critique of Pure Reason:* "It must be possible for the 'I think' to accompany all my representations; for otherwise something would be represented in me which could not be thought at all, and that is equivalent to saying that the representation would be impossible, or at least would be nothing to me." Hegel comments in his *Science of Logic* that "It is one of profoundest and truest insights to be found in the *Critique of Pure Reason* that the *unity* which constitutes the nature of the *concept* is recognized as the *original synthetic* unity of *apperception*, as the unity of the *I think*, or of self-consciousness." *Science of Logic*, p. 584; *WdL*, II, p. 221. He paraphrases (to the point of bad quotation) some lines from Kant (§16, B137) to make his point: "Consequently it is this *unity of consciousness* which alone constitutes the relation of the representations with the object and therewith their *objective validity* and on which rests even the *possibility of the understanding*." (*Science of Logic*, Ibid.)

119. It is not a logical, or "analytic" truth that the "I" that thinks one thought is the same "I" that thinks another thought. (For example, from the statements that "Someone ate my porridge," and "Someone sat in my chair," one cannot infer that it was the *same* person who did both. It is therefore a "synthetic" truth that one person – say, Goldilocks – did both things.) Therefore, the statement that "the I that represents X is the same I that represents Y" is itself a "synthetic" truth, and, as being necessary, is a synthetic a priori truth.

120. In the introductory section of the chapter on "Reason," Hegel remarks of the Kantian philosophy that it failed in what it set out to do when Kant claimed to arrive at a determinate list of twelve categories by taking the derivation of them to come out of the table of judgments found in logic textbooks and some basic principles of his own system: "But to pick up the plurality of categories again in

some way or other as a welcome find, taking them, e.g., from the various judgments, and complacently accepting them so, is in fact to be regarded as an outrage on science. Where else should the understanding be able to demonstrate a necessity, if it is unable to do so on its own itself (*an ihm selbst*), which is pure necessity?" ¶235, pp. 142–143; *PG*, p. 179. Hegel's basic charge seems to be that Kant should have been able to derive the categories and even the necessity for the manifold simply out of the synthetic unity of apperception itself. Kant argued that the "analytic unity of apperception" (I = I) *requires* a synthetic unity of apperception. That is, if the subject is spontaneously to be able to identify itself as the same "I," then it *requires* a set of different representations; that the subject is the same subject over time requires that he have a set of different representations such that the subject can spontaneously identify himself as the "I" that thinks X as identical with the "I" that thinks Y. Thus, from the synthetic unity of apperception (*the* category, in Hegel's parlance), we should be able to derive all the categories, and ultimately the necessity for the synthetic unity of apperception itself.

121. See ¶236, p. 143; *PG*, pp. 179–180 in which Hegel discusses what he takes to be the difficulties inherent in the Kantian dualism of appearances and things in themselves and in Kant's doctrine of individuals as given in intuition: "Individuality is the transition of the category out of its concept to an *external* reality, the pure *schema* which is both consciousness and because it is individuality and a unit excluding others from itself (*ausschliessendes Eins*) is a pointing towards (*das Hindeuten*) an other. But the other of the category is merely the *other categories mentioned at first*, namely, *pure essentiality* and *pure difference;* and in this category, i.e., just in the positedness of the other or in this other itself, consciousness is just as much itself." Hegel also speaks of the "negativities" here, indicating that in his mind, the Kantian philosophy generates its own problems within the terms that it sets for itself. In ¶237, p. 143; *PG*, p. 180, Hegel speaks of the "restless movement to and fro" between the idea of the thing in itself as something that consciousness posits as a necessary condition of knowledge and as something that is taken as not posited by consciousness but independent of it. In ¶238, pp. 144–145; *PG*, pp. 180–181, Hegel claims that the dualism between consciousness and the thing-in-itself is untenable precisely because it fails to make good on the kinds of claims it makes for itself. In ¶239, p. 145; *PG*, pp. 181–182, he claims that the reason for Kantian (and Fichtean) idealism's failure (the contradiction involved in talking about unknowable things in themselves) is that it "asserts the *abstract concept* of reason as that which is true," which leads it to an equally abstract conception of reality. The reason behind that charge, not mentioned in ¶239, is that it relies on a conception of representations as lying within the subject's mind, a conception which in turn leads to skepticism about the knowability of things in themselves.

122. Hegel is probably referring obliquely to Kant's idea of the "fact of reason" (among other things) in his discussions in the introductory chapters of the section on "Reason" in which he is almost certainly discussing Kant and Fichte. He speaks of (Kantian and Fichtean) idealism simply as giving an "assurance" (*Versicherung*) that what it says is true without giving a full set of reasons to underwrite this "assurance." See ¶¶234–235, pp. 141–143; *PG*, pp. 177–179.

123. It should be noted that "appearance" is given a specific sense as the necessary way in which the world could appear to minds having the dual structure of "intuitive faculty and conceptual faculty," and is to be distinguished from "appearance" in

the sense of "what appears to our particular human mind with its empirical structure of sensibility and understanding."

124. Hegel is therefore not simply trying to show that the Kantian philosophy is at odds with what he regards as the "true" account of morality and knowledge. Such a rejection of Kantian theory would be unacceptable for Hegel, given the terms he sets for his own theory. Thus, Hegel's criticism cannot lie, as David Hoy says in his "Hegel's Critique of Kantian Morality," *History of Philosophy Quarterly* 6 No. 2 (1989), p. 221, in the claim that "[F]or Hegel Kant's reflective procedures imply the wrong phenomenology of moral experience." Hegel cannot consistently with his own project simply juxtapose the "correct" phenomenology of moral experience to the "mistaken" Kantian account. He must show how the Kantian account breaks down on the terms that it, not Hegel's alternative "phenomenology," sets for it. As Hegel explains in the *Science of Logic:* "Further, the refutation must not come from outside, that is, it must not proceed from assumptions lying outside the system in question and inconsistent with it. The system need only refuse to recognize those assumptions; the *defect* is a defect only for him who starts from the requirements and demands based on those assumptions . . . The genuine refutation must enter into the opponent's power and meet him on his own ground (*sich in den Umkreis seiner Stärke stellen*); no advantage is gained by attacking him where he is not." *Science of Logic,* pp. 580–581; *WdL,* II, pp. 217–218. As Hoy notes elsewhere, "In present day parlance, Hegel is showing how the theory and practice of Kantian morality deconstructs itself." (p. 220)

125. See ¶429, pp. 256–257;*PG,* p. 306. This paragraph contains an oblique set of references to the transition from the Enlightenment to its completion in Kantian philosophy. Hegel there speaks of how the universality of the "substance" (the presupposition of the harmony of nature, sentiment and reason that had guided much Enlightenment thought) had failed to generate the content which it had claimed to be able to do, and how this is now taken up as "pure *consciousness*" (that is, the Enlightenment ideas become transformed by Kant into a theory of subjectivity), and that this "pure consciousness" is the *Sache selbst,* the "real thing," that which is authoritative for us as determining what counts as a good reason for belief and action. He then argues that this conception of pure consciousness is capable of testing the various claims to knowledge by submitting them to its own autonomously established criteria – or, in his words, "it is *formal* universality, to which the determinate content can measure up, since in that universality, the content is considered only in relation to itself," thus indicating that he is talking about Kant's idea of the categorical imperative as being a formal criterion of the validity of a maxim. He then claims, without argument, that this can only be a testing of content (for example, a maxim formed out of some occurrent desire, such as "I shall wear my trousers rolled") in terms of whether it is internally non-contradictory – whether, as he says, it forms a "tautology."

126. See ¶432, p. 259;*PG,* p. 309: "In both the moments just considered . . . the positing of immediate determinateness in the ethical substance and then the knowledge of them as to whether they are laws have been sublated."

127. See ¶435, p. 260; *PG,* p. 310.

128. See ¶434, p. 260; *PG,* pp. 309–310. On Rousseau's critique of the Enlightenment, see Judith Shklar, *Men and Citizens: A Study of Rousseau's Social Theory* (Cambridge: Cambridge University Press, 1985).

129. Hegel hints at this argument in ¶¶434–435, p. 260; *PG,* pp. 309–310, in which

he talks about how the idea of reason as legislative and reason as testing laws are each one-sided. In ¶436, pp. 260–262, *PG,* pp. 310–311, he sketches out what such a unification of the two one-sided moments would look like.

Chapter Five

1. See ¶438, p. 263; *PG,* p. 313: "Reason is spirit, when its certainty of being all reality has been raised to truth, and it is conscious of itself as its world, and of the world as itself . . . But essence existing *in* and *for itself,* which at the same time represents itself as actually consciousness and as itself, is *spirit.*"

2. See ¶438, p. 263; *PG,* p. 313: "But this determination of the category, of being-for-self opposed to being-in-itself, is equally one-sided and is a sublating *(aufhebendes)* moment. The category is determined thereby for consciousness as it is in its universal truth, as an essence existing *in-and-for-itself.*"

3. See ¶439, p. 264; *PG,* p. 314: "This substance is just as much the universal undertaking *(Werk)* created by the action of all and each as their unity and equality, for it is the *being-for-self,* the self, the doing *(das Tun).* As *substance,* spirit is unwavering upright *(gerechte)* equality-with-self; but as *being-for-self,* it is a fragmented essence, self-sacrificing and gracious *(gütige),* in which each accomplishes his own undertaking, rends asunder the universal being, and takes from it his own share."

4. Hegel expresses this in his later *Philosophy of Right* in speaking of the ethical order *(Sittlichkeit)* with reference to *Antigone,* the same example used in the *Phenomenology of Spirit:* "If we consider ethics from the objective standpoint, one can say that in it the ethical person is for himself incognizant *(sei sich unbewusst).* In this sense, Antigone declares that no one knows from where the laws come: they are eternal. That is, they are that which exists in and for themselves *(die an und für sich seiende),* determinations that flow from the nature of the thing *(Sache).*" ¶144, *Remark.*

5. Hegel quotes some lines from *Antigone* in two separate places in the *Phenomenology of Spirit* to make this point: "They are not of yesterday or today, but everlasting,/ Though where they came from, none of us can tell" (¶437, p. 261, *PG,* p. 311); paraphrased later as *"sure and unwritten law of the gods, that eternally lives, and no one knows whence it came."* (¶712, p. 431, *PG,* p. 497.) Hegel's quotation is apparently his own free translation from the Greek (and this of course is a translation of Hegel's free translation).

6. See ¶444, p. 266; *PG,* p. 317.

7. This development occurs in two chapters of the *Phenomenology.* In the chapter called "The ethical world. Human and divine law, man and woman," Hegel develops what he takes to be the best case for that view of Greek life as perfectly consistent and harmonious which was so deeply felt by some of his contemporaries. In the following chapter, "Ethical action. Human and divine knowledge, guilt and destiny," he develops what he takes to be the internal contradictions in the positive image of Greek life sketched out in the preceding chapter.

8. Hegel puts it this way in his later Berlin lectures on the philosophy of history: "That which is substantial in law, what is an affair of state, the universal interest is what is essential to the individual; but it is this only as mores *(Sitte)* in the mode of objective will, so that morality in the authentic sense, as the interiority of conviction and intention, is not yet present. The law is there, and in terms of its content, it is a law of freedom and rationality, and it is valid in terms of its

immediacy, because it is the law. Just as the natural element is present in beauty as the sensuous element, in ethical life (*Sittlichkeit*) the laws have the mode of necessities of nature (*Naturnotwendigkeit*)." *Werke,* vol. 12, p. 308.

9. See ¶447, p. 267; *PG,* pp. 318–319.

10. In the lectures on the philosophy of history, Hegel notes: "We can assert of the Greeks in the first and true formation of their freedom that they had no conscience; with them the custom prevailed of living for the fatherland without further reflection. The abstraction of a state, which for our understanding is what is essential, was unknown to them. Rather, to them the end was the living fatherland: this Athens, this Sparta, this Temple, these altars, this mode of living together, this circle of citizens, these mores (*Sitte*) and customs. To a Greek, the fatherland was a necessity, without which he could not live." *Werke,* 12, p. 309.

11. See ¶447, p. 267; *PG,* p. 319.

12. See ¶448, pp. 267–268; *PG,* p. 319.

13. See ¶462, pp. 277–278; *PG,* pp. 329–330.

14. See ¶449, p. 268; *PG,* p. 319.

15. See ¶450, p. 268; *PG,* pp. 319–320.

16. In his lectures on the philosophy of history, Hegel noted: "If we wish now to summarize what the *Greek spirit* is, we find that the fundamental determination of it is that freedom of spirit is conditioned by and is in essential relation to a natural prompting (*Naturerregung*). Greek freedom is prompted through an other; it is thereby free through the stimulation's being transformed and produced out of itself. This determination is the middle term between a people's lack of self (*Selbstlosigkeit*) (as we saw in the Asiatic principle, in which the spiritual and the divine only exist in natural modes) and the infinite subjectivity as pure certainty of itself, of the thought that I am the basis for everything that is valid. The Greek spirit as the middle term begins from nature and inverts it into a posit (*Gesetztsein*) out of itself; this spirituality is not yet absolutely free and not yet complete *from* itself (*vollkommen aus sich selbst*), not yet the prompting of itself." *Werke,* 12, p. 293.

17. See ¶450, p. 268; *PG,* pp. 319–320.

18. See ¶¶451–452, pp. 268–271; *PG,* pp. 320–323.

19. See ¶453, pp. 271–272; *PG,* p. 323.

20. See ¶455, pp. 272–273; *PG,* pp. 323–324.

21. See ¶457, pp. 274–275; *PG,* pp. 325–326.

22. Without the incorporation of some ideal of "free individuals" into its picture, Greek life might look as if it were *lacking* in some important feature which modern life has, in which case it would not be the allegedly superior alternative which it is supposed to be. Those who extol the virtues of Greek life would then have to admit that actually they are faced with the choice between Greek harmony, with its lack of free individuality, and modern life, caught in its alienation but nonetheless having a place within its social space for such individuals.

23. Hegel makes this explicit in his lectures on the philosophy of history: "This makes the Greek character into *beautiful individuality,* which is brought forth from spirit when it restructures the natural into an expression of itself . . . It is not free self-determining spirituality but naturalness cultivated into spirituality – spiritual individuality." *Werke,* 12, p. 293.

24. See ¶457, pp. 274–275; *PG,* pp. 325–327.

25. In developing the best case for the Greek form of life that he can make, Hegel also tries to show how this idealized version of Greek life can be understood to be

fulfilling those *desiderata* of modern life which he treated in the chapters on "Reason", without its having modern life's problems of self-justification. See ¶461, pp. 276–277; *PG*, pp. 328–329.

26. See ¶465, pp. 279–280; *PG*, pp. 331–332.
27. See ¶472, pp. 284–285; *PG*, p. 337.
28. See ¶470, p. 284; *PG*, p. 36.
29. See ¶475, pp. 287–288; *PG*, pp. 339–342.
30. See ¶478, p. 291; *PG*, p. 343: "This therefore counts henceforth as an essence existing *in and for itself*. To be so *recognized* is its substantiality. But it is an *abstract universality* because its content is *this rigid unyielding self*, not the self that is dissolved in substance."
31. See ¶480, p. 291; *PG*, p. 344.
32. In his lectures on the philosophy of history, Hegel puts it this way: "After the sense of patriotism, which was the dominant impulse of Rome, was satisfied, corruption breaks out among the masses in the Roman state; through contrasting events, the magnitude of individuality in it becomes stronger in both intensity and means. We see from now on the opposition (*Gegensatz*) contained in Rome itself beginning to stand out in another form, and the epoch that concludes the second period is the second mediation of the opposition. We earlier saw this opposition in the struggle of the patricians against the plebeians; now it is in the form of particular interests against the patriotic disposition itself, and the feeling (*Sinn*) for the state no longer holds this opposition in a necessary equilibrium." *Werke,* 12, p. 373.
33. See ¶481, p. 293; *PG*, p. 345.
34. Hegel notes in his lectures on the philosophy of history: "What was thus present for consciousness for such people was not the fatherland or any such ethical unity; they were pointed to giving themselves singly and alone over to fate and to achieving a complete indifference to life, which they then sought either in freedom of thought or in immediate sensuous enjoyment . . . for the systems of that time, stoicism, epicureanism and skepticism, although in themselves opposed to each other, were aiming at the same thing, namely to make spirit in itself indifferent to everything which reality offered." *Werke,* 12, p. 384–385.
35. In his lectures on the philosophy of history, Hegel notes: "We have seen subjective interiority (*Innerlichkeit*) as the universal principle of the Roman world." *Werke,* 12, p. 342. In another place in those lectures he says, "We saw the Romans start with the principle of abstract interiority, which is realized as personality in private law." p. 384.
36. Hegel broke from almost all of his contemporaries in seeing modern life as arising in principle at the end of antiquity with Christianity. Unlike those who saw history as falling into three periods – antiquity, the Middle Ages, and the modern world – Hegel saw the so-called "Middle Ages" as continuous with modern life in its insistence on the newly discovered role of human subjectivity and self-reflection that emerges with ancient antiquity. Like Nietzsche after him, he saw Christianity as the point at which history took its turn toward modern life. Hegel of course gave this a positive interpretation, in contrast to Nietzsche's rather negative view of the matter.
37. See ¶483, pp. 293–294; *PG*, p. 346.
38. See ¶487, pp. 296–297; *PG*, p. 350. Hegel calls these two realms of freedom of reflective thought and the alienated social world "pure consciousness" and "actuality."

39. See ¶¶488–489, pp. 297–299; *PG*, pp. 350–352. Hegel also mentions Diderot's dialogue, *Rameau's Nephew*, in this context to distinguish the "type" of which he is speaking. His point is that by the eighteenth century in France, the idea of being a "type" of person had come to be seen as a point of derision – one was supposed to be an "individual," not a "type." Or, to put it another way, one's autobiography was supposed to be more Rousseauian, to be the autobiography of a unique individual and not the retelling of some more general story.

40. The German term that Hegel uses, *"Bildung,"* carries the meanings of both formation (from the verb *bilden,* to form) and education. To become cultivated is to become *gebildet,* that is, "cultured" and "formed." The English term, "culture," is derived originally also from the idea of cultivation. Originally one was said to "culture" crops in the sense of cultivating them, and later one was said to cultivate one's mental faculties (that is, to "culture" them).

41. See ¶491, pp. 299–300; *PG*, p. 353.

42. See ¶493, pp. 300–301; *PG*, p. 354. Hegel speaks there of the "unchangeable essence" (meaning that set of practices that defined nobility) and the "passive spiritual essence" (meaning the individual who gives himself over to the "universal" standards of what it means to be cultivated), which by doing so gives itself over to "being for others" (honor in the eyes of others) and thereby becomes an individual, described by Hegel as a "becoming a being-for-himself (*Fürsichwerden*)".

43. See Orest Ranum's account of the ideals of European and particularly French aristocracy in his *Paris in the Age of Absolutism* (New York: Wiley, 1968). pp. 132–166.

44. Hegel's discussion here is somewhat anachronistic, since at least for the feudal period there is no *state* proper to which the aristocrat could be attached, something of which Hegel was well aware. (He makes a point of it in his later lectures on the philosophy of history.) However, Hegel seems to be using "state" here in a sense to mean something more general like "political community," which can take the form of the modern "state" or the form of a set of feudal relationships.

45. Quoted from Helen Gardner (ed.), *The Metaphysical Poets* (London: Penguin Books, 1957). p. 232.

46. Hegel sees both the aristocrat and the bourgeois as aspects of *Bildung,* cultivation and educative self-formation. He quite abstractly and obscurely describes the way in which the spirit of *Bildung* (the way in which European life accounts for itself in this period) in ¶492, p. 300; *PG*, pp. 353–354, in which he speaks of the way in which this form of life divides into "organically related groupings of people" (*Masse*) that represent the apparently contradictory accounts that people in this period give of themselves, with spirit itself serving as the unity that binds these accounts together in that this "spirit" consists of similar accounts of the same form of life, which, however, to themselves seem very different.

47. See ¶495, p. 302; *PG*, pp. 355–356.

48. See ¶496, pp. 302–303; *PG*, pp. 356–357.

49. See ¶498, p. 304; *PG*, pp. 357–358.

50. See ¶499, p. 304; *PG*, p. 358. Hegel says that one has "being-for-self" as a principle, and the other has "being-in-itself" as a principle. That is, one takes a good reason as having to do with the *subjective* point of view (being-for-self); the other takes a good reason as having to do with the *objective* point of view (being in-itself).

51. See ¶¶500–501, p. 305; *PG*, pp. 358–359.

52. See ¶500, p. 305; *PG*, pp. 358–359.

53. ¶503, p. 306; *PG,* p. 360.
54. The "privileges" were that set of laws relating to the estates of early modern Europe that expounded what was due to members of that estate; needless to say, there was great dispute as to the origin and legitimacy of these laws, as to whether they were natural, traditional or issued by the prince. In the later accounts, "privileges" came to be distinguished from "rights" in the sense that the "privileges" were considered *in principle* to apply only to members of a certain estate, whereas "rights" were considered to apply in principle to all people.
55. This seems to be the point of the condensed discussion in ¶506, pp. 307–308; *PG,* pp. 361–362.
56. See Orest Ranum's account of this transition in chapter eight, "The Last Heroes" of his *Paris in the Age of Absolutism,* pp. 8–151
57. Hegel explains this move from the Valois to the Bourbon aristocracy in ¶508, pp. 308–309; *PG,* pp. 362–363. He there speaks of language as the *"existence* of the pure self as a self; in it the *individuality* of self-consciousness as existing for-itself as such steps into existence, so that it is *for an other."* All other forms of expression (the wearing of fashionable clothes, the adoption of certain mannerisms, etc.) are such that the (noble) self can refuse to identify with them. On this account, the noble cannot be "distinguished" as a noble by such externalities. It is only in his *speaking* in the proper way that the true self (as a noble self) can be *taken to be* such by others. But the detached self that stands back and reflects on his self-presentations to others cannot therefore be wholly absorbed by these others. As Hegel notes, not entirely perspicuously: "In that he has been *noted* (*vernommen*) has his *existence* itself immediately *faded away* . . . and his existence is just this: as a self-conscious *now,* not to be present (*da zu sein*) as he is present, and, through this disappearance, to be present" – or, in other words, to be a detached, reflective self who presents himself to others, but who, as detached, cannot identify himself with the interpretations that these others put on him and who thereby immediately distances himself from all such interpretations.
58. See ¶509, p. 309; *PG,* p. 363. Hegel refers to the agents as "moments" of this spirit, indeed as the "self-knowing category," which for him is shorthand for the Kantian synthetic unity of apperception. His point seems to be that the creation of the "pure self" in European aristocratic culture was the social condition that set the stage for the Kantian articulation of the conception of the self-determining subject. Only when the subject had been "purified," as he puts it here, into the abstract conception of simply a thinking, acting *subject* could the Kantian philosophy be possible.
59. Hegel admired *Le Cid* (1636), which had been the sensation of its day in Parisian aristocratic circles. He speaks approvingly of the way the "collision of love and honor plays a brilliant part" in the play. *Aesthetics,* Vol. I, p. 241; *Werke,* 13, p. 312.
60. ¶511, pp. 310–311; *PG,* pp. 364–365.
61. Hegel says in ¶511, pp. 310–311; *PG,* pp. 364–365 that ". . . .through that it raises the individuality, which otherwise is only something supposed (*Gemeintes*), into its existing purity in its giving the monarch his own *name;* for it is only the name in which the *difference* of the individual from all others is not merely *supposed* but on the contrary is made actual by all."
62. See ¶512, pp. 311–312; *PG,* pp. 365–366.
63. See ¶¶516–517, pp. 313–314; *PG,* pp. 367–368.
64. Hegel's treatment of this part of the account occurs in the section of the *Phenome-*

nology titled, "The Spiritual Kingdom of Animals." In ¶521, pp. 316–317; *PG,* pp. 371–372, he makes reference to the idea of the "sincere consciousness," which was the logical development of the account offered in the "spiritual kingdom of animals."

65. *Rameau's Nephew* also makes reference to the debate about polyphonic music which had circulated in European circles in Hegel's youth. (This occurs in the discussions about melodies that are suited for the singing voice and the way this was not realized in the "older" music that showcased complicated harmonic effects.) Rousseau was one of the most well known opponents to the "older," polyphonic music, calling it "the remains of barbarism and bad taste that only persist, like the portals of our gothic churches, to the shame of those who have the patience to construct them." [In his *Lettre sur la Musique Française,* quoted in Arthur Loesser, *Men, Women and Pianos: A Social History* (New York: Dover Publications, 1954), p. 87.] The nephew in the story also opposes himself to polyphonic music, the music of which his uncle, Rameau, had been one of the masters. Like Rousseau, the nephew prefers a simple melody that "fits the words" because he takes it to be more "natural" than the complex polyphonic compositions of the previous generations and therefore to be a more complete expression of the "natural soul." Part of the object of Diderot's attack in *Rameau's Nephew* is this eighteenth-century conceit of the "natural" person, who expresses his common natural "humanity" (in this case by playing only simple melodies with little accompaniment), especially since this is put in the mouth of a completely "non-natural," self-consciously self-constructed individual such as the nephew (the antithesis of a "natural soul"). Diderot is implicitly making an analogy with the simplicity of "natural" tunes, and the clarity of "natural" ideas of virtue. On the accounts given by some in his day, both should be easily recognizable by a "natural soul." However, the "pure self" who is the nephew cannot then have any good reason for endorsing the natural melodies, except the nihilistic one that such an account is the best one to give to those equally "pure selves" who like to tell themselves that they are only being "natural" in their musical and ethical tastes. At one point in the dialogue, the "I" says: "When I pronounce the word "tune" I have no clearer idea than you and most of your kind when you say "reputation, blame, honor, vice, virtue, modesty, decency, shame, ridicule."" *Rameau's Nephew* (transl. L.W. Tancock) (Harmondsworth: Penguin Books, Ltd., 1966), p. 98. Hegel would have most likely recognized those passages as being critical of Rousseau, even though his own taste in music apparently also ran to the simple. In visiting Vienna, Hegel did not once hear either Schubert or Beethoven, feasting himself instead on some farces, theatrical pieces and Italian operas – he actually judged Rossini's *Barber of Seville* to be superior to Mozart's *Figaro!* Concerning Hegel's visit to Vienna, see Horst Althaus's biography of Hegel, *Hegel und die heroischen Jahre der Philosophie* (Munich: Carl Hanser Verlag, 1992), p. 438. On the strengths and deficiencies of Hegel's understanding of music and his preference (like Diderot himself) for music accompanied by texts rather than purely orchestral music, see Stephen Bungay, *Beauty and Truth: A Study of Hegel's Aesthetics* (Oxford: Clarendon Press, 1984), pp. 133–141.

66. In ¶¶523–524, pp. 318–319; *PG,* pp. 373–374, Hegel discusses the dialogue in a way that will be unintelligible to those who have not themselves read the dialogue. The most directly relevant pages in *Rameau's Nephew* (Tancock's translation) for Hegel's discussion are pp. 122–123 and p. 108, which has to do with the discussion of someone's being a "type," an *Espèce* – which itself has to do with the way in

which Hegel thinks that this type of "cultivation" has led to the formation of the modern concept of individuality.

67. See ¶526, pp. 320–321; *PG*, p. 375.

68. See ¶540, pp. 328–329; *PG*, pp. 384–385.

69. See ¶541, p. 329; *PG*, p. 385. Hegel notes at the end of the paragraph: "Pure insight, however, is at first without content and is rather the pure disappearance of it; but by the negative movement towards what is negative to *it*, it will realize itself and give itself a content."

70. See ¶542, p. 330; *PG*, p. 386.

71. See ¶543, p. 330; *PG*, p. 386.

72. See Immanuel Kant, "What is Enlightenment?" (transl. by Lewis White Beck) in Lewis White Beck (ed.) *Kant: Selections* (New York: Macmillan, 1988). pp. 462–467. Hegel speaks of the Enlightenment's attempt as that of making "faith's" self-consciousness having "only to become this *for-itself*." ¶544, p. 331; *PG*, p. 387.

73. Hegel refers is to the way in which unbelief spread like wildfire in the sophisticated urban setting of Paris during the Enlightenment by comparing it to a "silent expansion or to the *diffusion,* say, of a perfume in the unresisting atmosphere." He also calls it a "penetrating infection." See ¶545, p. 331; *PG*, p. 387. In that paragraph, he also makes oblique reference to the ways in which the religious establishment tried to stop the spread of Enlightenment and how these attacks therefore just made things worse for the proponents of "faith" – for example, the clerical counterattackers produced their own sets of satirical plays on the *philosophes,* mirroring the way in which the *philosophes* had produced works lampooning religion, the result of which was to intensify the atmosphere of satirical criticism which in turn fueled the dynamic of the *philosophes'* movement even more. (Hegel may have garnered his knowledge of these things from the discussions of them in *Rameau's Nephew.*)

74. See ¶548, pp. 333–334; *PG*, pp. 389–390. Hegel says somewhat darkly that "[a]s pure insight it is without any content; the movement of its realization consists in its becoming itself its content, since an other cannot become its content because pure insight is the self-consciousness of the category." Hegel is referring back here to his discussion at the end of the chapter on "Reason" concerning Kant's conception of the synthetic unity of apperception as the principle in terms of which the various grounds of knowledge are to be derived. The Enlightenment project of basing everything on "pure insight" is, so he is circuitously saying, *implicitly* a demand for a self-originating principle (like that of the synthetic unity of apperception). Thus, he says that "its completion has consequently this sense, that it is to know (*erkennen*) the content that was at first objective to it. Its result becomes . . . an insight which knows the absolute negation of itself as its own actuality, knows itself or its self-knowing concept" – that is, the Enlightenment project of constructing a "pure insight" finds itself completed in Kantian philosophy. In its Kantian, idealist form, it is more able to reassure itself that its own skepticism is not warranted; in that way, it comes to be "absolute negation," self-reassurance that its own skeptical doubts can be answered.

75. See ¶549, pp. 334–335; *PG*, pp. 390–391.

76. Hegel makes a subtle terminological shift in ¶549, p. 335; *PG*, p. 391 to indicate that it is the German pietists, and particularly Zinzendorf's "Brethren" that he has in mind. He says: "But the absolute essence of faith is essentially not the *abstract* essence, which would lie beyond the faithful consciousness; rather, it is the spirit of the religious community (*Gemeinde*), it is the unity of the abstract essence and

of self-consciousness." In the next sentence, however, he says, "That it be this spirit of the community (*Gemeine*) requires as a necessary moment a doing (*das Tun*) on the part of the community (*Gemeine*)." The shift from *Gemeinde* (community, usually religious) to *Gemeine* is significant, since the latter term is used nowadays almost exclusively to denote Zinzendorf's Herrnhut brethren. In Hegel's time, the term had a slightly broader meaning, but it is plausible that Hegel shifts terms from one sentence to the next to indicate that he is referring to a particular type of religious community.

77. See ¶549, p. 335; *PG*, p. 391: as Hegel puts it, the *account* that the pietist community gives of how one is to know God (the absolute essence) ". . . is not the only ground of the essence; rather it is only a moment. The essence is at the same time in and for itself."

78. See ¶550, pp. 335–336; *PG*, pp. 391–392.

79. See ¶554, pp. 337–338; *PG*, p. 394–395.

80. See ¶556, pp. 339–340; *PG*, pp. 395–396.

81. See ¶557, p. 340; *PG*, pp. 396–397. Hegel calls this conception of God a "vacuum, to which no determination, no predicate can be attached." In that paragraph, Hegel also sarcastically notes that "pure insight" – the idea that what counts as authoritative is only that which a detached individual (detached ironically or by listening to the voice of reason) can come to hold – must also hold that whatever content *it* has comes from its "negative," that is, from "pure insight's" generating skeptical attacks on religion on the basis of the way in which religion had typically accounted for itself, it tries to reassure itself that it is therefore not an empty practice as it accuses "faith" of being. Hegel identifies the deist God as the *"être suprême"* in ¶562, p. 343; *PG*, p. 400.

82. Hegel's discussion in ¶557 parallels Voltaire's writings on superstition. Voltaire notes: "Almost everything that goes beyond the worship of a supreme being, and the submission of one's heart to his eternal commands, is superstition." Quoted in Peter Gay, *The Enlightenment: An Interpretation: The Rise of Modern Paganism*, p. 396. (The quote comes from Voltaire's entry on superstition in his *Dictionnaire Philosophique*.)

83. See ¶558, pp. 340–341; *PG*, pp. 397–398. Hegel notes: "Being *grounded* on the insight of the nothingness of all the other formations of consciousness, and hence of everything beyond sense-certainty, this sense-certainty is no longer mere opinion (*Meinung*) but rather absolute truth."

84. See ¶¶559–560, pp. 341–342; *PG*, pp. 398–400. Hegel's contentions in these paragraphs have to with the abstract relations between the knowledge that "sense-certainty" claims to give us and the way things are in themselves. On the one hand, the things of nature are considered to be known by observing reason as they are in themselves, yet on the other hand, nature is so constructed that it exhibits an order (a weakly *divine* order for deists) such that all the parts contribute to the whole.

85. See ¶561, p. 343; *PG*, p. 400.

86. See ¶560, pp. 342–343; *PG*, pp. 399–400.

87. See ¶563, pp. 343–344; *PG*, pp. 400–401. Hegel speaks somewhat indirectly here, claiming that faith has the "divine right" of "absolute self-identity (*Sichselbstgleichheit*) or of pure thought," whereas the Enlightenment has the "human right . . . of non-identity (*Ungleichheit*)." The idea of "non-identity" with which Hegel is arguing here has to do with his general conception of "negativity" as the way in which skeptical doubts are generated. A set of beliefs that takes itself to be in

order, to have no contradictions within itself, is said to have "self-identity" or "self-equality", as *Sichselbstgleichheit* might be translated. Hegel's idea is that something has self-identity (such as A = A) when it has no internal contradictions or incoherences. When skeptical doubts are generated out of the way it takes itself (as opposed to those skeptical doubts that are imposed from outside, by views simply different from it), it is said to have "non-identity," in that the original set of views now finds that it is embroiled in contradictions. It is of course Hegel's thesis that all views (except the final, absolute viewpoint) generate skeptical doubts when they are reflected upon; they all are endowed with "negativity," and they all produce their "determinate negations," the specific doubts oriented toward those particular types of views. He calls this in ¶563 the "right of self-consciousness," by which he means that such skepticism can arise only when a form of life has developed a social practice whose function is to give an account of our reason-giving accounts, that is, when the form of life has become "self-conscious." He continues this line of argument in ¶564, p. 344; *PG*, p. 401.

88. See ¶565, pp. 344–345; *PG*, pp. 401–402. Hegel claims the "Enlightenment itself . . . is just as little enlightened about itself . . . The Enlightenment *is* only this movement, it is the yet incognizant activity of the pure concept." In ¶574, pp. 349–350; *PG*, pp. 407–408, Hegel makes the same claim: the Enlightenment as the "self-alienated concept . . . does not recognize the *same essence* of both sides, of the movement of self-consciousness and of its absolute essence – it does not recognize the *same essence* of that which in fact is its substance and existence (*Bestehen*)."

89. See ¶568, pp. 346–347; *PG*, pp. 404.

90. See ¶572, pp. 348–349; *PG*, pp. 405–406.

91. See ¶574, pp. 349–350; *PG*, pp. 407–408. Hegel says that as "absolute concept," the Enlightenment "posits that movement [of abstractions] over and against itself as the *essence*," that is, it *takes* its own claims (the inferential links or "move-ments" among the various abstractions it makes) not as self-authenticating but as requiring authentication by a metaphysical "other," and it is led to take itself in this way because of its particular representationalist self-construal of what would count as an authentication of itself. It thus sets its own criteria for legitimation of itself as lying outside of itself: "it posits the being-other (*Anderssein*) or the determinateness on it (*an ihr*)." It is significant that Hegel says that this otherness is posited as is *"an ihr,"* not *"an sich"* or *"an sich selbst;"* I take him to be signaling there that the kind of authentication of the claim to knowledge is *taken* to be outside of the social practice of the claim-making activity itself.

92. See ¶578, pp. 351–352; *PG*, pp. 409–410. Hegel notes there that the conceptions of God, Nature, or Matter are thus equivalent to the concept of "pure being," the most abstract of all abstractions and the conception which so clearly has a "nega-tivity" within itself (in the sense that any attempt to think about it automatically produces a whole series of paradoxes).

93. See ¶¶579–580, pp. 353–354; *PG*, pp. 410–412. Hegel argues that what is common to this kind of deism and materialism is "pure thought thinking itself," which he quite metaphorically calls a "simple rotary (*achsendrehende*) movement" that divides itself into different "moments," depending on which case it is trying to make.

94. See ¶580, pp. 353–354; *PG*, pp. 411–412.

95. See ¶580, pp. 353–354; *PG*, pp. 411–412. Hegel says that pure insight "is the

consciousness of this *metaphysics,* but not yet the comprehension (*Begreifen*) of it; it has not yet come to the *unity* of *being* and of the *concept* itself."

96. See ¶581, p. 355; *PG,* p. 413: "This insight is thus itself a *true knowing,* and self-consciousness has equally immediately the universal certainty of itself, its *pure consciousness* in this relationship in which, therefore, *truth* as well as the present and *actuality* are united. The two worlds are reconciled and heaven is transplanted to earth below."

97. ¶582, p. 355; *PG,* p. 414.

98. See Robert Pippin's discussion of Rousseau's conception of self-determination and its pivotal role in the modern conception of self-determination in his "The Modern World of Leo Strauss," *Political Theory,* 20, 1992, pp. 448–472.

99. See ¶584, pp. 356–357; *PG,* p. 415.

100. ¶585, p. 357; *PG,* p. 416: "In this absolute freedom, therefore, all estates (*Stände*) which are the spiritual essences into which the whole is articulated are abolished; the individual consciousness that belonged to any such estate and willed and fulfilled itself in it has set aside (*aufgehoben*) its limitation; its end (*Zweck*) is the general end, its language universal law, its work the universal work."

101. See ¶588, p. 358; *PG,* p. 417: "Universal freedom, which would have separated itself in this way into its constituent parts and by the very fact of doing so would have itself into an *existent* substance, would thereby be free from *particular* individuality, and would apportion the *plurality* of *individuals* to its various constituent parts."

102. See ¶589, p. 359; *PG,* p. 417: "Neither by the mere idea of obedience to *self-given* laws which would assign it to only a part of the whole, nor by its being *represented* in law-making and universal action, does self-consciousness let itself be cheated out of *actuality,* the actuality of *itself* making the law and accomplishing not a particular work but the universal work itself. For where the self is merely *represented* and is present only as an idea (*repräsentiert und vorgestellt*), there it is not *actual;* where it is represented (*vertreten*) by proxy, it *is not.*" Hegel (perhaps also following Rousseau) might be alluding to Hobbes' idea that "And because the sovereignty is either in one man, or an assembly of more than one . . . there can be but three kinds of commonwealth. For the representative must needs be one man, or more: and if more, then it is the assembly of all, or but of a part." *Leviathan,* 121. Rousseau says: "I therefore maintain that since sovereignty is merely the exercise of the general will, it can never be alienated, and that the sovereign, which is only a collective being, cannot be represented by anything but itself." *On the Social Contract,* Book II, Chapter I; translated and edited by Donald A. Cress (Indianapolis: Hackett Publishing Company, 1983), p. 29.

103. See ¶589, p. 359; *PG,* p. 418: "Just as the individual self-consciousness does not find itself in this *universal work* of absolute freedom as existing substance, so little does it find itself in the *deeds* proper and *individual* actions of the will of this freedom. Before the universal can perform a deed it must concentrate itself into the one of individuality and put at the head an individual self-consciousness; for the general will is only an *actual* will in a self, which is a one. But thereby all other individuals are excluded from the entirety of this deed and have only a limited share in it, so that the deed would not be a deed of the *actual universal* self-consciousness."

104. See ¶591, p. 360; *PG,* p. 419: "The government is nothing else but the self-established focus, or the individuality, of the general will. The government, which wills and executes its will from a single point, at the same time wills and executes a specific order and action. On the one hand, it excludes all other individuals from its act, and on the other hand, it thereby constitutes itself a government that is a specific will, and so stands opposed to the general will; consequently, it is absolutely impossible for it to exhibit itself as anything else but a *faction*. What is called government is merely the *victorious* faction, and in the very fact of its being a faction lies the direct necessity of its overthrow; and its being government makes it, conversely, into a faction and guilty."

105. ¶591, p. 360; *PG,* p. 418.

106. See ¶593, p. 361; *PG,* p. 420: "Absolute freedom as *pure* self-equality of the general will thus has within it *negation;* but this means that it contains *difference* in general, and this again it develops as an *actual* difference. For pure *negativity* has in the self-equal general will the element of subsistence or the *substance* in which its moments are realized . . . These individuals who have felt the fear of death, of their absolute master, again submit to negation and difference, arrange themselves in the various spheres (*Massen*), and return to an apportioned and limited task, and thereby to their substantial actuality."

107. This is Eric Hobsbawm's point about the cult of Napoleon constituting what he calls the first secular myth of the modern world. See Eric Hobsbawm, *The Age of Revolution: 1789–1848* (Markham: Penguin Books Canada Limited, 1962). pp. 98–100.

108. See ¶596, p. 364; *PG,* p. 423.

109. That Hegel's understanding of German idealism as completing the French Revolution "in thought" was not just idiosyncratic to him but was also shared by most of the other figures in German idealism is argued by Dieter Henrich in his essay, "Französische Revolution und klassische deutsche Philosophie: Uberlegungen zur Bestimmung ihres Verhältnisse" in Dieter Henrich, *Eine Republik Deutschland* (Frankfurt a.M.: Suhrkamp Verlag, 1990) pp. 71–101.

110. In *Eine Republik Deutschland,* Dieter Henrich argues that German culture remained largely unaffected by the court culture that shaped so much of French life. Its culture was shaped more by village pastors who espoused an unaffected form of life. This fits in well with Hegel's account of the way in which German pietism prepared the way for a completion in thought of the social revolution in France.

111. See ¶599, p. 365; *PG,* pp. 424–425, where Hegel speaks of the immediacy of the moral worldview's giving way to "negativity" and thereby needing an account of itself – in other words, of pietism giving way to Kantian philosophy.

112. Later, after the defeat of Napoleon and the seeming end of the French Revolution, this idea, which had preceded the Revolution, gathered further momentum, and it helped to extend the "moral worldview" in Germany. Interestingly, Hegel claimed (no doubt rashly) to have predicted the later 1812 downfall of Napoleon in these sections of the *Phenomenology* written around 1807. In a letter written to his friend Niethammer in 1814, he said (quoting his *Phenomenology*): "There are great things that have happened around us. It is a terrible spectacle to see an enormous genius destroy himself . . . Incidentally, I have, as I like to praise myself, predicted the whole upheaval. In my work (completed on the night before the battle of Jena), I said on p. 547, "absolute freedom (it was previously depicted; it is the purely abstract, formal freedom of the French

republic, which, as I showed, came out of the Enlightenment) leaves its self-destroying actuality and passes over into *another land* (I had there one *land* in mind) of self-conscious spirit where, in this non-actual world, freedom has the value of truth. In the thought of this truth spirit refreshes itself in so far as *it is* and *remains thought* and knows this being enclosed in self-consciousness as the perfect and complete essence. There has arisen the new formation of spirit, that of moral spirit.'" (quoted in Heinrichs, *Die Logik der ⟨Phänomenologie des Geistes⟩*, p. 357, note 208). The quoted passage is from the *Phenomenology of Spirit*, ¶595, p. 363; *PG*, p. 422. In saying that Germany accomplished in thought what the French had done in practice, Hegel is also possibly referring to a belief at the time that Germany had created a culture without a political base to it – what the later nationalist Gustav Freytag called the "miraculous creation of a soul without a body." (Quoted in James J. Sheehan, *German History: 1770– 1866*, p. 145.) In any event, though, Hegel did not think that pietism was the coherent expression of this new self-understanding of self-determining agency, even though it did share with it the idea of turning inward to subjectivity to find therein the springs of thought of action and thus was part of the general "moral worldview." Hegel shared Kant's personal antipathy to pietism, as both were themselves burdened by it in their youth. Hegel was, alas, not so prescient in his failure to predict the continuing force of pietist nationalist sentiment as a component of the movement of reaction in the 1820's in Prussia, a development which was to be the basis of so much personal nervousness for him during his sojourn in Berlin from 1818 to 1831. On that, see John Edward Toews, *Hegelianism* (Cambridge: Cambridge University Press, 1980). pp. 245–248. Nonetheless, he maintained a kind of historical optimism that the incoherence of the pietist form of self-understanding would eventually have to give way to the force of modern institutions and the logic of the forms of self-understanding that best explicated what they were about.

113. See ¶603, p. 367; *PG*, p. 427: "Both of these, the pure thought and sensuosity of consciousness, are *in itself One consciousness,* and it is precisely pure thought for which and in which this pure unity is." See also ¶602, pp. 366–367; *PG*, pp. 426–427.

114. See ¶600, pp. 365–366; *PG*, p. 425.

115. See ¶602, pp. 366–367; *PG*, p. 426–427. Hegel notes that "*individual conviction* and the knowledge of it constitute an absolute moment in morality."

116. For example, Kant says in his *Doctrine of Virtue* that in the laws of virtue, the categorical imperative is taken more specifically: "Only that in ethics, this is thought as the law of your own will, not of will in general, which could also be the will of another." *Metaphysik der Sitten* (ed. by Karl Vorländer) (Hamburg: Felix Meiner Verlag, 1966). p. 229.

117. In ¶602, pp. 366–367; *PG*, p. 426–427, Hegel notes that it "lies in the concept of morality . . . it is a demand of reason."

118. Hegel's development of the various postulates of the moral worldview along with these passages' overall resemblance to the Kantian moral project might suggest that we take them as reconstructions of Kant's arguments for the postulates of practical reason. However, Hegel's postulates have only very general family resemblances to Kant's postulates of practical reason, and there is thus little point in comparing the two. Hegel's point is to reconstruct the "moral worldview" in general. Kenneth R. Westphal offers a very close comparison of the relevant Kantian texts and doctrines with the Hegelian counterclaims in his

"Hegel's Critique of Kant's Moral World View," in Willem A. deVries (editor) *Philosophical Topics*, 19, 2 (1991), pp. 133–176. Westphal claims, convincingly, that "Hegel lets Kant have his arguments and focuses on his conclusions and the world view they articulate. He argues that Kant's conclusions form an inconsistent set and that some of his conclusions are themselves incoherent. Consequently, be the arguments what they may, they must be faulty." (p. 137) Westphal argues that Hegel is thereby justified in calling these things "postulates," even though they have little to do with what Kant specifically labeled the postulates, since they concern what Kant's philosophy must posit in order to make the claims it does. (See pp. 137–138) However, the target in several of these sections seems not only to be Kant per se, but also Fichte, whom Hegel considered as having taken the Kantian program to its logical conclusion. Westphal disagrees, claiming that it is fair to see Kant as the sole object of attack. However, at least in some cases, it is clear that it must be Fichte of whom Hegel is speaking. For example, in ¶626, p. 380; *PG*, pp. 440–441, Hegel says of "morality" in the moral worldview: "But it is the essence of morality to be only the *perfectly pure; imperfect* morality is therefore impure or is immorality." This is clearly a reference to Fichte's doctrine (and certainly not Kant's!) that an action motivated by anything else than duty is immoral. Allen Wood points out the decidedly non-Kantian aspects of Fichte's theory of morality in his "Fichte's Philosophical Revolution," *Philosophical Topics*, 19 (1991),pp. 1–28, see esp. pp. 16–18. For the case that Fichte is at least the partial object of criticism, see Johannes Heinrichs, *Die Logik der ⟨Phänomenologie des Geistes⟩*, p. 372, note 229 and pp. 374–375. Westphal's overall argument, however, rests on the view that the *Phenomenology's* "method" is to explain some given domain of phenomena, and it criticizes other theories when they fail to explain that domain; he notes that Hegel wishes to examine views internally, which he takes as "examining how well that view accounts for the phenomena within its intended domain." (p. 142) Thus, in his view, Hegel's criticism of Kant has to be with whether Kant's proposed revision of our experience of morality really fits the phenomena in question. This downplays too much, however, the element of *negativity* in Hegelian philosophy, of seeing not how accounts "fit" the phenomena but of how accounts generate within their own terms skepticism about themselves.

119. In ¶602, pp. 366–367; *PG*, p. 426–427, Hegel concludes by saying that the "existence thus demanded – that is, the unity of both – is therefore not a wish nor, regarded as an end, one whose attainment were still uncertain; it is rather a demand of reason, or an immediate certainty and presupposition of reason."

120. In his "Hegel's Critique of Kant's Moral World View," Kenneth Westphal makes this point against some recent neo-Kantian attempts at revising Kantian ethical thought to include non-Kantian elements. See pp. 160–165.

121. Hegel makes these references in ¶603, pp. 367–368; *PG*, pp. 427–428.

122. ¶603, pp. 367–368; *PG*, pp. 427–428. Hegel notes: ". . . for in it is contained the opposition through which the self is consciousness, or is first really an actual self and at the same time a universal."

123. Hegel notes that formally this is the same problem as confronted the Greek form of life in terms of the conflicts between the various "powers" of that which was known and the unknown laws of the netherworld, although the specific nature of the problem is much different. See ¶604, p. 369; *PG*, p. 429.

124. See ¶604, p. 369; *PG*, p. 429

125. Hegel says that they must be seen as "existent in and for themselves" instead of being relative to something else. ¶604, p. 369; *PG*, p. 429

126. See ¶606, p. 370; *PG*, p. 430.

127. See ¶626, p. 380; *PG*, pp. 440–441. This point is also made by Kenneth Westphal, in his "Hegel's Critique of Kant's Moral World View," pp. 153–157.

128. Hegel speaks of this union of the personal and the impersonal points of view as leading to a conception of the "master and ruler of the world" as being necessary to "produce the harmony of morality and happiness" in ¶606, p. 370; *PG*, p. 430.

129. See ¶606, p. 370; *PG*, p. 430. Hegel says that this point of view is a "consciousness . . . in which the universal and the particular are purely one."

130. See ¶607, p. 371; *PG*, pp. 430–431.

131. See ¶609, p. 371; *PG*, p. 431.

132. See ¶611, p. 372; *PG*, p. 432. Hegel says that the "moral worldview" is only a "thinking, not comprehending" account. For it to be a "comprehending" account would be for it to recognize the "negativities" (the ways in which the account undermines itself) and the necessity to develop a new, integrated account which resolves those dilemmas.

133. See ¶¶612–614, pp. 372; *PG*, pp. 432–433.

134. See ¶616, p. 374; *PG*, p. 434.

135. See ¶617, p. 374; *PG*, p. 434–435.

136. See ¶618, p. 374–375; *PG*, p. 435–436.

137. See ¶619, p. 375–376; *PG*, p. 436–437.

138. See ¶620, p. 376; *PG*, p. 437; ¶623, p. 378–379; *PG*, p. 439.

139. See ¶622, pp. 377–378; *PG*, p. 437–438. Hegel notes: ". . . the self-conscious sensuosity which ought to be sublated is exactly this mediator (*Mitte*) between pure consciousness and actuality."

140. See ¶622, pp. 377–378; *PG*, p. 437–438. Karl Ameriks in his "Kant and Hegel on Freedom: Two New Interpretations," *Inquiry*, 35, 219–232, argues that recent attempts at saving Kant's theory of freedom by invoking the "two aspect" account of action fail. The "two aspect" account, brilliantly articulated by Henry E. Allison in both his *Kant's Transcendental Idealism* (New Haven: Yale University Press, 1983) and his *Kant's Theory of Freedom* (Cambridge: Cambridge University Press, 1990), holds that, for example, in knowledge "the ideality of space and time rests just in their being epistemic conditions of our experience, and not in their being in any ontological contrast to some more fundamental set of noumenal things or properties." (Ameriks, p. 221). In practical philosophy, the "two aspect" view holds that we need not describe action either as the result of noumenal willing or of a causal series; we can describe our actions as spatio-temporal events, *and* we can describe our actions in terms of the reasoning that justifies the action. These latter modes of description are not competing accounts of action, since the same action may be described both ways. Ameriks holds that this way of taking Kant will fail to get Kant out of his dilemmas, since "either this adoption [of a maxim] is solely a temporal act, and then, with a non-noumenal metaphysics, it is absolutely determined after all; or else the Kantian must move back to a noumenal ground to save the claims of freedom." (Ameriks, p. 222.)

141. This seems like an extraordinary, ad hominem charge against Kant and the Kantians. Kenneth Westphal in his "Hegel's Critique of Kant's Moral World View," pp. 145–146 defends Hegel on this point. Westphal notes that Hegel

bases this on his argument that it is mildly incoherent to say, as many do, that the wicked prosper and the virtuous languish, since on Kantian grounds, we have no good way to distinguish the virtuous from the wicked (that is, to distinguish those who are really trying from those who are not). Since there is no good way to make the distinction, if the distinction is made, it must be made arbitrarily. What better explanation is there of this arbitrary division except that some people are envious are those who are happier?

142. ¶631, p. 382–383; *PG*, p. 443–444.

143. See ¶631, pp. 382–383; *PG*, pp. 443–444.

144. See ¶¶634–635, pp. 385–386; *PG*, pp. 446–448.

145. See ¶638, p. 387; *PG*, p. 449: ". . . it regards itself as the *in-itself* or *essence;* but as conscience, it apprehends its *being-for-self* or its self . . . a simple *self,* which is just as much *pure* knowing as it is a knowing of itself as *this individual* consciousness. Consequently, this self constitutes the content of what was previously the empty essence."

146. See ¶640, p. 388; *PG*, p. 450: "Conscience is what is communal to the self-consciousnesses, and this is the substance in which the deed has subsistence and *actuality,* the moment of becoming *recognized* by others." See also ¶641; *PG*, p. 451.

147. See ¶641, pp. 388–389; *PG*, p. 451.

148. See ¶646, p. 393; *PG*, pp. 455–456.

149. See ¶647, pp. 393–394; *PG*, p. 456.

150. See ¶650, p. 395; *PG*, pp. 457–458.

151. ¶652, p. 395; *PG*, p. 458: "Here again we see *language* as the existence of spirit. Language is self-consciousness existing *for others,* self-consciousness which as such is immediately present at hand, and as *this* self-consciousness is universal. It is the self that separates itself from itself, which as pure I = I becomes objective to itself, which in this objectivity equally preserves itself as *this* self, just as it coalesces directly with other selves and is *their* self-consciousness. It takes itself just as it is taken by others, and the taking is just existence which has become a self."

152. See ¶653, pp. 395–396; *PG*, pp. 458–459.

153. See ¶652, p. 395; *PG*, p. 458.

154. See ¶656, pp. 397–398; *PG*, pp. 460–461.

155. See ¶655, p. 397; *PG*, p. 460.

156. See ¶656, pp. 397–398; *PG*, pp. 460–461.

157. ¶656, p. 398; *PG*, p. 461.

158. The term was common in the eighteenth century and in Hegel's own day. The phrase, "the beautiful soul" was also used by a number of writers with which Hegel would have been familiar – for example, by Schiller in his essay, "Über Anmut und Würde," by Goethe in *Wilhelm Meisters Lehrjahre,* and by Rousseau in his novel, *La Nouvelle Héloïse,* which concerns a romantic, religious community of "beautiful souls."

159. The connection between Hegel's idea of the beautiful soul and Rousseau's conception of the *belle âme* is laid out by Jean Starobinski in his *Jean-Jacques Rousseau: Transparency and Obstruction* (translated by Arthur Goldhammer) (Chicago: University of Chicago Press, 1988).

160. See ¶658, p. 400; *PG*, p, 463: "The hollow object it has itself produced now fills it therefore with a consciousness of emptiness. Its activity is a yearning which, as

it becomes an object devoid of essence, merely loses itself, and, transcending this loss and falling back on itself, finds itself only as something lost. In this transparent purity of its moments, as an unhappy so-called *beautiful soul,* its light dies away within it (*verglimmt sie in sich*), and it vanishes like a shapeless vapor that dissolves into thin air." It is clear from what Hegel says in the paragraph on Novalis in his later lectures on the history of philosophy that it is indeed Novalis whom Hegel had in mind in his discussion of the decline of the beautiful soul. He says of Novalis in the paragraph on him in the lectures: "Subjectivity exists in a lack but is driven towards something solid and thus remains a *longing.* This longing of the *beautiful soul* is presented in Novalis's writings. This subjectivity persists as longing, does not come to substantiality, dies out like an ember (*verglimmt in sich*), and holds itself solidly to this standpoint – the weaving and plotting of lines within itself; it is interior life and the ladenness with minutia (*Umständigkeit*) of all truth. The extravagance of subjectivity often becomes madness; it abides in thoughts, so it is caught in a vortex of the reflecting understanding, which always is negative against itself." *Werke,* 20, p. 418. In his later lectures on aesthetics, Hegel says of Novalis, "Novalis, for example, one of the nobler minds who felt himself to be in this standpoint, was driven into a void with no determinate interests, into this dread of actuality, and was wound down as it were into a spiritual consumption. This is a longing which will not let itself go in actual action and production, because it is frightened of being polluted by contact with finitude, although all the same it has a sense of the deficiency of this abstraction within it." *Aesthetics,* I, p. 160; *Werke,* 13, p. 211. (Novalis died of consumption, i.e., tuberculosis, in 1801.)

161. See the *Philosophy of Right,* §140. In the section on "Irony" in his introduction to his lectures on aesthetics, Hegel claims that the romantic conception of irony had its roots in the works of Friedrich von Schlegel. "This had its deeper roots in one of its aspects in Fichte's philosophy, in so far as the principles of this philosophy were applied to art . . . Now so far as concerns the looser connection of Fichte's propositions with one tendency of irony, we need in this respect emphasize only the following points about this irony, namely, that [*first*] Fichte sets up the *I* as the absolute principle of all knowing, reason and cognition – an *I* remains throughout abstract and formal. *Secondly,* this *I* is therefore in itself just simple, and, on the one hand, every particularity, every determinateness, every content is negated in it – since everything is submerged in this abstract freedom and unity – while on the other hand, every content which is to count for the *I* is only posited and recognized (*anerkannt*) by the *I* itself . . . But in that case, the *I* can remain lord and master of everything, and in no sphere of ethical life (*Sittlichkeit*), law, things human and divine, profane and sacred, is there anything that would not first have to be posited by the *I,* and therefore could not equally well be destroyed by it . . . Now *thirdly,* the *I* is a *living,* active individual, and its life consists in making its individuality for itself as for others, in expressing itself, and bringing itself into appearance. For every man by living tries to realize himself and does realize himself . . . Moreover this virtuosity of an ironical-artistic life apprehends itself as a *divine genius* for which anything and everything is only a creation lacking an essence (*wesensloser Geschöpf*) to which the creator, knowing himself to be disengaged and free from everything, is not bound, because he is just as able to destroy it as to create it. In that case, he who has reached this standpoint of divine genius looks down from his high rank on all

other men, for they are declared to be dull and limited, inasmuch as law, ethical life, etc. still count for them as fixed, essential and obligatory. So then the individual, who lives in this way as an artist, does give himself relations to others; he lives with friends, lovers, etc.; but by his being a genius, this relation to his own determinate actuality, his particular actions, as well as to what is universal in and for itself, is at the same time null; he behaves to all of it ironically . . . This then implies that not only is there to be no seriousness about law, ethical life, and truth, but that there is nothing in what is lofty and best, since, in its appearance in individuals, characters, and actions, it contradicts and destroys itself and so is ironical about itself." *Aesthetics*, I, pp. 65–67; *Werke*, 13, pp. 93–97.

162. Hegel calls the former non-ironic standpoint a "universal consciousness" and the latter ironic standpoint an "individual consciousness". See ¶660, p. 401; *PG*, p. 464.

163. See ¶660, p. 401; *PG*, p. 464: "For the consciousness which holds firmly to duty, the first consciousness counts as *evil*, because of the disparity between its *being within itself* (*Insichseins*) and the universal; and since, at the same time, this first consciousness declares its action to be in conformity with itself (*als Gleichheit mit sich selbst*), to be duty and conscientiousness, it is held by the universal consciousness to be *hypocrisy*." After this passage, Hegel refers to the ironist consciousness as the "evil consciousness," assuming for the point of his exposition the point of view of the non-ironist consciousness.

164. See ¶663, pp. 402–403; *PG*, pp. 465–466.

165. See ¶664, p. 403; *PG*, p. 466.

166. See ¶665, pp. 403–404; *PG*, pp. 466–468.

167. See ¶666, p. 405; *PG*, p. 468.

168. See ¶667, pp. 405–406; *PG*, pp. 469–470.

169. Emmanuel Hirsch in his "Die Beisetzung der Romantiker in Hegels Phänomenologie" (1924, reprinted in Hans Friedrich Fulda and Dieter Henrich (editors) *Materialien zu Hegels ⟨Phänomenologie des Geistes⟩*, pp. 245–275, argues that the hard-hearted moralist is none other than Hegel's old friend, Hölderlin. This same line is defended by Moltke Gram in his "Moral and Literary Ideals in Hegel's Critique of the "Moral World-View" " in *Clio*, 7. No. 3, 1978, pp. 375–402. (There is no citation of Hirsch in Gram's piece, showing that Gram comes to this conclusion independently of Hirsch.) Gram especially argues against the idea that Hegel could have had Schlegel in mind as the hard-hearted moralist, since he argues that such a view would completely misrepresent Schlegel's concept of irony. But, if my reconstruction is correct, then Schlegel would not be the *hard-hearted* moralist at all; Schlegel would be clearly the *romantic ironist*. If we assume for the sake of argument that we must then find some other literary model for the hard-hearted moralist, it would seem to me that it would not be, as Gram suggests, Hölderlin (who is more of a beautiful soul like Novalis), but Rousseau, the archetypal romantic moralist who both condemns the evils of his age while pretending always to be outside of it, and all the while taking part in it.

170. See ¶671, p. 409; *PG*, p. 472: "The reconciling Yes, in which the two I's fall away from their opposed *existence,* is the *existence* of the I which has expanded into a duality, which therein remains identical with itself, and in its complete externalization and opposite possesses the certainty of itself: it is the appearing God in the midst of those who know themselves as pure knowledge."

Chapter Six

1. In the *Phenomenology*, however, unlike the later "system," art and religion are compounded into one topic, and philosophy is not treated as a separate subject. Instead, we have a concluding chapter on "Absolute Knowledge." The clear distinction of the three types of practice of "absolute reflection" is central to Hegel's later work as articulated in his Berlin *Encyclopedia*. As such these reflections on the essential self-identity of the members of the community (and consequently on their highest interests) can be seen from two aspects: (1) they can be seen from the standpoint of how they articulate the central core beliefs of a form of life; and (2) they can be seen as individual social institutions and formations, expressing only a particular point of view. Philosophy takes itself to be concerned only with the former, not the latter. But why these three forms? In his later mature system, Hegel strangely insists on employing the categories of subjective spirit (those used in his philosophical psychology) in order to classify the three forms of absolute reflection. Thus, art is intuition (*Anschauung*), religion is taken as representation (*Vorstellung*), and philosophy corresponds to thought (*Denken*). The three forms of absolute reflection thus correspond to the three basic ways in which mentality operates. (Willem deVries, *Hegel's Theory of Mental Activity* gives an excellent account of these three forms of mentality or subjective spirit). However, as Stephen Bungay in his *Beauty and Truth* argues, this seems mistaken from a Hegelian point of view. Bungay notes, for example, that Hegel often argues that some art is connected with representation (*Vorstellung*). Moreover, the modes in the "Psychology" designate not psychological modes of access to a common object (as art, religion and philosophy are said to do) but different forms of spirit. Moreover, absolute spirit is supposed to move on the level of what in the *Science of Logic* is called the "Concept," not on the level of the "Psychology." Thus, the division of absolute spirit into its form should follow the way in which concepts are divided. As an alternative, Bungay proposes that we see the distinction in the following way: Since the content of absolute spirit is self-reflection, we should see (1) in *art* that content is *universal;* (2) in *religion* that content is *particular* – that is, different according to socio-historical context; (3) in *philosophy* it is *individual* since universal themes are understood in a particular way. The difference would thus mirror the difference between universal, particular and individual concepts. See Bungay, *Beauty and Truth*, pp. 31–34.

2. See ¶672, p. 410, *PG*, p. 473: "In the previous formations (*Gestaltungen*) . . . religion as consciousness of *absolute essence* as such has indeed made its appearance, although only from the *standpoint of the consciousness* that is conscious of absolute essence; but absolute essence *in and for itself,* the self-consciousness of spirit, has not appeared in those forms."

3. To speak of *symbols* here might be misleading, since Hegel uses the term "symbol," in a very special way in his *Aesthetics* to denote the kind of art that one finds in Egypt. I am using "symbol" in its more contemporary, non-Hegelian sense here.

4. See ¶673, p. 410, *PG*, p. 473.

5. See ¶673, p. 410, *PG*, p. 473: "But the supersensible, the eternal, or whatever else it may be called, is devoid of self; to begin with, it is only the universal, which is a long way yet from being spirit that knows itself as spirit."

6. See ¶675, p. 411, *PG*, p. 474: ". . . the supersensible, *empty* beyond which is neither to be known nor feared it knows neither as a self nor as a power."

7. See ¶673, p. 410, *PG*, p. 473: "The immediate existence of *reason* which for us issued from that pain and its characteristic formations has no religion, because the self-consciousness of them knows or seeks *itself* in the *immediate* present."

8. See ¶680, p. 414, *PG*, p. 477: "The whole of spirit, the spirit of religion, is again the movement away from its immediacy toward the attainment of the *knowledge* of what it is *in itself* or immediately, the movement in which finally the *formation* in which it appears for its consciousness will be perfectly identical with its essence, and it will behold itself as it is."

9. See ¶682, p. 415, *PG*, pp. 479–480: "Spirit is actual as absolute spirit only when it is also for itself in its *truth* as it is in its *certainty of itself,* or when the extremes into which as consciousness it divides itself are for each other in a spiritual formation (*Geistesgestalt*)."

10. See ¶684, p. 417, *PG*, p. 481: "The series of different religions which will come to view, just as much sets forth again only the different aspects of a single religion, and moreover of *every single* religion, and the representations (*Vorstellungen*) which seem to distinguish one actual religion from another occur in each one."

11. This also distinguishes philosophy – as a form of absolute spirit – from science. Plato's or Aristotle's works have a kind of resonance for us that much Greek science does not and cannot have. Likewise, Newton's science is of interest to us as science only to the extent that parts of it continue to be accepted by the scientific community. Those parts that have been superseded are no longer of scientific interest.

12. *Lichtwesen* is translated by Miller as "God as Light".

13. See ¶686, p. 419, *PG*, p. 484: "In virtue of this determination, this formation is the pure, all-embracing and all-pervading *luminous essence* of sunrise, which preserves itself in its formless substantiality. Its otherness is the equally simple negative, *darkness.*"

14. See ¶689, p. 420; *PG*, p. 485.

15. Hegel's understanding of the Egyptians at the time of the writing of the *Phenomenology* was completely uninformed by anything now recognizable as modern Egyptology, since the latter did not really come about until after his death. At the time of the writing of the *Phenomenology,* for example, Champollion had not yet deciphered the Egyptian hieroglyphs. His knowledge of the ancient Egyptians as evidenced in the *Phenomenology* seems to rely heavily on Herodotus. Hegel later apparently became familiar with more up to date Egyptology, including Champollion's work. See *Lectures on the Philosophy of Religion: The Lectures of 1827,* (Peter Hodgson, ed.; translated by R.F. Brown, P.C. Hodgson, and J.M. Stewart, with the assistance of H.S. Harris) (Berkeley: University of California Press, 1988), p. 326, note 341, editor's comment.

16. See ¶691, p. 421; *PG*, p. 486.

17. See ¶695, p. 423; *PG*, p. 488.

18. See ¶696, p. 423, *PG*, p. 488: "Over against this outer self of the formation (*Gestalt*) stands the other formation which proclaims its possession of an *inner* side (ein *Inneres*). Nature, withdrawing into its essence, sets down its living, self-particularizing, self-entangling manifold existence to the level of an unessential husk, which is the *covering for the inner* aspect; and this inner aspect is, in the first instance, still simple darkness, the unmoved, the black, formless stone."

19. *Aesthetics*, I, p. 111; *Werke*, 13, p. 151.

20. Greek art is distinguished from Christian art. In the latter, truths about spirit cannot in principle be captured completely in the work of art, since the simple

pursuit of beauty itself is not enough to capture the Christian truth. (A well-done, beautiful painting of Jesus loosing himself from the cross and running away cannot capture Christian "truth," however well it is executed.) Modern art is distinct from Christian art in that it takes the principles of thought to be determinative of the truth, and hence imports itself as an external criterion into both religion and art in a similar way to which Christian religion imported itself into art. Hegel's complex doctrine of art also had him ranking the periods of world history in terms of the categories of absolute spirit. Thus, the ancient world is best captured in its art, the medieval world in religion, and modern life (post 1789) in philosophy. An excellent and clear discussion of this theme in the mature *Aesthetics* is found in Stephen Bungay, *Beauty and Truth.* pp. 56–71.

21. See ¶707, p. 428, *PG,* p. 494: "The *essence* of the god is however the unity of the universal existence of nature and of self-conscious spirit, which in its actuality has the appearance of standing over and against the former. At the same time, being in the first instance an *individual* formation, its existence is one of the elements of nature, just as its self-conscious actuality is an individual national spirit. But the former is in this unity that element reflected into spirit, nature transfigured by thought and united with self-conscious life."

22. See ¶709, p. 429, *PG,* p. 495: "The artist then learns in his work that he did not produce an essence *like himself.* From it, it is true, there comes back to him a consciousness in the sense that an admiring crowd reveres it as the spirit which is their own essence. But this animation, since it returns to him his self-consciousness only as admiration, is rather a confession to the artist that the animated work is not the same as him (*nicht seinesgleichen zu sein*). Since his work comes back to him simply as joyfulness, he does not find therein the pain of his cultivation and begetting, nor the effort of his work." Miller's translation of *Beseelen* and *Beseelung* as "inspire" and "inspiration" is terribly misleading in this context, since it makes the English passages suggest that what is at issue in the work of art is whether it comes from the inspiration of the artist. That is, it makes it seem as if Hegel is bringing in a romantic worry about artistic inspiration into his discussion of Greek art.

23. See ¶710, p. 430, *PG,* p. 496: "This higher element is language – an existence (*Dasein*) that is immediately self-conscious existence. Just as the *individual* self-consciousness is *immediately* present in language, so it is also immediately present as a *universal* infection; the complete particularization into being-for-self is at the same time the fluidity and the universally communicated unity of many selves; language is the soul existing as soul."

24. Hegel expresses this as saying that "in other words, self-consciousness in the becoming-objective (*Gegenständlichwerden*) of its essence, remains immediately with itself (*bei sich*)." ¶710, p. 430, *PG,* p. 496.

25. For example, in the lectures on the philosophy of religion, Hegel says: "Here this natural will is the negation, and the human being comes to itself and is free spirit in overcoming this naturalness; one has reconciled one's heart or natural individuality – which is other than rationality or the rational – with the rational, and so one is present to oneself." *The Lectures of 1827,* p. 311. In the *Encyclopedia,* Hegel says: "The *subject* is the *activity* of the satisfaction of drives, of formal rationality, namely, the translation from the subjectivity of the content, insofar as it is an end (*Zweck*), into objectivity, in which the subject comes together with itself (*sich mit sich selbst zusammenschliesst*) . . . An action is the subject's end, and it is his activity that executes this end; only in that in this manner the subject is *in* even

disinterested action, i.e., through his interest, is it an action in general . . . However, drive and passion is nothing other than the vitality (*Lebendigkeit*) of the subject, according to which it itself is in its ends and their execution." *Encyclopedia,* §475.

26. See ¶710, p. 430, *PG,* p. 496: "It retains within itself the individuality of self-consciousness, and this individuality is at the same time taken as universally there. Devotion, kindled in all the agents, is the spiritual stream which in the multiplicity of self-conscious agents is conscious of its act as the same as the act of all and as *simple being.* Spirit, as this universal self-consciousness of all, has its pure inwardness, no less than the being-for-others and the being-for-self of the individuals in a single unity."

27. See ¶710, p. 430, *PG,* p. 496: "This language is distinct from another language of the god which is not of universal self-consciousness. The *oracle,* both of the god of the religions of art and of the preceding religions, is the necessary first form of the god's utterance; for the *concept* of the god implied that is the essence of both nature and spirit, and therefore has not only natural but spiritual existence as well. In so far as this moment is at first merely implied in his *concept* and not yet realized religion, the language is for the religious self-consciousness the language of an *alien* self-consciousness."

28. See ¶712, p. 432, *PG,* p. 497: ". . . in the religion of art because the god has taken on consciousness and hence individuality in general, the language peculiar to the god is the spirit of an ethical people is the oracle, which knows its particular affairs and what is advantageous concerning them. However, the universal truths, because they are known as that which exists in itself (*das Ansichseiende*), are claimed by *knowing thought (wissende Denken)* for itself, and their speech is no longer alien to it but is its own." ¶712, p. 431, *PG,* p. 497; "What is higher than both, however, is not only to make deliberation into the oracle for contingent action but in addition to know that this deliberate action is itself something contingent on account of its connection with the particular aspect of the action and of its advantageousness."

29. In his lectures on the philosophy of religion, Hegel says: "In the cultus, honor is bestowed upon the god, but revering God turns into the reverence proper to humanity itself, the reverence that makes the consciousness of one's affirmative relationship and unity with the gods valid in one's own self." *Lectures on the Philosophy of Religion 1827,* p. 351.

30. See ¶718, pp. 434–435; *PG,* pp. 500–501.

31. In the lectures on the philosophy of religion, Hegel notes: "Bacchus and Demeter, wine and bread, are external for the human being. The way to make oneself identical with them is to consume them, to assimilate them into oneself."

32. See ¶718, p. 434, *PG,* p. 500: "The sacrifice of the divine substance, in so far as it is an *act,* belongs to the self-conscious aspect; that this actual deed be possible, the essence must in itself have already sacrificed itself . . . This renunciation therefore which the essence has already accomplished *in itself,* is presented by the acting self in existence and for his own consciousness, thus replacing that *immediate* actuality of the essence by a higher actuality, namely, that of *himself.*"

33. See ¶722, p. 437, *PG,* p. 503: "For the mystical is not concealment of a secret or ignorance but consists in the self knowing itself to be one with the essence and this therefore is revealed."

34. Hegel seems to be aware of the rather vague nature of some of the things that he says at this point in the *Phenomenology* about Greek religious life, but he also

seems to believe that such vagueness matches up with the rather abstract nature in which the religion appropriate to that form of life understood itself. The forms of self-reflection practiced by such cults are after all only *abstract* and are therefore only very general reflections on self-identity. It would falsify them to make them more determinate than they are, to give any more determinate articulation to expressions like "being one with the essence of things."

35. In speaking of the Greek games in his lectures on the philosophy of history, Hegel noted, "If we observe now the inner nature of these games, we note above all that the game is opposed to seriousness, to dependence and need. There was no seriousness to such wrestling, running and sparring; in them lay no necessity of defense, no need of battle. What is serious is labor in reference to some need; I or nature must perish; if one is to subsist, the other must fall. Compared to this seriousness, however, the game is the higher seriousness, for in it nature is incorporated into spirit, and although in these contests the subject has not advanced to the highest seriousness of thought, yet in this exercise of his corporeality, man shows his freedom, namely, that he has transformed his body into an organ of spirit." *Werke,* 12, pp. 297–298.

36. As Hegel puts it in his lectures on the philosophy of religion, "Thus, for example, Pallas Athena is not the goddess of the city. What is represented in Pallas Athena is the living, actual spirit of the Athenian people according to its essentiality" (*Lectures on the Philosophy of Religion,* p. 350); and, "Pallas is the people or nation itself; but the nation is the god imbued with life, it is this Athena who delights in herself." (p. 352.)

37. "A major point of their mythology is the gods, with Zeus at their head, have gained the mastery for themselves by a war, by violence. The spiritual power has cast down the giants, the titans, from the throne; the sheer power of nature has been overcome by the spiritual, the spiritual has elevated itself above it and now rules over the world. Thus this war with the titans is not merely a fairy tale but is the essence of the Greek religion. The entire concept of the Greek gods lies in this war of the gods." *Lectures on the Philosophy of Religion,* p. 333.

38. See ¶707, p. 428, *PG,* p. 494: "The form of the gods (*Göttergestalt*) has, therefore, its nature-element within it as a sublated element, as a dim memory. The desert-like essence and confused strife of the free existence of the elements, the unethical realm of the titans, is conquered and banished to the fringes of an actuality that has become clear to itself, to the obscure boundaries of the world which finds itself in spirit and is there at peace."

39. "A third aspect of epic individuals may be deduced from the fact that what epic has to describe is not an action as such, but an event (*Begebenheit*). In drama what is all-important is that the individual shall actually be working for his end and shall be presented precisely in this activity and its consequences. Undisturbed concern for realizing one end disappears in epic. Here indeed the heroes may have wishes and ends of their own, but the chief thing is not the devotion of activity to their own end but what meets them in their pursuit of it. The circumstances are just as effective as their activity, and often more effective." *Aesthetics,* p. 1069; *Werke,* 15, pp. 361–362.

40. "Here we have before us in domestic and public life neither barbarism nor the purely intellectual prose of an ordered family and political life, but that originally poetic middle stage that I described above. But a chief point in it concerns the free individuality of all the figures. For example, in the *Iliad* Agamemnon is the King of Kings, the other princes are under his scepter, but his position as overlord does

not become the dry connection of command and obedience, of a master and his servants. On the contrary, Agamemnon must be very circumspect and shrewd enough to give way, because the individual princes are not his lieutenants and generals, summoned at his call, but are as independent as he is himself; they have assembled around him of their own free will or have been induced by some other means to join the expedition. He must take counsel with them, and if they are dissatisfied they stay away from the fight as Achilles did. This freely willed participation in the struggle, or the reverse, preserves the independence of the individual unimpaired, and this is what gives the whole relationship its poetic form . . . The relation between Agamemnon and the princes is repeated in the relation between the princes and their people. The latter follow of their own will; there is no compelling law to which they are subject . . . Order prevails in the home as well, though it is not an organization of servants but a matter of disposition and *mores*. Everything looks as if it had become so immediately (*unmittelbar so geworden*)." *Aesthetics*, pp. 1053–1054; *Werke*, 15, pp. 341–342.

41. See ¶720, p. 436, *PG*, p. 502.): "This spirit confronting the self-conscious people is therefore not the luminous essence, which being devoid of a self does not contain within it the self-certainty of the individuals but is only their universal essence and the lordly power in which they disappear. The cult of the religion of this simple shapeless (*gestaltlosen*) essence therefore gives back to its dependents (*angehörige*) in general merely this: that they are the people of their god, who secures for them only their enduring existence (*Bestehen*) and their substance as such; not, however, their actual self, which on the contrary is rejected. For they revere their god as the empty depth, not as spirit."

42. "Of course in relation to the wrath of Achilles moral pedants may very well ask us to consider what trouble this wrath produced and what damage it did, and then to draw an inference fatal to the excellence and greatness of Achilles on the ground that he could not be perfect either as hero or man when on the occasion of his wrath he had not self-mastery enough to modify the strength of his feeling. But Achilles is not to be blamed, and we need not excuse his wrath at all on the score of his other great qualities: the point is that Achilles is the man that he *is*, and with that, so far as epic goes, the matter is at an end." *Aesthetics*, p. 1067–1068; *Werke*, 15, p. 360.

43. "In this sense we can maintain that what rules in epic, though not, as commonly supposed, in drama, is fate. In drama, owing to the sort of aim which a character is determined to carry out in given and known circumstances, with all the resulting collisions, he creates his fate *himself*, whereas an epic character has his fate *made for* him, and this power of circumstances, which imprints an individual formation (*Gestalt*) on his deed, allocates his lot to him, and determines the outcome of his actions, is the proper dominion of fate . . . epic poetry moves in the element of a total state of affairs necessary in itself, and nothing is left to the individual but to submit to this fundamental situation, that is, to what *is*, be it adapted to him or not, and then suffer as may or must." *Aesthetics*, pp. 1070–1071; *Werke*, 15, p. 364. "But in epic, circumstances and external accidents count just as much as the character's will, and what he achieves passes before us just as what happens from without does, so that his deed must prove to be conditioned and brought about just as much by his entanglement in external circumstances . . . Now when equal worth is given to external circumstances with their attendant accidents independent of the individual, it seems that indisputable

playroom is given to that vein of accident, yet what epic should present to us is what is genuinely objective, i.e., the fundamental substance of existence. We can meet this contradiction at once by pointing out that *necessity* lies at the heart of events and happenings." *Aesthetics,* p. 1070; *Werke,* 15, pp. 363–364.

44. See ¶729, pp. 440–441, *PG,* p. 507. The singer of the epic is the individual artist whose task is to articulate this remembrance for the community and to give it shape so that the members of the community can see their essential self-identities in it as something which was previously only taken for granted. As Hegel puts it, "[t]he *minstrel* is the individual and the actuality out of whom as subject of this world this world is produced and borne. His pathos is not the stupefying power of nature but mnemosyne, recollection (*Besinnung*) and developed inwardness, the remembrance of formerly immediate essence."

45. See ¶729, pp. 440–441; *PG,* p. 507. In this way, Hegel thinks, the whole thing appears as an analogy to a syllogism, with a universal term – the gods – being linked to an individual term – the minstrel – through a particular term – the heroes of legend.

46. "Here what is especially required is that in the actions of gods and men the poetic relation of their mutual independence shall be preserved, so that neither can the gods be degraded to lifeless abstractions nor human individuals to being obedient servants." *Aesthetics,* p. 1072; *Werke,* 15, p. 366.

47. See ¶730, p. 441, *PG,* p. 508: "The undertaking which is the object of these general endeavors has two sides: the side of the *self,* by which the undertaking is accomplished by a totality of actual peoples and the individualities standing at their head; and the side of the universal, by which it is accomplished by their substantial powers."

48. See ¶732, p. 443, *PG,* p. 510: "The content of the world of representation (*Vorstellung*) freely unfolds itself in the *middle term* for itself, gathering itself round the individuality of a hero who, however, in his strength and beauty feels his life is broken and sorrowfully awaits an early death."

49. In the *Phenomenology of Spirit* itself, Hegel says: "This necessity, however, is the *unity* of the concept which brings under control the contradictory substantiality of the separate moments, a unity in which the inconsistency and arbitrariness of their actions receives its earnestness and worth in the actions themselves." ¶732, p. 443, *PG,* p. 510. But in his *Lectures on the Philosophy of Religion,* p. 339, Hegel notes: "The higher power, absolute unity, stands above the gods as a pure power. This is power is what is called destiny, fate or simple necessity. It is without content, is empty necessity, an empty unintelligible power that is devoid of the concept. It is not wise, for wisdom falls within the circle of the gods and includes concrete characteristics that belong in the sphere of the particular and pertain to single gods. Destiny is devoid of purpose and wisdom, it is a blind necessity that stands above all, even above the gods, uncomprehended and desolate. The abstract cannot be comprehended."

50. "For it is only the wars of nations foreign to one another that are of a genuinely epic kind, whereas dynastic battles, civil wars, and commotions are more suited to dramatic representation. Thus, for instance, Aristotle long ago recommended tragedians to select material with the war of brother against brother as its subject matter." *Aesthetics,* p. 1060; *Werke,* p. 351.

51. In an apparent reference to the dictum in the *Phenomenology* that "substance must become subject," Hegel notes intriguingly in his lectures on aesthetics that the

basic principle of drama is that the unity of substance and subject is of primary importance. This principle is basic to both tragedy and comedy. See *Aesthetics,* pp. 1193–1194 and p. 1201; *Werke,* 15, p. 520 and p. 530.

52. This becomes clear in ¶733, pp. 443–444, *PG,* pp. 510–511, and it is much more explicit in his discussion of it in his *Aesthetics.*

53. "At its first level we find the art of the actor in Greece. Here the art of speech is bound up with sculpture: the actor comes on the stage as a objective picture in total embodiment. But this statue is vitalized; it assimilates and expresses the content of the poetry." *Aesthetics,* p. 1186; *Werke,* 15, p. 511

54. In speaking of music in his *Aesthetics,* Hegel explains this in terms of the distinction between artistic result and artistic activity: "In sculpture and painting we have the work of art before us as the objectively and independently existent (*für sich dastehende*) *result* of artistic activity, but not this activity itself as produced and alive. The musical work of art, on the other hand, as we saw, is presented to us only by the action of an executant artist, just as, in dramatic poetry, the whole man comes on the stage, fully alive, and is himself made into an animated work of art." *Aesthetics,* p. 955; *Werke,* 15, p. 218.

55. See ¶734, p. 444, *PG,* p. 511: "In regard to form, the language ceases to be narrative (*erzählend*) because it enters into the content, just as the content ceases to one that is represented (*vorgestellt*)." ¶733, pp. 443–444; *PG,* p. 510; "Lastly, these characters *exist* as actual human beings who impersonate the heroes and portray them, not in the form of narrative, but in the actual speech of the actors themselves. Just as it is essential for the statue to be the work of human hands, so is the actor essential to his mask – not as an external condition from which artistically considered we must abstract."

56. "A truly tragic suffering, on the contrary, is only inflicted on the individual agents as a consequence of their own deed which is both legitimate and, owing to the resulting collision, blameworthy, and for which their whole self is answerable." *Aesthetics,* II, p. 1198; *Werke,* 15, p. 526.

57. With regard to this idea of reconciliation, Hegel makes an exception for *Oedipus at Colonnus,* which he characterizes as "an inner atonement (*Aussöhnung),* which because of its subjectivity, already borders on our modern treatment." *Aesthetics,* II, p. 1219; *Werke,* 15, p. 551.

58. Zeus is, Hegel wryly notes, only a commander of a variety of unruly gods: "They stand too under the supreme *command (Oberbefehl)* of the one, rather than under his supreme *sovereignty (Oberherrschaft)*." ¶728, p. 330, *PG,* p. 507.

59. ". . . in fact the chorus confronts us as a higher substantial consciousness, warning against false conflicts, and weighing the outcome. Nevertheless, the chorus is not at all a moral (*moralische*) person, disengaged like a spectator, a person reflecting on the thing purely from outside, in himself uninteresting and tedious, and introduced simply for the sake of his reflections. On the contrary, the chorus is the actual substance of the ethical life and action of the heroes themselves; in contrast to these individuals it is the people as the fruitful soil out of which they grow . . . and by the existence of which they are conditioned." *Aesthetics,* II, pp. 1210–1211; *Werke,* 15, p. 541.

60. Hegel makes some extremely oblique references to Shakespearean tragedy in this context comparing Oedipus with Macbeth and Hamlet. Given his later thoughts on tragedy as he worked them out in his *Aesthetics,* this comparison is misleading. In Greek tragedy, the oppositions come from the form of life in its social and institutional formations. In modern life, on the other hand, tragedy comes from

oppositions found within the subjectivity of the character himself or between characters. Thus, in Hegel's mature view, whereas Antigone is paradigmatic for Greek tragedy, Hamlet is paradigmatic for the modern tragedy of internal subjective conflict. See ¶737, pp. 446–447; *PG*, pp. 513–514. See also Stephen Bungay, *Beauty and Truth*, pp. 165–178 for an insightful treatment of the difference between Hegel's view of Greek and modern tragedy.

61. See ¶738, p. 447, *PG*, p. 514: "The nether law sits with Zeus on the throne and enjoys equal honor with the god who is revealed and is knowing."

62. See ¶740, p. 448, *PG*, p. 516: "The action, in being carried out, demonstrates their unity in the natural downfall of both powers and both self-conscious characters. The reconciliation of the opposition with itself is the Lethe of the underworld in death; or the Lethe of the upper world as absolution, not from guilt (for consciousness cannot deny its guilt, because it committed the act), but from the crime; and also the peace of mind following atonement for the crime."

63. "At its plastic height in Greece, tragedy remains one-sided by making the validity of the substance and necessity of ethical life its essential basis and by leaving undeveloped the individuality of the dramatis personae (*handelnden Charaktere*) and the depths of their personal life (*subjektive Vertiefung*). Comedy on its side brings to view in a converse mode of plasticity, and to perfection, the subjective personality in the free expatiation of its absurdity and its absurdity's dissolution." *Aesthetics*, p. 1222; *Werke*, 15, p. 555.

64. Hegel apparently did not conceive of a fundamentally nihilistic form of tragedy in which the characters would either not receive what was due to them by justice or in which the representation of the "eternal order of things" or "the social scheme of justice" is seen as not in and of itself consistent – that is, in which the order of things is seen as fundamentally irrational. Hegel himself clearly thought that this could not produce genuine *tragedy:* "Fate drives individuality back within its limits and destroys it if these are crossed. But an irrational compulsion and innocent suffering would inevitably produce in the soul of the spectator mere indignation instead of ethical peace." *Aesthetics*, II, p. 1216; *Werke*, p. 548.

65. ¶741, p. 449, *PG*, p. 516.

66. See ¶741, p. 449, *PG*, p. 516: "The expulsion of such essence-less representations (*wesenslose Vorstellungen*) which was demanded by the philosophers of antiquity thus already begins in tragedy in general through the fact that the division of the substance is controlled by the concept and consequently individuality is what is essential, and the determinations are the absolute characters."

67. In speaking of Aristophanes' plays, Hegel notes: "The keynote resounding in all these portrayals is the self-confidence of all these figures, and it is all the more imperturbable the more incapable they are of accomplishing their undertaking. The fools are such naive fools, and even the more sensible of them also have such an air of contradiction in what they are devoted to, that they never lose this naive personal self-assurance, no matter how things go." He also says: "Aristophanes presents to us the absolute contradiction between (a) the true essence of religion and political and ethical life, and (b) the subjective attitude of citizens and individuals who should give actuality to that essence." *Aesthetics*, p. 1222; *Werke*, 15, p. 554.

68. In his *Aesthetics* and in his *Lectures on the Philosophy of Religion*, Hegel is a bit more wide ranging in views about tragedy and comedy, raising *Oedipus at Colonnus* to almost equal status with *Antigone* and putting more value on the rest of Aristophanes' plays.

69. See ¶746, p. 451, *PG*, p. 519: "This *Demos*, the general mass, which knows itself as lord and ruler, and is also aware of being the intelligence and insight which demand respect, is constrained and befooled through the particularity of its actual existence and exhibits the ludicrous contrast between its own opinion of itself and its immediate existence, between its necessity and contingency, its universality and its commonness . . . there is exposed more immediately the contrast between the universal as a theory and that with which practice is concerned; there is exposed the complete emancipation of the purposes of the immediate individuality from the universal order, and the contempt of such an individuality for that order." ¶745, p. 451, *PG*, pp. 518–519. "With the vanishing of the contingent determination and superficial individuality which representational thought (*Vorstellung*) lent to the divine essentialities, all that is left to them as regards their *natural* aspect is the bareness of their immediate existence; they are clouds, an evanescent mist, like those representations."

70. See ¶752, pp. 454–455, *PG*, p. 523: "We see that his unhappy consciousness constitutes the counterpart and the completion of the comic consciousness that is perfectly happy within itself . . . The unhappy consciousness, on the other hand, is conversely the tragic fate of the certainty of self that aspires to being in and for itself. It is the consciousness of the loss of all *essentiality* in this *certainty of itself*, and of the loss even of this knowledge about itself – the loss of substance as well as of the self, it is the grief that expresses itself in the hard words, that *god is dead*."

71. See ¶754, p. 456, *PG*, p. 524: "All of the conditions for its production are to hand, and this totality of its conditions constitutes its *becoming*, its concept, or the arising of that as *existing in itself (das ansichseiende Hervorgehen desselben*)."

72. See ¶755, p. 457, *PG*, p. 525: "Spirit has in it two sides which are presented above as two converse propositions: one is this, that substance externalizes (*entäussert*) itself from itself and becomes self-consciousness; the other is the converse, that self-consciousness externalizes itself from itself and makes itself into thinghood (*Dingheit*) or a universal self . . . the externalization of self-consciousness expresses this: that it is *in itself* the universal essence or – since the self is pure being-for-self which in its opposite remains with itself (*bei sich bleibt*) – that is just because substance is self-consciousness *for the self*, that it is spirit."

73. See ¶757, p. 458; *PG*, pp. 526–527.

74. In the *Phenomenology*, Hegel does not discuss Judaism in this transition, although it forms an essential part of his later mature lectures on the philosophy of religion in Berlin. This lack of discussion is a bit puzzling, since in earlier manuscripts Hegel discussed Judaism at length. However, his earlier understandings of Judaism – for example, in his early *The Spirit of Christianity* – involved a more or less typical prejudicial attitude toward Judaism as a religion of egoism, legalism, and harshness in contrast to Christian humility and love. Later, Hegel was to characterize Judaism however as the "Religion of Sublimity," and the earlier language dropped away altogether. Judaism becomes the mediating religion between the gods of Greece and the God of Christianity. Greek gods represent only determinate ethical powers in the form of beauty; God in Judaism is represented as one deity, as a self-determining subject, not as a deity subject to a deeper necessity. Likewise, nature is disenchanted in Judaism, and the possibility of the study of nature as a law-like structure is initiated. ("Or, the world is now prosaic, it confronts us essentially as a collection of things, it is rendered profane. Now nature is divested of divinity . . . At this stage, therefore, there are prosaic things, just as the world contains prosaic things for us also, as understanding beings –

external things in the manifold nexus of understanding, of ground and consequent, of quality and quantity, subject to all these categories of the understanding. Here then is what we call natural or necessary connection; and for that reason
the category of "miracle" emerges here for the first time too, as opposed to the
natural connection of things." *Lectures on the Philosophy of Religion,* pp. 364–
365.) What is lacking in Judaism, so Hegel argues, is that it retains the concept of
a transcendent God beyond appearance. Christianity, on the other hand, makes
God fully present in appearance (in our hearts) and thus conceptually seems to
mark a step forward. But this seems to be a way in which Hegel may have
misunderstood Judaism even from within his own principles; for example, his
characterization of the difference between Christianity and Judaism completely
ignores the idea of the *covenant* between God and humanity in Judaism.

75. See ¶759, pp. 459–460, *PG,* pp. 528–529: "In this religion the essence is known as
spirit, or this religion is the consciousness about itself that it is spirit. For spirit is
the knowledge of oneself in the externalization of oneself; the essence that is the
movement of retaining its self-identity in its otherness . . . Consequently, in this
religion the divine essence is *revealed.* Its being revealed manifestly consists in its
being known as what it is. But it is known precisely in its being known as spirit, as
an essence that is essentially *self-consciousness* . . . This – according to its *concept,*
to be that which is revealed – is the true formation (*Gestalt*) of spirit, and this its
formation, the concept, is likewise alone its essence and its substance. Spirit is
known as self-consciousness and to this self-consciousness it is immediately revealed, for spirit is this self-consciousness itself. The divine nature is the same as
the human, and it is this unity that is intuited."

76. See ¶761, p. 461, *PG,* p. 530: "Here therefore God is *revealed* as *He is; He is* thus
there (da) as He is *in himself (an sich)*; He is there as spirit. God is attainable in
pure speculative knowledge alone and *is* only in that knowledge, and is only that
knowledge itself, for He is Spirit; and this speculative knowledge is the knowledge
of the *revealed* religion. Speculative knowledge knows God as *thought* or pure
essence and knows this thought as being and as existence, and existence as the
negativity of itself, hence as self, as the self that is at the same time *this* individual
and also the universal self."

77. See ¶765, p. 463, *PG,* p. 532: "This form of representation constitutes the determinateness in which spirit, in this its community, becomes conscious of itself.
This form is not yet spirit's self-consciousness that has advanced to the concept
as concept: the mediation is still incomplete. This combination of being and
thought is therefore defective in that spiritual essence is still burdened with an
unreconciled split into a here and a beyond. The *content* is the true content, but
all its moments, when posited in the elements of representation, have the character of not being comprehended (*nicht begriffen*), of appearing as completely independent sides which are externally related to each other."

78. On the whole, the illustrations are the same as in his mature lectures on the
philosophy of religion, but in the latter work the details are much more worked
out.

79. See ¶774, p. 467; *PG,* pp. 536–537.

80. See ¶¶775–776, pp. 467–469; *PG,* p. 537–538.

81. See ¶781, p. 473, *PG,* p. 543: "Spirit is thus posited in the third element, in
universal self-consciousness; it is its *community.*"

82. See ¶778, p. 470, *PG,* pp. 539–540: "This lack of identity (*Ungleichheit*) is
therefore twofold, and two relationships arise whose common moments are those

just given. In one of them, the divine essence counts as that which is essential, while natural existence and the self count as that which is unessential and which is to be sublated. In the other, on the contrary, *being-for-self* counts as that which is essential and the simple divinity as that which is unessential. Their still empty middle term is *existence (Dasein)* in general, the bare community of the two moments." Hegel also notes: "This opposition is resolved not so much through the conflict between the two moments which are represented as separate and independent essences. It lies in their *independence* that each *in itself* must in its own self *(an ihm selbst)*, through its concept, resolve itself. The struggle begins where both cease to be these mixtures of thought and of independent existence and where they confront each other only as thoughts" ¶779, pp. 470–471, *PG*, p. 540.

83. See ¶784, p. 475, *PG*, pp. 544–545: "Besides this immediacy, therefore, the *mediation* of representational thought is necessary. *In itself* the *knowledge* of nature as the untrue existence of spirit, and this universality of the self developed in itself *(in sich gewordne)* is the reconciliation of spirit with itself. For the self-consciousness that does not think in terms of the concept, this in-itself receives the form of an *existent (eines Seienden)* and is *represented* to it. Comprehension is, therefore, for that self-consciousness not a grasping of this concept which knows sublated natural existence to be universal and therefore reconciled with itself; but rather a grasping of the *representation,* that by bringing to pass its own externalization, in its historical incarnation and death, the divine essence has been reconciled with its existence. The grasping of this idea now expresses more definitely what was previously called the spiritual resurrection in this same context, or the becoming of God's individual self-consciousness as a universal self-consciousness, or as the community."

84. This is the issue that immediately after Hegel's death split so many of his students into contending camps, somewhat misleadingly called the "left" and the "right" Hegelians. Hegel himself saw no fundamental tension between taking humanity as spirit to be self-grounding and his belief that in coming to understand spirit in this way, we would also see it as sacred. Some of his students, (for example, Feuerbach) took this instead as evidence that we should therefore discard all notions of divinity, of what is sacred, and focus instead only on the results of human practice. Others thought that in order to continue the Hegelian identification of the divine and the human, something like a more orthodox Christian position had to be maintained, and they sought to use Hegelian dialectic as a means of maintaining a more orthodox conception of God as *both* metaphysically "transcendent" and "immanent" at the same time. Both strategies depart from Hegel's own understanding, and they both remain the two most often taken interpretations of Hegel's thought. Some will no doubt suspect that it was only Hegel's own sensibility that held the doctrine together during his lifetime, that only Hegel himself was capable of maintaining *religious* awe and reverence for self-grounding, rational, human life, and that others simply could not countenance that sort of reverence or needed some more metaphysical reassurance for it than Hegel himself did. Another more "metaphysical" way of understanding Hegel's conception of the relation between the divine and self-conscious spirit would be to see them as "folding" into each other in much the same way that beauty and divinity "fold" into each in Greek art. For the Greek artist, the sculpting of a beautiful statue of a young woman was sufficient to make that statue a representation of Aphrodite; it captured perfectly what Aphrodite was. They "fold" into each other in that think-

ing correctly about one implies that one is thinking correctly about the other; as it were, hitting one target insures that you also hit the other. (After Greek art, on Hegel's conception of it, the qualities of the divine and those of beauty split apart again, since Christian truths are not exhaustively captured by a focus on beauty). Thus, Hegel might well be thinking of the divine and self-conscious spirit as "folding together" for moderns in the way that Greek religion and art "folded together" for the Greeks. For the moderns to reflect on and stand in reverence of self-conscious spirit would thereby be to reflect on and stand in reverence of the divine. The two would be different, but correct thought about one would imply correct thought about the other.

85. See *Lectures on the Philosophy of Religion*, pp. 482–484.

86. See ¶787, p. 477, *PG*, p. 547: "But the community is not yet perfected in this its self-consciousness; in general its content exists for it in the form of *representation*, and this duality still attaches even to the *actual spirituality* of the community, to its return out of its representational thought, just as the element of pure thought itself was burdened with it. The community also does not possess the consciousness of what it is . . . But the *positive* meaning, namely, that this negativity or pure *inwardness* of *knowledge* is just as much the *self-identical essence* – or that substance has here succeeded in becoming absolute self-consciousness is for the devotional consciousness an other."

87. See ¶787, p. 478, *PG*, p. 548: "Its satisfaction thus itself remains burdened with the opposition of a beyond. Its own reconciliation therefore enters its consciousness as something *distant,* as something in the distant *future,* just as the reconciliation which the other *self* achieved appears as something in the distant *past.* Just as the *individual* divine person has a father *existing in itself* (*ansich*seienden) and only an *actual* mother, so too the universal divine person, the community, has for its father its own doing and knowing, but for its mother, eternal love which it only *feels* but does not intuit in its consciousness as an actual immediate *object.* Its reconciliation therefore is in its heart, but its consciousness is still divided and its actuality is still disrupted."

88. See ¶¶789–792, *PG*, p. 550–552 for Hegel's summary of the movement of the *Phenomenology* that leads up to this claim. As Hegel puts it in condensed form, "In this knowing, then, spirit has concluded the movement in which it shaped itself in so far as this shaping was burdened by the difference of consciousness, a difference now overcome." ¶805, p. 490, *PG*, p. 561 – the phrase, "the difference of consciousness" refers to the idea that what it had taken as authoritative for itself (the "essence") was understood to be an independent *object* of consciousness, something "different" from consciousness, of which the subject only has "representations."

89. In ¶788, , p. 479; *PG*, p. 549, Hegel uses the word *"überwinden,"* "overcome" instead of his technical term, *"aufheben"* to speak of how the "spirit of revealed religion" has not "overcome" its "consciousness." Miller's various translations of *Aufheben* as "supersession," "do away with," "canceled," "not self-subsistent," "subordinated," "put aside," "stripped," "puts an end to," and "suspended" obscure this point.

90. See ¶802, p. 488, *PG*, p. 559: "Substance as subject has the *at first only internal* necessity of presenting itself as that which it is *in itself,* as *spirit.* The completed objective presentation is at the same time the reflection of substance or the becoming of substance into self – consequently, if spirit has not completed itself *in itself,*

has not completed itself as world-spirit, it cannot reach its completion as *self-conscious* spirit. Therefore, the content of religion expresses earlier in time than does science what *spirit is,* but only science is its true knowledge of itself."

91. See ¶788, p. 479, *PG,* p. 549: "The spirit of the revealed religion has not yet overcome its consciousness as such, or what is the same, its actual self-consciousness is not the object of its consciousness; spirit itself in general and the self-differentiated moments within it fall into representation and into the form of objectivity (*Gegenständlichkeit*). The *content* of this representation is absolute spirit; and all that now remains to be done is to sublate this mere form, or rather, since this belongs to *consciousness as such,* its truth must already have yielded itself in the formation (*Gestalt*) of consciousness." Hegel also notes: "These are the moments of which the reconciliation of spirit with its authentic consciousness is composed; for themselves they are single, and it is solely their spiritual unity that constitutes the power of this reconciliation. The last of these moments is, however, necessarily this unity itself and, as is evident, it combines them all into itself." ¶793, p. 482, *PG,* p. 552.

92. See ¶796, p. 485, *PG,* p. 555: "Through this movement of action, spirit has stepped forth as a pure universality of knowing, which is self-consciousness, as self-consciousness that is the simple unity of knowing. It is first spirit only in that it *is there* (*da ist*), that is, when it raises its existence into *thought* and thereby into an absolute *opposition,* and out of this opposition and even through this opposition returns into itself."

93. See ¶795, p. 483, *PG,* p. 553: "This unification has, however, already occurred *in itself* and that too in religion in the return of representational thought into self-consciousness, but not according to the authentic form, for the religious aspect is the aspect of the *in-itself,* which stands over against the movement of self-consciousness. Consequently, the unification belongs to the other aspect which in the contrast of the two sides is the aspect of reflection into self and therefore the one that contains both its own self and its opposite, and not only *in itself* or in a universal sense, but *for itself* or in a developed and differentiated way."

94. See ¶795, pp. 483–484, *PG,* p. 554: "The beautiful soul is its own knowledge of itself in its pure, transparent unity . . . Through this realization, this objectless self-consciousness sticking to itself sublates the *determinateness* of the concept with its *fulfillment;* its self-consciousness gains the form of universality and what remains to it is its true concept, or the concept that attained its realization; it is it in its truth, namely in the unity with its externalization – the knowing of pure knowledge, not as the abstract *essence* which duty is – but of knowledge as essence which is *this* knowledge, *this* pure self-consciousness, which is therefore at the same time a genuine *object,* for the concept is the self existing for itself (*für-sichseiende Selbst*)."

95. See ¶796, p. 484, *PG,* p. 554: "This concept gave itself its fulfillment on one side in the *acting* spirit that is certain of itself, and on the other, in *religion.* In religion it won for consciousness the absolute content *as content* or in the form of *representation,* the form of otherness for consciousness; on the other hand, in the prior formation the form is that of the self itself, for it contains the *acting* spirit that is certain of itself. The self carries out the life of absolute spirit."

96. See ¶797, p. 485, *PG,* p. 556: "Thus, what in religion was *content* or a form of representing an *other,* is here the *self's* own *act.* For this concept is, we see, the knowledge of the self's act within itself as all essentiality and all existence, the

knowledge of *this subject* as *substance* and of the substance as this knowledge of its act."

97. See ¶798, pp. 485–486, *PG*, p. 556: "This last formation of spirit – the spirit which at the same time gives its complete and true content the form of the self and thereby realizes its concept and which remains in its concept in this realization – this is absolute knowing; it is spirit that knows itself in the formation of spirit, or a *comprehensive knowing* . . . Spirit *appearing* in consciousness in this element, or what is here the same thing, brought forth by consciousness, *is science*."

98. As Hegel puts it in condensed form, "Spirit has attained the pure element of its existence, the concept . . . The different content exists as *determinate* content in relationships (*Verhältnisse*), not in itself, and its unrest is its self-sublation (*sich selbst aufzuheben*) or *negativity*." ¶805, p. 491, *PG*, p. 562.

Chapter Seven

1. Hegel's shortest characterization of the three types of thought that he develops in the *Logic* (Being, Essence and Concept) is made in his Berlin lectures on aesthetics to mark the difference between poetic and prosaic thought. First, there is what he calls "ordinary thought" ("Being"), which is "content to take what is and happens as just this mere individual, i.e., in terms of its meaningless contingency . . . [This is] a mere view of a world of successive or juxtaposed accidents which may have a great range of external life but which is totally unable to satisfy the deeper need of reason." (*Aesthetics*, II, p. 975; *Werke*, 15, p. 243) (translation altered). Second, there is "Essence," "the restricted thinking of the understanding and its categories, such as cause and effect, means and ends, i.e., in general with relations of externality and finitude. In this way of thinking, every particular either appears falsely as independent or is brought into a mere relation with another and therefore is apprehended only as relative and dependent." (*Aesthetics*, II, pp. 974–975; *Werke*, 15, p. 242) Hegel also calls these categories the understanding's "representations (*Vorstellungen*) and reflections" (*Aesthetics*, II, p. 976; *Werke*, 15, p. 243). Finally, there is what he calls "speculative thinking" ("Concept") which "does away with the understanding's representations and ordinary intuition," (*Aesthetics*, p. 976; *Werke*, 15, p. 244), that is, with the categories and types of thought appropriate to both "Being" and "Essence": "Thinking, however, results in thoughts alone; it evaporates the form of reality into the form of the pure concept, and even if it grasps and apprehends actual things in their essential particularity, it nevertheless lifts even this particular into the universal ideal element, wherein alone thought is "with itself" (*bei sich selber*). Consequently, contrasted with the world of appearance, a new realm arises which is indeed the truth of actuality, but this is a truth which is not made manifest again in *actuality* itself as its formative power and as its own soul. Thinking is only a reconciliation between reality and truth within *thought* itself." (*Aesthetics*, p. 976; *Werke*, 15, p. 244).

2. Allen Wood seems to see the result of the *Phenomenology* in this way. In his view, in the *Phenomenology* Hegel simply failed to reconcile two views that he held: "This leaves an unresolved tension in Hegel's ethical thought: the *systematic* superiority of ethical life versus the *historical* superiority of morality. Instead of resolving the tension, Hegel provides a critique of the moral standpoint, exhibiting the limitations of finite spirit as a whole and pointing to the awareness of absolute spirit in religious consciousness. It is not until Hegel's return to univer-

sity teaching a decade later that he attempts to present a picture of modern ethical life with which moral consciousness has been fully and positively reconciled." Wood, *Hegel's Ethical Thought*, p. 133. However, this way of contrasting Hegel's earlier and later views rests on attributing to Hegel some ideas that are only controversially his. It is certainly not clear that Hegel claimed that ethical life was "systematically" superior in the *Phenomenology*. Indeed, the various contradictions in Greek ethical life, of which *Antigone* was an expression, were part of the internal incoherence in the Greek accounts of themselves which led to the downfall of the Greek form of life. If anything is *systematically* superior from the standpoint of the *Phenomenology*, it is that form of life governed by secularized Judeo-Christian *morality*. Taking Hegel as holding to the systematic superiority of ethical life runs in that stream of interpretations which see him as basically subscribing to the kind of love of ancient Greek life characteristic of his generation; however, it severely underplays the way in which he broke from that kind of blind adoration of Greece. Wood is however clear that in Hegel's mature system he holds "morality" to designate a modern form of life that has a certain superiority to ancient forms of ethical life.

3. Hegel noted in his remarks on the proposed revision of the *Phenomenology of Spirit* in 1831 (right before his death) that the *Phenomenology* was a "peculiar (*Eigentümliche*) early work, not to be done over again (*umarbeiten*) . . . In the preface: the abstract absolute dominated at that time." Cited by J. Hoffmeister, *Phänomenologie des Geistes*, p. 578.

4. See Robert Pippin, "Kant, Hegel and Ethical Reasons," *Philosophical Topics*, vol. 19, no. 2 (1992). pp. 99–132. Pippin points out that Hegel's imagery here is that of "absorption, elevation and purification, rather than [that] of opposition, struggle and renunciation . . ." thus suggesting that Hegel is departing sharply here from both Christian and Kantian models of a struggle within the self for control. Instead, Hegel is using the language of the *Phenomenology*, of reconciliation with oneself rather than overcoming oneself. Pippin also points out that this is not a theory of the "true self" as opposed to the "false self." Some of Hegel's language is misleading in this regard, especially when he gets to the section on *Sittlichkeit* in the *Philosophy of Right;* sometimes Hegel speaks of the defining ends of modern agency as "my essence," which might misleadingly suggest that I am thereby discovering some *given* element of myself in pursuing those ends. This has led some commentators to see Hegel's talk of "finding one's essence" as identical with self-determination. This can only work if one has a "true self" view – that is, as seeing self-determination as being identical with following the given dictates of one's true self rather than following the ends dictated by one's false self. Stephen Houlgate in his *Freedom, Truth and History: An Introduction to Hegel's Philosophy* (London: Routledge, 1991) seems to take this strategy for reconciling Hegel's theses about self-determination with his talk of our "essence."

5. "Personality implies that as *this* person: (1) I am completely determined on every side (in my inner optings [*Willkür*], impulse, and desire, as well as by immediate external existence) and so finite, yet (2) nonetheless I am simply and solely a relation to myself and therefore in finitude I know myself as something infinite, universal and free." *Philosophy of Right*, §35.

6. The contemporary and popular distinction between first-order and second-order desires was developed independently by Gerald Dworkin and Harry Frankfurt. First-order desires are those desires for some kind of object (in the most general sense), whereas second-order desires are desires for desires. Thus, to take one of

the exemplary cases, the addicted smoker may desire a cigarette (first-order) but also desire that he not have a desire for a cigarette (second-order). This has been often taken as expressing the ideal of being a person and having a capacity for freedom, the idea being that it takes a second-order desire to transform an entity into an agent (or a "person"). There is nothing particularly special, however, about second-order desires, except that they are second-order, and it is not clear why being *second-order* gives them any special authority. They may be more reflective – but then again, they may not, or their reflective character may not be a good feature of them. A squeamish professional killer who has a second-order desire that he has a first-order desire to kill people, or desires that he did not have the desire to let his victims escape is not someone whose second-order desires should carry any special moral weight for him. The Hegelian point is that it is not important that our desires are ordered as first or second in some hierarchy of desires; it is how they fit in with the system of volitions that constitutes the agent's self-identity. The desires should be part of a justifiable inferential complex, and that means being structured by a certain type of conceptual and social space. Being first-order or second-order is not of any particular importance from the axiological or ethical standpoint; being a part of a justified nexus of practical reasoning is.

7. Hegel remarks on this process of idealization in the long Addition to §381 of his *Encyclopedia*: "*Ideality* must be designated as the differentiating determinateness of the concept of mind, that is, ideality as the sublation (*Aufheben*) of the being-other (*Anderssein*) of the idea, which out of its other is both returning and is returned into itself . . . This sublation of externality belonging to the concept of spirit is that which we have called *ideality*. All activities of spirit are nothing more than the different modes of leading the external back to interiority, which is spirit itself, and only through this leading back, through this idealization or assimilation of the external does spirit both come to be and is spirit."

8. "A person by distinguishing himself from himself relates himself to another person, and it is only as owners that these two persons really exist for each other." §40, *Philosophy of Right*.

9. One can contrast this with a pre-modern understanding that would see the most basic mode of self-understanding in terms of family membership (as being the son or daughter of so-and-so). In the pre-modern understanding, one finds one's self-identity already determined and given by a given network of familial and social ties; in the modern understanding, one finds one's self-identity more generally in the acquirings and exchanges into which one enters. The pre-modern period gives a different "social space" and the agents in it thus occupy different "points." The modern conception of ourselves as juridical individuals gives us a basic, although very abstract sense of ourselves as self-directing in a way that the pre-modern period could not. It sees us most generally as self-directing "persons" and not primarily as the son or daughter of so-and-so.

10. There is another, "external" reason for making the transition from "Abstract Right" to "Morality" which involves the necessity of the system of rights developed in "Abstract Right" to be administered by impartial judges. To be an impartial judge, however, requires that one have the right motives, so that one abstracts away from one's personal point of view to administer the rules of "Abstract Right" from the impersonal point of view. Thus, we need a system of *moral* agents who can take up the attitude of acting from the impersonal point of view. This is an external criticism in that it imports something from outside "Abstract Right" in

order to show its deficiencies. That is, it takes the analysis of what "we" mean by terms such as "right," "wrong" and the like, and show that a system of abstract rights cannot do justice to the meaning of these concepts. To be sure, without such impartial principles, one cannot distinguish revenge from punishment, but the question remains as to whether the agents of "Abstract Right" are required to make such distinctions. (What about their accounts of what is authoritative for them in "Abstract Right" make it necessary to introduce such distinctions?) Hegel's view is that it is the failure of the account of self-determination that motivates the agents to enrich their account with that of "Morality," not the failure of their accounts to match up with the sense of "right" employed in the full blown social order. When one views a Hegelian argument backward – reading it from the end of the theory to its beginning – it does indeed appear as a form of analysis. When read from the beginning to the end, it is however a "synthetic," dialectical argument. This kind of analytic reading (what I called the "backwards" reading) is offered in a clear form by Kenneth Westphal, "The Basic Context and Structure of Hegel's *Philosophy of Right*," in F. Beiser (ed.), *The Cambridge Companion to Hegel*, pp. 234–269.

11. Robert Pippin discusses this as the conflict between reasons of prudence and ethical reasons in "Hegel, Ethical Reasons, Kantian Rejoinders." Pippin is concerned there to show that ethical (*sittlich*) reasons are not reasons of prudence but involve a prior understanding of what it is for an end to be an end of a self-determining agent. Pippin's point is that the self-identity of the agent cannot be itself a matter of "prudential choice," and it is therefore prior to any other (at least fundamental) "prudential choice." What counts as a prudential choice (as fitting in with an agent's "life plan") will depend on a prior conception of the agent's self-identity.

12. In more contemporary terms, Gerald Dworkin develops such a "thin" view of autonomy as "a second-order capacity of persons to reflect critically upon their first-order preferences, desires, wishes, and so forth and the capacity to accept or attempt to change these in light of higher-order preferences and values. By exercising such a capacity, persons define their nature, give meaning and coherence to their lives, and take responsibility for the kind of person they are." Gerald Dworkin, *The Theory and Practice of Autonomy* (Cambridge: Cambridge University Press, 1988) p. 20. Dworkin does not, however, develop out of this "thin" conception of autonomy anything like the Hegelian critique of "morality" in terms of *Sittlichkeit*.

13. Hegel's reasons for placing his discussion of autonomous action in the section labeled "morality" has to do with the modern relation between autonomy and morality brought to the forefront in Kant's ethics. Hegel sees this as not merely an idiosyncrasy of Kant's own thought but as expressing a deeper truth about modern life. Our conceptions of moral agency and autonomous agency are deeply bound up together, and it is part of Hegel's concern to develop how the modern conception of being a self-determining agent leads to what he calls "morality." Hegel wrote a series of fragmentary remarks for his own use (for example, in lecturing) to go with his copy of the *Philosophy of Right*. In one he says, apparently with regard to §123, "Because of formally abstract subjectivity – abstract determination, only the taking up of the determinations present in a natural mode. This abstract subjectivity is the same as Kantian practical reason – This formal character (*das Formelle*) is none other than interest, the activity of subjectivity in general. *Autonomy is that formal self-determination*." (Italics added by me.) This

indicates clearly that he had a notion of self-choice, or autonomy in mind in writing these passages.

14. See *Philosophy of Right*, §105.

15. He does this in the sections of the *Philosophy of Right* called "Plans and Responsibility" (*Der Vorsatz und die Schuld*) (§§105–118) and "Intention and Welfare" (*Die Absicht und die Wohl*) (§119–128).

16. As Hegel puts it, "At the moral standpoint, the abstract determinacy of the will in the sphere of right has been so far overcome that this contingency itself is, as reflected in upon itself and as self-identical, the inward infinite contingency of the will, i.e., its subjectivity." §104, Addition.

17. "The transition to intention (*Absicht*) lies in my acknowledging (*anerkenne*) only what my representation of the matter (*meine Vorstellung*) was." *Philosophy of Right*, §118, Addition.

18. See §118, Addition, in which Hegel makes this point about "the self-consciousness of heroes (like that of Oedipus and others in Greek tragedy) . . ."

19. In his marginalia to his copy of the *Philosophy of Right*, Hegel makes a number of notes referring to modern and classical Greek drama, providing further evidence that this is what he had in mind in his discussion of planning and intending.

20. To mark this distinction, Hegel distinguishes between a deed (*Tat*) and an action (*Handlung*). The *action* includes only what I have determined for myself (by my plan or intention); the *deed*, however, includes also what happens as a result of what I do. The modern paradoxes thus turn on the distinction between whether I am only responsible for my action or for my deed. See §118, Addition.

21. See §118, Addition: "The principle: 'ignore the consequences of action' and the other: 'judge actions by their consequences and make these the criterion of right and good' are both principles of the abstract understanding."

22. In his lectures on the subject, Hegel says: "The action also has consequences, and the question is whether the action is to be judged according to them. As an external existence the action has the most multiple relationships; these are its consequences. On the one hand that externality is the development of the action itself; to that extent, the consequences of the action are to be imputed to me. They are nothing other than the manifestation of the nature of the action . . . The consequences have another side. Because the action is an external existence, many things external to it are bound up with it. The action can thus develop into very distant consequences, which do not any longer belong to me. On the one hand, one can lay down the rule that one ought not to trouble oneself with the consequences of actions, and, on the other hand, the opposite can as well be laid down as a rule . . . A collision arises here between the objective and the subjective, a collision which can become fearsome. The "is" and the "ought" stand here over and against each other. The noted collision cannot be absolutely overcome; on the contrary, it is enduring. Only an approximation can enter here." *Die Vorlesungen von 1819/1820*, pp. 94–95.

23. Hegel also holds this to be true with regard to the so-called paradox of moral luck. That paradox involves the idea that there is much for which an agent is commonsensically held to be responsible, but, on this account, for which he cannot be held responsible. Thus, two people with the same intentions can produce different consequences because of bad luck. (Two hunters fire at movement in the bushes; the first one hits the target, which turns out to be another hunter, whereas the other misses.) The so-called paradox is that both willed the same thing, and thus on this account both should be equally responsible, yet we commonsensically

hold that one is more responsible than the other. Hegel holds them to be differentially responsible, and, no doubt, would also hold that this is the reflective common-sense thing to do. Each should perhaps experience regret, make atonement, and so on, but, on Hegel's account, one is nonetheless more responsible than the other (and, correspondingly, he should feel more responsibility than the other). Hegel's view thus seems to be that the modern account does not absolve the agent of responsibility for the consequences of her actions but does *mitigate* it. He says in the Addition to *Philosophy of Right,* §119: "In spite of this, however, we must not make this a distinction between good and bad luck, since in acting a man must lay his account with externality. The old proverb is correct: "A flung stone is the devil's." To act is to expose oneself to bad luck. Thus bad luck has a right over me (*ein Recht an mich*) and is an embodiment (*ein Dasein*) of my own willing."

24. See *Philosophy of Right,* §123.

25. See *Philosophy of Right,* §122.

26. See *Philosophy of Right,* §124.

27. This argument occurs in the extremely condensed line of thought in §§125–126 of the *Philosophy of Right.*

28. Hegel clearly thinks that this kind of preliminary conception of morality cannot be the last word; his marginalia to *Philosophy of Right,* §125 show this: "Happiness – there is a real boredom in with these words, well-being and happiness – because of such indeterminate, empty reflection."

29. See *Philosophy of Right,* §126.

30. See *Philosophy of Right,* §135: "But since the universal existing in and for itself, in distinction from such a particular content, has not so far been further determined than as "the right," it follows that these ends of particularity, differing as they do from the universal, may be in conformity with it, but they also may not."

31. "Right and welfare stand opposed to each other here; both can correspond to each other and also both may not. It is the question of which must yield in the collision of one with the other: right is necessarily that substantiality which lies at the basis of things, and I may not assert and further my welfare at the cost of what is right. However, the right of particular willing, placed at the highest rank, is particular existence, life . . . This right which life attains is the right of emergency (*Notrecht*). It is not a matter of equity (*Billigkeit*) which is being spoken of here but of a right." *Die Vorlesungen von 1819/1820,* p. 100. He continues, "In emergency the contradiction between the right of particularity and that of the abstract universal will appears. Both are essential moments . . . The truth of both moments is now the good in general, the identity of the universal and the particular wills." Ibid., p. 101. The same point appears in the published text of the *Philosophy of Right* in the final paragraph to the section on "intention and welfare" (§129).

32. In both his lectures in 1819/1820 and in the published text of the *Philosophy of Right,* Hegel brings out the potential contradiction between the two by setting up a collision between the claims of distress or emergency and the claims of right. He says in the lectures, "Right and welfare stand opposed to each other here; both can correspond to each other and also both may not. It is the question of which must yield in the collision of one with the other: right is necessarily that substantiality which lies at the basis of things, and I may not assert and further my welfare at the cost of what is right. However, the right of particular willing, placed at the highest rank, is particular existence, life . . . This right which life attains is the right of emergency (*Notrecht*). It is not a matter of equity (*Billigkeit*) which is being spoken of here but of a right." *Die Vorlesungen von 1819/1820,* p. 100. He

continues, "In emergency the contradiction between the right of particularity and that of the abstract universal will appears. Both are essential moments . . . The truth of both moments is now the good in general, the identity of the universal and the particular wills." Ibid., p. 101. The same point appears in the published text of the *Philosophy of Right* in the final paragraph to the section on "intention and welfare" (§129).

33. "The right of particularity is thus a very essential right. That my welfare is my intention (*Absicht*) constitutes the concrete sphere of particularity. The principle of particularity is in general the principle of modernity (*neueren Zeit*) and constitutes the principle of higher quality compared with the older periods. This counts for all directions of life, for science, for the state and for religion. The principle of antiquity is plastic in thought and in action; the principle of modernity is romantic. Consequently the principle of love as belonging to particularity has a much higher significance in modernity than in antiquity." *Die Vorlesungen von 1819/1820.* p. 98. Compare this with the similar extended remark to §124 in the published *Philosophy of Right*.

34. In his lectures on the philosophy of history, Hegel argues that in an ironic sense the Athenians were correct to try Socrates for corrupting the youth of Athens because Socrates was trying to introduce a concept of reflective morality into a form of life that could not both allow for it and maintain itself. Socrates, Hegel says, "is celebrated as a teacher of morality, but we should rather call him the *inventor* of morality. The Greeks had an ethical life (*Sittlichkeit*), but Socrates wished to teach them which moral virtues and duties they had. The moral person is not merely the person who wills and does the right, not the innocent person, but he who has the consciousness of his action." *Werke*, 12, p. 329.

35. See *Philosophy of Right*, §130.

36. See *Philosophy of Right*, §129.

37. See *Philosophy of Right*, §132.

38. Hegel makes this point in his lectures on the history of philosophy: "It is a great determination of the highest importance in the Kantian philosophy that self-consciousness has led back into itself what counts as its essence, as law, as what it is in itself (*Ansich*) . . . It is a great advance when the principle is established that freedom is the last hinge on which man turns, this final point that allows nothing to be imposed on it; thus man allows nothing, no authority to count for him, insofar as it goes against his freedom." *Werke*, 20, p. 367.

39. See *Philosophy of Right*, §135, Remark.

40. Perhaps the most influential contemporary statement of a version of Kantian ethical theory that distances itself from Hegel's characterization of Kant is that represented by John Rawls. See his "Themes in Kant's Moral Philosophy," in Eckart Förster (ed.) *Kant's Transcendental Deductions: The Three Critiques and the Opus postumum* (Stanford: Stanford University Press, 1989). pp. 81–113.

41. See *Philosophy of Right*, §137. (Knox translates *"an und für sich"* somewhat misleadingly in that passage as "absolute.")

42. See *Philosophy of Right*, §136.

43. Robert Pippin in his "Idealism and Agency in Kant and Hegel," *The Journal of Philosophy*, makes an extended argument to the effect that the Kantian conception of agency, despite Kant's immensely sophisticated efforts to ameliorate it and defend it, cannot account for why anyone would on Kantian grounds do anything. "It is widely claimed now that Kant maintains that I am certainly free and responsible in nonmoral actions, that the mere experience of an intensely experienced

desire or aversion need not motivate an action unless I "let" it, unless I "elect" to regard that desire *as* a determining ground of action, or take it to be worthy of acting on, "incorporate" it into a maxim . . . Suppose that I am inclined to pursue a policy generally aimed at my own happiness. Suppose that this happiness is not viewed in a crudely hedonistic sense . . . , and I am not determined . . . by the mere presence of some inclination, to adopt that policy. In that case, what sorts of considerations, on Kant's view, *could* be relevant to the adoption of such a policy (and preserve the Kantian conditions of free agency)? . . . Indeed, if nothing about our empirical character could count as a reason for acting unless already incorporated into a maxim, it is hard to see the possibility of an *original* rationale for any such maxim or policy." pp. 538–539.

44. Hegel thinks that all forms of casuistry, of learning how to apply general principles in particular cases, are forms of such hypocrisy and dissemblance. In the *Philosophy of Right,* he discusses probabilism, a doctrine mostly associated with the Jesuits of the eighteenth century, which teaches that an action is permitted if it some authority for it can be found (for example, in some text); the authority then is said to give the desired action a "greater probability" of being right. In his lectures, Hegel is much more caustic, referring simply to "casuistry" in general as a form of hypocrisy. Hegel sarcastically refers to a "lifeboat case" in which we are supposed to decide which of the various valuable people get thrown overboard and argues that it is unjustified to expect that any moral theory could provide determinate answers to such cases. It is up to the individual ("particularity") to decide such cases, and "[t]he decisive particularity is in general that which one calls character; a person can only act insofar as he is a particular. The demand for casuistry of that kind contains the assertion that the person want to be spared the trouble of having a character . . . Mature, substantial action demands a forgetting of oneself in respect to one's particularity. The reflection that always wants to know whether one here and there acts admirably leads to flabbiness and self-conceit." *Die Vorlesungen von 1819/1820.* p. 119. The overall charge is thus that such casuistry simply presents such "hard cases" in a way so that the individual can then simply take the option he wanted in the first place (for example, which person he throws overboard) and cover the whole thing up with a patina of morality. This will be the case since a variety of authorities can always be found, each of whom contradicts the other, and the individual is simply left to choose which of the authorities he prefers. This is a form of hypocrisy, Hegel argues, because it presents what is really a matter of private choice as being based on objective reasons.

45. "Self-consciousness, in the vanity of all otherwise valid determinations and in the pure interiority of willing, is just as much the possibility of making the universal existing in and for itself into the principle of its action and then realizing it in its actions, as it is of making mere "opting" (*Willkür*), its own particularity over and above the universal, into a principle and realizing it in its actions – that is, to be *evil.*" *Philosophy of Right,* §139.

46. Socratic irony ". . . consisted for the first part in this, that a false, one-sided assertion is granted, and then the person who has proposed such an assertion is led through the development of the assertion to the point where its nothingness is demonstrated." *Die Vorlesungen von 1819/1820.*

47. "You respectfully accept a law as existing in and for itself. So do I, but I go further than you, because I am above this law and can make it this or that (*so oder so*). It is not the thing which is excellent, but I who am excellent; as the master of law and

thing alike, I *only play* with them as my whim; in this ironical consciousness, in which I let the highest perish, I only enjoy myself (*nur mich genieße*)." *Philosophy of Right*, §140, Remark.

48. In a somewhat elegiac sense, Hegel notes that, "Only in times where actuality is an empty, spiritless and unstable existence may the individual be permitted to flee back out of the actual into his inner life. Socrates arose in the time of the decay of Athenian democracy: he sublimated the existing and fled back into himself in order to find the right and the good there. Also in our times it is more or less the case that the reverence for that which is existing (*dem Bestehende*) is no longer at hand and the person wants to have what is valid as *his* will, as that which is recognized (*Anerkannte*) by him." *Philosophy of Right*, §138, Addition.

49. This is the point of Hegel's often misunderstood dictum that "The actual is the rational, and the rational is the actual." Rather than being a call to quietism or just a philosophically decorated form of smug conservatism, it is the claim that if there is to be a fully rational form of self-understanding, then it must be one that is anchored in *actual* social institutions which provide the agent with a non-contradictory form of self-understanding. A philosophical theory of *ethical ends* cannot therefore appeal to institutions that do not or cannot exist, nor can it appeal to an idealized self-understanding that has no institutional support. Purely "moral" theories typically appeal to something like that, but such theories only end up as exhortations to people to become what they ought to be, generally without any concrete prescription for how they are to do that and which are often at odds with the prevailing real possibilities for people.

50. "In the whole of ethical life the objective, as well as the subjective, is present; both are however only forms of the same thing." *Philosophy of Right*, §144, Addition. (my translation.) "Ethical life is just as well *in itself*, objective, as it is *for itself*, or subjective." *Die Vorlesungen von 1819/1820*, p. 122.

51. "That which is right and that which is moral cannot exist for themselves; they must have the ethical as their support and foundation, for the right lacks the moment of subjectivity, while morality in turn possesses for itself that moment alone, and consequently both moments lack actuality by themselves (*für sich*) . . . Right exists only as a branch of the whole or like the ivy which twines itself round a tree firmly rooted in and for itself." *Philosophy of Right*, §141, Addition.

52. The "Idea" is Hegel's term for a "rational whole," a kind of "conceptual map" of the world through which we *articulate* to ourselves what it is that we hold to be authoritative reasons for ourselves and why we hold them to be authoritative.

53. "The difference of this presentation from that taking the form of a *doctrine of duties* lies only in that in the following, the ethical determinations are demonstrated as necessary relationships (*Verhältnisse*) . . . An immanent and consistent doctrine of duties can consist in none other than that of the development of the *relationships* which are necessary to the idea of freedom and which consequently are *actual* to their whole extent in the state." *Philosophy of Right*, §148, Remark.

54. Michael Inwood in his *Hegel* argues that "There are, then, two distinct ways in which intellectual autonomy can be won, firstly by retreating from the apparently alien world into pure thinking, and secondly by advancing on the world and imposing one's thoughts upon it or, rather, discovering them in it." (p. 480) Because of this, Inwood concludes that self-determination for Hegel cannot reside in desire but only in thought. Hegel solves this problem, Inwood concludes, by seeing that thoughts are embedded in social phenomena: "When a man adheres to the laws and customs of his own society, he is in a sense "willing his own will,""

following the autonomous dictates of his own will, since the institutions of his society embody the thought which he at bottom is." (p. 486) This sees Hegel, however, in terms of a more "Augustinian" picture, that is, as understanding desire and thought to be antagonistic to each other. Hegel's project, however, is not couched in terms of the *subjugation* of one element of human nature by another but in terms of their *reconciliation* with each other.

55. In his lectures on aesthetics, Hegel notes that the peculiarly modern problem seems to be the clash between the moral point of view, with its claims to universality, and the personal point of view, both in regard to its desires and plans but also with regard to ordinary ethical virtues. He notes, "These are oppositions which have not been invented at all by the subtlety of reflection or the pedantry of philosophy; in numerous forms they have always preoccupied and troubled the human consciousness, even if it is modern cultivation (*Bildung*) that has first worked them out most sharply and driven them up the peak of harshest contradiction. Spiritual culture (*Bildung*), the modern understanding, produces this opposition in man which makes him an amphibious animal, because he now has to live in two worlds which contradict one another. The result is that now consciousness wanders about in this contradiction, and, driven from one side to the other, cannot find satisfaction for itself in one or the other . . . But for modern culture and its understanding this discordance in life and consciousness involves the demand that such a contradiction be resolved . . . If general culture (*allgemeine Bildung*) has run into such a contradiction, it becomes the task of philosophy to sublate the oppositions, i.e. to show that neither the one alternative in its abstraction, nor the other in the like one-sidedness, possesses truth, but that they are both self-dissolving; that truth lies only in the reconciliation and mediation of both, and that this mediation is no mere demand, but what is in and for itself accomplished and is ever self-accomplishing." *Aesthetics,* I, pp. 54–55; *Werke,* 13, pp. 80–82.

56. On this point, see also Pippin, "Hegel, Ethical Reasons, Kantian Rejoinders," p. 111.

57. *Die Vorlesungen von 1819/1820.* p. 125

58. It is of course open to Kantians to allow social roles to supply determinate ends for action, but for the Kantians these social roles will themselves be just as "given" as anything coming from inclination. Now, it might be open to the Kantian to select out those roles as essential to modernity that can meet the procedural test of the categorical imperative. Thus, being a classical warrior or a medieval monk might not (by hypothesis) pass the test, but other things (like being a Prussian *Bürger*) might. We would then *identify* with those roles that pass the testing procedure of the categorical imperative, since they would conform to our nature as rational agents. However, this would still only provide a wide assortment of roles as *permissible* but not obligatory (for example, being a German professor would be permissible, a role that Hegel happily assumed, even though he obviously did not think it essential to being a rational agent in modernity). Kant thought that he could show that justice and beneficence were in fact such obligatory ends, but without some empirical assumptions, so the Hegelian argues, he can do no such things. To use the language of John Rawls, the Kantian smuggles in conceptions of the *reasonable* into his conceptions of the *rational* in order to get the obligatory ends. Rawls distinguishes the two in the following way: the Reasonable involves a shared notion of fair terms of cooperation, whereas the Rational involves each participant's rational advantage, what they are trying to advance. The former is

shared, but the latter may not be. Rawls makes this distinction in his "The Basic Liberties and Their Priority," in Sterling M. McMurrin (ed.) *The Tanner Lectures* (Salt Lake City: the University of Utah Press, 1982). pp. 3–87. In "Kantian Constructivism in Moral Theory: the Dewey Lectures," 1980, *The Journal of Philosophy*, vol. LXXVII, No. 9, pp. 515–572, Rawls argues that the Reasonable presupposes the Rational because it presupposes that each person is moved by a specific conception of the good and that the Reasonable also subordinates the Rational because the Reasonable puts limits to the final ends that can be pursued (see p. 532). Reasonable principles correspond to the principles of justice, whereas rational principles correspond to the more formal principles of rational choice. For the Hegelian, reasonable principles will be derived from the basic kinds of self-identities that we must as rational agents assume in modernity. If the "Reasonable" is to count for us as reasonable, as something that can be affirmed in the face of skepticism about it, then it must be shown to derive its authority from the way it avoids or answers the dilemmas involved in earlier historical conceptions. A Rawlsian theory of justice thus presupposes something like Hegelian *Sittlichkeit* in order for it to count as a "reasonable" conception.

59. See *Philosophy of Right*, §120, §132.
60. Thus, Hegel cannot be content simply to describe and compare various types of goods within the modern form of life, such as the contemporary political thinker, Michael Walzer, does in his *Spheres of Justice: A Defense of Pluralism and Equality* (New York: Basic Books, 1983).
61. In the addition to §158 in the *Philosophy of Right*, Hegel says, "The first moment in love is that I do not wish for myself to be an independent person and that, if I were, then I would feel defective and incomplete. The second moment is that I reclaim (*gewinne*) myself in another person, that I count for something (*gelte*) in her, and which she in turn achieves in me. Love, therefore, is the most tremendous contradiction; the understanding cannot resolve it since there is nothing more stubborn than this punctuality of self-consciousness which is negated and which nevertheless I ought to possess as affirmative. Love is at once the propounding and the resolving of this contradiction."
62. Hegel makes it clear that he does not consider marriage as having only one determinate purpose to it (such as the rasing of children or the social channeling of sexual desire): "Marriage, as a concrete, substantial relationship, contains multiple moments in itself, of which no one alone constitutes the single end of marriage." *Die Vorlesungen von 1819/1820.* p. 130.
63. "The natural relation is transfigured into a spiritual relation, without its being thereby given up . . . On the other hand this natural relationship is however not to be viewed as something wrong and debased, to which one merely would be subjugated due to the imperfection of human nature. There are two extremes of looking at the matter, which could come forth here. The latter point of view appears under the title of platonic love; Plato by the way did not speak of this love. Certainly he spoke of an incorporeal love, which is other that of which we are speaking here." *Die Vorlesungen von 1819/1820,* pp. 131–132.
64. "What the person ought to be he does not possess from instinct; rather he must first acquire it for himself. On this is founded the child's right to become educated. People under patriarchal (*väterlichen*) governments are in the same position as children; they are fed from central stores and are not regarded as independent and as adults (*Majorenne*). The services which may be demanded from children should therefore have education as their sole end and be related to that."

Philosophy of Right, §174, Addition. "It is to be noted that on the whole children love their parents less than the parents love their children, for the children are facing their independence and are growing stronger and are thus leaving their parents behind, whereas the parents have in the children the impartial objectivity (*objektive Gegenständlichkeit*) of their bond." *Philosophy of Right,* §175, Addition.

65. There are plenty of passages in which Hegel could be said to express what would now be regarded as sexist ideas, but this one should suffice: "Women are capable of education, but they are not made for activities which demand a universal faculty such as the more advanced sciences, philosophy and certain forms of artistic production. Women may happy ideas, taste and elegance, but they cannot attain to the ideal. The difference between men and women is like that between animals and plants. Men correspond to animals, while women correspond to plants because their development is more placid and the principle that underlies it is the rather vague unity of feeling. When women hold the helm of government, the state is at once in jeopardy, because women regulate their actions not by the demands of universality but by arbitrary inclinations and opinions. Women are educated – who knows how? – as it were by breathing in ideas, by living rather than by acquiring knowledge. The status of manhood, on the other hand, is attained only by the stress of thought and much technical exertion." *Philosophy of Right,* §166, Addition.

66. In his marginal comments to his copy of the *Philosophy of Right,* one finds the following entries for §167, in which Hegel is obviously struggling to bring this view of family life in line with his thoughts on freedom and equality: "Free undivided love – the honor of personality – the man according to his individuality – the woman to be *respected as equal to himself* (*sich gleich achten*) and placed – not higher – as in chivalry as it were having its religion in the woman . . . Equality, self-sameness (*Dieselbigkeit*) of rights and of duties – The man should not count for more than the woman." He also goes on to lambast here as he does elsewhere any form of polygamy as equivalent to the slavery of women, and he has a note to the effect that women in the orient are slaves because they cannot direct the affairs of the house. For Hegel, only the modern *Hausfrau* is free in that she has a determinate sphere over which she reigns.

67. "One is not incidentally thinking here of the normal psychology, according to which the individual powers of the soul are viewed as indifferently lying next to each other. According to this point of view it can appear as if women would be denied certain spiritual capacities. In no way should one think in terms of such a bad segmentation. The difference can only concern the mode and manner of expression. One sex presents the spiritual form in its simple purity, while the other sex presents the opposite, the coming apart of the unity." *Die Vorlesungen von 1819/1820,* p. 137.

68. "Men can be thus in general more one-sided than women . . . The women do not content themselves on the other hand with such abstract knowledge. The same holds for the French, who in general have more femaleness (*Weibliches*) in their characters than do the Germans." *Die Vorlesungen von 1810/1820.* p. 138. Despite Hegel's protestations that he is arguing for an equality between the sexes, one does not get the impression that he is exactly praising the French here, nor does he seem to be seeing them simply as different but equal to the Germans in their possession of more "femaleness" in their characters.

69. In his *Hegel's Ethical Thought,* Allen Wood points out that "[t]he implication of

this solution may be more radical than we would like to realize. Hegel's remarks about the alleged natural incapacities of the female sex are easy to deride, and it is easy to agree with the platitudes that men should be more sensitive, women more self-confident. But we have never really seen what human personalities would be like if they were not socialized through the traditional system of gender stereotypes. We do not know what role gender differences might play in personalities balancing the substantial principle with the reflective. Moreover, the modern social order as it actually exists is not one in which such personalities could develop or thrive. It is understandable, if not admirable, that many fear the unknown path to new possibilities than the present contradictions they are living." p. 246. (Wood also makes some very illuminating comparisons between Hegel's thought and some contemporary feminist thought.)

70. A similar point is effectively made by Allen Wood who sees Hegel's views as ineffectively trying to combine three ideas: (1) reconciling "substantive" and "reflective" principles by the division of the sexes, (2) the principle of the modern world being that of subjective freedom, (3) everyone's being equally persons and subjects. Wood points out that these three ideas conflict with each other since subjective freedom clashes with women's being confined to the home, yet taking women out of the home (stressing the second and third points) would leave the "substantive" principle undervalued. See Allen Wood, *Hegel's Ethical Thought*, pp. 244–246.

71. Indeed, the attempt to keep women confined to a certain realm of the household may be seen by Hegelians to involve an attempt by men to create and maintain social ("spiritual") divisions on the basis of *natural* characteristics that women have. The struggles between men and women are thus like those of the master and vassal, with each struggling for recognition, the "masters" in this case trying to keep the "vassals" as parts of nature instead of letting them see themselves as self-determining agents, understanding the "vassals'" personal projects as having validity only to the extent that they fit into the "master's" projects (and getting the "vassals" to accept that as a definition of themselves).

72. Kant claims that "Sexual community (*commercium sexuale*) is the reciprocal use which a person makes of another's sexual organs and faculties (*usus membrorum et facultatum sexualium alterius*) . . . The natural sexual community is either that of merely animal nature (*vaga libido, venus vulgivaga, fornicatio*) or according to law – the latter is marriage (*matrimonium*), i.e., the combination of two persons of different sexes to a life-long reciprocal possession of each other's sexual properties." Immanuel Kant, *Metaphysik der Sitten* (Hamburg: Felix Meiner Verlag, 1922), §24.

73. The person of "[b]ourgeois (*Bürgerliche*) freedom ought to be so: to become unlimited in his inclination, his choice (*Willkür*), in the practice of his skills, etc." *Die Vorlesungen von 1819/1820*, p. 150.

74. "These different agents (*diese Differenten*) are after all at the same time identical; however they are not conscious of this identity. For the unity and universality is only an inner one; the relationship of the individuals is not a relationship of freedom but rather of necessity. They are related to each other against their knowledge and against their will . . . I must accommodate myself, for I can not satisfy my needs without the help of the others, and I am in that way in dependency on others. This is in general the sphere of dependency and exigency (*Not*)." *Die Vorlesungen von 1819/1820*, pp. 147–148. "If one calls that freedom, one is on the one hand correct, for it is freedom but only the freedom of particularity; on

the other hand, one does not know that this freedom is also at the same time the highest dependency." Ibid., p. 150. Hegel says something similar in the *Philosophy of Right*, §186, but does not put as much stress on this matter as he does in the lectures, where he repeats the point again and again.

75. "There are two moments in this mediation: I attend to my welfare, attain my interests in mediation with others, who just as well attend to their welfare; at the same time there enters the moment of universality as the seeming-to-be (*Schein*) of rationality. This universality constitutes the moment of return, the seeming-to-be of freedom; this is the reconciling side of this sphere. According to the aspect of particularity, it is in general the sphere of mere choice (*Willkür*) and of contingency – of ethical, moral as well as external contingency. In this way, at the same time this is the sphere of exigency (*Not*) in that each individual is dependent on others. This is here the sphere in which everything particular has its appearance (*Ergehen*) and its free play; beneficent and malevolent inclinations find their place here in the same manner. Here poverty and corruption can break through. In this sphere of dependency and exigency is accordingly that which is reconciling in the seeming-to-be of rationality." *Die Vorlesungen von 1819/1820*, pp. 148–149.

76. "A difference of the estates is in general necessary; the difference is grounded on the needs and the manner of their satisfaction mutually specifying each other." *Die Vorlesungen von 1819/1820*, p. 163.

77. See Gianfranco Poggi, *The Development of the Modern State: A Sociological Introduction* (Palo Alto: Stanford University Press, 1978). Chapter III: The *Ständesstaat*, pp. 36–59.

78. Mack Walker argues that in making this distinction, Hegel accurately captured the historical status of German society in the post-Napoleonic period and the way that it had been transformed by the Napoleonic wars of that time. In particular, Hegel saw how the new *mobile* class of intellectuals and merchants challenged the old order which had been rooted in a sense of place, of "hometowns" from which few wandered and into which few came. Intellectuals, merchants and the kind of person filling in the bureaucratic posts of the state in the post-Napoleonic period had both the tools and inclination to move from place to place, and they brought their more cosmopolitan mores with them rather than adapting to the mores of the new place. This made them "universal" rather than "particular" – that is, a group of people whose mores and outlooks were themselves mobile, that is, capable of being taken from place to place and were thus not tied in to the more particular ethos of particular hometowns. Interestingly, Walker himself arrives at the same thesis on independent grounds. See Mack Walker, *German Hometowns: Community, State and General Estate, 1648–1871* (Ithaca: Cornell University Press, 1971). p. 197.

79. "Ethical life (*das Sittliche*) insofar as it is reflected into the individual through his naturally determinate character is *virtue*, which, insofar as it points to nothing more than the simple fitness of the individual to the ethical relations to which he belongs, is integrity (*Rechtsschaffenheit*)." *Philosophy of Right*, §150. *Rechtsschaffenheit* is often translated as "rectitude." It also has the nineteenth century connotations of "righteousness."

80. Hegel notes in his "Remark" to §128 of the *Philosophy of Right* that agriculture, particularly in England, has come in his own day to adopt factory modes of production, but he argues that this will not change the fundamental virtues of the agricultural estate. Some of what he says shows that he did not perhaps understand just how much work went into agriculture – he sometimes speaks as if the

peasants just planted things and waited for nature to do the rest. The overall argument, though, is that the kinds of dispositions that *naturally* come from working with the land and with animals are those that involve a certain amount of patience, trust in nature to provide and so on. These natural dispositions become virtues when they are linked to a set of ethical ideals tied in with that estate. He also remarks on this in *Die Vorlesungen von 1819/1820*, p. 164.

81. See Mack Walker, *German Hometowns: Community, State and General Estate, 1648–1871*, p. 197.

82. It is perfectly natural to translate *Polizei* as "police," but this has some rather unfortunate connotations. Mack Walker explains the function of the "police" in Hegel's day in the following way: ". . . police, meaning not just public discipline and security – the American blue-uniformed arm – but sanitation, foodstuffs, public amusements, economic regulations, information media, perhaps the maintenance of roads . . . trade guilds too were apt to become involved in preparing and enforcing police decisions." *German Hometowns*, pp. 45–46. Thus, the phrase *Polizeistaat*, which we would translate as "police-state," has some rather different connotations for us than it would for a reader in Hegel's day.

83. "The individuals must first of all thus acquire the skills to satisfy their desires through participation in the universal capital." *Die Vorlesungen von 1819/1820*, p. 192.

84. "Further, a totally different schism appears in the poor, a schism between them and the general temper (*des Gemüts*) of civil society. The poor person feels himself excluded and mocked by all, and out of this there necessarily arises an inner indignation. He has the consciousness of himself as infinite and free and with that arises the demand that external existence should correspond to this consciousness. It is not a natural distress (*Naturnot*) in civil society with which the poor person must struggle; the nature that the poor person has over and against them is not a mere being but my will. The poor person feels himself being related to arbitrariness (*Willkür*), to human contingency, and in the last analysis, this is what is gives rise to indignation, that he is put in this schism because of arbitrariness. Because the freedom of the individual has no existence, the recognition (*Anerkennung*) of universal freedom vanishes. Out of these conditions comes that shamelessness which we find in the rabble." *Die Vorlesungen von 1819/1820*, p. 195.

85. See also Stephen Houlgate, *Freedom, Truth and History: An Introduction to Hegel's Philosophy*, pp. 109–114.

86. "The rich person sees everything as purchasable on its own (*käuflich für sich*), because he knows himself as the power of the particularity of self-consciousness. Wealth can therefore lead to the same kind of derision and shamelessness that goes with the poor rabble . . . Both sides, poverty and wealth, constitute the decay of civil society." *Die Vorlesungen von 1819/1820*, p. 196.

87. This insistence on international commerce is not made very sharply by Hegel in his published *Philosophy of Right* (although it is there in §§246–247 if one looks for it). In some of his other lectures, Hegel apparently noted some of the problems attendant to international trade. Stephen Houlgate (in *Freedom, Truth and History: An Introduction to Hegel's Philosophy*, p. 114) sees these remarks as indicating that Hegel did not think that international trade was any long-term solution to the problem of poverty; Houlgate takes Hegel's talk about international trade to be only offering a pragmatic solution to the problem. However, Hegel quite clearly thought that international trade was more than just a stopgap measure for a

distinct social problem. In his 1819/1820 lectures, Hegel goes into much more detail on the matter. There he also sees it as improving on colonization (definitely a stopgap measure) as a means of fulfilling the teleology of civil society construed as an ethical end. "Civil society strives thus in general to go beyond itself, at first in the external manner of establishing colonies. This going-out-of-itself has a passion for gain as its ground. The higher element in all this is that trade is the way in which nations come into relation with each other in a rightful, legal (*rechtliche*) manner. Barbarians at first stand in the relation to each other of being enemies; they are for themselves and constitute themselves as single points excluding others from them. Those who come into relations of trade first come to know (*erkennen*) each other as legal persons, as property owners. In this external empirical way, people arrive at universality and recognition (*Anerkennung*). Becoming acquainted with other nations is one of the most important moments in the education (*Bildung*) of the modern world. Through it, people are brought out of their narrow-minded representations (*Vorstellungen*) . . . The sea and the navigation of it constitutes, as it were, the poetry of trade; in it there arises a kind of bravery to which trade in itself progresses. There arises through trade the representation of the universality of mankind; the particularity of nations, their mores (*Sitten*) and their culture vanish. There remains only the universal thought that all these foreigners are people . . . Through trade and need there arises a world-interest; world history shows the aspect of the ethical whole in all this, whereas world trade shows that aspect of the way in which people are related as such (*Seiten des Verhältnisses*). At the same time bourgeois society transcends its principle because it puts its own gains, its own property into danger. In that way, the drive for gain turns into its opposite, bravery." *Die Vorlesungen von 1819/1820*, pp. 199–20.

88. Roland Mousnier, *The Institutions of France under the Absolute Monarchy 1598–1789* (Chicago: University of Chicago Press, 1979). p. 129.

89. Because of this, Hegel would probably think that "fraternity" – or, for that matter, "sorority" – would be an inadequate metaphor for the kind of communal self-identity at stake here. "Solidarity" or "camaraderie" would be the better terms.

90. "Without being a member of an authorized corporation (and it is only by being authorized that a communality is a corporation), an individual is without the honor of an estate (*Standesehre*), and because of his isolation is reduced to the self-seeking side of his business, and his subsistence and enjoyment are not fixed. Consequently, he must seek to gain *his recognition* through external statements of success in his business, statements which are unlimited. He cannot live in according to his estate, for there is no estate for him – for in civil society something exists as a communality only if it is legally constituted and recognized. Therefore, there can be for him no universal way of life fit for him." *Philosophy of Right*, §253, Remark.

91. Historically, as Hegel notes, many states have arisen out of the agreements among corporate (and other) groups, although not in the peaceful, deliberative way so dear to the social contract theorists; rather they have arisen out of bloody religious conflicts, wars of conquest, and disputes among dynasties. The binding agreements that formed the basis of these states were more like treaties or suits for peace than they were like contracts.

92. Because of all the false lore about Hegel that has been passed down from textbook to textbook about Hegel's philosophy of the state, it is unfortunately still almost *de rigueur* to begin any discussion of Hegel's theory of the state with a set of

disclaimers: Hegel was not a proto-Nazi, he did not encourage mindless worship of the state, he was not a proto-communist, he did not call for the abolition of individualism in the face of the state and so on. At one time, such ridiculous views of Hegel were rampant. Although there are still a lot of things like this being taught about Hegel in courses covering the history of political theory, there is a mountain of scholarly work that shows that the popular authoritarian, proto-Nazi, German nationalist, state-worshipping Hegel is a creature purely of myth. As a representative sample of such work in English, see Shlomo Avineri, *Hegel's Theory of the Modern State* (Cambridge: Cambridge University Press, 1972); Robert Pippin, *Modernism as a Philosophical Problem* (Oxford: Blackwell's, 1991); Steven Smith, *Hegel's Critique of Liberalism: Rights in Context* (Chicago: University of Chicago Press, 1989); Jacques d'Hondt, *Hegel in His Time: Berlin, 1818–1831* (translated by John Burbridge with N. Roland and J. Levasseur) (Peterborough: Broadview, 1988); Terry Pinkard, *Hegel's Dialectic: the Explanation of Possibility* (Philadelphia: Temple University Press, 1988); Stephen Houlgate, *Freedom, Truth and History* (London: Routledge, 1991); Peter J. Steinberger, *Logic and Politics: Hegel's Philosophy of Right* (New Haven: Yale University Press, 1988). The classic study of how the patently false view of Hegel-the-authoritarian-Nazi got its roots is found in Walter Kaufmann's, "The Hegel Myth and its Method," *Philosophical Review* LXIII (1954), pp. 3–18.

93. The term, "state," unfortunately conjures for us the more modern sociological idea of a territorial unity possessing a monopoly on power. Hegel, however, thinks that there can be states (in his sense) that have no power (*Macht*). "With constitutions it is further a matter of a people's becoming completely independent so that their independence can maintain itself by itself. There can be different kinds of combinations through which a state, which does not have power, can maintain itself as independent and still endure (*Bestehen*). In such weak states, which live on political sufferance (*politische Gnadenbrot essen*), such deficient constitutions can endure. Such a state can particularly hold out at the level of civil society. If the state actually holds together with such constitutions, then one cannot say that it does so only through other states. The main thing is that in such states an orderly and rightful private economy (*Privathaushaltung*) is conducted." *Die Vorlesungen von 1819/1820*, pp. 236–237.

94. "The question can be raised as to who is to make the constitution. This question seems fully meaningful and to be of the highest importance. Looked at more closely, however, it is meaningless. It bases itself on the view that there could be a people (*Volk*) without a constitution. Such a people would be only an abstract multiplicity. But such a thing does not exist." *Die Vorlesungen von 1819/1820*, pp. 228–229.

95. "The state in its constitution must permeate all relationships. Napoleon, for example, wished to give the Spaniards a constitution *a priori*, which went badly enough. A constitution is not just something manufactured (*Gemachtes*); it is the work of centuries, it is the idea, the consciousness of rationality to the extent that this rationality is developed in a people. No constitution is therefore simply made by its subjects. What Napoleon gave the Spaniards was more rational than what they had earlier had, and yet they recoiled from it as from something alien, since they were not yet educated up to its level. With regard to their constitution, a people must have a feeling for their rights and their condition, for otherwise there may be a constitution externally present at hand for them, but it has no meaning and no value." *Philosophy of Right*, §274, Addition.

96. Hegel compares it to Rousseau's general will, noting, however, that Rousseau's conception suffers from the defect of making the general will some kind of mysterious compound out of a collection of individual wills. This makes it seem as if the political community is somehow something to which individuals in, say, civil society consent in order to protect their property or their liberties. That would completely undermine the legitimacy of the political community, since it would make the political community's legitimacy contingent on how well it served those functions – it makes it, that is, a means to an end, rather than a common pursuit. Indeed, it is "social space" organized as ethical life – the collection of social practices and institutions that comprise the "ethical ends" – that makes individual willing possible in the first place, and thus the ethical end of the political community cannot be said to be the result of such independent willings. See *Philosophy of Right*, §258.

97. Hegel speaks in many places about how one should not confuse the issue of the legitimacy (or, in his words, validity, *Gültigkeit*) of the state with its historical origins. The legitimacy of modernity in general can only be understood in terms of how it makes up for the insufficiencies of its historical predecessors. That issue, however, is treated in the *Phenomenology of Spirit*, which shows us how we came to the standpoint where something like the "system" and in particular, the *Philosophy of Right* is possible for us. Hegel does say of the modern state: "It cannot be merely rigid, inherited rights through which the whole is held together. These are historically feudal states. The grounds which count in them are of a wholly positive kind: it has been valid and thus it is valid. Since civil society took shape within the feudal states, the universal has been made to count as such." *Die Vorlesungen von 1819/1820*, p. 209.

98. Shlomo Avineri, who is otherwise a reliable reporter of Hegel's views, seems to get this point wrong. For Avineri, Hegel "opposes any system which would like to achieve a separation of powers by investing each political *institution* with a separate and exclusive *function*." *Hegel's Theory of the Modern State*, p. 186. Avineri relies on Hegel's statement in §272 that ". . . each of these powers is in itself the totality of the constitution, because each contains the other moments and has them effective in itself, and because the moments, being expressions of the differentiation of the concept, simply abide in their ideality and constitute nothing but a single individual whole." But Hegel is only intending to say here that each moment *implies* the other. You cannot have a legislative power without some power to enforce the law, you cannot have an executive without some law to execute, and so on, and that the legitimacy of each moment comes out of its being a moment of the whole that is the political community – the state – not in its being simply a pragmatic stopgap measure to keep government working.

99. It is in his lectures of 1819/1820 that Hegel refers to a kind of *Schadenfreude* as connected with the separation of powers. See *Die Vorlesungen von 1819/1820*. p. 233

100. Compare, for example, the statement in the *Philosophy of Right*, §209: "A person [*Mensch*] counts as such only because he is a person, not because he is a Jew, Catholic, Protestant, German, Italian, etc."

101. Compare, for example, his comment: "The superficial and empty point of view and interpretation of the concept of a constitution has provoked much mischief. If one inquires in the individual German states (*Ländern*) whether the bourgeois (*Bürger*) and peasants want to belong to one Germany, in most cases the question will simply not be understood." *Die Vorlesungen von 1819/1820*. p. 230.

This occurs in the context of speaking of how a people must be "ready" and "formed" for a rational constitution and how the Spanish were not yet ready for the constitution which Napoleon gave them. The idea that "Germans" ought to belong to a unified German state simply because they are ethnically Germans is thus for Hegel simple irrationality. What is important is not their "Germanness" but whether they have developed an appropriately modern *self-consciousness*.

102. See Shlomo Avineri's discussion of this, *Hegel's Theory of the Modern State*, pp. 168–171.

103. *Philosophy of Right*, §318.

104. Shlomo Avineri does a nice job of showing how little this charge has to do with Hegel's actual proposals. See *Hegel's Theory of the Modern State*, pp. 161–167.

105. "The particular conceptual determination of the estates is thereby to be seen in that in them the subjective moment of universal freedom, the sphere's own insight and own will, which in this exposition is called civil society, comes into *existence in relation to the state*. That this moment is a determination of the idea developing itself to totality, is an inner necessity not to be confused with *external necessity* and *utility*, follows, as everywhere, from the philosophical point of view." *Philosophy of Right*, §301.

106. For this reason, in his lectures on aesthetics, Hegel argued that the appropriate form of drama for modern life is neither pure tragedy nor pure comedy but *tragicomedy,* in which there is both the seriousness of purpose present in tragedy and the free play of subjectivity present in comedy, and in which the tragic and comic elements serve to "balance" (*ausgleichen*) each other. He notes, "Instead of acting with comical perversity, the individual is filled with the seriousness characteristic of solid concerns and stable characters, while the tragic fixity of will is so far weakened, and the depth of the collisions so far reduced, that there can emerge a reconciliation (*Aussöhnung*) of interests and a harmonious unification of individuals and their aims. It is in a conception like this that particularly our modern plays and dramas have the basis of their origin. The depth of this principle is the intuition that, despite all differences and conflicts of characters and their interests and passions, human action can nevertheless produce an actuality fully harmonious within itself. As long ago as their day the ancients had tragedies like this, in that individuals were not sacrificed but saved . . . But in these cases the accommodation (*Ausgleichung*) comes from outside by command of the gods, etc., and does not have its source within the parties themselves, while in modern plays it is the individuals themselves who are led in the course of their own action to this cessation of strife and to the mutual reconciliation (*Aussöhnung*) of their aims and characters." *Aesthetics*, II, pp. 1203–1204; *Werke*, 15, pp. 532–533.

107. In speaking of the development of the "principle of thought" (which for him is the basic idea of self-determination, since only thought is fully self-determining), Hegel says, "With this formally absolute principle we arrive at the *last stage (Stadium) in history, at our world, at our time (Tage)."* *Werke*, 12, p. 524. This is of course ambiguous, since the "last stage" might be taken to refer always to "our time," whenever our time happens to be.

108. *Werke*, 12, p. 134. (The formula occurs in several places; this is from the lectures on the philosophy of history.)

109. This rests on Hegel's seeing all non-Western cultures as lacking a properly *reflective* form of life, that is, as failing to develop the kinds of reflective institutions which give rise to "spirit" and thus in principle offering no kind of alternative

account of our reason-giving activities. Hegel does not argue that the Chinese and the Indians, for example, do not engage in reason-giving activities, but only that they have not developed the kinds of reflective institutions that would be necessary in order to generate the kinds of skepticism that are necessary to move history forward. Thus, although China and India change over time, they cannot, in Hegel's view, have any *history*. That Hegel may be charged with simply misunderstanding the complexity of Chinese and Indian culture and expressing a kind of nineteenth century hauteur and arrogance toward non-Western cultures is for us later readers something that goes without saying. But Hegel was also drawing on the available literature of his day, which was scanty and was itself certainly colored by these, shall we say, somewhat ethnocentric views of the relation between Western and non-Western cultures. (What Hegel says, for example, about Africa displays the astounding ignorance possessed by almost all Europeans of his time towards that continent.) A more serious consideration of the alternative accounts given by Chinese and Indians (or whether they really are *alternative* accounts) would obviously require a rewrite of the Hegelian philosophy of history, but it would not require a rewrite of the Hegelian thesis that from the dialectical standpoint, what we are interested in are the ways in which forms of life come to give accounts of what they take to be good reasons for belief and action and the ways in which those accounts generate their own forms of skepticism.

110. The famous and influential interpretation of Hegel's philosophy by the Franco-Russian philosopher, Alexandre Kojève, mistook this point. Kojève used "History" in the same way in which the early moderns used "Nature." Kojève takes "History" to be that background of human action and passion that ensures through its own mechanism that the various actions humans take will automatically balance out so as to produce the best result. (See Alexandre Kojève, *Introduction to the Reading of Hegel* (translated by James H. Nichols, Jr.) (Ithaca: Cornell University Press, 1969). This corresponds to the idea of "Nature" in early modern thought as a beneficent, self-correcting background. This idea of "Nature" grows out of the way in which God was used in medieval ethical thought. God made the universe for a purpose, and every part has a purpose. We are conscious of our part, even though we cannot perhaps fathom exactly how we are contributing overall to divine purpose. God has given mankind a set of determinate, absolute duties; moreover, God in his supreme wisdom has given us these duties in the knowledge that if each person performs the duties of his station, the result will be good (even if we limited finite creatures cannot discern that good.) The seeming disorder in the world may thus be understood as mere appearance; the divine plan has ordained things so that the greater good is achieved, even if we cannot see it. Later moralists replaced God's plan for the world with the idea of Nature working itself out so as to give individuals certain desires and passions, the overall arrangement of which is supposed to produce an overall harmony among humans, provided that we learned to listen to the "voice of nature" in ourselves. (On this transition in the development of modern ethics, see Jerome Schneewind, "The Divine Corporation and the History of Ethics," in *Philosophy in History: Essays in the Historiography of Philosophy,* edited by Richard Rorty, J.B. Schneewind and Quentin Skinner (Cambridge: Cambridge University Press, 1984). pp. 173–191.) Kojève used "History" in much the same way. "History" was a self-correcting enterprise that ensured that the right outcome would be ordained even if we limited humans could not see how it was

working out. The mechanism by which history worked was the struggle for recognition, but Kojève took this to be the result of a "natural" desire within humans to gain such recognition from others. Kojève quite consciously used this idea of "History" in order to avoid being a complete relativist. Michael S. Roth in his *Knowing and History: Appropriations of Hegel in Twentieth Century France* (Ithaca: Cornell University Press, 1988), pp. 81–146 (his chapter on Kojève) also discusses how the views of later French thinkers such as Foucault were attempts to avoid such a conception of "History" as a self-correcting enterprise in favor of a more thoroughly relativist position. (See Roth, pp. 189–224.) Kojève's naturalization of the Hegelian conception of history has been revived by Francis Fukuyama, *The End of History and the Last Man* (New York: The Free Press, 1992). Like Kojève, Fukuyama posits a basic desire in "human nature," the desire for recognition, and then argues that the institutional setups of modern liberal democracies satisfy that desire in a rational way that avoids the kinds of irrational conflicts embodied in earlier, alternative setups. Both Kojève and Fukuyama therefore transform Hegel's project into a version of pre-Hegelian attempts at locating some fixed, transcendent standard to use for evaluating different historical phenomena.

111. There is an often-cited passage from Hegel's lectures on the philosophy of history that shows that Hegel entertained the possibility that world history might now begin a different story than it has up until now. The passage concerns his reflections on North America: "North America will be comparable with Europe only after the immeasurable space which that state offers is filled up and its civil society will be pressed back on itself . . . America is therefore the land of the future, where, in the times that lie before us, a world historical significance will reveal itself – perhaps in a conflict between North and South America. It is a land of longing for all those who are weary of the historical armory of old Europe . . . *It is for America to break off from the basis (Boden) on which until today the history of the world has set itself out* . . . and as a land of the future, it is not of concern to us here, for, as regards history, we only have to regard that aspect of history which has been and that which is." *Werke*, 12, p. 114. (italics added by me.) Were Hegel writing today, perhaps he would be instead talking about Asia.

112. Dieter Henrich claims on the basis of reading unpublished manuscripts that Hegel's thesis concerning the "end of art" apparently did not appear in his lectures on the subject until 1828, three years before his death. See Dieter Henrich, "Art and Philosophy of Art Today: Reflections With Reference to Hegel," in Richard E. Amacher and Victor Lange, *New Perspectives in German Literary Criticism* (Princeton: Princeton University Press, 1979). p. 114, note 1.

113. "Thought and reflection have spread their wings above fine art. Those who delight in lamenting and blaming may regard this phenomenon as a corruption and ascribe it to the predominance of passions and selfish interests which scare away the seriousness of art as well as its cheerfulness; or they may accuse the distress of the present time, the complicated state of civil and political life which does not permit a heart entangled in petty interests to free itself to the higher ends of art . . . consequently, the conditions of our present time are not favorable to art . . . the point is that our whole spiritual culture is of such a kind that [the artist] himself stands within the world of reflection and its relations, and could not by any act of will and decision abstract himself from it; nor could by special education or removal from the relations of life contrive and organize a

special solitude to replace what he has lost. In all these respects art, considered as its highest vocation, is and remains for us a thing of the past." *Aesthetics,* pp. 10–11; *Werke,* p. 25.

114. For Hegel's relation to his own time, see John Edward Toews, *Hegelianism,* which draws out the various tensions and social forces that occupied the Hegelian school during Hegel's Berlin period and immediately thereafter.

115. "Preface" to the *Philosophy of Right,* p. 11 and p. 13.

116. Hegel speaks of objective spirit as a "second nature" in *Philosophy of Right,* §4.

117. In his lectures on the philosophy of history, Hegel made this point in the following way: "A principle of thought was thus found for the state . . . the principle of certainty, which is the identity with my self-consciousness, but not yet with that of truth, from which it must be differentiated. This is a great discovery about that which is most inner (*das Innerste*) and about freedom. The consciousness of the spiritual is now essentially the foundation and *philosophy* has come to be dominant." *Werke,* p. 527. Here Hegel distinguishes the "certainty" that one finds in willing the ethical ends of family, civil society and state from the kind of reflection on whether this kind of "social space" is subject to the same kinds of skeptical attacks as were earlier forms of life. That reflection belongs to absolute spirit, which is concerned with what he calls in this passage, "truth."

Works cited

Henry E. Allison, *Kant's Transcendental Idealism* (New Haven: Yale University Press, 1983).

Henry E. Allison, *Kant's Theory of Freedom* (Cambridge: Cambridge University Press, 1990).

Horst Althaus, *Hegel und die heroischen Jahre der Philosophie* (Munich: Carl Hanser Verlag, 1992).

Karl Ameriks, "Kant and Hegel on Freedom: Two New Interpretations," *Inquiry*, 35, 219–232.

Richard Aquila, "Predication and Hegel's Metaphysics," in Michael Inwood (ed.), *Hegel* (Oxford: Oxford University Press, 1985). pp. 67–84.

Erich Auerbach, *Mimesis: The Representation of Reality in Western Literature,* transl. Willard Trask (New York: Doubleday Anchor, 1953).

Shlomo Avineri, *Hegel's Theory of the Modern State* (Cambridge: Cambridge University Press, 1972).

Werner Becker, *Hegels Phänomenologie des Geistes* (Stuttgart: W. Kohlhammer, 1971).

Frederick C. Beiser (ed.), *The Cambridge Companion to Hegel* (Cambridge: Cambridge University Press, 1993).

Stephen Bungay, *Beauty and Truth: A Study of Hegel's Aesthetics* (Oxford: Clarendon Press, 1984).

Colin Campbell, *The Romantic Ethic and the Spirit of Modern Consumerism* (London: Blackwell, 1987).

Ernst Cassirer, *The Philosophy of the Enlightenment,* transl. Fritz C. A. Koelln and James P. Pettegrove (Princeton: Princeton University Press, 1951).

Roger Chartier, "The World Turned Upside Down," in Roger Chartier, *Cultural History,* transl. Lydia G. Cochrane (Ithaca: Cornell University Press, 1988).

Anthony Ashley Cooper, The Earl of Shaftesbury, *"An Inquiry Concerning Virtue or Merit"* (1711), reprinted in Jerome Schneewind, *Moral Philosophy from Montaigne to Kant* (Cambridge: Cambridge University Press, 1990). vol. II.

Willem A. deVries, *Hegel's Theory of Mental Activity* (Ithaca: Cornell University Press, 1988).

Willem deVries, "The Dialectic of Teleology," in Willem A. deVries (ed.), *Philosophical Topics,* vol. 19, no. 2, pp. 51–70.

Willem deVries, "Hegel on Reference and Knowledge," *Journal of the History of Philosophy* (26), pp. 297–307.

Denis Diderot, *Rameau's Nephew*, transl. L.W. Tancock (Harmondsworth: Penguin Books, Ltd., 1966).

Gerald Dworkin, *The Theory and Practice of Autonomy* (Cambridge: Cambridge University Press, 1988).

Dietrich von Engelhardt, "Die biologischen Wissenschaften in Hegels Naturphilosophie," in Horstmann and Petry, *Hegels Philosophie der Natur*, pp. 121–137.

J. C. Evans, *The Metaphysics of Transcendental Subjectivity*, (Amsterdam: Verlag R.R. Grüner, 1984).

Francis Fukuyama, *The End of History and the Last Man* (New York: Free Press, 1992).

Helen Gardner, (ed.), *The Metaphysical Poets* (London: Penguin Books, 1957).

Peter Gay, *The Enlightenment: An Interpretation: The Rise of Modern Paganism.* (New York: W.W. Norton, 1966).

Peter Gay, *The Enlightenment: An Interpretation: The Science of Freedom* (New York: W.W. Norton, 1969).

Moltke Gram, "Moral and Literary Ideals in Hegel's Critique of the 'Moral World-View'," in *Clio*, 7 no. 3, 1978, pp. 375–402.

Norman Hampson, *The Enlightenment* (New York: Penguin Books, 1968).

Paul Hazard, *European Thought in the Eighteenth Century: From Montesquieu to Lessing*, (Cleveland: Meridian Books, World Publishing, 1963).

Hegel, *Phänomenologie des Geistes,* (ed. J. Hoffmeister, (Hamburg: Felix Meiner Verlag, 1955).

Hegel, *Phenomenology of Spirit,* transl. A.V. Miller, (Oxford: Oxford University Press, 1977).

Hegel, *Philosophy of Right,* (transl. T.M. Knox, (Oxford: Oxford University Press, 1952).

Hegel, *The Berlin Phenomenology,* transl. M.J. Petry (Dordrecht: Reidel, 1981).

Hegel, *Lectures on the Philosophy of Religion: The Lectures of 1827* Peter Hodgson (ed.), transl. R.F. Brown, P.C. Hodgson, and J.M. Stewart, with assistance of H.S. Harris (Berkeley: University of California Press, 1988).

Hegel, *Werke in zwanzig Bänden,* ed. Eva Moldenhauer and Karl Markus Michel (Frankfurt a.M.: Suhrkamp Verlag, 1971). Cited as *Werke.*

Hegel, *Aesthetics: Lectures on Fine Art,* transl. T.M. Knox (Oxford: Oxford University Press, 1975).

Hegel, *Science of Logic,* transl. A.V. Miller (London: Allen and Unwin, 1969).

Hegel: Philosophie des Rechts: Die Vorlesungen von 1819/1820, ed. Dieter Henrich (Frankfurt a.M.: Suhrkamp Verlag, 1983).

WORKS CITED

Johannes Heinrichs, *Die Logik der <Phänomenologie des Geistes>* (Bonn: Bouvier Verlag, 1974).

Dieter Henrich, "Französische Revolution und klassische deutsche Philosophie: Überlegungen zur Bestimmung ihres Verhältnisse" in Dieter Henrich, *Eine Republik Deutschland* (Frankfurt a.M.: Suhrkamp Verlag, 1990), pp. 71–101.

Dieter Henrich, "Art and Philosophy of Art Today: Reflections With Reference to Hegel," in Richard E. Amacher and Victor Lange, *New Perspectives in German Literary Criticism* (Princeton: Princeton University Press, 1979).

Johann Herder, *Ideen zur Philosophie der Geschichte der Menschheit,* in Herder, *Werke* (Frankfurt a.M.: Deutscher Klassiker Verlag, 1989), vol. 6.

Emannuel Hirsch, "Die Beisetzung der Romantiker in Hegels Phenomenology," reprinted in Hans Friederich Fulda and Dieter Henrich (eds.), *Materialien zu Hegels <Phänomenologie des Geistes>* (Frankfurt a.M.: Suhrkamp Verlag, 1973).

Eric Hobsbawm, *The Age of Revolution: 1789–1848* (Markham: Penguin Books Canada, 1962).

Jacques d'Hondt, *Hegel in His Time: Berlin, 1818–1831,* transl. John Burbridge with N. Roland and J. Levasseur (Peterborough: Broadview, 1988).

Rolf-Peter Horstmann, *Wahrheit aus dem Begriff: eine Einführung in Hegel* (Frankfurt a.M.: Anton Hain, 1990).

Rolf-Peter Horstmann and Michael J. Petry (eds.), *Hegels Philosophie der Natur: Beziehungen zwischen empirischer und spekulativer Naturerkenntnis* (Stuttgart: Ernst Klett Verlag, 1986).

Stephen Houlgate, *Freedom, Truth and History: An Introduction to Hegel's Philosophy* (London: Routledge, 1991).

David Hoy, "Hegel's Critique of Kantian Morality," *History of Philosophy Quarterly,* 6 no. 2 (1989), pp. 207–232.

David Hume, *Treatise on Human Nature,* ed. L. A. Selby-Bigge, (Oxford: Clarendon Press, 1978).

Georg G. Iggers, *The German Conception of History: The National Tradition of Historical Thought From Herder to the Present* (Middletown: Wesleyan University Press, 1968).

Michael Inwood, *Hegel* (London: Routledge, 1983).

Michael Inwood (ed.), *Hegel* (Oxford: Oxford University Press, 1985).

Michael Inwood, *A Hegel Dictionary,* (Cambridge, MA: Blackwell, 1992).

Immanuel Kant, "What is Enlightenment?," transl. Lewis White Beck in Lewis White Beck (ed.), *Kant: Selections* (New York: Macmillan, 1988).

Kant, *Metaphysik der Sitten,* ed. Karl Vorländer (Hamburg: Felix Meiner Verlag, 1966).

Walter Kaufmann, "The Hegel Myth and its Method," *Philosophical Review,* LXIII (1954), pp. 3–18.

Dale Van Kley, *The Jansenists and the Expulsion of the Jesuits from France: 1757–1765* (New Haven: Yale University Press, 1975).

Alexandre Kojève, *Introduction to the Reading of Hegel,* transl. James H. Nichols, Jr. (Ithaca: Cornell University Press, 1969).

Leonard Krieger, *Kings and Philosophers: 1689–1789* (New York: W.W. Norton, 1970). pp. 143–152.

Trevor H. Levere, "Hegel and the Earth Sciences," in Horstmann and Petry (eds.), *Hegels Philosophie der Natur,* pp. 103–120.

Arthur Loesser, *Men, Women and Pianos: A Social History* (New York: Dover, 1954).

Franz H. van Lunteren, "Hegel and Gravitation" in Horstmann and Petry (eds.), *Hegels Philosophie der Natur,* pp. 45–53.

Alasdair MacIntyre, "Hegel on Faces and Skulls," in Alasdair MacIntyre (ed.), *Hegel: A Collection of Critical Essays* (Garden City: Doubleday, 1972).pp. 219–236.

Roland Mousnier, *The Institutions of France under the Absolute Monarchy 1598–1789* (Chicago: University of Chicago Press, 1979).

G.E. Mueller, "The Hegel Legend of 'Thesis-Antithesis-Synthesis,'" *Journal of the History of Ideas,* 19 (1958), pp. 411–414.

Thomas Nagel, *The View From Nowhere* (Oxford: Oxford University Press, 1986).

Blaise Pascal, *Pensées,* transl. A.J. Krailsheimer (Baltimore: Penguin Books, 1966).

M.J. Petry, *Hegel's Philosophy of Nature* (London: Allen and Unwin, 1970).

Terry Pinkard, *Hegel's Dialectic: The Explanation of Possibility* (Philadelphia: Temple University Press, 1988).

Robert Pippin, "Idealism and Agency in Kant and Hegel" *Journal of Philosophy* (1991), pp. 532–541.

Robert Pippin, "The Modern World of Leo Strauss," *Political Theory,* 20, 1992, pp. 448–472.

Robert Pippin, *Kant's Theory of Form* (New Haven: Yale University Press, 1982).

Robert Pippin, "Kant on the Spontaneity of Mind," *Canadian Journal of Philosophy,* 17, 1987, pp. 449–476.

Robert Pippin, *Hegel's Idealism: The Satisfactions of Self-Consciousness* (Cambridge: Cambridge University Press, 1988).

Robert Pippin, "Kant, Hegel and Ethical Reasons," *Philosophical Topics,* vol. 19, no. 2 (1992), pp. 99–132.

Robert Pippin, *Modernism as a Philosophical Problem: On the Dissatisfactions of European High Culture* (Cambridge: Blackwell, 1991).

Robert Pippin, "'You Can't Get There from Here': Transition Problems in Hegel's Phenomenology of Spirit," in Beiser (ed.), *The Cambridge Companion to Hegel,* pp. 52–85.

Gianfranco Poggi, *The Development of the Modern State: A Sociological Introduction* (Palo Alto: Stanford University Press, 1978).

Otto Pöggeler, "Die Komposition der Phänomenologie des Geistes," in Hans Friederich Fulda and Dieter Henrich (eds.), *Materialien zu Hegels <Phänomenologie des Geistes>* (Frankfurt a.M.: Suhrkamp Verlag, 1973). pp. 329–390.

Orest Ranum, *Paris in the Age of Absolutism* (New York: Wiley, 1968).

John Rawls, "Kantian Constructivism in Moral Theory: The Dewey Lectures," 1980, *The Journal of Philosophy*, vol. LXXVII, No. 9, pp. 515–572.

John Rawls, "Themes in Kant's Moral Philosophy," in Eckart Förster (ed.), *Kant's Transcendental Deductions: The Three Critiques and the Opus postumum* (Stanford: Stanford University Press, 1989). pp. 81–113.

John Rawls, "The Basic Liberties and Their Priority," in Sterling M. McMurrin (ed.), *The Tanner Lectures* (Salt Lake City: University of Utah Press, 1982). pp. 3–87.

Jay Rosenberg, *The Thinking Self* (Philadelphia: Temple University Press, 1986).

Michael S. Roth, *Knowing and History: Appropriations of Hegel in Twentieth Century France* (Ithaca: Cornell University Press, 1988).

Jean-Jacques Rousseau, *The Confessions of Jean-Jacques Rousseau,* transl. J.M. Cohen (London: Penguin Books, 1953).

Jean-Jacques Rousseau, *On the Social Contract,* Book II, Chapter I; transl., ed. Donald A. Cress (Indianapolis: Hackett Publishing, 1983).

F.W.J. Schelling, *Allgemeine Deduktion des dynamischen Prozesses oder der Kategorien der Physik,* in Schelling, *Werke,* vol. 2.

F.W.J. Schelling, *System des transzendentalen Idealismus* in F.W.J. Schelling, *Werke,* Manfred Schröter, ed. (Munich: E.B. Beck Verlagsbuchhandlung, 1927).

Jerome Schneewind, "The Divine Corporation and the History of Ethics," in *Philosophy in History: Essays in the Historiography of Philosophy,* ed. Richard Rorty, J.B. Schneewind, and Quentin Skinner (Cambridge: Cambridge University Press, 1984).

Sally Sedgwick, "Hegel on Kant's Antinomies and Distinction Between General and Transcendental Logic," in *The Monist,* 74, no. 3, 1991. pp. 403–420.

Wilfrid Sellars, "The Language of Theories," in Wilfrid Sellars, *Science, Perception and Reality* (London: Routledge, 1963).

William R. Shea, "Hegel's Celestial Mechanics" in Horstmann and Petry (eds.) *Hegels Philosophie der Natur,* pp. 30–44.

James J. Sheehan, *German History: 1770–1866* (Oxford: Clarendon Press, 1989).

Judith Shklar, *Men and Citizens: A Study of Rousseau's Social Theory* (Cambridge: Cambridge University Press, 1985).

Steven Smith, *Hegel's Critique of Liberalism: Rights in Context* (Chicago: University of Chicago Press, 1989).

Ivan Soll, *Introduction to Hegel's Metaphysics* (Chicago: University of Chicago Press, 1969).

Jean Starobinski, *Jean-Jacques Rousseau: Transparency and Obstruction,* transl. Arthur Goldhammer (Chicago: University of Chicago Press, 1988).

Peter J. Steinberger, *Logic and Politics: Hegel's Philosophy of Right* (New Haven: Yale University Press, 1988).

James Hutchison Stirling, *The Secret of Hegel: Being the Hegelian System in Origin, Principle, Form, and Matter.* (Edinburgh: Oliver & Boyd, 1898).

Charles Taylor, *Hegel and Modern Society* (Cambridge: Cambridge University Press, 1979).

Charles Taylor, *Hegel* (Cambridge: Cambridge University Press, 1975).

Charles Taylor, "The Opening Arguments of the *Phenomenology*" in Alasdair MacIntyre (ed.), *Hegel: A Collection of Critical Essays* (Garden City: Doubleday, 1972). pp. 151–188.

John Edward Toews, *Hegelianism* (Cambridge: Cambridge University Press, 1980).

Donald Philip Verene, *Hegel's Recollections: A Study of Images in the Phenomenology of Spirit* (Albany: SUNY Press, 1985).

Mack Walker, *German Hometowns: Community, State and General Estate, 1648–1871* (Ithaca: Cornell University Press, 1971).

Michael Walzer, *Spheres of Justice: A Defense of Pluralism and Equality* (New York: Basic Books, 1983).

Karl Joachim Weintraub, *The Value of the Individual: Self and Circumstance in Autobiography* (Chicago: University of Chicago Press, 1978).

Kenneth Westphal, "The Basic Context and Structure of Hegel's *Philosophy of Right*," in F. Beiser (ed.), *The Cambridge Companion to Hegel*, pp. 234–269.

Kenneth Westphal, "Hegel's Critique of Kant's Moral World View," in Willem A. deVries (ed.), *Philosophical Topics* (vol. 19, no. 2), pp. 133–176.

Allen Wood, *Hegel's Ethical Thought* (Cambridge: Cambridge University Press, 1990).

Allen Wood, "Ficht's Philosophical Revolution," in Willem A. deVries (ed.), *Philosophical Topics* (vol. 19, no. 2, 1992), pp. 1–28.

Index

445

447